CONCEPTS AND PRACTICES IN
LOCAL GOVERNMENT FINANCE

OTHER WORKS BY AUTHORS

Lennox L. Moak

With Frank Cowan, Jr.

Manual of Suggested Practice for Administration of Local Sales and Use Taxes (Chicago: Municipal Finance Officers Association, 1961), 311 pp.

A Survey of the Use and Non-Use of Service Charges in the Performance of Refuse Collection and Disposal Functions in 380 Local Governments of the United States and Canada (Chicago: Municipal Finance Officers Association, 1962), 87 pp.

A Survey of the Use and Non-Use of Sewer Service Charges in 339 Local Governments in the United States and Canada (Chicago: Municipal Finance Officers Association, 1962), 66 pp.

With Kathryn W. Killian

A Manual of Techniques for the Preparation, Consideration, Adoption, and Administration of Operating Budgets (Chicago: Municipal Finance Officers Association, 1963), 347 pp.

With Kathryn W. Killian

A Manual of Suggested Practice for the Preparation and Adoption of Capital Programs and Capital Budgets by Local Governments (Chicago: Municipal Finance Officers Association, 1964), 152 pp.

With Kathryn Killian Gordon

Budgeting for Smaller Government Units (Chicago: Municipal Finance Officers Association, 1965), 194 pp.

Administration of Local Government Debt (Chicago: Municipal Finance Officers Association, 1970), 463 pp.

Albert M. Hillhouse

Municipal Bonds—A Century of Experience (New York: Prentice-Hall, 1936), 579 pp.

With Carl H. Chatters

Local Government Debt Administration (New York: Prentice-Hall, 1939), 528 pp.

With Carl H. Chatters

Tax-Reverted Properties in Urban Areas (Chicago: Public Administration Service, 1942), 183 pp.

With Muriel Magelssen *et al*

Where Cities Get Their Money (Chicago: Municipal Finance Officers Association, 1945), 229 pp.

With S. Kenneth Howard

State Capital Budgeting (Chicago: Council of State Governments, 1963), 177 pp.

With S. Kenneth Howard

Revenue Estimating by Cities (Chicago: Municipal Finance Officers Association, 1965), 16 pp.

CONCEPTS AND
PRACTICES IN

LOCAL
GOVERNMENT
FINANCE

LENNOX L. MOAK
ALBERT M. HILLHOUSE

*Municipal Finance
Officers Association
of the United States
and Canada*

© 1975 by MUNICIPAL FINANCE OFFICERS ASSOCIATION
of the United States and Canada
1313 East 60th Street, Chicago, Illinois 60637

First reprinting, August 1975

Library of Congress Catalog Card Number: LOC 75-1913
ISBN Number 0-89125-001-8
Printed in the United States of America

To the memory of Carl H. Chatters
A great student and practitioner in local government finance.

Foreword

Over the years, MFOA has issued hundreds of bulletins, special reports, several books and a large volume of technical literature covering every conceivable aspect of governmental finance. The point has now been reached, with the publication of this book, where these diverse elements have been integrated into a single volume. *Concepts and Practices in Local Government Finance* is a valuable operational and reference tool synthesizing an enormous amount of general and practical information for all persons, practitioners and academicians, dealing in local government finance administration.

This book complements *Management Policies in Local Government Finance*, published simultaneously by the International City Management Association. Drawing together communications analysis, fiscal policy and management guidelines for government finance, the ICMA book blends all aspects to give readers a better understanding of the economic environment of their own government.

To gain the most comprehensive view of the public finance field, readers should use both volumes. It is recognized, however, that some will prefer one book over the other for their specific needs. Because of this, there is some overlap in coverage between the two volumes, particularly with respect to the basic areas of budgeting, debt administration, cash and security management, purchasing, insurance and accounting. However, scope and treatment are unique to each book—one stressing operational and procedural concepts, the other emphasizing policy and decision making.

Concepts and Practices in Local Government Finance covers the environment of local government and the various local finance policies. Generally-accepted principles and methods are set forth concisely and evaluated for the reader along with evaluations of new approaches to investment policy, decision making and productivity measurement.

The authors, Messrs. Moak and Hillhouse, have cooperated in the welcome genesis of this authoritative and comprehensive volume, which began in inspiration several years ago with the work of Frederick L. Bird and the late Carl H. Chatters.

Lennox L. Moak is Director of Finance of the City of Philadelphia, his second tour of duty in that position. His other professional merits also credit him with being the first Budget Officer of the State of Louisiana in 1940. He has served as Director, Eastern Division, Pennsylvania Economy League and also served as Director of Personnel in New Orleans in 1942. He is Senior Lecturer at the Fels Institute of the University of Pennsylvania, and has been a lecturer in public finance at the Wharton School and the School of Fine Arts at the University of Pennsylvania during most of his 25 years in Philadelphia. He has written extensively in local government finance, including several books published by MFOA: *MFOA Operating Budget Manual*, *MFOA Capital Program and Capital Budget Manual* and *Budgeting for Smaller Governmental Units* (these with Kathryn Killian Gordon); and *Administration of Local Government Debt*, (MFOA, 1970).

Hillhouse is known to every student of local government finance for his landmark publication, *Municipal Bonds—A Century of Experience* (Prentice-Hall, 1936) and his co-authorship of *Local Government Debt Administration* (Prentice-Hall, 1939), as well as his *Where Cities Get Their Money* (MFOA, 1945). Following his service as Director of Research at MFOA 1934-1938, Hillhouse became Professor of Public Finance at Cornell University and continued his active teaching career until he retired as Professor Emeritus of Public Finance, The Graduate School of Business and Public Administration, Cornell University, in 1968. His research interests at Cornell have been in areas of measurement and performance evaluation as well as the more traditional concerns of local government finance.

The Municipal Finance Officers Association is grateful to the authors, and to Frederick L. Bird and the late Carl H. Chatters for the outstanding work over many years that brought about the publication of this fine book. MFOA is also indebted to the Earhart Foundation of Ann Arbor which provided financial support necessary for the preparation of the manuscript, and to the Fels Institute for releasing the time of Mr. Moak to enable him to complete this volume. We also extend devoted thanks to Kathryn Killian Gordon who assisted in the editing and final preparation of the manuscript for publication.

It is hoped that this volume will serve as a valuable reference for all persons involved in the administration of local government finance that makes possible the many public services governments provide.

DONALD W. BEATTY
Executive Director

Municipal Finance Officers
  Association of the United States
  and Canada

January, 1975

Preface

This volume has been prepared with a view to providing a general treatise on local government finance, with special emphasis upon the administrative aspects of each area covered. It is directed largely to the person who has some acquaintance with local government administration, but who has not had an opportunity to become widely acquainted with the financial aspects of carrying forward the programs of such governments.

Obviously, space limitations have precluded development in depth of any of the subjects treated. Yet, the authors have sought to provide an introduction which will be useful to public officials and employees and to serious students of local government finance.

The initiative for this volume came from conversations more than a decade ago between Richard A. Ware, President of the Earhart Foundation, Ann Arbor, Michigan, and the late Carl H. Chatters. When the completion of the project was in doubt in 1971, it was Ware who again took the initiative in revitalizing it.

Financing for the undertaking has come basically from the Earhart Foundation. Grants have paid for most of the time involved in writing and editing, as well as for most of the clerical and related costs. The City of Philadelphia has contributed some of the clerical assistance involved in typing drafts of the manuscript.

In the preparation of this volume, the authors have drawn upon both the literature and their own experiences in local government operations, and particularly the financial aspects of their experiences. The present volume is signed by two of the four authors who participated significantly in various phases of the development of this volume. The other two authors were:

- The late Carl H. Chatters who was the first Executive Director of the Municipal Finance Officers Association of the United States and Canada (1932-1945). After service in a number of other important capacities, he became City Comptroller, City of Chicago in 1955, in which position he served until shortly before his death in 1960. Chatters was co-author with Hillhouse in *Local Government Debt Administration*, published by Prentice-Hall in 1939. He prepared the application and secured the grant for the present volume; however, he died only a few months after work was commenced.

● Frederick L. Bird who was formerly director of the Municipal Department of Dun & Bradstreet. Bird has a wide knowledge based on experience with local government operations, with special emphasis on debt when he retired. Bird was most helpful in the early drafting of materials relating to debt. Following retirement, however, he was unable to continue active participation in this work.

The bulk of the remainder of the original drafts of this volume was prepared by Hillhouse during the last several years of his teaching. He used many of these materials in a public administration course at Cornell University prior to his becoming professor emeritus in 1968. Although the volume was brought substantially to publication stage in 1966, various problems intervened which precluded its publication at that time. Moak took over the updating and final editing of the volume in 1971 with planned publication early in 1973. However, his return to a second term as Director of Finance for the City of Philadelphia in January, 1972, slowed the completion of the book. At the final stage Hillhouse reviewed the manuscript and participated in some of the final revision work.

We wish especially to acknowledge assistance provided by a number of other people:

● Messrs. William G. Klenk, II, City Controller, Robert L. Greenberg, City Treasurer, Bernard B. Eiss, Director of Accounting, and Edward DeSeve, Deputy Director of Finance—all of the City of Philadelphia—for assistance in reading and criticizing various portions of the draft.

● Robert L. Funk of the Municipal Finance Officers Association for a very critical review of the manuscript.

● Kathryn Killian Gordon, long-time associate with Moak in writing several volumes published by MFOA on budgeting and capital programming, for updating and/or preparation of tabular materials and for editing much of the copy.

● Christina C. Ward, Secretary to Mr. Moak, for timely criticism and assistance at many phases of the preparation of the manuscript and seeing it through the printer.

● Ellen Brennan, Librarian, Eastern Division, Pennsylvania Economy League, Inc., for providing reference and library services in connection with most of the research during the past three years.

Finally, we wish to acknowledge the release of time for Mr. Moak by the Fels Institute of the University of Pennsylvania. Without the Institute having made this time available, it would not have been feasible to have brought this book to completion without substantial additional delay.

LENNOX L. MOAK   ALBERT M. HILLHOUSE
Philadelphia, Pa.   *Ithaca, New York*

November, 1974

Contents

LIST OF TABLES

LIST OF EXHIBITS

1

Nature of Local Government Finance

Local government finance, in the decades following World War II, has been thrust into new importance. Local governments in 1957 expended slightly over $30 billion, whereas in 1971 their total expenditures exceeded $105 billion. The primary reason has been the rapid growth of metropolitan aggregates of population. For better or for worse, we have become a nation of city people in heterogeneous urban concentrations. The urban community is rapidly becoming "America." Among other things, this means the compounding of mass transit problems, the pressure for new water supplies and for added drainage and sewage disposal facilities, and the urgent need for many other primary services. Abundant evidence has been amassed to demonstrate the impact such needs are having upon our national life.

Among this myriad of urban problems is that of urban finance. Local government officials and administrators need to consider such basic policy questions as:

The approach to be used to support the ever increasing demands upon urban governments

The structural framework which will enable urban finance to rise to its responsibilities

The allocation of the economic wealth in the metropolitan area to local governments so that they may play a viable role in rendering services

The appropriate division of responsibility for meeting urban needs among federal, state, and local governments

The allocation of resources to finance those functions of government that are to be performed at the local level

Complicated structural, legal, and political ramifications implicit in any financial rearrangements are all a part of the issue surrounding the future of urban finance.

Problems arise both as to the amassing of resources and the delivery of services. In some cases the effects of the division of labor among the levels of government are sharply defined and leave little doubt as to the need for change. For example, the geographic boundaries of numerous local governments are too limited to permit efficient revenue collection, especially for taxes such as those imposed on income or retail sales. In some instances, the state constitutes a better collection district or agency; in others, the federal government. On the other hand, local governments are generally close to the people. Their officials are best acquainted with the special circumstances of the community; they have

1

often proved themselves to be the best agency for the administration of programs which may be largely supported by state and federal transfer payments, i.e., subsidies. The alternatives open to state and federal governments in many situations are: (a) to use the local governments as agents at the final execution stage or (b) to establish a network of state or federal offices in hundreds of urban centers. To the extent that the first alternative has been chosen, both state and federal governments are finding themselves with a larger dollar stake in urban finance.

DEFINING THE NATURE AND SCOPE OF LOCAL GOVERNMENT FINANCE

There are three major ways to present the nature and scope of local government finance:

1. Direct—By defining its scope as a subject area, the size of the units involved, and its special characteristics: This approach affords a comprehensive listing of those jurisdictions, activities, overall revenues, and expenditures included and excluded within local finance and is a necessary first step towards knowledge of the subject.
2. Comparative—By placing it in sharp contrast with state finance and with federal finance: This approach allows evaluations to be made as to trends in the allocation of functional responsibilities and growth trends in financial statistics among the various levels of government.
3. Historical—By developing patterns of urban finance: A great deal is to be learned about local government finance by examining the major conditions which have influenced the development of its special features.

Since there are distinct advantages to all three approaches, each will be considered at some length.

The Direct Approach

As defined, the direct approach involves a long look at the scope and characteristics of local finance and the size of the units involved.

The Scope of Local Government Finance. Local finance embraces the affairs of a wide range of local governments, some geographically dispersed, others concentrated within expanding metropolitan areas. The subject, then, is as broad as the local finance laws, regulations, and practices of the 50 states, within both rural and urban areas. Encompassed within its scope are the finances of all local governments (counties, municipalities, and townships), special purpose districts (e.g., school, irrigation, reclamation, fire districts), and local authorities.

Local government finance is public finance exemplified and applied at one level of government. But the boundaries of the local level are fluid and subject to change, as may be illustrated by the following observations:

1. Local governments may find themselves divested of an old function through absorption by the state government

2. A former state source of revenue may also become a local source, or be given exclusively to certain classes of local units
3. Certain types of local borrowing, e.g., for school capital construction, may become guaranteed obligations of the state government
4. The federal government, through special purpose aids (categorical assistance), may share a local government expense now deemed in the national interest
5. The federal government or the state government may come to the aid of local government through general revenue-sharing

The scope of local government finance might also be explained in terms of the specific finance activities embraced within the four main traditional divisions of *revenues, expenditures, debt,* and *financial administration:*

1. Revenue administration, including the assessment of property for taxation and the many faceted elements of administration of nonproperty revenues
2. Programming and budgeting—for both operating and capital purposes
3. Administration of the financial elements of approved expenditure programs
4. Central processing of payrolls and accounts payable
5. Treasury management, including custody and payment of moneys on proper authorization as well as investment of funds available for short and long periods
6. Accounting
7. Auditing
8. Financial reporting
9. Debt administration, including the planning, issuance and servicing of the debt
10. Intergovernmental finance
11. Financial operations of publicly-owned utilities and other proprietary operations of the local government
12. State supervision and control of local government finance

In addition to these purely financial elements, it is customary to include with the finance group:

13. Supervision of insurance and fidelity bonds
14. Administration of retirement systems and elements of the fringe-benefit programs of local government employees
15. Procurement of materials, supplies, and equipment
16. Management of inventories
17. Advertising, receipt and tabulation of bids, and issuance of contracts for public works

Viewed more theoretically, local government finance contains all the main elements of the general area of public finance. To be more specific, it is concerned with:

1. The selection, levy, incidence, and effects of local taxes
2. The size of the local finance segment in the public sector

3. The economic impact of local taxation, expenditures, and borrowing upon the private sector of the economy
4. The contributions which local government finance, in the aggregate, may make to the countercyclical actions of the federal government and other federal fiscal policies
5. The effects of local government finance in developing equity in our society through the redistribution of money and/or services among citizens
6. Expenditure decision-making, involving the determination of priorities in using the funds available to local governments
7. Administration of the financial affairs of local governments

Table 1

A COMPARISON OF PAYMENTS FOR PERSONAL SERVICES IN 1970-71 IN THE 50 STATES AND THE 48 LARGEST CITIES

Millions of Dollars	Number		Cumulative Number	
	States	Cities	States	Cities
3,000 - 3,999	—	1	—	1
2,000 - 2,999	1	—	1	1
1,000 - 1,999	1	—	2	1
900 - 999	3	—	5	1
800 - 899	1	—	6	1
700 - 799	1	—	7	1
600 - 699	—	—	7	1
500 - 599	4	2	11	3
400 - 499	8	1	19	4
300 - 399	5	2	24	6
200 - 299	8	3	32	9
100 - 199	9	6	41	15
90 - 99	2	3	43	18
80 - 89	3	3	46	21
70 - 79	2	—	48	21
60 - 69	1	3	49	24
50 - 59	1	8	50	32
40 - 49	—	5	50	37
30 - 39	—	5	50	42
20 - 29	—	5	50	47
10 - 19	—	1	50	48
Total	50	48		

Sources: Based on information from the Bureau of the Census, *State Government Finances in 1971*, p. 27 and *City Government Finances in 1970-71*, pp. 87-100.

Table 2
A COMPARISON OF CAPITAL OUTLAYS IN 1970-71
IN THE 50 STATES AND THE 48 LARGEST CITIES

Millions of Dollars	Number		Cumulative Number	
	States	Cities	States	Cities
1,000 - 1,999	3	—	3	—
900 - 999	—	1	3	1
800 - 899	—	—	3	1
700 - 799	1	—	4	1
600 - 699	1	—	5	1
500 - 599	2	—	7	1
400 - 499	1	—	8	1
300 - 399	8	—	16	1
200 - 299	10	—	26	1
100 - 199	13	5	39	6
90 - 99	—	—	39	6
80 - 89	1	2	40	8
70 - 79	6	1	46	9
60 - 69	2	3	48	12
50 - 59	2	1	50	13
40 - 49	—	2	50	15
30 - 39	—	13	50	28
20 - 29	—	7	50	35
10 - 19	—	11	50	46
0 - 9	—	2	50	48
Total	50	48		

Sources: Based on information from the U.S. Bureau of the Census,
State Government Finances in 1971, p. 27 and
City Government Finances in 1970-71, pp. 87-100.

Size of the Units Involved in Local Finance. If size is a criterion of financial importance, one could begin with the population size of cities. In 1970,[1] there were 153 cities whose populations exceed 100,000; six of these cities number one million or more inhabitants; and some 48 of this group exceed the 300,000 population mark, ranging from Birmingham, Alabama, with 300,910 residents to New York City with 7.9 million. Legalistically, New York, Chicago, Los Angeles, and other cities are mere "political sub-divisions" of the state, but they

---

[1] Bureau of the Census, U. S. Department of Commerce, *Statistical Abstract of the United States, 1973,* (Washington, 1973), pp. 14-15, 22-25.

Table 3
A COMPARISON OF THE TOTAL DEBT OUTSTANDING IN 1970-71
IN THE 50 STATES AND THE 48 LARGEST CITIES

Millions of Dollars	Number		Cumulative Number	
	States	Cities	States	Cities
10,000 - 10,999	—	1	—	1
9,000 - 9,999	—	—	—	1
8,000 - 8,999	1	—	1	1
7,000 - 7,999	—	—	1	1
6,000 - 6,999	—	—	1	1
5,000 - 5,999	1	—	2	1
4,000 - 4,999	—	—	2	1
3,000 - 3,999	1	—	3	1
2,000 - 2,999	2	—	5	1
1,000 - 1,999	8	3	13	4
900 - 999	2	—	15	4
800 - 899	2	—	17	4
700 - 799	2	1	19	5
600 - 699	3	1	22	6
500 - 599	3	1	25	7
400 - 499	3	3	28	10
300 - 399	4	6	32	16
200 - 299	3	11	35	27
100 - 199	7	14	42	41
90 - 99	1	1	43	42
80 - 89	1	3	44	45
70 - 79	1	—	45	45
60 - 69	—	1	45	46
50 - 59	—	1	45	47
40 - 49	3	—	48	47
30 - 39	2	1	50	48
20 - 29	—	—	50	48
Total	50	48		

Sources: Based on information from the U.S. Bureau of the Census,
State Government Finances in 1971, p. 40 and
City Government Finances in 1970-71, pp. 87-100.

rival many of the state governments in population size. New York City's population outranks 43 of the states (excluding only the states of New York, California, Pennsylvania, Illinois, Ohio, Texas, and Michigan). Chicago (which is less than half the size of New York City) outranks any one of 28 states. The United States has 10 cities with a population of over 750,000 and 10 states with a population of under 750,000. There are 42 cities each of which has a population greater than that of Wyoming, and 47 cities each of which outranks Alaska in population.

As to financial size, the preceding three tables show that among our cities there are some giants whose expenditures rival those of state governments. The comparison in each table is between the 50 states and the 48 largest cities, as to total expenditures for personal services and capital outlay in 1971 and the amount of total debt outstanding.

New York City with $3.86 billion for personal services exceeded all of the states' expenditures in this category. No additional cities, but eleven states expended $500 million or more for personal services. And, although one-half the states spend $300 million or more in this category and about one-half the 48 cities spend $60 million or less, 15 cities actually spend more for personal services than seven of the states.

The states of California, New York, and Pennsylvania all surpassed New York City in 1971 with capital outlays of $1 billion or more. However, seven cities—New York ($985 million), Los Angeles ($190 million), Chicago ($140 million), Sacramento ($140 million), Philadelphia ($169 million), Washington ($123 million), and Baltimore ($129 million)—exceeded the capital expenditures of 11 states. However, whereas capital outlays in more than half of the states exceeded $100 million, capital expenditures in over half of the 48 cities ranged between $7 million and $39 million.

Comparing total debt outstanding, four cities and 13 states show a debt figure of $1 billion or more. New York City with a $10 billion debt figure outranked all other cities and all 50 states; New York State followed closely with an $8 billion debt figure. The total debt outstanding in four-fifths of all the states and four-fifths of the largest cities exceeded $100 million. Only five states and three cities showed a debt figure of $50 million or less.

As a revenue collector, only New York City rivals some of the populous states. According to their 1971 revenue collections (total general revenue as defined by the Bureau of Census excluding intergovernmental revenues), the first ten governments (states and cities) were:

	(billions)
New York State	$7.11
California	6.52
New York City	3.96
Illinois	3.51
Pennsylvania	3.47
Michigan	3.02
Texas	2.71
Ohio	2.23
New Jersey	1.82
Florida	1.80

The provision of urban renewal funds by the Congress and the establishment, within the federal government, of the Department of Housing and Urban Development are both evidence of the growing recognition in Washington that

Table 4
LOCAL GOVERNMENT FINANCE IN THE TOTAL PUBLIC FINANCE SECTOR
1970-1971
(amounts in billions of dollars)

Item	All Governments Amount	All Governments Percent	Federal Amount	Federal Percent	State Amount	State Percent	Local Amount	Local Percent	Percentage Distribution Among Levels of Government Federal	State	Local
Revenue from All Sources	342.5	100.0	202.5	100.0	97.2	100.0	100.9	100.0	n.a.	n.a.	n.a.
Intergovernmental Revenue	—		—		23.8	24.5	34.5	34.2	n.a.	n.a.	n.a.
Revenue from Own Sources	342.5	100.0	202.5	100.0	73.4	75.5	66.5	65.9	59.1	21.4	19.4
General Revenue from Own Sources	275.7	80.5	156.9	77.5	61.3	63.0	57.5	57.0	56.9	22.2	20.9
Taxes	232.3	67.8	137.3	67.8	51.5	53.0	43.4	43.0	59.1	22.2	18.7
Charges and Misc. General Revenue	43.4	12.7	19.6	9.7	9.7	10.0	14.1	13.9	45.2	22.4	32.5
Current Charges	29.3	8.6	12.4	6.1	7.1	7.3	9.8	9.7	42.3	24.2	33.4
All Other	14.1	4.1	7.2	3.5	2.7	2.8	4.2	4.2	51.1	19.1	29.8
Utility Revenue	7.3	2.1	—		—		7.3	7.2	—	—	100.0
Liquor Store Revenue	2.1	0.6	—		1.8	1.9	0.3	0.3	—	85.7	14.3
Insurance Trust Revenue	57.5	16.8	45.7	22.5	10.3	10.6	1.5	1.5	79.5	17.9	2.6
Total Expenditure	369.4	100.0	226.2	100.0	98.8	100.0	105.2	100.0	n.a.	n.a.	n.a.
Intergovernmental Expenditure	—		27.5	12.2	32.6	33.0	0.6	0.6	n.a.	n.a.	n.a.
Direct Expenditure	369.4	100.0	198.7	87.8	66.2	67.0	104.6	99.4	53.8	17.9	28.3
Current Operation	214.7	58.1	102.9	45.5	35.8	36.3	76.0	72.3	47.9	16.7	35.4
Capital Outlay	48.8	13.2	15.7	6.9	14.7	14.9	18.4	17.5	32.2	30.1	37.7
Assistance Subsidies	25.4	6.9	15.3	6.8	5.5	5.6	4.6	4.3	60.2	21.7	18.1
Interest on Debt	22.5	6.1	16.6	7.3	1.8	1.8	4.1	3.9	73.8	8.0	18.2
Insurance benefits and Repayments	58.0	15.7	48.2	21.3	8.3	8.4	1.5	1.4	83.1	14.3	2.6
Exhibit: Expenditure for Personal Services	120.1	32.5	49.5	21.9	19.9	20.2	50.6	48.2	41.2	16.6	42.1
Number of Civilian Employees	13.3	—	2.9	—	2.8	—	7.6	—	21.8	21.1	57.1
Total Debt Outstanding	556.9	—	398.1	—	47.8	—	111.0	—	71.5	8.6	19.9

Source: U.S. Bureau of the Census, Governmental Finances in 1970-71, pp. 4, 6, and 28; Public Employment in 1971, pp. 1–3.

cities are of high-ranking importance. Despite this, and despite the weight of the facts, attitudes toward urban finance persist which have deep roots in hierarchical thinking. The federal government is larger than any state, and the state is geographically larger than any of its "political subdivisions." A city is a political subdivision; therefore, it stands on the lower rungs. One cannot deny that urban finance is overshadowed by the magnitude of the federal government's taxes, budget, and debt—all concentrated in a single government; yet, the importance of local government finance needs re-examination. When considering the relative importance of federal, state, and local expenditures, it is noted that federal expenditures constituted 54 percent of the total expenditures of all governments in 1971 and local governments expended 28 percent. As may be seen in the detailed figures for 1971 contained in Table 4, federal revenue sources, as a percentage of total public revenues, exceed both state and local revenues, which roughly approximate each other for each of the sources specified. However, on the expenditure side, the percentages show that federal and local spending surpass state spending in the categories of current operation, capital outlay, and interest on their debt. Expenditures for personal services by the federal government and all local governments are equal, both as to amounts and the percentage of the total which those amounts represent. In addition, local governments account for 57 percent of total public employment. As to total debt outstanding, the federal government accounts for the lion's share—71 percent and local governments for 20 percent. In the overall, local governments account for somewhat less than one-third of the revenues generated and the moneys expended in the public sector.

The drive for "city-states," especially where the metropolitan areas straddle state boundaries, will no doubt one day force a re-evaluation of the place of local government finance. The scope of the big city's responsibilities for public services and the staggering numbers of its clientele make obsolete the older hierarchical ranking. Yet, this relic of legalism is embedded in the law, in our church structure, and in common thought patterns.

Attitudes toward cities require radical adjustment. In many of our large cities, the director of finance in charge of a centralized department of finance has a dollar responsibility which can be outranked only by high finance officials in the United States Treasury Department, the Director of the Budget, the Department of Defense, and the top finance officials in about ten states. Moreover, his responsibility as regards revenue collection, budgeting, debt management, purchasing, accounting, and auditing often exceeds that in most of the attractive finance jobs in the federal government because of the high degree of specialization in such federal positions and the scattering of expenditure control thoughout the OMB (Office of Management and Budget), the Treasury Department, and the General Accounting Office.

Special Characteristics of Local Finance. Local government finance has many distinguishing characteristics including the following:

The property tax remains the main source of revenue for most local governments but has lost its former dominant position in many individual local government revenue programs.

Many of the larger urban municipalities have adequate economic resources within their geographic boundaries but are restricted by state statutes or the state constitution in their power to tax these sources. The result is often inadequate locally-collected revenues to support a high standard of local services. An unwise and prodigal use of unlimited powers of taxation can lead to differentials between the city and its neighbors, which in turn can result in economic disadvantage to the city.

Local finance is partially dependent upon, and is usually supplemented by, financial help from higher levels. Such assistance has become increasingly necessary.

Municipalities now spend more than they collect. With the dispensers of aid showing increased interest in improved programming and budgeting and in more sophisticated expenditure controls, local officials must, of necessity, give greater attention to improved expenditure administration.

Local finance policy must ordinarily be conceived, planned, and executed within (1) a restrictive constitutional and statutory framework, (2) an administrative supervisory network from state capitals, and (3) controls imposed by the federal government as a condition of the receipt of loans or other financial assistance.

Local finance is vulnerable to adverse financial decisions made at higher levels. To take two illustrations:

1. Lucrative revenue sources may be pre-empted by the state government or materially affected by federal use of the same sources
2. A city's property assessment base may be reduced without warning by new property tax exemptions voted by the legislature or by the acquisition of property within city limits by the federal or state governments

Local finance has historically been the favorite "beat" of the reformer, who has roads open to him in seeking to accomplish his goals. He may proceed through the local legislative body, the state legislature, the Congress, or the courts. In the latter he may find success through legal action before indulgent judges turned policy-makers.

Local finance is much less glamorous than state or federal finance. It is often difficult to attract top-level talent.

Fragmented local government structures produce fragmentation in discharging community responsibilities:

1. In general, each unit proceeds policy-wise and administratively as if it were the only local unit in the area.
2. The fallacy of this layer-cake approach to the utilization of public finance resources is underscored by its rejection in the investment market. There, the municipal bond analysts proceed with a total community financial analysis, attempting to provide meaningful summaries of overlapping and underlying district factors.

Despite this tendency to proceed unilaterally, the finances of local units are interdependent. For example, a city's credit rating will be affected by the financial condition and outstanding debt of its geographical associates. And, the citizen will be concerned about the totality of his bill for all local governmental services.

Because local finance has had to overcome serious obstacles, and because there are so many local governments and in such variety, this area of public finance has been a fertile field for innovations. Many new financial improvements have sprung from this area: the standardization and improvement of governmental accounting, the initial formulation of the current budget process, the later performance or program budget, the capital budget process, and the revenue bond investment program—to mention a few.

Local finance is an area where highly trained individuals (such as the municipal bond attorney, the investment banker, the civil engineer, the planning consultant, and the finance consultant) have had a large hand in shaping policies and the trend of events.

The Comparative Approach

This approach details the similarities and differences which exist between local, state, and federal finance, respectively.

Comparison with State Finance. State finance and local finance are so closely connected that it is not always possible to write of each separately. Rather, there exists a form of partnership—a combined state and local finance system—in which the state is the general and managing partner and the localities, the limited partners. It is feasible, however, to contrast certain aspects of the combined system.

1. The state, a larger geographic area, is a more effective tax collection district for most nonproperty taxes than even the largest of the local governments within a state.

2. Because of the geographical dispersion of state institutions (such as hospitals, mental and penal facilities, and colleges and universities), the states have developed a type of functional finance supervision (central office-field agency relationship), which is relatively unimportant at the local level. Local governments are more compact geographically which makes possible a greater centralization of finance activities than possible in most states.

3. The local tax base is narrower, despite permissive legislation in some states granting broad revenue powers to their local subdivisions. Local governments still depend heavily upon the property tax for their main support. This may mean inadequate financial resources; it also tends to make property tax exemptions by the state legislature a serious problem at the local level.

4. Most local governments are subject to a degree of continuing legislative control rarely experienced in state finance. First, the former is governed by two legislative bodies—the local council or board and the state legislature. Secondly, the local council or board is a continuing governing body meeting regularly, whereas the state legislature is in session

intermittently, and then usually adjourns after a few months. Third, constitutional and statutory restrictions on local finance are greater and usually based on formulae which often cannot take into account the full significance of the variables which exist among the governments subject to each such regulation. (The most serious example of the latter are the state debt limitations in some jurisdictions.)

5. States are dispensers of grants-in-aid and, as such, set the standards for the various types of state aid. With only a few exceptions, local governments make no grants-in-aid to other governments. However, they have access to both state and federal aid, while the states have only one outside aid source to which they may turn.

6. The state government imposes prohibitions and restrictions and, in many service areas, mandates certain requirements. The state has the supervisory and enforcement powers; while the local units must assume the duty of compliance. Since the states are not "political subdivisions" of the federal government they are not subject to mandated expenditures—except as a part of the contract involved in acceptance of the provisions of federal law, e.g., employment security or of federal categorical grants. Such federal financial supervision or regulation over state governments, as may be exercised, grows out of a mutually agreed contractual relationship. Otherwise, the state, in contrast to local governments, need not seek permission in finance matters.

7. If a state has a progressive tax system[2] and well developed grant-in-aid programs, the distributive impact of its tax and expenditure policies is probably more significant than that of all the local governments in the state combined.

8. Special assessment levies and special assessment bonds are found at the local but not at the state level.

9. Local governments operate more proprietary enterprises than the states. As a result, they make extensive use of the type of revenue bond which is supported by enterprise earnings. The states have gone further than local governments with the special tax obligation (also classified by some as a revenue) bond.

10. A good many states prepare budgets which cover two one-year periods.

---

[2] A "progressive" revenue system is ordinarily defined as one which requires contributions by individuals (or the family as an economic group) on a basis that results in higher percentages of money and/or economic income as such income increases.

A "neutral" revenue system is ordinarily defined as one which requires contributions by individuals (or the family as an economic group) substantially in proportion to their money and/or economic income.

A "regressive" revenue system is ordinarily defined as one which requires contributions by individuals (or the family as an economic group) on a basis that results in lower percentage levies as income increases—or, conversely, imposes a higher burden in relation to income upon the lower income persons.

It is to be noted that these concepts do not take into account the benefits derived from the operations of governmental finance. Many students hold that it is not appropriate to consider only the revenue side of the governmental equation but also the economic benefits derived from the operations of government.

Only a small number of local units have experimented with current budgets beyond a one-year period.

11. Many local governments have adopted fairly comprehensive capital budgets. In state governments, with some important exceptions, the capital budgeting process is still underdeveloped.

12. A municipality has access to Title XI of the Federal Bankruptcy Act, but state governments do not.

13. Since local governments go out of existence (principally school and other special-purpose districts), the problem of debt succession arises in municipal finance. To date, this problem has not arisen at the state level.

Comparison with Federal Finance. In general, the differences between federal finance and local finance are much wider than those between state finance and local finance. The most important differences are:

1. The federal government has greater access to more lucrative taxes, including the income tax, and can more effectively administer certain taxes because of its national scope. The penalties for federal tax evasion are greater and are more respected by the citizenry. Local revenue sources tend to provide more stable yields than federal revenue sources.

2. The operation of the federal tax system is uniform throughout the nation and, therefore, has a neutral effect upon the location of business enterprises and individuals. On the other hand, local taxes are applicable only to very limited geographical areas with the result that differentials in the kinds of taxes used and the rates at which they are imposed can have a significant influence upon the locational decisions of individuals and businesses.

3. The federal government with income, estate, and gift taxes possesses more effective means for the redistribution of income and wealth.

4. Because local governments make use of a different range of revenues (user-charges, business and occupational licenses, etc.), the problems of tax incidence are not the same. The benefit principle has more applicability at the local level.

5. Local governments spend more money than they collect from taxpayers. Consequently, the theory of expenditures and expenditure control takes on special significance. With a probable increase in state and federal grants-in-aid and revenue-sharing, the role of local governments as administrative and spending units will probably be increased. Nevertheless, the sheer size of federal government expenditures, and the potentiality for better control within a single governmental unit, place the control problem at the federal level in a priority all its own.

6. The concept of balancing the budget is different at federal and local levels. By long custom, local and state governments attain a balanced budget when revenues cover current operating and debt service requirements. The balanced budget concept is not violated if the government borrows more for capital improvements than it retires. By way of contrast, the federal government budget is "balanced" only when total outgo, including capital expenditures, is no greater than income.

7. At the local level the capital program and capital budget are instruments for planning both long-term and short-term capital improvements and the means of financing such improvements. Because of the compactness of the geographic area, these processes have a more visible impact upon the physical attributes of the locality and upon future growth than do most federal capital outlays have on the nation. At the federal level, no formal capital program and capital budget processes exist outside the regular budget operations. Vast amounts of capital expenditures are made for military and other purposes but these are usually financed from current revenues. A capital program for the federal government is condemned by some economists on the basis that it would tend to weaken, or destroy, the requirement for budget balancing except under emergency conditions. To date no substitute has been found for the constraints which this politically accepted goal has imposed. The arguments against multiple budgeting at the federal government level do not apply at the local level.

8. Federal government borrowing is not tied to particular capital improvements, or even necessarily to capital expenditures. When the federal government borrows, it is to meet a deficit no matter how it has arisen. The market does not inquire whether the new issue is for a hydro-electric plant, a postal system deficit, or other purposes. By way of contrast, the investment market usually examines closely the purposes of local bond issues.

9. The federal government itself issues only general obligation bonds and notes; however, various federal agencies may issue revenue bonds upon authorization of the Congress. Local governments may directly issue general obligation bonds and revenue bonds, when authorized by proper authority.

10. The largest increases in federal debt usually come in war periods and during serious depressions. By way of contrast, local long-term debt tends to show the greatest increase in periods of prosperity.

11. The federal debt limit is more flexible than the debt limits under which local governments generally operate. The federal government has a wider variety of debt instruments than any single local unit and makes a much greater use of short-term debt. Local bond issues must face both credit and market acceptability. As for federal issues, there is no question as to the credit risk; analysis is focused on the instrument and the market. Interest on federal debt is taxed under the federal income tax laws, whereas interest on the great majority of local debt is exempt under such laws. Local debt is less usable as a fiscal-monetary instrument because it is more subject to market conventions and requirements and because the market channels do not involve direct use of the Federal Reserve banks. Finally, local debt is usually external debt (i.e., external to its own geographic boundaries); whereas federal debt is primarily a domestic debt burden.

12. Because of the high rate of migration of residents into and out of most urban communities, the method of financing capital improvements at

the local level raises a question of equity not found at the federal level. The question is that of pay-as-you-spend vs. pay-as-you-use.

13. The countercyclical potentialities of local finance in the aggregate are not unimportant but are comparatively more difficult to harness. Federal finance contains more powerful taxing, spending, and other fiscal weapons because of its sheer size, its wider geographic reaches, its direct link with the Federal Reserve banking system, and the greater ease of action and flexibility possible in a single unit of government.

14. The problems of state-local relations do not raise the same political and legal questions as federal-local relations or, indeed, federal-state relations. The first mentioned arise out of the legal status of creator and created, the sovereign and the subordinate unit. The issue of home rule arises, but home rule is frequently more a conceptual ideal and slogan than a reality. Many federal-local relations are established contractually. But, the bypassing of state governments in federal aid to local governments and the entrance of the federal government into areas formerly controlled by the states, raise important political questions concerning the viability of the federal system and the future role of the states.

15. Local units are generally the supervised rather than the supervisory government. The upper level approach, including the setting of standards and policy guidelines, belong more to the states and the federal government. It currently appears that the federal government will, in time, assume even larger responsibilities for local services as they are viewed more in the light of national welfare interests. On the other hand, the local governments are closer to the people and, within areas where there is local autonomy, they are more responsive to public demands. Still, the framework for social decision-making is more narrow.

16. From sheer size, governmental accounting, the problems of post-audit, financial reporting, and budgeting in a mammoth organization mean that administrative problems at the local and federal levels are developing quite differently. The differences were not so marked prior to World War II. At an earlier date, many of the municipal developments were more easily emulated in the federal government.

17. Because of the fiscal policy impacts of federal finance, professional economists are much more interested in federal than local finance. This, of course, accounts for some of the differences in emphasis in the literature of these two segments of public finance.

18. As a subject matter area, local finance usually embraces such activities as purchasing, stores, property insurance, bonding, and personal property management, which are generally not considered a part of federal finance.

19. As to location of the finance function within the federal government structure, finance offices are found at many levels of the hierarchy. To take one illustration, budget offices exist at the departmental and the bureau levels and are subordinate to the Office of Management and Budget in the Executive Office of the President. In some agencies,

budget offices are required at lower rungs in the structure, including field offices and armed services command posts. This centralization with successive decentralization is the result of the staggering size and the long pipelines through which finance activities must be handled. Nothing comparable exists in local government; however, the very large municipal governments are beginning to develop characteristics similar in some respects to federal procedure.

In stressing differences, it is necessary to remember also that, in many cases, we are concerned with distinctions that arise from the magnitude of federal financial operations. Many parallels between federal and local finance exist even though found in different contexts.

To the student interested in the comparative approach, the field offers many opportunities. Our big cities and their metropolitan complexes are widely dispersed geographically. Local finance in each of the 50 states is governed within a different statutory and constitutional framework. There are likenesses, but a diversity of approach also exists. Much could be learned from a wider use of the comparative method.

The Historical Approach

One cannot completely grasp the nature and scope of local finance unless one understands in broad outlines its development.

Development of Local Government Finance Patterns. There are three main features in the background of local finance which stand out:

1. The separation of education from local government and the professional attempt (with great success) to insulate it from other municipal service functions
2. The widening market for local government bonds
3. The dominant position of the property tax in the local revenue structure

The split between the "city hall" and the professional educators and the latter's rise in influence have altered the structure of local government and have given the school supporters a special access to borrowing power and to state grants-in-aid which is not available (to the same degree) to other service functions. The results constitute one of the most difficult forms of cleavage in the local government structure. Also, the schools formed the prototype of the special purpose district which, no doubt, helped to influence the patterns of creation of other special districts. From a scientific viewpoint, the secession of the education function has also meant the growth of a body of school finance literature which has ignored much of the parallel developments in other areas of local finance.

It is interesting, however, to note that as public school districts in the major urban cities, e.g., Philadelphia and Detroit, encountered severe financial difficulties following aggressive unionization in the late 1960s and early 1970s, the school district officials turned, in large measure, to the mayors of those cities to help find a way to keep the schools open. So the separation is now undergoing change in some areas.

The widening market for local government bonds is a second basic feature in the development of urban finance. The tax exempt feature of this debt has been most advantageous to government at the local level. It has given the local units the important independence which they now enjoy. Ready access to the investment market has meant great strength in local capital financing as opposed to the possible alternatives of a dependent reliance upon loans from state governments, or upon federal loans, or upon a federally-supported municipal bond bank system designed to create a secondary reserve market for municipal bonds.

But, it has been the dominant role of the property tax in the local revenue structure which has made it the greatest influence in shaping local finance as we know it today. So much of the development of local finance can be written in terms of all the restrictive measures which have been devised to protect the property owner, and the efforts, in reaction or counteraction, which were made to break these restrictions so that local governments might meet the growing service demands placed upon them. The main restrictive measures have been:

Property tax limitations
Debt limitations
State supervision (and often control) of local budgets
The requirement of bond referenda

In the face of the unwillingness of legislators and citizens directly to afford needed constitutional relief, methods of circumvention had to be discovered if local governments were to meet their responsibilities. An array of layer upon layer of "new approaches" and their paraphernalia are the result. Some have different and often ingenious forms:

1. Referenda which would permit the voters by mandate to exceed constitutional or statutory limits

2. Fragmentation of local government, with complex patterns of taxing districts in layers, each with a new tax and debt limit—except in those jurisdictions where debt and/or tax limits were applied to the total underlying and overlapping local government structure

3. Use of the local authority device which shifted the method of financing to a user tax or to enterprise earnings

4. Creation of new variations of the revenue bond which has pushed capital financing even further away from property tax support

5. Wider use of special fund bonds which require no pledge of the property tax

6. Creation of authorities to issue debt based on lease-back arrangements which in turn involved indirect pledging of taxes to support debt that was issued in revenue form

7. Growth of nonproperty tax revenues

8. Shift of some local government functions to the state level where taxing powers are broader

9. Increasing use of state grants-in-aid and, more recently, federal grants-in-aid as a supplement to local revenue sources—methods which are slowly transferring local governments more markedly into spending units, as opposed to collecting and spending units

Embedded in this development of local finance by action and reaction lie much of the detail of the peculiar nature and slowly expanding scope of local finance. These details will constitute the background for any movement to rationalize the local government structure and create a more defensible system of financing the important service responsibilities of local government.

Relativity of the Subject

The relativity of municipal finance was adequately expressed many years ago by Professor Robinson:

. . . What are in practice regarded as the proper objects of local expenditure and the proper sources of local revenue vary from country to country with geographical conditions, historical associations, and political traditions; and vary from period to period in the same country with changes in economic and social conditions and changes in the relative efficiency of the local and central governing authorities.

There are indeed certain kinds of public expenditure which are so clearly national in scope that they must on grounds of efficiency and economy always be left to the central authority whether in a federal or unitary state (e.g., National defense services). On the other hand, the public provision of certain services (such, for instance, as a town gas supply) is so obviously of local interest that even in the most highly centralized State it would be left to some local authority. Apart from these extreme cases, there are a vast number of forms of Government expenditure which are both of national and local importance, and the division of the responsibility for such expenditure between the central and local authorities will in practice, as we have already said, depend upon a variety of constitutional, political and geographical conditions.[3]

SOME OTHER CONSIDERATIONS

Although the foregoing portion of this chapter serves to provide a general description of the nature of local government finance, it is in order to introduce several other dimensions before moving on to the more definitive aspects of the general subject. Accordingly, represented below are comments relating to:

1. The economist's approach to local government finance
2. The political scientist's approach to local government finance
3. The general relationship of local government finance to the private sector
4. The "status" of local government finance in academic curricula

---

[3] Robinson, M. E., *Public Finance*, (New York: Harcourt, Brace and Co., 1922), pp. 102-103.

The Economist's Approach to Local Government Finance

As a part of public finance, local finance is not without interest to the macro-economist, but, in his aggregative approach and in sector analysis, he usually treats state and local finance together. The national account data and other statistics lend themselves to this approach. If he is concerned with counter-cyclical measures, he again looks at state and local finance as a unit. Some would contend that state and local finance, with federal government incentives, should be accorded a positive role in counteracting depression forces or, alternatively, measures might be planned which would neutralize their role. At least one major study has been made as to how many local governments and special authorities have capital improvements in sufficient magnitude to justify enlisting their co-operation, along with that of the 50 states, should a coordinated public works program be used as one major countercyclical measure.

Some of the macro approach is present in municipal finance thinking, but, on the whole, state and local finance lie within the area of micro-economics. The state and local finance administrator is interested in such problems as tax incidence; the effects of particular taxes upon individual industries or businesses; the use by municipalities of certain nonproperty tax revenues; grant-in-aid- programs; the problems presented by state-collected, locally-shared taxes; the tax-exempt feature of state and municipal securities; other state-local and federal-state fiscal relationships; and questions of equity as to specific proposals in the tax structure.

Within general welfare economics, many problems involving local finance directly, or peripherally, invite attention: the distributive vs. the service function of state and local finance; the use of municipal-enterprise pricing policies for welfare purposes; methods of policy decision-making as between the majority and minorities; the economic problems of the central city at the metropolitan core; the role of state and federal aid in economically depressed local governments and in school finance within federally-impacted areas. The services of local governments are frequently very close to the "have nots," but when areas are poverty-stricken on a general economic basis, one finds that their economic capacity to raise revenue will also have been seriously weakened.

The Political Scientist's Approach to Local Government Finance

The International City Managers' Association a quarter century ago helped to put this matter of the political scientist's approach into focus when it observed:

The student of government has a very real interest in problems of public finance, for control of the pursestrings has always been an important source of political power. Generally speaking, the political scientist's interest in municipal finance centers around such subjects as control of public expenditures, the distribution of tax burdens among different groups, and the uses of taxation as means of social control or regulation. The political scientist is more interested in finance administration than the economist, but his interest is likely to be focused upon the essential features of structure and relationships, not upon operating procedure. For example, he is more concerned with the distribution of fiscal powers between the legislative and administrative branches than with the number and nature of funds in the accounting system, the specific uses of cost accounting data, or methods of enforcing tax collections.[4]

To this we would add a few more specifics. Among the political scientist's interests might also be found:

1. The alignment of various community forces in the resolution of financial issues

2. The legal framework within which local finance must operate, especially the political and other forces at work to write into the statutes new and more effective restrictive and control devices and, simultaneously, other contending forces interested in discovering ways to escape or to break down both old and new restrictions

3. The influences of finance upon the structure and growth of local government

4. The bureaucracy of finance administration

5. The fiscal contacts among grass-roots governments and the intergovernmental relationships between the three main levels of government

6. Within the comparative field, a contrast between the approaches used by a unitary state and a federal state, respectively, in the solution of local financial problems

Other Approaches

The municipal bond attorney, the municipal bond dealer (investment banker), the institutional investor, the certified public accountant, the consulting engineer, the municipal finance consultant, the city planner, the taxpayers' association, the general public—these and others bring their own special viewpoints to bear on local finance. To take one example, the municipal bond attorney's role is to see that the bond instrument meets all legal tests and, by strict adherence to this role, regardless of his immediate client, he protects all interests concerned.

Relation of Local Government Finance to the Private Sector

An explanation of the varied viewpoints above would underscore how closely related local finance is to the private sector. The supplier of goods and services may be just as interested in city hall as a customer as in a private corporate customer. There are manufacturers who produce almost exclusively for municipal purchasers of equipment and supplies. Construction and consulting engineers, contractors, and architects have municipal clients as well as individual and corporate clients. A firm of certified public accountants may have a staff which specializes in governmental accounting and auditing as well as

---

[4] International City Managers' Association, *Municipal Finance Administration*, 4th ed., (Chicago: International City Managers' Association, 1949), p. 1.

commercial accounting staffs. Dun & Bradstreet, Standard and Poor's, Moodys' Investor Service, *The Bond Buyer*, and *The Blue List* link the issuing municipality, the intermediary dealers, and the ultimate investor. What is debt in the public sector is an investment in the private sector and vice versa to the extent that local and state governments own private securities in pension and other funds.

Finally, there is the average citizen's approach. One need only contemplate a few examples of the variegated patterns of business and civic life to which the citizen must adjust himself in order to understand that municipal activities may have become somewhat lost for him. At best, they are taken for granted. Not only is the local government structure complicated (general and special purpose districts, semi-independent utility boards or commissions, and local authorities) but also the activities of voluntary membership groups, religious nonprofit organizations, and a host of industrial and commercial firms add complexity through their different patterns of ownership and operation. Our mixed enterprise system (private, voluntary nonprofit, and public) contains both variety without duplication and variety with duplication:

Variety Without Duplication. Services furnished to citizens by either a public or private agency (but not both) include:

A city water plant, a metropolitan authority sewage disposal plant, and a privately owned electric plant or other public utility

A nationwide telegraph system, a statewide telephone company, and a local privately owned television cable system

A privately-endowed local history and genealogical library open to the public, and a general municipal library

Variety With Duplication. Services which are performed on both a public and private basis include:

The United States Postal Service and the Railway Express Agency (a private corporation competing with the Postal Service for parcel shipments)

The governmental police (FBI, state police, the county sheriff and his deputies, the city police, school traffic guards) and private guards (at banks and other commercial establishments)

A state agricultural college dairy and milk bar and privately owned dairies and milk outlets

A privately owned commercial park with bathing facilities, a membership country club, a membership athletic club, and institutional athletic and recreational facilities (YMCA, YMHA, or CYO) vs. a city park with beaches and public pools, a state park in the environs with similar facilities, or a public school swimming pool

Small wonder that much of this leaves the average citizen baffled or indifferent, and that local government and local government finance remain for him something either too commonplace for serious study or too mysterious to tackle—or is so submerged among other components of his life that they never enter for long into his stream of action-thinking.

Status in Academia

State and local finance in some universities suffered heavily with the vast expansion of federal finance during the Great Depression and World War II and with the influx of Keynesian economics. Emphasis shifted to fiscal policy, and a new generation of economists brought public finance back into the mainstream of economics and economic theory. Neglect of state and especially local finance must be viewed as a by-product of an otherwise healthy and stimulating renaissance for economics.

With the lively emphasis today on urban studies, the economic base of our metropolitan centers, and the integration of planning and economics into a regional science, one can expect local finance to make a new place for itself in the academic hierarchy, especially in universities located in urban settings.

At present, there is diversity as to the location of local finance in the curriculum. It is a separate public administration course in some universities, especially where training for the "city" management profession is emphasized. In others, state and local finance has regained a place as a part of the public finance concentration in the economics department. In addition to separate courses, segments of the subject matter appear in the state and local government course in political science departments, and in a course on the law of local government in some law schools.[5] The training of CPA candidates usually includes work in governmental accounting, which, of necessity, must cover some aspects of municipal budgeting and financial administration. An optional problem on municipal accounting has for some years appeared on the CPA examination, and recently a non-optional problem. At a few metropolitan universities, the analyses of state and municipal bonds and the principles of sound debt management are stressed in a specialized investment course.

CONCLUSION

Any student who chooses local government finance as a graduate area, or as a career, should realize that it is a demanding but most challenging field. The last three decades, especially the years since World War II, have witnessed many new developments and emphases in local finance: the municipal income tax, a proliferation of other new sources of revenue, the creation of new local authorities with user-benefit revenues, increasing resort to revenue bonds to evade debt limits and to satisfy investor demands, direct aids from the national and state capitals, and other sometimes desperate and opportunistic measures. The older overlapping and underlying local government complex has now been further augmented by larger metropolitan area finance problems and by new complications, arising from the earmarking of revenues to achieve specific, but limited, objectives. It is not clear how some of these financial problems can be resolved. By contrast, it is clear that some of the new developments can only result in

---

[5] In some continental European countries, public finance has been a part of the law curriculum. At one time in the United States, public finance was a part of political science, and still is in some universities, e.g., University of Pennsylvania.

further obstacles to more permanent solutions. What seems to be the general direction of municipal finance raises serious policy questions which are at the very heart of state and local government and their roles in the federal system.

Progress is being made today in studying local government structural problems and relationships in metropolitan areas, but parallel work needs to be done on finance. Wherever and whatever the forms of urban government, financial considerations intrude and, often, so much so as to constitute a controlling factor. Unfortunately, research developments in metropolitan finance have lagged, and new approaches have not kept pace with new demands. This situation presents a real challenge. Current solutions and proposals require a thorough re-examination within an overall and more rational framework which will give appropriate weight to equities and other fundamental principles. To make a substantial contribution toward such a re-examination should be the basic purpose of intensive new research.

2

Organization for Financial Administration

Organization problems, including those in local finance administration, have long held a particular fascination for many. But much that has been written about structuring for finance administration is in simplistic terms and leaves untouched the more knotty questions. To illustrate: independence of the postauditor from the administration is often stated as a "sound principle," but this leaves unanswered the crux of the matter—not only the location factor but all the other special conditions and circumstances which determine whether the auditor's independence can be protected or will be subjected to periodic emasculation and erosion.

This whole subject area is of more than academic interest. Many activists, both within and outside the city hall, are confronted again and again with the necessity of making and defending structural proposals. This is especially true for political leaders, finance administrators, research staff members for legislative committees, political parties, citizen groups, and for drafters of city charters.

ORGANIZATIONAL PATTERNS

Are there general patterns which are useful in classifying local finance organizations found in actual practice? Is it possible to isolate the reasoning which lies behind these major patterns? This section is concerned with answering these questions by a description of typical prevailing patterns of organization and the reasons therefor.

Patterns Found in Practice

Location of the finance function in the overall local government structure varies from one city to another. In an individual government, all or many of the finance activities may have been pulled together into a functional department under a director with this head, in turn, reporting directly to the chief executive or to some other central supervisory authority. Again, the finance activities may have remained scattered and may appear on an organization chart to defy any rational explanation. In general, however, after excluding the postaudit function, it is possible to speak of four pattern groups:

1. *A unified or centralized department:* The concept applies to a department headed by a single official to whom the other finance officers are responsible, and who supervises the performance of all finance activities under the city government. Usually the head of the department is appointed by the chief executive.

2. *A modified, centralized finance department:* This pattern embraces those situations where there is a substantial concentration under a chief finance officer, but one or several finance activities are outside this concentration. In some of the council-manager cities (e.g., Fort Worth) and strong-mayor cities (e.g., Chicago), budget preparation and purchasing are directly under the city manager or mayor, with both offices independent of the finance director. Such an arrangement is designed to give the chief executive better tools for his role in planning and programming and in budgetary matters. In practice, budget preparation can function under the manager or mayor, with budget execution and control remaining in the finance department where the budgetary accounts are kept. In another situation, the assessor and the treasurer may be elected officials or appointees of the mayor or other officers and constitute the only finance officers outside the centralized department.

3. *A decentralized finance structure under an overall finance supervisory authority:* Within this group would fall any structure where finance activities are carried out by a number of separate offices (headed by either elected or appointed officials), but in which some board or other agency, or an individual other than the chief executive, is given some powers of supervision over the various finance officials—powers, however, not sufficient to achieve substantial integration and coordination.

4. *A decentralized finance structure without any formalized overall finance supervisory authority:* This group designation applies to any finance administration where no centralization has taken place. Instead, all the finance activities are carried on by individual offices or agencies—such as the purchasing office, treasurer's office, sinking fund trustees, and a board of assessors—whose heads are not all selected by nor responsible to a single finance official, nor under the general supervision of an overall finance authority. This older pattern of independent finance offices, built on the concept of checks and balances, can still be found.

Many examples could be cited of a combination of elected and appointed officials with various degrees of decentralization. For example, an appointed comptroller (or controller) might have under him approximately half the finance activities, with the remainder under an elected assessor, an elected treasurer, and an appointed budget director.

Reasons Behind the Major Patterns

Differences in basic patterns are the products of conflicting concepts or "principles." In those situations where decentralization is still the pattern, with several separate independent or quasi-independent finance offices or boards, the concept of checks and balances constitutes the most important consideration.

This old and once dominant concept, although now less pervasive in application, presumably persists because no other and stronger rationale has effectively challenged it. A number of separate, elective finance offices are provided with the purpose of having at least one to check upon another. It takes participation of two finance officers, independent of each other, to get many important things done, for example, two signatures to draw a check and warrants drawn by one officer in order to authorize another to receive money and to disburse funds. Undoubtedly, the strength left in this old concept has partially blocked the tendency toward unification. An elected treasurer or an independent (elected or appointed) comptroller, exercising preaudit functions is retained with the expectation (a false one in the authors' view) that by virtue of his separateness he can maintain better internal control over other finance officers.

On the other hand, the necessity for an independent postauditor outside the administration and completely divorced from preauditing is well accepted and remains the most useful application of this once dominant "principle" of checks and balances. An elected auditor should have only postaudit duties and should not be subject to direction by the administration. His audit reports should go not only to the administration but also to the governing body and the public. If the postauditor is appointed, he should be chosen by the governing body on the recommendation of its finance committee. None of the executive officers whose accounts are to be audited should have anything to say about the selection of the postauditor.

The concept of checks and balances (exclusive of postaudit) conveniently fits in with the views of those who distrust the civil service, appointed officials, and a strong executive. Some see in a multiplicity of elected officials the flowering of local democracy. Still others oppose a centralized finance department on their own interpretation of the practical limits upon the span of supervision and control.

On the other hand, there are those who stress the need for building an organization under which citizens will know who is responsible for achievements and failures. Maximum citizen control is best obtained by a focus of responsibility and the delegation of commensurate power and authority. There is also the belief that efficiency in administration is promoted by grouping like activities together and by building a carefully defined system of responsibility in the hierarchy of relationships. Coordination, supervision, and control are thereby facilitated. Where a unified or centralized department of finance is the pattern two or more of the above reasons will have converged to form the underlying rationale.

Form and Reality

The foregoing discussion is largely limited to considerations of form. Within itself, the prescription in law or administrative regulation of an excellent form of organization does not guarantee that the finance function will be permitted to operate according to the prescribed organization. Local government is frequently very highly politicized at the top levels. Indeed, only in this manner can public policy be determined on a basis fully responsive to the views of the community.

With some frequency one encounters realities of organization and power relationships which are significantly different from the legally prescribed arrangements. Thus, an assistant to the mayor may develop a power base which enables him to intrude at various times into the orderly functioning of a legally prescribed finance organization. Or, conversely, a mayor who is determined to have a strong finance officer can provide such strength in the face of a legally prescribed weak system of finance organization.

The point here is that the legal prescription of a strong, integrated finance organization will facilitate the attainment of the reality of a strong integrated finance organization. But, it cannot guarantee that such will occur.

The Role of Finance. A brief review of the role of finance throws additional light on the strength of the reasoning behind centralization. Writers on administration have fairly consistently treated finance as a staff function and as an auxiliary agency function. Each finance officer, or director of a group of finance activities, is called upon to provide some staff services to the chief executive and, often, to the legislative body. Such services include reports and information and the interpretation of such information; advice on proposed policy decisions or alternatives; assistance in the preparation of memoranda, reports, or proposed ordinances for which the chief executive or some council committee has the responsibility; and, sometimes, just plain "leg work" for the chief executive or a legislative committee. All can be summed up as staff work or staff assistance to someone above in the hierarchy who needs or requests help meeting his responsibilities.

The finance office, in addition, furnishes certain auxiliary agency services to the operating departments and bureaus. Such services include centralized accounting, disbursement of funds, custody of funds, centralized purchasing, and technical assistance in budget preparation. Since services involve particular activities, or segments of activities, they are often the work of whole units of the finance organization rather than the labor of a single finance officer and his immediate assistants.

The preceding explanation of the role of finance, however, is incomplete. Finance goes beyond staff and auxiliary agency services. In the authors' view, one important aspect has been overlooked. Finance is essentially a means to an end or ends, that is, the end-objectives of local government. Since attainment of the end-objectives, in all their multiplicity, entails the expenditure of funds, financial resources are required. But, in the acquisition of resources, finance is not a neutral tool or means. Finance may generate consequences not directly related to service which, over the long run, tend to shackle; or, it may enhance greatly the capacity of the government to meet its responsibilities. The amassing of resources, therefore, must be carefully planned, programmed, and controlled as well as the expenditure of funds in pursuit of defined goals.

Stated another way, finance as a *flow* is divided into two parts—income and outgo. Generally speaking, the income flow is a financial husbandry responsibility; the outgo involves auxiliary service responsibilities. On both sides, the finance office performs staff services. The mustering of resources, in fact, responsibility for the entire income flow, constitutes activities not classified under either auxiliary agency or staff service activities.

Such activities include (among others): assessment of property; the billing and collection of taxes and other revenues; the borrowing of funds; the investment of idle cash and sinking fund resources; protection of the local unit's credit in the investment market; execution of financial requirements mandated by the state; and, at times, performance as a financial agent for the state at the local level.

The primary purpose of local government is service, but it should be remembered that governments are engaged in extracting money from the taxpayer's pocket by compulsion. This process is no less real than the rendering of services and can have economic consequences of great importance to the community. The fact that the service function is connected in purpose with the husbandry of resources does not lessen the fact that each of them is a distinct entity. In more technical terms, local government not only performs a service function through most of its departments but also an income redistribution function through some of its finance activities.

A clear recognition of the distinctions among each of the three types of finance activities—financial husbandry, auxiliary agency services, and staff services—would, in the authors' view, have an important impact upon the acceptance of the reasons for a unified or centralized finance department. Financial husbandry is of primary concern to the chief executive. Financial resources raise major policy issues. They must be planned as an integrated whole; undivided responsibility for policy execution should be centered in a chief finance officer and the necessary authority provided to him. Effectiveness in policy-making and execution is lessened if the responsibility for financial husbandry is parceled out.

If parts of financial advice and information come from different finance officers, the chief executive must spend valuable time in coordinating that which should have been integrated at the next lower level. Staff services, too, need to be focused if the chief executive is to function effectively. If the major role of finance were the rendering of auxiliary services to the other departments, there would probably be less need for a unified, centralized finance department. Presumably, departments would not suffer greatly if they got their internal finance services from several different finance offices independently. This is not to say that the chief executive is not interested in the effective performance of auxiliary services. It does imply that the problems of integration and coordination in this area are of a lower order of importance.

Guidelines From Public Administration. What guidelines found in the present state of public administration can be drawn upon? Within the main goals of administration a useful framework will be sketched here, but in a very abbreviated form. Three major guideline groupings will suffice: (a) conditions for effective executive leadership; (b) efficiency in the use of personnel, equipment, and other resources; and (c) the responsibility of local government to its citizens.

If the first goal is to be achieved, namely *the creation of conditions under which executive leadership can function effectively*, attention in devising a finance structure will be paid to the following guidelines:

1. Creation of a feasible span of control for the chief executive
2. Provision for staff to assist him in financial planning
3. The establishment of controls designed to assure that there will be compliance with the approved plans

4. The addition of a system of checks and balances to prevent dishonesty and other practices which would embarrass the administration
5. Achievement of a proper balance among controls over the heads of operating departments, creation of a system of technical assistance to them from the central finance staff, and provision of auxiliary finance staff at the departmental level

If the second goal, *efficiency*, is to be attained, the organization for financial management will be laid upon a foundation which, at a minimum, includes:

1. Specialization and division of labor
2. A grouping together of related activities within the structure in order to achieve maximum coordination
3. A built-in system of controls to assure that the planned channeling and utilization of resources are followed
4. The establishment of centers within which standards and actual performance can be readily compared

The third goal is partly political and partly administrative. If *responsibility to the citizens* is to be realized, efforts must be made to build into the organizational structure certain safeguards, namely:

1. Direct lines of authority so that citizens can readily identify those responsible for financial achievements and failures
2. A system of financial controls, dependent, in part, upon the distribution of financial sub-activities, which would strengthen the chain of responsibility
3. An office to produce integrated financial reporting so that the government's finances can be viewed as a whole
4. A postauditor who is independent of the administration and protected by safeguards to ensure preservation of his independence
5. An agency, an ombudsman, or some type of independent appeal board, before which the citizen can seek relief from arbitrary finance regulations and decisions

At this point, a *caveat*, however, is very much in order. The above in no way embody "the laws of the Medes and Persians." They are guidelines to be considered but they also frequently require modification to fit particular situations. Given the starting point (i.e., the structure which already exists), the above may prove too ideal. Yet, it is useful to know the approximate elements of a model which is built upon certain goal assumptions and supported by accumulated experience in public administration.

FACTORS IN ORGANIZATIONAL DECISION-MAKING

Structural proposals which are power-motivated often clash with guidelines based on administrative-oriented goals, but again the two may coincide. Still, something may be sacrificed on both sides and some sort of mix attained with the resultant compromise. Efficiency and the interests of the citizens may be subordinated, yet, at times, may fare well when a balance is struck. In analyzing factors which may affect organizational structuring, it is necessary, therefore, to consider the approximate relative weight between these two components in the probable resultant mix.

But, there are other factors which carry weight, and one or more of these may be the dominant factor or factors and outweigh what we have previously conceived to be the main ones. However, it should be noted that, under some circumstances, some of these factors may lose their identity or become almost competely overshadowed by larger issues.

Basic Governmental Structure

The existing form of the executive branch, or the desired form, is a factor which determines basic governmental structure. There are three major patterns with several variations:

1. Strong chief-executive type
   a. Strong-mayor type: The mayor is elected and ordinarily has the authority to veto acts of council, appoint and remove department heads, prepare and administer a budget. The mayor in some cities appoints a CAO (chief administrative officer) to assist him.
   b. Council-manager (often referred to as the city-manager form): The manager is appointed by the council and acts as chief administrator for the city. He appoints department heads, advises the council, and executes council policy.

2. Commission form: The elected body is both legislative and executive; each commissioner serves as head of one or more departments.

3. Weak-mayor type: Executive power is distributed among independent boards and/or a number of elected officials—all with overlapping terms; power resides primarily in committees of council.

No obstacles to an integrated finance organization need arise in the strong chief-executive type. Even in a commission form, a unified finance department is possible if one of the commissioners can serve as commissioner of finance. Where there is a weak-mayor structure, or a combined legislative-administrative body, it is theoretically possible to have a centralized finance department with the chief reporting to a board or a legislative committee. Usually, however, the absence of a strong executive is symptomatic of an atomistic structure. Where there are independent or quasi-independent finance boards, the chances for an integrated finance organization may be even darker.

The existence of elected as well as appointed finance officers within the same structure is almost always a relevant factor. This makes the establishment of a centralized department more difficult. Much depends on personalities. An elected finance officer may be willing to function within such a department and to cooperate fully; again, he may insist on acting independently. In this case, the result is usually fragmented financial reporting and sometimes frictions and delays in administration.

Type of Legislative Body

The type of legislative body will sometimes be a factor in making organizational decisions. Members may be elected at-large or by wards or districts. The city council may be a small or large body. There is more of a chance for a small body to function primarily as a policy-making group. A large council tends to divide itself into committees, some of which may arrogate to themselves duties which are essentially administrative. For example, the finance committee of the council may set the guidelines for the operating budget and supervise its preparation.

A legislative budget staff may supplement, or even supersede, the regular budget staff. The balance of power between the majority and minority parties or well-defined factions will partly determine the council's effectiveness. The council, in some instances, may be controlled by the mayor who is also the leader of the majority party; yet, the president of the council may have a degree of independence through leadership in his own right. One or more of these circumstances may dictate the location of the operating budget office and/ or the capital budget staff and the need for a possible duplication of budget staffs. Such circumstances may also affect the location of and the method of achieving independence for the postauditor.

Absence of Key Finance Activities

Units of local government differ as to the range of finance activities. Some are special-purpose districts with a limited number of service responsibilities and, sometimes, with but a single source of revenue. This may be true even for a district which is sizable when measured by any of the usual criteria. Other situations limit the finance activities. Within a particular state, the state government (by mandate or by option) may have taken over certain activities—such as retirement fund investments and administration, sinking fund management, postauditing, or even the marketing of municipal bonds. In many jurisdictions, the county now has responsibility for the assessment and collection of property taxes so that the other local units need no organization for property tax administration. Also, here and there, some local units have limited their finance activities by contract. The assessment of property for taxation, the collection of taxes, and purchasing are three activities which lend themselves to a contractual shift to another, and often larger, overlapping local government. In general, a narrowing of the range of finance activities affects only the internal structure of the finance organization and not its place in the overall structure. If the range, however, is markedly delimited, the need for a centralized department of finance may disappear. The manager or mayor might easily deal separately, for example, with an accountant-auditor and a treasurer.

Size of Local Government

The size of the local government is a most important limiting factor. All the activities may be there, but in such small, or in such large, volume that economy and efficiency require a marked departure from that which is theoretically sound. For example, a town may be so small that centralization of finance activities and the hiring of one full-time paid finance officer may not be practicable. At the other end of the scale, a metropolitan city may be so gargantuan as to require the centralization of some finance activities, while at the same time encouraging each department head to hire financial staff to perform the functions of preauditing, budget planning, and capital programming at the operating levels.

Finally, the individual catalyst cannot be overlooked. The presence within the community of an activist citizen group, or of a single, able individual who has a continuing interest in city government reform, may constitute a catalytic factor. A committee of the League of Women Voters; a newspaper reporter or radio commentator with a year-in, year-out overview of city hall; an able young lawyer who wants to make himself known; or a well-known citizen from a family with a tradition for civic responsibility—any one of these may be a factor to be reckoned with.

Organization for a Small Government. Any definition of what constitutes a small governmental unit is, of course, wholly arbitrary. Therefore, we shall not attempt any one definition. Rather, three hypothetical cases are used to illustrate at least some situations.

Case 1. The town or village manager is the budget officer, the purchasing agent, the countersigner of checks, and the negotiator and administrator of all contracts. For a flat sum, agreed upon by contract, the county assesses property and collects the property tax. The remaining activities are in one finance officer who keeps the books, audits the bills, draws the warrants or checks for all payments (including payrolls) which go to the manager, and performs all the treasury activities. Postauditing is the responsibility of a state agency.

The smaller the unit the less important is the question of organization, except for purposes of internal audit or internal check. A small town or village with fewer than 50 employees has no great organization problem. If there is a manager, he will "run the show."

Case 2. In the absence of a strong executive type of government, a finance committee of the council, or other governing body, performs the budgeting and preauditing activities. Assessment of property is the responsibility of a part-time assessor. The remaining finance activities are under the supervision of, and are the ultimate responsibility of, a part-time treasurer (a local banker or business man). The routine work is done by a full-time clerk who keeps the books, initiates purchases subject to preaudit approval, collects the property tax and other revenues, and prepares reports for the state. Postauditing is the responsibility of an accounting firm.

Case 3. A council committee prepares the current budget. This committee, with the help of a planning consultant, is responsible for the capital budget. Two high-grade clerks fill the role of village (or town) treasurer and village (or town) clerk, respectively. The latter functions as a preauditor, purchasing agent, and bookkeeper-accountant. If there is a utility, the clerk will also keep the utility accounts and prepare the bills. The treasurer collects all taxes and revenues, including the utility bills, and performs all the other treasury activities. The assessment of property is performed by the county under contract, and postauditing is the responsibility of a state agency.

In the overall, several generalizations about finance organizations in small units appear to be reasonably accurate:

1. Where there is a full-time chief executive, he should be given the budgeting, purchasing, and ultimate preauditing activities. In a small unit he has time for multiple roles. These responsibilities provide him with the tools for financial planning and some of those used in financial control and strengthen his position as a strong executive.
2. In the absence of such an executive, a legislative committee must assume the overall planning and financial control duties.
3. Where feasible, the assessment and collection of property taxes should be entrusted to the county (if not already placed there by statute) and paid for under contract.
4. The residual finance activities will have to be performed either by one or two part-time or full-time persons or by some combination of a part-time supervisor and several full-time employees.
5. The postauditing function should be performed outside the financial administration by a professional accountant or firm, or by a state agency.

Organization for Middle-sized and Larger Governments. Middle-sized and larger units of local government may set up a unified department of finance. (The term "unified" is preferred to "centralized" because it more clearly implies integration.) The only finance activity which should regularly be excluded from the unified department is the postauditing function.

All of the reasons which are offered in support of a unified finance department are basically elaborations of one or more of the guidelines from administration. Many illustrations could be cited. Replacement of several independent finance officers with a director of finance is more suitable to the chief executive's span of supervision and control. A single department simplifies the task of building a finance team. Finance activities are so closely interrelated that they function more effectively when brought together under one head.

We would add two further observations. Financial planning as a whole is more feasible under an overall director of finance, and the prospect for comprehensive planning becomes more challenging. Second, a larger finance organization under one officer should mean that a higher salary could be offered and, other things being equal, it should be more feasible thereby to attract a high caliber person to advise and assist at top management levels.

Appraisal of a Unified Department

A strict adherence to the rationale behind a unified finance department is not recommended. Two general areas of modification are suggested.

First, centralization can be overdone. Too often it has been viewed as a desirable end in itself. "All accounting should be centralized" and "all money should be centrally collected" have become cliches often repeated as if they were immutable laws. The idea of centralized accounting is proper, but it must be modified when parts of the accounting can be performed more easily, or more accurately, or to better administrative advantage in other departments or bureaus.

None of this decentralization, however, prevents the entire financial process, insofar as it involves the examples cited in the preceding, from being integrated parts of a whole, whether the work is done entirely by the finance department or by other persons and agencies, as long as the organizational pattern channels the information and decision-making where they should be. Neither does decentralization need to imply lack of supervision, or uniformity, or lack of control. The most impelling reason for centralization is to facilitate integration and to make all the parts work together without undue friction. If better integration can be obtained by some degree of decentralization, this should be done.

In the second place, a qualification can be made concerning the chief executive's span of control and its effect upon centralization of finance activities. It is generally recognized that an executive's span of control can be widened by the use of staff assistants. This is precisely what some city managers and strong mayors are doing when they have the budget director and purchasing agent report directly to them. This requires the supervision of two more finance officers in addition to the finance director. On the other hand, by drawing upon one or more key employees in these two offices, and, at times, by using these two officers themselves as staff, the chief executive is able to widen his range of supervision and control. One city manager indicated that he wanted the budget director and the budget staff attached to his immediate office because this structure supplied him with more staff for special assignments without taking them out of their area of budgeting, program planning, and expenditure control.

Arguments for location of the budget function in the overall administrative structure will be presented in Chapters 5 and 6. It is sufficient to say here that, although many of the principal budgetary decisions should be made by the chief executive or principal administrative officer, numerous budget decisions involve considerations of a lesser importance which can be appropriately delegated to the chief budget officer, wherever situated in the governmental hierarchy.

CRITERIA FOR EVALUATING A FINANCE ORGANIZATION

Empirical tests can be used to determine whether a finance organization is suited to its tasks. A poor structure may work because of good personnel and their exceptional coordinating skills. On the other hand, if the personnel are good and the organization still functions with difficulty, the soundness of the structure is open to doubt. Some of the indicators which might point to a poor structure include:

1. Conflicts in advice to the chief executive on finance matters
2. Overlapping information reported either to top management or to the public; also, actual or seeming contradictions in figures because of different reporting bases and differences in terminology

3. The appearance of a "no-man's land" in the finance function for which
    no planning has been done and where no operating responsibility has
    been assumed
4. The existence of undue emphasis on certain finance activities and under-
    emphasis on others of equal or greater importance
5. Hiring of extra personnel for peak loads in one finance activity when
    it is known that another has, at the same time, surplus personnel capable
    of providing the required services
6. Duplication of machine equipment, or the use of machines successfully
    in one finance activity and the persistence of manual operations in
    another
7. Delays in operations, such as in the distribution of payroll checks, the
    billing for services rendered, and the making of contract payments
8. Frequent jurisdictional disputes over finance activities and the need for
    repeated clarifications of lines of authority
9. Low morale which grows out of frustration, loss of time, ruffled feel-
    ings, and the wear and tear on personnel because of the obstacles to
    getting things done
10. An established pattern of a multiplicity of clearances before a decision
    can be taken
11. Continuing uncertainties in the minds of other departments dependent
    upon finance decisions as to who is responsible for certain activities in
    the finance organization

Limitations on Classification of Finance Activities

Unfortunately, there are some major obstacles to a clear understanding of
organization problems. One stems from the failure to question the validity of
the conventional listing of finance activities. Upon careful scrutiny, this classification is seen to be faulty. First, it fails to recognize "mixed activities," i.e., those
which are partly finance activities and partly operating head and/or non-finance
staff responsibilities. The classic examples are operating (current) budgeting and
capital budgeting. The programming, administrative planning, and physical planning aspects of budgeting loom large. To claim that both types of budgeting
are finance activities, rather than mixed activities, is to fail to recognize the roles
which operating heads (and the city planning staff in capital budgeting) perform
by virtue of their operating or staff responsibilities and specialized knowledge.

Second, the conventional classification contains at least two other important
errors, namely, in the listing of purchasing and personal property control as
finance activities. In the authors' view neither is a finance activity, not even a
mixed activity. Purchasing involves spending for goods and contractual services
and is an important area for control because it is open to favoritism and graft.
Two reasons apparently lie behind the conventional classification of purchasing
as a finance activity: Tight financial controls extend over this area, and competitive bidding is used. We emphasize, however, that financial controls cut across
all aspects of spending. Their presence is not sufficient to classify this spending
activity area as a finance activity or even a mixed activity. If this were the
case, all spending activities would have to be classified as finance or mixed ac-

tivities. Further, the requirement of competitive bidding (similar to public works contracts) is part of the marketing function (buying and selling) rather than finance, and requires technical talents different from the accounting/finance talents common to finance activities. If purchasing is a finance activity, consistency would require that public works contracting and competitive bidding for the rental or sale of public property be so classified.

As for personal property control, cities have found from experience that movable property items are subject to appropriation for personal use and theft for conversion to cash. Like cash they require tight control. Despite the analogy, it is difficult to justify classifying this activity under finance. Record-keeping on such items is for location control in order to fix management's responsibility for each individual item. It is a type of custodial supervision. A physical inventory of these assets is for verification of the records and is a part of location control. It matters not for classification purposes whether the accounting division participates in, or audits, this inventory and uses the data for either balance sheets or financial control; nor would it matter if the accountants did the inventory and the personal property staff used the results as a part of their custodial supervision. Control of location and temporary custody of excess personal property stock still constitute a separate management activity. Taking inventory of physical assets is a basic part of financial record-keeping and financial control. Use by the operating staff for management purposes of records kept by the accounting division, or use by the accounting division for financial purposes of records kept by others, with appropriate audit and other checks as to accuracy, would not make the activity which is subject to such record-keeping a finance activity or a mixed activity.

Considerations of internal control may still dictate that these functions be performed under the supervision of the principal finance officer; however, this should be done with recognition of the non-financial character of purchasing and property control.

Considerations for Classifying Finance Activities

Three considerations appear to constitute a suitable basis for classification of activities within the "finance" category:

First, the activity must be directly concerned with money or securities, or with the records of financial accounts, or with the custody of financial contracts and documents.

Second, the activity must be such as to require the specialized training which is usually classified as "accounting and finance."

Third, the classification must recognize that there are mixed activities, namely, those for which finance-trained staff have a joint responsibility with operating heads, or with staff which has other professional training, for some major aspect of the management function (namely, planning, the drafting of formal proposals, the defense of such proposals before a legislative body or the chief executive, and the execution of the approved program).

Table 5

CLASSIFICATION OF ACTIVITIES AS FINANCE, MIXED, AND NON-FINANCE
APPLICATION OF THREE CRITERIA

Activity	1. Analysis of Activity	2. Training & Experience Req'd	3. Sole or Joint Respon.	Classification
Retirement System Administration	welfare of civil servants and dependents; money income and outgo; investments	personnel and finance	joint responsibility of personnel and finance	mixed activity
Debt Administration	money income and outgo; sale of securities in market; investment; record-keeping	finance and accounting	sole responsibility of finance	finance activity
Licensing (with important revenue income)	investigation and physical inspection; standards; money income	professional or semi-professional (health, engineering, construction, etc.) and finance	joint responsibility of operating personnel and finance	mixed activity
Purchasing	planning of requirements; buying of goods and contractual services; devising standards and testing products	operating experience; knowledge of products and their usage; experience in the market; engineering	joint responsibility of operating departments and central purchasing agent	non-finance activity
Special Assessments	drawing of district lines; mapping; spreading of benefits; money income and outgo; debt administration	real estate; engineering; public works; finance and accounting	joint responsibility of special assessment board and finance	mixed activity
Personal Property Control	record-keeping and supervisory locational control; custody of surpluses	general administration	sole responsibility of property control officer	non-finance activity
Capital Budgeting (Capital Improvement programming)	physical planning and programming; financial planning; preparation of document; defense; execution	city planning and finance	joint responsibility of city planning and finance	mixed activity
Financial Reporting	preparation of financial schedules and statistical data; coordination and integration of finance as a whole; processing of document	accounting and finance statistics; and experience with document preparation	sole responsibility of finance	finance activity

Table 5 illustrates application of the above criteria and the results to selected activities.

From this re-examination of the conventional classification we make several observations:

1. There may be one or more good practical reasons why purchasing, data-processing, personal property control, printing and mimeographing, and other non-finance activities are made a part of a centralized department of finance. One reason might be that location there is better than creating a new auxiliary service department or placing the particular activity somewhere else in the structure. Such a pragmatic reason is defensible, but an attempted justification by resort to a scientific classification is not.

2. Since financial record-keeping and financial control (preauditing, financial reporting, cash and security custody, and postauditing) cut across the whole range of administrative activities, these two activities are finance *per se* and cannot, no matter how important, be combined with some other activity to justify classifying the activity subject to record-keeping and financial controls as a mixed activity.

3. Ideally, in locating a mixed activity, an attempt will be made to weigh the relative responsibilities and to bring both components into a structural position which permits maximum coordination. Location according to the weightier side of the coin is workable only if the other side accepts and can function well under the arrangement. Location elsewhere than in a centralized department of finance should not be blocked by any dogma as to what is, or is not, a finance activity. The operating budget is sometimes directly under the chief executive for planning, document-preparation, and defense purposes; but, after the budget is approved, many aspects of budget execution are within the finance department. The capital budget is sometimes the major responsibility of the city planning department with finance playing a secondary role. In other cities, capital budgeting is a joint cooperative effort, or there is a regular capital budget staff but co-opted from both departments.

4. Thinking in terms of dichotomies presents difficulties. A precise grouping—such as, "it is either finance, or it isn't"—is usually indefensible. Two other dichotomies are of little assistance; in fact they may add confusion to the classification problem. First, finance has sometimes been compared to the alimentary canal, because it has an income (intake) side and an outgo (spending or discharge) side. Some finance activities are primarily, or solely, on one side. For example, the income side includes, exclusively, assessment and property tax administration and most of revenue collection (but not all because expenditures sometimes generate revenues). But other activities cut across both sides, notably financial record-keeping and financial controls (to take major examples). The second dichotomy involves line and staff functions. Finance is usually regarded as a staff function, but a case can be made that some finance activities (particularly on the income side) are line operations and supply no staff service either to the departments or to the chief

executive. From these two sets of dichotomies we can make only one generalization, namely, that it is on the outgo side and the staff side where mixed activities usually are found and where the more difficult structural-location problems arise.

Titles May Obscure Definition of Duties

Another basic obstacle to the understanding of organization problems arises from semantics. For example, some finance officers are misnamed. A city may have long had an official known as the "City Auditor" with responsibility for accounting and a range of other financial activities. This title may be a factor in defeating an attempt to get an independent postauditor. With little understanding of the difference between so-called preauditing and postauditing, many voters will be confused. "If the City Auditor already audits, why do we need another auditor?"

Again, a city may have essentially a centralized finance department under the direction of a city comptroller, city controller, or even a city clerk. The absence of a title such as "Director of Finance," however, may be used as a wedge to give the comptroller or controller a narrower range of responsibilities; to make him into solely a postauditor, or to subordinate him to a new official with a broader "director" title.

Titles, such as director of finance, city assessor, city treasurer, city purchasing agent, city budget officer, and city auditor (usually chiefs of bureaus or divisions) are common in the larger cities. Several of these titles (assessor, treasurer, and auditor) date back to an earlier day when these officers were elected.

The term "Annual Financial Report of the City of ————" is sometimes applied to the report of only one of two or three finance officers. In fact, the one who prepares the report may be more nearly the chief finance officer than any other; but, the title may hide the fact that the city has neglected to produce a complete financial report covering all of its financial activities and, basically, has an inadequately integrated finance function.

Some local groups have, at times, seized upon the model charter, or some model law, published by the National Municipal League, and supported it as an ideal solution to their local government structural problems. This is a misuse of a document which was intended to be adapted to particular local situations. Yet, "model" suggests the best or, at a minimum, the epitome of expert wisdom.

Within the post-World War II period the federal government has gone far in adapting "internal auditing" as practiced in important business corporations to the needs of top management at the federal departmental and agency level. If the movement spreads to large city and county governments, the term "auditing" will most likely create confusion as to where this activity might best be located. It can be an activity which is more investigative and efficiency-oriented than financial in nature.

Superficial Reactions to Organization Problems

We come now to another type of obstacle to a full understanding of organizational problems. Some look upon such problems through quite unsophisticated eyes. This is often manifested by emphasis on uncomplicated organization charts and on "textbook" solutions. This may mean that attention is concentrated upon goal-oriented principles, with almost complete neglect of the political, or power group, forces present in given situations.

Others, particularly among practitioners, regard the whole question of structure as relatively unimportant. This may be, in part, a reaction against reformers and others who overemphasize the importance of structural change. The practitioner may state his position in terms of good personnel versus structure, for example, "with good personnel, I can make any organizational setup work." This may be true, but it essentially begs the question.

There are many situations in which good personnel make a poor structure work, but at the cost of stress and strain upon key personnel who have the responsibility for getting things done. With the same quality personnel and a better structure, the chances for efficiency, with less human wear and tear, are improved. One suspects that practitioners who take this attitude are more likely the ones who come into administration at the top, or who never had to work very long at the lower or middle management levels. The man at the top can reach down and completely disregard subordinate lines of authority and responsibility with at least temporary immunity. But personnel lower in the structure will disregard such lines only at great risks. They have to account for such action—first to their immediate supervisor but, possibly, also to one or more administrators higher in the command chain.

There are some who take an even more superficial view of organizational problems. They apparently associate change with progress. They are so busy with proposals "to move the furniture around" that they fail to analyze critically the ends to which their proposals ultimately lead. They may even state, and regard, their solutions in terms of "good" and "bad," but without a clear recognition of the goal assumptions upon which their concepts of an ideal or model rest.

Internal Organization Problems

By far, the larger number of organization problems and those that continue to arise must be classified as internal organization problems. They demand the time of the finance officer and their solution is essential to smooth operations.

"Organization," writes Millett, "is the structural framework within which the work of many individuals is carried on for the realization of a common purpose."[1] He also states that the fundamental characteristic of organization is a hierarchy, a formalized structure of relationships. Organization also implies authority, delegation of authority, responsibility, planning, direction, integration or centralization, and control.

Delegation and Division of Labor. There should be a delegation of authority and responsibility from the chief executive to the chief finance officer. The finance officer, in his turn, should share responsibility, authority, and prestige with his deputies, staff assistants, and bureau or division chiefs. If he does not, he becomes an administrative Atlas trying to carry on his own shoulders

---

[1] Millett, John D., *Management in the Public Service*, (New York: McGraw-Hill, 1954), p. 153.

the problems of his entire department. Failure to delegate authority implies ignorance, egotism, lack of confidence—or all three. He may well break himself physically and his department fail in many ways if he tries to carry the burden alone. Authority and responsibility should be exercised at several different levels in an organization.

One organizational arrangement which may be cited provides for two deputies to the chief finance officer. The first deputy has all the authority of his chief except as he is limited in writing. A second deputy, or assistant, is responsible for the day-to-day operation of the department, that is, the work assignments, personnel supervision, formulation of departmental rules, and internal office arrangements. The work is divided among bureaus and divisions so that it may flow freely. Certain staff activities, attached directly to the office of the chief finance officer, are supervised directly by the second deputy. This immediate staff consists of a secretarial staff, a small internal security unit, a director of personnel, an assistant, and a chief clerk who handles payroll, supplies, stores, vaults, and the departmental budget. It seems best to have a methods analyst report to the chief finance officer since such work cuts across all activities within the department. Changes in methods and systems are always viewed with alarm by those already doing the work, so the changes will probably have to be dictated from above. This cannot be done if the methods or systems analyst is attached to any one bureau.

Role of the Department Head. The nature and scope of the duties of the head of the finance department are determined by any number of factors, including the size of the city, the form of government, and the legal provisions under which he operates. In a smaller city, he may have many specialized and technical functions to perform. However, the director of a department with 100, 200, or 300 employees cannot be familiar with the details of every operation; otherwise, the major matters of overall policy, internal policies, and general supervision would be neglected. The division and bureau heads who supervise technical and routine matters must know the details of these operations intimately, but the chief finance officer cannot be expected to do so.

The logical organization of a department is absolutely necessary, but only the personality and tact of its director will make the department operate successfully. Otherwise, it is like a piece of machinery without any grease or oil to cut the heat of friction.

Organization Reduced to Writing. An important step in the organization of a department of finance is the preparation of a statement of the functions and duties of the department as required by the constitution, statutes, city charter and city code, or by administrative decision. The director, through his deputies and bureau chiefs, should check regularly to see that all required duties have been performed and are being performed. Since public officials are liable for nonfeasance as well as malfeasance in office, they may be required to account to the courts for things they have failed to do as well as for things which they have done improperly.

Following the preparation of the statement of departmental duties, the work should be clearly assigned in writing to the various bureaus and divisions of the office. Then, the principal deputies should be given written instructions outlining their duties and their limitations. As a rule the deputies, unless instructed otherwise, would normally exercise the full powers of their principal. A clear statement should be prepared as to who is entitled to authorize exceptions and variations from the general operating rules. Some exceptions will have to be handled directly by the director. Others could be decided by his deputies and still others by the bureau heads. The department head himself should spend much of his time on policy planning.

Clear Lines of Authority. An organization pattern permits the director of finance to transmit orders and receive information and suggestions. It also provides a means of following through on all instructions, procedures, and legal requirements. The pattern should remove all doubt as to which bureau or division performs any stated task. It will also permit ready assignments of new tasks and the transfer of existing tasks between bureaus and divisions. A proper organization structure reduces friction within the department, between the department of finance and other departments, and between the department and the public.

The organization, when tentatively complete, should be tested by assigning every employee to a unit and seeing that he works solely under the direction of his designated supervisor. There should be no doubt in any employee's mind as to whom he reports. After each employee has been assigned to a division or bureau, his place in the organization should be made clear to him, and he should be given instructions that any questions or comments from him go to his designated supervisor and that he takes orders only from this supervisor.

The internal arrangements are planned to speed the flow of work, give proper attention to the public, serve other departments conveniently, and provide the employees with freedom from unnecessary interference.

Channels of Communication. Organization, among other things, must settle who in the department will deal with the public, and on what matters. It must show who from outside and inside the department will deal directly with what employees, and on what subjects. Discussions with the press should take place only through a recognized, authoritative channel designated by the director, unless he makes an exception. Persons dealing with the department of finance should go through channels—that is, through the director or the deputies designated by him. Unless other channels have been established, other city departments should deal with the director's office only through the director or persons designated by him. No superior officer of the municipality—the mayor, city manager, or city councilman—should deal directly with departmental employees. Questions or directives should go through normal channels of communication, that is, the head of the department. Since there are many financial relations between a city, other units of local government, the state, and the federal governments, channels for communication with these governments must also be designated.

Relationships. The director of finance is responsible to the chief executive. His formal reports will ordinarily be to the chief executive; however, in the larger governments, it is not feasible to channel all communications in this manner. Especially important in this regard are his relations with the press. Regular releases by the director of finance should be made available to the chief executive in advance of being provided to the press; however, on a day-to-day basis, the director will doubtless be obliged to handle many items directly with the press—under general guidelines which should have been previously established for press relations within the government.

The director has contact with all departments and agencies of the government. His contacts with other departments are broader and more frequent than any other official with the possible exception of the mayor or chief administrative officer. His attitude should be one of cooperation, not obstruction. The director, however, must act according to professional standards in his decisions about the classification of accounts, disclosures on audits, many payroll matters, and all events involving the financial integrity of public employees, contractors, or suppliers. He deals with the employees of other departments only through channels, except in his capacity as auditor or investigator. Since the director does have a different kind of relationship with other departments than most other officials (because he may restrain expenditures or purchases), he must be careful not to interfere in operating matters or to substitute his judgment or his directions for the authority of another department head.

Nor should it be overlooked that the department of finance has the responsibility of supplying the various municipal departments and agencies with monthly, weekly, or daily data so that they will not need to keep unnecessary detailed records of expenditures and appropriations. They should know, at least monthly, the detail of the charges against the various appropriation accounts for which they are responsible. This can be done by supplying copies of ledger sheets, by reports made through electronic equipment, or by terminals in more sophisticated systems. In any case, the departments must know in detail what the central records show, both for the purpose of checking the work of the department of finance and for ease of departmental operations.

CHANGES IN ORGANIZATIONAL STRUCTURE

Usually, when a new finance officer assumes his responsibilities, he finds a going organization through which he finds it appropriate to carry forward the functions of the unit—at least initially.

Some finance officers will continue the inherited organization throughout their term of office even though there may be a need for change. However, within a reasonable period of time, and certainly not more than a year from assumption of responsibilities, the organization then in being is the responsibility of the *present director of finance*. (The only exception being where provisions of charter or state law inhibit change.)

The point is that, to the extent that the director of finance has authority to modify his organization and elects not to do so, it is fair to presume that he has studied the matter and has concluded that the undisturbed elements of organization are superior to any alternative of which he is aware.

This is not to argue for change for the sake of change. However, it is to attempt to bring clearly into focus the fact that the director is as much responsible for elements of organization which he continues as he found them as he is for the new or modified elements of administration which he causes to be installed. In other words, where he has authority to make changes, he has a positive responsibility to examine alternatives at reasonable intervals and to make adjustments in the light of his findings as to the kind of organization that will best serve in the performance of the functions for which he is responsible. Of course, he is obliged to operate within the framework of the charter or other laws or ordinances that may bear upon internal organization; however, this does not absolve him of responsibility for advocacy of a change in any such provision that he deems to constitute an unwise restraint on the development of proper organization.

The Motivations for Change

Generally, proposals for change in the financial organization come from the director of finance, his subordinates, or persons outside the finance organization. It is not feasible to provide ironclad characterizations of the motivations of each of these persons; however, it may be useful to comment upon some of the forces at work.

Changes which originate with the director himself usually arise from some combination of the following:

1. Efforts to improve the capacity of the director to accomplish his mission
2. Accommodation of a personnel change—either the placement of someone deemed by the director to be especially useful to him or the displacement of someone deemed to inhibit the attainment of his objectives
3. Assignment of new activities, e.g., additional collection functions because of the adoption of a tax which requires enforcement
4. Emergence of the need for a radical change in the procedures used in the department, e.g., installation of new automatic data processing techniques
5. The need to shake up an organization that has become too "set in its ways"

In the case of change initiated by subordinates of the director of finance, each of the foregoing may be present; however, two additional motivations are frequently present:

6. Readjustment of power relationships among subordinates
7. Improvement in the compensation of one or more of the proponents of change

Changes which originate from outside the finance agency may involve most of the foregoing. In addition, more comprehensive considerations may be involved, especially overall decisions as to which functions will be included in the central finance department or agency and which will be assigned to other units of the government. These "outside" changes may come as a result of actions within the city council, state legislature, or the amendment of the home rule charter.

In most of the changes initiated by subordinates of the director of finance or by those outside the finance agency, power relationships are frequently the major motivation. Some person or group may wish to modify the power relationships in the government—either to the advantage or disadvantage of the finance agency. Sometimes, these proposals are in the interest of improved administration within the finance agency or between the finance agency and the executive or council. Others may arise largely from personality considerations—for or against some individual or group of individuals within the government.

In almost all situations, the director of finance is likely to become involved in the process, even when he may prefer to remain aloof. Especially when the proposals for change come from outside the finance agency, he must be prepared to make a careful analysis of the probable impact of proposed change and to place his case before the chief executive and, sometimes, before the council, a charter revision commission, or the general public.

The Absence of Permanent Solutions

That solutions to problems are rarely "permanent" is a somber fact often overlooked, especially because of the enthusiasm generated, sometimes necessarily, if proposed changes are to be accepted. Too much is usually expected from structural changes. They remove, or resolve, old problems but frequently create new ones. From a larger sphere comes a paraphrased analogy: "To win a battle is not to win the war, and to win the war is not necessarily to win the peace." Despite the fact that not all the consequences can be prophesied, proponents of change can do no more than attempt to weigh the expected advantages during the next decade or so and balance them against any possible foreseeable disadvantages.

The cold reminder that time and circumstances may obliterate, in whole or in part, what seemed to be a victory by placing internal structure within charter, law or ordinance is a sobering thought to those who seek to predetermine the details of administration through these devices. In general, the law is doubtless best which deals only with the key elements of administrative organization and leaves to the administrators the task of timely revisions in structure to meet changing conditions.

CONCLUSION

Electronic data processing equipment and methods are forcing major changes in the organization for financial management. Perhaps the centralized department of finance will evolve into a centralized department of administration, which means that the latter will absorb the former as a subordinate unit. Initially, responsibility for the data processing activity has been placed where the best use can be made of expensive equipment and where technical know-how exists. This has often been the case with activities which have been added to the department of finance.

As for the future, it is not possible to predict, of course, the outcome of more automation in city hall, but we would expect some lasting, and perhaps drastic, changes.

Space restrictions have prevented pursuit of this subject of organization for financial management in all of its ramifications. Empirical research as to structural patterns under different circumstances, and reasons for deviations, must be left to others; similarly, the building of models with explicit statements of underlying goal assumptions has not been undertaken. Ours has been an analytical and questioning approach. The authors have striven to produce a chapter suggestive rather than conclusive with the objective of putting to rest the conventional approach too often used or, at least, supplying warnings of its dangers. Simplicity of structure, neatness of organization chart, and adherence to administrative principles based on rational goals—these are not always reliable guides. History, tradition, struggles for power, the size of local government, structure of the executive branch, the type of legislative body, and other factors may enter into the ultimate decision as regards structural proposals.

3

Financing Local Government

At the core of successful urban financial administration lies the sometimes awesome concept of local financial policy.[1]

Elements of Local Financial Policy

The principal elements of local financial policy are:
1. A determination of the general level at which services are to be performed by the local government
2. The relative emphasis which the local government will place upon the different revenue sources available to it in financing governmental operations
3. The degree to which capital improvements are to be financed from current revenues, as distinguished from the anticipation of future revenues through incurring debt
4. The pattern of current wages, deferred wages (pensions), cash fringe benefits, and time-off fringe benefits which will prevail
5. The characteristics of any debt issues in terms of overall life, pattern of maturities, and the alternate uses of general obligation and revenue bonds
6. The degree to which the local government will vary its levels of expenditure and taxation in view of changes in the local economy
7. The extent to which services will be performed by contract rather than by force account

There have been no comprehensive studies of the extent to which principal local government finance officers participate aggressively in the development of local financial policy. However, the limited direct evidence and considerable indirect evidence suggest that many local government finance officers have not functioned at their best in the role of developing and adjusting local financial policy.

---

[1] One is tempted to use the phrase "fiscal policy," however, inasmuch as that term is widely identified with tax and budgetary approaches to adjust the economy, in contrast to "monetary policy," it seems best to use the more restrictive term of "financial policy."

Frequently, this has been due to the absence of a sufficiently broad assignment to the finance officer to enable him to function effectively in developing the varied aspects of financial policy. In other cases, finance officers have failed to grasp the opportunities which do present themselves—sometimes, because of personal preference and, sometimes, because of inadequate professional background.

In other circumstances, the chief executive or governing body of the local government may show little interest in the subject or may even be antagonistic to efforts by administrative officials to develop a general policy framework within which annual, or day-to-day, financial decisions can be made.

The greatest opportunity for participation in the development or modification of local financial policy lies with the officer (or officers) responsible for developing the annual long-term operating program, the annual operating budget, the capital program, and the capital budget. However, those local financial officers responsible for other financial functions—e.g., procurement, treasury, or capital loans—have a great opportunity for significant contributions when aspects of local financial policy to which their duties immediately relate are under consideration.

Of course, the ultimate responsibility for local financial policy lies with the chief executive and the governing body of the community. However, the well-trained public finance officer can be expected to bring to financial policy development a great breadth and depth of knowledge and understanding of both the short-term and long-term consequences of such policies upon the economic, social, and political well-being of the community and its citizens.

If financial policy is to be well developed, it should be done on a professional basis. Where elements of such policy are carefully identified and documented, public officials and the general public can better understand the significance of decisions concerning various aspects of local government finance.

Conversely, in the absence of a well-defined policy, a host of decisions (that are, in fact, closely related) may be made with little understanding of their consequences.

This is not to argue that financial policy has to be formally approved in writing by the chief executive or the legislative body. Rather, it is to urge that a widespread understanding of the basic financial policies to be pursued will usually provide adequate stability, as well as flexibility, to the decisions of the chief executive and the council.

Financial policies must conform to the laws under which the local government operates; however, such laws should not be considered as unchangeable. Local governments, acting in concert with each other and their representatives in state legislatures and Congress, can frequently bring about desirable changes in such laws. Perhaps the most significant action in this respect, in recent years, was the adoption in 1972 of federal revenue-sharing.

However, finding sufficient revenues to meet expenditure needs is a perennial problem. It is desirable—but not necessarily feasible—that local governments be able to finance public services at whatever minimum level is deemed necessary for the welfare of the people. However, the revenue systems of many local governments are not adequate to meet these standards.

FACTORS UNDERLYING LOCAL GOVERNMENT
REVENUE STRUCTURES

The basic determinants of local revenue structures are:

1. Legal capacity of the local government to levy taxes and service charges
2. Fragmentation of local government
3. Economic characteristics of the community served by the local government

These basic determinants of the local government revenue structure, in combination, form the economic, legal, and political factors underlying the development of local revenues from local sources. Also important in this regard are the structure of the local government and the prevailing systems of transfer payments (revenue-sharing and categorical grants) to local governments.

Limited Taxing Authority. In the first place, most municipalities have only limited taxing authority. Being instrumentalities of the states, they are not legally free to draw on their taxable resources as they see fit, but have only the taxing powers that are delegated to them by state constitutions and statutes. The states have relinquished, largely or entirely, one major source of revenue to local governments—real and personal property taxes—but usually with restrictions.

In some instances, state laws severely curtail the extent to which the property tax can be levied. Moreover, state laws generally provide for full or partial exemption of many types of real and personal property.

In a few states, home rule provisions give municipalities the power to levy nonproperty taxes without special authorization; but, commonly, such action is dependent on specific legislative authorization. In recent decades, there has been considerable legislation authorizing local governments to levy nonproperty taxes, and many of the larger cities have developed substantial revenues from these sources.

As the bottom layer of a multilevel system of government, local governments (even if given broad legal taxing power) are at a disadvantage in competing with the federal and state governments for use of the nation's taxable resources. Local revenue sources are difficult to expand because of the sheer weight of federal taxation, the states' rapidly increasing requirements and superior ability to draw on productive sources; and the unsuitability of most such sources for local administration, except in the larger and less competitively situated municipalities. The development of adequate local revenue systems is considerably inhibited by interlocal and interstate economic competition. Moreover, local governments, with their limited territorial jurisdictions, are quite vulnerable to competitive tax factors. In any event, local administration of complex major taxes tends to be either inefficient or expensive. It also tends to generate irritating problems of compliance.

Fragmentation of Local Government. The development of adequate local governmental revenues is handicapped by the haphazard and fragmented structure of local government. Many economic and social urban communities in the United States have the potential in taxable wealth to meet the full revenue requirements for local public services. However, because of the manner in which local government in these communities is organized it is not possible to realize adequately and equitably the full revenue potential. This arises from the fracturing of the governmental structure both horizontally and vertically within these communities. This produces a financially restrictive condition not only in standard metropolitan statistical areas, as defined by the Bureau of the Census but also in hundreds of smaller urbanized areas whose populations and economic resources have expanded beyond the limited confines of their central cities. In 1971, there were 264 SMSA's, embracing a total of 22,185 local governments.[2]

The balkanization of local government magnifies inequalities among municipalities in taxable resources, with the result that the local tax effort required to produce a given standard of services tends to range widely—from very low to very high. The variation among the political subdivisions within individual states and within individual metropolitan areas in their capacity to raise revenue is vastly greater than the variation among the states—a fact often noted as a point of weakness in the federal system.

A study of the patterns of growth of local governments in metropolitan areas shows that the process of fragmentation has frequently resulted from unwise legislation which sought to protect some local or transitory interest. The conditions which gave rise to the initial creation of the unwise local governmental arrangements may have long since ceased to exist; however, provisions of law make it difficult—sometimes almost impossible—to secure a rationalization of local governmental structure.

Economic Considerations. Underlying the problems of local government finance in many communities is an economy which cannot adequately support local government services. The pattern of gross difference between the wealthy and the poor governmental units is too well established to require documentation here.

If a local government is fortunate enough to have a high income constituency (or even with a low income constituency to have a high level of taxable economic activities) it may develop sufficient economic base to carry on successfully. The major problems occur in the low income situations. There is frequently no immediate answer other than resorting to aid from higher levels of government.

Mobility Is Expensive. The high mobility of our population contributes to the problems of financing our local governments. Where urban growth is well ordered, it is likely to produce sufficient taxable resources to finance the accompanying governmental needs. However, the decentralization into ever-widening metropolitan areas has generally been accompanied by lower levels of effective control over development patterns.

---

[2] U.S. Bureau of the Census, *1972 Census of Governments: Governmental Organization,* Vol. 1, (Washington, D. C.), p. 10. In 1972 the 264 SMSA's had 4,758 school districts, 444 counties, 5,467 municipalities, 3,462 townships, and 8,054 special districts.

In mushrooming new suburban communities, entire physical plants have to be financed in addition to the financing of expanding urban services; the fringe areas shift from rural to urban status without proper regulatory and protective controls; and there is frequently little or no offsetting reduction in expenditures in the central cities with declining populations. The latter find their traffic, safety, and welfare problems intensified by the increasing population mobility and, in order to check the inroads of obsolescence, they must resort to costly rehabilitation programs. Meanwhile, the lack of area-wide and effective planning for land use, transportation, sanitation, and other needs is contributing to vast accumulation of financial liabilities. Moreover, many central cities in the metropolitan areas have become the residence of the poor, who, in turn, tend to generate an abnormally high per capita expense burden.

Finding remedies for municipal revenue deficiencies has many ramifications, involving not merely a search for adequate and suitable revenues for the existing structure of local government but also a consideration of how the deficiency might be relieved by a more efficient distribution of functions, by more judicious intergovernmental fiscal relations, and by constructive changes in the structure itself. Of most immediate practical concern, however, are the characteristics of existing municipal revenue systems and the alternatives for modifying and augmenting these systems constructively.

In striking a balance, one must also observe that in many of the older core cities of the metropolitan areas, the political leadership has been responsible for some of its own problems—especially in granting salary and fringe benefits to city employees which are high in relation to the prevailing levels in the private sector in these same cities. Also, many of these cities are guilty of permitting personnel and other practices which result in low efficiency.

CRITERIA OF A GOOD REVENUE SYSTEM

The efficiency and vitality of local self-government depend a great deal on how local government is financed. As municipalities seek to strengthen and broaden their revenue systems, they need to observe certain considerations to the best of their ability, among them the following:

1. *The revenue system should be adequate to meet a local government's reasonable needs.* This means that the yield of important sources of revenue should not be unduly sensitive to cyclical economic fluctuations and, therefore, a hazard to fiscal stability. Local governments have little opportunity for deficit financing (except in capital project financing) and, thus, must ordinarily maintain balanced budgets. An income tax, for example, either as a local tax or as a shared state tax, is cycle-sensitive and may not produce the same stability of yield as some other taxes. This is particularly true if liberal exemptions and deductions from income are allowed.

2. *A revenue system that stirs tax consciousness among all the voters is much to be desired.* If all are clearly aware that they have some share in financing the cost of their local government, they are likely to be more responsible in making decisions on the purposes and methods of spending. On the other hand, political leaders may, at times, find it more convenient to enact revenue measures that tend to obscure the realities.

3. *Features of the local revenue system that are harmful to the local economy are shortsighted.* The system should have as little adverse effect as possible on economic growth. Also, frequently condemned as unjust and shortsighted, however, is the use of discriminatory local tax exemptions and preferences for economic promotion.

4. *There is wisdom in avoiding very high tax rates.* Very high rates can create economic distortion, weaken revenue sources, and generate administrative problems. They can be partially avoided in large cities through the use of more than one major source of revenue; in most small local governments, they are less successfully avoided without great local ingenuity and good state-local cooperation.

5. *Ease of administration is an important test of the suitability.* To be acceptable for a given municipality, any source of revenue must be susceptible of fair, efficient administration without undue administrative expense or undue cost and inconvenience resulting from taxpayer noncompliance. In this regard, both the size and the administrative competence of the governmental unit are also decisive factors.

6. *Facets of equity must be brought into a sense of balance.* On the one hand, many students of the problem look only at the incidence of the taxes and, accordingly, can point to many kinds of local revenue measures which are regressive in character; that is, the contributions of lower income groups are greater proportionately to their incomes than those of middle and higher income groups.

    To counterbalance this consideration, however, there is another major facet of equity which is frequently overlooked by those who advocate tax rates that are proportionate, or even progressive, in relation to income. This much overlooked consideration relates to the services being received. Thus, the lower income groups are frequently the major recipients of, or the cause of, local government expenditures. Hence, if taxes were levied in relation to benefits received, the rates upon the lower income families as a group would be substantially higher.

Of even greater importance is the fact that several levels (local, state, and federal) of "progressive" taxation pyramided one on top of the next can produce very adverse cumulative effects. There is a respectable body of thinkers who believe that proportionate taxation at the local level is sufficient, leaving to the state and federal governments (perhaps only the latter) the responsibility for serious attention to progressive taxation and income redistribution.

The resolution of these conflicting concepts of equity is a political problem of the first order. This work does not attempt to offer a solution, but merely to call attention to these competitive concepts of equity.

SOURCES OF REVENUE—A RETROSPECTIVE VIEW

An understanding of the present status of local government revenue is facilitated by looking at the broad outlines of the picture as it has developed during this century.

Growth in Total Local Government Revenues, 1902-1972

The growth in local government revenues is shown in Table 6 for the period through 1971-72. From that table, it may be seen that total local government revenues have increased about 100 times in a period of 70 years—from $0.9 billion in 1902 to $113.2 billion in 1971-72.

Of course, a large portion of this growth has been due to the restatement of the value of the dollar. Also, a large part has been due to the large increase in urban population during the period. Yet, when local government revenues are related to Gross National Product, it is found that these revenues have increased from 3.7 percent of GNP in 1902 to 7.7 percent of GNP in 1940 and to 10.2 percent of GNP in 1971-72.

This, of course, means that today local government finance is roughly three times as important in our national economy than it was 70 years ago. Some of this has been accounted for by transfers of elements of our economic activities from the private sector to the public sector, e.g., transit and some utility operations. However, in the main, it has been in the form of expansion of the levels of service provided through local governments.

Growth in Locally Generated General Revenues, 1922-1972

The growth in locally generated general revenues from 1922 to 1972 was from $3.55 billion to $64.45 billion—an increase of 1,715 percent. Even with this great increase, the locally generated general revenues did not keep pace with total local general revenues so that the percentage of total local general revenues from local sources decreased from 91.7 percent to 62.3 percent.

Of the locally generated general revenues, service charges and miscellaneous sources continued to increase—from $0.48 billion in 1922 to $15.52 in 1972. Service charges accounted for only 13.5 percent of locally generated general revenues in 1922 and for 24.0 percent of such revenues in 1972.

The remainder of locally generated general revenues are taxes. Total tax revenues increased from $3.07 billion in 1922 to $48.93 billion in 1972, an increase of 1,494 percent. But as a percentage of total local revenues, local taxes decreased from 74.2 percent to 43.2 percent during this half century.

Growth in Locally Generated Special Revenues, 1902-1972

The U.S. Bureau of the Census treats three items as other than general revenue and general expense of local governments, i.e., utilities, liquor store operations, and insurance trust fund operations (largely pensions).

Table 6
TRENDS IN SOURCES OF LOCAL GOVERNMENT REVENUES
SELECTED YEARS, 1902 – 1970/71
(amounts in billions of dollars)

Year	Total Revenue From all Sources	Utility Revenue	Liquor Store Revenue	Insurance Trust Revenue	Total General Revenue	Intergovernmental Revenue		General Revenue from own Sources	Charges and Miscellaneous General Revenues	Tax Revenue	Property Taxes	Sales and Gross Receipts	Income Taxes	Other Taxes
						Federal	State							
1902	0.91	.06	—	*	0.85	*	.05	.80	.09	.70	.62	*	—	.08
1922	4.15	.27	—	.02	3.87	.01	.31	3.55	.48	3.07	2.97	.02	—	.08
1932	6.19	.46	0.10	.04	5.69	.01	.80	4.88	.61	4.27	4.16	.03	—	.09
1942	8.11	.89	.11	.09	7.12	.06	1.78	5.29	.66	4.63	4.27	.13	.03	.19
1952	19.40	2.07	.11	.26	16.95	.24	5.04	11.67	2.21	9.47	8.28	.63	.09	.47
1962	43.28	4.15	.15	.62	38.36	.75	10.93	26.68	5.72	20.96	18.42	1.47	.31	.76
1971-72	113.16	7.79	.28	1.63	103.47	4.46	34.56	64.45	15.52	48.93	40.88	4.24	2.24	1.58
Percentage Distribution														
1902	100.00	6.60	—	*	93.40	*	5.50	87.90	10.00	76.90	68.10	*	—	.90
1922	100.00	6.50	—	.50	93.50	.20	7.50	85.70	11.60	74.20	71.70	.50	—	1.90
1932	100.00	7.40	—	.60	91.90	.20	12.90	78.80	7.80	69.00	67.20	.50	—	1.50
1942	100.00	11.00	.50	1.10	87.80	.80	21.90	65.20	8.20	57.10	52.70	1.60	.40	2.50
1952	100.00	10.70	.60	1.30	87.40	1.20	26.00	60.20	11.40	48.80	42.70	3.20	.50	2.40
1962	100.00	9.60	.40	1.40	88.60	1.70	25.30	61.60	13.20	48.40	42.60	3.40	.70	1.80
1971-72	100.00	6.90	.20	1.50	91.40	3.90	30.50	57.00	13.70	43.20	36.10	3.70	2.00	1.40

*Statistically insignificant amounts.
Sources: Bureau of the Census, *Historical Statistics of the United States, Colonial Times to 1957*, p. 729; *Governmental Finances in 1962*, p. 20; *Governmental Finances in 1971-72*, p. 20.

In 1902, utility operations accounted for 6.6 percent of total local government revenues. This percentage increased until the 1940/1950 period and in 1952 accounted for 10.7 percent of total local government revenues. Since 1952 this sector has continued to increase in absolute terms; however, in relative terms it has moved back toward the percentages which existed in the 1902/1922 period— i.e., under 7 percent of total local government revenues.

Local liquor store operations have never loomed as a significant factor in total local government finance; however, the operations of local insurance trust funds, primarily for pensions of public employees, is assuming an increased importance in total local governmental revenue operations. The earnings of such trust funds (excluding contributions made by employees and governments) accounted for less than 1/100th of 1 percent of local government revenues in 1902, for 1.1 percent in 1942 and for 1.5 percent in 1972.

State and Federal Support of Local Government, 1902-1972

The dependence of local governments, especially public education but also redevelopment, housing and other local functions, upon federal and state payments has increased very materially during recent years. Thus, in 1902 only about 1/20th of local government revenue was derived from state and federal sources. By 1972, the state was providing 30.5 percent and the federal government providing 3.9 percent of local government revenues. (Actually, considerable portions of state support of local government was in the form of pass-through federal moneys; however, available data do not identify these pass-through amounts.)

The impact of the 1972 General Revenue-Sharing Act is not reflected in the foregoing statistics. When data are available for 1973 and subsequent years, the federal share will increase dramatically—perhaps to more than double the percentages in 1971-72.

Recent Trends, 1957 to 1971-72

Recent trends in the development of the overall revenue structure of local government in the United States can be seen in Table 7. This table provides a composite view of the trends in all local governments—counties, municipalities, townships, special districts, and school districts. In the period 1957 to 1970-71, total revenues more than tripled. Changes in relative degree of reliance upon various revenues are reflected in the percentage data. In 1957, locally generated revenues accounted for 62 percent of total revenues; in 1971, this percentage had declined to 57 percent of the total. The property tax (long the mainstay of local revenues) is still the largest single revenue source. It has, however, declined —from 43 percent of the total in 1957 to its current level of 36 percent. Intergovernmental revenues account for 34 percent of local moneys—having increased from 26 percent in 1957. Historically and currently, state grants constitute the lion's share of these funds—25 percent in 1957 and 31 percent in 1971—a fourfold increase in dollar amounts. However, if one looks at the trend, federal grants have increased ten times—from $0.3 billion to $3.4 billion—and can be expected to increase even more significantly over the next few years.

A considerable portion of the money which is passed by the state governments to their local governments is actually derived by them from the federal government. Moreover, with the initiation of general revenue sharing by the federal government in 1972, large amounts of additional funds are now flowing directly from the federal government to local governments.

VARIATIONS IN REVENUE SOURCES

The revenue systems of individual local governments often vary widely from the composite picture of the general revenues of all local governments in the United States.

Variations by Specific Types of Local Government

A review of Table 8 provides a distribution of total general revenues (excluding utilities, insurance trusts, and some other enterprise income which are included in Table 6) and reflects the tremendous differences in the use of, and emphasis upon, different sources in the revenue structures of specific types of local government.

Table 7
TRENDS IN REVENUE OF LOCAL GOVERNMENTS, BY SOURCE,
FOR SELECTED YEARS, 1957 to 1971
(amounts in billions of dollars)

		1957		1966-67		1970-71		Increase 1957-1971	
		Amount	Percent	Amount	Percent	Amount	Percent	Amt.	Percent
	Total Revenue	28.9	100.0	65.4	100.0	101.0	100.0	72.0	249.5
1.11	Utilities	2.9	10.0	5.5	8.4	7.3	7.2	4.4	151.7
1.12	Trust Funds & Other	0.5	1.3	1.1	1.3	1.5	1.4	0.9	180.0
1.2	Total General Revenue	25.4	87.8	58.7	89.7	92.0	91.0	66.5	261.8
1.21	Intergovernmental	7.5	25.9	20.4	31.1	34.5	34.1	27.0	360.0
1.211	Federal	0.3	1.0	1.9	2.9	3.4	3.3	3.1	1033.3
1.212	State	7.2	24.9	18.5	28.2	31.1	30.8	23.9	331.9
1.22	General Revenue from Own Sources	17.9	61.9	38.3	58.5	57.5	56.9	39.6	221.2
1.221	Taxes	14.3	49.4	29.3	44.8	43.4	43.0	29.1	203.4
1.2211	Property taxes	12.4	42.9	25.4	38.8	36.7	36.3	24.3	195.9
1.2212	Other taxes	1.9	6.5	3.9	5.9	6.7	6.6	4.8	252.6
1.222	Charges & Misc.	3.6	12.4	9.0	13.7	14.1	13.9	10.5	291.6

Sources: U.S. Bureau of the Census, *1957 Census of Governments: Compendium of Government Finances*, Vol. III, No. 5, p. 17; *Governmental Finances in 1966-67*, p. 20; and *in 1970-71*, p. 20.

Table 8
TRENDS IN GENERAL REVENUE OF LOCAL GOVERNMENTS, BY SOURCE AND TYPE OF GOVERNMENT FOR SELECTED YEARS, 1957 to 1971
(amounts in billions of dollars)

	1957		1966-67		1970-71	
	Amount	Percent	Amount	Percent	Amount	Percent
Counties						
Total General Revenue	5.6	100.0	12.6	100.0	20.3	100.0
Intergovernmental	2.1	37.5	5.1	40.4	8.5	41.8
Federal	0.1	1.8	n.a.	—	n.a.	—
State & other	2.0	35.7	n.a.	—	n.a.	—
General Revenue from own sources	3.5	62.5	7.6	60.3	11.8	58.1
Taxes	2.8	50.0	5.8	46.0	8.7	42.8
Property	2.6	46.4	5.3	42.0	7.6	37.4
Other taxes	0.2	3.5	0.5	3.9	1.1	5.4
Charges & Misc.	0.7	12.5	1.8	14.2	3.1	15.2
Municipalities						
Total General Revenue	9.3	100.0	19.2	100.0	30.6	100.0
Intergovernmental	1.8	19.3	5.1	26.5	9.7	31.6
Federal	0.2	2.2	n.a.	—	n.a.	—
State & other	1.6	17.2	n.a.	—	n.a.	—
General Revenue from own sources	7.5	80.6	14.1	73.4	20.9	68.3
Taxes	5.9	63.4	10.4	54.1	15.1	49.3
Property	4.3	46.2	7.2	37.5	10.0	32.6
Other taxes	1.6	17.2	3.2	16.6	5.1	16.6
Charges & Misc.	1.6	17.2	3.7	19.2	5.8	18.9
Townships and Special Districts						
Total General Revenue	2.2	100.0	5.1	100.0	7.7	100.0
Intergovernmental	0.4	18.1	1.2	23.5	1.9	23.6
Federal	0.1	4.5	n.a.	—	n.a.	—
State & other	0.3	13.6	n.a.	—	n.a.	—
General Revenue from own sources	1.7	77.2	3.9	76.4	5.8	76.3
Taxes	1.1	50.0	2.1	41.1	3.2	42.1
Property	1.0	45.4	2.0	39.2	3.0	39.4
Other taxes	0.1	4.5	0.1	1.9	0.2	2.6
Charges & Misc.	0.6	27.2	1.8	35.2	2.6	34.2
School Districts						
Total General Revenue	8.9	100.0	23.3	100.0	35.3	100.0
Intergovernmental	3.9	43.8	10.5	45.0	16.3	46.1
Federal	0.1	1.1	n.a.	—	n.a.	—
State & other	3.4	38.2	n.a.	—	n.a.	—
General Revenue from own sources	5.1	57.3	12.8	54.9	19.0	53.8
Taxes	4.5	50.5	11.0	47.2	16.5	46.7
Property	4.4	49.4	10.9	46.7	16.1	45.6
Other taxes	0.1	1.1	0.2	0.8	0.3	0.8
Charges & Misc.	0.6	6.7	1.8	7.7	2.6	7.3

Sources: U.S. Bureau of the Census, *1957 Census of Governments: Compendium of Government Finances*, Vol. III, No. 5, p. 17; *Governmental Finances in 1966-67*, p. 30; and *in 1970-71*, p. 30.

Among the five types defined by the Bureau of the Census, school districts in 1971 accounted for the greatest part of total general revenues (38%), followed closely by municipalities (33%) and counties (22%), and then by special districts (4.6%) and townships (3.5%). In 1957, however, municipalities, with 37% of total revenues, held first position with school districts taking second place.

Intergovernmental revenues ($34.5 billion in 1971) accounted for 46 percent of total revenues in school districts, 42 percent of county revenues, 32 percent of revenues in municipalities, and 24 percent in special districts and townships. Of the intergovernmental revenues, the $16.3 billion allocated to school districts is almost twice the $9.7 billion given to municipalities. In the period 1957 to 1971, intergovernmental payments to municipalities, as a percentage of total general revenues, showed a tremendous increase—from 19 percent to 32 percent—an overall increase of 64 percent.

Property taxes, totaling $36.7 billion in 1971, accounted for 39 percent of general revenues in townships and special districts; 46 percent of school district revenue; and 37 percent and 33 percent of general revenues in counties and municipalities, respectively. Over the period 1957 to 1971, property taxes as a percentage of general revenues have declined in each type of local government.

Other taxes—sales, income, and gross receipts—are now (and have been) five percent or less of total revenues in townships, school districts, and counties. However, in municipalities they represent 17 percent of general revenues.

Even more significant differences in the use of different revenue sources among the various types of local government can be seen in the category of charges and miscellaneous revenues. Over the period 1957 to 1971, the percentages in this category have remained stable in municipalities and school districts; they have increased somewhat in townships and special districts; and have shown a marked increase in counties. These charges currently represent 34 percent of revenues in special districts and townships; 19 percent in municipalities; 15 percent in counties; and 7 percent in school districts.

It may be concluded from the foregoing that in school districts and counties the most important sources of revenue are the property tax and state and federal aid. Municipalities depend on intergovernmental revenue and the property tax and, to a lesser (but still substantial) degree, on income, sales, and gross receipts taxes along with special assessments and other charges. Special districts rely mainly on special assessments and other charges. Townships depend primarily on property taxes.

Variations Within Municipalities

Variations within classes of local governments, both interstate and intrastate, are particularly conspicuous in the case of municipalities. Interstate variations depend not only on state aid policies and the available local alternatives to the property tax but also on the allocation of functions. Some states, for example, administer all or much of the welfare function, while others assign it to the municipalities or counties and transfer revenues to aid its financing. Within many states, there is a fair degree of uniformity in municipal revenue systems, but there are increasingly numerous exceptions. Such exceptions occur in states which give their municipalities power to experiment with nonproperty taxes and charges for services, and also in states in which there is a lack of uniformity in the major functions performed by municipalities—particularly in those functions which receive state aid.

Variations of wealth and tax effort between municipalities naturally contribute both to inter- and intra-state differences.

To illustrate, in New York intergovernmental revenue supplied 52 percent of the general revenue of Buffalo but only 29 percent of that of Mount Vernon in 1971, the main reason being that schools were a city function in the former and a separate district function in the latter. Binghamton, although it operated no schools, derived 42 percent of its general revenue from intergovernmental sources, chiefly because it administered intergovernmentally-aided health, hospitals, and welfare—county functions in the instance of the other two cities.[3]

Table 9 contains a percentage distribution of general revenue of municipalities developed from their own sources during 1970-71. From this table, it may be seen that when one considers all municipalities in the United States, 72.3 percent of locally generated general revenues were from taxes, 17.1 percent from current charges and the remaining 10.6 percent from miscellaneous sources. Of the 14 cities selected for comparison, it is noted that Hartford depends upon taxes for 92.8 percent of its total locally generated revenue in contrast to only 55.1 percent in the case of Seattle.

The contrast in terms of relative degrees of reliance upon various local taxes is of interest. Thus, for all municipalities, the distribution is found to be as follows:

	Percent
Property taxes	66.5
General sales and gross receipts	11.0
Selective sales and gross receipts	7.4
Other taxes (including income)	15.1

Within the individual cities, the contrast is even sharper. Thus about the only local taxes levied in Boston, Hartford, Syracuse, and Indianapolis are property taxes. In each of these cities more than 97 percent of local taxes are derived from property taxes.

At the other extreme, the City of Philadelphia had the lowest degree of reliance upon the property tax—30.7 percent—followed by Phoenix at 33.7 percent. General sales and gross receipts taxes accounted for more than one-third of local tax revenue in four cities—New Orleans, Denver, Houston, and Phoenix. In Philadelphia, "Other Taxes," especially the wage and net profits taxes, accounted for 68.7 percent of local municipal tax revenue.

Of material significance is the very low degree of reliance upon non-tax sources in Boston, Hartford, Syracuse, Philadelphia, Chicago, Indianapolis, and Houston. On the other hand, about one-third of all locally generated general revenue was developed from nontax sources in Jacksonville, New Orleans, Denver, Las Vegas, Phoenix, and Los Angeles. In Seattle, about 45 percent of locally generated general revenue was developed from nontax sources.

---

[3] United States Bureau of the Census, *City Government Finances in 1970-71*, (Washington, D. C.: United States Government Printing Office, 1971), p. 42.

Table 9
PERCENTAGE DISTRIBUTION OF GENERAL REVENUE FROM OWN SOURCES
ALL MUNICIPALITIES AND SELECTED CITIES, 1970-71

Region Municipality	Total	Current Charges	Miscellaneous Sources	Taxes	Distribution of Taxes by Source				
					Total Taxes	Property	General Sales & Gross Receipts	Selective Sales & Gross Receipts	Other Taxes
All Municipalities	100.0	17.1	10.6	72.3	100.0	66.5	11.0	7.4	15.1
New England									
Boston, Massachusetts	100.0	15.8	3.6	80.6	100.0	98.7	—	—	1.3
Hartford, Connecticut	100.0	2.9	4.3	92.8	100.0	99.5	—	—	0.5
Middle Atlantic									
Syracuse, New York	100.0	16.5	9.4	74.1	100.0	97.4	—	4.8	0.8
Philadelphia, Pennsylvania	100.0	12.7	9.6	77.8	100.0	30.7	—	0.6	68.7
Southern									
Jacksonville, Florida	100.0	23.5	13.2	63.3	100.0	61.2	—	33.0	5.8
New Orleans, Louisiana	100.0	23.8	11.2	65.0	100.0	38.3	41.0	12.1	8.6
Central									
Chicago, Illinois	100.0	11.2	7.5	81.3	100.0	61.0	14.7	13.9	10.4
Indianapolis, Indiana	100.0	9.2	10.0	80.8	100.0	98.7	—	—	1.3
Mountain									
Denver, Colorado	100.0	21.4	13.8	64.8	100.0	40.0	41.1	5.6	13.3
Las Vegas, Nevada	100.0	15.4	15.4	69.2	100.0	38.8	23.5	8.2	29.5
Southwest									
Houston, Texas	100.0	12.0	13.5	74.5	100.0	40.0	41.1	5.6	13.3
Phoenix, Arizona	100.0	15.1	17.3	67.6	100.0	33.7	38.5	15.2	3.6
Pacific									
Los Angeles, California	100.0	14.8	16.9	68.4	100.0	52.7	19.6	9.4	18.3
Seattle, Washington	100.0	24.1	20.8	55.1	100.0	44.8	9.7	24.5	21.0

Source: Developed from Table 5, Bureau of the Census, *City Government Finances, 1970-71*, pp. 87-100.

THE USE OF DEBT IN FINANCING

Although all financing (except where local governments default on their debt) is ultimately payable from their revenues, a large portion of the dollars used to pay the expenditures of local governments in any single year is derived from the issuance of debt. Of course, except in unusual circumstances, the use of debt issues (other than revenue anticipation notes) is restricted to paying a portion of capital outlay expense for the year.

In the aggregate the equation goes like this:

"A"	+	"B"	+	"C"	=	"D"
Resources at beginning of year		Revenues received in year		Proceeds of debt issued in year		Total Resources available in year

−	"E"	−	"F"	−	"G"	=	"H"
	Payment of principal of debt		Payment of interest on debt		Payment of expenses		Resources at end of year

Despite the efforts of the Bureau of the Census in compiling comprehensive data in the various editions of its census of governments and annual volumes on governmental finance, it has not been feasible to secure sufficiently accurate data on the totality of local governments in the United States to permit the development of each of the items "A" through "H" for consecutive years.

However, the approximate data developed for 1971-72[4] is as follows:

			(amounts in billions)
A.	Cash resources at end of 1970-71		$53.3
B.	Revenues received in year	$114.8	
C.	Debt issued in year		
	1. Short-term (net increase)	0.1	
	2. Long-term debt issued	13.6	128.6
D.	Total cash resources available		$181.9
E.	Payment of principal on long-term debt	5.9	
F.	Payment of interest on long-term debt	4.8	
G.	Expenditures	113.8	124.5
H.	Indicated cash resources at end of year		57.4
	Actual cash resources reported		58.4
	*Discrepancy		$ 1.0

* The discrepancy arises in part because the reports of the Bureau of the Census for years other than the "census of government years" is based upon samples of local governments. It is probable that the samples resulted in an erroneous reporting of the increase in short-term debt, which from other sources is known to have increased considerably during this year.

4 U. S. Bureau of the Census, *Government Finances in 1970-71*, p. 29; *1972 Census of Governments*, Vol. 4, "Government Finances," No. 5, "Compendium of Government Finances," (Washington, D. C., 1974), pp. 26, 28, 35.

The picture for 1971–72 indicates that total outstanding debt increased by $7.79 billion. Doubtless the increase would have been greater except for the fact that this was the first year of distribution of moneys under federal general revenue sharing, which enabled many local governments to reduce the amount of their short-term debt. In national economic effect, the substitution of $13.6 billion of new long-term debt for the $5.9 billion of long-term debt retired produces a relatively small total increase in long-term debt outstanding—only 4.9 percent for local governments in a period of considerable inflation.

On the other hand, from the standpoint of the local governments, the debt retirements are normally scheduled through the payment of serial bond maturities. In these circumstances, all of the issuance of the $13.4 billion of new long-term debt represented the degree to which local governments rely upon new debt issuances to pay larger portions of their (capital) expenditures. In 1971–72, with expenditures (excluding interest) of $113.8 billion, the new debt issued amounted to more than 10 percent of the total.

Hence, in considering the overall pattern of financing local government in the United States in any year since World War II, debt must be taken into account.

As in the case of other elements of local government finance, the degree to which different types of local governments rely upon debt financing varies widely—as do regional patterns in this field.

At the end of World War II (1945) the total outstanding local government debt was $13.6 billion. At the end of the 1971-72 fiscal year this had risen to $120.7 billion (plus an undetermined amount of short-term debt anticipation notes.) Therefore, during this period, the debt had increased by $107.1 billion.

CONCLUSION

The wide variety of financing for different types of local governments and the wide regional differentials make it difficult to offer generalizations which are meaningful. Yet, it is apparent that as we rely more heavily upon the local governments for delivery of public services, it is inevitable that we will increase the amount and the degree of reliance upon transfer payments from the state and federal governments to help balance local budgets.

It is also clear that if we are to be able to take advantage of the broad economic strength in most SMSA's—as an offset to the uncontrolled expansion of state and federal transfer payments—we must get on with the matter of reorganization of the structure of local governments from present balkanized areas into reorganized governments capable of dealing with revenue and other problems on a local regional basis.

4

An Overall View of Budgetary Process

The use of budgeting for control purposes has long been a paramount objective of many; however, over the years, other emphases have emerged. Budgeting developed at the national level as part of a long struggle in England by the Parliament for effective participation in control of public affairs—a struggle for prior Parliamentary approval of the finances of the realm as a check against the levy of oppressive taxes and embarkations upon unnecessary and wasteful ventures. In the United States, modern municipal budgeting was a part of the reform movement in the first quarter of the twentieth century to strengthen and to professionalize the office of the chief executive. Legislative control in many of the big cities had degenerated into rule by corrupt party bosses. Management by the executive branch was weak.

RETROSPECTIVE REVIEW

The local budget process as we now know it had its genesis in the work of the New York Bureau of Municipal Research[1]—one of the very early voluntary organizations concerned with the application of scientific principles of manage-

---

[1] The New York Bureau of Municipal Research, a privately supported non-profit organization, between 1907 and 1915 produced a number of studies in which it gradually developed an approach to improved budgeting at the municipal and state levels of government. The first of these, *Making a Municipal Budget*, 47 pages, was published in 1907. A careful study of that document reveals a statement of desirable budgetary processes that portended virtually all of the concepts that have been included in the literature of budgeting since—programming, planning, performance accounting, and others. These concepts were more fully developed in later publications of the Bureau, e.g., *The Elements of State Budget Making*, 63 pages, published in 1916.

Other similar organizations were spawned in Philadelphia, Baltimore, Los Angeles, San Francisco, Buffalo, Detroit, and other cities—usually with the same title of Bureau of Municipal Research. These organizations, frequently staffed initially in part by staff members of the "mother church" expanded on the development of these concepts with application to their respective governments.

Finally, in 1929, Arthur Eugene Buck, a staff member of the New York Bureau during most of his professional life, brought the essence of the state of the art together in his *Public Budgeting*, 612 pages, (New York: Harper & Brothers). Again, a study of that basic work reveals adherence to concepts still being advocated by most prominent authors in the field of state and local government budgeting.

All this is by way of pointing out that leaders in the field have long known the best ways in which to do the job. The problem is to get the practitioners in the field to put into effect these now time-honored principles and procedures.

ment to the conduct of local government affairs. In this early period, almost no city of any size in the United States operated under systematic budget procedures. From time to time, appropriations were made to individual departments and agencies; and revenue measures were enacted sporadically, with a view to financing most of these operating expenditures. Sometimes, cities relied heavily upon the proceeds of long-term loans to meet current obligations, on the assumption that, with the rapid growth of the city, these could be repaid out of incremental revenue yields.

Moreover, most appropriations tended to be in "net amounts"; i.e., for those departments and agencies which collected fees or other non-tax revenues, the appropriations were supplemental to the direct revenues which the office, department, or agency was automatically permitted to spend—usually without periodic appropriation.

This rather haphazard system developed a broad range of critics, interested not only in bringing some order out of the process but also in causing offices, departments, and agencies to develop plans for expenditure related to their assigned functions and goals.

Currently, the budget is a proposed plan of expenditures and revenues and the authorization to spend is usually contained in a separate resolution of the council, known as the appropriation ordinance. Even today, however, the governing bodies of many municipalities still "adopt the budget," without a full understanding of which of the thousands of lines in the budget document constitute limitations upon what can be spent and which are only explanatory.

As the budget process at the national, state, and local levels has evolved, greater emphasis has been placed upon such concepts as "programs," "performance," and "planning." The current epitomization of the acme of perfection is supposed to be the "PPBS," i.e., the program, planning, budgeting system. However, even this system has come in for widespread criticism as its limitations have come to be more clearly recognized, especially as they relate to local government budgeting.

PPB(S) is compatible with the history of budget reform intended to link program information in budgetary decision making. At the same time, much of PPB(S) grew out of a series of concepts and techniques that were developed largely independent of budgeting. These are operations research, economic analysis, general systems theory, cybernetics, computers, and systems analysis. The Department of Defense, despite whatever shortcomings one wishes to cite, was well grounded in these analytic techniques that had emerged mainly during and following World War II . . . Though PPB(S) was an apparent success during the early 1960s, the Indochina war and cost overruns in Defense were to bring into question the entire efficacy of the Defense system.

Federal civilian agencies were required by 1965 to establish their own planning-programming-budgeting systems with the guidance of the Bureau of the Budget. Much was lost in the translation from the military side to the civilian side of the government . . .

State and local governments also tried PPB(S) during the 1960s and met with only a modicum of success . . . the general tenor of the early 1970s was that PPB(S) was an interesting but unsuccessful experiment.[2]

Contrast of Local Budgeting with Federal Budgeting

Those students who were first introduced to budgeting at the federal level through economics texts and discussions of fiscal policy and the federal budget and now, for the first time, approach municipal budgeting are in need of some reorientation. Budgeting at the two levels of government is not the same.

1. At the federal level the terminology is more complex. There, the literature refers to three types of budgets: administrative budget, consolidated-cash budget, and an economic budget. The last two are used in fiscal policy and economic analysis. Economists devised the term "administrative budget" to designate the budget of primary interest to administrators and appropriation committees as opposed to the budgets most useful in economic analysis. A fourth term, "development budget," although not applicable in our federal government, applies to those countries which have adopted "five-year" or similar plans to stimulate and direct the economic growth rate. Such a budget makes projections of planned programs and capital improvements in both the public and private sectors.

    At the local government level in this country, the operating budget and the capital budget are properly classified as "administrative budgets."[3]

2. The local government budget is not considered an important instrument for fiscal policy, using the term "fiscal policy" as the economist uses it and not as synonymous with "financial policy," which is often the case in municipal finance literature. Only the federal budget is of sufficient size to make planned surpluses or deficits a feasible form of economic manipulation in order to effect broad economic results—and even there experience does not give us much basis for thinking that political institutions are full masters of their destiny. Some economists have an interest in planned public works (with state and local government participation) as a special countercyclical measure when downward trends threaten depression proportions; other economists see this as a clumsy and relatively inflexible approach to fiscal policy.

3. The concept of a "balanced budget" in state and local governments is quite different from this concept at the federal level. In the latter, "balance" is defined as the point where income and outgo are equal. However, the definition must go further in order to state what is involved—total federal operations or some segment less than the totality. Thus, there may be an overall balance and, at the same time, substantive

---

[2] Robert D. Lee, Jr. and Ronald W. Johnson, *Public Budgeting Systems*, (Baltimore: University Park Press, 1973), pp. 147-148.

[3] The administrative budget is roughly comparable to the general fund budget, including most revenues and expenditures and excluding specially designated funds, such as trust funds.

internal imbalances, e.g., the social security fund may show a surplus while other portions of the federal budget relating to the more traditional functions may show an offsetting deficit. Moreover, annual outlays for capital projects are considered as part of the federal annual budget; whereas, a markedly different treatment is accorded them at the state and local levels of governments.

In state and local governments, "budget-balancing" is discussed in much different terms. Generally, a budget is considered balanced if the income is sufficient to meet current costs of operation and the interest and scheduled payments on the principal of the debt.

The fact that the total amount of debt is increased during the year does not, at the state and local levels, produce an "unbalanced budget" in prevailing terminology and concepts. The same results, if applied to the federal budget, could produce the claim of an "unbalanced" budget. Conversely, a reduction in long-term debt at state and local governmental levels is not considered a contribution to the "balancing" of the budgets of these governments. In the federal terms, any reduction in the debt is automatically considered a budget-balancing truism.

4. Borrowing by the federal government is to meet cash requirements, without designation as to whether the proceeds are to be used for operating or capital purposes. Federal bond issues or other debt issues are not generally linked with a specific capital improvement project. Borrowing by local governments is usually for specific capital projects. Net federal debt reduction is achieved only through a cash surplus. Local governments are simultaneously retiring some debt while providing for payment of capital expenditures from proceeds of new debt. Some central governments have capital programs and a few have capital budgets which relate borrowing to these rather than the operating budget; but, borrowing by our federal government is undifferentiated as to operating or capital requirements.

Role of the Budget in Planning and Programming

As previously indicated, the control aspects of budgeting long overshadowed the role of the budget in planning and programming. Control and accountability are still very important, but, with the coming of program budgeting and of capital budgeting, a more balanced view has appeared. Both types have made it clear that budgeting is an integral part of a wider management spectrum.

Viewed from its broadest perspective, budgeting is a pervasive element of the overall management process. Although the concept is often associated exclusively with the narrower aspect known as the "annual operating budget," the process encompasses the entire field of long-term programming—both for operational and capital purposes. Once those responsible for the administration of the government substantially agree upon the elements of a long-term operating program, those portions of expenditure which are capital in nature can be gathered together rationally in the form of a long-term capital program.

Unfortunately, before the shift in budget emphasis, the terms "planning, programming and budgeting," in combination, became rather firmly embedded in administrative language. Continued usage implies that budgeting is separate from planning and programming and follows after the other two. This is too narrow a concept.

Budgeting, to be genuinely successful, requires a set of well-defined programs extending over a period of years—namely, a comprehensive physical development plan, an analysis of financial policy, a projection of work programs, and a capital needs program. By this measure, relatively few local (or other) governments have accomplished a genuinely successful job of budgeting.

The core of the budgeting process is the allocation of resources among competing demands. This process of allocation takes place at several levels:

1. A decision as to the portion of the economic resources of the community that is to be assigned to attainment of governmental goals and programs vs. retention by private persons—both individual and corporate—of control over the economic and human resources available to the community

2. Within this given portion of the community's economic resources (coupled with resources made available by other governments) a determination of the emphasis which will be placed upon different programs and activities carried out by the particular governmental entity

3. Within the municipal governmental programs and activities, the assignment of resources to the various organizational units and the determination of the relative degree to which these resources will be applied to engaging personnel, purchasing services, acquiring materiel, acquiring property of a permanent nature, and other kinds of expenditure

4. Within each organizational unit, the choice of specific program elements to which available resources will be applied—within the limits of discretion available to such unit

5. In the case of capital financing, the extent to which payment will be made from current resources and the extent to which the government will anticipate future revenue through the issue of debt

Planning and programming reappear again and again during the budget cycle. Some writers lay great stress upon the cyclical character of these activities. Much of formal planning and programming comes at the budget formulation stage. If cutbacks are required at the legislative review stage, reprogramming is necessary to meet legislative objections. Approval by the governing body of the operating and capital budgets for the year establishes a guide for subsequent planning and programming. In general, at the execution stage, plans and programs have to be adjusted periodically.

Plans and programs are molded by a variety of other conditions. For example, some assert that planning for a whole community rather than separate overlapping local governments is superior; however, in many situations this is more a statement of an ideal than a feasible course of action. Again, a wealth of experience with the long-term capital program now exists, but only a minimum of experience has been gained with the long-term operating budget. Total long-term programming is still a proposal, although the concept is implicit in a rational budget process.

Classification of Budgets

One who would master budget literature is inevitably faced with a variety of terms that are used to connote diverse concepts. Here, we have attempted to sort out those terms which classify budgets by types. With successive application of different sets of criteria (various ways of looking at the same thing), a single budget in a given city, for example, could be at one and the same time: an executive budget, a main or general budget, an annual or current budget, an operating budget, a program budget, a performance budget, an authorized budget, and a lump-sum budget.

Classification by types stems from applying such criteria as: who is responsible for preparation of the budget, who is expected to be the primary user, etc. The gamut includes the following classifications:

1. As to responsibility for preparation:
    Executive
    Legislative

2. As to primary user:
    Administrative
    Economic (including consolidated-cash budget, the nation's budget)

3. As to time-span:
    Current or annual
    Long-term

4. As to source of financing:
    Current revenue
    Loan funds

5. As to expenditure character:
    Operating
    Capital or capital improvement program
    Emergency
    Extraordinary

6. As to expenditure classification emphasized in planning and in appropriations:
    Objective or means-oriented
    Program or goal-oriented

7. As to organizational comprehensiveness:
    Main or general
    Auxiliary, special or annexed
    Departmental
    Project

8. As to method used in incorporating public service enterprises into the general budget:
   Gross
   Net

9. As to degree of appropriation breakdown:
   Line-item
   Lump-sum

10. As to method of enforcing "balancing":
    Cash-basis
    Accrual-basis
    Modified cash-accrual basis

11. As to general classification:
    Traditional
    Performance
    Program
    PPBS-Program planning budget system

BUDGETING IS A DYNAMIC PROCESS

Those who would comprehend the broad significance of the budgeting process must avoid the notion that the budget is a fixed document. Of course, it can be set in concrete; however, most attempts to do so result in major fissures in the structure as the approved budget is carried into execution. The annual nature of the process should not be construed as constituting a lack of flexibility —either within the fiscal year to which the annual operating budget relates or as regards the longer period of years to which the budget planning process should, in fact, relate.

Even so, the historical base is likely to be among the most pervasive in the determination of the content of one budget in relation to its immediate predecessor. This flows naturally from two factors: (1) once a program, an element, or subelement of a program has been "legitimatized" by having been included in the approved budget and appropriation ordinance, it becomes an element of public policy; and (2) there is almost always a clientele being served by any given program; a set of public employees and officials who have a special stake in its continuance; and, frequently, an outside group (exclusive of the clientele) which has an interest in the continuation of each program element.

However, despite these considerations (which must not be underestimated in their importance) changing public interests, public needs, and technology all combine to introduce elements of dynamics into the process. Although relatively little change may be apparent from one annual budget to the next, a careful comparison of the contemporary budget with that of a decade or two decades ago will usually reveal that substantive changes have occurred.

Therefore, it is imperative that all those associated with public administration understand that the process is dynamic, not static.

Long-Term Perspective and Plan

Unfortunately the average operating budget is developed with the primary —if, indeed, not the whole—focus on the budget year. We have long since learned that the capital programming process should cover a period of years. We have not learned that, in proper perspective, the capital program itself should be an outgrowth of an even more comprehensive process which we may appropriately label: "the long-term operating program."

The long-term operating program has not caught on in the U. S. In some respects, this has been a reaction against the "five-year plans" of socialist nations. Actually, a long-term operating program should be developed for as long a period as the capacity and interest of the administration can be marshalled. It needs to emphasize the aspects of services intended to be rendered, the manpower, materiel, and structures required for implementation—reduced to the common denominator of dollars.

For an administration prepared to accept the discipline implicit in this kind of planning and administration the long-term operating program can provide one of the greatest tools of public administration. The problem is that public officials must spend so much of their time confronting and coping with the immediate problems of administration that they cannot—or will not—devote the time and energy necessary to develop the kinds of comprehensive plans that are needed for effective and efficient administration of public affairs.

SOME UNRESOLVED BUDGETARY PROBLEMS

There are many unresolved budgetary problems—some at the theoretical level and some at the administrative level. Attention in this section is drawn to a number of such problems as they appeared in the early 1970s.

The Budget Cycle

How shall the budget cycle be defined? Among the options are:
1. *The fiscal year to which the budget relates:* Obviously, this is too narrow because it fails to take into account the preparatory and post-evaluative phases, except where the budget is prepared after the beginning of the fiscal year and the process is cut off sharply at the close of the year.
2. *The preparatory phase plus the fiscal year:* Doubtless most persons concerned with budget administration tend to use this as the definition of the cycle, i.e., the time span extending from the initial preparation of the new budget through the year covered by the budget. They would largely ignore subsequent activities.
3. *The full period from initial preparation to final postaudit:* In a very real sense, the budget cycle for a given year commences with the preparation of request forms in the budget office through all phases until all services, materials, supplies, equipment, and other elements of expenditure authorized under the budget have been expended and the postaudit of those expenditures completed. This means that the period

frequently extends over three or more calendar years.

Specifically, such a concept would include the postaudit not only in a financial sense but also the postaudit of performance to determine whether the objectives sought in justifying the appropriations have, in fact, been accomplished.

Perhaps, as we become more sophisticated in our work with budgeting, we are likely to extend the concept of the cycle closer to that indicated in the third alternative. However, the definition of the cycle must be practical. The fact that there may be substantial delay in the completion of a single contract under a budget is not a basis for failing to complete the review of operations shortly after the close of the fiscal year in an administrative sense. The remaining tagends are not likely to have a substantial impact upon judgments as to the success or failure of the year's operations.

Impact of Collective Bargaining and Arbitration

One of the major unresolved issues with respect to local government budgeting is the impact of collective bargaining and, where applicable, mandatory and binding arbitration. The amounts of money eventually to be paid out are very important; however, from the strategy of both budgeting and collective bargaining, the relative timing of the various actions involved may be even more transcending.

For some of the larger local governments, the requirement for conduct of the budgeting activity and collective bargaining activities simultaneously has been the rule for a number of years. This has tended to become a more widespread pattern since the mid-1960s.

Generally, the law imposes upon administrative and legislative officials the responsibility for performance of specified elements of the budgetary function according to a specific time schedule. The law frequently provides that failure to complete the process by a given date carries very stiff penalties: (1) the invalidation of appropriations, (2) nullification of the tax levies needed to balance the budget, or (3) both of the foregoing.

As collective bargaining laws have come to be more widespread, it is customary to provide a schedule for the conduct of such bargaining. And, where mandatory, binding arbitration is the rule, a further schedule is set forth in the law. But the collective bargaining and arbitration laws ordinarily do not contain *enforceable* requirements which will cause these processes to be completed prior to the time that the proposed budget must be made public by the chief executive. Indeed, experience during recent years has resulted in failure, particularly in the case of a number of large school districts, to reach agreement until the fiscal year to which the budget relates has been largely completed.

Under these circumstances, it is not feasible for the finance officer or the chief executive to submit a meaningful and accurate budget. Public officials, *of necessity*, are obliged to violate the principles of good budgeting. They cannot set forth the amounts which they actually estimate will be required to secure a viable contract or to fund a binding arbitration award. To do so results in placing in the hands of the adversary unions facts that will increase the amounts eventually provided in compensation and fringe benefits. Obviously, the union officials will take the position that the amounts which are set forth in the budget constitute a form of offer. As such they become the floor to any settlement and that all bargaining or arbitration must take place between the amounts already allowed and the most recent demands of the unions.

As a direct result, public officials undertake one of two broad courses: (1) reduction of service levels by the amounts required to meet the cost of labor settlements, or (2) inclusion in the budget of appropriations for various items of expenditure which are "soft" items, i.e., items which can be converted to satisfy the cost of labor settlements.

Both of these courses are highly disruptive of sound principles of public administration. On the other hand, they constitute about the only practical alternatives now available. Perhaps the most damaging aspect of the operation is that, if it is extended for a period of years, the entire budget-making process will become a charade—with executive and administrative personnel "justifying" program elements and program levels which cannot be carried into effect and with councilmen confused as to what is real and what is sham. Eventually the entire budgeting system is discredited before everyone—public officials, citizens, and unions.

It may be that a new system will have to be adopted under which the budget is not adopted until new labor contracts have been negotiated or the awards made in order that budgeting may return to the real world. The developing situation appears quite intolerable.

Operating Budget Time Span

Early in this chapter reference has been made to the need for an operating program covering a number of years, in the same manner that the capital program is intended to be a reasonable projection of capital improvement needs over a span of years. Although this has been discussed in the literature for a decade or more, only limited success has been achieved in the development of such a multiple-year approach to the process. For many years, departments in Kansas City, Missouri, were required to maintain a seven-year work program. Each year's departmental budget request identified requirements currently being met and those for which the need was apparent but for which current appropriations were inadequate. For the period 1952-1966, the city of Philadelphia provided a good prototype for such a system. It developed at least the financial framework within which budgeting was to be carried out during discrete four-year periods.[4]

The Philadelphia experiment worked during moderate inflationary periods; however, with the onslaught of major inflation after 1966 the process proved unequal to the task.

Yet, this does not necessarily spell doom for the process of long-term operating programs. As a matter of fact, if long-term capital programs are to have

---

[4] See Lennox L. Moak and Emma Bowman, "A Long-Range Operating Program," *Public Administration Review*, Vol. XX, No. 1-Winter, 1960, pp. 38-40.

any validity, it is necessary that they be complemented by long-term operating programs—because the expression of capital needs in a long-term capital program should be the logical outgrowth of a long-term operating program—in which the capital facility is only one of the elements essential to attainment of the service program for the community.

The capital program has already supplied essential experience. The feasibility of planning and programming on a five- to six-year basis (but with partial execution and accounting control on a twelve-months' basis) has been demonstrated. The management concept can reach its full potentiality only when budgeting is accorded a longer time span.

Relating Revenues to Obligations

If we were to take a comprehensive view—in terms of fiscal effect—of the budgets of all states or of all local governments, we would find that the period since World War II has been a "deficit" period, inasmuch as outstanding debt has tended to rise more rapidly than cash and security holdings (including insurance trust funds for unemployment compensation and employee retirement). This has been especially observable at the local government level.

The concept that a budget should be balanced, whether or not embodied in a charter or statutory provision, is a potent force on both the revenue and expenditure sides. Balancing has at least three meanings:

1. The budget is balanced at the stage of formulation and adoption if the revenues for the year are estimated to be equal to the proposed expenditures for the year. In this situation, the cumulative carryover surplus or deficit from the prior year is ignored.
2. The budget is balanced if the sum of opening surplus plus revenues for the year is equal to the sum of the expenditures plus opening deficit; or, if there be no opening deficit, to the amount of expenditure authorizations.

In the two foregoing situations, capital outlays financed from the proceeds of bonds are not included as expenditures; however, interest on the debt and provision for repayment of a portion of the principal is included.

3. The budget is balanced if the sum of the opening surplus plus revenues for the year is equal to the expenditures plus opening deficit, provided that expenditures include the full amount of capital outlays in the year.

The third concept is that which is used by the federal government; however, it is not applied in state and local government budgeting.

The second concept of balancing is that which prevails in most local and state governments in the United States. In a sense, this is unfortunate, especially where large amounts of opening surplus are being dissipated in financing new and higher levels of current expense that will demand funding in the next year and in successive years.

The real test of balance comes at the fiscal year's end at which time the balance concept is met if revenues have covered expenditures, or if there is a surplus. A deficit violates the concept. To achieve the end result, balancing receives special attention during several phases of the budget cycle: the final executive review to formulate the proposed budget; the legislative review; the mid-year review during the execution stage, and several times during the final quarter of the fiscal year.

Enforcement of the balancing concept is a result of pressures from several sources. Widespread public belief that an unbalanced budget amounts to fiscal immorality is one; and, almost always, there are council members who reflect this underlying attitude. The investment market is a second and powerful pressure. Municipal bond dealers and their investment clientele frown on deficits and funding bonds, and a city which persists in operating with a deficit will lose face and will be penalized in the market. Finally, many state governments, in order to protect the good general reputation of their local governments, exercise supervisory powers which work to prevent operating budget deficits in the few governments which might spoil this reputation.

The ideal of the fiscal analyst is for a local government to have a light debt and to have a continuing year-end surplus in its operating funds. This idyllic situation rarely exists, even in AAA rated debt.

Over long periods of time, e.g., five or ten years, budget balancing in most local governments is inevitable. Although a few may go bankrupt, the long history of local governments suggests that, in one way or another, the budget will be balanced over a period of years. Despite this obvious fact, the annual headlines concerning the budget surplus or deficit tend to impose upon local government administrators an inordinate concern with "a balanced budget."

In due course, it is hoped that a more mature view of the situation will be adopted by all sides so that temporary imbalances will not be "viewed with alarm," and it will be recognized that a surplus is frequently more difficult to manage than a modest deficit.

The Multi-fund Structure of Budgeting

The multi-fund structure is a potent fracturing force within the budgetary process of some local governments. Basically, the fund structure is an accounting mechanism. However, if the fund structure contains dedicated tax or revenue funds which are limited to specified purposes, flexibility in planning and programming is narrowed. And the range of revenues and expenditures within which adjustments can be made to accommodate changing conditions and requirements is limited. This is especially true if tax revenue receipts are contractually dedicated for debt service over a long period of time and surpluses are locked in for the extra protection of bondholders. Some earmarking results from state legislative action, but a great deal more arises from the contractual pledges of specific revenues for the support of revenue bonds or special tax bonds.

In some respects, the flexibility arising from the concentration of all revenues into a general fund is very attractive. In other situations, the attractiveness of improved bond ratings for certain bonds, or even the legal capacity to issue such bonds, presents the finance officer with very difficult decisions.

The Fractionation of Local Government Structures

Many local governments, particularly municipal governments, have internal structures which act to fractionate not only the structure of the government but also its financial affairs. Many such separate elements of the local government tend to fall wholly or partially outside the central budgetary process—leaving the process seriously truncated. In the language of the old "principles of budgeting," comprehensiveness has been violated. Not only has the chief executive lost control of specific governmental activities, but, perhaps more importantly, overall planning and programming have been defeated. Secondly, even if the budget is comprehensive, activities which are essentially parts of a single program are often scattered among separate departments or bureaus. The usual result is divided responsibility for fragmented parts of a program that would best be planned, programmed, and executed as a whole. The most practical solution may be structural changes which bring together, within a single organizational unit created for that sole purpose, all closely related program activities. Responsibility for each program is thereby clearly fixed.

If program or goal-oriented budgets are to have more than a modicum of usefulness, a lot of sham and faking will have to be recognized as such. Every city wants to get on the band wagon and to claim that its budget system has been modernized. But program budgeting worthy of the name requires a difficult change-over from object budgeting. Activities must be regrouped within the governmental structure to cross over organizational lines and form programs; ways of stating program goals need to be improved; the accounting system has to be adjusted to new appropriation/expenditure classifications; adequate measures of goal achievement have to be devised; and legislators and administrations (at all levels) need to be educated to the full potentialities of this revolutionary budget concept.

Multiplicity of Governmental Units

Whenever local government in a logical area for local self-government is carried on by a number of overlapping/underlying local governments, one finds that budgeting is fractured vertically. The total community approach is lacking, often with resultant uncoordinated capital improvement programs, competition for tax sources, some buck-passing of the responsibility for services, jealousies and even jurisdictional disputes among law enforcement and inspection agencies, and (equally serious) a splintering of citizen interest and local loyalties. How can one citizen maintain loyalty to, and interest in, a county, a city, a school district, and perhaps several special purpose districts? In some urban areas, a citizen may be a taxpayer in a half-dozen or more local taxing units simultaneously.

If progress in local government budgeting is to be maximized, we must begin to reduce or remove the fracturing forces. Operating and capital budgets should be integrated. Within a single government, all organizational units should be brought together under one budget. Within a single community, the capital improvement needs of all local governments should be presented in a single, cooperative capital budget. State legislatures should put an end to any further balkanization at the local level as a result of special districts and local authorities and begin the slow process of rationalizing the whole local government structure. School district consolidation has pointed the way.

State and Federal Aid

Currently, the most difficult aspects of comprehensive budgeting are the state and federal grant-in-aid programs. Such programs may result in a great deal of confusion arising from "split-level" budgeting.

Until recently, almost all grant-in-aid programs have been of the "categorical grant" variety. Usually, they either required a "maintenance of effort" formula insofar as the local government was concerned, or they required varying degrees of "matching grants" by local governments.

Typically, the state or federal agency responsible for the administration of the grant programs does not know the level of its own funding in time to permit the local government budget officer to estimate adequately the impact of such programs on the local budget. He is, therefore, obliged to proceed very much "in the dark" as to just which elements of the budget are likely to be funded by state and federal governments. Further, in most fiscal years, unexpected and enticing state and federal grant programs—which require local participation—may become available immediately after the enactment of the local budget.

There is no single answer to this problem; however, if state and federal grants were all concentrated into "block grants" and if the magnitude of these grants were known in sufficient time to enable the local budget officer to take them into account in his budgeting process, considerably better budgeting at the local level would become feasible.

Other Budgeting Considerations

Since the end of World War II, we have witnessed, at all three levels of government, an explosion of ideas about the budgetary process. But, the future looks bright only if there is a more widespread understanding of the serious handicaps to applying these "breakthroughs" at the local level, and only if state supervisory agencies make determined efforts to overcome the somewhat formidable obstacles to further progress. The most serious barrier is an attitude of self-satisfaction and apathy. Sights need to be set higher. In fact, we need a major reform movement with enough driving force to apply widely that which is already known.

In the postwar period, no state has faced up to the urgency of an "operation bootstrap" program in the areas of local government budgeting and accounting. This holds true even for states with the better supervisory agencies. Witness the tragi-comedy of a state agency bragging about its new accounting and budget manuals for local governments when the accounting and budgeting theories embodied in these documents are decades behind the times. The United Nations through its technical assistance budget program is teaching the latest budget practices to the newly created central governments in less developed parts of the world; but our most highly developed states in this country have lower aspirations for their local governments, many of which now face markedly increased expenditure programs and require the most modernized administrative approaches.

Similarly, we must frankly recognize that accounting, as expounded in the standard texts and as usually taught, has not caught up with the budgetary breakthroughs. Some texts make no mention of capital budgeting and only pious reference to program budgeting. Illustrations and problems do not advance the new, but perpetuate the old. Their treatments of budgeting and budgetary accounting unfortunately constitute for most accountants their first, and most important, introduction to the subject.

Much of the budgeting literature is less critical of actual practices than should be the case. Equally important, perhaps, is the failure to recognize the innovations under experimentation in the federal government and their possible application in the local government area. Larger cities, especially, would do well to keep abreast of these developments. Learning is a two-way street. For several decades, municipal budget reform set the pace for the states and the federal government. Since 1945, some federal agencies have finally put into effect that which was articulated by the local private "bureaus of municipal research" more than a half-century ago.

5

The Annual Operating Budget

The best known of the budget concepts is that of the annual operating budget. Basically, the function of the annual operating budget is to rationalize the projected allocation and application of resources over the year comprehended by the budget.

Unfortunately, many view the annual operating budget in much less comprehensive terms. For them, the process is likely to be limited to the balancing of probable monetary resources during a single year with the projected outlays being authorized for a wide variety of competing purposes, with only a glimmer of understanding of the interrelationships among the various programs, activities, and organizational units.

In another context, the budgeting process has the function of bringing about a clear-cut statement and rationalization of overall management activities and objectives.

An Authorization to Spend

Fundamentally, the annual operating budget provides a basis upon which the governing body may adopt an ordinance or resolution which constitutes an *authorization to spend*. Obviously, the budget also provides limits beyond which spending may not properly proceed; however, the adoption of the budget ordinance or resolution by the governing body is a *positive* act. Without this act, under our theory of government, the executive is without authority to incur obligations and the finance officers without authority to make payments in respect thereto.

Unfortunately, many persons tend to emphasize the negative, i.e., the control, aspects of the budget. This can produce negative psychology surrounding the process with significant adverse effects in the execution of the budget.

Objectives of the Annual Budget Process

Most seasoned students of the annual operating budget process at the local governmental level include the following in any listing of its specific objectives:

1. To provide for comprehensive involvement of departmental and sub-departmental units of the government in planning the programs to be

81

executed during the ensuing year; the quantification of requirements for personnel, materiel, contractual and other services; and the resolution of these into current dollar requirements

2. To require the executive branch of the government to produce a program of operating expenditures (including debt service requirements) which can be balanced by the recommended revenue program

3. To provide to each successive level of management—and especially to the chief executive or administrative officer—the means by which competing requirements for limited resources can be effectively evaluated

4. To provide a system for measuring the objectives expected to be attained within the fiscal period and to facilitate the scheduling of work and the coordination of nonpersonal service requirements with the personal services intended to be engaged

5. To facilitate understanding by the governing body and the body politic of the proposed plan of operations for the year and to allow revision of the proposed plan prior to legislative approval

6. To provide a basis for the enactment of the annual appropriation ordinance and such accompanying revenue measures as may be required

7. To provide a basis upon which planned activities for the ensuing year may be adjusted to conform to appropriations

8. To provide a basis for financial audit and, hopefully, for performance audit, both during the fiscal year and after the close of the fiscal year

For services and outlays, the budgetary process opens up a convenient channel through which administrators all along the line can communicate upward their proposed plans and programs for consideration. The budget calendar, justification forms, review steps, and other requirements of the process exist to expedite and to make more effective the formulation of recommendations and the ultimate acceptance and execution of plans and programs. Revenue estimating is bound up with planning the revenue side of the budget as well as the choosing of measures which may be needed to augment revenue receipts.

ORGANIZATION FOR BUDGETING

Two questions are the concern of this section: (1) the circumstances which determine the location of the budget function within the overall structure of a local government and (2) the patterns of internal organization of the central budget staff in larger local governments.

Many local governments operate under a legislative budget; however, in most local governments, the chief executive or administrator has a dominant role in the preparation and administration of the budget. Under a legislative-type budget, a council budget committee has responsibility for preparation of the budget. A budget staff is frequently attached to this committee, and operating heads and their staffs deal directly with the committee and committee staff. Such a central budget staff is outside the executive branch but "within the administration" since the council is functioning both as an administrative body and a legislative body.

An executive-type budget exists where the organizational structure places initial responsibility for budget formulation upon the chief executive. He comes to the council with his proposals, but the council has the final policy-making responsibility.[1] This division of responsibility for the budget between the legislative and executive branches is found in the strong executive-type cities, i.e., the strong mayor cities and the council-manager cities, which also have strong legislative branches.

If the administrative pattern is a strong executive type, the question remains as to where the central budget staff shall be located. The basic choice is between:

1. A budgeting unit directly responsible to the chief executive
2. The assignment of the budgeting function to a finance officer in charge of comprehensive financial policy, accounting, and other financial functions

The choice of the former results in the definition of the budgeting function as a somewhat isolated staff function under the chief executive; the choice of the latter places the official responsible for budgeting in the mainstream of overall administration.

As has been indicated, local government budgeting developed as a part of the reform movement to provide a comprehensive approach to the formulation and execution of the budget under a strong chief executive. With a budget officer appointed by the chief executive and reporting directly to him, centralization is at its maximum, unless the chief executive himself is the budget officer—as is frequently the case in smaller council-manager type governments.

Operational work programs and performance standards which have been added to financial estimates make budgeting a well-rounded management process as well as a financial process. This consideration argues for physical location of the budget function outside the finance department. A budget office or division within a department of general administration, co-equal in rank with other staff functions, is a theoretical possibility. However, very few local governments have established departments of administration into which the major staff functions have been grouped.

If the preparation of the capital program and the capital budget are the responsibility of the central budget staff, or the joint responsibility of the budgeting and central planning staffs of the government, a case can be made for a combined budget, planning, and research division reporting directly to the chief executive.

On the other hand, there are strong arguments for a concentration of all financial functions, including budgeting, in the hands of a capable officer who is the chief finance officer of the government. With such an arrangement, the finance officer can bring about a degree of coordination of finance and finance-

---

[1] A notable exception is New York City in which the Mayor's proposed budget is automatically law except to the extent modified through joint action of the City Council and the Board of Estimate and they are limited to reductions (no increases or transfers) in the Mayor's budget.

related operations which is not feasible where the budgeting function is separate from the other finance functions.

Regardless of the location of the central budget staff, considerable decentralization of the budget function is desirable in medium-sized and larger local governments. Small budget and planning staffs will be required in the major operating departments; however, the central budget staff should continue to assist all the departments and other staff agencies in the preparation of their budget estimates and justifications.

Internally, the central staff may be organized around two activities: (a) the preparation phases of budgeting and (b) the administration of approved budgets. Within the budget unit, there may be a budget analysis and review unit with each examiner having responsibility for one or more functional departments and/or staff agencies. Even the handling of estimates going into the capital program and capital budget may be assigned to him so that this examiner has before him all the estimates—both operating and capital—applicable to the individual programs or organizational units for which he has responsibility. During the year, the same examiner (or group of examiners) may be responsible for exercising budget controls in respect to the departmental budgets assigned to him (or them).

Frequently associated with the budgeting process is an administrative management unit which usually operates without a fixed internal division of labor. Specialists will receive *ad hoc* assignments as required and work alone, in pairs, or as a part of a larger team.

Although most of the activities of the central budget staff are concerned with expenditures, this staff is also responsible for many aspects of the revenue side of the budget, the financing of capital improvements, and the issuance of new debt.

SIGNIFICANT STEPS IN THE ANNUAL BUDGET PROCESS

Despite the broad concepts normally characterizing the budget process, bricks and mortar, planks and nails, and other very ordinary ingredients go into the making of the annual budget. The basic steps involved in a well-ordered annual budget system may be divided into three broad classifications:

1. The preparation of the executive budget
2. Legislative and public consideration and action on the budget
3. Administration of the budget

The cycle within which these processes take place is frequently spread over the greater part of 24 months (and sometimes over even longer periods of time) when one considers the time which elapses from the distribution of budget request forms to the departments and the preparation of preliminary revenue estimates to the publication and circulation of a financial report pertaining to any given fiscal year and the completion of postauditing activities.[2]

---

[2] For a comprehensive treatment of this topic, see Lennox L. Moak and Kathryn W. Killian, *A Manual of Techniques for the Preparation, Consideration, Adoption, and Administration of Operating Budgets*, (Chicago: Municipal Finance Officers Association, 1963), pp. 60-332.

Preparation of the Executive Budget

Inherent in every budget process is a budget calendar—the schedule, stipulated in law or by administrative regulations—which apportions time for completion of the various budgetary activities culminating in the adoption of the budget and the beginning of the fiscal year. The kickoff of the cycle relating to each annual operating budget is usually triggered by the distribution from the central budget agency of the forms, instructions, worksheets, etc., required to be processed in the preparation of the budget.

Depending upon local practice, these may or may not be accompanied by a message from the chief executive or administrative officer of the government setting forth the broad configurations within which the budget for the coming year is to be prepared. Thus, if an economic recession is at hand, or if the chief executive is pledged to a "hold-the-line" policy, the message may indicate that there is little or no room for program expansion during the coming year—and may even indicate that there is a need for reduction. Alternately, if national economic indicators are favorable, or if the local government has experienced tremendous growth in resources, the emphasis may be on expanded services. A prerequisite to this type of executive message is some formalized degree of forecasting with regard to economic conditions, revenues, the financial impact of current operations, and the future needs of operating units already known to, or anticipated by, the chief executive.

The Departmental Opportunity. The instructions to departmental and other officials to submit budget requests are likely to be accompanied by carefully designed forms upon which the various departmental units are asked to provide information concerning their programs, activities, and dollar requirements for the succeeding year as seen by the heads of the administrative units. Standardized budget request forms allow for completeness and uniformity in the information sought and for the pre-entry of prior years' data on the forms submitted to the various operating units.

In large departments or units, this distribution is a signal to bring into action the heads of the principal organizational or program units within the department or agency. In a government which is heavily committed to programmatic presentations, this may be the signal for the interagency planning units to begin detailing their component parts of the program budget. Elements of budget preparation at the departmental level include:

1. Designation of the person or persons to be responsible for the performance of budget functions
2. Determination, from the department's long-term work program, of its short-range objectives and the personnel and materiel requirements to meet these objectives. Such a determination may be based on open-end budgeting, work measurement and unit costing, and priority listings

In order to place some check on the tendency towards expansion of the outgo side of the budget, innovations in preparing expenditure estimates have been proposed which can be referred to as: alternative budgeting, lower-base or retrenched-base budgeting, and *ab initio* budgeting. Under the first proposal, each operating department submits two sets of estimates: one which meets departmental requirements and another which shows what could be accomplished program-wise if a lower aggregate budget were apportioned to the departments, each with a reduced figure. Retrenched-base budgeting contemplates that the chief executive would begin with a drastically cut aggregate total from the prior year and require each department to prove what would really be lost by way of services and efficiency if the lower base were adhered to. The *ab initio* budgetary proposal stresses the necessity for each department to defend annually the level of every activity, and even the existence of the department. This is in contrast to concentrating on justifications for increases or decreases from last year's base budget. (*Ab initio* budgeting is also called zero-based budgeting.)

Innovations such as these can serve useful purposes because administrators may, at times, ignore the benefits to be derived from leaving money in the hands of the taxpayers. They are likely to overlook the fact that money left in the hands of the citizens may be more effectively used by them than the manner in which the public official would use the same money. Administrators may also be driven more by the incentive to increase the quality and quantity of services to be financed by additional dollars than to stretch the dollar in order to hold the line, or even to reduce taxes.

The end product of this complex first step is the presentation to the central budget agency of requests, supporting data, and selected historical information deemed useful in evaluating the operating unit's estimate of its own budget needs. In the case of budgets constructed along major organizational lines, this period is frequently referred to as the *departmental opportunity*. Certainly, if this phase goes by without the department having taken full advantage of the opportunity afforded, the likelihood of its pressing for program expansion or adjustment for the ensuing year is greatly diminished.

Central Budget Agency Review. Once the departmental work in the preparation of the initial draft of the budget has been completed, the papers are forwarded to the central budget unit. The initial function of this agency is to check the departmental submissions for their completeness and accuracy. When these routines have been completed, the central budget unit compiles the requests of all the agencies into a preliminary document which will provide an overall view of total dollar needs.

Concurrent with, or preceding, this process, this unit develops information concerning projections of available revenues at prevailing rates for the ensuing year. Along with its revenue projections, the budget unit prepares preliminary projections of changes in wage and benefit costs likely to result from wage negotiations (or arbitrations) in process or in prospect. Another responsibility of this unit is to determine the amounts required for such non-departmental items as debt service and interfund transfers.

In initiating a substantive review of departmental budget requests, the central budget unit seeks to:

1. Segregate changes in the work program and their cost in terms of personnel and materiel
2. Identify policy changes inherent in budget requests

Revenue projections are then compared with the totals of the departmental requests to determine the magnitude of difference between projected resources and the indicated needs of the departments. Depending on the size of the governmental unit, the central budget unit may, at this juncture, conduct hearings so that the heads of the various operating units may defend their overall proposals or explain items in question.

On the basis of these information gathering processes, the head of the central budget unit (or other responsible official) informs the chief executive of the overall budgetary picture. At this point, such budget officer may take up particular expenditure proposals in order to ascertain the preliminary views of the chief executive concerning them. Moreover, at this juncture, it is likely that the chief executive will indicate the overall limits to which he is willing to go in proposing new revenue sources or increasing the rates applicable to existing local revenues.

In light of this conference, the head of the central budget unit will proceed to a reworking of the tentative budget with a view to bringing projected expenditures into line with available resources so that the chief executive may submit a balanced budget to the governing body.

Once this step is completed, the principal budget officer may again meet with the chief executive to advise him of the actions taken to bring the budget into balance. As a result of this conference, in which the chief executive may assign a different set of priorities, the principal budget officer informs the departmental spending units of the preliminary decisions that have been reached.

Conferences with the Chief Executive. Depending upon the choice of the chief executive, an opportunity may be afforded to the heads of departments and other principal agencies to confer with him with a view to explaining or defending all, or selected portions, of the budget of the department or agency. Ordinarily, if such conferences are held, the principal budget officer is present for the discussion which may be wide-ranging or may be restricted to a few points requiring clarification prior to final executive decision.

At the conclusion of all of these conferences, the principal budget officer once again develops a summary of the tentative budget as it then stands and confers with the chief executive. Final decisions are made and the principal budget officer thereupon develops the final budget in line with the directives from the chief executive.

The Revenue Side of the Budget

Budget literature tends to emphasize only the outgo side. Concern is focused upon various techniques and principles concerned with the allocation of resources which are available to the government. The neglect of the revenue side of local government budgeting is perhaps partly due to the limited flexibility which local governments have generally possessed in adjustment of their revenue base.

Obviously the local government accounts must be brought into balance—either annually (as is generally required by law) or in a matter of a few years at most.

Among the most important decisions for public officials is that group of determinations revolving around two questions:

    a. How much of the local economy should be assigned to financing the activities of the local government?

    b. With the answer to the first question, the question becomes: How shall the costs be assessed among the different elements of the community?

On the general question of equity, when revenue changes are under discussion, the least that equity requires is for the budget staff and the policy-makers to strive to prevent the new revenue measures from making the total revenue system less equitable than at present. If each incremental change cannot be used to improve equity, the minimal goal should be that inequities not be augmented.

The complexities of equity account, in part, for the frequent neglect of this factor in evaluating revenue proposals. Alternatives are often between different taxes (e.g., a local sales tax and a property tax increase) or between increases in rates for two service charges. The incidence and effect of each proposed new burden has to be studied and weighed. To take one example, automatic use of the property tax as the "deficiency tax" may be expedient but not necessarily equitable. If the property taxpayer has been contributing his fair share of the tax burden, why should he contribute more because service demands have increased? Suppose identifiable segments of property taxpayers could establish no increased ability-to-pay and no new service benefit? Payers of a particular tax do not always constitute a homogeneous group.

If the revenue side of the budget is to receive proper emphasis, perhaps the most important precondition is recognition by the chief executive and the legislative body that revenue estimating and equity research constitute activities which merit a place in the organizational structure and a well-trained person or group of persons in this field.

The Balancing Concept. The desire, and often the legal requirement, for preparation of a two-sided document which is balanced in the aggregate forces a decision as to the overall total of the budget. Either side, depending on particular circumstances, may prove to be dominant in determining the budget level. Scarcity and needs/demands are both relative terms. In prosperous periods, expenditures may, for several years, exert a steady upward pull upon the budget aggregate. In other times and under other circumstances, the revenue side may hold the aggregate level steady or even apply a downward pressure. Deliberate misstatement of either revenues or expenditures in order to anchor the budget level may be a temporary expedient, but such a tactic is open to serious question. In most cases, it is customary to refer to a surplus or deficit situation limited to the general fund. Operations of special revenue funds and of trust funds are largely ignored in such discussions—even though a consolidated view of the operations of the government would result in a much different statement of financial results.

In like manner, the typical discussion of the general fund budget is in terms of current resources on the one hand and current expenditures and debt service requirements on the other. Capital expenditures financed from the proceeds of loans are considered to be outside the mainstream of the current budgeting process.

THE BUDGET DOCUMENT

The operating budget may be a single document or several documents, as is the case in the larger local governments. Regardless of its size, the essential elements of the "budget document" generally include the following:

1. The "budget message" of the chief executive officer—setting forth in broad outline the thrust of the proposed budget and an overall explanation by the chief executive officer of the major pertinent elements of the proposed budget
2. The official estimate of revenue—this section of the budget document sets forth the recent history of revenues by major categories and also includes the recommendations of the chief executive as to the revenue measures required to finance the proposed budget of expenditures
3. A summary of the proposed expenditures for the budget year, with appropriate comparisons between the expenditures of one or more prior years and the current year
4. The detailed information relating to the proposed level of expenditures and explanation of the reasons for deviations between the proposed budget and current and prior levels of expenditure
5. Supplemental schedules which will facilitate an understanding of the interrelationships of various elements of proposed expenditures—for example, by recasting the expenditures of departments and organizational units along program lines

The choice as to the detail involved in item (4) above lies with the chief executive and the principal budget officer. The pattern of presentation will vary significantly from one local government to the next. Thus, in one jurisdiction, emphasis may be placed upon an explanation of the number of positions that are to be financed under the proposed budget; in another, emphasis may be on programs and outputs.

Essentially, the purpose of the detailed expenditure data is to provide to the governing body and to the public the kinds of information which will enable them to understand all aspects of the proposed budget. A well-constructed presentation of budget detail will provide information concerning the quantity of services to be rendered and any changes of service in the proposed budget.

Presentation to and Consideration by the Governing Body

It is customary that the chief executive officer of the government submit a *budget message* to the governing body. This may be done in person by address to the governing body, or it may be done solely through the written message. The oral presentation is frequently used, inasmuch as it affords the chief executive an opportunity not only to address the governing body but also to reach the media and, through the media, the citizens of the community.

The budget message customarily contains a summary of the budget with special attention to any emphases contained therein as they bear upon programs of the government and upon revenue measures being sponsored.

Initial consideration of the budget by the governing body—either as a whole or by an appropriate committee—is ordinarily in public session. Heads of departments and agencies are invited to explain their requests for funds and the principal finance officer is asked to provide an overall view of proposed expenditures as well as an explanation of the revenue measures called for to balance the budget.

Ordinarily in the course of the legislative hearings, citizens are afforded an opportunity to present their views concerning any aspect of the budget or of revenue measures in which they may have an interest.

At the conclusion of the public hearings, the governing body—or the majority caucus in the case of bipartisan governing bodies—holds executive sessions during which attention is given to components of the budget and the proposed revenue measures. The principal budget officer (or his representative) may be invited to attend these sessions. If invited to attend, his role is usually that of providing additional information, rather than that of being an advocate for the point of view of the administration.

(Ordinarily, where there are significant differences between the governing body and the chief executive as to the content or size of appropriations, informal conferences are held in person or by proxy with a view to achieving an accommodation mutually acceptable.)

On the basis of the determinations of the executive session, the governing body thereupon makes such amendments as it deems fit to the expenditure portion of the budget and to the proposed revenue measures. The final product is reported in public session to the governing body and is likely to be adopted in the form thus presented.

Distinction between the Proposed Budget and the Appropriation Ordinance. Obviously, the governing body does not attempt to adopt all budget details as "the budget." However, where there is a resolution of the legislative body "approving the budget" the question arises as to just what it has approved.

On the other hand, a separate appropriation ordinance listing specific amounts for specific agencies of the government by specified categories of expense, e.g., major object classes or programs, provides a much more comprehensible and usable form of authorization to spend than does a resolution which merely "approves the budget."

Moreover, when one comes to the administration of the budget through preaudit and on through postaudit, a definitive appropriation ordinance provides an effective benchmark for administration and postauditing.

To become a blueprint for operations, the proposed budget document has to be revised to accord with legislative changes made at the review and enactment stage. This is often done by the publication of revised pages which the operating heads and others insert in the original document.

As a final step, some cities provide for the possibility of executive veto and legislative reconsideration of the budget as adopted. The executive veto may be in several forms:

1. The entire budget: This is rarely effective
2. An entire item: This is of limited effectiveness, unless the appropriations are in very detailed form
3. Reduction of an item: This is the most desirable and provides the executive with the greatest effectiveness in use of the veto

ADMINISTRATION OF THE APPROVED BUDGET

Execution of the budget is both a substantive operational process and a financial process. It is getting things done within a time schedule by the application of all means authorized for attaining program goals, but within monetary limitations and, ideally, within standard cost limits. Since this stage covers the full fiscal year, it is usually the longest in the municipal budget cycle and overlaps with both the formulation and legislative stages of the succeeding year's budget.

Responsibility for Administration

Patterns of administration of the approved budget vary widely from one government to another. In some governments, administration amounts to little more than establishing budgetary accounts and recording expenditures as they are processed for payment. Ordinarily, however, responsibility for execution of the budget rests primarily upon the chief executive. By delegation from him, the central staff agencies and operating heads assume portions of this responsibility. Operating heads, in turn, share segments of their responsibility with their subordinates with the result that budget execution encompasses management at all levels.

Steps in Administration. In more advanced budgetary systems, the first step in administration is the *allocation* of elements of the appropriation.

The process of *allocation* is one by which the appropriation is subdivided according to programs, minor organizational units, or classes of expenditure, e.g. motor fuel. Thus, through the allocation process, the appropriations to a health department may be subdivided to show a stipulated amount for the outpatient clinic in the children's hospital or to segregate funds for the mental health unit. Or, in the case of a police department, the allocation process may result in the segregation of that part of the appropriation to be used to purchase motor fuel.

The basic function of the allocation process is to assign elements of larger appropriations to specific categories of expense in order that the funds may be reserved for that category.

Following the process of allocation, it may be determined that provision should be made for an *allotment* system under which the appropriations that have been allocated can be further subdivided into time elements, e.g., monthly or quarterly allotments of appropriations for personal services or for some item or group of items in the nonpersonal service categories.

Where the expenditure (or commitment) of appropriations is contingent upon future events, such as the availability of grants from other governments or the projected opening of a new capital facility (library or recreation center), the portion of the appropriation in question may be retained in the unallocated or unallotted category. In this manner, the original plan for the expenditure can be carried out more easily. Thus, if the facility is not completed at the projected date, the funds initially intended for this purpose are restricted until such time as there is a requirement for their use as originally approved.

In very highly developed budget systems, account is also taken of the work actually performed in relation to that which was planned. Accordingly, the system of budget controls is equipped to relate promise to performance. If the projected levels of performance do not materialize, then discussions are first held with the departmental spending unit and, if necessary, with the chief executive as to the pattern within which the funds for the remainder of the year will be made available.

Accountants play a major role in the implementation of financial controls. Budgetary accounting supplies the control mechanism for enforcing allotment and appropriation limits—namely, encumbrance accounting (the recording of actuals against estimates) and periodic internal budget reports. Cost accounting, or adaptations of financial accounting which produce cost figures, plus statistical reporting, permit the production of work unit costs and comparison with performance and cost standards. Project budgets for construction, work schedules, cost centers, performance standards, standard costs per work unit, and reports— all of these constitute the accountant's stock-in-trade. Much of accounting is highly centralized. In some of the larger cities, however, partial decentralization has taken place in order to keep encumbrance and cost accounting close to operating centers.

In the control of specifics, legislative bodies have long used such devices as the line-item appropriation, insertion of conditions for the use of funds, the requirement of periodic budgetary reports, and the independent postaudit. Such bodies also often retain a hand at the execution stage through the requirement that proposed transfers between appropriation items must have legislative approval. In some jurisdictions, the state legislature imposes mandatory expenditures upon local governments and a state supervisory authority must be satisfied that the legal aspects of budgeting have been met. This involves budget reports to the state and, sometimes, reviews by the state agency.

Not all controls, however, are budgetary. Certain supplemental expenditure controls are drawn upon:

1. Position control (restrictions on filling of vacancies, moratoria on promotions, etc.), once assigned to the personnel unit and under the chief executive, is so powerful a tool that to an increasing degree it is being taken over by the budget director
2. Property management can lower the need for new capital outlays by improving equipment care and maintenance
3. Purchasing through quantity and quality controls likewise helps to stretch the dollar
4. If postauditing includes efficiency or administrative audits, these are valuable to the budget staff, as are special administrative studies and related analyses by a research division

Administration of the budget may also involve approval by the central budget office of requisitions to purchase equipment or other items in order to assure that appropriated amounts are being used to acquire the materials or items of equipment for which justification was made in the first place.

Departmental officials, with some justification, consider most of these elements of central budgetary administration as an intrusion upon their freedom to conduct the affairs of their departments or agencies within the overall framework of the appropriations made available. It is in this area that the "art" of budgeting perhaps reaches its fullest development. Obviously, no competent department head wants all of the decisions regarding his operations second-guessed by a central budget office—frequently by lower-grade budget examiners. On the other hand, left without the discipline of central review, some departmental officials would pursue a path that was contrary to their own justification of funds and, simultaneously, embarrass the administration in its relations with the governing body and the public.

It is easy, however, to overemphasize the control aspects of the execution stage. Much planning and programming also takes place at this stage. Frequent reviews of changing conditions and appraisals of recent past performance require new planning and programming, or adjustments therein. By this approach, future action is made more intelligent. The mid-year review and the one during the period when the succeeding year's budget is being formulated and finalized are scheduled reviews; but, reappraisals and revised planning and programming occur at many points in time. Flexibility in operations requires this. Reappraisal is sometimes thought of as a stage which comes subsequent to the fiscal period's end and after annual accounting and statistical statements have documented the full results of the prior year's budget operations. In practice, however, it is difficult to identify such a period in the budget cycle.

Program budgeting, performance budgeting, and PPBS have introduced further devices for budget management, if properly used. These kinds of budgets set goals and work programs. The council can attempt to hold the executive branch accountable for these production or performance targets. Likewise, the chief executive can measure his departmental operations on a performance basis and heads of departments can, in turn, fix responsibility upon their subordinates for performance.

The older type of control asked: "Has management lived within the dollar limits set?" This newer type seeks to put the question thusly: "Did management perform as promised?" and "Was performance within the cost standards laid down?" There is, of course, no magic in the old or the new types of control as such. The adequacy of the system is properly measurable only by its contribution to attainment of the goal of delivering public services at a reasonable cost.

Adjustments to the Budget. Few are gifted with 20/20 foresight—either on the side of the operating units or on the side of the central budget agency. Accordingly, most operating budgets require modification through amendment during the course of the year. It is the function of the central budget office to maintain sufficient knowledge—both through the accounting process and through contacts with the individual departments and other budget units—to be aware of impending requirements for formal amendments to the budget during the course of the year. Some amendments require immediate attention; many can be more easily handled in a single *omnibus* amendment once each year—ordinarily, during the last three or four months of the year.

Of course, departmental officials should take the initiative when problems come to their attention; however, regardless of the action or inaction of departmental officials, the central budget agency has the ultimate responsibility for the management of the budget and must therefore recommend any necessary actions in order that there be no payless paydays or lack of funds to buy critical materials or equipment when required.

During the final quarter of the fiscal year, revised estimates must be made of the anticipated closing status of the unappropriated surplus account. This type of close watch is essential if appropriations from this account have been proposed or enacted for the next year.

To summarize, execution of the budget requires a complex mix of leadership, shared responsibility, operational directives, controls, new and adjusted planning and programming, and frequent reviews and reappraisals.

6

Capital Programming and Capital Budgeting

Capital programming and capital budgeting, when appropriately executed, are important financial planning tools. Although some local governments have been involved in these processes over a period of more than half a century, some confusion still exists concerning their actual definition.

The National Committee on Governmental Accounting has defined the concepts of a *capital program* and a *capital budget* in this manner:[1]

CAPITAL PROGRAM. A plan for capital expenditures to be incurred each year over a fixed period of years to meet capital needs arising from the long-term work program or otherwise. It sets forth each project or other contemplated expenditure in which the local government is to have a part and specifies the full resources estimated to be available to finance the projected expenditures.

CAPITAL BUDGET. A plan of proposed outlays and the means of financing them for the current fiscal period. It is usually a part of the current budget. If a Capital Program is in operation, it will be the first year thereof. A Capital Program is sometimes referred to as a Capital Budget.

Despite the frequent confusion in the literature and in administration between the capital program and the capital budget, this volume follows the concepts as defined by the National Committee on Governmental Accounting.

Project planning has been in force for centuries as witnessed by the overall design and specific public improvements in cities, both ancient and modern. The early history of municipal development, however, has been marked by the uncoordinated construction of public works.

The Great Depression of the Thirties and World War II in the Forties did more to focus attention of governmental officials on the necessity for long-range programming of public works construction and on capital budgeting than any other events in the Twentieth Century. Prior to 1930, only a few governmental jurisdictions had engaged in long-range capital programming and capital budgeting . . .

---

[1] National Committee on Governmental Accounting, *Governmental Accounting, Auditing, and Financial Reporting*, (Chicago: Municipal Finance Officers Association, 1968), p. 155.

Now, more than ever, the necessity for long-range capital programming and for capital budgeting is absolutely clear . . .

The real crux of the matter revolves around the determination as to which projects are so vitally necessary that they can be deferred no longer and thus must receive first consideration in the allocation of limited financial resources.[2]

Among the earliest attempts by local governments in the United States to program public improvements were those of the Minneapolis Board of Education in 1916 and the city of Kalamazoo, Michigan, in 1920-21. Cincinnati took a giant step forward in 1926 when its charter established a City Planning Commission, without whose approval no public improvement could be undertaken. In 1926, a Capital Improvements Committee was created in that city and its procedures were required to include: cooperation with school district and county planning; detailed project requests; council review of committee recommendations and adoption of a capital program; and control of capital spending according to the program, as adopted, unless amended by the council. Another milestone was the 1936 charter of New York City which set forth the basic procedures to be followed in capital programming in that city, including accounting for the status of previously authorized projects, public hearings, and a five-year capital program. The 1951 Home Rule Charter of Philadelphia became the first charter to distinguish clearly between the concepts of capital programming and capital budgeting.

State of the Art

Although the concept has spread, Moak and Killian in 1963-64 found that, among sixteen larger cities selected for study, the state of the art of capital programming and capital budgeting was well advanced in some, moderate in others, and only barely perceptible in some.[3] Their studies in 1964-65 of 20 smaller cities revealed, as might be expected, a lesser degree of development than in the larger cities, although some progress was being achieved and the programming processes in one or two cities were very well developed.[4]

Moak, in a report to the Housing and Home Finance Agency,[5] involving 28 smaller cities (with minor overlap with Moak and Killian's 20 smaller cities), found only a few examples of good practice. The report states that, in most instances, the so-called capital program had been developed by consultants under

---

[2] Terhune, George A., *Capital Budgeting Practices in the United States and Canada,* MFOA Committee on Budgeting Report No. 3, (Chicago: Municipal Finance Officers Association, August 31, 1966), p. 1.

[3] Lennox L. Moak and Kathryn W. Killian, *A Manual of Suggested Practice for the Preparation and Adoption of Capital Programs and Capital Budgets by Local Governments,* (Chicago: Municipal Finance Officers Association, 1964), 152 pp. The volume does not present a direct generalization of findings as to the state of the art; however, a careful reading of the description of the processes found in each city will suffice to support the comment.

[4] Lennox L. Moak and Kathryn Killian Gordon, *Budgeting for Smaller Governmental Units,* (Chicago: Municipal Finance Officers Association, 1965), 194 pp.

Section 701 grants, with little evidence of comprehensive local involvement by either administrative officials, governing bodies, or important lay groups in the community.

These findings of actual field studies are in sharp contrast to the impression which one gathers from the results of questionnaires in which local governments are invited to indicate whether or not they have capital programs within the sense here used. A 1966 survey reported that 88 percent of the 548 jurisdictions participating were involved in capital budgeting.[6]

The Rationale of Capital Programming

The capital program has introduced a relatively long time span for planning and programming and has sponsored a close integration of financial and physical planning where the process is carried out appropriately. The use of the capital budget (the first year of several years included in the capital program) requires detailed planning and programming for those capital project commitments soon to be made. Establishment of project priorities is an essential part of capital programming.

Capital outlays financed from debt have always been outside the balancing concept inherent in operating budgets. But, several steps have been taken over a period of time, to bring this area of expenditure under budget control. Strong proponents of full or partial pay-as-you-spend policies have succeeded in some jurisdictions. States here and there have adopted statutes which require a down payment out of current revenues on each project financed from bonded debt. The use of serial bonds has the effect of bringing more and more debt retirement under orderly budget control. Although the capital program was originally devised as a long-term planning instrument, an aggregate ceiling on annual capital outlays sometimes results in forcing into the operating budget capital items, e.g., equipment and other small capital outlays which could legally have been financed by borrowing. The result is at least a partial pay-as-you-go basis. In addition, the concept of a project budget is a form of budgetary control over capital outlays at the critical execution stage.

The subject of capital programming and capital budgeting needs to be looked at in its total managerial context. Although the finance director has an important part in the process, these matters are not solely his responsibility. The programming process involves participation at all operating levels up through the chief executive and requires staff agencies other than finance to play significant roles—the planner, engineer, and urban renewal coordinator.

As has been outlined in the preceding chapter, the annual budget process can best be carried on as part of a process which we have designated the long-term operating program—a program which takes into account the projected kinds and levels of services expected to be performed at certain times within the period of years spanned by the program.

---

[5] Moak, Lennox L. et al., *A Report to the Housing and Home Finance Agency*, prepared during 1964-65 and unpublished.

[6] Terhune, George A., *op. cit.*, 14 pp.

The annual operating budget, in such a system, becomes a set of steps taken within a broader framework both as to time and objectives.

In like manner, the capital budget and the capital program are (or should be) intimately associated with the long-term operating program because the *raison d'etre* of a capital project is to facilitate the accomplishment of an *operating* objective. Thus, a library is built to facilitate the objective of providing library services which appear in the operating program—as is the case with health centers, sewage treatment plants, streets, and courthouses.

Therefore, although many local governments look upon the capital program and capital budget processes as "independent" of the mainstream of overall administration, they should be construed as activities which relate directly to the operating program and operating budget. Any less comprehensive view of these processes invites the construction of projects as ends within themselves, rather than as elements of the entire process of providing governmental services.

Despite these important relationships, there are special characteristics of capital projects which justify their being segregated in a capital program. Even though some of these characteristics may now be open to question, the following have contributed to the development of the rationale:

1. Because of their life span (durability) capital projects have a long-range effect upon the community and the lives of its citizens. They, therefore, need to be planned within a long-range perspective—their size, suitability of design, durability of materials, location, etc. all have to be gauged not for a brief twelve months but over a much longer period. The five- or six-year span of the capital program, together with its retrospective and prospective aspects outside the period covered, offers a means for taking a longer term view of this essentially long term process.

2. Since capital projects affect land use, traffic circulation, the density of population, and the future physical look of the municipality, they require a special expertise, namely, that of the architect-city planner. In application of the principle of a division of labor, the programming of capital improvements has been separated from other aspects of municipal programming and assigned to those especially equipped to do the job.

3. Many current operating decisions are subject to reversal, in whole or in part, at the end of (or even during) the current budget. In contrast, capital decisions are irreversible for an extended period; mistakes last longer and are apt to be more costly.

4. The ability to postpone most capital projects (usually much more easily than current services) has also meant that, without special programming in this area, important municipal expenditures would often be neglected. The capital budget process tends to restore any imbalance.

5. In a small community, the nonrecurring character of large capital requirements was an argument for a process which envisaged planning ahead for the extraordinary. Initially the same argument was advanced in large municipalities, but, by 1930, it was accepted that capital outlay requirements, at least in overall amounts, tended to recur with some regularity.

6. The "lumpiness" of capital outlays, i.e., the tendency for them to be concentrated within relatively short periods followed by periods when capital construction stagnated, also suggested the need for a process which would assist in leveling out the peaks and valleys—resulting in a more orderly approach to meet capital requirements and a more rational and manageable schedule to pay debt service requirements.

It must be recognized that, within the above broad rationale, different individual or group participants have found that the capital budget process can be used to accomplish different objectives. Strong pressures with diverse emphases sometimes generate "pulling and hauling" and even serious conflicts. However, some generalizations are possible:

1. A strong administrative bureaucracy may believe that the bulk of capital program and capital budget projects should arise from operational proposals as opposed to centralized planning. These administrators stress the contributions of capital projects to program objectives and view the capital budget as another, but slightly longer, administrative budget. They tend to stress flexibility since beyond a two- or three-year period, the quality of program planning deteriorates and project proposals tend to be hazy—except for estimates for projects already begun but which will remain under construction for several years. In this instance, the administration's attitude toward long-range planning may be neutral (and even negative toward centralized planning).

2. Some city planners see the capital program and budget process as a convenient "staging area" between the long-term comprehensive (master/general) plan and the final implementation of capital proposals within a given budget year. It becomes both a method for implementing the comprehensive plan and a practical and convenient instrument for keeping the plan up-to-date. They seek adherence to the overall plan and place a high premium on the stability of projects within the general scheme of priorities. Constant priority shifts are regarded as a partial negation (or violation) of long-term centralized planning.

3. Other city planners, more aesthetically oriented, may view the capital program and budget process as an opportunity for accomplishing some of their designs for beautifying the city. They envisage the physical rebirth of an environment now dominated by ugliness, disorder, and disharmonies. Any lack of planning over the decades must be reversed. The city is for people; therefore, it must be made more attractive as a place to live.

4. Still others—planners, economists, and business groups—see the capital program and budget as a process through which protection and improvement of the community's economic base can be accomplished. Urban renewal, with federal assistance, is attractive to this group, as well as to the preceding group.

5. Taxpayer groups and councilmen may see in these processes an instrument for establishing a fairly even level of capital outlays from year

to year, in order to achieve over a period of years, a more stable property tax rate.

6. Engineers on the city's staff may regard these processes primarily as scheduling devices through which projects can be constructed in the most effective and efficient sequential relationship.

7. To the finance director, the capital program and budget process offer opportunities for achieving a more orderly debt service structure, for determining any associated pay-as-you-spend policy, and for projecting the effect of new capital proposals upon future operating budgets.

8. To still others, these processes offer the one means of conforming with the requirement that a "plan" be submitted as a prerequisite for state or federal assistance for certain capital projects.

THE CAPITAL PROGRAMMING PROCESS

The legal foundation of this process usually lies in the city charter, an ordinance, or both. (In at least one state, New Jersey, the foundation was an order by a state department applying to all municipalities—but not to school districts or other units of government lying outside the area of responsibility of the department.) The process, however, is amplified, regularized, and set in a formal framework by regulations, a calendar, standard forms, and sometimes a manual. Although not the same from one municipality to another, some aspects of the process can be generalized.

At different cyclical stages, capital programming activity is concentrated on different organizational levels. The central review staff is active throughout because it has the responsibility to initiate and to keep the process moving according to schedule. Proposals are made at the program supervisor level; these are then screened and supplemented at the bureau and departmental levels. Departmental proposals, in turn, are reviewed, adjusted, cut back, and often added to, at the central review and chief executive level. All during the formulation stage, the process moves proposals upward in the hierarchy and in the direction of more definitive recommendations. Many segments of the process go on simultaneously.

The process next involves public hearings and legislative review. Proposals culminate eventually in firm capital investment decisions which are embodied in project appropriations and/or bond authorizations. In most jurisdictions, the process loses its separateness at the legislative review and execution stages and becomes merged with the current budget and other current processes (such as accounting and procurement).

Participants in the process are numerous, including program supervisors, bureau and department heads and their immediate staffs, city planners, the finance director, the city engineer, the central review staff, the chief administrator and chief executive, the public, and the council. Each has a special contribution to make and each brings to the process a special expertise. Operating heads and their staffs are in the best position to weigh alternatives and capital project contributions to program effectiveness and efficiency. Engineers are experts in cost-benefit analyses, sufficiency ratings, and cost estimating. In preparing alternate finance measures and estimating their effects upon the future financial status of the city, the finance director is the expert. To projections of demographic, economic, and social changes in the community, city planners and others bring experience and advanced techniques. Planners are also specialists in land utilization, traffic flow and circulation, and improvement of the physical pattern and looks of the city. These specialties give them an important role in capital decisions. The central review agency performs an integrative function and, as staff for the chief executive or administrator, brings to problems an overall, total municipal viewpoint—lacking even at the departmental level. The public, as the consumer, brings to the whole process a grass-roots "demand" approach. Pressures from various segments of the public can serve to enlighten elected officials as to what is wanted. The chief executive and the council have political leadership responsibilities. Their expertise lies in assessing the politically feasible, in adjudicating among competing pressures, and in gaining consent.

It should be emphasized, however, that the above generalizations are subject to many variations and exceptions. The impression should not be left that the capital programming process has become standardized. On the contrary, a great deal of experimentation and improvisation goes on.

Estimating Capital Requirements

Estimation of capital requirements begins with program and activity supervisors. A call for estimates by the central review staff and the distribution of forms start the process. Whether or not a ceiling should be placed on requests which come up from the operating levels is a controversial matter. The authors recommend that no ceiling be set, even though this means that the central review staff will have a more difficult task in reviewing, negotiating, and, where needed, reducing or eliminating requests. Imaginative approaches to program efficiency and effectiveness should be encouraged; to begin with a negative approach is to stifle administrative initiative and to dampen interest in the managerial usefulness of capital programming.

The quality of the capital proposals emanating from the operational, grass-roots level, especially the thoroughness and effectiveness with which alternate solutions to program needs are examined and approved, will condition the subsequent review process. The weighing of alternatives in a given program may involve:

1. The choice between a capital construction project or an increase in current operating services—for example, between a new school building to meet increased enrollment or added transportation to carry pupils to underutilized school buildings elsewhere in the city.
2. Replacement of, as opposed to continued use of, an old building. In such a case, a cost-benefit analysis can often be applied.
3. A choice among several arterial thoroughfares as to which shall be widened and rebuilt. Here, sufficiency ratings constitute a workable approach.

4. Other choices may have to be faced: a high-cost, low-maintenance structure vs. a low-cost but high-maintenance structure; differences in size; possible locations; alternate designs; and the quality of construction materials used. In this instance, emphasis is placed on the contributions which each of the competing alternatives can make to a particular program's objectives. This goal-contribution approach is more relevant than the standards approach based on norms supplied by professional associations in the different functional areas.

Inept estimating of capital requirements at the operating level will probably be discovered at some successive level (by the bureau chief, department head, or the central review agency). Because officials are sometimes not aware of feasible alternatives or may lack the necessary experience, higher levels soon learn where they must render technical assistance in capital decision making. Successive levels of review and reexamination of alternate choices constitute a sifting and refining process.

Not all program requirements, however, go through the several levels. Projects may be proposed and tested for their soundness at intermediate stages or at the highest executive level. Examples include: a project designed to develop the city's economic base; an urban renewal project; a central district face-lifting proposal; a priority which arises because of the availability of state or federal aid; or a capital outlay mandated by court order or a state regulatory body. At times, program-oriented projects, such as the above, may compete successfully with the everyday programming requirements.

The final task in the measurement of needs is a careful testing of the overall level of capital requirements. This responsibility devolves upon the central review agency.

Level of Capital Outlays

The determination of the levels of capital program expenditures is a combination of economic, political and legal factors.

Economic. Obviously the economic conditions in a community tend to place upper limits upon the amounts of community improvements which can be financed from local resources within a given period of time. Because capital improvements are usually of a character that will benefit the community over a period of years, large portions of capital outlays are financed from loan funds. But, within any given set of economic circumstances, the prudent lender places distinct limits upon the amounts which will be advanced to the local government in the form of short- and long-term loans. Experience has shown that local governments which borrow very heavily may become indebted to an extent that seriously impairs their ability subsequently to meet debt service payments.

Moreover, within the sphere of economic considerations must be included the impact of the projected improvements upon the cost of operating and maintaining the facilities. The cost of amortization of street improvements lies largely in the debt service element of cost; the cost of amortization of the library, hospital, or recreation center carries with it major increases in costs for operation and maintenance if these are net additions to plant.

Political. Given the separation in point of time between the provision of new capital facilities and the impact upon the operating budget in the form of debt service and operating costs, there is an opportunity in the capital field to attempt to take short-term political advantage of the politically acceptable capital project. The community may, in fact, have limited capacity to operate the facilities which it already possesses. But the political considerations to an administration about to run for reelection may be of such over-powering importance to the public officials that distorted scheduling results.

Legal. The desires of the public officials are usually tempered by their legal limit to incur debt. In most circumstances, the legal limits are likely to be rather stringent insofar as general obligation debt is concerned. On the other hand, there is a marked degree of freedom in many places insofar as revenue debt or pseudo-revenue debt is concerned.

In preparing their capital programs, many local governments operate under a ceiling; that is, an aggregate annual amount, usually set at a level intended to be applicable for an extended period of time. This is generally not an annual decision because its basic purpose is to stabilize local tax rates. Periodically, a dollar ceiling for capital outlays may be established by the legislative body on the advice of the finance director. Projects which are not tax-supported (i.e., self-liquidating or revenue-producing projects) are customarily exempt from this overall limit. Urban renewal projects, which involve some addition to the tax burden but which attract substantial federal aid, are sometimes given a separate ceiling. But, the central review agency should be required to counter this "ability-to-pay" level with a recommended "reasonable capital requirements" level. What the community can afford and what is required in order to live up to reasonable program standards may be widely different amounts.

For the above task, capital budgeting techniques are inadequate. Through research, it should be possible to establish a reasonable rate of growth for capital investment for a community; to measure the level of capital investment normally required by different kinds of programs; and to arrive at objective tests to judge the existence of capital deficiencies in particular areas.

It should be noted that this section deals with "needs" and "requirements"; that the term "demands" is not used. In the area of public expenditures, the budgetary process takes the place of the market; in public decisions as to capital investments, the economic concept of a demand schedule is not operationally useful.

Because of constraints upon the aggregate of capital outlays, and their connection with financial policy, these periodic "level" decisions are critical. Therefore, powerful interests both within and outside city hall will attempt to bring influence to bear. On the one side, are those striving to keep tax rates stabilized; on the other, those working for community growth, those attempting to make the community a more desirable place in which to live, and those who place high importance on certain program services.

Ideally, on the administrative side, the planners, the engineer, and the finance director will all have a hand in determining a dollar ceiling. The planners will have worked on proposals to improve the economic base of the community. If the productive capacity and viability of the community can be improved, potential rises in the tax base and tax resources can be projected. In the finance department, forecasts of present and possible new revenues and debt resources will be made and translated into a level proposal; the effects of such a proposal on the community's future financial status will also be studied. The engineer will be asked to forecast replacement deadlines and to give other technical advice. Under certain circumsances, the chief executive or chief administrator might ask all of the above staff to submit their proposals and the justification for each proposal independently. With this approach, the chief executive or the manager can be prepared to defend his recommendations as opposed to alternate level proposals from pressure groups or the council and to be ready with projections of the probable effects of each proposal, if two or three possible levels are serious contenders.

Funds available from current revenues for capital program outlays have customarily been arrived at by a residual approach. Revenue resources and current expenditures are projected and the estimated annual excess of revenue receipts over current expenditures becomes the amount available each year for capital outlays. This is not, however, a necessary approach. The calculation could begin with the level of capital project financing needed and the revenue proposals or current expenditure reductions ("belt-tightening") which would produce the necessary financial margin to support capital projects. The demand for current services need not always take first priority, solely because most capital outlays are postponable. It would be at least rational to require all expenditures, current and capital, to compete on an equal basis for scarce financial resources.

Establishment of Priorities

The scheduling of requested capital projects according to priorities contributes substantially to the achievement of program goals in one or more ways:

1. If projects are scheduled to begin and reach completion in a year-by-year framework, waste can be avoided. For example, if sewers are built underground before streets are paved, it will not be necessary to dig up the pavement. When a new building is constructed, the timing of all auxiliary utilities is important, especially if immediate occupancy is required. New arterial systems should precede relocation of fire stations. Sometimes a local government must meet a deadline to comply with a mandatory order from the state—for example, the construction of new sewage disposal facilities to end water pollution. Again, the availability of state or federal aid may depend upon site acquisition or other capital outlays by a certain date.

2. Implementation of a predetermined program emphasis over several years requires priority scheduling. Let us assume that, in a small city, improvement of the community's economic base is to be a primary goal and is

to be sought by a combination of public capital investments and the attraction of outside private capital. This policy emphasis necessitates a proper ordering of, and effective timing for, these particular projects vis-a-vis other public capital projects.

3. A priority schedule is also a useful device for centering attention (and hopefully action) during the "cutback process" on projects which are postponable or dispensable (that is, less urgent and/or less essential). In the formulation of the capital budget which is to be recommended to the council, cutbacks are "musts," if the total is to be brought within available resources. Cutbacks may also occur at the legislative review stage.

The establishment of priorities involves, first, programming projects by years over a five- or six-year time span. Next, within the first year when bond authorizations or appropriations embody capital decisions, the individual projects should be ranked, at least by groups. Ranking by years is ideal according to an "urgency" or postponability scale and, within the first year, on an "essentiality" scale. Theoretically, within a given year, all projects are approximately equal as to urgency or postponability, but vary as to essentiality. For example, two bridges may have been condemned and closed. Replacements are equally urgent and both projects are scheduled in the first year. One replacement, however, may be more essential than the other. These scale concepts, however, are often of limited use operationally. Priority ranking is a complex value judgment, difficult to pursue within a dual-scale framework.

Priority ranking takes place at several organizational levels. It parallels the work of establishing capital requirements. Since it is known in advance that all requirements cannot be met because of scarce financial resources, priority schedules accompany project requests whenever recommended proposals are submitted to the next higher organizational level.

Projects are ranked as they contribute to the same program goal at the program supervisor level. At the bureau and departmental levels, the establishment of project priorities cuts across programs and also organizational units. Priority recommendations are usually prepared on a standard form with columns by years. Projects are scheduled by years. At the departmental level, a ranking (or indication of the priority of a single project or group of projects) is desirable so that persons reviewing proposals at higher levels can know the priority assigned by the departmental personnel. This accommodation is important in those instances in which fewer than the total number of projects requested can be included in the capital program.

At a later stage, review by the chief executive and the central review staff provides an even more overall perspective and the whole ordering of projects as to time and priority is reviewed and adjusted. Projects must be weighed in light of their contribution to programs which, in themselves, are not of equal rank. We emphasize that the project contribution-to-program approach, rather than the departmental or functional approach, should dominate even at this level. It is not a question of which department or which function is to have the greater emphasis in the capital improvement program, but rather which programs—no matter where located—must be bolstered by capital projects and when.

But the complexity does not end even here. Operating program needs may also have to compete with certain projects which are oriented to protection or development of the city's overall economic base (or that of one major segment, especially the central business district), or to a community face-lifting or other aesthetically oriented projects. These, in themselves, are legitimate programs but are often conceived and promoted at a higher level than most operating requirements.

The central review staff, in assisting the chief executive, must perform an adjudicative function and an integrative function. Decisions must be reached as to competing priorities and these must be compiled into a master schedule and justified.

Most will admit that the process for establishing priorities works imperfectly. The causes are not always the same for there are many possibilities. Scientific research has been generally lacking in this phase of financial administration; standards and criteria are crude.[7] Because program and policy goals in some municipalities are nebulous, if not completely lacking, the central review staff may be obliged to work without clear guidelines. Since some municipalities follow the practice of almost never eliminating project proposals but rather allocating them to later years, projects of very low priority may gain status and "mature" into a priority ranking which they hardly warrant. Frequently, there is a tendency to give high priority to projects with substantial outside aid and projects which bring no additional tax burden (i.e., projects supported from non-tax sources). These considerations introduce disturbing and sometimes irrational elements into the priority system. Objectivity is often diluted by the inability of the central staff to divorce its recommendations from the anticipation of political reactions. The desire for a good "batting average," unfortunately, may outweigh the staff's special responsibility to bring objectivity to the process.

Capital Equipment

Practice varies among local governments as to treatment of capital equipment in the capital programming process. In keeping with the business practice of capitalizing the cost of equipment and furnishings for new buildings, many governments include such equipment and furnishings in the estimated capital costs of new building projects.

The medium-sized and larger communities, however, generally exclude all other classes of capital equipment. Several reasons lie behind this practice. First, to include capital equipment is to clutter up and make more complex a process already dealing often with large numbers of site purchases and construction projects over a five- or six-year period. Second, equipment needs and replacement policies are often already well administered under the operating budget practices (property and purchasing controls), and require none of the technical expertise of the city planners. Third, most cities expect to pay for all capital equipment

---

[7] For a more detailed discussion of developing criteria for the investment of public funds see W. H. Brown, Jr. and C. E. Gilbert, *Planning Municipal Investment: a case study of Philadelphia*, (Philadelphia: University of Pennsylvania Press, 1961), 293 pp.

needs out of current revenues. It is true that the capital programming process does not dictate a borrowing policy, but bonded debt is often the major source of funds for the capital program. In the fourth place, since most local governments have to plan their capital improvement programs within an upper limit, it is important that all of this margin be reserved for project sites and construction costs.

In some smaller local governments the tests of value and estimated useful life of a piece of equipment are used in deciding what capital equipment shall be included in the capital program. For example, the rule may be that any unit of equipment which costs $10,000 or more and has a useful life of at least five years will be contained in the capital program. This policy has some rational basis. In a small municipality, capital equipment needs of this size (or a comparable size) may be nonrecurring and, therefore, require advanced scheduling. Furthermore, in a small municipality, the capital program process might perform a portion of the function which, in a larger municipality, would be performed by a property control officer.

Large and small local governments alike seem to agree that the usual accounting distinction between current and capital expenditures is not the dividing line for inclusion in, or exclusion from, the capital program. The accounting distinction has no compelling significance at the planning and programming stage—only at the stage where expenditures are actually recorded in the books.

Urban Renewal

Urban renewal projects under federal and state sponsorship have been brought into the capital program process, but not without adjustments in the process itself.

In some jurisdictions, the organization for urban renewal has been superimposed on the existing structure by adding a new redevelopment body, a coordinator, and inter-departmental committees. Because of new channels of communication and new focal points for decision making, modifications in the older capital program process have been inevitable. Urban renewal projects have been partially forced outside the regular channels of decision making and have become highly centralized because negotiations with the Department of Housing and Urban Development, and compliance with federal regulations, are time-consuming and cut across the capital program and budget calendar.

The magnitude of federal funds has been sufficient, in some municipalities, to shift the emphasis from meeting the capital requirements of operating programs to improving the "economic base" of the community and, more particularly, to rehabilitating the central business district. This may mean capital deferrals in important operating areas, but deferrals are not a new phenomenon to municipal administrators. Despite the obvious neglect of other capital requirements, to "ride the wave" of urban renewal while federal money is available could be a deliberate policy for two reasons. First, there is no certainty as to the number of years that this type of aid will continue. Secondly, if the program proves to be short-lived, the greatest gain to an individual municipality will no doubt result from maximum utilization of the funds while they are available. It remains to be seen whether urban renewal will add to, or tend to level out, the "lumpiness" of municipal capital outlays. The recent enactment of special revenue sharing legislation for development and proposals for similar enactments covering other broad categories could bring these activities more closely into line with good capital programming procedures.

Another important factor is the tendency to give the highest priority to capital projects which will qualify under the "non-cash contribution" provisions of the federal law. In order to provide an attractive investment possibility to potential redevelopers in the renewal area, the temptation is strong to concentrate public capital improvements in that area. The justification is that the cost to the city is nominal since the federal government assumes the major cost burden. Granting higher priorities to projects which are only a minor burden to the property taxpayer (or none at all) is, of course, nothing new in capital budgeting. Because of the practice of establishing ceilings, or levels, for capital budgets in terms of tax-supported revenues, a self-liquidating (revenue-producing) project or one financed substantially from outside funds may have a greater likelihood of being authorized than a tax-supported project.

Financing the Capital Program

Available financial resources for capital outlays over the program period have to be estimated and a determination made as to how these resources can best be utilized. This determination results in a financial plan. Several alternatives are open:

1. An all-borrowing policy, or a substantial reliance on debt financing, is one approach. The annual available resources could be used entirely for debt service (interest and retirement of principal), with the size of the annual resources setting a limit upon the amount that could be borrowed.

2. A capital reserve plan is a second approach; that is, the annual resources available could be accumulated in one or more capital reserve funds, the amounts invested, and when any fund becomes adequate to pay for a proposed project, the fund would be expended. If a municipality has a capital requirement which can wait, accumulation of the necessary capital funds over a period is a feasible approach, assuming a relatively stable construction dollar.

3. A partial pay-as-you-go policy is a common approach. Some of the annual resources will be used to finance capital improvements directly; the remainder will go for supporting a debt program. Even if a local government generally pursues a borrowing policy, an initial down payment out of current revenues is a possibility. A customary five to ten percent down payment is a limited pay-as-you-spend policy and assures that the voters authorizing the improvement will make a cash contribution and that all of the burden will not be postponed.

4. A substantial (even if not full) pay-as-you-spend policy could be adopted. This means utilizing most of the annual available resources for land purchases and construction without any intermediate financial

steps. A largely pay-as-you-spend policy would be justifiable for a large city which (a) had caught up with abnormal backlogs; (b) found itself in a period when the construction dollar was relatively stable; (c) had a debt service burden not in excess of about 10 percent of its annual revenues; and (d) had capital outlay requirements which recurred annually in a fairly level *amount*. If capital outlay requirements in a given year exceeded the normal recurring level, borrowing to the extent of that excess could be resorted to in order that the level of taxes not be markedly disturbed.

In typical patterns of general obligation debt financing, a degree of pay-as-you-acquire financing tends to be present, even when full financing appears to be in debt form. Thus, if a $10,000,000 bond issue is sold at 6 percent average interest costs, with repayments scheduled on the basis of $500,000 annually commencing one year from date of sale, it is likely that it will take two or three years to complete the project. Assuming a three-year period, the total payments made on principal and the actual net interest during construction would be $3,210,000 by opening date. This is, in effect, a down payment although it is recorded as a debt service payment. In other words, any payment on the principal prior to availability of the facility for use and any net payment of interest during construction (gross interest paid less interest earned on temporary balances) constitute the equivalent of a pay-as-you-acquire allocation to the financing of the project.

Numerous considerations are involved in the selection of one of the foregoing patterns, or some combination thereof:

1. In periods of national emergency when most of the national resources are needed for federal war expenditures, it is feasible to develop reserve funds for later financing; however, political realities tend to preclude this possibility in most other circumstances

2. The pay-as-you-spend concept has three distinct advantages: (a) it preserves great flexibility to the community for future periods of economic recession or depression by not piling up large fixed charge costs; (b) it avoids the payment of interest charges; and (c) it imposes upon public officials the full political responsibility for levy of the taxes necessary to pay the local share of such projects

3. The pay-as-you-use approach has the advantage of permitting the costs to be spread out over a generation of current users of public facilities, thereby imposing upon each a significant proportion of the costs of each project

4. In an inflationary period, one must take into account the extent to which prepayment for capital outlays is warranted, when the opportunity for repayment of the principal and interest in dollars that are less dear can be arranged

5. During periods of rapid price rise, the time delay necessary to accumulate down payments or full pay-as-you-spend resources invites higher costs which may wipe out most, if not all, of the advantages of nonpayment of interest

For that portion of the capital program to be financed from the issuance of debt, substantial planning processes are in order. A general review of these processes is provided in subsequent chapters.

The Central Review Agency

Who should perform the central review function for capital requirements is still a matter of controversy. As a budget function it is claimed, in some municipalities, by the budget office. As a planning function, it is often lodged in the city planning department. A third alternative is to create a separate capital budget staff, perhaps with a part of its staff co-opted from both finance and planning. Finally, an *ad hoc* capital improvement program committee might be used representing planning, finance, certain operating departments, the administration, other jurisdictions, and, in some cases, the legislative body, and the public. On analysis, the planning function seems the more dominant one, which suggests that, if the finance staff and the planners both report to the same chief administrator or executive, the weight of the reasoning is in favor of placing the primary responsibility for integration and for preparation of the document upon the planners. The finance staff would have primary responsibility for the finance side of the program and the planners, responsibility for the physical (or capital improvement) side.

Among the more successful agencies in capital programming has been the city planning commission composed of appointees of the mayor or the council with *ex-officio* representation by the director of finance and selected officials responsible for line operations. (Such a provision is made in Philadelphia and Cleveland.)

Activities which a central review agency must perform, regardless of its location, include:

1. Focusing upon the totality of project proposals submitted from different sources and eliminating any project requests not eligible for inclusion in the capital program
2. Mapping of all project locations, reviewing all proposals in order to prevent overlapping, and checking as to whether the proposals are in conformance with the comprehensive plan
3. Relating the projects in the capital program with the objectives contained in the long-term operating program, where such exists
4. Careful exploration of the impact of each capital project on the annual operating budget, both in terms of debt service and in terms of the cost of operating and maintaining completed projects
5. Bringing to bear upon the more difficult problems the combined expertise which can be mustered within the administration—including engineering, financial, planning, and statistical talents.
6. Conferring and negotiating with operating heads in order to explain central agency viewpoints not in agreement with the department's recommendations
7. Preparing a recommended schedule of priorities to assist in the ultimate appropriation of scarce resources among competing capital claims

8. Assembling and integrating into a unified document proposals which meet with the chief executive's approval; preparing project justifications and drafts of the executive budget message; and writing all press releases to be issued
9. Recommending the means of financing approved projects
10. Assisting the chief executive at public hearings and at the legislative review stage
11. Conducting a "soft-sell" campaign within the administration, year-in and year-out, for advanced planning approaches, primarily through the rendering of able technical assistance in project decision making
12. Reappraising capital investment decisions upon the completion of individual capital projects with the objective of broadening the experience base for future capital programming

The Capital Program as a Reporting Document

In some municipalities, the capital program has become an effective medium for reporting to the council, the many civic organizations, and to leading citizens upon a very important aspect of municipal government. Capital projects so vitally affect land utilization, traffic circulation, and the future physical appearance of the city that they generate real community interest. In addition to the document as an external reporting device, the capital budget process itself produces a series of internal reports: from the project (or activity) supervisor to the program supervisor; from the program supervisor to the department or bureau head; and from the latter to the chief administrator or executive, or his staff agencies.

A message, enlivened by charts, diagrams, and financial summary tables, usually introduces the program document and explains the consideration given the projects proposed and the means of financing suggested. Typically, the document reflects accomplishments (projects completed), a comparison between accomplishments and the program as envisaged, and individual project proposals which are new with their attendant costs and anticipated impact on the operating budget. Code numbers are used to key individual projects with the textual material and with maps (usually by sections of the city) so that the reader moves with ease from one portion of the document to the next. The artistic ability of the architect-planner is often quite evident throughout.

Where the capital program is one major division of a combined operating and capital budget document, the capital section customarily comes second and carries its own executive message.

The grouping of projects under program headings so that capital outlays conform to the style of presentation of the program-performance budget, in general, has not yet been developed. Project justifications, however, on a unit construction-cost basis and, sometimes, on a cost-benefit basis can be found.

Public Hearings and Legislative Review

In the capital decision-making process, one function of the local legislative body is to ensure that all elements of the community are given a fair opportunity to present their views on capital projects. This is done at public hearings. Hearings should be timed so that the public can influence legislative decisions and action. The public should be given ample notification of the time and place of the hearings; have adequate newspaper coverage of the main proposals; have access to a study of the document itself; and be furnished information upon request.

The president of the legislative body should preside at the hearings at which the chief executive and his staff may be asked to explain the proposals and to answer questions. Even if a semi-independent planning commission representing the citizens has already held hearings on the capital program and capital budget, the council, as elected representatives, should also hold public hearings in order to assess for themselves the people's reactions. Its responsibility in this area should not be delegated or preempted. Formal legislative review follows these public hearings. It is at this stage that the current and the capital budget cycles merge and the council should look at both sets of proposals at the same time.

The legislative body should not be brought into the capital programming process prior to completion of the executive budget. Compromises in this direction tend to invite persistent legislative attempts to influence decisions all along the way, with a resultant weakening of the executive's responsibility for budget formulation. Since they have the final decision, councilmen should wait for the legislative review stage, at which point their voices will be heard. The council has important responsibilities in capital investment decision-making: (1) to arrive at an upper level of capital outlays, periodically—but generally not each year; (2) to establish overall policy regarding the extent of borrowing and the degree of partial pay-as-you-go; (3) to hold public hearings annually and make certain that all diverse views have an opportunity to be heard; (4) to appraise the merits of any conflicts between the expert's views and those of the layman; (5) to assess opposing viewpoints among citizens and citizens' groups in an attempt to determine wherein lie the best interests of the community; (6) to furnish political leadership and gain consent where major issues as to the future development of the community are at stake; (7) to make appropriations for all approved projects; and (8) to require reports so that this body may keep a watchful eye on the execution stage.

Councilmen, however, often fail in their responsibilities. Where a councilman is not elected at-large but represents a ward, his interest in the capital program and budget may center too highly in assuring that his district gets a fair—or a lion's—share of projects. Priorities get reshuffled—particularly for small projects such as playgrounds or larger projects with special vote-getting appeal. And, legislative bodies sometimes attempt to retain too much control over the execution stage by making partial appropriations and requiring a return to the council for funds at every new stage of the project.

Approval of the Capital Program

In many municipalities, the council is not required to act upon the capital program as such; if any direct action is taken, it is likely to be with respect to the capital budget year, i.e., the next ensuing year. In many situations, the council does not even act upon a capital budget for the year. Rather, it uses the means of authorizing bond issues as the mechanism for making appropriations for the capital projects which are to be financed by the local government.

It has been found that where the governing body is obliged actually to adopt the five- or six-year capital program, this action is likely to have a beneficial effect in contrast to those communities where no legislative action is required upon the capital program. In the latter instance, the council is likely not to take the document seriously; in some instances, e.g., New York City, they give but little consideration to the "program" years as contrasted to the "budget" year.

By contrast, in communities where formal action is required, the members of the council develop a concern not only for the projects of the "budget" year but also for the "program" years as they come to realize that projects incorporated into the late years of the program become the basis for the subsequent capital budget as that year arrives. Also, their constituents (at least in respect to the projects most dear to them) see the promise of improvements at stated times in the future and make their wishes known to their councilman.

The effect of adopting the capital budget for the ensuing year may appear to be unimportant; however, experience has proven otherwise. If the capital budget becomes the sole means by which the legislative body may authorize capital projects and other related expenditures, this process becomes a vital one to all members. On the other hand, if the actual appropriations are made through special ordinances—either in conjunction with the authorization of loans or otherwise—the importance of the capital budget is downgraded. Only by use of the capital budget as the appropriation device can one be assured that the whole range of capital projects for the next year is likely to be considered *in toto*—rather than piecemeal.

Execution of the Capital Budget

The participants in the capital budget process at the planning stage and the actual execution stage are usually different. The user agency and the central review staff are involved in the former. But, at the execution stage, the department or staff responsible for letting and supervising outside construction contracts is primarily involved—or the city's own construction agency, if the project is done by force account. In large measure, the capital budget is executed through those processes centering around land acquisition, contract awards, and project cost control during construction. The real estate bureau, the purchasing agent, the city engineer, the city architect, the project foreman or supervisor, the project cost accountant, and the cost accounting division of the finance department— these are some who may participate in the execution stage.

The legislative body may also retain a hand at this stage, and this may prove unfortunate. In some jurisdictions, every project must come before the council for approval as regards: (1) an appropriation for preliminary drawings; (2) if approved, an appropriation for final drawings; and (3), if approved, an appropriation for land acquisition and either the initial year's construction costs or total construction costs. This type of continuing control invites minute decisions as to design (a field outside the expertise of a legislative body) and often interminable delays in construction. The council may also, at the execution stage, insert small projects and make priority shifts, if a time lag develops in progress on approved projects and it appears that allocated funds will not be actually spent or obligated during the budget year. It sometimes happens that a small project, so inserted, will appear in a published capital program only as a completed project.

Cost-consciousness should enter into capital programming early in the process of estimating capital requirements and continue through the several review stages; and, it should not be neglected in the final construction stage.

Reappraisals and Annual Revisions

"Reappraisal" is an essential step in any administrative process. In capital programming, it is not necessarily annual but normally comes at the completion of each capital project. A reappraisal includes reexamining the original decision and testing whether actuality measured up to expectations; and if not, why not? Reappraisals establish guides for the future. If participants in capital budgeting learn from their successes and from their mistakes, the city's proficiency in capital investment decision-making will improve.

A number of questions can be posed and answered at the reappraisal stage. Is the municipality satisfied with the contractor's performance? If there was a delay in the delivery date, are there measures which could be taken to avoid a similar delay in future projects? Were there clauses which should have been included in this type of contract? If construction costs were higher than the contract price because the city requested structural variances, were these requests justifiable? What elements (such as the design, types of materials, size, and functional attributes) should not be duplicated in a similar project? What of the appropriateness of the location? Was the project properly coordinated with other levels of government? These questions do not pretend to exhaust the list.

Sometimes the council may agree to a "pilot project." Under these circumstances, the project may be subjected to reappraisal not only at the completion stage but periodically during the first year or two of usage.

An important stage in the capital programming cycle is the annual revision of the capital improvement program. Continuity in advanced planning is thereby built-in; as one year materializes, another is added at the far end so that a five- or six-year projection is always available. A second purpose is also served. As projects move closer to the year of implementation, they can be reexamined, thus keeping the whole process flexible. If a capital improvement program were approved only at five or six-year intervals and strictly adhered to, rigidity and perhaps loss of interest would result. Also, after two or three years had elapsed, advanced planning would have shortened to only two or three years.

Reappraisals are basically backward looking, but have the objective of improving future performance. In contrast to reappraisals, annual revisions are periodic and forward looking.

Some argue that a three-year capital improvement program is long enough; that beyond three years any vision into the future is blurred. Even conceding this fact, the annual addition of one year and revision of the prior year's program constitute a maturing process as projects move closer to the present.

Opposed to the view of a shorter capital program, a good case can be made in some fields for a perspective substantially longer than six years as to the problems involved in capital programming. For example, any basic water supply or sewage disposal program must look far beyond such a limited time period. In the transit field, six years or more is necessary to construct a single major rapid-transit artery and a 15 to 25 year, or even longer thrust, is essential in long-term planning. The question, to some degree, revolves around the size of the local government and the nature of the problem being confronted.

Admittedly, flexibility is not desired by all participants in the capital programming processes. Forward planning, both physical and administrative, would be improved by greater definitiveness in the decisions made and greater stability of the projects in the priority schema. Insistence on stability and on firm decisions would probably, however, shorten the time span for advanced capital programming. The assumption is implicit here that a five- or six-year framework justifies itself, even if it does no more than facilitate and improve the year-by-year decisions as to which capital projects shall be incorporated into the current edition of the capital program. Flexibility seems to be a *sine qua non* if advances in the acceptability of forward planning are to be achieved.

COOPERATIVE CAPITAL PROGRAMMING

This term is used to include instances where two or more local governments cooperate in long-term capital programming and budgeting. The governments are usually overlapping and underlying units, such as the county and city; the city and its co-terminus, but independent, school district; or the county, city, and school board. A major new thrust in this direction is currently occurring at the insistence of the federal Department of Housing and Urban Development. That agency has assigned to regional planning agencies responsibility for the development of regional capital programs, with a particular view to coordination of the work of many governments operating within a region. This process is still in its infancy; however, as it develops much can be expected of it, especially in the avoidance of overlapping water, sewer. transit, and other facilities which have taken on a regional character.[8]

Ideally, overlapping and underlying local governments should get together and integrate or coordinate their capital improvement programs. This normative injunction, however, is rarely obeyed. Yet, there is enough experience with cooperative capital budgeting to know that it can work. The requisites seem to be: an organization willing to perform the overall central staff function; an incentive (or incentives) strong enough to make cooperation attractive; and a willingness on the part of the community's political leaders to keep the issue out of partisan politics.

---

[8] For a discussion of some of the problems involved. see the Pennsylvania Economy League, Eastern Division, study for the Delaware Valley Regional Planning Commission, entitled *The Issue of Regional Capital Programming*, Sept., 1969, 34 pp.

As an example of a consolidated approach to the problems involved in capital programming, perhaps Cincinnati affords the best single example. For about 25 years, the three major overlapping governments—the city, board of education, and county—worked out their capital improvement programs together. Each year, representatives of the three governments met as a Joint Improvement Program Committee and considered, as a body, the needs of the community as a whole and its ability to finance capital improvements.

The first step was taken before the committee met. Each government studied its needs and ranked proposed projects in the order of their necessity. Then, the costs were estimated. The first point at which the committee began to function was in estimating the community's ability to pay for capital improvements. Under the total capital improvement program to be financed from bonds, the three governments volunteered not to interfere with one another financially and the combined program was kept within the limits of reasonable maximum tax rates. Each year, the committee called upon the Cincinnati Bureau of Governmental Research (a private agency) to assist in estimating revenues. The Bureau was not a member of the committee, but a privately-supported organization not connected with any one of the governments. The Bureau did much of the yeoman's work in estimating the ability of the community, as a whole, to finance capital improvement programs and furnished the data upon which the committee would base its correlation of needs with resources. The principal features of the technique were as follows:

1. The trend of assessed valuations was ascertained from tax lists and duplicates of taxable property and future trends were estimated for each year of the program.

2. Normal operating expenditures for the city, the schools, and the county were predicted and translated into total tax rates for operating purposes.

3. Annual debt charges (for both principal and interest) on all existing debt of all three units were computed and converted into tax rates.

4. By adding the tax rates for operating costs and for existing debt, the community's probable total tax rates for the years immediately ahead were projected as they would be if no new bonds were issued and if no expansion of activities were undertaken. Ordinarily, upon that assumption, the predictions would show declining tax rates, in proportion to increased taxable values and reduction in old debt.

5. A reasonable maximum tax rate was agreed upon, or assumed, and this total could not be exceeded by the three local units combined. This had to be either an arbitrary figure, a personal preference, a reflection of community opinion, or a mixture of these elements.

6. Once a reasonable maximum rate was set, the next step was to subtract from it the rates needed for operation and for servicing debt already outstanding. The differences were the rates available for paying the interest and principal on new debts each year. By applying these rates to the assessed valuation, an annual revenue figure was obtained and then translated into a capital figure (debt principal) for which this

revenue would be sufficient as annual debt service. Then, the committee could determine how much could be borrowed by all the authorities together, without exceeding the maximum tax rate agreed upon.

The next and final step was for the committee to bring the capital improvement programs of the three units into harmony with available resources. When costs and resources had been estimated, demands were generally found to exceed resources. This usually meant that the improvement programs had to be scaled down or postponed so as to accord with ability-to-pay. Accordingly, the committee had to ascertain which needs must be taken care of eventually, and in what order. The committee considered not only the budget year ahead but also looked toward the future and planned some years in advance. The committee did not attempt to pass upon the merits of any particular improvement. When the total program for any year happened to exceed what could safely be financed in that year, members of the committee discussed the problem as representatives of the community as a whole, rather than as champions of their respective governments.

By looking ahead a few years, the committee was able to outline a program under which all needs could be met in the order of their urgency. Committee members worked out the proportions which they agreed constituted a fair and proper program for the whole community. Any one of the governments could ignore the program and issue bonds up to the statutory limits, regardless of the consequences upon the tax rate or upon local services. However, each government kept in line. Each knew that, in the long run, the community was better off with an orderly program of public improvements, and that an orderly program was attainable only by continuing the work of the Joint Improvement Program Committee and by general acceptance of the committee's recommendations.

Unfortunately, when the long-time director of the Cincinnati Bureau of Municipal Research retired, the program of cooperation shortly faltered. Perhaps this offers a justification for the belief that even the best conceived and operated cooperative undertakings are not sufficient in the long run. Perhaps the new thrust through regional planning agencies and the regional COGS ("Councils of Governments") with forceful assistance from HUD will provide the impetus not only to the development but also to the continuation and improvement of such processes of cooperation among governments within a region. Yet, adoption of federal special revenue sharing may act to nullify this potential.

CONCLUSIONS

Improved capital programming and capital budgeting techniques have been painfully slow in coming, although some progress has been made. In some places, recognition of capital budgeting as a central staff review and integrative function has been accomplished. Here and there, efforts have been successful in building into the capital programming and capital budgeting process devices for resolving conflicts which arise from contending pressures for capital projects. The cost-benefit analysis, as developed in engineering economics, has been applied in certain classes of municipal capital decisions. More recently, economists have been devoting attention to capital investment decision-making in both the business and public sectors, and the literature is growing. One important case study of book length, *Planning Municipal Investment: a case study of Philadelphia*, previously cited in this chapter, throws light on a number of issues and suggests areas for further empirical investigation, especially the extent to which certain factors condition capital program "success:" the existence, or lack, of a comprehensive plan; the kind and strength of community interest and support which urban renewal and other centrally planned programs have aroused; the framework for program formulation; the experience of administrative heads and their connection with special clienteles; the cohesiveness of the administrative group; the method of electing councilmen; and current economic conditions.

Improved techniques, however, have not kept pace with the requirements for better capital investment decision making which the volume of new capital projects (generated by population concentrations, technological advances, and the availability of new types of financing) has made more urgent. The authors venture to suggest one major technical advance, and that is the compilation of accurate information regarding capital assets. Without this, many of the overall decisions as to capital investment policy are made "in the dark." Our proposal is in two closely interrelated parts: the classification by program of all proposals for capital projects and the use of depreciation as an integral part of fixed asset accounting.

Fixed asset accounting, with appropriate treatment of depreciation, provides helpful information during periods of low levels of inflation. However, in periods of marked inflation, e.g., 1973 and 1974, historical data tends to lose much of its comparability because of the marked changes in dollar statement of costs at one time to those prevailing in the two or three prior decades.

The use of depreciation here recommended is primarily as a means of measuring the rate at which the governmental plant, in the aggregate or in large functional segments, is maintaining its value, increasing in value, or decreasing in value. It is recognized that conventional methods of depreciation may not be adequate for these purposes in periods of major, prolonged inflation; however, there is work to be done here in fashioning a suitable tool for improved decision-making.

7

Revenues I:
The Property Tax

This chapter is concerned with the property tax—its role in the overall financing of local governments and elements of its administration.

Although the property tax is under its greatest attack in history, especially as the mainstay of local support for public education, the stubborn fact is that this tax has for centuries demonstrated its capacity to withstand severe and protracted attacks. Because of its past and present importance and because of its almost universal use as the principal element of income of local governments, there is more study, research, political controversy, and literature generated each year on this tax than any other local government revenue source.

It not only continues to stand as the most important single source of local governments in the United States but also the valuation of the property subject to taxation continues to be the primary base upon which debt limits of local governments are constructed. Accordingly this chapter is devoted to a brief review of some of the more salient points considering its role and elements of its administration. Other elements of local government revenue will be discussed in Chapter 8.

THE ROLE OF THE PROPERTY TAX IN
LOCAL GOVERNMENT FINANCE

In an historical context, the all-pervasive importance of the property tax is indicated by the following:

> . . . we note from the general chronicles of English history that even before the Norman conquest there were such taxes and the Danegeld . . . Following the conquest, William the First developed his famous Doomsday Survey . . . It was an elaborate assessment of everything in the King's realm . . . The Angevine kings collected the "scutage" or shield-money . . . It seems that for several centuries property taxation worked well enough to be retained as almost the whole tax system.[1]

---

[1] Groves, Harold M., "Is the Property Tax Conceptually and Practically Administrable?" *The Property Tax and Its Administration*, ed. Arthur D. Lynn, Jr., (Madison, Wis.: The University of Wisconsin Press, 1969), p. 19.

Table 10
PROPERTY AND OTHER LOCAL GOVERNMENT TAXES
SELECTED YEARS, 1902-1972

Year	Total Taxes	Property Taxes	Sales and Gross Receipts Taxes	Income Taxes	License and Other Taxes
(Amounts in Billions of Dollars)					
1902	.70	.62	—	—	.08
1922	3.07	2.97	.02	—	.08
1932	4.27	4.16	.03	—	.09
1942	4.63	4.27	.13	.03	.20
1952	9.47	8.28	.63	.10	.47
1962	20.96	18.42	1.47	.31	.76
1971-72	48.93	40.88	4.24	2.24	1.58
(Percentages)					
1902	100.0	88.5	—	—	11.5
1922	100.0	96.7	.7	—	2.6
1932	100.0	97.3	.7	—	2.0
1942	100.0	92.2	2.8	.6	4.3
1952	100.0	87.4	6.7	1.1	5.0
1962	100.0	87.9	7.0	1.5	3.6
1971-72	100.0	83.5	8.7	4.6	3.2

Sources: Bureau of the Census, *Historical Statistics of the United States, Colonial Times to 1957*, p. 729; *Governmental Finances in 1962*, p. 20; *Governmental Finances in 1971-72*, p. 20.

American local governments have traditionally relied heavily on the property tax for the greater part of their revenues, but this reliance is gradually diminishing. In reviewing the overall degree of reliance by local governments upon property taxes in providing total revenues, as indicated in Tables 9 and 10, one is struck by the fact that from 1922 through 1952, the percentage of total revenues derived from the property tax decreased from 72 percent to 43 percent. Following a period of some stabilization, the percentages decreased further by 1972—when property taxes accounted for only 36 percent of total local government revenues.

Thus, one sees that, in terms of its relative importance as a source of support of local government, the property tax has been cut in half in the 50-year period, 1922-1972. However, in the same period, the absolute amounts derived from the property tax rose from about $3.0 billion in 1922 to $40.9 billion in 1972. Moreover, in 1972 it was still the largest single source of income for local government. The only category of similar importance was intergovernmental revenue payments which accounted for $39.0 billion.

Table 11
GENERAL REVENUE SOURCES OF LOCAL GOVERNMENTS
1971-72

	General Revenue	Intergovern- mental Revenue	General Revenue from Own Sources	Non-Tax General Revenue	Tax Revenue	Property Taxes	Non-Property Taxes
(Amounts in Billions of Dollars)							
All Local Governments	103.47	39.02	64.45	15.52	48.93	40.88	8.05
Counties	23.40	9.82	13.58	3.64	9.94	8.57	1.37
Municipalities	34.94	11.43	23.50	6.45	17.06	10.99	6.07
Townships	3.93	.90	3.04	.35	2.68	2.45	.23
School Districts	38.45	17.66	20.78	2.50	18.28	17.94	.34
Special Districts	5.07	1.52	3.55	2.58	.97	.93	.04
(Percent of Total)							
All Local Governments	100.0	37.7	62.3	15.0	47.3	39.5	7.8
Counties	100.0	42.0	58.0	15.6	42.5	36.6	5.9
Municipalities	100.0	32.7	67.3	18.5	48.8	31.5	17.4
Townships	100.0	22.8	77.2	8.9	68.2	62.3	5.9
School Districts	100.0	45.9	54.0	6.5	47.5	46.7	.8
Special Districts	100.0	29.9	70.1	50.9	19.1	18.3	.8
(Percent of Taxes)							
All Local Governments					100.0	83.5	16.5
Counties					100.0	86.2	13.8
Municipalities					100.0	64.4	35.6
Townships					100.0	91.4	8.6
School Districts					100.0	98.1	1.9
Special Districts					100.0	95.9	4.1

Sources: Bureau of the Census, *Governmental Finances in 1971-72*, p. 30.

Property Tax Component of Local Government General Revenues

In reviewing the local tax component of local government revenues, as shown in Table 10, it appears that the property tax reached its zenith in 1932, when measured as a percentage of total *tax* revenue. In that year, 97 percent of total local government tax revenue was derived from property taxes.

Moreover, it is important to note that, whereas the property tax has declined markedly in total local government revenue systems, its position as an element of the local government tax structure continues very dominant. Thus, although there was a noticeable decrease in the percentage of total taxes derived from the property tax in the years 1932 to 1952—from 97 percent to 87 percent, the decrease in the period 1952 to 1972 was less marked—from 87 percent to 84 percent. Property taxes accounted for approximately 78 percent of all locally generated general revenues in 1902; 81 percent in 1942; 71 percent in 1952; and 63 percent in 1972.

For Different Types of Local Governments

The property tax has widely differing degrees of importance in both the entire revenue structure and the tax structure of local government revenues, depending upon the type of local government under consideration. The availability of state and federal aid and the use of nonproperty taxes, such as income taxes and sales taxes, necessarily results in a lessened dependence on the property tax. Property taxes will be more significant in school districts, counties, and smaller municipalities than in large cities which have a greater diversity of taxing sources available to them or special districts which depend very heavily on service charges. Consequently, as shown in Table 11, property taxes in 1971-72 represented 62 percent of the total general revenues in townships, 47 percent for school districts, 37 percent for counties, 31.5 percent for municipalities, and 18 percent for special districts. As a share of locally generated tax revenues, they represented over 91 percent for townships; 98 percent for school districts; approximately 86 percent for counties; 64 percent for municipalities; and 96 percent for special districts.

Regional Differentials

In recent years the movement to nonproperty taxes has become marked in some states while continuing at the almost non-existent level in others. The data for 1970-71 is presented in Table 12 and for 1971-72 in Table 13. The degree of dispersion in reliance upon nonproperty taxes in 1972 can be summarized as follows:

Percentage of Total Local Tax Revenue Derived From Nonproperty Taxes	Number of States	Cumulative Percentage of States
55–59	1	2
40–44	1	4
35–39	–	4
30–34	2	8
25–29	6	20
20–24	3	26
15–19	6	38
10–14	7	52
5– 9	8	68
0– 4	16	100

Looking at property taxes as a part of the general revenue systems of local governments, it may be seen that in 1971 Alabama depended upon this source for only 12 percent of local governmental general revenues. By contrast New Hampshire was at the 69 percent level. Property taxes provided less than one-third of total local general revenues in the South Atlantic region and the South Central states. They tend to equal one-half of all general revenues in the North

Table 12

RELATIVE IMPORTANCE OF PROPERTY TAX IN GENERAL
REVENUE SYSTEMS OF LOCAL GOVERNMENTS, BY STATES
1970-71
(amounts in millions of dollars)

Region/State	Total General Revenue (1)	Total Taxes (2)	Property Taxes (3)	Property Taxes as a Percent of	
				Total General Revenue (4)	Total Taxes (5)
New England					
Connecticut	1,291	847	842	65.2	99.4
Maine	275	184	182	66.2	98.9
Massachusetts	2,555	1,660	1,647	64.5	99.2
New Hampshire	239	167	165	69.0	98.8
Rhode Island	293	175	173	59.0	98.9
Vermont	134	86	84	62.9	98.4
Middle Atlantic					
New Jersey	3,437	2,138	1,932	56.2	90.4
New York	14,447	6,416	4,745	32.8	73.9
Pennsylvania	4,396	2,185	1,523	34.6	69.7
East North Central					
Illinois	4,791	2,607	2,234	46.6	85.7
Indiana	2,000	1,065	1,060	53.0	99.5
Michigan	4,173	1,877	1,730	41.5	92.2
Ohio	3,954	2,149	1,793	45.3	83.4
Wisconsin	2,231	971	958	42.9	98.7
West North Central					
Iowa	1,249	644	639	51.2	99.2
Kansas	935	477	463	49.5	97.1
Minnesota	2,163	833	811	37.5	97.4
Missouri	1,579	858	694	43.9	80.9
Nebraska	669	358	334	49.9	93.3
North Dakota	226	120	116	51.3	96.7
South Dakota	250	170	161	64.4	94.7
South Atlantic					
Delaware	229	57	49	21.4	86.0
Florida	2,675	1,051	857	32.0	81.5
Georgia	1,520	558	495	32.6	88.7
Maryland	1,953	878	633	32.4	72.1
North Carolina	1,492	434	411	27.5	94.7
South Carolina	612	182	172	28.1	94.5
Virginia	1,508	714	501	33.2	70.2
West Virginia	412	149	130	31.6	87.2
East South Central					
Alabama	972	248	118	12.1	47.6
Kentucky	803	278	204	25.4	73.4
Mississippi	687	184	167	24.3	90.8
Tennessee	1,209	469	340	28.1	72.5
West South Central					
Arkansas	445	143	133	29.9	93.0
Louisiana	1,158	408	237	20.5	58.1
Oklahoma	742	302	254	34.2	84.1
Texas	3,686	1,729	1,508	40.9	87.2
Mountain					
Arizona	778	332	264	33.9	79.5
Colorado	1,001	508	426	42.6	83.9
Idaho	235	105	102	43.4	97.1
Montana	262	163	158	60.3	96.9
Nevada	289	121	91	31.5	75.2
New Mexico	369	85	75	20.3	88.2
Utah	352	158	141	40.5	89.2
Wyoming	165	71	69	41.8	97.2
Pacific					
Alaska	171	43	33	19.3	76.7
California	13,534	6,524	5,748	42.5	88.1
Hawaii	178	113	89	50.0	78.8
Oregon	874	454	439	50.2	96.7
Washington	1,497	553	466	31.1	84.3

Source: U.S. Bureau of The Census, *Governmental Finances in 1970–71*, pp. 31–33.

Central region and about two-thirds in the New England states. In addition, property taxes represent more than 95 percent of tax revenues in the New England states and the North Central region. At their lowest, they constituted less than 45 percent of tax revenues in Alabama and only 56 percent of tax revenues in Louisiana.

Table 13 presents data for 1971-72 by states in the order of degree of reliance upon property taxes as a percentage of total locally generated general revenue. From this table it may be seen that Connecticut led the list with 88.8 percent of locally generated revenue derived from the property tax—compared to U. S. average of 63.8 percent. Alabama was at the bottom in terms of degree of reliance upon the property tax—with only 22 percent of its locally generated revenue being derived from the property tax.

Table 14 presents still another dimension in terms of relative reliance on the property tax, based upon the size of municipalities. From that table, it may be seen that in 1970-71 municipalities with 1970 populations of one million or more used the property tax for 27.3 percent of their general revenue. As the size of the municipality decreased, the degree of reliance upon the property tax tended to increase.

For the Future

It is not feasible to predict with accuracy the position which the property tax will have in the revenue structures of local governments in the future. For decades, various students of taxation have predicted the demise of the property tax as a major source of support of local governments. Thus, in 1956 one writer predicted that by 1976 the property tax would ". . . become an all-but-forgotten relic of an earlier fiscal age."[2]

Regional Taxation. The sharing of selected tax sources on a regional basis is a relatively recent phenomenon in the property tax field. It has been attempted in the Minneapolis-St. Paul area as a result of a July, 1971 enactment of the Minnesota state legislature effecting the sharing of 40 percent of the valuation of future industrial-commercial growth by every unit of government.[3]

The major features of the Minnesota law provide:

1. A comprehensive revision of the Minnesota school aid formula designed to insure equality for students throughout the state, regardless of other factors, by committing the state to pay 65 percent of school operating expenses instead of the prior 43 percent
2. A substantial infusion of state nonproperty tax revenues to local governments

---

[2] Mitchell, George W., "Is This Where We Came In?" *Proceedings of the National Tax Association,* (1956), p. 494.

[3] The following information is based on an article of the Advisory Commission on Intergovernmental Relations, *State Local Finances: Significant Features and Suggested Legislation,* (Washington, D. C.: United States Government Printing Office, 1972), pp. 7-8 and "The Minnesota Approach to Solving Urban Fiscal Disparity" by Charles R. Weaver in *State Government,* Vol. 45, No. 2 (Spring 1972), pp. 100-105.

3. An increase of state income, sales, and other taxes in order to shift from local dependence on the property tax with a prohibition against further sales or income taxes being levied by local governments

4. A limited pledge of the state's full faith and credit on the general obligation bonds of local governments

5. A sharing of 40 percent of future growth in the industrial-commercial property tax base

6. A partial shift in financing county highways to a wheelage tax and authority for the Metropolitan Transit Commission to levy a limited property tax

7. An upgraded local government fiscal information system

8. A joint executive-legislative Tax Study Commission

9. A State Board of Assessors charged with establishing the qualifications of assessors and certifying assessments throughout the state

10. Reform of the property tax classification system

11. A 17-member Quality Education Council to fund local school district experimental programs

The advantages cited for this experiment are (1) it does not sacrifice local control; (2) it imposes no additional tax; and (3) sharing of the tax base keeps decisions as to spending local. Objectors to the experiment allege that: (1) it is unfair to communities planning industrial-commercial development within their boundaries through means of zoning; (2) it is unfair to newly emerging communities which would have to share their tax base; (3) it would deter communities from accepting commercial-industrial development within their boundaries; and (4) it may be a "foot-in-the-door," resulting in the abolition of local governments in favor of a metropolitan unit.

This passage of this legislation in Minnesota, however, was not the result of normal legislative procedures. At the time, the state aid system for financing public school education was under severe attack in the federal court. This case, *Van Dusartz vs. Hatfield*, contested the constitutionality of local variations in educational spending caused by variations in taxable wealth. Immediately after the recent legislation was enacted, the case was withdrawn prior to final decision.

This case was one of a number of recent public school finance cases filed against states in both state and federal courts. In general, the Supreme Court held in *Rodriguez vs. San Antonio* that states are not obligated to provide for the eliminations of these types of variations. In this case, the Court ruled that the Texas system of school financing did not violate the equal protection clauses of the U. S. Constitution despite admitted severe inequity in the abilities of districts to provide funds.

Although this case closed the avenue of the federal courts to those seeking "reform" of public school financing, a number of state courts, including those in California and New Jersey, have recently held that inequities caused by variations in local ability to support education are unconstitutional by application of standards in state constitutions.

A GENERAL DESCRIPTION OF THE PROPERTY TAX

The phrase "property tax" is ordinarily used to describe a group of taxes which are levied on the value of different kinds of property determined by the individual states to be subject to taxation—usually on an *ad valorem*, i.e., according to value, basis.

As used by local governments, the property tax usually takes two forms:

1. *The Real Property Tax:* The tax levied on the assessed valuation of taxable land and improvements thereupon
2. *The Personal Property Tax:* A tax which is, or has been at one time or another, applicable to the assessed value of taxable *tangible* personal property, e.g., furniture and equipment, automotive equipment, animals, and inventories, and taxable *intangible* personal property, e.g., money, stocks, bonds, and other assets representing a property right that is not tangible in character.

During the long history of the property tax in financing government, the primary theoretical justification has been that, inasmuch as the ownership of property constituted a fair index of wealth, it was appropriate to require contributions in support of public services in proportion to the accepted measures of wealth, i.e., ownership of property.

In almost all jurisdictions each municipality is given the right to use the property tax. The theory behind this approach is severalfold. For one thing it was designed so that each municipality would live within its own resources. Furthermore, real property benefited from the community, and as such, it was considered logical that it should contribute to the cost of municipal government . . .[4]

In the relatively simple economy of the American colonies and of the nation until after the Civil War, this presumption seems to have had great validity. Indeed, it is to be noted that, from 1890 to 1922, the antecedent of the present *Census of Governments* series was entitled *Wealth, Public Debt, and Taxation.*

This was due, in large measure, to adherence to the concept of wealth being associated with the ownership of property, especially real property.

With the passage of time, personal property has become an increasingly important element of total property. Moreover, with the development of modern business organization and practices, intangible personal property burgeoned as the most important subelement of the personal property class.

The Growth of Exemptions

In early America, it was customary for almost all real and personal property to be subject to taxation. The list of exemptions was indeed small. Thus, in the personal property tax field, household furnishings, personal jewelry, livestock,

---

[4] Wright, Edward T., editor, *Sources of Municipal Revenue*, (Springfield, Ill.: Charles C Thomas, 1971), p. 11.

farm implements, and inventories of businesses were subject to taxation. In like manner, exempt real property was largely limited to churches, cemeteries, the few schools and other institutions of learning, property belonging to government, and remarkably few other categories.

This policy of broad application of the definition of taxable property continued generally through the 19th century, although there was evidence by the end of the century that the categories of exemptions were being expanded. As municipalities grew, it became increasingly difficult to secure realistic appraisals of household effects and also of intangible wealth. Moreover, increased municipal expenditures and overall increases in tax rates resulted in very high tax rates on intangible wealth. Along with this development, recurring recessions and depressions and local crop failures gave rise to demands for exemption from taxation of agricultural implements, livestock, and household furnishings. By the end of the 1920s, exemptions had been extended in most states to very large portions of tangible personal property.

During the depression of the 1930s, the legislatures in a number of states adopted laws under which "homesteads," i.e., owner-occupied residential properties, were given exemption to specified amounts of assessed value. This tendency was most pronounced in the lower tier of southern states but was also used in some other states.

By 1940, many states had removed from taxable status almost all tangible property and had adopted legislation under which the remaining elements of personal property were taxed at relatively low rates—largely in recognition of the fact that a 5 mill tax on a $1,000 par value security produces a high tax in relation to the income potential of most such securities. (For example, a 5 mill tax—$5 per $1,000—is the equivalent to a 10 percent income tax on a security that yields only 5 percent annual return). Moreover, as increasing amounts of wealth came to be in the intangible form, it became increasingly difficult to ascertain the amounts of such property owned by most persons.

A recent study of the United States Senate's Subcommittee on Intergovernmental Relations regarding exemption of real property from taxation indicates that:

> In about half the states there are exemptions of various types of property to relieve certain persons from part or all of the burden of property taxes. The most common are homestead exemptions and veterans exemptions. A more recent development is the exemption for the aged—persons 65 and older . . .

> Many states have legislated special tax breaks for industry. Generally the intention is to promote industrial expansion, although in some cases these special exemptions seem to have outlived their usefulness and comparative benefits to the public . . . Exemptions for new industry are common in the South. Mining exemptions are frequent in the West.

> Besides . . . there is exemption from property tax liability of a large amount of property that is owned by governments and religious, educational, philanthropic, or other non-profit organizations . . . The sorts of properties exempted . . . are often concentrated in the center city, which has to bear

the burden of providing regular public services to the areas and to buildings from which no revenue is collected.

One partial solution to this is to impose direct charges for specific services provided to exempt properties, a practice already adopted by a few localities.[5]

The Assessment of Property for Taxation

In the assessment process, the assessors prepare a tax roll of all properties to which the legislative body applies a tax rate. Real property is classified as to use; personal property is classified as to its tangible vs. intangible aspects.

The principal functions of the assessment process are:

1. To assure that all properties appear on the roll, with a proper notation as to the taxable status of each property
2. To ascertain values, especially for the taxable properties, under which each property can be made to bear its equitable share of the tax load

The first of these elements requires the development and maintenance of a comprehensive, accurate set of assessment records.

For decades, the assessed valuation of both real property and personal property relied largely on the periodic rendition by owners of lists of the property which they owned that was subject to taxation. Personal rendition is still the primary method by which personal property is taxed, ordinarily because the tax assessor has few alternate sources of information—or, if he has them, he may be reluctant to use these sources, e.g., access to federal personal income tax tapes.

A huge body of literature is available which discusses the various aspects of the assessing process and the problems associated with assessment. It is not feasible in a summary volume on local government finance to detail these many problems and the procedures which have been developed to cope with them.

It is, however, appropriate to note that the basic objective of the assessment process should be to determine values which are internally consistent in order that taxpayers can be subject to the same effective millage rates. If a reasonable degree of internal consistency is achieved, it matters little in terms of tax equity whether the assessment process results in a typical pattern of 30 percent of market value or 50 percent or 100 percent.

On the other hand, a general rule of 100 percent of market value helps to increase equity among taxpayers because of the resistance of taxpayers to accept a valuation of more than 100 percent. Where valuations are but a small percentage of market value, the coefficient of dispersion tends to be high; where the ratio of assessed to market value is high, the coefficient of dispersion tends to be low.

The application of any required tax rate levy will then produce needed revenue and also (if tax rate limits permit) provide ample revenue to the local government. But, many local governments operate under legal restraints as to

---

[5] Subcommittee on Intergovernmental Relations of the Committee on Government Operations, United States Senate, *Property Taxation: Effects on Land Use and Local Government Revenues*, (Washington, D. C.: United States Government Printing Office, 1971), pp. 4-10.

the tax rate. In those circumstances the general ratio of assessed valuation to market value becomes very important. Also, the debt limit is typically expressed in terms of a percentage of taxable property values. If the law fails to adjust borrowing limits to a realistic basis, various circumventions occur, including the creation of "debt authorities," the creation of special districts in order to avoid either tax or debt limits, or the development of various types of subsidiary debt.

The assessment of property on an equitable basis is a very complex and difficult task. It is easy for critics of the assessor to pick out wide variations between the presumed assessment ratio and the actual ratios between assessed and market value as shown by sales prices. Careful assessment officials seek to avoid extremes and to keep assessed valuations reasonably current in relation to market valuations.

Yet, during periods of abnormal prices or price changes of real estate, assessors generally seek to avoid moving rapidly with the trends, which may be of short duration. Thus, during a period of marked depression, such as the 1930s, the market value of real estate may decline very rapidly. Situations may occur in which there is no buyer available. Or, if one is available, sales are at abnormally low prices arising from general distressed economic conditions. With the property tax as a mainstay of local government finance in such past periods, assessors have tended to try to hold the line on assessments on the assumption that conditions will right themselves in due course.

In like manner, during World War II and the period immediately following, the scarcity of available homes produced very high market prices. In such periods, assessors generally tend to mute the effects of sharply changing trends by holding their changes in assessed value to lesser rates than those prevailing in the market. Much the same situation is being observed in the early 1970s during a period of protracted major inflation.

Certain types of property almost defy rational assessment. Thus, a huge manufacturing or petroleum refining plant presents a problem frequently beyond the expertise of the local assessor. In such cases, assessments should be made only with the assistance of consulting specialists familiar with the values of the plants involved.

Assessment of railroad properties, including rolling stock, presented problems of such magnitude in the past that many states took over the assessment of these kinds of property in order to secure a degree of internal uniformity among taxpayers in the same categories. In a few instances, the properties were generally exempted by state governments. These governments tended to impose substitute taxation, e.g., gross receipts taxation on utilities in Pennsylvania.

Assessment is typically a local function; however, it is currently carried out as a state function in Hawaii. Several other states have state performance under consideration. Varying degrees of state supervision occur in relation to locally selected assessors—ranging from rigorous regulation in some instances to non-existent supervision in other states.

Local assessors are elected in 23 states. In the remainder, selection is by appointment or some combination of appointment and election.[6]

---

[6] The State of Texas has the distinction of allowing duplicate assessment in all cases, i.e., separate assessment organizations for county governments and for school districts. More-

Suggested improvements in the assessment field often cite the need for trained assessors subject to state regulation in order to attain equalization of assessed valuations. The key needs are: (1) a workable assessment law that lends itself to good administration; (2) large assessment districts; (3) a competent, professional staff with a well structured internal organization and, competent personnel, adequate pay, protection against dismissal for doing a good job, and (4) adequate financial support. State supervision is frequently cited as a necessity in achieving the foregoing, including substantive equity between taxpayers both within a taxing district and also between taxing districts.

ADVANTAGES AND DISADVANTAGES OF THE PROPERTY TAX

The principal advantages claimed for the property tax are:

1. It provides a major portion of the locally derived tax revenue of local governments and cannot easily be replaced by other forms of taxation.

2. The tax has a great degree of stability. Especially in periods of economic adversity, it continues to be a consistently high producer of income—with lesser amounts of downward adjustments than would be the case for income, sales or gross receipts taxes.

3. Many local government services are for the benefit of property and the occupants of property. The property tax, therefore, provides a manner in which contributions can be required of the owners and/or occupants of property in some degree proportionate to the services being rendered, e.g., police protection, fire protection, refuse collection and disposal.

4. The property tax has a valuable social effect in that the owners of properties which are nonproductive or of marginal value are encouraged to develop the properties or to sell them to others. Thus, a man and wife or a widow who occupies a house suitable for a large family may be encouraged to vacate the house which can then serve a broader social purpose through occupancy by a large family.

5. The ownership of property is an index to a part of a person's wealth and, therefore, falls more heavily upon the wealthy family with large holdings than upon the poor person who owns property, or occupies only small amounts of taxable property.

---

over, each incorporated municipality may have its own independent assessment for municipal purposes—and most do this. Although there is provision in the law allowing contracts between these governments for performance of the assessment function, such contracts tend to be the exception, rather than the rule.

The result is that most urban properties are assessed by three distinctly separate and independent sets of assessing officials. Inasmuch as there appears to be little coordination among these separate assessors, a property may have three significantly variable assessments. Such a system is obviously both irrational and unduly expensive where a careful job of assessment is carried out.

Among the disadvantages frequently cited are:

1. The tax is regressive in the sense that it tends to absorb (in the case of residential property) a greater proportion of the income of low income families than higher income families.
2. The increasing list of exemptions tends to accentuate the inequities inherent in the tax.
3. The yield is not as flexible as some other kinds of taxation. As a result, in periods of inflation, assessments fail to rise in relation to actual changes in value.
4. The problems of administration are very substantial. Administration tends also to become rather expensive in relation to yield where efforts are made to perform the assessment function on a current and equitable basis.
5. The tax tends to discourage improvements because in the process of making improvements, or even of careful current maintenance, values are held above levels than would otherwise exist and these, in turn, require higher tax payments.
6. Differentials between adjacent taxing districts result in unnatural competition both for the location of new residential developments and for the location, or relocation, of economic activities necessary to the sustenance of the entire economic/social community.

When applied to personal property, the property tax has not been a particularly substantial producer of revenue during recent decades—largely because so much personal property has been removed from the tax rolls. The discovery and equitable assessment of personal property is difficult. Invasion of privacy as well as the general desire to avoid this kind of taxation helped to result in the limitation of the tax to selected intangibles in most states. Problems of inequity were widespread and no feasible means of overcoming these seemed to be inherent in the broad application of the personal property tax.

Even where the tax is retained as a tax on intangibles, there is considerable evidence that the amount of evasion is tremendous. Many argue, with considerable merit, that the personal property component of the property tax is not so inequitably applied that it should be abandoned.

COLLECTION AND ENFORCEMENT OF THE TAX

Once the assessment roll is completed and the rate determined, it is the responsibility of collection officials to prepare and distribute bills. Many jurisdictions have the collection cycle on a basis of single annual payments; others permit periodic partial payments; some allow discounts during portions of the normal payment periods.

Following the established due date, it is customary to require payment of interest on delinquent amounts and, in some jurisdictions, to add a significant penalty, usually after a period of several months of delinquency has elapsed.

The record of collection of property taxes has generally been very good in almost all jurisdictions, except in periods of major economic dislocation. If there is a general depression, delinquencies begin to pile up. Also, as people have become more sophisticated concerning the value of interest in relation to tax payments, some local governments are finding that, in periods of high interest rates, a considerable number of taxpayers will take advantage of the relatively low interest rates normally payable on delinquent taxes and allow periods of considerable delinquency, because they conclude that they can "borrow" from the local government at lower rates than in the commercial money market.

Historically, local governments have enforced collection only against the value of specific properties through filing tax liens and eventually selling the property at tax sales. Recently, some cities have been considering the possibilities of proceeding against the full assets of the owners of delinquent properties, especially in areas in which owners of slum properties are quite willing to allow the city to take the property once the owners have derived all the benefit they can from ownership.

The process of sale of tax liens and, eventually, the sale of the properties themselves is a tedious one and rather expensive in most jurisdictions. In some of the older cities, the rates of abandonment of properties has now become sufficient to cause very major concern as to how these problems should be handled on a long-term basis. No fully satisfactory answers have yet been developed.

Of major importance in any real property tax enforcement program is to identify the properties upon which delinquencies are being allowed to accumulate and to take action at an early date—before the delinquencies equal a significant percentage of the residual value of such properties.

As parts of urban areas fall into decay, it is likely that it will be necessary for the local governments concerned to develop urban land banks into which properties can be placed until, in due course, general redevelopment becomes feasible. The high public investment in various public facilities in areas precludes allowing them to lie fallow over decades.

IMPROVEMENTS IN THE PROPERTY TAX

Improvements are needed in property tax administration. Taxpayers are demanding better equalization. Court decisions are affecting the tax. Some state governments are renewing their interest in property tax administration. Assessors are reassessing their own procedures. One author has summarized recent developments as follows:

> Changes in property tax laws are continually being made during the various state legislative sessions. The majority of these laws are concerned primarily with clarifying existing laws and providing various types of property tax relief.

> Within the general area of clarifying existing laws, equalization has received much attention. Georgia, Arizona, and Nebraska are striving for uniformity through statewide reassessment programs which are near completion; New Mexico is in the initial stage of its program.

The courts also have been active in the area of equalization, regarding primarily the use of fractional valuations among various classes of property within a state and those valuations in use which differ from what is specified in state statutes. Statutes in twenty-three states require assessment of property generally at full value . . .[7]

Although the statutes in twenty-three states require assessment at full value, only three states are presently at that level (Florida, Kentucky, and Oregon).

THE USE OF ALTERNATIVES

Increased use of state and federal levels in the performance of governmental functions is a first alternative to use of the property tax. A closely related alternative is increased state and federal financing of local governments. Another remedy might be the imposition of user charges to finance certain public services, e.g., transportation, parking facilities, recreational activities, rather than general taxes. Also, taxes on nonproperty are an alternate solution. Another alternative is a tax on the value of land alone or heavier tax rates on land values than on buildings since land value is a consequence of collective investment, community development, and population growth. This type of tax (1) does not interfere with decisions as to land use, (2) encourages improvements since these would not result in increased taxation, and (3) turn back the ever increasing tide toward negative land use, particularly in core cities. It has its pitfalls: there are administrative problems as regards valuing land and buildings separately; revenues under this system might not adequately replace current property tax earnings. Again, there can be a tax on land value increments so that the government can recoup what is an unearned increment to an individual owner. This type of taxation has the same pros and cons as land value taxation.

CONCLUSION

The foregoing is intended only as a very summary statement of the importance of the property tax and the identification of a few aspects of the problems in its administration. In this volume, the authors have attempted to do no more than to introduce a subject about which perhaps more has been written than any other aspect of local government finance. Future trends with respect to the use of the tax are unclear. However, based on the old adage: "An old tax is a good tax," one can probably expect to see it around for a long time, and probably as a continued producer of a significant segment of local government revenue.

---

[7] Corusy, Paul V., "Improved Property Tax Administration: Legislative Opportunities and Probabilities," in *The Property Tax and Its Administration*, Arthur D. Lynn, Jr., editor, being the edited proceedings of a symposium of the Committee on Taxation, Resources and Economic Development of the University of Wisconsin, (Madison, University of Wisconsin Press, 1969), pp. 53-78.

8

Revenues II:
Nonproperty Taxes and
Nontax Revenues

A disruptive sequence of depression, war, and postwar inflation caused a quasi-revolution in local government revenue systems. Basically, the trend has been away from the property tax to other forms of local general revenue. Whereas local governments in the 1920s, 1930s, and 1940s relied on the property tax for, by far, the greater portion of local general revenues, the property tax today accounts for less than forty percent of total general revenue of local governments in the United States.

The sources of revenue examined in this chapter may be classified into three broad categories: (1) locally generated nonproperty taxes; (2) locally generated nontax revenues; and (3) transfer payments by the state and federal governments. In a sense all of these constitute a search for viable alternatives to the historic reliance upon the property tax. Since the search for alternatives is relatively recent in origin, is still in progress, is in many respects experimental, and reflects the far from uniform fiscal policies of many thousands of governments, its explorer enters a financial jungle which can be mapped here only along main trails that are fairly well-defined.

LOCAL NONPROPERTY TAXES

Significant reliance on nonproperty taxes by local governments is a relatively recent phenomenon. This reliance had its genesis largely in the Great Depression of the 1930s when property owners were frequently confronted with property taxes well beyond their capacity to pay—with consequent tax sales, taxpayer revolts, etc.

In some very important ways, the shift to nonproperty taxes accompanied a basic shift in our economy from a rural to an urban economy and from an economy characterized by individual family ownership of small manufacturing plants to a system of national corporations. In a rural-agricultural society, the ownership of property was long understood to be a major indicator of wealth and, therefore, of one's ability to pay taxes. In these periods, that portion of the population working for money wages was small.

With the major changes following World War I, accentuated by those following World War II, the nation moved from a rural-agricultural to an urban-industrial economy. The payment of "in-kind" wages decreased, and the

Table 13
SOURCES OF LOCALLY GENERATED
GENERAL REVENUES OF LOCAL GOVERNMENTS
1971-72*
(amounts in millions of dollars)

	Total Locally Generated General Revenue	Non-tax Sources	Taxes	Property Taxes	Other Taxes
All Local Governments**	63,886	15,413	48,472	40,734	7,738
Connecticut	1,068	112	956	948	8
Rhode Island	220	23	197	194	2
Vermont	112	11	101	99	2
Maine	234	27	208	204	4
Massachusetts	2,177	287	1,890	1,875	15
New Hampshire	218	28	190	187	3
Wisconsin	1,383	291	1,093	1,081	12
Montana	228	44	185	178	7
New Jersey	2,863	406	2,457	2,224	233
South Dakota	218	38	180	168	11
Indiana	1,521	358	1,163	1,141	21
Iowa	891	223	669	659	10
Kansas	684	172	513	496	17
Oregon	670	167	503	486	17
North Dakota	155	41	114	110	4
Illinois	3,744	670	3,074	2,660	414
California	9,287	1,963	7,324	6,427	897
Minnesota	1,305	377	928	901	27
Utah	226	54	173	153	20
Nebraska	516	144	372	347	25
Michigan	2,938	830	2,109	1,930	178
Idaho	162	54	109	107	2
Hawaii	154	28	125	98	28
Wyoming	121	43	79	77	2
Colorado	757	178	579	478	101
North Carolina	760	258	503	464	39
Texas	2,731	826	1,904	1,652	252
Arizona	520	126	394	313	81
Ohio	3,148	822	2,326	1,878	448
Missouri	1,293	322	971	748	223
New York	9,217	1,750	7,466	5,307	2,159
West Virginia	258	90	168	145	23
Pennsylvania	3,059	650	2,409	1,695	714
Maryland	1,222	273	949	673	277
South Carolina	377	158	219	207	12
Virginia	1,036	230	806	548	258
Oklahoma	502	177	325	263	62
Washington	1,028	378	649	533	116
Florida	1,898	704	1,194	957	237
Delaware	111	44	67	55	12
Georgia	1,129	493	635	561	74
Arkansas	302	143	159	147	12
New Mexico	163	75	88	77	11
Mississippi	374	184	190	173	18
Tennesse	830	292	538	381	158
Nevada	222	83	139	98	41
Kentucky	494	187	307	215	92
Louisiana	703	245	457	257	200
Alaska	95	48	47	35	12
Alabama	564	288	276	124	152

*Arranged in descending order of degree of reliance upon property taxes.
**Excludes District of Columbia.

Table 13
(continued)

| | | Percentage Distribution | | | | Property Tax as Percent of All Taxes |
	Total	Non-tax Sources	Taxes	Property Taxes	Non-Property Taxes	
All Local Governments**	100.0	24.1	75.9	63.8	12.1	84.0
Connecticut	100.0	10.5	89.5	88,8	.7	99.2
Rhode Island	100.0	10.4	89.6	88.5	1.1	98.8
Vermont	100.0	10.2	89.8	88.2	1.6	98.2
Maine	100.0	11.4	88.6	87.0	1.6	98.2
Massachusetts	100.0	13.2	86.8	86.1	.7	99.2
New Hampshire	100.0	12.9	87.1	85.6	1.5	98.3
Wisconsin	100.0	21.0	79.0	78.1	.9	98.9
Montana	100.0	19.1	80.9	77.7	3.2	96.0
New Jersey	100.0	14.2	85.8	77.7	8.1	90.6
South Dakota	100.0	17.5	82.5	77.3	5.2	93.7
Indiana	100.0	23.6	76.4	75.0	1.4	98.2
Iowa	100.0	25.0	75.0	73.9	1.1	96.7
Kansas	100.0	25.1	74.9	72.4	2.5	96.7
Oregon	100.0	25.0	75.0	72.4	2.6	96.5
North Dakota	100.0	26.5	73.5	71.3	2.2	97.0
Illinois	100.0	17.9	82.1	71.0	11.1	86.5
California	100.0	21.1	78.9	69.2	9.7	87.7
Minnesota	100.0	28.9	71.1	69.1	2.0	97.2
Utah	100.0	23.7	76.3	67.5	8.8	88.5
Nebraska	100.0	28.0	72.0	67.3	4.7	93.5
Michigan	100.0	28.2	71.8	65.7	6.1	91.5
Idaho	100.0	33.1	66.9	65.7	1.2	98.2
Hawaii	100.0	18.4	81.6	63.7	17.9	78.1
Wyoming	100.0	35.1	64.9	63.6	1.3	98.0
Colorado	100.0	23.5	76.5	63.2	13.3	82.6
North Carolina	100.0	33.9	66.1	61.0	5.1	92.3
Texas	100.0	30.3	69.7	60.5	9.2	86.8
Arizona	100.0	24.3	75.7	60.3	15.5	79.7
Ohio	100.0	26.1	73.9	59.7	14.2	80.8
Missouri	100.0	24.9	75.1	57.9	17.2	77.1
New York	100.0	19.0	81.0	57.6	23.4	71.1
West Virginia	100.0	34.9	65.1	56.1	9.0	86.2
Pennsylvania	100.0	21.2	78.8	55.4	23.4	70.3
Maryland	100.0	22.3	77.7	55.0	22.7	70.8
South Carolina	100.0	41.8	58.2	55.0	3.2	94.5
Virginia	100.0	22.2	77.8	52.9	24.9	68.0
Oklahoma	100.0	35.3	64.7	52.4	12.3	81.0
Washington	100.0	36.8	63.2	51.7	11.5	81.8
Florida	100.0	37.1	62.9	50.4	12.5	80.1
Delaware	100.0	39.8	60.2	49.9	10.3	82.9
Georgia	100.0	43.7	56.3	49.7	6.6	88.3
Arkansas	100.0	47.4	52.6	48.6	4.0	92.4
New Mexico	100.0	45.8	54.2	47.2	7.0	87.1
Mississippi	100.0	49.2	50.8	46.2	4.6	90.9
Tennesse	100.0	35.2	64.8	45.9	18.9	70.8
Nevada	100.0	37.3	62.7	44.3	18.4	70.7
Kentucky	100.0	37.8	62.2	43.5	18.7	69.9
Louisiana	100.0	34.9	65.1	36.6	28.5	56.2
Alaska	100.0	50.6	49.4	36.5	12.9	73.9
Alabama	100.0	51.0	49.0	22.0	27.0	44.9

Source: Bureau of the Census, *Governmental Finances in 1971-72*, pp. 31-33.

importance of money wages increased. Ownership of property, especially non-residential property, increasingly passed into the hands of corporations. Today, evidence of ability-to-pay is represented to a much greater degree by money income than by title to real property. (Title often connotes only a minor interest in the dollar value of real estate, with the remainder represented by mortgage notes, leasehold notes, etc.)

This evolution in the realities of the economic life of the community has had a natural expression in terms of local governments attempting to shift portions of the burden for the support of local government to revenue sources other than property taxes. Local governments now rely to a considerable degree on a variety of nonproperty taxes.

The development of local nonproperty tax sources has been at highly uneven rates in different parts of the nation. In a few states—notably Alabama, Louisiana, Maryland, New York, Pennsylvania, and Virginia—they have been widely used by local governments; in others—such as Connecticut, Indiana, Iowa, Maine, Massachusetts, and Wisconsin—little headway has been made.

During 1971-72, local governments in more than one-fifth of the 50 states depended upon sources other than the property tax for more than half their locally generated general revenues. The data for the states are contained in Table 13. From that table, it may be seen that these eleven states were led by Alabama with 78 percent from sources other than the property tax, Alaska with 63.5 percent, and Louisiana with 63.3 percent.

At the other extreme, there were 11 other states which depended upon sources other than the property tax for 25 percent or less of their locally generated general revenue. In this group, Connecticut was lowest with only 11.2 percent, followed by the other five New England states. Each depended upon nonproperty tax sources for less than 15 percent of their locally generated general revenue in 1971-72.

Local Nonproperty Taxes. Looking at nonproperty taxes as a percentage of total local government taxes, it is found that in 1971-72 the states with the highest percentages were:

Alabama	55.1	Nevada	29.3
Louisiana	43.8	Maryland	29.2
Virginia	32.0	Tennessee	29.2
Kentucky	31.1	New York	28.1
Pennsylvania	29.7	Alaska	26.1

Again at the other extreme were the New England states, depending upon nonproperty taxes for less than 2 percent of total local taxes. These were joined by 9 other states which depended upon nonproperty taxes for less than 5 percent of total local taxes—Wisconsin (1.1); Idaho (1.8); Indiana (1.8); Hawaii (2.0); North Dakota (3.0); Iowa (3.3); Kansas (3.3); Oregon (3.5) and Nebraska (4.0).

Need spurred a widespread search for new revenue in the 1930s in all units of local government but the major use of new taxes originated in the larger cities. Under permissive state legislation beginning in 1934, New York City adopted taxes on the gross income of utilities, on the gross receipts of business, and on retail sales—initially, as a temporary and emergency measure for financing public welfare payments. But, these later became an important part of the city's regular revenue system. In 1938, New Orleans became the second large city to levy a general retail sales tax. In 1937, upstate New York cities were authorized to levy a tax of not more than one percent on the gross income of certain utilities; most of them did so within a few years. Philadelphia, after a year's unsatisfactory experiment with a two percent sales tax, in 1939 pioneered in the levy of an earned income tax under taxing powers granted by the state in 1932.

World War II reduced the pressure for public welfare financing; but, the postwar urgency for meeting both accumulated and expanding service and facility needs, under inflationary conditions, brought an immediate revival of the search for new local revenues. Originally, these tax enactments resulted from enabling legislation limited to particular cities; but, during this period, the use of productive new taxes spread to the smaller units of local government, as shown in Table 14.

The degree of reliance upon nonproperty taxes tends to decrease with the size of the city; however, the degree of reliance upon nontax revenues tends to increase as the size of the city becomes smaller, as is shown in Table 14.

Moreover, as has been previously shown in Table 8, the degree of reliance upon nonproperty tax revenues has been highly variable among types of local government. Thus, with only a few exceptions, the taxing power of local school districts has been very widely limited to the property tax. To a lesser degree, this is true of township and county governments and of special districts (which levy no nonproperty taxes but supplement the property tax with other charges and user fees).

Broad local home rule powers provided the basis for widespread adoption of nonproperty taxes in two states. Toledo, Ohio, initiated an income tax in 1946, under a home-rule doctrine that sanctioned the local use of taxes not used by the state, and this tax subsequently was adopted by many Ohio municipalities. In California, five cities enacted retail sales taxes in 1945-46 creating an overlapping with the state sales tax under home rule powers and, within a few years, the local sales tax was virtually on a statewide basis.

Legislation of more or less limited character authorizing the local levy and administration of nonproperty taxes has been enacted in numerous states; but Pennsylvania and New York, with their enabling acts of 1947, provided blanket local nonproperty taxing authority. New York's permissive tax law of 1947, since variously amended, authorized cities and counties to tax retail sales, restaurant meals, utility services, alcoholic beverages, admissions, motor vehicle use, vending machines, and hotel room occupancy. Pennsylvania's beguiling "tax anything" law, with its authority for cities, boroughs, school districts, and first-class townships (extended to all townships in 1965) to tax "persons, transactions, occupations, privileges, subjects, and personal property" not subject to a state tax, later received narrowing and restricting amendments and emerged as a new Act 511.

Non-real estate tax sources are used almost universally by local governments in Pennsylvania. Such taxes of one type or another are levied by

Table 14
PERCENTAGE DISTRIBUTION OF GENERAL REVENUE OF 18,048 MUNICIPALITIES BY SOURCE AND SIZE OF MUNICIPALITY 1970-71

	All Municipalities	Population (000)						
		Over 1,000	500-999	300-499	200-399	100-199	50-99	Under 50
Number of Municipalities	18,048	6	21	21	17	88	231	17,664
Total General Revenue (in Billions)	$30.58	$10.22	$4.65	$1.97	$1.04	$2.67	$2.93	$7.09
Percentage Distribution								
Total General Revenue	100.0	100.0	100.0	100.0	100.0	100.0	100.0	100.0
Intergovernmental	31.7	41.8	33.1	28.1	29.7	27.9	23.1	22.6
State Government	24.1	36.3	19.2	17.8	18.6	18.3	17.3	17.8
Federal Government	6.1	5.0	12.2	7.7	8.3	7.4	4.5	3.0
Other Local Governments	1.4	0.5	1.7	2.6	2.8	2.1	1.3	1.8
General Revenue From Own Sources	68.3	58.2	66.9	71.9	70.2	72.1	76.8	77.4
Taxes	49.3	46.7	49.7	45.8	50.5	52.8	55.9	49.8
Property Taxes	32.8	27.3	30.1	29.7	34.3	40.9	42.8	36.1
Other Taxes	16.5	19.4	19.6	16.1	16.2	11.9	13.1	13.7
General Sales and Gross Receipts	5.4	6.4	5.3	4.9	5.8	3.8	5.5	4.7
Selective Sales and Gross Receipts	3.7	3.5	4.6	4.7	4.6	3.4	2.8	3.4
Other taxes	7.4	9.5	9.7	6.6	5.8	4.6	4.8	5.6
Non-Tax Revenues	18.9	11.5	17.2	26.1	19.7	19.3	20.9	27.6
Current Charges	11.7	7.6	10.9	16.6	11.9	11.9	12.8	16.1
Miscellaneous General Revenue	7.2	3.9	6.3	9.5	7.8	7.4	8.1	11.5

Source: U. S. Bureau of the Census, *City Government Finances in 1970-71*, p. 7.

all counties, cities, first class townships, and second class school districts, and by about 97 percent of the remaining smaller classes of taxing jurisdictions. The city of Philadelphia and numerous other taxing jurisdictions in 1967 raised over one-half of their tax revenues from non-real estate tax sources—in some cases as high as 90 to 95 percent. The other cities, and the boroughs and second class townships raised better than one-third of their aggregate tax revenues from these sources.[1]

Still another method of fostering local nonproperty taxes is the tax supplement. Local governments are authorized to levy a tax, as a supplement to an existing state tax, with a maximum rate usually specified. The local government makes the decision to impose the tax, but the state government administers it in conjunction with the state tax—thus enabling local units that are too small to sustain its administration to use the tax and avoiding duplication in administration, rate competition, and the burden of enforcement, except for a pro-rata share of the cost of administration. This method of administering the tax is being used mainly for the sales tax (presently in 18 states), although in isolated instances it is also being used for gasoline, cigarette, amusement, and income taxes.

A related device that a state may use to provide for state administration of a locally-levied tax is the tax credit. Taxpayers are permitted to offset their payment of a specified local tax against their liability for an identical state tax.

One of the most recent developments in the field of local taxation is a subject long discussed but only recently tried. This is the sharing of selected tax sources on a regional basis. As noted in Chapter 7, the pioneer example of this kind of sharing is the Minneapolis-St. Paul area as a result of the July, 1971 enactment of the Minnesota state legislature to the effect that 40 percent of the valuation of future industrial-commercial growth would be shared by every unit of government.[2] Two major features of the Minnesota law, with respect to nonproperty taxes, are to provide:

1. A substantial infusion of state nonproperty tax revenues to local governments through revenue-sharing

2. An increase of state income, sales, and other taxes (in order to reduce local dependence on the property tax) with a prohibition against further sales or income taxes being levied by local governments

Types of Nonproperty Taxes

The aggregate nonproperty tax revenue of all local governments in 1971-72 amounted to $8.1 billion, with the distribution shown in Table 15.

---

[1] Pennsylvania Economy League, Inc. (State Division), *Where the Money Comes From*, Report No. 2, "Non-Real Estate Taxes," (Harrisburg: Pennsylvania Economy League, Inc., 1969), p. 23.

[2] Because much of this arrangement is linked to the property tax, a full discussion of regional taxation is contained in Chapter 7.

Table 15
NONPROPERTY TAXES OF LOCAL GOVERNMENTS
1971-72
(amounts in millions of dollars)

Revenue Source	Amount	Percent
Total nonproperty taxes	8,054	100.0
Individual income	2,241	27.8
Corporate income	n.	
Sales and gross receipts	4,238	52.6
General sales and gross receipts	2,675	33.2
Selective sales and gross receipts	1,562	19.4
Motor fuel	57	0.7
Alcoholic beverages	68	0.8
Tobacco products	168	2.1
Public utilities	911	11.3
Other	358	4.3
Motor vehicle and operators licenses	221	2.7
All other	1,354	16.8

Source: U. S. Bureau of the Census, *Governmental Finances in 1971-72*, p. 20.

Individual income taxes represented 27.8 percent of these nonproperty tax revenues; general sales and gross receipts taxes accounted for 33.2 percent and selective sales and gross receipts taxes for 19.4 percent.

Developments regarding nonproperty taxes become more comprehensible if one keeps in mind that, other than property, there are only three bases on which taxes can be levied—sales, income, and privileges. The following sections examine the major local taxes related to these bases.

General Retail Sales Tax

The sales tax, known in some form since the 19th century, was introduced into the states—originally by Mississippi in 1932—in the depression of the 1930s as traditional sources of revenue declined and expenditure needs (particularly in the welfare field) increased. According to a recent Tax Foundation report, it is today the largest single source of state revenue and is utilized in all but five states:

> In the 1960s the pace of retail sales tax legislation stepped up sharply as financial pressures on the states continued. Eleven states adopted the tax in the period of 1960 through 1969 bringing the total number of states levying the sales tax to 45 . . . Three percent is . . . the most common rate, but higher tax rates apply in 23 states. The top rate is six percent (in Pennsylvania). . . .[3]

This same report notes that sales tax receipts in 1969 accounted for less than 25 percent of total revenues in 12 states; 25 to 40 percent of total revenues in

---

[3] Tax Foundation, Inc., *State and Local Sales Taxation*, (New York: Tax Foundation, Inc., 1970), p. 10.

24 states; and over 40 percent in 8 states. The sales tax appeared in the 19th century as a levy on all stages of the production process at extremely low rates and did not produce significant amounts of revenue. It has since been accepted as an addition to the price paid by the buyer for the purchase of goods or services. It may be included in the seller's price or stated separately.

Local general sales taxes are a postwar phenomenon. Only those of New York (1934) and New Orleans (1938) antedate World War II. The impetus has been, and is, the search for a supplement to the property tax. For local governments taken together, the property tax dwarfs all other revenue sources; however, in 1971, sales taxes accounted for 2.5 percent of total general revenues in all local governments; 5.9 percent of revenues in cities over 300,000 population (the 48 largest cities); 4.8 percent of revenues in municipalities in the population range of 50,000 to 299,000; and 4.7 percent of revenues in municipalities with under 50,000 population.

There are no sales taxes, state or local, in the states of Delaware, Montana, New Hampshire, or Oregon. In 1972, the general retail sales tax was being used by 4,340 local governments in 25 states— the local users including 3,409 municipalities and boroughs, (the largest among them New York, Chicago, and Los Angeles), 47 school districts (all in Louisiana), 583 counties, and the San Francisco Bay Transit District.

In Alaska, there are only local sales taxes and the rates range from one to three percent. In 24 states, the local tax overlaps a state tax and the local rates are low (the great majority one percent) but the overlapping can result in an effective tax rate of 7 percent—as is the case in four Colorado municipalities. In five states (Alaska, Arizona, Louisiana, Oklahoma and Oregon), all local sales taxes are locally administered. In Alabama, a few municipalities (by local option) and all counties (by state law) which levy a consumer sales tax require that it be collected by the State Department of Revenue; but, most of the local sales taxes are gross receipts license taxes levied on the seller and locally administered. Colorado also offers a system of local option. California, after several years of growing dissatisfaction with a multiplicity of locally-administered taxes, switched to a policy of state administration (with few exceptions) in 1955 and Utah made this change in 1963.

Data concerning rates and general administrative patterns, as developed by the Advisory Commission on Intergovernmental Relations, is presented in Exhibit 1.

Local sales taxes, like their state counterparts, are primarily taxes on retail sales of tangible personal property, but the tax base may include one or more specified services, such as public utility services.[4] The consolidated administration of state and local sales taxes within an area requires that the base for the taxes

---

[4] Local general retail sales taxes have concentrated mainly on consumer expenditures for goods and have taken only limited advantage of the tax revenue potential in the rapidly increasing volume of expenditures for services. Restaurant meals, transient lodgings, and amusements are the more common inclusions; others that have limited use to date, or have been given consideration, include laundry, dry cleaning, barber shop and beauty parlor services, printing, photography, storage, repair services to tangible property, and various professional services.

Exhibit 1
STATUTORY PROVISIONS GOVERNING IMPOSITION OF GENERAL SALES TAXES BY LOCAL GOVERNMENTS, JANUARY 1, 1972

State and type of local government	Statutory authority	Number using	Scope	Rate limits	Voter approval	Administration
Alabama						
Municipalities	Business and occupational license	190	Sales & use	None	No	Local Option[1]
Counties	Specific[2]	24	Do	2%	Yes[2]	State[1]
Alaska						
Municipalities	Specific	63	Sales	3%[3]	Yes	Local
Boroughs	Do	5	Do	3%[3]	Do	Do
Arizona						
Municipalities	Business and occupational license	33	Do	None	No	Do
Arkansas						
Municipalities	Specific	1	Sales	1%	Yes	State
California						
Municipalities	Specific	380	Sales & use	1%[4]	No	State
Counties	Do	58[5]	Do	1%[4]	Do	Do
Special Districts	Do	1	Do	0.25% or 0.5%	Do	Do
Colorado						
Municipalities[6]	Home rule[6]	64	Both[6]	None[6]	Do[6]	25 Local 39 State[6,7]
Counties	Specific	9	Sales	[6]	Yes	State
Georgia						
Special district[8]	Do	2[8]	Sales & use	1%[8]	No	Do
Illinois						
Municipalities	Do	1,245	Do	1%	Do	State
Counties	Do	98	Do	1%	Do	Do
Kansas						
Municipalities	Do	. . .	Sales & use	0.5% or 1%	Do	Do
Counties	Do	. . .	Do	0.5% or 1%	Do	Do
School Districts	Do	. . .	Do	0.5% or 1%	Do	Do
Louisiana						
Municipalities	Do	84	Do	1%[9]	Yes	Local
Parishes	Do	12	Do	1%[10]	Do	Do
School districts	Do	47	Do	1%	Do	Do
Minnesota						
Municipality	Do	1	Do	None	Yes	Do
Missouri						
Municipalities	Do	50	Sales	0.5% or 1%	Yes	State
Nebraska						
Municipalities	Do	2	Sales & use	0.5% or 1%	No	Do
Nevada						
Counties	Do	8	Do	0.5%	Do	Do
New Mexico						
Counties	Do	3	Sales	0.25% or 0.5%[11]	Yes[11]	Do
New York						
Municipalities	Do	19	Sales & use	3%	No	State
Counties	Do	41	Do	3%	Do	Do
North Carolina						
Counties	Do	64	Do	1%	No[12]	Local option
Ohio						
Counties	Do	24	Do	0.5%	[12]	State
Oklahoma						
Municipalities	Do	263	Sales	[13]	Yes	Local[14]

Exhibit 1 (continued)

State and type of local government	Statutory authority	Number using	Scope	Rate limits	Voter approval	Administration
Oregon						
Municipalities [15]	Do	. . .	Do	None	No	Local
South Dakota						
Municipalities	Do	5	Sales & use	None	Do	State
Tennessee						
Municipalities	Do [16]	14	Sales & use	1½%[17]	Yes	State [18]
Counties	Do [16]	84	Do	1½%[17]	Do	Do [18]
Texas						
Municipalities	Do	659	Do	1%	Do	State
Utah						
Municipalities	Do	150 (approx.)	Sales	0.5%	No	State
Counties	Do	27	Do	0.5%	Do	Do
Virginia						
Municipalities	Specific	229 (approx.)	Sales & use	1%	No	State
Counties	Do	96	Do	1%	Do	Do
Washington [19]						
Municipalities	Do	249	Sales & use	0.5%[20]	Do	Do
Counties	Do	33	Do	0.5%[20]	Do	Do
Wisconsin						
Counties	Do [21]	. . .	Sales	0.5%	No	Do

[1]The State Department of Revenue is authorized, on request by a municipality, to collect local sales and use taxes. The municipal tax must parallel the State tax except for the rate. The Department of Revenue presently administers 150 of the 190 municipal sales taxes. The statutes applicable to individual counties usually (in 20 counties) require State administration.

[2]Specific statutory authority is given to individual counties. Voter approval is required in most cases.

[3]First class cities, incorporated villages, and first and second class boroughs; otherwise 2 percent.

[4]A city tax may be at any rate up to 1% (usually between 0.85% and 1%) and must be credited against the countywide 1% tax. Effective 7/1/72, counties are allowed to increase their rate to 1¼%, and correspondingly, the State levy is decreased from 4% to 3¾%.

[5]Includes the city-county of San Francisco.

[6]Home rule cities only. H.B. 1141, Laws 1967 provides that counties, second class cities and incorporated towns, with voter approval, may also levy sales taxes but the total State and county, city or town rate cannot exceed 7%. Such taxes must begin either January 1 or July 1 of any year and are administered by the Director of Revenue. The director must be notified at least 120 days prior to the effective date. This law does not affect or limit the power of home rule cities to levy local sales and use taxes.

[7]Home rule cities may contract with the State for administration and collection, without charge, if local tax conforms to certain specifications (one requirement is that home rule cities do not impose a use tax).

[8]Governing bodies which enter into rapid transit contracts with the Metropolitan Atlanta Rapid Transit Authority may levy sales and use taxes at the rate of 1% for the first 10 years, and ½ of 1% thereafter if the tax is also imposed in Fulton and DeKalb Counties. Taxes must parallel State tax except for rate and are State collected. Fulton and DeKalb county tax eff. 3/1/72.

[9]Baker, Baton Rouge, New Orleans, and Zachary, 2%.

[10]East Baton Rouge 2%; Jefferson 1½ percent.

[11]The general limit is ¼%; certain specific counties are authorized to levy a ½% rate without voter approval.

[12]Not required unless a specified percentage of voters petition.

[13]Incorporated cities and towns are authorized to levy and collect taxes (except property taxes) to the same extent as the State legislature. The State sales tax is currently 2 percent.

[14]Municipalities and the State Tax Commission are authorized to enter into contractual agreement for State collection (all municipal sales taxes are presently State collected). Municipalities are required to enforce their own sales tax laws, even if the Commission collects the tax.

[15]Cities with population of 9,000 — 10,500 only, but none is presently using this authority.

[16]Where the county elects to levy such tax, half the proceeds originating in a city or town are shared with such city or town, and any city or town is pre-empted from enacting such tax unless it does not reach the maximum rate in which case the city or town may levy the difference between the rate established by a county and the maximum rate allowed.

[17]The rate is limited to ½ of the State sales tax rate until 6/30/72, and may not exceed 7/12 of the State rate thereafter, and the maximum tax on a single transaction is limited to $7.50.

[18]Optional.

[19]Effective 7/1/72, class AA counties, or cities and municipal corporations within such counties, may impose sales and use taxes of 3/10 of 1%, subject to voter approval to finance public transportation systems.

[20]County rates must be ½ of 1%, city rates may not exceed ½ of 1%. If the county in which the city is located imposes a tax, the rate of the city tax may not exceed 0.425%. County tax must allow credit for full amount of any city tax.

[21]S-B. 95 approved August 27, 1969 authorized counties to levy ½ of 1% sales taxes on same items subject to the State sales tax. If enacted, taxes will become operative on January 1 of the year following enactment.

Source: Advisory Commission on Intergovernmental Relations, *State-Local Finances: Significant Features and Suggested Legislation*, (Washington, D.C.: United States Government Printing Office, 1972), pp. 194-196.

imposed by both levels of government within the area be either identical or nearly so. Significant differences act to negate many of the advantages of consolidated administration—both from the standpoint of the taxpayer and the tax administrator.

Exemptions are dictated by various considerations and, thus, follow no uniform pattern. In some instances, there are exemptions for food, or food and drugs, in order to lighten the burden on the poor. This complicates administration and may substantially reduce yield; however, it goes far toward eliminating the regressiveness of the tax and gives more flexibility for using higher rates. To help protect vendors in commercial centers against the loss of outside business, exemptions are generally granted on sales for out-of-town deliveries. In most instances, there is a compensating use tax on goods purchased outside the jurisdiction of the local government but brought within it for consumption—an attempt at checking one form of noncompliance, but its effectiveness is rather limited.

In assessing the economic impact of a retail sales tax, observers frequently fail to note that a very considerable portion of such taxes fall upon business, rather than upon individuals. This leads to erroneous conclusions in evaluating the impact of the tax.

As shown in Table 16, the local retail sales tax, even at low rates, is an especially good revenue producer for commercial centers—in 1971 (excluding schools in each instance), a one percent rate yielded 15 percent of Chicago's tax revenues and 20 percent of the tax revenue of Los Angeles; and a two percent rate yielded 41 percent of the tax revenue of New Orleans.

Table 16

**REVENUES FROM SALES TAXES AND GROSS RECEIPTS TAXES
IN THE 10 LARGEST CITIES IN WHICH THEY WERE USED
1970-1971**

City	Population Rank 1970	Sales Tax Rate (1968) (Percent)	Tax Revenues (in millions)		Sales Tax a Percent of Total Tax Revenues
			General Sales & Gross Receipts	Total Taxes	
New York	1	3	$493.6	$3,262.9	15.1
Chicago	2	1	66.2	440.3	15.0
Los Angeles	3	1	66.0	337.6	19.6
Houston	7	n.a.	28.6	109.8	26.1
Washington, D.C.	9	4	77.6	434.2	17.9
St. Louis	10	n.a.	8.7	110.6	7.9
San Francisco	12	1	30.8	248.9	12.4
Dallas	14	n.a.	21.6	101.2	21.3
New Orleans	15	2	26.3	64.2	41.0
San Antonio	17	n.a.	9.0	34.8	25.8

Source: Tax revenue information is from the U.S. Bureau of the Census, *City Government Finances in 1970-71*, pp. 87-100.

An added advantage of the sales tax is that some taxes are obtained from nonresidents. The tax yield is not inelastic, but varies less widely during business fluctuations (especially with inflation) than do the yields of net income taxes on individuals and businesses. The tax also has the virtue of creating wide tax consciousness. It needs safeguards, however, against inequity, maladministration, and damaging economic effects:[5]

1. The theory that what a consumer spends is a good measure of his tax-paying ability has obvious limitations; thus, unless food for off-premises consumption is exempt, the tax is harshly regressive.

2. For efficient, and equitable administration of the tax, there are requirements which are beyond the reasonable capacity of small municipalities and are frequently not adequately met by larger jurisdictions. For administrative purposes, the retailers are the taxpayers. The success of what is, in effect, a self-assessed tax depends on their making complete and accurate collections, keeping acceptable records, and making satisfactory returns. Attaining such results calls for professional sales tax administrators backed by unambiguous regulations and equipped with competent staffs which include well-trained technicians to do thorough, periodic audits of all large taxpayers and a representative sampling of small taxpayers. The administrator must treat the taxpayers with consideration and provide good informational programs, but be able to detect and penalize carelessness and dishonesty. A fair arrangement, not always provided, is to allow the retailers to retain a small percentage of collections as compensation for costs.

3. Major complications in the administration of taxes, due in part to the multiplicity of different local administrative arrangements and in part to differences in ordinances and regulations as to substantive and procedural aspects of the local sales tax.

4. When sales taxes are imposed in one jurisdiction but not in others in the same local trade area, they tend to disturb intercommunity economic relations.

5. A good enforcement program, including audits of taxpayer records, is essential and somewhat costly.

Experience seems to indicate that these administrative and economic weaknesses can be avoided or mitigated by making the local tax a supplement to the state tax (where there is a well-administered one) and, in any event, making judicious use of the county in the local sales tax setup.[6] A county-wide tax

---

[5] Useful guides to local sales tax administration are Lennox L. Moak and Frank Cowan's *Manual of Selected Practice for Administration of Local Sales and Use Taxes*, (Chicago: Municipal Finance Officers Association, 1961), 311 pp. and John Due's *State and Local Sales Taxation, Structure and Administration*, (Chicago: Public Administration Service, 1971), 336 pp.

[6] Low administrative cost is one of the big advantages of state collection of local sales taxes. For example, in California, the state cost (and charge to local governments) is 1.1 percent of collections; the charge is 3.1 percent of collections in Alabama, and no charge is made to local governments in Arkansas, Colorado, or Virginia.

comes closer to covering the local trade area than a tax levied by one municipality within the county—thus alleviating the uneven competition between taxed and untaxed merchants. And, in states where the tax is exclusively local, use of the county as the administrative agency avoids a potential multiplicity of municipal agencies. The levy of a county tax need not deprive municipalities within the county from using the tax. In Illinois, for example, where over half the counties use the authorized supplement to the state sales tax, the county tax applies only to unincorporated areas. In California, where all but two counties levy a conforming one percent supplement, the taxpayers in the municipalities in these counties may credit their taxes up to a rate of one percent against the county taxes.

Gross Receipts Taxes

Gross receipts taxes are imposed on businesses and occupations and measured by the gross receipts of the undertakings. The Bureau of the Census groups them with general sales taxes in reporting municipal revenue. This method of taxing business, or the privilege of engaging in business, is used variously by many municipalities. In some areas, the tax on gross receipts has replaced former flat-rate privilege license taxes; in others, it has been the product of new, permissive tax legislation.

In a few instances, this tax is a broad-based general business tax, notably New York City's general business and financial tax, which is imposed on every person and corporation engaged in trade for profit, professional and commercial activities within the city. Utilities otherwise taxed and banking institutions are exempt. Generally the scope of the tax is far less inclusive. Southern cities that have unusually broad license taxing powers may use gross receipts as a measure for only part of the subject of taxation. (Its use in Alabama for local retail sales taxes is noted later in this chapter.) Often, the tax is imposed only on some kinds of business. For example, numerous local governments in Pennsylvania impose a gross receipts mercantile tax on wholesalers and retailers (the Philadelphia School District and the City of Philadelphia have more broadly based taxes), and this form of tax is applied by some municipalities exclusively to public utilities.

Usually, gross receipts tax rates are low and often uniform for businesses within the same class. In New York City, the rates are 2/5 of one percent of the gross receipts of nonfinancial business generally, 3/20 of one percent for certain low mark-up businesses, and 1½ percent of the gross income (i.e., gross receipts minus cost of goods sold) of financial business—this last category creating a hybrid tax rather than a true gross receipts tax. The usual rates for Pennsylvania's local mercantile taxes are one mill on wholesale gross receipts and 1.5 mills on retail gross receipts (except in Philadelphia, Pittsburgh, and Scranton).

When levied at uniform rates on all kinds of enterprise, the gross receipts tax bears no relationship to the profitability of the enterprise being taxed. As between enterprises operating at high and low profit margins the tax is discriminatory because it fails to take account of the factor of profitability. This is a crude type of tax which can be quite harmful if imposed at more than very low rates, especially on enterprises with low profit margins in relation to gross sales. Tax specialists have pointed out that a carefully designed gross receipts tax imposed at different rates on different classes of business could substantially eliminate discrimination among classes of business and reduce the discrimination within classes, but such refinements seem too complex for widespread local use.[7]

Selective Sales Taxes

Numerous municipalities that do not use the general retail sales tax levy excise taxes on specific commodities or services and some use both the general sales tax and separate special excises. The most productive of these taxes nationally are those on public utilities, tobacco products, amusements, and motor fuels.

Public Utility Taxes. Local nonproperty taxes on utilities are used in a number of states. Many smaller cities use such taxes. They may be collected by the utility from customers or, as privilege taxes, they may be levied on the gross income of the utility.

Public utility taxes have the advantage of being good revenue producers, without requiring heavy administrative expense. The legal, and frequently political, basis for utility gross income or gross receipts taxes is that the tax is imposed for the privilege of exercising a franchise, using the city streets, and occupying a monopoly position. But, in fact, the tax is almost always passed on to the consumer—unless economic circumstances or public utility regulation forecloses this under selected circumstances. If the utility is to have a viable financial operation, it must be able to attract suitable capital to meet its ever-recurring capital needs. To do so, it requires appropriate earning capacity. Therefore, the net return on investment must sooner or later be brought into an acceptable range.

For decades, it was customary for many political leaders to demand such taxes from privately-owned public transit companies and railroad companies. Payment of such taxes was feasible only so long as the earning power of these companies kept them viable. Once the combination of circumstances rendered their operation unprofitable, it was, of course, not economically feasible to continue extraction of these taxes. Where the process was continued too long, it hastened bankruptcy actions such as the one which engulfed the Penn-Central and most other railroads in the Northeast during the early 1970s.

Where a single corporation, e.g., the New Orleans Public Service, Inc., controls the primary public energy source distribution (electricity and gas and also local transit), or where a telephone company has a genuine monopoly, this tax can be successfully used for very protracted periods of time. Yet, excessive tax levies can produce successful competition, e.g., from fuel oil or other energy sources or, perhaps, from other means of electronic communication.

Tobacco Taxes. Tobacco taxes have been used by state governments since the original enactment of a cigarette tax in Iowa in 1921. With the enactment

---

[7] For a demonstration of methodology for such a tax, see James W. Martin and Mary Evins, "Devising a Rate Structure for the City Business Tax," *National Tax Journal*, Vol. 3, No. 1 (March, 1950), pp. 64-74.

of such a tax by North Carolina in 1969, all of the 50 states and the District of Columbia were active in the field. As of November 1, 1972, the state-wide taxes per standard package of 20 cigarettes were distributed as follows:[8]

1— 5 cents	5 states
6—10 cents	15 states
11—15 cents	22 states
16—20 cents	8 states
21+ cents	1 state

At the same time, 20 states were taxing tobacco products other than cigarettes.[9]

Cigarette taxes were levied locally in only 10 states,[10] and in only five of these was the use of local cigarette taxes extensive. The local use of the tax was broadest in Florida where there is a state-wide levy for allocation to local governments. In Alabama 169 municipalities and 10 counties were levying the tax in 1972; in Colorado, 70 municipalities; in Virginia, 19 municipalities and 2 counties. New York City was the only local government in New York with a local tobacco tax (which yielded $52.8 million in 1972).

The Bureau of the Census reported that in 1971-72, the total yield of local tobacco sales and gross receipts taxes was $168 million, or 2.1 percent of all local nonproperty taxes. (See Table 15)

For metropolitan centers, where a considerable amount of tax comes from nonresidents, each one cent of cigarette tax has a yield in the range of $1.25 to $1.60 per capita. The justification frequently offered for these increasingly discriminatory taxes on cigarettes is that they are sumptuary taxes, designed to penalize the purchase of a harmful commodity. The extent to which consumption can be controlled by taxation and by accumulating evidence of the harmfulness of smoking remains to be seen; but, at some rate (not yet reached), declining consumption could lessen the attractiveness of the cigarette tax for revenue purposes. Aside from this future uncertainty, the tax presents serious difficulties of evasion and enforcement in local administration and can be used best as a local supplement or credit to a state-collected tax.

Admissions and Amusement Taxes. These taxes have been regarded widely as particularly well suited for local use. They are readily administrable; they tax so-called nonessential expenditures; they obtain revenue from nonresidents using local facilities; and they are to some extent benefit taxes—recouping the expense of such special services as police, fire protection, traffic regulation, and inspection. In practice, such taxes are a very minor source of municipal revenue except in special situations. The local revenue potential is limited by their use by the federal and state governments, by the inroads of television on motion picture theatres, and, more often than not, by the narrow scope of the coverage.

---

[8] Tobacco Tax Council, Inc., *The Tax Burden on Tobacco, Historical Compilation,* Volume 7, (Richmond, Tobacco Tax Council, 1972), p. 9.

[9] Ibid., p. 38.

[10] Ibid., p. 75.

A well-coordinated system of taxes on all forms of entertainment, rigidly and evenly enforced, would be reasonably productive and would avoid the present unfair discrimination; but no municipality, so far as is known, has developed such a system. A composite list of amusement and admission taxes would include almost every form of amusement, cultural activity and sport. In many situations, the taxes also apply to various kinds of social and golf clubs as a percentage of initiation and membership fees. The admissions tax is usually a percentage of the admission or service charge imposed on the seller, with provision that it be passed on to the buyer as an indicated part of the total charge. Usually, the tax on devices and facilities is a specified annual amount per unit.

There is some local use of these taxes in approximately 14 states but they have had their most extensive use in Ohio, Pennsylvania, and Washington. In Pennsylvania, Philadelphia has had an admissions tax since 1937 and over 800 other Pennsylvania local governments have adopted such taxes under the broad permissive legislation of 1947 and 1965. The most frequently used rates are 5 and 10 percent. Washington repealed its state tax on admissions in 1943 to make it available to cities and Ohio took similar action in 1947; in both states the tax is in wide local use, at a 5 percent rate in the former and a 3 percent rate in the latter. In New York, which includes a 5 percent tax on admissions among its permissive local taxes, the tax is used by New York City but by only a few other cities. Among other states in which there is more or less limited use of admissions and amusement taxes certain variations in method are worth noting. In Illinois, Chicago and several other cities tax the gross receipts from admission charges (at 3 or 4 percent). In Maryland, local governments are permitted to add a supplement to the state admissions tax, though few do so. In several states, local governments tax admissions under their general sales and gross receipts taxes, and New Orleans (in addition to taxing admissions under its general sales tax) adds special taxes on admissions to places of amusement.[11]

Motor Fuel Taxes. The benefit principle in taxation is given a wide recognition in the levy of highway user taxes—the motor fuel tax and the motor vehicle license tax. The theory is that each highway user should pay a tax that (1) results in collections which are at least roughly related to the cost of providing him with highway service; (2) covers, in the aggregate, the overall cost of highway service less some imprecisely determined allowance for collective benefits; and (3) allows all such revenue to be applied to highway purposes. So literally is this theory applied that most states provide tax exemption for fuel not used in highway transportation, and the federal government and the great majority of state governments tamper with sound budget practice by earmarking highway user taxes.

The taxation of motor fuels at the state level began in 1919 when Colorado, New Mexico, North Dakota, and Oregon adopted such taxes; in 1946, Alaska became the last state to approve this type of tax. State gasoline tax rates in

---

[11] For a more detailed discussion of amusement taxes see the Advisory Commission on Intergovernmental Relations, *Tax Overlapping in the United States 1964*, (Washington, D. C.: United States Government Printing Office, 1964), pp. 202-212.

1972 ranged from 5 cents to 9 cents per gallon, with a 7 cent rate by far the most common.

In most of the states, there is a remission to the local governments of considerable portions of the state-collected motor fuel taxes—based on the amount collected within the county or municipality.[12] In 1971, total state intergovernmental disbursements for highways was reported at $2.5 billion—43 percent of the local general expenditure for highway purposes.

The local levy of motor fuel taxes was prevalent in many states in the 1920s and 1930s. However, as these taxes became more and more widespread in some of the states, there was a tendency to make the taxes state-wide with state administration and redistribution among local governments upon various formulae. Today, it appears that only a few counties and municipalities are involved in locally administered motor fuel taxes—21 municipalities and 12 counties in Alabama; some local governments in Florida; New York City; Washington, D.C.; and (as a temporary tax) Newark, New Jersey. In Carson City and five counties in Nevada, three counties in Mississippi, and four counties in Hawaii, local taxes are supplements to the state tax and are collected by the state with remissions to the local governments. The top combined federal-state-local tax rates in these seven states and the District of Columbia ranged from 11 to 15 cents.

For the few local governments for which information was available, local rates in 1972 ranged from 0.75 cents in some Alabama municipalities to 7 cents in Newark, New Jersey. (Washington, D.C., levied an eight cent tax; however, its city/state character makes it different from the others and the tax there may be viewed largely as a state-type of motor fuel tax.) New York City imposes a one cent tax on fuel with lead content above specified limits.

Most municipalities would need a considerable increase in their highway user revenues to have them cover all, or even a very substantial part, of the cost of construction, maintenance, and policing of their street systems. Aside from user charges (tolls) and special assessments, which may be feasible and desirable in some situations, the possible sources for the necessary increase are motor fuel sales and motor vehicle license taxes, administered locally or by the state. For urban centers, the former of these two taxes has the advantage in that it obtains some revenue from commuters and other nonresident users of the local streets. Local administration of this tax is handicapped, however, by the ease with which it can be avoided, except in jurisdictions with large areas, by making purchases outside of the municipality's corporate limits. Any effort to raise the tax rate to an adequate level is likely to be thwarted by increasing avoidance. More satisfactory alternatives are to place administration of the tax on a countywide basis, with an appropriate formula for local distribution, or for the state to recognize municipal street system requirements in its levy and allocation of motor fuel taxes. Some existing allocation formulae are based on proportionate shares at the time of the original assumption of the taxes by the state governments. With

---

[12] For a state-by-state compilation of these formulae see the Advisory Commission on Intergovernmental Relations, *State-Local Finances: Significant Features and Suggested Legislation*, (Washington, D. C.: United States Government Printing Office, 1972), pp. 73-112.

population shifts, these patterns of distribution have become highly inequitable among municipalities and other participating local governments.

Business License Taxes. The levy of gross receipts taxes on businesses and occupations has been discussed earlier in conjunction with retail sales taxes, with which the Bureau of the Census classifies them in its reporting of municipal revenues. Numerous cities that have never developed this form of tax have imposed separate flat-rate license taxes primarily for revenue purposes on so many kinds of businesses and occupations as to create a species of the overall business tax. These accretions of licensing provisions may have several different rate schedules and measurement bases within the same city; and, unless they have received systematic and frequent overhauling, they are likely to be unfairly discriminatory and to bear little relation to benefits received or the ability to pay. One early review of local business license taxes identified 20 different measurement bases in actual use and commented that most were very crude and should be abandoned.[13]

In the municipalities of some southern states, license taxes produce more revenue than property taxes. In Alabama, for example, where broad licensing power has been in effect since 1909, it has been used by the cities and towns for the levy of their sales (gross receipts) taxes, the occupational license tax, and such special taxes as the gasoline tax, tobacco tax, amusement tax, and beer and liquor tax. In the words of a local leader, "The sum of our levies based upon this licensing authority exceeds 50% of all our revenues. Without the broad interpretation of this statute by our Supreme Court our cities and towns would not be able to operate." For some business license classifications, the analysis continues, maximum rates and measurement bases are set by statute— such as flat charges based on population for railroads, telegraph, telephone, and motor carrier companies; various percentages of net premiums for insurance companies; a percentage of gross receipts for utilities; and flat amounts related to capital structure figures for banks and savings and loan companies. Otherwise "our business privilege licenses are bound only by the court's determination of reasonableness."[14]

Although such extensive use of business and occupational license taxes has been confined to a few southern states, a number of cities in other states obtain substantial revenues from this source. Among the 48 largest cities, business privilege licenses yielded from 69 cents per capita in Indianapolis to $23.32 per capita in Pittsburgh in 1970-71; $5.56 in Chicago; $9.87 in Kansas City, Missouri; $21.71 in Los Angeles; $14.09 in Philadelphia; $11.61 in Portland, Oregon; $18.73 in St. Louis; and $20.81 in Seattle. Many of these systems for taxing business have evolved with differential bases and rates and it is not uncommon to find, in a single city, special licensing provisions for each of more than 100 different kinds of business and occupations. There is little justification for this method

---

[13] A. M. Hillhouse and Muriel Magelssen, *Where Cities Get Their Money*, (Chicago: Municipal Finance Officers Association, 1946) 229 pp.

[14] Comments from "The Revenue Structure of Alabama Municipalities," an address before the Tennessee Municipal League, May 25, 1960, by Ed. E. Reid, Executive Director, Alabama League of Municipalities.

of taxing business because its piecemeal development tends to overlook overall principles of equity, benefit, and ability to pay, and the regulatory purpose tends to be submerged in considerations of what the traffic will bear. If businesses, professions and occupations are to be specially taxed locally for productive revenue purposes, a more satisfactory means is inclusion in a comprehensive local tax or development of a carefully classified gross receipts tax.[15]

Alcoholic Beverage Taxes.   Although alcoholic beverages provide the base for large amounts of public revenue, the local share is small. A compilation by the Distilled Spirits Institute in 1971 shows a grand total of $7.9 billion in receipts from this source—of which the federal share was 63 percent and the state share 34 percent.[16] The local share was $267.5 million, or 3.4 percent.

No alcoholic beverage revenue is produced locally in the states of Alaska, Connecticut, Delaware, Indiana, Maine, Michigan, New Hampshire, Oregon, South Carolina or Washington. In some of the other states, local shares are only through remission of portions of state yields to local governments.

At the local level in other states, alcoholic beverages are taxed in two ways: by selective sales or excise taxes and by license permits or fees. In 24 states, local governments benefit only from license fees; in another four states, license fees and selective sales taxes are used; in eight states, there is a combination of license fees and sales taxes (general, selective, or both) on alcoholic beverages; and in three states, the general sales tax on alcoholic beverages is the source used.

License fees are more productive than selective sales taxes—$93.2 million vs. $37.5 million in 1971. Alcoholic beverage sales are included in the base of local general sales taxes in 12 states and account for $114.7 million in local government revenues from alcoholic beverage sources—23 percent of that total amount is generated in California and 55 percent in New York.

Three states—Maryland, Minnesota, and North Carolina—permit municipalities and/or counties to operate liquor stores. These generate significant amounts of nontax revenues for some local governments. For example, in 1971, liquor store profits in both Winston-Salem and Greensboro, N.C., exceeded $1 million.

In Pennsylvania, the state remits a portion of the state-collected license fees to the municipalities and townships in which the holders of liquor licenses operate. (Pennsylvania operates a state monopoly on bottle sales of all alcoholic beverages, except beer).

---

[15] See James W. Martin, "Devising and Administering Municipal Gross Receipts Business Licenses," *Municipal Finance*, May, 1955, vol. 27, pp. 134-140. An enlightening discussion of one large city's complex medley of business taxes and its problem of extricating itself from a still remaining "hodge-podge" of many and varied methods of licensing some businesses and occupations is given by John H. Poelker, Comptroller of the City of St. Louis, in "Revenues from Licenses and User Charges," *Municipal Finance*, August, 1962, vol. 35, pp. 55-59.

[16] The information in this section is based on a report of the Division of Research and Statistics, Distilled Spirits Institute, *Public Revenues from Alcoholic Beverages*, (Washington, D. C.: Distilled Spirits Institute, 1972), p. 4.

In all, local governments in 40 states raise revenue in some form from the taxation of alcoholic beverages, but in 1971 the aggregate of such revenues for local governments exceeded $10 million in only seven states—California, $26.5 million; Georgia, $20.1 million; Illinois, $22.4 million; Minnesota, $14.6 million; New York, $63.6 million; North Carolina, $19.9 million, and Tennessee, $22.2 million. Twenty-eight states specifically share some part of their alcoholic beverage revenues with their local governments, usually according to a formula based upon population or location of the licensed premises. Revenues that are returned by the state are generally earmarked for a great variety of purposes— school construction, veterans' benefits, etc.—and, in many cases, shared revenues are also restricted as to their use. County and municipal license fees are collected and retained by the local government in nine states; but, they are more generally collected by the state and returned to the locality, less the cost of administration —except in Colorado where only a percentage is returned and in Nebraska where these revenues are designatd for the school fund. Liquor store profits are locally controlled only in Oregon; in Maryland and Minnesota, they are earmarked for certain funds.

Alcoholic beverage license taxes serve a regulatory purpose, but their primary purpose is production of revenue. The nature and extent of local participation in this source of revenue are determined by the various methods of alcoholic beverage control which the states developed after repeal of the prohibition amendment. Thirty-two states depend on licensing systems, 17 states maintain state monopolies for the distribution of liquor, and North Carolina has county-operated liquor stores supervised by the state.

In the license-control states, license taxes are typically levied on manufacturers, importers, wholesalers, and the several classes of retailers. The local licensing power is exceedingly varied. In three states (California, Connecticut, and Delaware), licensing is exclusively a state function, but with local sharing of tax proceeds in California. In Hawaii, the counties issue all licenses; and, in a few states, e.g., Idaho and Illinois, a local license is prerequisite to a state license. More commonly, there is provision for local licensing which duplicates some part of the state system. Generally, this authority extends to retailers within the respective local jurisdictions, with or without such special qualifications as licensing for on-premises consumption only; but, sometimes it applies to wholesalers and manufacturers as well. Usually, the state specifies maximum local fees, often as some proportion of the state fees. Of the monopoly states, seven (Alabama, New Hampshire, Ohio, Oregon, Pennsylvania, South Carolina, and Washington) maintain exclusive control through their stores and licensing provisions; but, in the others, the monopoly is not complete. Counties and municipalities may be authorized, sometimes exclusively, to license retailers of beer, or light wines and beer; in a few instances, they are permitted to duplicate state licenses; and, in Wyoming, the state monopoly is restricted to wholesaling, with the the local governments responsible for all retail licensing except that of railroads.

Income Taxes

At the end of 1971, local income taxes were levied in these states:

Alabama	1	city
Delaware	1	city
Kentucky	33	cities; 1 county
Maryland	1	city; 24 counties
Michigan	14	cities
Missouri	2	cities
New York	1	city
Ohio	328	cities and villages
Pennsylvania	3,400	cities, boroughs, townships, and school districts

In addition, Denver has an occupational privilege tax, Newark, N.J., a payroll tax, and San Francisco a payroll expense tax. Also, there was ½ of 1 percent payroll tax on employers in the Tri-County Metropolitan Transit District serving the Portland, Oregon, area; and a 3/10th of 1 percent tax in the Lane County (Oregon) Mass Transit District.

The tax is a flat-rate tax, levied at a low rate on a base that varies somewhat among the states. The rates range from 0.2 percent in some small Ohio and Pennsylvania local governments to 3.5 percent in New York City (the tax rate in Washington, D.C. is 10 percent). One percent is the legal maximum in Pennsylvania, except in Philadelphia, Pittsburgh, and Scranton. In Wilmington, the tax is based only on income over $4,000 and the rates range from one-fourth of one percent to 1.5 percent. In Ohio municipalities, the tax ranges from one percent to 1.5 percent. Michigan state law prescribes a one percent rate for residents and a 0.5 percent rate for nonresidents, except in Detroit which has a 2 percent rate. Local governments in Maryland which have enacted the tax receive from 20 percent to 50 percent of the state income tax.

In its broadest application, the tax applies to: (1) the gross income from salaries and wages of residents earned both within and outside the city; (2) the gross income from salaries and wages of nonresidents earned within the city; (3) the net profits of professions and unincorporated businesses of residents from activities wherever conducted; (4) the net profits of professions and unincorporated businesses of nonresidents from activities conducted within the city; and (5) the net profits of corporations from activities conducted within the city. The tax on salaries and wages generally provides no personal exemptions or deductions—except in Wilmington—although tax credits in the case of overlapping jurisdictions or nonresidents are sometimes specified.

In Pennsylvania, all of these components are included in the tax base except the tax on corporations, which is generally debarred because local governments may not enter tax fields occupied by the state. An exception to the general Pennsylvania rule was the Philadelphia School District, which from 1969 to 1972 levied a three percent corporate net income tax. This was abandoned because of its apparent adverse influence upon corporate locational decisions. The Philadelphia School District also levies a tax upon selected portions of the unearned income of individuals.

The local income tax has created problems of double taxation in two ways, its levy by overlapping governments and its application to personal income both at the place of origin of the income and at the domicile of the taxpayer, i.e., a person may live in City A and work in City B, both of which levy income taxes, and be subject to the tax in both places. In Pennsylvania, there are numerous instances of income taxes being levied by both the municipality and school district serving an area. A statutory rate limitation of one percent is maintained by a required sharing of the rate where there is tax duplication—either equally, by mutual agreement, or on some other basis. In Louisville, and overlapping Jefferson County, both of which levy a 1.75 percent tax, the county allows taxpayers subject to the city tax a credit against the county tax. To avoid the potential for double taxation, Pennsylvania municipalities, other than Philadelphia,[17] provide for tax crediting that gives priority to the place of residence. Under this arrangement, the municipality of employment loses its power to tax nonresidents if the municipality of residence imposes the tax. In Ohio, the cities have worked out various tax crediting or reciprocity arrangements that give priority to the place of employment.[18]

Administration of the tax depends heavily on collection at the source and places the burden of compliance on private business. The usual procedure is for the employers to remit withholdings to the collector on a monthly or quarterly basis and to file withholding statements (with copies being sent to employees) at the end of the year, at which time any necessary tax adjustments are made. For recipients of taxable earnings not subject to withholding (residents elsewhere, employees of the federal government or of concerns not withholding the tax, self-employed persons, unincorporated businesses, and corporations), the tax is self-assessed in much the same manner as the federal income tax. Tax reporting forms are supplied for annual submission (commonly required also from persons subject to withholding), and annual estimates of prospective income, as a basis for quarterly payments, are sometimes required. When only a part of the profits of a business is subject to a local taxing jurisdiction, the allocation formula generally used is one which allocates profits on the basis of tangible property, payrolls, and gross sales.

The multiplication of users, particularly when it results in numerous local units within a limited area levying the tax, complicates administration and poses perplexing compliance problems for taxpayers and employers. Because of the haphazard relationship between where people live and work, an employer's

---

[17] The city of Philadelphia enjoys a preferential status in that nonresidents working in the city or residents working outside the city may take a tax credit against any other local income tax levied in Pennsylvania. As a result, few suburban local governments in the SMSA impose a local income tax.

[18] For a further discussion of this complicated problem of interlocal tax coordination see the report of The Advisory Commission on Intergovernmental Relations on tax overlapping, *op. cit* pp. 225-227 and Robert A. Sigafoos, *The Municipal Income Tax: Its History and Problems*, (Chicago: Public Administration Service, 1955), 169 pp.

Table 17
LOCAL INCOME TAX RATES AND PER CAPITA RECEIPTS
FOR SELECTED CITIES
1970-1971

	1970 Population (in thousands)	1970-71 Income Tax Rate	Income Tax Revenues (millions)	*Per Capita* Yield
New York City	7,896	0.7 – 3.5[1]	$449.7	$56.96
Detroit, Mich.	1,514	2.0	88.2	58.29
Philadelphia, Pa.	1,950	3.3125	226.1	115.95
Baltimore, Md.	906	50% of State Tax	31.0	34.23
Washington, D.C.	757	2.0 – 10.1[1]	130.1	171.99
Cleveland, Ohio	751	1.0	41.5	55.21
St. Louis, Mo.	622	1.0	37.2	59.71
Columbus, Ohio	540	1.5	32.3	59.88
Pittsburgh, Pa.	520	1.0	13.3	25.49
Kansas City, Mo.	507	1.0	15.8	31.21

1. The tax is graduated; higher rates are levied on salaries in excess of a stated amount—$30,000 in New York City and $25,000 in Washington, D.C.

Sources: Tax Foundation, Inc., *Facts & Figures on Governmental Finance* (New York Tax Foundation, Inc., 1973), p. 250 and U.S. Bureau of the Census, *City Government Finances in 1970-71*, pp. 87-100.

labor force may come from a dozen or more communities, or the business may be of such nature that individual employees work a few hours a week in each of these communities. When some, or all, of the local governments in the area levy income taxes, at different rates, under different local ordinances, and subject to certain crediting and reciprocity arrangements, the complexities of tax withholding and enforcement are significant. An added disadvantage of this tax is that it frequently involves opposition from low-income groups and nonresidents.

The earned income tax has features that can make it the most acceptable of the major local nonproperty taxes. As a flat-rate tax, generally without allowance for deductions or exemptions, it has a broad base that yields substantial income from low rates; it lends itself well to collection at the source; it is proportional rather than regressive (although it does have the limitation of excluding unearned income from its base); and it is paid as income is earned, thus avoiding the problem of bulk payments. Also, it can obtain considerable amounts of revenue from the commuter population. Income tax yield data in 1971 for the 10 largest cities using the tax are given in Table 17. For the four cities with a one percent rate, revenue ranged from $25 *per capita* to $60 *per capita.* Higher rates yielded $57 *per capita* in New York City, $61 *per capita* in Cincinnati, and $116 *per capita* in Philadelphia.

The good features of the local income tax are no justification for its indiscriminate use, marked by inept administration and myriad problems of overlapping jurisdictions and taxpayer and employer compliance. Effective, equitable administration of the tax calls for a well qualified administrator and adequate, competent auditors and field staff—facilities which are beyond the reach of individual small governments. In larger cities, the tax can be made to work well; but, as a source of revenue for small places, its acceptability depends on the development of some tenable form of centralized county or area-wide administration.

LICENSES AND PERMITS

Most local governments have broad responsibilities in the supervision of various kinds of business and other activity within the community. Thus, building construction is regulated by building codes with part of the enforcement consisting of the examination of plans and issuance of building permits, along with varying degrees of inspection to see that the construction is basically in accordance with the plans. In like manner, licenses are issued for food vendors and permits are required for parades, circuses, and a host of other activities.

In most situations, a fee is charged in conjunction with the issuance of the license or permit. If the fee charged is less than, or generally in the magnitude of, the cost of the administration of the government's activities in the field, the payment is entitled to be classified as a license or permit fee. If, however, the issuance of the license or permit requires payment of an amount that is substantially greater than the cost of associated administration, the excess portion is properly classified as a tax in that it is for the general welfare and is not related to the amount or cost of the services being rendered with regard to the activity being regulated.

Because the two types of receipts are normally not segregated, it is not feasible to estimate the amount of revenue derived strictly from license and permit activity nor the amount from the tax aspect of this revenue source. Yet, annual income of several dollars *per capita* can be derived from license and permit fees, as such, in most general purpose local governments.

SERVICE CHARGES AND MISCELLANEOUS GENERAL REVENUE

Following World War II, the need for moneys to support rapidly expanding governmental services has, as detailed in the foregoing sections, engendered a search for nonproperty tax revenues in order to relieve the burden formerly placed on the property tax. This need has also caused an interest in the use of nontax revenue sources. The latter ordinarily impose no mandatory obligation on all citizens, or all nonresident workers, or all persons in a given occupation, such as taxes do. Yet, in some cases, e.g., a refuse collection charge, or a sewer charge when billed with an essential service like water, the charge is not altogether devoid of its mandatory aspects. Service charges are intended to transfer the cost of governmental services to the beneficiaries or are a byproduct of governmental functions, e.g., fines.

The Bureau of the Census classifies 17 separate sources of nontax revenues under the groupings of "current charges" and "miscellaneous general revenue."

> Many people think of taxation as the sole source of public support. There are several other government sources of revenue, however, some of which have been, at certain times and places, very important . . . Even as recently as the late 1920s there were cities that derived more revenues from special assessments than from general property taxes. And at present there are sizable cities that secure more revenue from the earnings of public service enterprises than from property taxes. On the whole, however, nontax revenues are of far less importance now than formerly.[19]

As detailed in Table 18, nontax revenues represented 15 percent of the general revenue of all local governments in 1970-71. And, as previously shown in Table 14, these sources, taken together, constituted only 12 percent of the total local general revenue of municipalities with a population of 1 million or more but accounted for 28 percent of general revenues in municipalities under 50,000 population. Their relative importance in the various types of local government may be seen from the fact that, in 1972, current charges and miscellaneous general revenue represented 15 percent of the total local general revenue of counties; 19 percent of such revenue in municipalities; 9 percent of revenues in townships; 7 percent of school district revenues; and a ponderous 51 percent of the revenues of special districts (as previously shown in Table 11).

Current Charges

Current charges, based on the benefit principle, generally bear a direct relationship to the cost of providing the service, thus freeing tax funds for other services. Current charges in 1970-71 accounted for 11 percent of all local general revenues. As defined by the Bureau of Census, they are amounts received from the public for performance of specific services benefiting the person charged and from sales of commodities and services—except by city utilities. They include fees, assessments, and other disbursements for current services, rents and sales derived from commodities or services furnished incident to the performance of particular functions, the gross income of commercial activities and the like—such as parking lots and school lunch programs.

Education sources accounted for 2.7 percent of total local general revenues: the gross income of "School Lunch Sales" was 1.6 percent; "Institutions of Higher Education" (consisting of payments for tuition), another 0.4 percent; and other sources, 0.7 percent.

---

[19] Groves, Harold M., *Financing Government*, Sixth Edition, (New York: Holt, Rinehart, and Winston, 1958), p. 399.

Table 18
NON-TAX REVENUES DETAILED FOR ALL LOCAL GOVERNMENTS
1970-1971
(amounts in billions of dollars)

Revenue Source	Amount	Percent of Total General Revenue
Total General Revenue	91.9	100.0
Charges & Misc. General Revenue	14.1	15.3
Current charges	9.8	10.7
Education	2.5	2.7
School Lunch Sales	1.4	1.6
Institutions of Higher Education	.4	0.4
Other	.6	0.7
Hospitals	2.6	2.8
Sewerage	1.0	1.1
Sanitation Other than Sewerage	.3	0.4
Local Parks and Recreation	.3	0.3
Natural Resources	.1	0.1
Housing and Urban Renewal	.6	0.7
Air Transportation	.5	0.5
Water Transport and Terminals	.2	0.2
Parking Facilities	.2	0.2
Other	1.4	1.6
Miscellaneous General Revenue	4.2	4.6
Special Assessments	.6	0.6
Sale of Property	.3	0.3
Interest Earnings	1.8	1.9
Other	1.6	1.7

Source: U.S. Bureau of the Census, *Governmental Finances in 1970-71*, P. 20.

Hospitals administered by the government concerned generate some revenues and, thus, accounted for 2.8 percent of total general revenues in 1971.

Sanitation, by definition of the Bureau of the Census, comprises revenues received for activities connected with the collection and disposal of garbage and other waste. *Sewerage* revenues are derived from the provision of sanitary and storm sewers and sewage disposal facilities and services. These two sources in 1971 accounted for 1.5 percent of total general revenues.

Local Parks and Recreation include revenues generated by museums, art galleries, swimming pools, municipal parks, and special facilities for recreation, such as auditoriums, stadiums, and harbors. This category produced 0.3 of total general revenues in 1971.

Natural resources revenues are generated by concessions in parklands and bird sanctuaries and accounted for 0.1 percent of total general revenue in 1971.

Housing and Urban Renewal Revenues are produced by city housing rents and payments made by private developers and, in 1971, they accounted for 0.7 percent of total general revenues.

Finally, there are included in the "Current Charges" grouping a catch-all category of "Other," accounting for 1.6 percent of all revenues, and three commercial activities.

1. *Air Transportation* involving airport charges and representing 0.5 percent of revenues
2. *Water Transport and Terminals* involving revenues from the operation of canals, docks, wharfs and related facilities and accounting for 0.2 percent of 1971 revenue
3. *Parking Facilities* including meter collections and charges for the public use of municipally-operated garages and accounting for 0.2 percent of total revenue

Miscellaneous General Revenue

There are three categories of locally generated revenues included in this general grouping which, taken together, accounted for 4.6 percent of total general revenue in 1971.

Interest earnings in 1971 accounted for 1.9 percent of total local general revenue. By definition of the Bureau of the Census, this source consists of earnings on deposits and securities, other than the earnings of insurance trust funds or employee retirement systems.

The sale of property involves receipts from the sale of real property and improvements thereon. It excludes receipts from the disposition of commodities, equipment, and other personal property and from the sale of securities. In 1971, this source represented 0.3 percent of total local general revenues.

Special assessments, like taxes, are imposed on a property. They are compulsory, for public purposes, and require formal assessment. They differ from taxes in that they are related to a specific benefit, need not be uniform throughout the jurisdiction, and generally allow no exemptions. Unlike a service charge, they are levied against property and the benefit may be remote, rather than direct. As defined by the Bureau of the Census, special assessments are compulsory contributions collected from the owners of property benefited by specific public improvements (paving, drainage or irrigation facilities, etc.) to defray the costs of such improvements, and they are apportioned according to the assumed benefits to the property affected. In 1971, such assessments accounted for 0.6 percent of total local general revenue.

Until the 1930s special assessments were extensively used particularly by rapidly growing municipalities in their efforts to meet the cost of needed public improvements. However, faulty administration, extensive defaults on special assessment bonds, and the partial financing of improvements through federal relief agencies, accounted for a rapid decline in the use of this means of financing during the 1930s. Following World War II the rapid developments in the construction field to meet housing demands coupled with the urgent need to use all existing means of financing brought a resurgence in the use of special assessments, particularly for streets and related improvements in older built-up sections of the city.[20]

In most states the introduction after 1945 of new land use controls resulted in requirements that developers install the principal immediate public improvements—water and sewer mains, streets, sidewalks, curbs, and street lighting—as a part of the development costs. The cost of these improvements were then funded into the total cost of development and passed on to the buyer as a part of his purchase price. As a result, this greatly decreased reliance upon special assessments for financing these costs. Also, widespread use of revenue bonds secured by water and sewer service charges has served to reduce the requirement for special assessments in those areas.

INTERGOVERNMENTAL REVENUES

Intergovernmental revenues may be categorized as to source and function. Local revenues in this category may be derived from either the federal or the state government (and occasionally from intergovernmental transfers among local governments). But, in 1971 the state was a far more important source—accounting for nine times more aid to local governments than by the federal government—$31.1 million compared to $3.4 million. Such revenues may be given in the form of grants-in-aid, shared taxes, or revenue-sharing.

The reporting system of the Bureau of the Census does not provide data as to the amount of state aid to local governments which is, in fact, flow-through federal money paid to the state governments and then passed on to local governments.

The function of grants-in-aid is two-fold: (1) to give to poorer municipalities a disproportionate share of these revenues to increase their capability for providing needed services in an attempt to effect stabilization, equalization, and support of such governments; and (2) to provide impetus to expansion of particular functions. Such grants are usually provided for specified purposes and the receiving unit of government is required to meet a set of imposed minimum standards.

Shared taxes, on the other hand, are based on rights and allocate to localities their portion of a tax collected or imposed by a higher level of government. Except for motor fuel taxes there are generally no requirements specified and shared taxes may be used for any purpose.

General revenue-sharing, as adopted by the federal government in 1972 apportions part of that government's total revenues to local governments with few, if any, restrictions as to project or purpose and such revenues increase as the personal income tax base of the federal government grows. Proposals for special revenue-sharing continue to be considered by Congress as a substitute for

---

[20] International City Managers' Association, *Municipal Finance Administration*, 6th edition, (Chicago: International City Managers' Association, 1962), p. 43.

portions of the huge array of categorical grants by the federal government to state and local governments. The first step was taken by Congress in 1974 by the enactment of special revenue sharing legislation in the field of urban renewal, model cities and certain other programs.

During the period 1957-1971, intergovernmental revenues, as a percentage of total general revenue, have increased from 30 percent in 1957, to 35 percent in 1967, to 38 percent in 1971.

In 1971, intergovernmental revenues represented 42 percent of total general revenue in counties; 32 percent of such revenues in municipalities; 21 percent of these revenues in townships; 20 percent in special districts; and 46 percent of such revenues in school districts (as previously shown in Table 7).

Intergovernmental revenues represented 42 percent of total 1971 general revenue in municipalities of one million population or more; 33 percent of such revenues in municipalities in the 500,000 population range; 28 percent of these revenues in municipalities within the 300,000 population grouping; 28 percent of revenues in the 100,000 group; 23 percent of those with 50,000 or more population; and 23 percent of revenues in municipalities with under 50,000 population. (See Table 14.)

Federal Aid

Direct federal aid to local governments began in the 1930s with relief programs and was extended to low-income housing construction and payments in lieu of taxes. During World War II, federal aid centered on public works and services and on government financed housing projects. Two important post-war aid programs enacted were the Federal Highway Act of 1944 and the Federal Aid Airport Act of 1949. In 1960, there were 46 federal aid programs to local governments underway and 7 programs of shared revenues. By 1970, the Congress was "dangling almost 500 large and small conditional aid carrots collectively worth about $25 billion a year before State and Local Governments."[21]

With its 1972 budget, the federal government recognized that

> . . . assistance in the form of categorical grants, even of great magnitude, has not removed . . . local fiscal problems, and in some cases these problems have been aggravated.

> At the same time, this form of assistance has had other profound effects on the nature of government at all levels. One unfortunate result is the proliferation of narrow, overlapping programs. Other results are program delay and uncertainty, restrictions on the authority and responsibility of

---

[21] These figures are taken from reports of the Joint Economic Committee, *Subsidy and Subsidylike Programs of the United States Government*, (Washington, D. C.: United States Government Printing Office, 1960), pp. 14-16 and the Advisory Commission on Intergovernmental Relations, *Revenue Sharing—An Idea whose Time has Come*, (Washington, D. C.: United States Government Printing Office, December 1970), p. 7.

governors and mayors, and the creation of nearly autonomous functional bureaucracies at each level of government.[22]

In view of these circumstances, the executive budget proposed the sharing of a portion of federal revenues with local governments without any program or project restrictions and the continuation of only a few of the existing grant programs. Revenue-sharing proposals recognize the responsibility of local governments to provide needed public services and attempt to increase their capacity to do so. This proposal also recognizes the responsibility of the federal government to support research and to develop innovating ways of carrying out public services.

State Aid

Of the $105.2 billion spent by local governments in 1971, $31.1 billion came from state sources. In 1967, state aid represented 32 percent of total local general revenues; in 1971, it was 34 percent of the total.

With the ever-increasing gap between local ability to provide services and the cost of such services, the states have stepped in with grants-in-aid and shared taxes. Other alternatives for state support include: (1) state assumption of performance of the services, thus obviating the need for local financing; and (2) increased state technical assistance in areas such as investment and marketing. When distributed on the basis of need, state aid should consider relative economic capacity, local tax effort, legal restrictions on taxing ability, and fixed service costs. This basis for distribution, however, can perpetuate inefficient units of local government. Nonetheless, the state should accept some measure of responsibility because: (1) the state uses local units as vehicles of administration; (2) the state sets minimum standards and procedures with regard to selected functions or activities; (3) there are legal limitations set by the state on local borrowing and taxation; (4) the state has a greater economic capacity; and (5) in some instances, the state acts to channel federal funds.

A 1969 analysis of state aid resulted in the following findings and conclusions:

There is a mismatch among governmental levels in the financial responsibility for the provision of public services. This imbalance is caused by (a) the widespread State practice of forcing the local property tax to serve as the primary underwriter of both the local school system and units of local general government and (b) the present Congressional policy that requires State and local governments to pick up approximately one-half of the nation's $10 billion welfare bill.

To redress the imbalance, the Commission calls upon the Federal Government to assume full financial responsibility for the public assistance function

---

[22] United States Office of the President, *The Budget of the United States Government, Fiscal year 1972,* (Washington, D. C.: United States Government Printing Office, 1972), pp. 32-33.

—including general assistance and medicaid—and for the States, as a long-range objective, to assume substantially all the non-Federal share of elementary and secondary education costs.

With the major exception of public education, State aid distribution formulas generally fail to recognize variations in local fiscal capacity to support public services. For such intergovernmental programs as public health and hospitals and highways, the Commission calls for States to include measures in their distribution formulas that reflect the ability and capacity of local governments to provide these services. This would add greater equalization to State-local fiscal relations and help assure that State dollars go to those local jurisdictions in greatest fiscal need.

In few if any States does State aid really constitute a "system." To assure a more responsive and effective state aid structure, the Commission believes certain organizational aspects of the State-local fiscal system to be imperative, suggests criteria for assessing local government viability, and calls for the adoption of State performance standards to accompany categorical State aid, such programs to conform to comprehensive and functional planning objectives.[23]

As is the case with the operating and capital budgeting fields, suggestions for improving state-local fiscal relations are rampant; the implementation of these suggestions is still lagging.

---

[23] Advisory Commission on Intergovernmental Relations, *State Aid to Local Government*, (Washington, D. C.: United States Government Printing Office, April, 1969), p. 13.

9

Administration of Governmental Enterprises

The great majority of municipalities in the United States own and operate one or more undertakings that are essentially of a commercial nature—supported by user charges rather than by taxes. Moreover, numerous special districts exist for this purpose. Included with varying degrees of representation are most of the basic public utility industries, numerous other enterprises with some of the characteristics of utilities, and various public facilities—some of them formerly tax-supported, which have been placed, fully or partially, on a commercial basis by the imposition of user charges.

Unfortunately the revenue classification system of the Bureau of the Census does not reflect full data on the results of operations of all governmental enterprises. The only enterprises for which data is reported are: (1) water, (2) electric, (3) transit, and (4) gas utilities. Information is also available as to liquor stores operated by local government. Revenues from other enterprises are reported under the general classification of service charges and expenditures in relation to these enterprises and are likewise so reported.

In 1971-72, locally owned public utilities are shown by the Bureau of the Census to have had revenues totaling $7.8 billion and expenditures of $9.7 billion.[1] The distribution was as follows:

	(Amounts in billions of dollars)	
	Revenues	*Expenditures*
Water supply	3.17	3.73
Electric power	2.91	3.35
Transit	1.24	1.60
Gas	.48	.43
Total	7.79	9.70

---

[1] U. S. Bureau of the Census, *Governmental Finances in 1971-72*, p. 26.

SCOPE OF GOVERNMENTAL ENTERPRISES

The kinds of governmental enterprises are numerous and diverse. Comments concerning a few of the more numerous types are made here to assist in defining the character of these operations.

Water Systems

Public ownership is dominant in the field of water supply. Publicly owned systems account for the greater portion of all municipal water systems and serve an even larger portion of individual consumers. Of the 48 largest cities, only Indianapolis and Oakland are served by private companies. Some municipalities maintain only distribution systems, buying their water wholesale from other public agencies,[2] while a number of publicly served communities do not administer their own systems, depending on service from an adjacent central city or a unified metropolitan district.[3] These features reflect the changing character of this most basic of all utilities. The fragmented character of governmental organization in suburban areas and the intensification of the supply problem in many sections of the country necessitate metropolitan, state, and even regional solutions.[4] For the majority of governmental units, however, the financial administration of water utilities is still a direct responsibility.

Wastewater Systems

The handling of wastewater (sewage) has become a major enterprise activity of many local governments. For centuries cities and towns dumped all wastewater (both from sanitary and storm sewers) into nearby streams or bodies of water. During the past few decades much attention has been given to cleaning up the waters of the nation. The current emphasis upon environmental considerations in our society is giving new impetus to improving the quality of wastewater discharged.

---

[2] The wholesaling agency may be a central city. Chicago, for example, provides water to over 72 suburban communities and the Detroit Metro Water System serves some 3 million customers in 60 communities. Or, it may be a specially constituted metropolitan district. Among such districts are the Metropolitan Water District of Southern California, the Passaic Valley Water Commission in New Jersey, and the Colorado River Municipal Water District in Texas.

[3] Districts which administer the entire water utility function, including retail distribution as well as supply and transmission include the Washington Suburban Sanitary District (which serves Montgomery and Prince George counties) in Maryland; the East Bay Municipal Utilities District in California; the Hartford County Metropolitan District, Connecticut; Suffolk County Water Authority, New York; and the Metropolitan Utilities District of Omaha. Comprising a special feature of water administration by a public body in a few states, mainly in Pennsylvania, are several hundred separately constituted, local public authorities which are little more than subordinate agencies of general purpose governments.

[4] For a useful analysis of these problems and their possible intergovernmental solutions see The Advisory Commission on Intergovernmental Relations, *Intergovernmental Responsibilities for Water Supply and Sewage Disposal in Metropolitan Areas*, (Washington, D. C.: United States Government Printing Office, 1962), 135 pp.

This trend has been accompanied by increased use of service charges designed to make wastewater services self-sufficient. To an increasing degree, these charges are calibrated upon the basis of the degree of pollution and the cost of treating the polluted waters. Under this concept, the amount of the fee is brought into more or less direct relationship to the cost imposed upon the system by major users, especially industrial users.

Also, there is a recognition of the need for larger systems to facilitate quality control and efficiency of operations. This is resulting in the organization for handling of wastewater services on a much broader geographical basis. In areas with highly fragmented local governments, cooperative agreements are being worked out. Either a large system is expanding its facilities to take care of waste-water heretofore handled by neighboring smaller systems; or, new special purpose governmental districts or authorities are being created to provide the services.

Energy Systems

In the ownership and operation of electric power and gas supply utilities, governments currently play a relatively minor role. The early development of electric power was on a local community basis and, beginning in the 1880s, governmental ownership became popular in many areas with the number of government-owned plants reaching a peak of 3,066 in 1923. Since then, with the advancing technology of the industry emphasizing the economy of large-scale production and facilitating long distance transmission, many small plants, public and private, have merged into large private systems. Although there was a resurgence of governmental ownership in 1930s, particularly with the advent of TVA, the number of publicly owned plants has been greatly reduced—and the great majority of these are small distribution systems.[5] A 1970 report of the Federal Power Commission indicates that there were 536 municipally owned electric utilities in that year—generating $2.2 billion in revenues. The number of electrical plants in that year was 3,519.[6] In terms of KWH generated, plants owned by local governments accounted for 4.7 percent of total power produced in 1970.

While gas supply utilities continue to be mainly privately owned, there has been a rapid increase in recent years in the acquisition of distribution systems by small local governments—induced by newly available natural gas from the spreading network of transmission lines. The great majority of government-owned gas supply utilities are small; yet, some serve cities of over 50,000 population. Among the larger systems are those of Long Beach, Houston, and Memphis.

---

[5] The largest municipal systems generating all, or part, of their power are those of Los Angeles; Seattle and Tacoma, Washington; Austin and San Antonio, Texas; Jacksonville, Florida; and Lansing, Michigan. The largest exclusively distribution systems are those of Memphis, Nashville, Chattanooga and Knoxville, Tennessee; and Orlando, Florida. Two large cities are served by publicly owned metropolitan systems—Omaha by the Omaha Public Power District, created in 1945, and Sacramento by the Sacramento Municipal Utility District, which began to distribute power at the end of 1946.

[6] Federal Power Commission, *Statistics of Publicly Owned Electric Utilities in the United States 1970*, (Washington, D. C.: United States Government Printing Office, February 1972), p. vii and U.S. Bureau of the Census, *Statistical Abstract of the United States: 1972*, 93rd edition, (Washington, D. C.: United States Government Printing Office, 1972), p. 507.

Table 19
DISTRIBUTION OF TRANSIT SYSTEMS BY POPULATION GROUPS*
1972

Population Group (1970)	Rail Transit (incl. Joint Trolley Coach and/or Motor Bus)	Trolley Coach and Motor Bus Operations Combined	Motor Bus (Exclusively)	Grand Total
500,000 and over	10	1	20	31
250,000 to 500,000	2	1	40	43
100,000 to 250,000	0	0	80	80
50,000 to 100,000	0	0	122	122
Less than 50,000	0	0	395	395
Suburban and other	3	0	371	374
Total	15	2	1,028	1,045

* Each system is counted only once. It is classified in the population group of the largest city it serves.

Source: American Transit Association, '72-73 *Transit Fact Book*, (Washington, D. C.: American Transit Association, 1973), p. 3.

Mass Transit

For decades urban transit was mainly in the hands of private enterprise, but generally declining use combined with rising costs have undermined its profitability and indicated a need for public ownership to restore, maintain, and improve the urban systems of mass transportation.

> Public mass transportation facilities are provided by few local governments (10 of the 48 largest cities own and operate public service transportation). The need for mass transportation is apparent, and local government in major metropolitan areas will become more involved with public transportation facilities . . . What form government involvement will take is unknown. There is the choice of direct ownership and operation, leasing public facilities for operation by private interests, and major subsidy of private operations.[7]

In 1972, there were 160 publicly owned systems. This represents 15 percent of the transit industry, distributed as follows among the various population groups as shown in Table 19.

To date, public ownership of urban transit has taken on a metropolitan character. The Chicago area (including Chicago and metropolitan Cook county) is served by the Chicago Regional Transportation Authority; five counties in the Philadelphia area by the Southeastern Pennsylvania Transportation Authority; the Boston area (including 79 cities and towns) by the Massachusetts Bay Transportation Authority; Los Angeles and three other counties by the Southern

[7] International City Management Association, *The Municipal Yearbook 1973*, (Washington, D. C.: International City Management Association, 1973), p. 96.

California Rapid Transit District; the St. Louis area (involving three counties in Missouri and three counties in Illinois) by the Bi-state Development Agency; and the San Francisco area (including eleven surrounding counties) by the San Francisco Public Utilities Commission and four separate transit districts. Public ownership and operation of transit systems is distinguished from water, gas, and electric systems because transit is ordinarily the only loss operation in the group.

Other Enterprises

Other government-owned and operated enterprises are air terminals, parking facilities, motor bus and motor freight terminals, ferries, toll bridges, and tunnels. In many local governments, sewage disposal systems (generally tax-supported in the past) have been placed on a utility basis with charges usually geared to water consumption and the characteristics of sewage discharged into the system. Governmental enterprises may also include housing, hospitals, markets, auditoriums, stadiums, radio stations, abattoirs, and such recreational facilities as golf courses, marinas, and swimming pools. School lunch programs can also be classified as an enterprise activity. In three states (Minnesota, North Carolina, and Maryland), there are municipal liquor stores. Finally, refuse collection and disposal have been placed on a service charge basis by numerous governmental units.

SOME CONSIDERATIONS IN THE ADMINISTRATION OF GOVERNMENTAL ENTERPRISES

The administration of local government enterprises involves not only the conventional concepts of public administration but also many aspects of private business administration.

Organizational Requirements

Regardless of the size of the local government operating an enterprise, the basic organizational requirements for its successful operation and financial administration are identical. There are several considerations of particular importance:

Effective Management. Effective management calls for integration of the appropriate functions of an enterprise under the direction and control of a single, responsible administrative head who is free to direct and develop the enterprise within the broad policy guidelines determined by the governing authorities. This applies not only to enterprises which are large enough to constitute separate departments headed by full-time managers but also to small enterprises in which it is necessary for the manager to have other duties (such as superintendent of public works) and to rely heavily on the part-time services of other divisions of government. The key to successful operation is a competent manager with adequate executive authority and protection against arbitrary, or political, removal or interference.

Competent management of governmental enterprises necessarily includes alert business management—which goes beyond the basic essentials of assuring skillful technical performance and dependable service. The manager has to run an efficient business office; have available an accounting and records system that provides him with adequate information for rate-making and cost control; work for good customer and public relations; and use endless ingenuity in keeping consumer charges under control. He is also responsible for improving service to the community and expanding facilities as needed while maintaining the system's financial integrity as a commercial enterprise.

When a governmental unit operates more than one utility, there may be substantial advantages in grouping them as divisions of a single department under a general manager. Unified administration enables small communities to develop better-managed, more self-contained utility departments and offers larger communities a considerable range for more economical and efficient utility operation by savings in overhead, economies of scale, consolidation of routine business operations, and unification of top-level business management. Water and sewage disposal make a logical combination when the latter is treated as a utility and various groupings of water, electric, and gas are common. Mass transit usually has its own separate organization, although its grouping with other transportation and terminal facilities might provide a sounder basis for developing a well-coordinated transportation system.

Effective, Integrated Operation. Reinforcing the requirement of operating a governmental enterprise as an integrated business is the related requirement of maintaining its fiscal identity. Since a utility provides service to other divisions of the government and, irrespective of its size, very properly makes at least some use of the services of the other divisions, this requirement of fiscal identity poses some problems. It can be met satisfactorily only by keeping standard utility accounts, separate from the general accounts of the government and by having them accurately reflect the monetary value of all interdepartmental service relations. In the unified management of two or more enterprises, maintenance of the fiscal identity of each calls for carefully segregated accounting records. The managers of the utility, governmental officials, and the public need the true financial facts about each enterprise.

Overall Supervision. Who shall appoint the manager and who shall exercise general control over policies of a governmental enterprise? These questions may be answered simply and effectively by vesting the authority in the mayor or manager of the governmental unit. It seems illogical, in fact, for a governmental unit to withhold from its chief administrative officer the responsibility for supervising its business enterprises. In any government with sound traditions of administration, there is no reason why, regardless of its form of government, overall supervision by the chief executive cannot be satisfactory.

Expert Advisors. A necessary adjunct to the foregoing organizational requirements is the use of independent expert advisors from the initiation of a public undertaking. Well-qualified consultants help to avoid costly mistakes, and maximize the results of operations. No major acquisition, expansion, or reconstruction project should be undertaken, no long-range capital program adopted; and no purchase of complex, expensive equipment transacted without the advice of consulting engineers—except, perhaps, in very large departments. The planning and marketing of sizable bond issues call for independent financial advisors and special bond counsel. In designing and revising rate structures and in installing accounting and records systems, the aid of technicians can contribute significantly to the quality of financial management and periodic, independent audits by public accountants, well versed in municipal utility accounting, are indispensable.

Capital Financing. The long-term financing of the operations of a governmental enterprise may be carried out within the overall general obligation funding capacity of the government. However, attention to the value of revenue bonds is also a necessity to avoid the overloading of the general obligation debt pledge.

Organizational Patterns

Depending on the organizational makeup of the governmental unit itself the framework within which municipal enterprises are conducted varies.

A Utility Board. A frequently employed alternative to direct supervision (particularly in communities that do not employ professional managers) is to place the responsibility for operation of a governmental enterprise in an appointive board or commission. In some instances, an elective board is used. The appointive board device has numerous variations but, typically, it consists of three to five nonsalaried members, appointed by the chief executive or chief administrator (with, or without, the consent of the legislative body), for three- to five-year overlapping terms, with one member serving as chairman.

The essential functions of such a board include:

1. Appointment of a competent manager and delegation to him of full managerial authority
2. Approval of the budget and overall supervision of expenditures
3. Consideration, with the manager, of plans for system expansion and improvement and all major matters of general administrative policy
4. Acting as liaison between the manager, the chief executive, the general governing body, and the public.

While board control marks some diffusion of executive responsibility, it frequently has compensating advantages. If a board is composed of individuals who have influence in the community and understand the needs of the enterprise, it can be an effective means for securing careful planning, continuity of sound policies, public enlightenment, and cushioning against political interference. Conversely, a board which is a little more than the captive of the enterprise manager or largely subservient to political forces in the community offers little that is constructive and may act as the protector of unwise management practices.

Authorities. The use of public authorities to acquire, develop, and operate governmental enterprises has become a favored policy in some sections of the country. Typically, under this device, a municipal enterprise, instead of being given departmental status, is constituted as an independent or semi-independent governmental entity administered by an appointive board with broad powers to acquire, construct, and operate facilities, enter into contracts, issue debt, determine the operating organization and personnel, establish and collect charges, make regulations for the use of facilities, and the like. It is free to exercise these powers with little supervision, other than that implicit in the appointing (and perhaps removal) process. Having no taxing power, an authority must depend on user charges to pay its operating expenses, finance its improvements, and service its bonds—unless it is supported by contracts with, or grants from, governments with taxing powers.

Under some circumstances, these instrumentalities serve well. They provide self-supporting public facilities and services to areas that fail to coincide with any single, general-purpose government. For example, the Port of New York Authority, the famous American prototype of public authorities, furnishes certain transportation and terminal facilities to a port district lying in two states.

A Separate Department. A department for the operation of governmental enterprises, while it has specialized technical and business functions, is one of the components of an integrated governmental structure. There are opportunities for relationships between this and the other components that are mutually beneficial and also help to advance the general programs of the government. The first organizational requirement is the effective development of these relationships. Their scope depends, to a considerable extent, on the nature and size of the public enterprise. A small water system or electric or gas distribution system may be able to operate successfully only by using the part-time services of officers and employees in other divisions of the government; but, many sizable systems find it both workable and thrifty to use the services of the government's revenue department for the collection of revenues and custody of funds, the department of finance for accounting, the central purchasing division for the purchase of supplies, the personnel department for aid in recruitment, and the municipal attorney for handling routine legal matters. Enlarging the responsibilities of these central staff agencies, with appropriate sharing of costs, permits the employment of more highly qualified officials, the introduction of more efficient equipment, and more flexible use of personnel. For example, medium-sized cities are finding that, by centralizing data processing for their governmental and utility functions, they can afford to install electronic computers which, with little increase over previous expense, not only perform all billing, payroll, and accounting functions more efficiently but can also produce new and valuable statistical data for management purposes.

A governmental unit fails to get full value from ownership of a public enterprise unless its operations are well coordinated with those of functionally related departments and its policies and programs are geared to advance those of the municipal unit. Examples of this type of coordination include:

1. The installation of extensions and underground services in conjunction with new paving programs planned by the department of public works
2. A water system's development can be planned to provide better fire protection, attract industry, and help rationalize the pattern of development in a new area
3. The work of community planning is facilitated when the liaison arrangements between the planning director and the utility's managing officials are good

How to make a public enterprise an instrumentality for furthering the government's general social objectives as well as an efficient purveyor of a commercial service is answered, partly, by well integrated administrative organization but, even more, by the degree of perspicacity of the local government's chief administrative officer.

FISCAL ADMINISTRATION OF BASIC ENTERPRISES

Governmental enterprises are public businesses engaged in the furnishing of certain commodities and services. This characteristic needs clear recognition in their organization and management. Their efficient administration demands continuity of policy and direction, foresighted planning, technical skill, and business ability. In respect to these qualities, the requirements for high standards in governmental and private operations are identical. The sound management of governmental enterprises, however, involves additional considerations. They must be fitted into the general governmental structure so as to take full advantage of opportunities for efficiency and economy inherent in the relationship and their financial and their operating policies must be aligned with the general policies of the government for serving the community. To meet these standards, a system has to overcome such hazards as political pressures, bureaucratic inertia, vagaries of the voters, lack of the incentive provided by stockholder demands for more profits, and the more generous pay and benefit structures frequently associated with public operation. Some governmental enterprises more or less succumb to these handicaps; but, there are enough excellently managed systems to demonstrate that a high degree of competence is feasible.

The Financial Bases of Governmental Enterprises

Private enterprise, in undertaking any of these types of activities, must have profit as a primary objective and must earn a reasonable return on its investment. Governmental units usually have broader goals and more flexibility. To justify a government's undertaking of any enterprise, there must be the prospect of social gain for the community and the provision of some commodity or service to consumers on a user charge basis. In serving a community's social needs, it may be justifiable to operate an enterprise at a profit, on a service-at-cost basis, or at a deficit to be offset by other revenue.

Profit or Loss

Local governmental enterprise operations may be carried on at a profit, on a break-even basis, or at a loss. However, definitions of these concepts are in part contingent upon the precepts used. If, for example, one is making a comparison with a privately owned and operated enterprise the question arises as to how certain costs of operation will be treated. Before discussing the factors which account for these different bases of operation, it is appropriate to consider elements of cost which may be associated with the concepts of profit, break-even, and loss.

Costs Associated with Private Enterprise Operations. The costs which are associated with the conduct of a private enterprise may be grouped into the following categories:

1. *Direct costs.* The direct costs of operation are deemed to include the following:
   a. Materials and supplies used
   b. Service purchased, including rentals
   c. Salaries, wages, and fringe benefits
   d. Interest (at taxable rates)
   e. Depreciation upon capital investments
   f. Other operating and maintenance costs
2. *Taxes.* All taxes except income taxes are considered costs of doing business in the case of private ownership and operation. (Income taxes are not considered a cost of doing business inasmuch as they are a tax on net income, when earned.)

Costs Associated with Governmental Enterprise Operations. The costs associated with governmental enterprise operations are substantially the same as the above with these exceptions:

Interest Differential. Local government enterprises are able to secure the use of money at rates which reflect the tax-exempt status of income from such interest in federal income taxes and usually state and local government income taxes in the state of operation. This interest differential is substantial, especially in enterprises which are highly capital intensive.

Federal, State and Local Nonincome Taxes. Typically the local government enterprise is excused from most of the federal, state, and local taxes which would apply to privately owned and operated enterprises. Some excise taxes and some selective sales taxes are still payable by the enterprise operated by local governments where the tax is initially paid by others and passed on to the local government enterprise; in most instances however, we may consider that these taxes are not payable. (Of course, no income tax is payable by the local government enterprise.)

In the light of the foregoing, the question recurs as to the definition of what constitutes profitability for the enterprise operated by the local government.

Parity Between Private and Governmental Enterprises. If one is making a comparison between a privately owned and operated enterprise and a similar enterprise owned and operated by a local government, it appears that considerations of parity would require that the local government make provision for the payment of the same kinds of taxes and interest rates that would be payable by the private owner (except for income taxes). Only when this is done can there be a genuine comparison between the relative efficiency of private and governmental ownership and operation.

Unfortunately, it has not been customary in the United States to develop data for governmental enterprises which facilitate such comparisons. Claims are, therefore, made as to the lower costs of public ownership when in reality much of this is likely to be nonpayment of taxes or of interest rate differentials. Thus, a "profit" of a governmentally owned and operated enterprise may not even be sufficient to meet these differentials.

Excess of Earned Income Over Direct Costs. The customary concept of profit in governmental enterprises is a simple comparison between earned income and costs payable by the enterprise, without taking into consideration allowances for taxes or differentials in interest rates. Where income exceeds costs, there is deemed to be a profit.

If the statement of costs include a full allowance for *all* of the services rendered by the various governments to the publicly owned enterprise, perhaps this concept of profitability is admissible. However, it must include costs for police and fire protection, use of streets, costs of services rendered directly to the governmental enterprise, general overhead allocations, and all other costs to the sponsoring government. Even this may, however, act to deprive other governments—local, state, and federal—of income to which they would otherwise be entitled. Therefore, other taxpayers are being obliged to put up the funds which might appropriately be furnished by the governmental enterprise through an equitable assessment of taxes and differentials on interest costs.

The Basic Alternatives as to Profitability. In the light of the foregoing, it is feasible to develop four categories of profitability:

A. *Fully Financed, Plus Profit*
   This alternative corresponds most closely to the profitable privately owned and operated business. If the local government chooses this, it means that the earnings of the enterprise will have to be sufficient to pay all of the costs and to make provision for development of income sufficient to make in-lieu payments for taxes (excluding income taxes) and interest rate differentials. Beyond these, there will also be the requirement for earnings to provide profit as defined in private business.
   If this alternative is chosen, it is necessary to develop procedures for providing a decision-making process for the disposition of the earned net income, i.e., the excess of income over direct costs associated with governmental operation of the enterprise.

B. *Fully Financed Costs, Without Profit*
   This alternative is essentially the same as the previous one, except that the policy is to develop earned income sufficient to meet costs of operating the enterprise plus amounts equal to the taxes which would be

payable if the enterprise were privately owned. As in the foregoing alternative, there is a necessity for developing procedures for disposition of excess income.

C. *Self-Sustaining Operation*
This alternative calls for earnings substantially equal to the costs of operation. It provides for no payment of tax equivalents and no provision for interest rate differentials.

This is the alternative most frequently associated with "successful" governmental enterprise operations.

Once again it is emphasized that the failure of the governmental enterprise to make these payments results in higher requirements upon other citizens. There may be sufficient social or economic reasons to forego these kinds of payments; however, such forebearance should be undertaken with a full recognition of the general tax implications of this course of action.

D. *Operation Under Acknowledged Subsidy*
The final alternative in this group is the situation in which the earnings generated by the enterprise are not sufficient to meet the direct cost of operating the enterprise. There are many circumstances in which governments have, as a matter of public policy, developed or taken over from private enterprise certain services which cannot be operated at a profit, e.g., mass transit. In other situations, e.g., medical services, the decision may have been to operate at a loss either for all of the population or for the lower income groups.

Not all of these four alternatives are available for application to all kinds of services. Thus, in the case of mass transit, the choice in most communities during recent years has been only that of (a) subsidized mass transit or (b) no mass transit. Where the economic and social considerations permit application of Alternative "A", "B", and "C", those responsible for making the decision as to which of these will be used should make very deliberate decisions—not meander into a policy.

In the case of Alternatives "A" and "B", there is a question as to where the excess moneys will be directed. Of course, they could be paid over to the governments which would receive them under private operation; however, this is not likely to happen. Those controlling the enterprise are likely to make the decision as to the application of the excess moneys.

If the agency responsible for operation is a multi-purpose agency, the decision may well be to use the excess money to subsidize some other service, either permanently or during such time as necessary to get it onto its feet. One of the most widely known of this kind of operation has been the Port Authority of New York and New Jersey. From time to time during its half century of operations, excess earnings from the Hudson River crossings have been used to help finance water borne commerce facilities, airport facilities, transit facilities, bus terminals, and more recently, a World Trade Center.

Or, in the case of the City of Philadelphia, a "rental" of $15.5 million is annually required of the city owned Philadelphia Gas Works. This rental is paid to the general fund of the city for use in general support of local services. And, in the same city, recent policy has included a requirement for a payment to the city general fund from the water and sewer funds of an amount roughly equivalent to the property taxes which would be payable if these services were privately owned and operated.

Wherever a service is operated under the concepts involved in Alternatives "A" and "B" above, it is necessary to realize that the incidence of taxation being paid by the users of the service(s) involved may be different than that which would exist if the same funds were being raised through general taxation. Such a realization does not constitute a determinant in respect to whether or not such revenue should be raised; however, it imposes upon decision-makers the obligation to be aware of the considerations.

Efficiency, in its commonly accepted sense, relates to such factors as the technical competence and economy with which an enterprise is operated and maintained; but, it also concerns economic efficiency in the use of an enterprise's resources. Therefore, if a pricing policy, directed arbitrarily towards profit-making, places an uneconomical restriction on the use of a commodity or service, there may be a waste of resources. But, unless some external social gain is at stake, setting prices at a level below those which people are willing to pay may also be economically wasteful, if it impairs the prospects for an enterprise sustaining and developing its full potentialities.

Service-at-cost is often advocated as the ideal pricing policy for public enterprises. This undoubtedly is a good rule when a profit policy would cause wasteful under-utilization of an enterprise's productive capacity; but, it lacks general applicability because, considering the nature of a government as a sort of multipurpose consumers' cooperative, the user charges for a particular enterprise may be related to some broader purpose than financing its operation. Public pricing policies should permit the optimum use of a facility or service and also produce the optimum social benefit for the community. The pricing policy of a water system, for example, may waive potential profits in behalf of such objectives as better health, more dependable fire protection, encouraging the maintenance of green lawns in an arid climate, or stimulating economic development. Pricing policies, too, can be used to prevent waste or help limit the demand for a supply which is limited and not economically suitable for much expansion. The wise use of tolls and charges for bridges, tunnels, expressways, and parking facilities offers constructive alternatives to the endless diversion of valuable urban land to roadways.[8] Again, the elasticity of demand for a service such as transit may make operation on a self-supporting basis unfeasible. The origin of many municipal enterprises, in fact, resulted from their lack of financial attraction for private enterprise.

There is no inherent virtue in operating an enterprise at a loss, with the community subsidizing the users; but, a governmental unit may be justified in doing so if there is a compensating overall community gain. An airport may

---

[8] The potentialities for this pricing device are presented cogently by Lyle C. Fitch in "Financing Urban Roadways," *Financing Highways*, (Princeton, N. J.: Tax Institute, 1957), pp. 136-154.

have only a remote possibility of breaking even financially, yet it may contribute importantly to maintaining and improving a governmental unit's economic position as well as providing for the convenience of its citizens. A local government may be able to develop a well coordinated transport program which, although some of its facilities operate at a loss, enhances population growth, business expansion, and land values and affords a viable alternative to the excesses associated with freeway development. Such interrelation of governmental activities precludes valid comparison of public and private enterprises in terms of profits, but makes no less essential a municipality's need to know precisely to what extent it is subsidizing an enterprise, why it is doing so, whether the policy is well advised, and whether the general benefits compensate for the direct loss.

Regardless of whether a governmental enterprise operates at a profit, at cost, or at a deficit, the choice should be based on carefully determined policy and be subject to periodic review. But, before the responsible authorities and the people can make meaningful decisions, they must know the financial facts. Many governmental units lack such information, not only for minor enterprises but also for major utilities. Their financial records are so inadequate and misleading that an undertaking believed to be self-supporting may actually be subsidized, and one believed to be operating at a loss may be paying its way.

Among the primary elements of financial policy will be those relating to the choice of alternatives that have been discussed above. However, associated with these are other elements of financial policy that require resolution. Among these are the items discussed below.

One of the requisites in the case of enterprises which issue their own debt is the building of a satisfactory credit basis. Even where capital funds are provided by others, it is still essential that a suitable cash flow be developed in order to conduct operations in an orderly manner.

Financing Capital Costs

The problems involved in the financing of the capital costs of enterprises are likely to be considerably different than those in general public improvements. Two aspects are considered here: the building of a credit base and the financing of extensions.

Building a Credit Base. Capital improvements for a governmental enterprise may be financed partially on a pay-as-you-use basis, i.e., from current revenues and accumulated reserves, for two reasons. First, this policy helps to build a credit base which facilitates borrowing, when needed, at favorable interest rates. Second, it is economical in its saving of interest costs and, when used with discretion, it is beneficial to present as well as future consumers. On the other hand, if a pay-as-you-use basis in an inflationary economy should result in a zero, or even negative, effective interest rate, then it may be advisable to forego payments for capital outlays from current revenue.

Private enterprises depend heavily on bonds as a source of funds; but, to satisfy investors as to the security of the bonds issued they find it necessary to keep long-term debt at a ratio of from 50 to 60 percent of net plant value. For the remaining long-term financing requirements, they rely on equity capital (preferred and common stock) and, to a limited extent, reinvestment of earnings. If an enterprise earns a reasonable return on its investment, there will be a good margin to provide coverage for the debt service. Governmental enterprises, if they use revenue bonds, need an equivalent of equity capital to provide secure coverage for debt service; if they use general obligation bonds of the government, the utility should avoid having to rely on assistance from taxes. For governmental enterprises, moreover, coverage for debt service means provision not only for the payment of interest but also for the steady and fairly rapid retirement of principal—the latter not a common practice in privately owned enterprises.

This equivalent of equity capital for governmental enterprises is achieved primarily by creating a capital surplus through reinvestment of earnings and through amortization of costs at rates which exceed actual depreciation. The combination of depreciation and net income must be sufficient to cover the cost of well planned debt retirement and that portion of the cost of replacements, extensions, and improvements that can be scheduled on a proper basis. Under this policy, long-term borrowing is used only to finance relatively large and infrequently recurrent types of improvements.

The arguments are endless as to the relative desirability of pay-as-you-spend vs. pay-as-you-use. If one is to depend upon revenue bonds, the greater the equity developed in the facility, the more attractive the bonds and, therefore, the lower the relative interest costs. In addition, the accumulation of annual surpluses for reinvestment normally provides a steady flow of revenues to working capital reserves and also provides a cushion against physical or economic emergencies. Since governmental enterprises vary greatly in size, type, and capital demands, each enterprise will find it necessary to adjust this policy to fit its own circumstances; but, in most cases, because even routine capital requirements vary from year to year, the most satisfactory practice is to make regular annual contributions to a working capital reserve, which is then available to help finance the capital program as needed.

Financing Extensions. The financing of extensions to provide needed service in new localities within the service area of a public enterprise calls for a well-defined policy designed to keep the system self-supporting and to be fair to existing, as well as new, customers. In defining such a policy, a basic question is the extent to which the new customers or the developers should be required to aid in financing the cost of the extension. For regulated enterprises, it is a fundamental legal principle that, when the revenues anticipated from an extension are sufficient to cover operating expenses and support the enterprise's investment, the extension should be made without any special charge; but, when the anticipated revenues indicate a deficiency in such coverage, the enterprise may remedy the deficiency by such means as requiring contributions to aid construction, refundable advances, or guaranteed rates in excess of the generally established rate schedules. The finances of publicly owned electric and gas utilities are regulated by public service commissions in only a minority of states and those of municipal water utilities in only a few states; but, the general principle cited above concerning the financing of extensions (adapted to governmental enterprise conditions and standards) is applicable to all governmental enterprises in the interest of equity and financial stability. However, surpluses from the existing system should be sparingly used to finance extensions unless studies show increased use warrants such investments.

In practice, the systematic application of these principles in financing extensions has been more difficult to develop for water systems than for some other basic enterprises, partly because water extensions have the dual function of providing water service to consumers and contributing to public fire protection and other public purposes. Serving the latter purpose may involve larger mains, more storage, and greater pumping capacity than would otherwise be necessary —costs which should be, but very often are not, reflected fully in the water system's charge to the sponsoring government. For a number of years, a Committee on Water Main Extension Policy of the American Water Works Association has been studying the principles that should govern water main extension policies and has agreed on a few general principles which apply equally well to other enterprises. They are, in summary, that extension policies should be nondiscriminatory; should be based on business principles that assure a self-supporting status for extensions; should provide for customer participation in the financing if the anticipated revenue is insufficient to justify the enterprise's undertaking of the entire investment; and should be supported by carefully formulated rules which are subject to periodic review.

Although the management personnel of many governmental water systems attempt to observe these principles, the diversity in method and procedure is very great. Some systems depend on special assessments or front-foot benefit charges; some pay all of the capital costs and some pay none; many allow free main footage of 50 to 150 feet per customer but, beyond that, require deposits which are refundable to the extent that new customers are connected to the extension. An increasing number rely, primarily, on relating the amount of the investment to the anticipated revenue in determining the required refundable advance, rate surcharge, or installment contract, although the multiples used follow an extraordinarily wide range. Thus, in some states, where governmentally owned systems are subject to state financial regulation, the contribution required of new customers is minimized by charging one-half of the extension cost to fire protection; and there are numerous other variations or combinations of method. The AWWA Committee, consequently, has found it difficult to agree on precise rules; but, its reports go incisively into the problems involved, review and analyze the various policies in use, and emphasize that financing policies as regards extensions must be fair to both prospective and existing customers. To meet this objective, a system's investment in an extension—which must be recognized as including not only the cost of the extension itself but also the incremental cost of the supporting production, pumping, storage, and transmission facilities—should not exceed the amount that can be supported from the anticipated revenue.[9]

Service outside the corporate limits is a special phase of governmental policy regarding extensions that concerns a good many water systems, numerous sewage

---

[9] See Committee Reports on Water Main Extension Policy, *Journal American Water Works Association*, August, 1949 and November, 1964.

disposal systems, and some other utilities. The question of how to finance such extension needs to be dealt with in conjunction with other considerations in providing extraterritorial service, as explained later; but it may be noted here that the general principles covering extension financing within a utility's primary service area are also applicable to outside services.[10]

One of the most difficult tasks in operating any business is the development and maintenance of satisfactory pricing policies for the enterprise. If the enterprise is in direct competition with other similar enterprises, the market place can be depended upon to provide suitable guidance in most circumstances.

However, when one is engaged in an essentially monopolistic undertaking—whether privately or publicly owned and operated—the development and maintenance of prudent pricing policies should proceed largely out of accepted statements of principles covering the various facets of the problem. Yet, governmental ownership and operation implies a greater degree of public policy consideration than is likely to be present in privately owned and operated enterprises.

Of course, the choice of the base for operations set forth in the alternatives discussed earlier in this chapter will provide an initial determination of at least one of the major elements of pricing. But, even within the framework of the discipline imposed by the choice of one of the alternatives, there are a host of points at which decisions are required.

For example, in pricing a parking service, relatively low turnover may improve the profitability of the operation. But, there may be a competing objective of providing high turnover through relatively short duration parking. Thus profitability of the enterprise may have to be reduced in order to serve the larger economic objectives of increasing the amount of shopping and other short-term visits to the central core of the city.

Then there are various special interest constituencies that press for special treatment—the elderly, the low income groups, parents of school children, racial and other minority groups—by policy makers. Frequently these have sufficient political power or attractiveness to cause policy makers to give special treatment to them.

In general, it is wrong to adjust rates for such groups at the expense of other users of the same services. If the rates are to be adjusted to take into account special considerations, it appears desirable that the subsidies being granted be made up through appropriations from general revenue of the government rather than by differential rates among different groups of users of the same services.

If the financial viability of the enterprise is to be sustained, it is essential that the managers of the enterprise have the authority to make reasonable rates within the broad statements of principles laid down by the "parent" government.

Debt Management

The principles of municipal debt administration will be reviewed in Chapters 13, 14, and 15, but the more pertinent features of their application to long-

---

[10] A program report by the Committee on Water Main Extension Policy, "Water Service for Suburban Areas," *Journal American Water Works Association*, July, 1953, provides a useful analysis of the problem.

term borrowing for governmental enterprises need comment here. The acquisition of a governmental enterprise and its subsequent expansion and development commonly involve the issuance of bonds, thereby raising questions as to the most suitable borrowing medium and the most appropriate means of using it.

Borrowing for the Lowest Interest Costs. For a basic enterprise serving a genuine social purpose (one which is needed for the welfare of the community), the common sense policy is to use, where possible, the type of borrowing medium which will produce the lowest interest cost. If, for reasons of equity or necessity, an enterprise is designed to be subsidized from taxes, there obviously is no alternative to using bonds pledging the faith and credit of the government. But, when an enterprise is designed to be self-supporting, there are three general alternatives in use in the United States: (1) bonds pledging the faith and credit of the government, but serviced from the revenues of the public enterprise; (2) bonds pledging both the government's faith and credit and the revenues of the public enterprise; and (3) revenue bonds supported solely from the revenues of the enterprise.

Since the relative level of interest rates is mainly dependent on the quality of credit, revenue bonds are not automatically the most appropriate choice. If an enterprise is well established and has demonstrated ample and stable earning power, a municipality may be able to finance its capital needs with revenue bonds at interest rates which are as low as those it can obtain on general obligation bonds (perhaps even lower if the municipality's general credit happens to be mediocre). But, if an enterprise (1) is a new undertaking, (2) has earning power which is not well established, (3) has a margin of self-support which is narrow, or (4) falls short in other ways of achieving a good credit ranking, revenue bond interest rates may range upward accordingly—placing an undue expense on consumers and a needless handicap on the development of the enterprise. Under such conditions, the use of the government's general credit is the economical means of accomplishing a community purpose. And, even greater economy is sometimes feasible by pledging both the government's general obligation credit and the enterprise's earnings.

Because of the prevailing local bond laws, many governmental units do not have these alternatives available. The law may impose unduly severe limits on general obligation borrowing, set inflexible patterns for general obligation bond retirement that are unsuitable for financing public enterprises, or require authorization of such borrowing by a special majority popular vote which permits the defeat of a borrowing proposal by a relatively small minority of the voters. Launching a new enterprise is a matter of basic policy which, in many communities, should be decided by the people; but, once the undertaking is a going concern, the governing body of the community should be given wide discretion to approve bonds for expansion and improvement, as needed. If such decisions are left to the electorate, the prospects for continued adequate and dependable service can become precarious. For these reasons, the use of revenue bonds may be a necessity.

Without doubt, the use of revenue bonds has permitted a notable development of governmental enterprises which would not have been feasible under the antiquated bond laws that control general obligation borrowing by local governments in a majority of the states. Revenue bonds, through the contractual obligations entered into by local governments with bondholders, also have made a significant contribution to businesslike management of public enterprises in communities where such management was deficient. The typical revenue bond contract goes far towards fixing the enterprise's financial policies and requiring such administrative refinements as budgeting, the use of technical consultants and independent audits, and periodic financial reporting. So long as these contractual requirements are in accordance with sound financial management and planning, the bondholders quite understandably try to assure a quality of performance which the government should have been providing voluntarily.

However, some local government revenue bond contracts contain provisions which are detrimental to good financial administration, handicap the growth of the public enterprise, and impose needless costs upon the governmental unit. Among these are:

1. Imposition of conditions which flout standards of good accounting practice
2. Imposition of conditions prerequisite to the issue of additional bonds that severely inhibit the authority of the local government in making timely expansions of the system
3. Provision for the issue of term bonds with requirements for call of portions thereof in advance of maturity according to a rigid schedule, thereby causing the issuer to pay long-term interest rates at the top of the yield curve for money which is essentially short-term

In any event, the use of revenue bonds should involve the use of high grade financial advisory services which should be independent of potential bond buyers.

Regardless of the type of bonds issued, their terms should be tailored to fit the needs of the enterprise. To achieve this end, several principles need to be observed: (1) the life of the bonds should be long enough, without exceeding the periods of usefulness of the facilities financed, to allow retirement from earnings without overburdening the customers; (2) since the enterprise's need for borrowing is likely to be recurrent, the planning of each bond issue must keep the way open for successful planning and marketing of future issues; and (3) each bond issue needs to be planned so that the annual principal and interest requirements of the enterprise's debt structure, as a whole, relate to the prospective amount and trend of revenue available for repayment. There are no hard and fast rules for accomplishing this, since each operation has its own special problems arising from such factors as rate of growth, financial condition, purpose of the pending bond issue, and prospective borrowing requirements. For example, if a water system serving a growing community is financing a major source of supply with ample reserves for the future which will obviate further heavy borrowing over a long period, it is justified in planning a rising annual debt service for purposes of equity between present and future users as well as security. Such a policy would be untenable, however, if large future borrowings were in prospect.

Aids to Planning. Aids to planning a safe correlation of debt service and earnings, particularly when the prospective margin of safety threatens to be narrow, include the following:

1. Since the facilities financed by long-term borrowing ordinarily are designed to pay their way in added income from the enterprise, the accepted practice is to capitalize interest during construction

2. For the same reason, the initiation of bond retirement or amortization may properly be deferred until the newly financed facility is well established in its operation—failure to do this has plagued more than a few revenue bond-financed enterprises

3. Although term bonds usually require a higher interest rate than serial bonds, they are a safer medium than the latter for utilities lacking a demonstrated earning capacity and stability to meet fixed annual maturity requirements

4. Since borrowers must be able to plan the impact of bond issues on their annual budgets, they should beware of the types of multiple rate bidding for their bonds that can grossly distort debt service requirements

5. Finally, a goal of every governmental enterprise should be adherence to policies which will give it sufficient flexibility in planning its borrowing to take full advantage of prevailing market conditions at all times

Programming and Budgeting

The concepts discussed here are basic to the conduct of any activity and include an analysis of the total needs of any given service, a decision as to the level of service, and, finally, the application of cost estimates to each of these—for the next budget year and in succeeding years.

A Five-Year Program. A public enterprise always has to be ready to meet the reasonable demands within its service area for service that is adequate, dependable, and of good quality, and it has to do this without large development in advance of need, which imposes an undue charge on its present customers. Thus, it should keep forecasting its operating needs several years ahead and translating these into personnel, material, equipment, and capital facility requirements along with their attendant costs and means of financing. The responsibility for looking ahead varies in difficulty with the physical, social, and economic characteristics of the service area and with the nature of the supply problem.

Such forecasting needs to be in a long-term context, with imminent requirements formalized in a five-year program to be revised and extended annually, which, in turn, will contribute to the sound formulation of each annual budget. Enterprises responsible for the supply of water or electric power may have to extend planning much further into the future. What is called for is not only a capital program but also an operating program for the next five years in which the operating requirements help to define capital needs. Involved are long-term projections of demand and consumption, of revenues, and of the major classes of expenditures. Such projections facilitate the determination of priorities for improvement projects; maintenance of orderly replacement schedules weighing of alternate policies and lines of action; avoidance of deferred maintenance accumulations; review of rate structures, judicious apportionment of capital facility financing between surplus, reserves, and miscellaneous resources, on the one hand, and borrowing on the other; and foresighted preparation for borrowing. Such programming would require good property inventory and depreciation records and also close collaboration with the government's planning agency in matters such as land use projections. The initial long-term program and each annual revision should require review and approval by the governing body (council or utility board) well in advance of submission of the enterprise's annual budget so that the portions applicable to the current budget can be incorporated.

The Annual Budget. The general principles of budgeting discussed in Chapter 5 are applicable to governmental enterprises, provided due allowance is made for their commercial characteristics. The annual budget formalizes in a financial plan that portion of an enterprise's continuing program of operations and development which is to be performed in the ensuing fiscal year, and should be formulated and adopted before the beginning of the year. The plan must be comprehensive—covering both the operating (revenue and expense) and capital portions of the year's program. And, the process should be accompanied by a careful projection of cash flow on at least a monthly basis and, perhaps, a shorter time series.

The current operations section of the budget shows the estimated revenues, expenses, and profit or loss for the year. Strictly from the point of view of the governmental enterprise, it is highly desirable to maintain both revenues and expenditures on an accrual basis in order to produce meaningful profit and loss statements. However, to comply with the requirements of law governing local budget-making and accounting, it is sometimes also necessary to maintain budgetary accounts on either a cash basis or a modified-cash basis.

In the rather formidable task of estimating operating revenues, the general procedure is to estimate total consumption for each class of service on the basis of the recent trend in actual consumption and the various factors influencing the prospective trend; to multiply these totals by appropriate rates; and make suitable adjustments for noncollectibles. A simple (and, normally, a fairly satisfactory) method of determining such rates is to compute a weighted average rate for each class by dividing the revenues of each class in number of gallons, kilowatt-hours, or other like measure. Such special factors as rate changes, demand charges, and minimum charges may necessitate additional analysis. Nonoperating revenues—such as interest earned, merchandising income, and the like —while usually relatively minor, call for as precise estimation as possible.

On the expense side, the estimates cover operations, depreciation, the tax or tax equivalent, and interest. Purchases of fixed assets are not included in current expenses because they are charged as expense items as annual amounts of depreciation. Also, the retirement of debt is not an expense item since the assets thus financed are being paid for through the depreciation charges.

Estimating operating expense is not only a means of identifying the amount of revenue required but also an invaluable management tool for supervising performance, controlling costs, and evaluating results. The effectiveness of this instrument depends on the precision with which it is devised and the capability of the accounting system to provide the required data. The overall operation comprises a group of related functions, each of which is an identifiable area of responsibility and a cost center. (In any sizable system, each center is usually a specific responsibility of a subordinate of the manager). In a water system, for example, these components probably would be: source of supply, power and pumping, purification, transmission and distribution, accounting and collection of user charges, and general administration. When the costs for each of these centers for the last completed fiscal year are accumulated and analyzed, it is clear that they divide into fixed costs and variable costs—the former directly affected only by major changes in the volume of consumption but the latter varying proportionately with the volume of consumption. When the combined variable costs for each cost center are placed on an appropriate measurement unit basis, they provide the means (combined with fixed cost data) for translating the forecast of production and consumption into estimated expense. By comparison with an enterprise's own past performance and the performance of other enterprises, fixed and variable unit costs can be developed and refined as standard unit costs—dependable yardsticks for budget-making and supervision.

If the revenue and expense section of the budget shows an anticipated surplus, the budget plan should include provision for its assignment to established reserves for working capital, debt retirement, and capital improvements—to the extent that such reserves are necessary to maintain financial stability and carry out the long-range program. If surplus is thus earmarked in the balance sheet, instead of being shown entirely as free surplus, there is considerable protection against political inroads on the earnings of the public enterprise. If surplus accumulation should exceed the requirements of the program, consideration of rate reductions is in order.

The capital section of the annual budget deals with the receipts and expenditures related to (1) new borrowing and the retirement of debt and (2) the construction or acquisition of fixed assets. With respect to debt, this section shows all debt to be issued during the year; the serial bonds to be retired during the year; in the event there are term bonds outstanding, the amount to be paid to retirement or sinking funds; and the amount and sources of funds to be provided for these purposes. With respect to fixed assets, this section of the budget shows the portions of major construction projects (provided for in the long-term program) to be carried out in the budget year, the minor additions, extensions, renewals, and replacements to be constructed, and the machinery and equipment to be purchased. The budget should show the overall cost for each undertaking with a supporting schedule providing such relevant data as the cost of labor and materials and other costs. In each instance, it should also show the source of funds for payment, (such as bond proceeds, surplus, special reserves, depreciation, etc.) and the estimated operating cost of the new, or expanded, facility.

Cash Flow Analysis. Supplementing its annual budget plan, an enterprise needs what some authorities call a cash budget,[11] namely, a forecast of cash

---

[11] Tenner, Irving, *Financial Administration of Municipal Utilities*, (Chicago: Public Administration Service, 1947), pp. 39-40.

receipts in relation to cash requirements for each month of the budget year. Anticipation that the annual revenue total will equal or exceed the annual expense total offers no assurance that cash receipts during the year will synchronize with disbursement requirements. On the one hand, service requirements have more or less seasonal fluctuations, there is always a time lag between the earning of revenue and its billing and collection, and miscellaneous receipts may follow an uneven time pattern. On the other hand, fixed charges and regularly scheduled requirements, such as payrolls, have specific payment dates; and, in its purchase of material and supplies, an enterprise will want to take advantage of discounts for prompt payment. To avoid delay in the payment of bills or the need for temporary borrowing and to make and take advantage of opportunities for temporary investment of idle cash, an enterprise should project its anticipated cash receipts at least by months; plan its disbursements, so far as feasible; and, through these means, take advantage of flexibility in its maintenance and purchasing programs in order to match the availability of cash supplemented by a sufficient working cash balance carried over from the previous year to avoid any cash stringency.

10

The Treasury Functions

For our purposes, the primary treasury functions are deemed to be:
1. Receipt for deposit of money paid to the city
2. Custody of money and securities of the government or supervision of any such custodial activities performed by others
3. Disbursement of moneys of the government upon proper authorization
4. Investment of available moneys

Whereas the foregoing constitutes a basic list of the principal treasury functions, it is not intended as a comprehensive listing of the functions which may be assigned to the officer bearing the title of "City Treasurer." The title itself is sometimes used to designate the principal finance officer—who has responsibility for the full gamut of financial functions, excluding postaudit. Attention here is focused upon the four functions mentioned above.

RECEIPT AND DEPOSIT

A few decades ago it was customary physically to remit most of the funds collected by the many offices, departments, and agencies of a city government to the city treasurer, who entered items of receipt into his accounts. His clerks counted all the money, prepared deposit slips, and then carried the money to depository banks.

Some city treasurer's offices still operate in this manner; however, the wide use of checks and branch banking and the development of separate departments and offices to specialize in revenue administration, together with advances in data processing, have acted to provide bypasses to the treasurer's physically handling the bulk of receipts in many local governments.

Even so, many transactions involving payments from other governments still flow through the treasurer's office.

Regardless of the manner in which the moneys actually reach depository banks, the great bulk of them is deposited in the accounts for which the treasurer has responsibility. Good financial administration requires that funds received by any unit of the government promptly pass to the treasurer's control

191

in order that responsibility can be more easily established, accounting improved, and performance of other treasury functions facilitated. Thus, even if deposits are made by other departments and agencies to bank accounts maintained by the treasurer, it is essential that notice of deposit (by deposit slips or otherwise) be furnished immediately to the treasurer in order that he may maintain a correct official record of deposits and maximize the use of funds.

Timely Deposit

To the extent feasible, all items should be deposited on the day of receipt in order that these moneys may be credited to the account of the local government as promptly as feasible.[1]

Further gains in time can be acquired by pre-sorting large checks according to the banks on which they are drawn and depositing all such local checks only in the bank on which they are drawn—usually saving one or more days for clearance. Also, when large payments are received in the form of checks on out-of-town banks, the use of special messengers is sometimes warranted to accelerate payment. When interest on short-term deposits is at five percent, the average worth of a business day per million dollars is $200. Thus, if a large check for $2,500,000 is received payable across the state, the normal delay in payment is two business days—or a value of $1,000. It may be worth having the bank send a messenger by airline to secure immediate payment.

It is the responsibility of the treasurer to keep all officials alerted to the importance of prompt handling and/or deposit of all checks which come to them for the government. Moreover, the treasurer should prescribe procedures under which he is notified immediately of deposits by other officials when these deposits are of such size as to be significant in his treasury management procedures.

CUSTODIAL FUNCTIONS

The treasurer has important custodial functions relating both to cash and to securities. The cash for which the treasurer is ultimately responsible consists of six kinds:

1. *On Hand:* This is currency, checks, and other forms of evidence of money in the hands of the treasurer which are immediately available for deposit

2. *Demand Deposit Accounts:* Ordinarily, this is money shown by the books of the city as being on demand deposit each day

3. *Temporary Investments:* The daily "cash" balance as shown by the treasurer's daily statement is likely to include both demand cash and cash invested in time deposits and repurchase agreements

4. *Imprest Funds:* Cash in change funds for cashiers

---

[1] To accelerate the processing of checks by the bank, the City of Philadelphia instituted the practice of doing its own encoding as to the dollar amount of the checks. Although the cost to the city is considerable, the aggregate added yield in interest (amount $175,000 per year) is far greater than the costs.

5. *Petty Cash Funds:* Money that has been segregated into petty cash funds held by either the treasurer or other officers or employees of the government which can be used in limited amounts for specified purposes
6. *Long Term Investments:* Usually restricted to pension funds in local governments

The treasurer may also be responsible for maintaining money belonging to others, such as the reserves required to be maintained under revenue bond indentures or under other trust arrangements, or, occasionally, cash held in escrow arrangements in litigation.

Whatever the form of money, the treasurer is likely to have responsibility for the safekeeping of the money, even though it may be deposited with others. His responsibility for safekeeping is not discharged, in most jurisdictions, merely by the deposit of moneys in banking institutions since he is ordinarily responsible for seeing to it that suitable collateral is posted to provide a guarantee for the safety of the moneys, as required by law.

Custody of Securities

The custody of securities owned by the government as investments, or held as collateral, plus other securities held by the treasurer due to his ex officio membership on various public boards and commissions, frequently constitutes a significant responsibility of the treasurer.

Access to the securities should be tightly controlled, whether the securities are held in the treasury vaults or in bank safety deposit facilities to which the treasurer has access. No one person should have control of the securities, even the treasurer himself. If the law does not require that a co-signer be present when the security vault is opened, the treasurer should make such a rule himself.

Many securities are fully negotiable, i.e., they may be sold by the bearer. To minimize the holding of negotiable securities, the treasurer should insist upon registered instruments when available, with registration in the name of the government—not in the name of the treasurer or other officer.

An alternative to providing custody by the treasurer is an arrangement with one of the commercial banks in the community, under properly formulated agreements. Under many such agreements, the treasurer may never see the securities themselves. The bank acting as trustee maintains possession, providing the treasurer with appropriate trust receipts. The bank can also arrange for collection and deposit of interest.

The treasurer's records should contain a complete list of all securities, arranged according to the funds to which they belong. Other records should show the maturity dates of all securities, arranged in the date sequence so that timely action may be taken to reinvest the proceeds available upon the date of maturity of the securities. The treasurer's records should also show the dates and amounts of interest due, again arranged in date sequence for ease in handling the proceeds when available. The chief finance officer should maintain somewhat similar records, especially as to due date, in order that he may exercise appropriate supervision and control.

Facilities for Custody

In earlier times, much of the money and securities held by the treasurer was kept in the safe or vault in his office. With the expansion of commercial banking functions, the modern treasurer is likely to maintain money as deposits; securities are likely to be held either in the vaults of banks or by banks under trustee agreements. Indeed, for many city treasurers, the largest amount of cash actually maintained is his own petty cash fund—and this likely to be kept by one of his clerks.

The maintenance of securities in banks may be in safe deposit facilities under (1) the control of the treasurer, (2) the joint control of the treasurer and some official of the government, (3) joint control with a designated officer of the bank, or (4) contracts executed with one or more banks under which they hold securities in trust for the treasurer.

In almost all circumstances where banks or other institutions are used to facilitate the performance of the functions of the treasurer, the responsibility for selection of the institutions to be used rests either wholly, or partially, upon the treasurer. And, he is usually responsible for ascertaining that suitable security arrangements are maintained and that banks perform obligations undertaken for the treasurer.

Security for Local Government Deposits

Deposits of local governments are usually limited to the banks which are willing to provide acceptable collateral—usually in the form of some mix of federal, state, and local government securities. The amounts of such security are usually determined by the par value of the securities, rather than their market value. In some instances, the amount of security is equal to the maximum deposit (demand, time and certificates of deposit)[2] in the institution, sometimes at more than the maximum deposit, and sometimes at a percentage less than the full amount of the deposits.

The rapid decrease in market value of low coupon debt securities during the 1974 tight money market demonstrated that the local government is fully protected in collateral if it demands market value, rather than par value in posting of collateral.

This practice has been the subject of much controversy over the years, especially between the banks and public officials. In a very realistic way, the practice has the effect of establishing a preferential position for the governmental depositor, in case of problems of liquidity in the banking institution. Accordingly, the private depositor (except for one covered by deposit insurance) is obliged to shoulder much greater risks than the governmental depositor.

Changes, from time to time, in the amount of the deposits of local governments have the effect of requiring banks to modify their security holdings

---

[2] Although many governments consider a certificate of deposit as equivalent to a time deposit, a certificate of deposit is actually a security held by the purchaser. It is not a deposit, as such.

which qualify as collateral. An act of the Pennsylvania General Assembly (Act 72 of 1971) provides that a bank, unless otherwise instructed by a public body, may pledge assets to secure all public deposits on a pooled basis in order that the total amount of the assets pledged is at least equal to the total amount of such assets required to secure all the public deposits of the bank.

New approaches have been taken recently by several states. For example, the State of Washington in 1969 created a Public Deposit Protection Commission which administers collateral requirements for the state and all local governments. Under the new procedure each participating bank must deposit with the Commission collateral equal to 5 percent of all public funds on deposit with it. In case of default by a participating bank, all participating banks are assessed to cover the loss in proportion to their public fund deposits—to a maximum of 5 percent of such public fund deposits.

Many students of the problem believe that no priority should be given to governmental depositors. Yet, local officials are very reticent to give up this protection against possible loss. They generally take the position that if a bank fails, the public official who made the deposit may be subject to major criticism— even though the official has no means of determining that the default was imminent. Moreover, local government treasurers are frequently subject to pressures from local banks to maintain all of their deposits in these banks. Where there are several local banks, the pressures are for spreading the deposits among all these banks. Again, the local official finds it difficult to differentiate between the quality of security offered by different banking institutions. Therefore, he seeks to take refuge in the requirement for full protection through marketable collateral.

The problem is a difficult one and has been the subject of different approaches by the legislatures of the several states. Some of the states have undertaken state guarantees of such deposits, thereby relieving the local government of all, or substantial portions, of the risk.

Reconciliation of Bank Statements

One of the important, although largely clerical, custodial functions of the treasurer is the periodic balancing of bank statements with statements of fund balances. Once again, as the size of the local government increases, the procedures involved in this process become more complex and time consuming. However, such complexities and time requirements do not abrogate the treasurer's responsibility to make appropriate reconciliations at stated intervals— monthly with respect to most accounts.

Various techniques are available to facilitate this procedure. One of these is the establishment of a separate bank account for each payroll period. Another is to establish separate accounts to handle each month's general disbursements. Moreover, one can arrange with the banks to perform a major portion of the routine work associated with bank account reconciliation.

DISBURSEMENT OF FUNDS

The magnitude of disbursements for payroll and other purposes is now so great that in all, except the smallest, local governments the disbursement activity has reached a highly routinized and even highly automated state.

In the more sophisticated systems, for routine disbursements, e.g., paychecks, the treasurer may do little more than to lend his signature plate to the automated processing unit which affixes his facsimile signature to the checks. In larger transactions, the treasurer or his employees may operate the signature machines; and, in the largest transactions, the treasurer may personally sign the check or other form authorizing disbursement.

Responsibility Continues

Regardless of the extent of automation or routinization, the treasurer is still responsible for ascertaining that each disbursement is in response to a proper authorization by the officer performing the preaudit responsibilities or by proper order of another authority, e.g., the courts. Funds disbursed in the absence of such authorization constitute illegal disbursements. The treasurer (or his employees or agents) should be held strictly accountable for lapses from the proper performance of their duties in this regard.

Not only must the treasurer himself act with integrity but he must also see to it that a proper system exists for full protection of public funds—and that the system works as intended.

Form of Disbursement

Currently, most disbursements are in the form of checks drawn on banks. In earlier times, it was customary for the preaudit official to issue a warrant which, strictly speaking, was an authorization to the treasurer to make payment to the person named in the warrant. Gradually, the warrant became a negotiable document, and the holder of the warrant frequently deposited it with his bank to arrange for collection. The warrants were gathered by the bank at the end of the day and presented to the treasurer who drew a check to the bank for the aggregate amount of the warrants which had been presented.

Eventually, this practice was supplanted by the use of the "warrant-check" which might be in two parts, with the preaudit officer signing the warrant portion and the treasurer signing the check portion. The warrant portion was detached by the treasurer who, thereupon, signed the check and issued it to the payee. With the increase in volume, especially of payrolls, the practice in many jurisdictions has become one in which the accounting office prepares the voucher and a draft of the warrant (or order to pay). If the preaudit office finds the voucher in order, it is returned to the accounting office which mechanically (from the same tape or other data processing medium) prepares the check and furnishes it to the treasurer along with the order to pay.

For the Future

New procedures are now being used experimentally, insofar as payroll and some other types of payment are concerned. They involve elimination of the check as an instrument of payment. In lieu thereof, upon proper authorization of the payee, the amounts due him are credited to his account by the bank upon order of the treasurer. The bank then advises the payee of the credit to his account.[3]

The whole purpose is to provide for the simplification of banking and accounting procedures. Although this procedure is not yet being generally used by local government, adaptations will doubtless be made in the handling of local government transactions both in the collection of amounts due to the local government and in selected kinds of payments.

PLANNING CASH MANAGEMENT

One of the most challenging activities associated with the treasury function is the planning of the ways and means to harness cash flow so that it makes its maximum contribution to financial management. The first step lies in forecasting cash income and cash outgo for the period ahead. For operating funds, the period under consideration is likely to be the fiscal year; however, in many circumstances, projections for operating funds may need to extend substantially into, or through, the succeeding fiscal year.

For capital funds, the period of projection may be for a matter of a few months; however, in most circumstances, it should extend for a considerably longer period in order for the treasurer to be able to plan for the availability of cash to meet requirements and to plan for interim investments.

For trust and agency funds, the periods of projection will vary from a few months to long periods of years. For sinking funds, if entrusted to the treasury for full or partial management, the period under consideration may be that of each bond issue for which sinking funds or reserve funds are required.

Projecting Receipts and Outgo

A first step is to make projections of the times when each element of cash receipt is likely to be realized during the fiscal year. This may be in terms of months for smaller governments; for larger governments, projecting receipts on a weekly (or even a daily) basis is indicated—at least for the period of the fiscal year. As the period stretches out into years, projection on the basis of monthly periods is sufficient for the early years, and projection on a semiannual basis is sufficient for the later years.

---

[3] The city of Wichita uses such a system. Another system currently in use is advanced authorization by individuals to utility companies and others to cause withdrawals to be made from time to time from the account of the debtor on demand by the utility or other firm. It is doubtful that this procedure will be utilized soon by local governments.

On the outgo side, projections for similar time periods are appropriate. Due account must be taken of periodic payments, e.g., payrolls, debt service payments, and payments to pension and retirement funds. Consideration should also be given to requirements for routine expenses as well as extraordinary expenses, e.g., the time of payment for a large purchase, such as the automotive fleet.

Expenses for public works projects frequently follow a pattern; however, this is different for different kinds of public works projects and may also vary due to unforeseeable situations, such as work stoppages.

Comprehensive estimates of cash receipts and outgo need to be supported by detailed estimates for each significant category of receipt and expense. Although many governments rely on aggregate amounts, more detailed supporting estimates are important in order to project accurately the probable cash balances to be on hand and to be required in order to meet obligations promptly as they fall due.[4]

Projections of receipts and outgo must be revised at least monthly in light of changing conditions—at least for short-term forecasts of up to two years.

When the cash flow has been well forecast, the forecast provides an indispensable tool for determining the need for, and timing of, revenue anticipation loans as well as investment programs—both temporary and long-term.

Therefore, the 12-month forecast of cash flow and cash balances must be revised each month in light of changing conditions as the budget year progresses. Forecasting is a major tool in helping the treasurer meet the following cash flow and cash utilization responsibilities:

1. To have sufficient cash available when it is required. If borrowing is necessary, the need for arrangement of loans can be anticipated in order that the cash proceeds will be on hand when needed.

2. To plan the cash stream so as to minimize and, if possible, to eliminate the necessity for short-term borrowing.[5]

3. To assure that any excess of cash income over cash outgo, not required as a working balance, is temporarily invested. The goal is

---

[4] The League of California Cities, *Treasury Cash Management and the Investment of Idle Funds*, April, 1956, 16 pp. In this publication dealing with cash flow and balances, the League recommended seven procedural steps and five useful forms. The schedules illustrated were: an analysis of monthly receipts and disbursements by fund over a 12-month period; an analysis of monthly receipts (by source) and disbursements (by major category) in the general fund for a 12-month period; a factor analysis sheet for each revenue source by months for three years, together with a 3-year moving average; an annual projection sheet for revenues (by source and in total) for three months in advance; and a contractor's estimated payment schedule by months over a 12-month period. This publication was reproduced in part by the Advisory Commission on Intergovernmental Relations in *Investment of Idle Cash Balances by State and Local Governments*. (Washington, D. C.: United States Government Printing Office, January, 1961), Appendix E.

A more recent publication is of interest here. John A. Jones and S. Kenneth Howard in *Investment of Idle Funds by Local Governments: A Primer* (Chicago: Municipal Finance Officers Association, 1973), 48 pp., have set forth important guidelines for local finance officers in this field.

[5] Although conventional wisdom calls for avoidance of short-term borrowings, the opportunity for earning interest at rates in excess of the rates payable cannot be overlooked.

optimum investment of idle cash and bond proceeds so that investment earnings can make an important contribution to the budget. One test of efficient financial administration is the ability to "put cash to work." The better the cash forecast, the longer the time frame of the investment; the longer the investment, the greater the rate of interest in most circumstances.

4. To schedule the investment of bond proceeds to meet the periodic demands of contractors as construction progresses since bonds must often be sold in full prior to letting the contract.

Good forecasting is, however, only the first background step essential in harnessing the cash stream. Over a period of time, much can be done to synchronize the collection calendar and the dates for large payments since good cash flow estimates also become a basis for determining whether the schedule for taxes and other payments due to the government is appropriate. In many instances, the government may have little option as to the scheduling of income; however, acting separately or in concert with other municipalities, officials can seek to have laws or administrative practices changed with a view to improving the cash flow from the standpoint of the local government.[6]

Consolidated Cash Accounts[7]

One of the greatest aids to effective cash management is the consolidated account, i.e., the system under which cash belonging to various funds is commingled into a single bank account—with entitlement to the various portions of the cash being reflected in the fund accounts of the local government.

There are some potential adverse effects of the use of consolidated cash accounts, e.g., the use of assets of one member fund to cover (temporarily) deficits of other member funds; however, if the rules are carefully developed and administered, these adverse situations can be controlled.

Planning cash management requires imagination and a positive attitude toward cash flow and cash use. If synchronization necessitates changes, long hours of staff study and negotiation may lie ahead before the support of policymakers is forthcoming. The time is long past when the treasurer can easily resort to a passive role, concentrating only on the receipt of cash as it happens

---

[6] As noted elsewhere, in the course of determining new schedules for payments to the local government, consideration must be given to the relative advantages to be gained by the local governments in accelerating the cash flow in contrast to the impact upon the persons who are to make the payments. Thus, given the favorable terms that are available to local governments through negotiating tax-free temporary loans, the advantages of accelerated payment to the municipality need to be considered in light of the impact of costs upon individuals and businesses that may be obliged to secure short-term loans at higher rates of interest in order to make the payments to the government according to the revised schedules.

[7] From a fund point of view, the consolidated cash account is only one account; but, from the treasurer's point of view, it is necessary to have a consolidated account at every bank even if just a minimal amount of money is kept in each account. The reason for this is to expedite the deposit of large receipts of money which was explained earlier. The deposit of the check in the bank upon which drawn makes the funds good that day.

to occur and the custody and protection of funds. In a sense, he is the banker of the local government. As such, his responsibility extends to maximizing net cash balances and earnings to be derived from the timely and correct investment of these balances.

Maintaining Knowledge of Collected Bank Balances

Essentially, the treasurer's statement must be issued in a form which reflects the balances shown in his books, i.e., a book balance, rather than a bank balance. The actual amounts of funds available to the treasurer for investment are those shown on the daily position statement as carried in the bank's books, adjusted for items of deposit which have not yet cleared the banks upon which they are drawn. These bank balances are referred to as "collected balances."

For example, a deposit of $700,000 may be made on February 1 for $300,000 principal and $400,000 interest on five series of bonds. As bonds and coupons are paid from time to time, the balance in the paying agency's account will be reduced, for example, to $30,000.

Several questions are then raised. Does the balance represent unpaid bonds or unpaid coupons and how much of each? Which bonds and which coupons have not been paid? Have the bonds and coupons been examined to verify that they were the bonds and coupons of the city and that they were the items due at this time? Occasionally, a verification of the accounts and a check of actual items unpaid will reveal overdeposits in the paying agency or that bonds or coupons have been charged in error to the city's account.

The paying agency balance should not be assumed to be correct without audit, nor should an unusual or continuing balance in the account be overlooked. The money in the paying agency account belongs to the public body that made the deposit, and, if there is a permanent balance representing bonds and coupons lost or destroyed and never presented, the depositing local government has the right either to use of the money for investment or, perhaps, even to withdrawal of the money—depending upon provisions of the laws of the state.

The treasury faces another situation when bonds and coupons are payable both at the office of the city treasurer and at the city's fiscal agent bank (or banks). In such cases, the local banks usually pay the bonds and coupons presented directly to them and charge the amounts to the proper account of the treasury. Coupons paid at a distant financial center, e.g., New York, are reimbursed daily by a correspondent bank of the government whose bonds and coupons are being paid; the paid bonds and coupons come to the local correspondent bank which, in turn, collects from, or through, the city treasury. Many variations of this practice occur.

The paying agent is entitled to a fee for handling bonds and coupons. Sometimes the "float," or balance, in the account is large enough to compensate the bank, especially when a deposit is made in full before the payment date. Sometimes, it is too large, and investment of a part of the "float" is warranted. However, when the bonds and coupons are paid only by daily reimbursement, a fee must be agreed upon and reviewed periodically.

SHORT-TERM LOANS

One of the elements of treasury management is to have cash on hand to meet requirements for disbursements as they occur. Ordinarily, if the cash flow situations provide heavy amounts of income early in the year, no problem is encountered. However, for those local governments having the reverse situation, it is usually necessary to secure short-term loans to provide ready cash in anticipation of the receipt of revenues later in the year.

The responsibility for planning the short-term loan program usually devolves upon the treasurer or one of the assistants to the chief finance officer. The choices in the timing of short-term loans are:

1. Issuance of tax or revenue anticipation notes as cash is needed and repayment of these notes as receipts permit
2. Issuance of the tax or revenue anticipation notes in large amounts near the beginning of the fiscal year and repayment near the end of the year, preferably with payments to a trustee as cash flow permits —with investment of the cash by the trustee for the benefit of the issuer government.

In pursuing the first course, local governments are able to hold down the gross amount of interest paid to a minimum. However, a local government can frequently secure the funds it needs at a lesser net interest cost by pursuing the second course, providing it has an aggressive program for the investment of the balances temporarily on hand.

In the arrangement of short-term loans, the smaller local governments are usually restricted to negotiation with local banks; larger local governments also have the alternative of public sale of revenue anticipation notes in the general market.

Closely associated with the short-term loan program for operating purposes is the need for short-term loans issued in anticipation of the sale of bonds. This is considered in a later chapter.

SHORT-TERM INVESTMENTS

One of the treasurer's major responsibilities is the investment of available cash.

More than a responsibility, it is a positive *duty* of the treasurer to secure from investments the last dollar of income that is earnable by the cash at his disposal—consistent, of course, with maintaining balances sufficient to compensate banks for services rendered and protecting security of funds.

The program of investment calls for aggressive planning with respect to the availability of cash balances, as has been discussed in a preceding section. In the absence of such planning, no treasurer can maximize the returns to the city from the investment program that is his responsibility.

The program of investment initially requires a decision concerning the pattern under which the banks will be compensated for their services in receiving and collecting items of deposit, in paying funds, in sorting checks, in providing bank account reconciliation services, in acting as paying agent for bonds and interest thereon. The bank should be considered as a service institution. Pricing arrangements for each of the services performed by the bank should be the subject of negotiation between the local government and its depository and paying banks. The cost to the bank together with a reasonable profit on transactions handled should be the subject of positive determination through joint conferences between the bank(s) and the treasurer.

The decision as to how the bank should be compensated, i.e., through compensating balances or by direct payment, is a separate decision. It may be appropriate to pay the bank by use of compensating balances; or, it may be more appropriate to compensate the bank through direct payment of a service fee. Until comprehensive analyses of the differential effects of the two methods, or a combination of the two methods, has been made, it is inappropriate to come to any conclusion. Moreover, the conclusion which is appropriate under one set of conditions may not be appropriate under another set of conditions, e.g., the 1970 tight money market vs. the comparatively easy money market of mid-1972.

Once the decision has been made concerning the extent to which compensating balances are required, good cash flow projections provide a basis for determining the longest period of time to be used in temporary investments. Under most conditions, the longer the period of investment, the greater the rate of interest return. Accordingly, it is desirable that investments—both short-term and long-term—be made for as long a period which may be considered safe.[8]

The major sources of cash available for investment on a short-term basis are:
1. Revenues realized in advance of the need for disbursement
2. Differentials between the proceeds of revenue anticipation loans or bond anticipation notes and immediate requirements
3. Proceeds of long-term bonds which are issued in advance of the time at which payments for capital purposes are required[9]

Each of these situations offers opportunities for earning interest, even when the balances are available for only a few days or weeks.

In the planning and execution of the investment program, the treasurer may have substantial latitude in terms of the type of securities purchased. Ordinarily, short-term investments should be made in securities which will

---

[8] Where the law permits, loans in anticipation of the issuance of long-term debt may prove less expensive than the initial issuance of the bonds, after due allowance for the interest to be derived from the short-term investment.

[9] Except in periods of very high short-term interest, e.g., mid-1973, the short-term rates are considerably lower than long-term rates. Therefore, it is not advisable to issue long-term debt substantially in advance of the need for funds.

mature as close as possible to the date on which the funds are needed. If the investments are of high liquidity, e.g., United States Treasury bills, there will be little problem in selling them even if the need arises for disposition prior to their maturity date. However, when maturity is beyond the date on which the cash is needed, one assumes the normal risks involved in changes in the interest market. Disposition of securities maturing at a date considerably in the future may be accompanied by losses, if the market has moved to significantly higher interest rates than those prevailing at the time of the original investment.

Among the factors to be considered in all investments are the matters of: safety of principal, liquidity, and yield anticipated.

Types of Short-term Investments

The principal types of short-term investments available to local governments are:

1. *Time Deposits:* The time deposit is a particularly attractive means of investment for the smaller units of government that lack the staff resources to make adequate evaluation of the other forms of short-term investment.

2. *Certificates of Deposit:* The certificate of deposit is basically an investment even though styled as a "deposit," however, the period of time for which the investment is being made is specified and subject to restrictions concerning liquidations in advance of the specified term. The difference between a certificate of deposit and a time deposit at a commercial bank are: (1) a certificate of deposit from a commercial bank is marketable; and (2) it is represented by a certificate of deposit which is negotiable. A time deposit, on the other hand, is evidenced by a receipt which is not negotiable and must be held to the end of the agreed-upon period of deposit.

3. *United States Treasury Bills:* United States Treasury bills are normally issued for periods of 91 or 182 days, with some issues running as long as a full year. These bills bear no stated interest rate. They are initially sold and subsequently traded at discount rates which determine their actual rates of return. The bills can be purchased or sold on any day in the market. Because such bills are offered frequently, one can ordinarily find maturities substantially conforming to the desired maturity date for his investments. Their complete security and liquidity provide attractive features. Because of their liquidity, one can usually purchase them from banks with an agreement for repurchase in a given number of days at a stated price, or yield. This makes the bills excellent for overnight, or other very short-term, investment.

4. *United States Treasury Certificates:* Treasury certificates of indebtedness are usually issued with a maturity of one year. These are not

quite as liquid as Treasury bills; therefore, one should normally purchase them with a view to holding them until maturity.

5. *United States Treasury Notes:* Treasury notes are normally issued with a maturity of not less than one year and not more than five years. The notes offer a good form of investment for bond proceeds where bonds are issued substantially in advance of the dates upon which cash is to be required.

6. *United States Government Bonds:* Treasury bonds are normally issued with an initial maturity of five or more years. Of course, as in the case of other federal securities, one may be able to find that which he needs, in terms of maturity, available from the supply in the market issued several months, or years, previously.

7. *Federal Agency Securities:* A wide range of federal agencies offer both short-term and long-term securities in the form of notes, debentures, consolidated notes or debentures, and certificates of indebtedness. Among the agencies with issues quoted on the market are: the Federal National Mortgage Association, the Home Loan Banks, the Federal Land Banks, the Intermediate Credit Banks, Banks for Cooperatives, the United States Public Housing Administration, and the International Bank for Reconstruction and Development. Yields for the same periods of time vary from security to security, and the investor may make his choice of those available in light of his requirements.

8. *Short-term Municipal Securities:* Although short-term municipal securities (i.e., notes of states and their governmental instrumentalities as well as municipal bonds about to mature) offer opportunities for investment, their tax-exempt character ordinarily results in yields which are substantially less attractive for the tax-exempt investor than those from taxable securities. Therefore, they are not attractive to the tax-exempt local government investor.

9. *Short-term Securities of Private Corporations:* There are a host of short-term debt securities of private corporations available in the market. These are either bonds about to mature or commercial paper of various kinds. Only those local governments with considerable sophistication in the field of investments—found either in their staff or in trusted advisors—should enter this field. Even then, such investments should be restricted to the securities of companies with an excellent *current* credit position.

Those who undertake investments in either short-term or long-term securities should be fully acquainted with the methods used in determining the actual net interest being earned. This is particularly true when securities are being purchased on a basis other than par, or when it is likely, or even a potentiality, that the securities are to be sold prior to maturity. The sophistications involved in the compound interest calculations required to determine price and yield should be mastered; however, the problems involved are much too numerous and complex to warrant even a preliminary explanation in this summary treatment of the treasury function.

LONG-TERM INVESTMENTS

Attention here is directed to the responsibilities of the treasurer in making long-term investments. The occasions for long-term investments include: (1) pension and retirement funds; (2) sinking funds; and (3) other trust funds being held by government on a long-term basis.

At earlier periods, when most bonds were issued as term bonds, treasurers (or the sinking fund officers) had very substantial amounts available to them for investment for the benefit of sinking funds. Because serial bonds have largely supplanted the term bond and because many term bond indentures either place the control of the funds in a trustee other than a public officer or require that excess funds accumulated be used periodically to retire portions of the bond issue in advance of the original maturity date, the treasurer's responsibilities relating to long-term investments are likely to be limited to (1) pension and retirement funds and (2) other trust funds for which he is the custodian. In many states, the administration of pension and retirement funds has passed to the state government; therefore, the long-term investment responsibilities of the local treasurer are further reduced. Even so, many local treasurers still have significant responsibilities in this area.

For treasurers responsible for making long-term investments, the safety of the investment—both in terms of principal and the certainty of interest payments—is a major concern, but adequate yields on investments are also very important. A review of the history of government holdings of tax-exempt securities shows that, prior to 1945, there was a marked tendency for local governments to invest substantial sums in tax-exempt securities. Thus, in 1945, the Board of Governors of the Federal Reserve System estimated that of the $15.7 billion of credit market instrumentalities which state and local governments had outstanding, these governments owned $1.8 billion—or approximately 11 percent. By 1961, the state and local government holdings of credit instrumentalities of these governments had risen to $2.8 billion, accounting for somewhat less than 3.6 percent of the $76.1 billion outstanding. By the end of calendar 1972 the state and local government holdings of credit instrumentalities of such governments were at $3.6 billion, accounting for only 2.4 percent of the $178.6 billion outstanding.[10]

Looking only at retirement systems, in 1941, the Bureau of the Census found that of the total of $1.9 billion of cash and security holdings of state and local government retirement systems, $1.3 billion, or 72 percent was in the form of securities of state and local governments.[11] By 1970-71, the assets of state and local government retirement systems had risen to $61.6 billion, of which only $2.1 billion, or 3.4 percent of total cash and security holdings was invested in state and local government securities, as shown in Table 20.

---

[10] Federal Reserve System Board of Governors, *Flow of Funds Accounts: Financial Assets and Liabilities Outstanding 1945-1972,* (Washington, D. C.: Board of Governors of the Federal Reserve System, 1973), pp. 117-119.

[11] United States Bureau of the Census, *Retirement Systems for State and Local Government Employees;* (Washington, D. C.: United States Government Printing Office, 1941).

Table 20
CASH AND SECURITY HOLDINGS OF EMPLOYEE-RETIREMENT SYSTEMS
OF STATE AND LOCAL GOVERNMENTS
1970-1971

Item	Amount (in billions)	Percent of Total
Cash and deposits	$0.6	1.0
Federal government securities	4.4	7.2
State and local government securities	2.1	3.4
Corporate bonds	34.6	56.2
Corporate stocks	9.5	15.4
Mortgages	6.9	11.2
Other private securities	3.5	5.7
Total	$61.6	100.0

Source: U.S. Bureau of the Census. *Governmental Finances in 1970-71*, p. 28.

It is, therefore, apparent that state and local government retirement funds have largely abandoned the practice of purchasing municipal bonds or other tax-exempt securities as a part of their investment programs. In general, this is a wise procedure, because the tax-exempt feature of "municipal" securities provides no advantage to the local government itself, inasmuch as it is obliged to make no payment of federal or state income taxes. However, on a few occasions, a local government can still purchase its own securities at an advantage.

Normally, local treasurers will do well to restrict their long-term investments to securities of the United States or agencies whose debt is secured thereby and to high grade corporate securities. Although some of the larger state funds are now invested partially in equities (primarily high grade stocks) and, occasionally, in mortgages on land and buildings, the degree of expertise required for successful investment in these fields is likely to be much greater than that possessed by, or available to, the average local government treasurer.

ACCOUNTING AND REPORTING

The treasurer's records may not be complicated, but they must meet certain rigid tests. Each item of cash received or deposited to the treasurer's accounts by others must be traceable to a record which will identify the source. If the detail of revenue by minor and major classifications is maintained by the treasurer, rather than by the revenue agency, the report of receipts should follow standard classifications established for other revenue transactions. Use of such standard classifications greatly simplifies reconciliation between the records of the treasurer and the sources from which the revenues are remitted to him. (Of course, if the treasurer is also charged with the administration of revenue measures, his accounts in this capacity will show great detail not appropriate for the records incident to his treasury functions.)

Receipts, deposits, disbursements, and other transactions should be recorded daily by the treasurer and summaries of these postings should be transmitted to the officer responsible for the maintenance of the general accounts of the municipality. All record keeping should reflect the fund to which the transactions relate, even when consolidated cash account procedures are in force.

Lists of disbursements for each fund and account should be maintained on a daily basis, with totals for each set of listings or summaries posted to the appropriate accounts. In a similar manner, records should be maintained concerning each bank account in order that reconciliations can be made promptly and that a suitable audit trail may be provided.

The treasurer's records should also include a master list of all securities arranged by funds along with any information to be used as a guide for collecting interest and maturing principal and as a basis for reinvestment.

The forms and accounting procedures used by the treasurer are usually prescribed by the principal accounting officer of the municipality. By means of controlled financial stationery, standard deposit slips and transmittal reports, and frequent internal audits, the treasurer can keep a close control over all collecting officers. The use of prenumbered authorization forms and stubs, or appropriate listings, enhances the possibility for strict accounting in smaller governments. Appropriate data-processing procedures accomplish this elsewhere.

Some duplication of records between the central accounting office and the treasurer is ordinarily inevitable. Moreover, some degree of duplication is desirable as a means of internal control. To the extent that the accounting system does not provide for initial classification by others, the treasurer will be obliged to provide the classification of both receipt and disbursement documents. This obligation may also extend to the listing of vouchers, warrants, or checks; however, in the larger municipalities, such listings will probably be produced by the central electronic data processing unit. The records of the treasurer have major relevance to cash; the records of the principal accounting officer are concerned with more definite classifications, e.g., categories of expense and the appropriation to which charged.

Ordinarily, the treasurer does not publish separate financial reports since this is the function of the principal finance officer of the government. However, it is appropriate for the treasurer to publish a brief report setting forth information pertinent to the functions which he performs and, in some instances, details of certain categories of financial transactions.

Internal management reports, including forecasts of cash position; daily and monthly receipts; daily, weekly, and monthly statements on actual cash position and bank balances and earnings; and other information on investment portfolio are appropriate treasury functions.

The functions of accounting and reporting by the treasurer, the auditing of treasury records, and other matters are covered in more detail in the standard works concerned with governmental accounting.[12]

---

[12] See R. M. Mikesell and Leon E. Hay, *Governmental Accounting,* 4th edition, (Homewood, Ill.: Richard D. Irwin, 1969), Chapter 17, "Cash Procedures and Accounting"; Edward

Bonding Local Officials

The head of the treasury function should ascertain from the statutes and court decisions in his state his liability for bank and burglary losses, for the acts of his subordinates, and for others under his functional supervision. He also needs to know which public officials handling money or securities have filed individual bonds for faithful performance of their duties, as required by some statutes, or are covered by blanket bonds.

The blanket form bond is superseding the older individual bond and the name, or position schedule, bond. Blanket coverage makes it unnecessary to advise the surety company when changes of personnel occur. There are variations in the form of blanket bonds. The bond may contain either an aggregate penalty clause or a multiple penalty clause. The privilege of cancellation or addition of positions on a *pro rata* basis during the year may also be included in the contract; or, the faithful performance bond may cover all officers and employees of the government.

Because of the variations in policy, local treasurers may find it useful to seek advice from a state office, an outside consultant, or from at least two surety company agents. The most important coverage sought is protection against dishonesty on the part of employees and officials (theft, forgery, embezzlement, etc.), either singly or in collusion. Another type of coverage is for faithful performance of duties which protects against both dishonesty and nonfaithful performance (malfeasance, misfeasance, and nonfeasance). Recovery for other than dishonest acts, unfortunately, has been infrequent, except where the statutes clearly define the duties of an office and a violation of statutory duties can be precisely proven. Some statutes require officials—both elected and appointed—to take an oath of office and to file an individual bond.

Surety bond coverage should be obtained on two- or three-year contracts by competitive bidding, but only reliable companies should be eligible to bid. A list of companies which are acceptable sureties on federal bonds and which hold certificates of authority for this purpose from the United States Secretary of the Treasury constitutes a useful guide.[13] Most of the larger companies belong to the Surety Association of America (New York City) and are known as the "conference" group. Bonds should be written to cover specific occurrences, where the law permits.

If the law does not permit such coverage, positions, rather than persons, should be the rule—generally limited to those positions in which employees or officials handle, or are responsible for, money or securities. The municipality should be protected against cumulative losses as well as losses in a single year, and premiums on surety bonds should be paid out of public funds.

S. Lynn and Robert J. Freeman, *Fund Accounting: Theory and Practice*, (Englewood Cliffs, N.J.: Prentice-Hall, 1974), Chapter 16 "Cash"; and the National Committee on Governmental Accounting, *Governmental Accounting, Auditing, and Financial Reporting*, (Chicago: Municipal Finance Officers Association, 1968), 234 pp.

[13] See the United States Department of the Treasury, Circular 570, reproduced in the *Federal Register;* Vol. 37, No. 133, Part II, July 11, 1972. The list gives some information on each company, including the new underwriting limit on any one risk.

11
Procurement

In its broadest context, procurement is concerned with the acquisition of all goods and services beyond those services provided directly by employees of the government. Thus it embraces materials, supplies, equipment, and all services performed under contract, whether for construction of new public works or provision of services in connection with regular operations of the government. This subject is the concern of this chapter and the closely related subjects of stores and property control are treated in Chapter 12.

Indicative of the dollar importance of procurement is the following conclusion reached by the Bureau of the Census:

> More than half of all public spending is for current operation. This includes most public payrolls, purchase of goods and services used in the performance of various governmental functions, and purchase of goods for resale by governmental activities.[1]

Local governments are frequently encouraged to follow business practices in their operations. Although the service objectives of local government preclude the universal use of the same kinds of measures of effectiveness that exist in private business, in the procurement field, direct comparisons between public and private practices are possible.

Timely and effective procurement provides smoother governmental operations, higher morale, and greater effectiveness of local government. Efficiency in the operation of the procurement function has a significant potential for cost reduction and financial savings in the operating and capital budgets.

OBJECTIVES OF PURCHASING

The objectives in purchasing are often stated so broadly as to lack specific content. What is meant by "getting the most out of the purchasing dollar"; or "facilitating the procurement of required materials, supplies, services, and other items of use;" or by "procuring the right things at the right price and in the right quantities?" The following seven categories offer a somewhat more precise characterization of procurement responsibilities:

---

[1] United States Bureau of the Census, *Governmental Finances in 1970-71*, (Washington, D. C.: United States Government Printing Office, 1972), p. 5.

1. To procure the materials, supplies, and equipment best suited to do the job which the operating units want done: Operating personnel work with men, material, and a functioning organizational structure. The kind, size, quantity, and quality, of equipment and material must fit the operational performance needs. Purchasing agents must know the job to be done and the characteristics of the materials and equipment which are possible choices for use in particular operations.

2. To procure the right number of units or quantities required: One aim in purchasing is to avoid over- and under-buying. Requirements need to be judged closely and scheduled so that surplus stocks and shortages are minimized and the rates of flow in and out of stores are controlled.

3. To ensure that goods and equipment are in the hands of the operating units when and where they need them: Delivery at the right time and place.

4. To obtain the goods, services, or equipment at the lowest price: Promotion of effective competition in public purchasing by competitive bidding, prevention of price rigging and identical bids, bulk purchasing and quantity discounts, standardization of common items, and other approaches are all factors in effectuating this major aim.

5. To obtain technical services as required: These are sometimes a necessary accompaniment of the product, such as assembly or installation, instruction of operators, initial servicing to assure proper functioning, and guarantees of quality and efficiency for one year or some other specified time period.

6. To explore feasible sources of supply for critical materials in order to avoid serious shortage in an emergency: This means avoiding sole supplier situations, testing for effective substitutes, and maintaining good relationships with important and effective suppliers.

7. To dispose of unneeded inventory: By careful identification of those items no longer needed, arrangements may be made for disposition of surplus through trade-ins, salvage, or sale as scrap.

CENTRALIZED PROCUREMENT

Before proceeding with the substantive aspects of procurement, it is appropriate to consider briefly the arguments for and against centralized procurement. So much has been written about the subject that it is not necessary to cover all of the points which have been advanced. The principal favorable considerations are:

1. Centralization, except in the case of smaller units of government, makes possible the hiring of a full-time professional purchasing agent. The purchasing agent is in a much better position to perform an effective job than a number of persons with a necessarily limited knowledge of the purchasing field, functioning at the departmental level.

2. The opportunity for quantity buying, either through bulk purchases or on term contracts, is enhanced through centralized purchasing. The cost to the local government of materials, supplies, and equipment can be lowered by standardization of the items and by widening the competition to wholesalers, jobbers, and manufacturers. The tendency under departmental purchasing of hand-to-mouth buying in the retail market can be eliminated, or greatly reduced.

3. Delivery services can be improved, if adequate replenishment schedules are carried out.

4. The quality of items purchased can be improved through standardization, use of standard specifications, and better inspection and testing of deliveries. Timely improvements in quality may also be made feasible by use of the professional knowledge of the purchasing agent and his constant study of new and advanced products which give improved performance per dollar expended.

5. Lists of qualified vendors can be developed and shortages and delivery of goods below the contract specifications can be avoided. The local government can also be put in a stronger position to cope with identical bids and other forms of collusion among bidders.

6. Responsibility for procurement is more easily pinpointed in case of irregularities. Such irregularities may be much more easily detected in a single office than in several agencies buying under the decentralized plan.

7. Greater financial control over expenditures for materials, supplies, and equipment can be established. The timely settlement of accounts, including encouragement of dealer discounts for prompt payment, can result.

8. Stores, inventories, and the purchasing process can be better coordinated where centralized purchasing exists because responsibility for storage and inventory control is usually given to the central purchasing unit.

9. Good inventory records and a systematic procedure, which are essential for effective purchasing, are generally more feasible under centralized purchasing arrangements.

10. Administrative costs under centralized purchasing can be lower than those under a decentralized structure; however, this is not always the case. One who would centralize on the basis of reduction of administrative costs will do well to examine the facts carefully. Centralization may or may not reduce paperwork; whereas it can make more effective use of the personnel who are performing purchasing activities, it may result in an overall increase of such personnel. It should be able to reduce selected overhead costs through operation of central storehouses; however, unless carefully controlled, this advantage can be more than offset by added distribution and accounting costs.

11. Centralized purchasing is more convenient for the vendor. Contracts for city business can be centered in one office. The number of separate bids, orders, and deliveries can be reduced, resulting in more efficient accounting and payment procedures.

The foregoing benefits are potentialities. These benefits do not automatically accrue from centralized procurement procedures. Only effective administration will produce the benefits implicit in the claims.

Centralized purchasing, however, is not always an unmixed blessing. There is always a possibility of friction between the purchasing department (with its eye on economy) and the using departments, which are primarily interested in timely availability and quality of goods. It is unfortunate if either side overstresses one aspect of purchasing. Dollar savings are important, as is quality, but choosing the right product for job performance may be even more important and, in the overall, more economical. The mere centralization of purchasing does not solve all problems.

> Unfortunately, there have been cases in which the centralization of purchasing merely meant the centralization of inefficiency and even graft. On the other hand, there have been cases where the purchasing department was too honest and efficient to suit an unscrupulous administration, and the work of the department was crippled through lack of sufficient budget appropriations or by divesting the purchasing agent of authority.[2]

The fact that most purchasing operations are centralized does not necessarily mean that all will be, or should be. Thus, the late Russell Forbes, long a leading authority and practitioner in the purchasing field, once wrote:

> If there are to be any exceptions to the authority of the purchasing office to make all purchases for the municipality, such exceptions should be made in terms of specified types of articles and not in terms of a using agency or agencies. If the city hospital, for example, insists upon the right to purchase its pharmaceuticals independently, there is no reason why the purchasing office should not buy the hospital's coal, stationery, and other standard commodities. And in most instances this office should also be able to purchase the pharmaceuticals according to specification. In making such special purchases the best practice is for the central purchasing officer to prescribe the procedure to be followed, subject to the approval of the chief executive.[3]

Planning and Quantity Buying

A centralized purchasing unit is in a position to ascertain total procurement needs in all using agencies, to consolidate these requirements, and, through bulk purchasing, to obtain lower prices than might otherwise be possible. However, to effect such savings good planning is required and, unfortunately, many local governments fail reasonably to anticipate their future needs.

In procurement, information of a very specific character is needed. The generalized categories used in the preparation and administration of budgets are of value only to help determine the broad categories of projected expenses,

---

[2] International City Managers' Association, *Municipal Finance Administration*, Fourth ed., (Chicago: International City Managers' Association, 1949), p. 390.

[3] Forbes, Russell, *Purchasing for Small Cities*, (Chicago: Public Administration Service, 1951), p. 2.

e.g., drugs, food, or clothing. The most effective technique for developing the type of information required is by analysis, over long periods of time, of the specific items used, quantities, and time of use during the year. Only through the highly sophisticated identification and classification of items can a genuine pooling of requirements be accomplished. Some of this information can be garnered by calling for departmental estimates when the annual budget is in preparation and at regularly prescribed intervals during the budget year. These estimates can then be reviewed carefully by the purchasing agent, and adjustments recommended as required.

Only by planning ahead can the maximum advantage be obtained from quantity buying. Hand-to-mouth purchases as requisitions flow in mean that the purchasing agent is little more than an order clerk. It is poor business to buy in retail lots, when the usage is in wholesale quantities. Quantity buying invites more effective competition from wholesalers and manufacturers.

Consolidation of estimated needs puts a premium upon more careful studies of price trends and taking advantage, wherever possible, of a soft market in a given commodity. When prices are down, an opportunity may occur to buy and store or to enter into requirements contracts or price agreements for future delivery over a specified period of time. The incentive for gauging the market is much greater where purchasing is centralized and quantity buying is practiced. But, entering the market for requirements contracts is the work of a professional. Forward buying as a protection against a rising market is not universally endorsed. Some contend that it is not the function of a purchasing agent to stock up in an attempt "to beat the market." The argument is advanced that speculation with public funds is undesirable—however propitious the circumstances and noble the intentions. However, quantity buying, cash discount allowances, and agreements for free technical services are often more generous. And, quantity buying will also reduce paper work. One city found that it was writing 250 individual purchase orders annually for subscriptions to various periodicals and magazines. Consolidation of all subscription needs into one contract with competitive bids produced savings not only in subscription prices but also in the writing of purchase orders. With quantity buying, it is also easier to ensure that state and federal tax exemptions are taken; that discounts available to charitable and educational institutions are not overlooked; and that bills are paid promptly so as to earn the cash discounts.

Savings from quantity buying under centralized purchasing are frequently set at an average of 10 to 20 percent, but this type of statement is difficult to verify. The best comparison can be made during the first year when the shift from decentralized buying occurs. Many individual examples of savings are reported in the journals which exceed the 10 to 20 percent range.

Competitive Bidding

A formalized system of procurement, mandated by law, is the main distinction between public purchasing and commercial procurement practices. In most jurisdictions, the law requires that every purchase order or purchase contract above a specified amount (with very limited exceptions) must be subject to competitive bidding. These laws generally include the requirements for advertising for bids, the mode of processing bids, the method of determining the "lowest and best bidder," and making the award. The result is a certain amount of inflexibility combined with rather cumbersome procedures. Many professional public purchasing agents, seeing the greater freedom of their confreres in the commercial field, chafe under these legal requirements. On the whole, however, such requirements are reasonable and justified. The profit motive in business forces the purchasing agent to buy competitively. In public purchasing, the law supplies a comparable force. Mandated competition was a long step forward in the development of public procurement practices.

The main positive objective of these legal requirements is to obtain lower prices by stimulating competition.[4] Unfortunately, compliance with the letter of the law is possible while violating, at least in part, the spirit. If calls for competitive bids are posted on a bulletin board and inserted only in the local newspaper, or newspapers, the legal requirement of advertising is met, but competition may be quite limited. The spirit requires: maintaining up-to-date lists of suppliers; wide circulation of written notices to possible bidders; telephone calls; initiative in maintaining contacts with former suppliers; and aggressiveness in the widening of competition. Good purchasing procedures require more than compliance with the law.

The minimum dollar value over and above which competitive bidding is required is often set too low. For smaller governments, purchases of $1,000 or more might be reasonable; for larger cities, $3,000 to $5,000 or more would be a more realistic figure. Therefore, the size of the local government and the volume of its purchases are important considerations. On the other hand, as the purchasing power of the dollar declines, the legally prescribed lines of demarcation tend to become obsolete and the minimum amounts have to be raised.

Certain guidelines have been suggested as useful in establishing practices in competitive bidding, some of which appear in laws governing this activity:

1. The opportunity to bid should be largely unrestricted. Any attempt to eliminate or to restrict competition, either through local preference or through manipulation of the specifications, so as to favor a particular vendor runs counter to this guideline. As for the latter practice, the best safeguard is to adhere to standard specifications which should be made known to all possible bidders and not only to a few favored ones. In unorganized city purchasing, there is an opportunity for collusion between city officials and merchants to write specifications so as to favor an individual or a small group of bidders. On the other hand, the disqualification of irresponsible bidders is essential. Sometimes there is strong pressure to give local merchants a preference. Buying outside is occasionally characterized as "taking bread out of the taxpayer's mouth." In fact, if outside competition will produce a lower price, it is a protection to the total community of taxpayers against a few "insiders" or a few merchants—no matter how honest.

---

[4] Yearly comparisons of the average number of bids per specification, published by some cities, should be interpreted with care.

Municipalities are on solid ground if they adhere to the practice of awarding bids to the lowest and best bidder. Preference to local bidders is earned only when it is definitely established, by comparison of all bids or offers received, that such is justified.[5]

The percentage of purchases made from local vendors tends to increase with the size of the local government—largely because the larger jurisdictions have a greater number of dealers in a greater variety of products needed by the local government.[6]

2. Each invitation to bid should include only related items. Bids should be called for on homogeneous or kindred items. If this guideline is not followed, difficulties arise in establishing the best bid. Also, the advantages of quantity purchasing and price discounts are defeated if small, unrelated lots have been consolidated. In the choice of items to be consolidated, the procurement officer must be fully aware of the general prevailing organization of business and arrange his bid offerings in order that each is likely to be directed to specific groups of general or specialty businesses, e.g., one should not consolidate the purchase of water pipe and dry goods in the same offering.

3. Each invitation to bid should specify the conditions of delivery as an integral part of the contract in order that competition is focused on the delivered price. The conditions may include the minimum size of a delivery, where provision is made for partial deliveries of items being purchased. The extent to which the local government is involved in central stores and warehousing operations and the size of the order will help to determine whether deliveries are to be made to a single location or to a number of using agency depots. But, all such conditions must be specified in the invitation to bid.

4. The opening of sealed bids should be public in order that bidders and other persons may be in attendance if they choose. It is highly desirable that the process be conducted in a manner which will enhance the bidders' confidence in the integrity of the process and its complete fairness to all bidders.

5. The use of prequalified buyers tends to simplify the procurement process; however, it has a number of implications which may act to reduce full competition.

6. If a contract is awarded to other than the lowest bidder, the reasons for declaring a higher bidder as the "best bidder" must be made clear to all concerned. Otherwise, many will conclude that favoritism is involved and the government will gradually lose the interest of other bidders. This is not to suggest that price should always be the only

---

[5] Although the foregoing statement once constituted the best theory in procurement, one cannot be entirely oblivious to the tax consideration. Thus, if it be assumed that the nonresident bidder can offer to supply a given quantity of materials and supplies for $9,900 whereas the local bidder offers a bid of $10,000, normal procedures require the acceptance of the $9,900—despite the fact that, if the local government should derive a tax benefit from the local bidder equal to $300, this would make him the lowest net bidder.

[6] See International City Managers' Association, *The Municipal Yearbook, 1957*, (Chicago: International City Managers' Association, 1957), pp. 195-211.

consideration. Past performance with a given bidder may indicate that, regardless of his promises, he fails to deliver at times critical to the government; therefore, it may be justifiable to exclude his bid in making the award.

7. Awards should always be made in strict accordance with specifications.[7] This is necessary to restrict the possibility of favoritism or collusion between the purchasing officials and one of the bidders. Also, this system gives a reasonable opportunity to all bidders (local and outside) to compete for city contracts on a fair basis. Limited exceptions to the formal competitive bidding rule are occasionally warranted. Where there is clearly only one source of supply, advertising and other formal procedures are a waste of public funds. Safeguards, however, must be established to prevent any abuse of this exception. Contracts for professional services and purchases in a genuine emergency are two additional exceptions.

8. Purchasing agents should not only do everything they can to stimulate competition but, where some form of collusion appears, they should also act with vigor to protect the local government. If a form of price rigging is suspected, or identical bids are submitted, all bids should be rejected. The identical bids or the other factual circumstances should be referred to the appropriate legal counsel or law enforcement officers for investigation—or, perhaps, for the drafting of additional legislation to deal with the subject.

Both state and federal anti-trust laws help to protect against collusion.

Negotiated Buying

What is gained on very small contracts by competition is often offset by advertising, administrative, and related costs. The result is a lot of motion, and no net gain to the taxpayer—and, perhaps, even a net loss. In general, there are five exceptions to formalized competitive bid requirements:

1. *Small amounts* which fall below the stated legal minimum for competitive bids. This exception is reasonable as long as it is not used as a device to evade competitive bid requirements by splitting requisitions. For small purchases, advertising and other costs of a formalized procedure may more than offset the possible price advantage.

2. *Emergency buying* arises in many situations, e.g., hospital operations or meeting requirements arising from explosions, storms, fire, etc. It is important that regulations be established which allow emergency buying, but under prescribed safeguards.

3. *A situation in which a second bid is lacking* occasionally arises. In the absence of any bid, or, in the absence of a second bid, the purchasing

---

[7] In smaller governments, specifications are frequently in the form of a specified product by use of trade or manufacturer's name, "or equal." This is an inadequate procedure because there may not be a product that fully qualifies as "or equal." The standard specifications developed by federal agencies and some private associations and societies offer a partial answer to these smaller—and even to some larger—governments. Large local governments can, over a period of time, develop their own standard specifications for many of the items used by them.

authority has the right to accept the single bid or to reject it and proceed to negotiated procurement of the necessary items.

4. *Contracts for professional services* are normally considered outside the responsibility of the procurement officer. Whenever the law imposes this responsibility upon him, he ordinarily negotiates such arrangements because differentials in price may be only a minor consideration in obtaining professional services.

5. *Purchases from petty cash funds* ordinarily are made without reference to competitive bidding. The law or administrative regulations should specify the conditions under which petty cash may be used and a review of petty cash purchases should be made from time to time to assure that this device is not being misused.

Negotiated bidding does not mean that competition has been eliminated in the procurement process. Quite the contrary. The purchasing agent should continue to use the competitive technique in most circumstances—albeit through less formal methods involving telephone (or other informal) quotations or, in the procurement of certain types of professional services, through the use of competitive proposals. Unquestionably, the procurement officer, or departmental officials acting with his authority, must utilize this freedom in the public interest and with the most careful discretion. The ease and economy of informal procurement procedures have resulted in strong advocates for broadening this approach. It has been proposed by some that formal competitive bidding be restricted to the procurement of products which have to be made to order or those which have no readily ascertainable market price.

In general, however, the weight of opinion—as well as the law—still supports the broad use of formal processes.

Term or Requirements Contracts

Instead of soliciting bids on single quantity purchases, suppliers are frequently asked to compete for a contract against which deliveries are to be made over a period of time—usually with an upper and lower limit as to quantities. Essentially, this type of bidding results in an agreement as to the price, or price basis, with deliveries by the successful bidder being made as needed by the government. Competition may be enhanced by this approach because the size of the contracts is larger. Moreover, there is a reduction in the advertising and administrative costs involved in determining the best bidder and arranging the contract. Two types of term contracts are in use:

1. Lump-sum or bulk contracts which require competing bidders to supply specified quantities over a given period, often the fiscal year: The dates and quantities of each delivery are determined by the government, generally under conditions which establish the total amounts to be purchased. The contract may be coupled with a price agreement that hinges the price to unit prices contained in published indices of commodity costs.

2. Standing contracts or price agreement contracts which are essentially price agreements which stipulate the maximum quantity which can be

ordered over a given period at the contract price: Examples would be a milk contract with stipulated prices for different grades or motor fuels contracts.

The main advantages of such contracts are the savings in storage and distribution costs, periodic payments for deliveries received, the opportunity for using departments to place orders directly according to the terms of the contract, the avoidance of frequent bidding during the year and, avoidance of losses from over-stocking, with subsequent disposition of surplus at salvage rates.

In periods of marked price stability, the use of requirements contracts is likely to result in considerable savings on a unit price basis. The vendor is able to make advanced commitments with his supplier on a bulk basis and to pass some of this forward to the local government.

On the other hand, in periods of marked price inflation—especially prolonged inflation—the vendor may be obliged to include in his bid a substantial hedge against cost increases to which he may be subjected over the life of the contract. A partial offset in both situations can be secured through price agreements which can be adjusted upon the basis of recognized independent market indices relating to the types of commodities covered by the agreements.

If term contracts are used, certain precautions must be followed:

1. More frequent inspection and testing will be required because deliveries made to the various user departments and institutions are spread over a long period of time. Higher inspection and testing costs under this approach, as contrasted with bulk buying and storage, may constitute an offset to other savings advantages.
2. Competition should be sought among wholesalers and manufacturers because of the size of the contracts and because these dealers are able to meet requirements promptly and in the quantities ordered. Reliance on retailers for wholesale quantities may prove to be unwise.

Purchasing contracts will generally include the following elements: the period covered by the contract; the goods and quantities to be delivered; the price; delivery conditions; and the requirement for, or absence of, a faithful performance bond. One or more of these matters may be omitted, or purposely left indefinite.

Standardization

Standardization of the specifications for purchased items is an objective, rational attempt to reduce the number and kinds of items which must be purchased for a given purpose. It begins with a careful study of the articles in use, their main ingredients and attributes, and the job they are expected to perform. In this process, the purchasing agent may discover, to use one illustration, that many different sizes and qualities of typewriter paper are in use throughout the government. Some differences may be justified; others may be accidental or the result of individual preferences—neither of which are any longer defensible. If the government is to take advantage of quantity buying, typewriter paper will have to be standardized. This same type of study will have to be made of scores of other items in common use. For example, a purchasing agent may find many different cleaning compounds in use—all with a common chemical base and substantially the same product.

Standardization can be easily applied in such commodities as gasoline, lubricants, stationery and office supplies, disinfectants, cleaning compounds, floor treatments, paint colors, paper towels, printed forms, etc. The extensive experience of the American National Standards Institute, Inc. should be drawn upon. It publishes the bi-weekly periodicals, *ANSI Reporter* and *Standards Action*, and has boards of review for standards in important product areas. Unless standardization is achieved, centralized purchasing will only result in processing an untold number of small orders—and at a price disadvantage.

Technical experts within the government can, and should, supply advice on standardization. Standards should represent the combined views of the using agencies and the procurement agency. This does not mean that each department must be satisfied with proposed changes, regardless of their precise requirements; major users (or the exclusive user) of a commodity should suffice.

Exceptions to standardization may include highly specialized and technical goods, e.g., library book acquisitions, selected scientific equipment, and many medical supplies.

Standardization can be used to achieve price savings, quality improvement, and lower administrative costs. With fewer items to buy, quantities can be increased—often with more wholesalers, jobbers, and manufacturers being brought into the bidding. With fewer items purchased, the preparation or adoption of standard specifications is facilitated, as are testing and inspection procedures. This should mean better quality. Similarly, fewer items permit fewer advertisements calling for bids, smaller stocks on hand, and better control of inventories resulting in lower administrative costs in the acquisition and distribution of stores.

Specifications

A procurement specification is a description of the product or material upon which bids are solicited in all of its essential attributes, including the requirements for physical performance. An adequate specification should meet the following major criteria:

1. It must be specific and complete, leaving no loopholes whereby an unscrupulous bidder may evade any of its provisions, thereby taking unfair advantage of the buyer and of the other bidders
2. It must accurately describe the article specified and the requirements for its physical performance
3. It must not overspecify—requiring materials of a better quality than are needed for the job or including elements not germane to requirements
4. It must prescribe the methods of inspection and testing which will govern the acceptance or rejection of the materials
5. It must be worded as simply as is consistent with clarity
6. It must stipulate any special methods of packing or marking which are required
7. It must conform, as clearly as possible, to nationally recognized specifications.

Good specifications can achieve several objectives concurrently:

1. Putting all bidders on an equal basis by making known that the contract will be awarded strictly in accordance with specifications and that the specifications will be enforced; that no one bidder can take unfair advantage of his competitors by lowering his price with prior knowledge that his delivery of an inferior product will be accepted
2. Minimizing disputes and disagreements as to whether or not the delivered product conforms to the specifications
3. Avoiding brand name buying which makes it difficult to determine what alternate brands or generically named items would be acceptable, thus achieving the improvement in price frequently associated with purchasing under generic terms

The responsibility for writing specifications is variously fixed: (1) the professional buyers in a large purchasing division may develop the specifications for the commodities which they purchase; (2) a section may be established within the purchasing division for this specific task; and (3) specification or standardization committees may be established with representatives from the purchasing division and the user departments. Regardless of the location for this responsibility, the close cooperation of user agencies is essential.

An enormous amount of work has gone into the preparation of standard specifications for hundreds of products by many highly qualified organizations. Large investments are made in the periodic revision of these specifications. This vast store of knowledge can easily be tapped. Federal government specifications include "federal specifications" and "military specifications." The former cover a wide variety of civilian-type items and the latter, materials and products used in national defense. The General Services Administration publishes an *Index of Federal Specifications and Standards* and keeps this up-to-date through supplements. All sizeable procurement offices should maintain and make frequent references to these publications as well as to those prepared by the United States National Bureau of Standards. Additional information can be obtained through the American National Standards Institute, Inc., the American Society for Testing Materials, the National Association of State Purchasing Officials, the National Institute of Governmental Purchasing, and the standards developed by various national trade associations.

Generally it is inadvisable to rely upon the specifications which are offered from time to time by companies which sell products used by the local government; however, on occasion, these can be useful—especially when those of several manufacturers are studied in concert.

Specifications should not be used when they serve no practical purpose. If for example, the local government has determined by testing and past performance that it wants any one of three standard, medium-priced cars—all available within a close price range, no useful purpose is served by drawing up elaborate specifications as to rated horsepower, wheelbase, or other elements. On the other hand, a short form specification is needed which gives the model, type, body design, basic essentials, and special equipment required. More detailed specifications are frequently required for trucks since a wider difference in service and quality exists between the various makes.

Specifications should be in terms which are as simple as feasible while not sacrificing clarity and preciseness to the degree required. Although it is easy to restrict competition through over design of the specifications, this is obviously not in the public interest. Nor are loose specifications which afford loopholes for the bidder wishing to do as little as possible in relation to the price being paid.

Where specifications are prepared by using departments, the central procurement agency should carefully review them for language which may cause them to be unnecessarily restrictive.

Inspection and Testing

The starting point for inspection and testing is usually the time of delivery; however, in some cases, e.g., ready-mixed concrete, inspection at the mixing plant may be necessary. A receiving report will verify the quantity, but not the quality, of the goods received. The receiving unit should have no information concerning either the quantity or quality of goods actually ordered. In fact, the central procurement agency should, from time to time, deliberately modify the quantities which have been requisitioned and then check carefully to determine that the receiving report relates to the quantities ordered rather than those requisitioned. The purpose is to require the receiving clerk to prepare an independent count. The condition of delivery, as revealed by general inspection, should also be entered in the report of goods received. Checking on deliveries is so elementary a safeguard that one cannot but appreciate the sarcasm in a New York Times editorial of several years ago:

> The city administration [New York City], cheated for years and out of many thousands of dollars by short-weight deliveries of rock salt for clearing the streets of snow and ice in winter, has hit upon a novel technique of self-protection. Whereas it previously accepted the seller's certification of how much he had delivered, the city will now decide for itself. This novel policy is announced by Sanitation Commissioner . . ., who, in the understatement of the year, says: 'We have concluded that the best way to tell how much salt is delivered is to weigh it on a scale.' Of this revolutionary management reform we can only say in admiration, what will they think of next.[8]

Among the functions of the materials inspector from the central procurement agency is test-checking the accuracy with which receiving units prepare their receiving reports. Proof of the quality delivered will depend upon sampling and laboratory tests. Opinions are insufficient; careful testing is necessary. A good purchasing agent will not be satisfied with quantitative verifications. His responsibility extends to the more subtle type of fraud, namely, deliveries of goods whose quality is below contract specifications.[9] User departments do not

---

[8] "The Buyer Bewares," *New York Times*, November 21, 1960.

[9] In a few instances, accepting commodities of a higher grade may be inappropriate. Thus, for institutional meals, acceptance of Grade "A" beef in lieu of standard grade may result in acceptance of meat with considerable fat that will only be boiled out in certain menus. Or, the acceptance of a high butterfat content milk may render it useless when skim milk is needed.

have the technical knowledge nor the facilities to perform this function. Whether the quantity or quality shortage is deliberate or the result of carelessness on the part of the supplier, the loss to the purchasing government is just as serious. The government has an obligation to unsuccessful bidders in the sense that their participation in bidding is likely to continue only if they are convinced of the fairness of the full range of procurement procedures affecting them. To accept goods which do not comply with the terms of the contract is a very serious breach of faith with such firms. If a city maintains a reputation for careful inspection and quality control, substandard deliveries will be discouraged.

For some deliveries random sampling should suffice; others will require a limited, test-check basis. Public health and safety requirements, as well as good purchasing practices, may govern the frequency of testing.

Some quality control should be carried out by field inspections as in the case of meat delivered to a city hospital. Without warning, from time to time, an inspector from the purchasing division will be on hand when the meat truck unloads to check its quality against delivery papers. An alternative is to place an inspector at the point of shipment to stamp all items approved. Some municipalities send their buyers out to do on-the-spot purchasing of fresh produce, fish, and other perishables for city institutions. For equipment and other products being manufactured for a large city, a field inspector may be sent to the plant since on-site inspection may be the best means for examining the quality of materials going into the goods. One year, the city of Chicago reported that its field inspectors had visited 76 plants in 15 states, involving commodities and equipment valued at nearly $15 million.

In addition, testing frequently serves a precontract purpose. For example, when samples are submitted with bids, compliance with advertised specifications must be determined in awarding the contract. Another instance arises when buyers are searching for new or better products and equipment. Then, demonstrations by sales representatives, laboratory tests, and experimental or performance runs may be necessary to establish quality and adaptability to the city's operations.

The larger municipalities normally have their own laboratory facilities for testing purposes. However, even they find it necessary to send samples of products to commercial or university laboratories for analysis and testing. The smaller units should rely more heavily upon commercial laboratories, larger units of government (including the state), and other facilities in their area.[10] Payment may be on a contractual or fee basis.[11] In the area of food products, the experience that has been accumulated by the Agricultural Marketing Service of the United States Department of Agriculture will be useful.

---

[10] The National Bureau of Standards, Washington, D. C., no longer finds it feasible to perform this type of service for states and municipalities.

[11] Information as to the availability of testing facilities may be obtained from the current edition of the *Directory of Testing Laboratories* of the American Society for Testing Materials, 1916 Race Street, Philadelphia, Pa., 19103.

Services by Suppliers; Sources of Supply

Delivery by the supplier at the time and place designated is often most important. In determining the "lowest and best bidder," consideration may have to be given as to whether or not the supplier has demonstrated in the past both willingness and ability to make timely deliveries under his contracts. In some cases, promptness in deliveries may be so essential that failures in this respect should bar such suppliers from future bidding.

Other technical services required of the supplier may be a part of the contract: equipment assembly, installation of the machinery, instruction of operators, engineering service until adjustments have resulted in a smooth operation, periodic inspections, and, finally, guarantees for a limited period. The original purchase contract might also include a price agreement for technical repair personnel where the equipment is highly specialized and only the manufacturer has the service capability.

Sources of supply should receive careful scrutiny by the purchasing agent. Where there is a sole supplier, suppliers only in a foreign country, or a very limited supply source for some critical material, research should be done on possible substitutes or an effort made to locate alternate sources. If these precautions are not taken, the city, in an emergency, may face a serious shortage or a price squeeze. Stockpiling is one alternative, but a very expensive one. Nonetheless, more careful planning of inventory in these materials, or price agreements, may be required.

Disposal of Property

The purchasing agent has the responsibility for securing the best "results" from materials, supplies, and equipment declared surplus by a unit, and from obsolete, worn-out, and unusable items. This responsibility may be carried out in several ways:

1. Items declared surplus by one unit may be put on a list and the list circulated to all operating units. Where feasible, reassignment of such items should be made.
2. The local government may have a deliberate policy of moving certain items systematically to a lower use. The best example is automobiles. One department, e.g., the emergency unit of a gas utility, requires vehicles which may be expected to function without fail and at maximum efficiency. The same is not true for all parts of the government. Thus, after one year, the vehicles may be transferred to uses in which requirements are not so stringent.
3. Many items have a salvage value—either as trade-ins or through sale by auction. The sale of these items has the effect of reducing the outlays for new purchases.
4. Surplus or obsolete items can sometimes be sold to other governments or to the public, where requirements are less exacting. A case in point is the fire truck that may be obsolete for the large city but adequate for many additional years of service in smaller communities.

5. Dismantling of special equipment on motor vehicles for re-use on new vehicles offers substantial potential for cost reduction. Or, some of the parts recaptured can be sold at attractive prices to dealers in used parts.

6. Waste materials, scrap, and salvage from wrecks or fires can be systematically collected and sold at intervals through auction, sealed bids, or negotiated sales.

The disposal of property can be performed more effectively under centralized purchasing. Unfortunately, it is a phase of purchasing and property control that is sometimes neglected.

Financing of Purchases

Among the principal methods of financing the purchase of materials, supplies, and equipment are:

1. *Direct Charge to the Departmental Appropriation.* This involves encumbering purchase orders against the appropriations available when the contract is being processed.

2. *Charges To Revolving Funds.* Where central stores or warehouse funds are used, initial charge may be made thereto. The costs of operation of such central stores operations—including handling, shrinkage, obsolescence, and delivery—are charged to the using departments as items are withdrawn from central stores.

3. *Use of Equipment Rental Funds.* With increasing frequency, equipment is "owned" by a separate fund. In some instances the fund is only a means for distributing cost of acquisition over a period of years. In other cases, the equipment rental fund is used not only to acquire equipment but also to provide for its full maintenance. Occasionally the concept is further broadened to include operating costs. In any event, where such funds are used, schedules of charges are maintained under which charges can be made to using departments for reimbursement of fair shares of the costs involved.

It is appropriate to mention also a device frequently offered by manufacturers or vendors of equipment, i.e., the lease-purchase agreement. Although the lease-purchase agreement sometimes offers the only viable method of financing acquisitions of certain types of equipment, one must realize that interest on the investment by the supplier-owner is at rates reflecting taxable interest. But some suppliers, e.g., lessors of computer equipment, appear to be able to provide low interest rates. Therefore, in determining the relative attractiveness of direct purchase vs. lease-purchase, attention must be given to the potentialities of direct financing—even through bank loans to the local government—over the same period involved in the lease-purchase agreement. With the increasing use of leased equipment in the private sector, the procurement agency, in concert with the principal finance officer, should determine, from time to time, the relative costs of lease vs. ownership of many kinds of equipment.

Cooperative Purchasing

There are a number of circumstances in which cooperative purchasing is likely to prove beneficial to the cooperating governments or units. However, not all cooperative purchasing arrangements produce results superior to procurement by the individual governmental units involved. When one is evaluating the relative advantages and disadvantages, the *total* cost of securing the items being procured—not just the unit price involved—must be taken into consideration.

Thus, if centralized purchasing results in delivery at favorable prices to a central point from which most of the cooperating parties must provide transportation to the point of use, the full cost of such transportation must be taken into consideration. Moreover, if the costs of warehousing, inventory records, payment to vendors, inter-agency settlements, obsolescence, delays in receipt of portions of shipments, inventory shrinkage, insurance, value of funds tied up, and cost of administrative time to develop and maintain relationships are all taken into consideration, some of the alleged advantages of joint purchasing arrangements may not prove to be particularly beneficial.

Servicing participating smaller governments which maintain joint arrangements with larger governments sometimes results in substantially increased costs to the vendor. The cost advantage to the local governments may be obtained only at increased costs to the larger partner in the operation.

The point here is that a *full* evaluation is required for a correct conclusion as to the advantages—not just comparisons of the unit costs quoted by the vendor to large and smaller users.

Despite the foregoing admonitions, many circumstances exist where genuine savings can be achieved through joint purchasing. When this is the case, the opportunities should be exploited to the fullest.

The kinds of cooperative arrangements that have been found beneficial include those along the following lines:

1. A county or large municipality with tie-in advantages for smaller governments
2. Use of state leagues of municipalities
3. State purchasing, with a provision for local governments to purchase under the state's contracts
4. Cooperative arrangement between two or more municipalities in the same area

For each item that is to be procured, purchasing under cooperative arrangements ordinarily requires advanced determination of the volume of requirements for each of the participating governments.

ADMINISTRATION OF PURCHASING

Centralized purchasing has been defined as "the method of organization and procedure by which procurement of all purchased materials and supplies is concentrated in or channeled through a single department, under the direction of one responsible person, rather than handled on a promiscuous, unorganized basis or as an incidental function in connection with other duties of various department heads or other officials."[12] The growth toward centralized purchasing in municipal government, which dates from about 1910,[13] has been slow but certain. Once tried, centralized purchasing has usually not been abandoned. As a by-product of the general trend toward greater centralization of responsibility and accountability, it received special impetus from the city manager movement since this form of organization stands for centralization.

By 1957, the International City Managers' Association reported that about 70 percent of the participating cities with a population of 10,000 or over had instituted some form of centralized purchasing.[14] Doubtless the percentage has increased; however, no comprehensive recent study of the practice appears to have been made. At that time, only a small percentage of the counties had centralized purchasing; however, the growth of the importance of county government as an administrative unit during recent years suggests that more and more of them are moving to centralized procurement.

Centralized purchasing seems to function successfully under almost any form of general-purpose, local government organization. The principal choices are among:

1. A separate department (or, in smaller governments, an office) reporting directly to the chief executive or to his chief administrator
2. A bureau in a finance department
3. A board of purchasing which is under the governing body of the local government

Strong arguments can be made for placing the purchasing function outside the principal finance department or agency (as outlined in Chapter 2). On the other hand, a good case can be made for locating purchasing in the centralized finance department. Purchasing seems to have a greater affinity to finance than to other central management functions. Perhaps it can best function with the finance group; however, this is not necessary, as has been proven by very successful purchasing departments in cities as large as Chicago and in numerous other governments where centralized procurement operates outside the financial group.

In smaller governments, where the volume of activity is insufficient to warrant the employment of a full-time purchasing agent, it becomes necessary to combine the performance of this function with other functions—the most logical apparently being the finance function. Frequently, purchasing is a responsibility combined with budgeting or an officer assigned to these operations.

---

[12] Heinritz, Stuart F., *Purchasing*, (New York: Prentice-Hall, 1947), p. 8.

[13] Between 1910 and 1924, some 172 cities with population 10,000 or more, 50 counties, and 36 states adopted some form of centralized purchasing. Pittsburgh in 1910 and Dayton in 1913 were early pioneers. The origins, however, predate the start of a trend. The first full-fledged municipal organization which survived the experimental stage was established in 1896 in Washington, D. C. Oklahoma, in 1910, was the first state to try centralized purchasing for the entire state organization, although Iowa in 1897 centralized the purchasing for all state charitable and penal institutions. See Russell Forbes, "Centralized Purchasing in Governments of United States and Canada," *The Annals* of the American Academy of Political and Social Science, May, 1924, Vol. CXIII, pp. 272-286.

[14] International City Managers' Association, *The Municipal Yearbook 1957*, (Chicago: International City Managers' Association, 1957), p. 195.

In the larger local governments, the purchasing activity becomes highly specialized with a number of different job classifications—specifications writer, buyer, inspector, etc.

Scope of the Purchasing Agent's Jurisdiction

Operations of central stores and warehousing; the reassignment of movable property and supplies which are surplus in one operating department to another department; disposal of unusable or obsolete property, waste, or salvage; and the negotiation of contracts for such technical services as printing, duplicating, telephone, light and other utilities, laundry services, etc.—these are all clearly a part of the purchasing function.

The need to shift insurance procurement to a competitive basis may have been a factor in assignment of the procurement of all types of insurance to the purchasing agency.

The role which the purchasing agent should play in the letting of contracts for professional services is a matter of considerable controversy. Some contend that professional services should not be subject to competitive bidding. This is especially true where a specialist or group of specialists are being engaged to perform a particular service. On the other hand, many kinds of professional service contracts today involve series of operations by the supplier which do not differ significantly from some types of public works contracts. Moreover, the differentiation between what is "professional" and what is not professional becomes more and more difficult.

If a genuinely professional engagement is being made, bidding on a price basis is likely to provide a quality of output that is not altogether satisfactory. The use of "requests for proposals" and a careful evaluation of them by the procurement officer and the using agency probably afford the best potential procedure available.

Personal property control is usually the responsibility of a property control officer, with records kept by him or by the accounting unit. The purchasing agent should work closely with such officer or property custodian.

The development of specifications for public works contracts is primarily the responsibility of the public works department or its consulting architects and engineers. However, the qualified purchasing agent should review the specifications for materials and equipment to avoid closed specifications. For that portion of public improvements done by the force account, the purchasing agent should be responsible for securing the materials needed. The invitation to bid should usually be made by the purchasing agent. Tabulation of bids should be the joint responsibility of the purchasing agent and the public works department, with formal awards made by the purchasing agent.

In larger cities, a real estate bureau is normally responsible for the purchase of real estate (land and buildings); the repair and rental of city-owned properties; the leasing of office or warehouse space; and, sometimes, the maintenance, repair, and operation of all city-owned buildings. But, the procurement of the materials, tools, and other items incident to these operations should normally be assigned to the purchasing unit.

Purchasing agents have often been required to assume all sorts of "house-keeping" duties. Because of the volume of work involved and its sometimes rather tenuous relationship to the procurement function, these duties would be better assigned to a special unit for administrative services. Such housekeeping activities include: janitorial and minor repair work for city buildings; central telephone service; central mail room and messenger service; the typewriter repair and service shop; other repair and carpentry shops; and the operation of a motor pool or central garage. The purchasing agent should purchase automotive equipment, parts, gasoline, lubricants, and other items for an automotive center; but, he should not have the operating responsibility. On the other hand, the operation of central duplicating and printing services has now become a fairly common responsibility of the purchasing division.

Qualifications of the Principal Procurement Officer

The principal procurement officer should be considered an important official in every local government. If he serves a small government, it is necessary that he be personally acquainted with the features of materials, supplies, and equipment. If he serves a large government, he should still have substantial knowledge concerning these matters, even though his principal responsibility will be that of administration.

Although much of the knowledge of the procurement officer is gained through practical experience on-the-job, broader training is now available in a number of major universities as well as inservice training through a variety of specialized training programs.

As the complexities of the procurement task expand, it becomes increasingly important that he take advantage of the numerous methods of keeping abreast with developments in the field. Membership in suitable professional associations is important for professional growth and for keeping abreast of new developments.

Most professional public purchasing officers are likely to be members of one or more of the following: National Association of Purchasing Agents; National Institute of Governmental Purchasing, Inc.; or the National Association of State Purchasing Officials. Membership in the Municipal Finance Officers Association affords considerable opportunity for securing information not only on purchasing but also in other fields closely related to procurement.

Character. Regardless of professional qualifications in terms of expertise, personal character traits are of major importance. The temptations in this area are great. Unless one is honest and irreproachable as to integrity, trouble lies ahead for him. He must also be resourceful, tactful, and courageous.

Professionalization

The National Institute of Governmental Purchasing, organized in 1944, has taken the lead in developing standards for personal qualifications in the field of procurement. The Institute provides for certification of purchasing agents who meet the standards established by it, which include a comprehensive examination upon technical and managerial aspects of procurement and supply management.

12

Stores, Property Control, and Insurance

Closely associated with central purchasing, discussed in the previous chapter, are three other topics: central stores, property control, and insurance.

CENTRAL STORES

This term is used broadly to include not only central warehousing but also storage tanks and uncovered storage yards for coal, gravel, pipe, and other bulk items.

Where the using agencies are within sufficient proximity, central storage and direct distribution may eliminate the need for substores within operating units of the government. In a large municipality, however, it is usually necessary to maintain operations at numerous locations, with the central stores function concentrated upon reserve stocks with direct distribution limited to relatively few items.

One of the principal purposes of central stores is to make quantity buying possible at the right time and at lower prices. For example, in the spring or early summer, pre-seasonal competition for carloads (or tank car lots) of coal, fuel oil, cinders, rock salt, and other winter supplies, with immediate deliveries taken, often results in the lowest prices for these important items. This practice, even with storage costs and carrying charges, often proves to be the best. The municipality has the storage yards; the suppliers are often pressed for space in stockpiling for winter months. Furthermore, pre-seasonal business enables the suppliers to make more efficient use of their delivery facilities.

Central stores are also required where the lead time involved in securing delivery is substantial or uncertain. Even for items which are normally bought under lump-sum or requirements contracts, limited stocks may have to be kept on hand at times—e.g., in preparation for a threatened rail or trucking strike or other emergency, or to counter against an expected price squeeze. Again, if central stores constitute the local government's only inventories, a supply of certain items for a month, or other lead time, may be wise.

Among the considerations in determining the levels at which stores are to be maintained would be rapid inflation, such as prevailed in the 1967-1974 period. In such cases, it may be advantageous to increase inventories as a hedge against inflation; however, one must also take into consideration the losses arising from depletion of cash and reduction in interest earnings.

There is a growing tendency to avoid storage costs, wherever feasible, and to shift to either staggered buying or to requirements contracts, i.e., purchase under term contracts with future deliveries in amounts estimated at the time the contract is issued. This avoidance of storage is feasible for many items. However, if the vendor must carry the storage costs, the overhead will appear in his bid price. Policy decisions should be made in light of a full evaluation of each of the foregoing factors, with a composite weighting.

Central stores means not only the maintenance and distribution of expendable items but also the central control and management of these items in order to reduce the accumulation of surplus inventories which eventually become obsolete and must be sold at minimal prices. Good management includes the accumulation and evaluation of costs, turnover, and other essential data.

The advantages of centralized vs. decentralized warehousing or storage are usually, but not always, in favor of the former. In a very large municipality, with widespread buildings and institutions, complete centralization is not feasible. Where it is feasible, lower overhead costs and operating costs should be possible because responsibility can be fixed in one supervisor; space and handling equipment can be better utilized; deliveries from one central point permit consolidation; protective measures (fences, night watchmen, etc.) are more economical; and physical inventories can be completed more efficiently. In most cases, better planning of total stock levels might also result.

Good warehousing facilities and a central stores organization, however, can easily prove to be a mixed blessing. Some cities have found that the following tendencies must be combated:

1. Overstocking, with resultant obsolescence
2. Stocking too many items, rather than restriction of inventory to items of substantial demand and easy accessibility
3. Failure to consider the proper relationship between the cost of stocking an item and the value of the item
4. Failure to take into account the full range of cost elements

When do central stores constitute an economical unit?

With the exception of a few bulk items, delivery under term contract is likely to prove more economical for many smaller governments. The enticement of more favorable unit prices in many items, e.g., stationery, frequently induces the purchase of larger quantities than circumstances warrant, thereby producing higher total costs while still reducing unit costs. For the larger governments, the problem is even more complex.

In all governments, comparative unit and total cost data should be periodically accumulated to demonstrate the relative advantages and disadvantages of the use of central stores vs. decentralized stores or reliance upon requirements contracts for specific items. Exhibit 2 provides a convenient checklist of the items to be considered in making such a comparison.

Exhibit 2
ELEMENTS OF COST TO BE CONSIDERED IN DECISION TO MAINTAIN CENTRAL INVENTORY vs. SUPPLY UNDER REQUIREMENTS CONTRACTS

Item	Costs Involved in Operation of Central Stores	Costs Involved Under Requirements Contracts
1. Cost of commodity FOB central stores warehouse	....	
Cost of commodity FOB point of use or departmental warehouse		....
2. Cost of central warehousing		
a. Labor	....	
b. Employee benefits	....	
c. Rental value of equipment in warehouse	....	
d. Inventory shrinkage	....	
e. Interest on value of inventory	....	
f. Obsolescence	....	
g. Insurance	....	
3. Delivery costs		
a. Rental value of motorized equipment including interest on investment	....	
b. Operation of equipment		
(1) Personal services	....	
(2) Employee benefits	....	
(3) Repair and maintenance	....	
(4) Materials and supplies, e.g., motor fuels	....	
c. Motor vehicle insurance, collision, property damage, and liability	....	
4. Overhead costs, including services provided by other bureaus or departments for ordering, invoicing, accounting, periodic inventory, and prorated general administrative costs	....	
5. Rental value of warehouse and land used	....	
6. Taxes payable to local government	.... *	.... **
7. Allowance for value of time lost arising from delay in deliveries	....	....
8. Other costs	....	....
Total costs	....	....

   * This line would be blank where the local government owns the warehouse. Where it rents such space, this item would be entered as a deduction.

   ** Taxes payable should be deducted for purposes of this calculation.

Inventories

Usually, inventories of some operating supplies are carried even when there is no system of central stores. Some inventories constitute a needed margin of safety where delays in deliveries would result in work stoppages or difficulties in operations. Inventories may also exist because quantity buying results in a reduction of unit costs despite storage and carrying charges, or because practicality dictates the minimum size of deliveries under take-down or term contracts.

Forecasting, based on experience and good records, is required to maintain inventories at the proper level. Proximity to suppliers, the dangers of obsolescence, perishability, the relationship between inventory needs and the rate of progress in certain work programs are typical determinants of policy. Determination of the minimum and maximum amounts of each important item to be stocked, after surveys of past experience have been made, has proved a useful device in timing purchases. Computations of the rate of inventory turnover—for the entire stock and for individually selected items—aid in inventory planning and control. A low turnover rate suggests overstocking; a very high turnover rate may point to the need for raising the minimum level of amounts stocked. Some purchasing agents require periodic reports on slow-moving inventory items—for example, for all items where quantities will not be consumed in a 60- or 90-day period—and a computation as to the length of time the present inventory stock will last.

If there are central stores, withdrawals should be requisitioned on a standard form. Purchases for central stores are not charged against departmental appropriations until actually withdrawn. The usual procedure for recording withdrawals is as follows: A stores resquisition, properly executed by the using agency, is presented to the storekeeper. Upon delivery of the goods, the employee of the using agency signs a copy and duplicate as proof of receipt. One copy becomes the basis for posting to the proper stock cards the amounts withdrawn and reducing the amounts shown as on hand. Individual items on the requisition are next priced and the total cost of the withdrawals computed on the receipted requisition. This copy goes to the accounting office for an expenditure charge against the proper appropriation account of the using agency.

Required minimums of items to be requisitioned may be an important factor in the cost of operating central stores. In the smaller municipalities, the various using agencies are within sufficient proximity to make departmental storerooms unnecessary and deliveries from central stores possible. Even here, the storekeeper must arrive at a minimum quantity for each item that may be requisitioned. The cost of processing each requisition must be balanced against the possible wastage if minimum quantities are raised. In large municipalities, central stores may service some departments directly but act as the warehousing operation for reserve stocks held for several department storerooms. In the latter case, the central stores requisition orders will be in larger amounts.

Controls through a requisition system must be supplemented by certain other controls. Where individual items are small, valuable, easily transported and sold, or used in the ordinary household, special control devices may have to be used. A continuous record should be maintained which is suitable for both stock and cost control. The record provides information as to the quantity purchased, issued, and on hand and the unit price of the item. It should also include a statement of the conditions for reordering, i.e., the point to be reached in declining inventory before reordering. The unit price represents the total purchase price, plus the freight charges, divided by the number of units purchased. The stock of an item on hand may have been purchased at different times and at different prices. In computing the unit purchase price, a consistent practice should be followed, involving a choice to be made among three possible methods: the first-in, first-out or FIFO method; last-in, first-out or LIFO method; or the weighted average method.

Even with a perpetual inventory, periodic physical inventories are necessary. At least annually every item in stores should be physically counted and checked so as to ascertain quantities on hand, their condition, any breakage, deterioration, or shortages. Any discrepancy between the physical count and the stock record should be properly investigated and the loss accounted for. Supervision of the inventory should be vested in an office which is not in the chain of command for stores.

The method of financing the central stores operation will determine whether an overhead factor is added to the unit price billed to the using agency. If central stores receives an appropriation to cover operating expenses, no overhead factor is used. If, however, the financing of central stores is from a working capital (revolving) fund, billings will include the unit purchase price, transportation costs, and an overhead factor which includes operating expenses and losses on inventories. If all costs are not billed, the revolving fund will gradually be depleted and cease to "revolve."

From time to time, special studies should be made as to the complete costs of stocking and distributing particular materials and supplies. The resultant costs may indicate that some items should be on a standing contract with direct deliveries to the using agency. The purpose would be to shift some of the storage and handling costs to the supplier.

PROPERTY CONTROL

Real estate—whether rental properties or the land and buildings used for a municipal purpose—is outside the purview of this volume. The finance function does not include the purchase, management, and sale of real estate, nor the maintenance of buildings and grounds. Borrowing for real estate acquisition and keeping records of fixed assets are treated within the chapters on debt management and accounting.

This section is concerned with movable property and equipment. Since the purchase and disposal of such items are a part of purchasing, it seemed convenient to treat in close proximity the other management aspects, namely, records and physical control, leasing equipment and property insurance.

In the age of electronic data processing systems, it is no longer defensible to plead that suitable records cannot be kept on a fully current basis.

Records and Physical Control

Records control and the overall responsibility for the efficient management of personal property and equipment, in a large municipality, require a property control division—usually in the finance department headed by a property control officer. He should have no operational control over line officials except to require conformance with systematic, uniform procedures; his role is rather to assist them toward a more efficient utilization of property and to establish accountability for physical control. He should establish procedures and maintain records on acquisitions, transfers, and loans between departments and decide the final disposition (sale, salvage, or junking) of equipment or other personal property.

A line will have to be drawn as to the value and kinds of items to be separately recorded. Items with either a short life of usefulness or small value should be recorded and controlled as a group. Or, items of small value may be expensed at the time of acquisition and, thereby, require no inventory control since the cost of such control may be excessive. For example, some municipalities do not inventory items costing less than $50.

Location of the property control function within a finance department makes the centralization of records more feasible. With modern data processing equipment, copies of the transactions and records involved can be promptly supplied to operating officials for their purposes.

Records control serves several essential purposes. It fixes upon those with actual physical control the responsibility for custody and care of each item of movable property. This includes responsibility for proper protection against the weather, theft, fire, and other hazards and for repairs and adequate preventive maintenance. Periodic reports on any changes in condition and on maintenance are supplemented by the annual physical inventory. The objective is to reduce losses and inefficiencies as much as possible. In smaller cities, a card for each item shows the specific operating unit to which the property has been assigned. In middle and large-sized cities, records are usually maintained on the more advanced data processing systems. Transfers are authorized only upon orders which become the basis for adjustments of the inventory record.

Records are a great aid to management in other ways; they establish a precise basis for insurance claims in case of fire or other loss and assist in planning and in making budget estimates for furnishings and equipment needs. On the cards are shown the make, age, acquisition cost, condition, and, for some equipment, the mileage or hours in actual use. This information, combined with physical inspection, furnishes a precise basis for reassignment (transfer) decisions, for judgments as to suitability of the make or the item for the particular job performed, and for devising replacement schedules. The property control officer should also work closely with the purchasing agent to study the needs of the operating units for equipment and property. Surpluses in one operating unit and shortages in another can be easily identified through records control.

Identification numbers and acquisition, transfer, and disposition orders constitute the connecting links between each item and the control records and also facilitate the taking of inventories. A uniform method of coding and identifying similar items within each property group and for affixing a decal, or other marking device, should be established. A code symbol might indicate the type or group with numbers in numerical sequence assigned within each type or group. The most common device for marking is the prenumbered decalcomania, or a prenumbered metal tag, but many others are in use. A number should be retired when the item for which it has been used is retired or disposed of.

Physical inventories are necessary in order to verify the accuracy of records periodically. This work may be cycled throughout the year so that it does not become a heavy burden at year's end. The actual affixing of identification numbers and taking physical inventories should be carried out by employees of the property control division, not the operating units. Physical inventories may reveal the lack of conformance to uniform, systematic procedures. If violations are serious enough, they may become a matter to be reported to the chief administrator.

Property control is an indirect control over expenditures. To the extent that a city protects, manages, and takes good care of its property, replacements and, therefore, replacement expenditures will not be necessary. It is just as important dollarwise to conserve property or physical assets as to take care of cash and other financial assets. Both represent dollar values.

Leasing Equipment

A municipality may, at times, be faced with the alternatives of leasing or purchasing equipment. Examples which are common are electronic data processing equipment, passenger cars, trucks, typewriters, and other office equipment. Occasional rentals may include heavy duty cranes or similar specialized equipment. If a municipality has used up its debt margin, or is faced with the policy that capital expenditures are to be kept at a fixed level and capital equipment is badly needed, leasing may be the only solution. But, generally, there is a choice.

We are not concerned here with short-term rentals (a month up to a year) of equipment to meet occasional needs. Nor are we discussing lease-purchase agreements which are more feasible, if at all, in the acquisition of buildings, as opposed to equipment.

The alternatives of lease vs. purchase of equipment should be compared primarily on an economic (i.e., cost-benefit) basis. Both estimates must be reduced to the same period. A lease is usually for a period of one to four years, whereas the purchase of a capital asset commits the municipality for a longer period. Having determined the estimated life that the capital equipment will be utilized, if purchased, leasing costs must be projected over the same period. The factors to be applied are set forth in Exhibit 3.

Even if the asset is purchased with current budget funds or an accumulated reserve, rather than borrowed money, an "imputed cost of capital" should be calculated on the purchase price. This money could have been invested or used for some other purpose and, therefore, has at least an alternate cost. It is essential that costs be brought to a present value basis in order that a proper comparison may be made.

It is possible with some fleet-leasing companies to get a "complete maintenance-leasing contract." The contract might include everything except the driver: all gasoline, oil and tires; maintenance, damage repairs and insurance; cost

Exhibit 3
RELATIVE COST OF RENTAL vs. OWNERSHIP OF EQUIPMENT

Item	Ownership	Rental
1. Depreciation	....	
2. Interest on depreciated value	....	
3. Rental		....
4. Insurance payable by lessee	....	....
5. Maintenance and repair costs	....	....
6. Cost of providing substitute equipment during down-time	....	....
7. Materials and supplies involved in operation of equipment, e.g., motor fuel	....	....
8. Non-vehicle costs due to inadequate operational efficiency of vehicle	....	....
Total	....	....

Notes: 1. Depreciation should be computed on basis of original cost less estimated or actual salvage cost.
2. Interest is on the undepreciated cost of investment in the equipment. Interest should be calculated on the same periodic basis as rental.
3. Rental is as paid.
4. Insurance includes actual amounts identified as insurance, or, in the case of self-insured operations, an amount estimated as equivalent to providing the same coverage.
5. Costs of maintenance and repair should be computed on a basis which excludes the proceeds of insurance reimbursement and the value of the manufacturer's reimbursement for costs developed by the government during the warranty period.
6. If substitute equipment is provided to cover the time that primary equipment is inoperable or unavailable for use, the cost of such substitute equipment should be entered here. If, under a rental arrangement, the lessor guarantees the availability of substitute equipment, an entry should be made under that column for the lease arrangement indicating a zero cost.
7. Materials used can vary with the age and individual efficiency of units of equipment. Only the age factor can appropriately be taken into account.
8. Non-vehicle costs due to inadequate operational efficiency include the extra costs which may arise from the use of over-age equipment. The direct equipment cost factor may not be influenced, but the ability of the men depending upon the equipment to perform their assigned responsibilities may be impaired—even though the equipment is not considered inoperable. Thus, the inefficiency of old equipment may result in a requirement of 10 hours to complete a task that otherwise could be completed in 7.5 hours. The extra costs of the 2.5 hours would have to be charged to the older equipment.

of painting, lettering, garaging and servicing—including road service. A municipal garage operation might be eliminated if most automotive equipment were under such a comprehensive contract.

If the local government has a well-run central garage, it already has the records to justify or challenge a new approach to its automotive equipment needs. The need for special bodies and equipment for trucks, however, may make the comparison of truck costs more complicated or inaccurate than a comparison of costs for passenger cars. A growing number of firms lease trucks and cars, but not very specialized vehicles, such as garbage-handling equipment. For such specialized types, leasing may not offer any economies because the limited demand does not allow for large-scale purchases which are the main source of the economies which the lessor firm can pass on.

There is also the possibility of purchasing equipment under what is known as a "life cost cycle" arrangement. In this instance, the supplier guarantees to maintain the equipment for its life cycle and to sell it to produce a fixed cost per month. This has the advantage of enabling the local government to use its tax-free interest position in current financing (where such rates are less than the taxable rates available to the supplier).

It must be stressed that if, under the lease alternative, new equipment is to be substituted each year, the comparison will have to be shifted to a different basis. The alternatives would then be the purchase of new equipment to be traded in each year vs. the rental of new equipment each year. Other investment comparisons are possible; for example, the lease of new equipment as opposed to the continued operation of present equipment with high repair and maintenance costs. Into this comparison, however, should be brought a third possibility, namely, purchase of new equipment for replacement of the old.

The fact that many business firms are leasing fleets of motor vehicles does not constitute proof that the same policy is wise for a local government. The large leasing companies once had the advantage of fleet discounts; however, recent actions of the Federal Trade Commission appear to have discouraged this practice. Among the factors which tend to favor leasing are: (1) the advantages gained from the tax benefit available in accelerated depreciation for the lessor; (2) advantages of improved insurance rates obtainable on a fleet basis; (3) the potential for greater efficiency in handling repair and maintenance (both in actual costs and in lesser amounts of down-time); and (4) the potential for obtaining a higher price through hard bargaining in the disposition of equipment.

On the other hand, where the local government purchases the equipment, it usually avoids state and local sales taxes (and federal excise taxes when these are applicable); ownership by the local government, ordinarily, means immediate full payment, without payment of interest costs; and, even if interest is involved, it is likely to be at lower rates than those obtainable by lessors (unless a public authority, in effect, lends the money to the lessor).

The specific plan offered the local government must be weighed against the alternative of purchasing. Not all the arguments advanced by leasing companies will stand up under careful analysis. For example, it is claimed that leasing provides a guarantee against inflation, that is, if used cars depreciate rapidly and new car prices remain high or are increased the lessee is protected against this spread in replacement costs. This is only true for the term of the contract. If, at the end of the contract, the leasing company finds that used car depreciation has been greater than expected, it will not renew the contract at the same rates. It is also claimed that leasing provides a fleet of well-kept vehicles with few maintenance worries. This is true; but if the municipality should replace its own vehicles on the same schedule as leased vehicles, the same advantage may accrue.

The leasing company may not have the financial soundness and managerial capacity to perform as promised. If the company fails, the lessor government may be put to major inconvenience and unanticipated expense in securing an alternative source of supply of the equipment necessary to maintain governmental services.

There is one other aspect of the problem. Because of the profit motive of the firms which lease equipment, leasing can easily push a municipality into a higher standard of equipment use, perhaps an unwarranted high standard. It may be necessary to have a new fleet of cars each year for police patrol work and for fire department specialists who must dash to the scene in automobiles; but, new cars each year for the entire police force could hardly be justified. Certainly, the rental of new cars each year for the entire municipal organization would be setting a public standard of living as high as the wealthiest taxpayer—and not the average taxpayer.

The same type of reasoning holds true for the size and make of the leased automobile. In general, the public standard should not be higher than that of the average taxpayer. The annual lease cost as opposed to a single capital outlay might tempt the municipality to step up to higher-priced cars. We endorse, as sound, a view expressed many years ago by a wise municipal consultant:

> "With very few exceptions there is no legitimate justification for going out of the lowest price range in acquiring passenger cars. There may be some reason in allowing the mayor or manager of a city of 100,000 people the use of a large car in the middle price range, and in a few other instances the fact that cars are used frequently for long journeys may warrant a similar liberality. For 99 cases of 100, cars in the lowest price range are fast and comfortable enough. The arguments that the author has heard for large cars for every kind of municipal work have been many and ingenious. They have scarcely ever survived analysis."[1]

Under a lease-purchase agreement for financing the acquisition of a building, the contract provides that the title will pass to the lessee upon the expiration of the term of the lease or, at any time during the term, upon payment of the balance due, after allowing a percentage of the lease payments to be credited toward the purchase price.

If there are advantages to the lease-purchase arrangement in the acquisition of buildings, these are likely to lie in a more prudent design, a more efficient means of construction, and a lesser amount of interest during construction. Yet, one must also take into account the importance of depreciation, especially accelerated depreciation, which is available to the private owner. In any event, the most careful analysis is required for a proper comparison.

In the entire leasing operation it must be kept in mind that the tax savings realized in leverage-leasing are available only to persons and corporations subject to federal income taxes.

---

[1] Reed, Thomas H., *Municipal Management*, (New York: McGraw-Hill, 1941), p. 347.

INSURANCE

The operations of government involve such a wide range of activities that a correspondingly wide range of risks arise. Some governments—especially larger ones—choose to be largely self-insured; others depend upon a wide range of insurance protection purchased. The choice is one warranting deliberate decision —a decision which should be comprehensively reviewed from time to time in light of changing conditions.

For many years, the typical local government was interested in insurance only for the protection of real and personal property from such hazards as fire and windstorm. During the past half-century, however, this emphasis has changed and other areas of asset protection and protection against damage claims by others have come to the fore.[2] The old doctrine of sovereign immunity has eroded and most local governments can now be held responsible for the acts of their employees, insofar as they affect other employees or the lives and property of other citizens. Further, it is now customary for local governments to arrange for life insurance and health insurance for employees and their dependents, the premiums being paid in whole, or in part, by the local government.

Accordingly, what was once a routine commodity has increased in dimension and complexity. The development and production of a sound insurance program is an activity warranting careful consideration in any local government today. Responsibility for the entire insurance program should be vested with a single official—usually the principal finance officer or the purchasing agent. A planned policy, program, systematic records and procedures, and accountability are made easier.

Risk identification is the first important step in the establishment of an insurance program and there are three methods in general use:
1. The insurance survey approach
2. The insurance policy-checklist approach
3. The enumeration and classification of all possible risks, not just those which are insurable[3]

Having identified its insurance risks, there are several methods of purchasing insurance coverage, including competitive bidding; buying through a broker or a board representing all, or a group of, local agents; dividing the business among several agents; and buying from only one agent. There is a trend toward competitive bidding but a frequently used method is to place the insurance through a broker who is designated by, and acts for, a group. The local government deals with one broker or a committee of brokers who also act as advisers to the government on insurance matters. The number of policies is kept at a minimum; for example, a single policy may be sufficient for each type of insurance, or even

---

[2] An informative presentation of current practice is detailed in a study by Jerry D. Todd, *Effective Risk and Insurance Management in Municipal Government*, (Austin: The University of Texas, Institute of Public Affairs, 1970), 138 pp.

[3] A discussion of these approaches is contained in a report by Harris, B. Felix, "Obtaining Lowest Premium Costs and Maximum Coverages," *Insuring Against the Hazards Common in Public Administration*, Special Bulletin 1953H, (Chicago: Municipal Finance Officers Association, 1953), pp. 11-12.

for several related risks. One advantage to the local government is that, in case of loss, there will be only one proof of loss, one adjuster, and one settlement; other advantages are avoidance of the purchase of duplicate coverage and voids in the pattern of coverage.[3] The local government gets a single, responsible source of coverage and/or premium information and the convenience of dealing with one person. Similar results are obtained if a placement board, rather than a broker, represents the local agents.[4]

The least desirable method is for the city to attempt to divide the business. The whole problem can then very easily become involved in politics—no one agent feels responsible for an overall program approach and, generally, there are inherent dollar inefficiencies in a fragmented program. When a loss occurs, it may be discovered that more than one policy applies, causing each carrier to implicate the other.

Competitive bidding is usual because, when competition is introduced, lower premium costs often result. Not all insurance rates are the same and, even if they are, if dividends or recredit adjustments are available, these vary—resulting in net cost differentials. Bid specifications have to be carefully drawn and minimum standards established for eligibility to compete. For example, a stock company may be required to have a Best's Insurance Guide rating or A or A-plus with a paid-up capital stock and surplus which is significant in relation to the risks involved. Service need not suffer because agents know that service, including fire prevention engineering service, will be considered in an award to the "lowest and best bidder."

Stock companies are mentioned above; however, mutual companies should be permitted to bid. In prior years, mutual companies were suspect because of their assessable nature; but now, virtually all of the larger mutuals are non-assessable and, while many small assessable mutual companies still exist, bids from them should not be entertained.

Fire insurance policies can be written on a three-year, prepaid basis at a ten percent discount. This can be an important factor; however, the true cost must be determined.[5] Having the same expiration date on all policies is a convenience which allows all renewals to be arranged at the same time. This is very important in those years in which a change is to be made in basic coverage covenants.

One important insurance decision relates to the extent of coverage. Some local governments exclude small risks, but many municipalities cover all buildings and their contents. There is a definite trend toward blanket policies which covers all properties. Yet sometimes it is desirable to secure independent coverage through separate policies for high risk, high value properties. This may be desirable because their inclusion could have a disproportionate effect on the entire premium; it may be necessary because the insurance company will not entertain the hazardous exposure. Such exposures can be handled separately with

---

[4] Harris, *op. cit.*, in which the author notes that the Placement Board Plan in Dallas has attracted wide attention.

[5] Bureau of Municipal Research and Service, University of Oregon, *Insurance Practices of Oregon Cities*, (University of Oregon, Eugene), Information Bulletin No. 94, 1954, 47 pp.

the same, or with another, insurer. As much equipment as possible should be insured as a part of the building. Wherever feasible, it may be desirable to attach equipment to floors or walls because anything affixed to the building comes under the building rates, which are generally lower.

Before construction contracts are awarded, plans for new construction should be reviewed for their insurance implications. Even slight changes in construction plans may produce substantial insurance savings. Substantial changes in existing structures—such as the installation of fire doors, automatic sprinklers, and alarm systems—may also result in worthwhile rate reductions. Good housekeeping may also reduce risk hazards which invite penalty charges on contents. If, for example, bulk alcohol is stored in a large hospital building the penalty may be very substantial; if stored in a small out-building, the cost may be negligible.

Fire and extended coverage are the basic municipal property coverages. Extended coverage, once subject to a variety of wordings, is now generally standardized to include losses from windstorm, hail, explosions, riots, riots attending a strike, civil commotions, and damage resulting from aircraft, vehicles, or smoke. Vandalism and malicious mischief coverage may accompany standard coverage. Boiler machinery insurance is usually purchased separately because of the necessity for regular periodic inspection service. This service, before a loss occurs, is most valuable in reducing interruptions in operations and possible serious disasters.

Local governments will usually, through a co-insurance clause, take advantage of greater coverage at a lower premium cost. This is an agreement between the insured and the insurance carrier that the insured will maintain insurance on his property equal to a certain percentage of its insurable value. By offering reduced rates to owners who insure their property close to its full value, the companies seek to combat a tendency of building owners to carry too little insurance. When the insured carries sufficient insurance to comply with the co-insurance clause, he will be entitled to collect the entire loss up to the face value of the policy. If, however, he fails to carry the agreed percentage in the co-insurance clause, he may collect, in the event of loss, only that portion which the amount of insurance carried bears to the amount of insurance he contracted to carry. The results under co-insurance can be illustrated by the three hypothetical cases contained in Exhibit 4. In the first two cases, partial losses are sustained; in the third, total loss of the property is incurred.

The possibility of incurring the co-insurance penalty or being under-insured, as described in the illustration above, has diminished. In these days of "blanket" policies and "agreed amount" clauses, the insured benefits by:

1. The "blanket" policy which provides the total amount of all buildings and the contents of any single structure, thereby negating the possibility of insufficient insurance

2. The "agreed amount" clause which simply states that the total amount of insurance carried satisfies the co-insurance requirement—no questions asked—thereby nullifying the co-insurance penalty cited in Case 2 above

The term "insurable value" in fire insurance means that value which can be insured—essentially, the superstructure of buildings. Insurable value may be

Exhibit 4
OPERATION OF 90 PERCENT CO-INSURANCE[1]

Item	Case 1	Case 2	Case 3
Actual cash value of property	$100,000	$100,000	$100,000
Amount of insurance required to be carried by the 90% co-insurance clause	90,000	90,000	90,000
Insurance actually carried	90,000	60,000	90,000
Loss sustained	36,000	36,000	100,000
Amount collectible from the insurance company	36,000	24,000	90,000
Amount paid for by insured	none	12,000	10,000

[1] Illustration adapted from *Insurance Practices of Oregon Cities*, p. 3.

considered on an actual cash value (cost of replacement less depreciation) or on a replacement cost basis.

The benefits of "agreed amount" and "blanket" coverage notwithstanding, the prudent insurance buyer will endeavor to upgrade his insurable values periodically and to keep abreast of constantly increasing construction costs. In fact, the insurance company may require such reappraisals annually.

On the other hand, exercise of discretion is called for where replacement costs are high but the remaining economic value of the structure is low due to age, condition, or obsolescence, e.g., an ancient outmoded civic auditorium.

Public Liability Insurance

Aside from fire and extended coverage, municipalities also carry public liability and motor vehicle liability insurance. These two types of insurance may be combined in a single policy, though many local governments prefer separate contracts.

Public liability protects the local government and its officials from liability for bodily injury and property damage arising from the general activities of the government, other than the operation of automotive equipment. For example, liability may arise from the sale of goods or products causing injury, such as internal injuries from the consumption of food or refreshments purchased in a public park or a school cafeteria. Other hazards include injuries within public buildings or on public property. Elevators, construction sites, an auditorium, a hospital or clinic, an airport, golf courses, playgrounds, streets and sidewalks, swinging bridges, and other properties provide hazards out of which damage suits may arise.

Public liability hazards may also arise out of contracts entered into by the government. Where a property (or concession thereon) is leased to another party, the desirability of requiring the lessee to purchase the insurance should be explored. In the case of contracts for new construction, however, it may be to the local government's advantage to cover all public liability hazards and so prescribe in the specifications calling for competitive construction bids. This would apply if the government enjoyed a very favorable public liability rate and was acting as general contractor. However, bid specifications frequently require the contractor(s) and subcontractor(s) to release the government from any responsibility for bodily injury or property damage resulting from performance of the contract. If the government is sued, the contractor or his insurer must defend the government and hold it harmless in the event of an adverse judgment.

Automobile liability insurance protects against claims arising from the operation of the designated motor vehicle fleet. Street equipment (graders, sweepers, rollers and the like) is considered as mobile equipment and is covered under the public liability policy. If a blanket policy is used, different rates will be applied to the various types of vehicles and equipment. The local government may also wish to be covered for exposure which arises when employees use their own cars, on a reimbursable basis, for official business. Ideally, the government should buy a Comprehensive Automobile Liability Policy which will protect it against losses caused by any automobile. This policy contains a provision that new equipment is automatically covered. Some local governments require the insurance carriers to keep the government advised as to progress in the settlement of claims and the final disposition of each claim. This information enables the government to maintain an experience record which becomes a guide for future insurance decisions.

In some states, local governments are immune from liability in the performance of their "governmental" functions but not when engaged in "proprietary" activities. Limitation on the governments liability may, however, only pass the hazard on to the injured or to the public official or employee if his negligence can be established. There is a growing tendency to cover not only the local government but also its officials and employees against liabilities arising from activities in both the governmental and the proprietary areas. This approach recognizes a moral responsibility on the part of the local government to provide reimbursement to its citizens or others for any loss resulting from the negligent action of a public official, employee, or agent. An "immunity waiver" clause will prevent the insurance company, without the local government's consent, from denying liability for claims for which the government is not legally responsible but for which it assumes an obligation. In some jurisdictions, doubt still lingers as to the legal authority of a local government to purchase liability insurance beyond its strict legal responsibility. Nonetheless, the law is gradually making it possible for local governments to shoulder their share of automobile liability hazards equally with private individuals and corporations.

Liability insurance is no substitute for: (1) training programs for automobile, truck, and equipment operators; (2) safety education, precautions, and devices; (3) persistent efforts to eliminate hazards; and (4) constant vigilance in carrying out repairs and preventive maintenance. A safety committee to review accidents involving governmental vehicles and injured employees has proven to be a good device.[6] Full advantage should also be taken of the engineering and safety facilities of the insurance carriers.

Self-insurance

Many local governments now undertake self-insurance for large portions of the risks involved. This is particularly true of the larger local governments which own many facilities widely dispersed over large areas. (Some use the phrase "no-insurance" to denote this situation.) A self-insurance policy may be accompanied by building up reserves for the payment of claims. In other circumstances, the local government merely assumes the liabilities which are paid from current appropriations, except where the loss is very large. In the latter circumstances, the local government relies upon its power to incur debt to meet large claims or to rebuild major facilities.

A common practice is for the government to buy liability insurance with a large "deductible" for each occurrence. All losses under the deductible are assumed by the government and paid out of a special fund or current appropriations. In the event of a catastrophe, the government looks to the insurance company for any judgments in excess of the deductible. As in the choice of deductibles under public liability, governments can also retain certain losses as respects its own property under its fire insurance program. The deductibles can be of any amount, but the larger governments can generally afford to retain larger deductibles. Once again, the affordable loss is assumed by the government but, in the event of a catastrophe, replacement funds are available from the insurance company and the government's budget is not disrupted. Under all types of insurance, coverage records should be kept on the loss experience, as compared with premiums paid, and these records made the basis for future decisions as to how protection can best be obtained.

Coverage in a state-operated insurance fund constitutes one alternative in a few states and Canadian provinces. South Carolina, North Dakota, and Wisconsin have had long and successful records with state funds and with municipal coverage thereunder. A number of other state funds have operated with varying degrees of success and, in some cases, offer sound opportunities to municipalities, or special classes of municipalities, for economies in premium costs.

---

[6] Hunrick, William, Jr., "Automobile and Public Liability Insurance," *Municipal Finance*, November 1950, Vol. 23, No. 2, p. 88.

13

Purposes and Problems in Local Government Borrowing

The total outstanding local government debt in the United States rose from less than $1 billion in 1890 to $16.4 billion in 1932. During the Great Depression and World War II, new issuance of debt was limited and in the years 1941-1945, the total amount of outstanding local government debt actually decreased from $16.8 billion to $13.6 billion.

Since 1945 this debt has risen very rapidly—to $18.8 billion by 1950; to $51.2 billion by 1960; and $120.0 billion by 1971-72. It is likely that the debt will continue to grow at a rapid rate—perhaps reaching $250 billion by 1980 or shortly thereafter.

Local government debt figures of this magnitude show that credit is a large and important municipal financial resource; but, they also raise numerous perplexing questions respecting debt policy, debt planning, debt management, and their underlying economic implications. On the one hand, local governments have an enormous responsibility for providing the public facilities and services that are essential to the well-being and economic progress of a predominantly urban population; but, on the other hand, their resources are variously limited and their power to use these resources is variously restricted. They lack the monetary powers of the federal government and the fiscal powers of the federal and state governments. They have only such power to incur debt as is granted to them by state constitutions, state statutes, or the charters under which they operate. The use of municipal credit has contributed and can continue to contribute markedly to advancement of the local and national economies; but, under these conditions, local governments face the necessity of employing credit as productively and discriminatingly as possible.

The judicious planning and management of municipal debt are inseparable from forward-looking, overall financial planning and management for any local government. They demand a substantial amount of professional competence and skill; but, much more than this, they call for a quality of judgment and policy determination that comes only from a sound understanding of the necessary programs and long-range objectives of a community, the extent of the resources of the community that can be made available for advancing these programs, and the ways in which borrowing can be made to contribute most equitably and effectively to the desired results. Among the general considerations that must underlie the decisions of the responsible local officials are: (1) the purposes for which it is appropriate to borrow; (2) how much debt the community may safely incur; (3) the means which are to be used for controlling authorization of debt; and (4) the most suitable means of borrowing in each case.

Wise decisions as to when and how to borrow have never been easy to make and, for many reasons, they have become more difficult in recent years. One reason for this is the increasing diversity and complexity of municipal undertakings involving the incurrence of debt. The kinds of major and minor revenue-producing enterprises that municipalities engage in have multiplied, user charges have replaced taxes for the support of some facilities, and borrowing has been expanding for urban renewal, industrial aid, and related means of economic rehabilitation and advancement. Another reason is the bewildering hodgepodge of local governments which is becoming less and less well identified with the economic communities they attempt to serve and, thus, less and less able to do the unified planning and financing that the communities need. A related reason is the increasingly intergovernmental character of certain basic types of capital projects, such as water supply, storm drainage and flood control, water pollution control, and all kinds of metropolitan transportation and terminal facilities. Local governments, as they come more and more to join with their neighbors in financing such projects or share in the formation of special districts and authorities for the purpose, face new and often intricate problems of debt policy and planning.

Borrowing may be well conceived as to purpose and yet produce unsatisfactory results because it is not well planned. The planning aspect is a many-sided subject that is reviewed in Chapter 14.

Some of the misguided policies that have periodically clouded the history of municipal debt in the past have been abandoned; but, the inventiveness of legislatures and local governments and their professional advisers in developing new ones seems almost unbounded. Thus, the municipal bond market is a veritable showcase for products of borrowing policy that range from examples of distinguished financial management to demonstrations of extraordinary mismanagement. The latter, to some extent, reflect a lack of professional competence and political courage.

Any realistic appraisal of the purposes and problems of local government borrowing, as can be seen, must concern itself with the technical aspects of planning and managing debt; the appropriate place of credit in the overall financial policies of local governments; and how well local governments are equipped by their structure and fiscal powers to make judicious and effective use of their power to borrow.

THE CLASSES OF BORROWERS

Analysis of the purposes and problems of municipal borrowing needs to start with some note of the relationship between local government structure and local government debt. Broadly speaking, there are two classes of local governments to be considered, general purpose (counties, cities, villages, towns, etc.) and special purpose (school districts, special districts, authorities, etc.).

This simple classification of borrowers, however, falls short of recognizing the increasing complexity of local government structure and its implications for the problems of local government borrowing.

Not only is the continuously evolving structure of local government contributing to the intricacy of local debt but the endless search for more ways and means of borrowing is also contributing to the intricacy of governmental structure. This complicating development has been, to some extent, inevitable because of urban and metropolitan growth; but, it is partly the result of piecemeal improvising instead of comprehensive planning, along with ramshackle structural additions to evade outmoded fiscal restrictions.

Realism requires the recognition that opportunities for patronage through appointment of personnel, special counsel, bond counsel, and other functionaries also contribute to the multiplicity of debt issuing local governmental entities.

In the review contained in Chapter 2 of the structure of local government in the United States and its relation to the problems of municipal finance, certain principles are stressed that have special relevance to the incurrence of debt. First, all local governments should have jurisdiction and fiscal powers that are commensurate with their responsibilities. Second, they need unified financial planning that is as comprehensive as the scope of their operations, with decisions to borrow becoming an integral part of these overall plans. Local government structure would be simpler and stronger and the use of credit more productive and less costly if these principles were more generally observed.

General purpose governments, because they may operate revenue-producing enterprises as well as tax-supported services, draw on a considerable variety of revenue sources, have several types of borrowing instruments at their disposal, and are particularly vulnerable to fragmented borrowing policies, (unrelated to overall financial plans) that may unbalance programs, waste money, and tie the hands of management with an assortment of earmarked funds and satellite authorities. Special purpose local governments perform either single functions or a few related functions and, therefore, have a relatively narrow range of well defined borrowing requirements which appear to be amenable to control under sound borrowing principles. The actual situation is not quite so simple. School districts, for example, traditionally have financed their borrowing requirements simply, through general obligation bonds; but, in recent years, some states have set up complex state and local mechanisms for school district capital financing that violate a sound principle of borrowing solely through procedures that produce the lowest interest cost.

Among the developments in local government structure that have helped to complicate the problems of finance—including borrowing—has been the rapid growth in recent years of special purpose districts and authorities because of the increasing inability of the established system of general purpose governments to satisfy community needs for facilities and services within their current legal restrictions. These arrangements can generate more fiscal problems than they solve. The ability of these special districts to borrow adequately, and at favorable interest rates, to meet the purposes for which they have been created, depends largely on whether the available borrowing instruments and sources of supporting revenue are appropriate for these purposes. There has been a growing tendency to disregard this consideration in the creation of new special districts and to make bonds which are supported solely by user charges serve purposes for which they are not well suited. For example, a new water district created to serve a rapidly growing community and restricted to the levy of user charges and the issuance of bonds secured exclusively by such charges may not be well situated to finance the reserve supply and excess capacity of the distribution system required for long-term economy and safety.

A related shortcoming in the structural background for borrowing is the very considerable and increasing number of subsidiary agencies of local governments, usually designated authorities, which have debts outstanding in their own names but lack sufficient autonomy to be classed as separate governments. Most of these agencies have been created solely, or principally, for the purpose of incurring limited obligation debt and many of them have no sound reason for existence, except to provide a vehicle for overcoming unwise debt limits.

In some cases, the independent authority performs a very legitimate purpose, e.g., operating a self-sustaining local enterprise or providing financing for certain types of community programs such as non-profit hospitals. On the other hand, in instances in which they are created only for the purpose of evading legal debt limits or the safeguards established in law for the sale of bonds, it is doubtful that these authorities should be continued. If continued, the continuation should be coupled with strong efforts to remove unnecessary restrictions on debt which gave rise to the unwise limits that was responsible for creation of the authority.

This proliferation of new local governments and pseudo-governments is diffusing the responsibility for debt policy and management. An economically and geographically integrated community, whether it be rural, urban, or metropolitan in character, ideally needs some kind of unified direction to plan, finance, and operate the basic public services and facilities that are community-wide in character. Without such an arrangement, it is virtually impossible to evaluate a community's available overall financial resources, draw on them equitably, apportion them judiciously as to purpose and priority, and apply them effectively. The structure of local government falls short of this requirement most conspicuously where it is needed most—in the erupting metropolitan areas, large and small, where the bulk of the nation's population lives. Local government in most of these areas is a jumble of independent general purpose and special purpose agencies, some of them with dependent subsidiaries, piled up in untidy overlapping layers, and with no correlation of their respective shares of the area's fiscal resources with their fiscal needs.

Some progress has been made toward metropolitan area government, both by the activation of metropolitan counties and the creation of special purpose metropolitan districts, and more progress is in the making. A good record in the consolidation of school districts in some states is encouraging. However, an enumeration of the major special purpose metropolitan districts now providing, variously, water supply, flood control, sanitation, park, transportation, terminal, and other facilities makes a rather imposing list—reflecting ingenious improvisation toward metropolitan government on a piecemeal basis. Continuation of the process would supply each metropolitan area not with unified metropolitan government for performance of the functions assigned or assignable on a metropolitan basis. Instead, the region will have a galaxy of separate special purpose metropolitan governments competing for use of the area's fiscal resources.

These structural shortcomings of local government create a dual problem for municipal debt planning and management. On the one hand, there is the responsibility of borrowers to follow approved principles in the incurrence of debt. On the other hand, there is the problem of how to reverse the deteriorating trends in the local governmental and legal environment within which debt must be planned and managed. This is only one aspect of the basic problem of how to adjust the structure and powers of local government for a better satisfaction of community requirements, but it is a demanding aspect because of the importance of public credit in a community's development and the lasting handicaps in its misuse. Since borrowing involves long-term contractural commitments, it can take a long time to undo mistakes.

THE PURPOSES OF BORROWING

The purposes for which local governments may borrow and the amounts of debt which they may incur are regulated variously by state constitutions, legislatures, and local charters. Some of these regulations are still influenced by the conviction of conservative civic leaders of a century ago, when local governments were having their first great fling at floating bond issues, that municipal indebtedness was evil and municipal borrowing a form of sin. But, within these legal restrictions, local governments generally have very considerable range for exercise of good judgment and foresight, or the opposite, in the formulation and execution of debt policy.

The Role of Borrowing

The question of the appropriate role of borrowing (the use of public credit) in the conduct of local government is essentially one of how local government capital expenditures should be financed—when they should be met from current or accumulated revenues and when from loans, which are in anticipation of future revenue. Part of the answer can be found in the nature of the responsibilities assigned and the revenues available to local governments. Each local government is responsible for the administration of designated public service functions. In the performance of some of these functions expensive capital facilities are required and, unless they are available when they are needed and to the extent they are needed, substandard, financially wasteful performance is virtually inevitable.

To meet the totality of operating and capital requirements as needed and to provide for emergencies that may arise from time to time there is likely to be considerable year-to-year fluctuations in the level of expenditures. But the revenue systems of most local governments are neither very broad nor very flexible. To keep tax rates and charges fluctuating in a correspondingly wide range would be demoralizing to the tax and rate payers. The primary purpose of municipal borrowing, therefore, is to permit timely financing of needed expenditures without causing such fluctuations when they cannot be otherwise avoided by careful planning. An alternative to borrowing is the accumulation of surplus and reserves. There are situations in which this procedure is very desirable; but, in practice, it has too many limitations to be relied on extensively.

There may be quite as much justification for a local government to pay in installments through long-term borrowing for a hospital, park, school building, or extension of a water system as for an individual to use the installment plan for buying a house, automobile, or other durable goods. This method of financing does cost more, however, because of the interest charge; it may tend to induce less careful and thrifty deliberation because the financial impact on the purchaser is deferred instead of immediate. Responsible, foresighted financial management calls, therefore, for finding the combination of cash spending and borrowing that will obtain the most value from the resources available without wide gyrations in the revenue requirements.

The foregoing comments emphasize the role of borrowing by local government as an instrument of financial policy. Its primary purpose is to enable local governments to meet their public service responsibilities continuously, effectively, and on a timely basis—without erratic fluctuations in taxes and charges. In serving this purpose, however, borrowing policy also should be directed to maintaining the long-term financial stability of local government and, to the extent that it is feasible, cooperation with the federal government for economic stabilization.

Some clarification of these goals is possible by review of the purposes for which local governments borrow. There are two general classes of borrowing to be considered (based upon the term of borrowing): (1) temporary loans and (2) long-term loans.

Short-term Borrowing

Local governments engage in temporary borrowing for three general purposes: (1) in anticipation of the receipt of revenue; (2) to meet emergencies not foreseen in the budget; and (3) in anticipation of the issuance of bonds for capital purposes.

Revenue Anticipation Borrowing. Many local governments, although operating with balanced budgets, engage regularly in temporary borrowing in anticipation of revenues to meet current operating requirements. The ability to do such borrowing helps to assure the uninterrupted functioning of the government operations and the regular and prompt payment of debt service and other fixed charges.

The need for revenue anticipation notes ordinarily arises from a delayed flow of revenue because major elements of revenue are due and payable late in the fiscal year. This has historically been true in those communities which are dependent upon an agricultural economy coupled with the calendar year as the fiscal period. Thus, where crops are, for the most part, harvested in the fall, it is necessary either to carry over very large cash surpluses from one year to the next or to borrow on temporary revenue anticipation notes until taxpayers are in a position to make payments.

The point of view of most students of public finance has been that the interest charges required under these procedures constitute an unwise public expenditure. Some, however, hold that, inasmuch as the interest rates payable by local governments are usually low, it is perhaps more economical to hold to the traditional revenue payment dates because the alternative of advancing the due dates has the effect of depriving citizens of the use of money which is more valuable, in terms of interest, than the interest being paid by the local government.

A major consideration in charting the course of action to be followed lies in the amount of such temporary borrowing and the impact of such borrowing upon the credit of the municipality. (See Chapter 14 for a further discussion of this point.)

Dependence upon revenue anticipation borrowing varies widely among local governments of similar type. Some cities, e.g., New York, Chicago, and Philadelphia, in recent years regularly borrow large amounts in anticipation of revenue. Others still have a pattern of revenue flow which enables them to avoid this practice. Thus, Los Angeles is reported to have had no revenue anticipation borrowing, other than interfund, since 1907.

One of the factors which can contribute to the amount of such temporary borrowing lies in the difficulty, both political and legal, in carrying over large amounts of surplus at year-end. Frequently, the law requires that all such surplus, except that required to meet bills from the prior year's operation, be budgeted as a resource for the ensuing budget year.

The regular use of temporary borrowing to finance operations arises primarily because the collection of revenue is not timed to coincide with cash demands for expenditures. This lack of synchronization may occur because the property tax does not become payable until the fiscal year is well advanced; because an important shared tax, grant, or reimbursement due from another government is not received until late in the year; or for other, similar reasons. Widespread action to provide for installment payment of property taxes well coordinated with the fiscal year was spurred by the financial stringency of the 1930s depression, but it failed to reach some areas. In Massachusetts, for example, no penalty attaches for nonpayment of taxes until two months before the close of the fiscal year; in Rhode Island, according to a study published in 1959, one or more of the quarterly tax payment dates in many of the cities and towns fall in the year following the one which the tax is designed to finance[1]; and, in Chicago, taxes for any year do not become due and payable until the following year—accounting for the large loans outstanding at the year-end.

Undue use of revenue anticipation borrowing is sometimes induced by unrealistic budgeting of property taxes. The full tax levy is accrued as revenue without allowance for losses through abatement and uncollectibility, or for very slow collections. Loans are carried against the uncollected portions of the levies and renewed from year-to-year for several years before some kind of deferred provision is made to offset the budgeting of fictitious revenue. The amount of routine revenue anticipation borrowing depends also on whether local governments operate on a hand-to-mouth basis or carry over from year-to-year enough cash surplus or reserve funds to maintain adequate working capital.

---

[1] Institute of Public Administration, *State-Local Relations in Metropolitan Rhode Island,* 1959, pp. 131-134.

Los Angeles' freedom from temporary borrowing, noted above, has been due largely to the maintenance of a revolving fund which can be drawn on in the months of low revenue receipts.

Avoidance of temporary borrowing in anticipation of revenue realization involves these steps:

1. More alert cash management
2. Better synchronization of revenue receipts with cash requirements through modification of due dates for principal elements of revenue
3. Acceleration of settlement by state and federal governments in the case of transfer payments—for both categorical grants and general revenue-sharing
4. Creation of suitable reserves for nonpayment of taxes payable within the year if significant delinquencies are a recurring factor
5. Development of more adequate working capital funds

In some cases, the use of interfund borrowing can avoid requirements for going to the market; however, under most circumstances, the moneys available for loan by one fund to another can be invested on more advantageous terms than the rates which are charged for temporary loans in anticipation of revenue receipts.

In any event, the state laws regulating the conduct of local finance should place adequate safeguards on revenue anticipation borrowing and also seek to make it unnecessary as a normal procedure.[2]

Temporary Borrowing for Emergencies. Budgets should be sufficiently flexible to provide for the minor contingencies which arise in the regular conduct of operations; but, from time to time, local governments find it necessary to finance sizable emergency expenses for which insufficient or no provision has been made in the budget. Emergencies of a major character may include disasters caused by such natural forces as flood, hurricane, fire and drought, or even an exceptionally severe winter that multiplies the normal cost of snow removal and leaves streets and highways in a dilapidated condition. An emergency might also arise from the rendering of a large judgment against a local government or failure of an important source of revenue to produce as planned. When an emergency is genuine, not merely the product of defective budgeting, and expenses of the government exceed available appropriated revenues and contingency reserves, the use of temporary borrowing is justifiable. To the extent feasible, such borrowing should be retired in the current or subsequent fiscal year; however, much of it may have to be converted to long-term debt.

The local finance laws of some states provide strict regulation of emergency borrowing. The National Municipal League's *Model Accrual Budget Law* proposes, "for other than a regular or recurring requirement, to protect the public health, safety or welfare," a limit of 3 percent of the operating appropriations in the budget; only upon recommendation by the budget officer and after approval by a three-fifths vote of the governing body; with retirement of the loan required before the end of the next fiscal year.

---

[2] Reasonable standards are proposed in the *Model Accrual Budget Law* and *Model Cash Basis Budget Law* published by the National Municipal League.

Temporary Borrowing for Capital Financing. Such borrowing takes the form of bond anticipation notes, capital notes, and special assessment notes. Temporary notes in anticipation of bond revenues are issued, and may sometimes be renewed, for limited periods after bonds have been authorized. Such notes are ordinarily retired from the proceeds of bond sales. By their use, the borrower may be able to reduce the cost of interest during the construction of large projects through temporary financing, as funds are required.

There are circumstances in which a local government is able to save money through the early sale of the entire bond issue and investment of the proceeds on a temporary basis, pending the need for the funds. However, a very careful scrutiny of this practice frequently discloses that the actual costs are less through the use of bond anticipation notes.

If bond anticipation notes are to be used, it is desirable to provide substantial flexibility to the local government as to the total time they may be outstanding, e.g., four or five years; however, it is essential that this flexibility not be permitted solely for the avoidance of payment of the principal that otherwise would have been paid had the bonds been issued when the project was begun. Thus, a provision may be included requiring retirements at the end of each year of five percent of the total amounts of bond anticipation notes outstanding—except in the case of revenue bonds where interest during construction is being funded into the long-term bonds.

Capital notes, usually maturing in one or two years, are used to finance capital projects when local governments wish to pay for them virtually from current revenues. With the same objective, bond anticipation notes sometimes are retired wholly, or in part, from current revenues. Special assessment notes are issued in anticipation of the receipt of special assessments levied to finance local improvements or in anticipation of the sale of special assessment bonds.

Long-term Borrowing

Long-term borrowing is ordinarily to finance the acquisition of land or capital improvements thereupon. However, numerous bond issues have been sold to pay for costs arising from emergencies, judgments, and even the funding of current deficits or accumulated unpaid operating expenses.[3]

The major portion of all local debt is long-term debt. In 1971 long-term debt accounted for approximately 90 percent of total outstanding debt. However, a considerable portion of the short-term debt was due to bond anticipation notes.

Purposes of Debt Issuance. Two measures of the outstanding debt of local governments are afforded by the data contained in Tables 21 and 22. The long-term debt outstanding for all local governments in 1971 was $99.3 billion—about one-eighth of which was issued within the year. Also, in that year

---

[3] In 1939, the city of Philadelphia issued a large amount of funding bonds through the lessee of its gas works (The United Gas Improvement Company), using the proceeds of the loan to liquidate floating debt and unpaid obligations accumulated during the years of depression.

retirement of long-term debt was equal to approximately 6 percent of the debt outstanding at the end of the previous year.

From Table 21 it may be seen that in 1971 the greatest amount of outstanding debt was for public education—$30.7 billion, or 31 percent of the total. The debt of local utilities amounted to $21.1 billion in 1971, accounting for 21 percent of the total debt figure. Water utility debt was $11.0 billion, 52 percent of total utility debt; electric utilities accounted for another $6.1 bil'ion, or 29 percent; transit systems, $3.6 billion, or 17 percent; and gas utilities $0.4 billion, or 1.9 percent of the total debt figure for utilities. All other debt—for highways, hospitals, parks, airports, water terminals, etc.—amounted to $47.5 billion, or 48 percent of the outstanding debt of all local governments.

Table 22 shows the distribution of local government debt among the various types of local governments. In 1971, the long-term debt in counties amounted to $11.8 billion, or 11 percent of the total local debt; that in municipalities, $42.1 billion, or 38 percent of the total; townships, $2.1 billion, or 1.9 percent; school districts, $22.3 billion, or 20 percent; and special districts, $21.0 billion or 19 percent—the remainder being accounted for by short-term debt issues.

A number of conclusions may be drawn from Table 22:

1. In the period from 1952 to 1971, the gross debt of local governments increased at a very rapid rate—by 382 percent, or at an annual compound rate of 8.59 percent.

2. Short-term debt rose much more rapidly than long-term debt in all

Table 21
DEBT AND DEBT TRANSACTIONS OF ALL LOCAL GOVERNMENTS
1970-1971

Item	Amount (in billions of dollars)	Per cent of Total
Total outstanding	111.0	100.0
Long term	99.3	89.5
Full faith and credit	62.5	56.3
Nonguaranteed	36.8	33.2
Short-term	11.7	10.5
Net long-term debt*	93.7	
Long-term debt by purpose	99.3	100.0
Local schools	30.7	30.9
Local utilities	21.1	21.3
All other	47.5	47.8
Long-term debt issued	12.0	
Long-term debt retired	5.7	

* Total outstanding less sinking fund and other debt reserves
Source: U.S. Bureau of the Census, *Governmental Finances in 1970-71*, p. 28.

Table 22
LOCAL DEBT BY CHARACTER AND BY UNIT OF GOVERNMENT, FOR SELECTED YEARS 1952 to 1971
(amounts in billions of dollars)

Item	1952 Amount	1952 Percent	1957 Amount	1957 Percent	1962 Amount	1962 Percent	1967 Amount	1967 Percent	1971 Amount	1971 Percent
Gross Debt	23.2	100.0	39.3	100.0	59.2	100.0	72.5	100.0	111.0	100.0
Short-Term	1.1	4.7	2.0	5.1	3.3	5.6	4.5	6.2	11.7	10.5
Long-Term	22.1	95.3	37.3	94.9	55.9	94.4	68.0	93.8	99.3	89.5
Full Faith and Credit	17.5	75.4	26.1	66.4	38.0	64.2	44.6	61.5	62.5	56.3
Nonguaranteed	4.6	19.8	11.2	28.5	17.9	30.2	23.4	32.3	36.8	33.2
County	2.0	8.6	3.5	8.9	5.4	9.1	6.6	9.1	12.7	11.4
Short-Term	0.1	0.4	0.2	0.5	0.2	0.3	0.3	0.4	0.9	0.8
Long-Term	1.9	8.2	3.3	8.4	5.2	8.8	6.3	8.7	11.8	10.6
City	12.6	54.3	19.1	48.6	26.9	45.4	31.9	44.0	48.9	44.1
Short-Term	0.5	2.2	0.9	2.3	1.8	3.0	2.6	3.6	6.8	6.2
Long-Term	12.1	52.1	18.2	46.3	25.1	42.4	29.3	40.4	42.1	37.9
Township	0.6	2.6	1.0	2.5	1.4	2.4	1.9	2.6	2.7	2.4
Short-Term	–	–	0.1	0.2	0.1	0.2	0.2	0.3	0.6	0.5
Long-Term	0.6	2.6	0.9	2.3	1.3	2.2	1.7	2.3	2.1	1.9
School District	3.8	16.4	9.1	23.1	13.9	23.5	16.7	23.0	23.5	21.2
Short-Term	0.1	0.4	0.2	0.5	0.2	0.4	0.4	0.5	1.2	1.1
Long-Term	3.7	15.9	8.9	22.6	13.7	23.1	16.3	22.5	22.3	20.1
Special District	4.1	17.7	6.6	16.8	11.7	19.8	15.4	21.2	23.2	20.9
Short-Term	0.4	1.8	0.6	1.5	1.0	1.7	1.1	1.5	2.2	2.0
Long-Term	3.7	15.9	6.0	15.3	10.7	18.1	14.3	19.7	21.0	18.9

Sources: Tax Foundation Inc., *Facts and Figures on Government Finance*, (New York: Tax Foundation Inc. 1971), p. 242 and U.S. Bureau of the Census, *Governmental Finances in 1970-71*, p. 30.

types of government—at an average annual compound rate of 13.25 percent for short-term debt and 8.23 percent for long-term debt.

3. The rise in long-term debt was at the greatest rates in counties, school districts, and special districts. City long-term debt increased much more slowly; albeit, it still accounted for the greatest actual amount of additional debt.

Looking at the $42.1 billion of long-term debt of municipal governments, one finds from Table 23 that $12.2 billion, or 29 percent of the total, was accounted for by the six cities with a 1970 population of one million or more. The 21 cities between 500,000 and one million population accounted for 13 percent, while the remaining municipalities accounted for 58 percent. The data for the six large cities is somewhat distorted by the presence of data for New York City, where debt for school and county purposes is included; and for Philadelphia, which includes debt for county as well as city purposes.

On a *per capita* basis, long-term debt amounted to $651 in cities of over one million population and $404 in cities of 500,000-1,000,000 population class.

As the size of the city decreased, so did per capita debt. Thus, cities with population of under 50,000 had per capita debt of only $234—less than 29 percent of the per capita debt for cities with a population of more than 1,000,000.

The major factors in the indebtedness of the 48 largest cities, as a group, are detailed in Table 24. In 1971, these were education (small by comparison, due to the existence of separate school district), highways, sewerage, airports, housing and urban renewal—ranging from 6.8 percent to 12.1 percent of the total long-term debt—and utility debt which accounted for 30 percent of the overall total. The long-term debt of this group of cities alone represents 19 percent of the total long-term debt outstanding for all local governments and almost one-half of total long-term debt of all municipalities.

Relation of Purpose to Future Benefits. Since debt is payable from future revenues, the relation of its purpose to the production of future benefits is significant. In this respect, local government borrowing may be for purposes

Table 23
INDEBTEDNESS OF MUNICIPAL GOVERNMENTS IN THE UNITED STATES, 1970-71
BY POPULATION-SIZE GROUPS

Item	All Municipalities	1,000,000 or more	500,000 to 999,999	300,000 to 499,999	200,000 to 299,999	100,000 to 199,999	50,000 to 99,999	under 50,000
Number of Municipalities, 1967	18,048	6	21	21	17	88	231	17,644
Aggregate Population, 1970 (in millions)	132.0	18.8	13.6	8.0	4.2	11.9	16.1	59.4
Gross Debt Outstanding*	48.9	15.2	6.2	3.4	1.8	3.9	4.5	13.9
Long-Term	42.1	12.2	5.5	3.0	1.5	3.3	3.9	12.7
Full Faith and Credit	24.0	8.0	3.7	1.9	0.9	2.0	2.3	5.2
Utility debt only	4.7	2.8	0.4	0.1	0.1	0.2	0.3	0.8
Nonguaranteed	18.2	4.2	1.8	1.1	0.5	1.3	1.6	7.6
Utility debt only	8.4	1.5	0.9	0.4	0.3	0.7	0.9	3.6
Short-Term	6.8	3.0	0.7	0.4	0.4	0.6	0.6	1.2
Per Capita Debt	371	813	457	423	427	330	277	234
Long-Term	320	651	404	375	345	279	241	215
Full Faith and Credit	182	428	270	242	214	169	141	87
Utility debt only	36	149	33	16	21	13	18	14
Nonguaranteed	138	223	135	133	131	110	100	128
Utility debt only	63	80	68	54	63	60	58	60
Short-Term	52	161	52	48	83	50	36	20

Source: U.S. Bureau of the Census, *City Government Finances in 1970-71,* pp. 7-8.
Outstanding debt in billions of dollars; per capita debt in dollars.

Table 24

**LONG-TERM DEBT OUTSTANDING IN THE 48 LARGEST CITIES
OF THE UNITED STATES, BY PURPOSE
1970-1971**

Item	Amount (in billions of dollars)	Percent of total
Total	20.7	100.0
General	14.5	69.9
Education	1.6	7.6
Highways	1.7	8.0
Hospitals	0.3	1.6
Sewerage	1.8	8.7
Parks and recreation	0.6	2.7
Housing and urban renewal*	2.5	12.2
Airports	1.4	6.5
Water transportation and terminals	0.6	2.8
Other and unallocable	4.1	19.8
Utility	6.2	30.1
Water	2.8	13.7
Electric	1.4	6.6
Gas	n.a.	n.a.
Transit	2.0	9.8

* These amounts do not include debt of local housing authorities.

NB: These amounts of debt are for the cities themselves. Generally, they do not include figures for independent authorities, e.g., the Port of New York Authority or the Delaware River Port Authority, which overlap one or more of the cities included in the group.

Source: U.S. Bureau of the Census, *City Government Finances in 1970-71*, p. 88.

that add clearly and materially to the debt-supporting capacity of a community; or, it may be for purposes of economic or social benefit whose future intrinsic value is not readily measurable and may be large or small in relation to the cost of the debt; or, it may be for purposes that add little or nothing to a community's future fiscal ability or social advantage. Included in this last class would be such items as long-term borrowing to finance operating deficits resulting from mismanagement and even borrowing that created tangible assets if such "assets" were for wasteful and foolish purposes. Extensive borrowing of this type fosters economic and financial trouble.

Some of the borrowing by local governments differs little in its purpose and economic effect from that by private corporations. Bonds are issued to finance the acquisition, construction, improvement, and extension of water systems, electric plants, and various other kinds of revenue-producing enterprises, and the earnings of the enterprises are applied to the payment of bond interest and principal. When the earnings are adequate for this purpose, such debt is called self-supporting or self-liquidating—to distinguish it from tax-supported debt. This classification of debt, however, merely identifies the method used for its support. The payment of debt incurred for a sewage disposal system, for example, draws on the financial resources of a community irrespective of whether the debt is supported by user charges or taxes, though the choice between taxes and user service charges may produce markedly different patterns of distribution of costs among different economic elements of the community. The point is that borrowing, if it is excessive or wasteful, does not have to be of the tax-supported type to become a community burden.

On the other hand, the statement that this debt draws upon the same economy as tax-supported debt is frequently not true. For example, a recent local study of the passengers who use the Philadelphia International Airport showed that only one-eighth were residents of the city. And, on the basis of origin and destination of passenger trips, only one in three started or ended in Philadelphia. Moreover, much of the debt relating to airports is financed by charges payable by airlines that depend upon both the national and international economies for their revenue.

Accordingly, where an airport serves the entire metropolitan area it is unfair to consider the debt as being applicable solely to the economic base of the central city if revenues supporting the debt are derived from a much larger universe. The same logic applies to local parking authority debt, bridge debt, and a number of other types of debt.

Debt may be for purposes that provide a compensatory addition to the financial ability of a community, regardless of the sources of the revenue for its support. Tax-supported debt for some purposes creates economic activity which generates taxes in excess of the cost of the facilities and related governmental support requirements. A well devised urban renewal project may produce a clearly identifiable net increment to the tax base, or it may avoid a general deterioration of the business district. This is recognized in California by the use of tax increment bonds.

Frequently, the facilities financed by borrowing add to, or preserve, community fiscal resources less directly or tangibly—in such ways as bettering conditions for the conduct of business, halting economic deterioration, adding to attractiveness for residential purposes, or increasing earning power by improving the health and education of the people. From the economic point of view, as Shultz and Harriss point out:

> If the full costs of borrowing are less than the expected benefits, then borrowing for construction is economically wise. The capital equipment added will create more real income than it costs. This is good investment. In practice, however, the calculation is very difficult. Precise—perhaps even rough—measurement of the full social benefit of a public investment is impossible, just as is the measurement of the value of the sacrifices the taxpayers must make to service the debt.[4]

Borrowing for General Improvements. Most of the basic, tax-supported functions of local government require capital facilities for their operation. The

---

[4] W. J. Shultz and C. L. Harriss, *American Public Finance*, (New York: Prentice-Hall, Inc. 1959), p. 522. *Ibid.*, 8th ed. (1965) p. 480.

physical plant of a typical local unit includes land, structures, and equipment. Since structures and equipment wear out or become obsolete, their replacement alone calls for a continuous flow of capital expenditures except in very small local governments. Sometimes neglect in the upkeep and maintenance of facilities·necessitates major repairs that a local government may classify as capital outlay. In addition to the expenditures needed to keep the physical plant in good condition, there are varying requirements for capital expenditures to upgrade or expand the physical plant. Upgrading may occur (even if a community is not growing), through replacements of a higher quality than the facilities which are replaced, or through the provision of added facilities, e.g., a park or sewage disposal system. In any growing community, the governmentally owned plant should expand to keep pace with the rate and nature of growth by replacements that are larger and often of a higher type than the facilities replaced. Moreover, an increase in municipal standards may involve acquisition of more land.

Determination of the part long-term borrowing should play in financing this diversity of capital expenditures is discussed in Chapter 14 as part of debt policy development.

Long-term Borrowing for Emergencies. Major emergencies may require not only temporary borrowing but also the spreading of costs over a period of years through the issuance of long-term debt. Justification for such a policy lies in the fact that new facilities represent an upgrading of the quality of the plant being replaced. In the absence of such consideration the practicalities of the situation are frequently such that spreading the costs offers the only feasible course of action. In a very real sense, where advance provision is not made through purchase of insurance or development of reserve funds, the handling of any major unexpected expense needs to be spread over a period of years. Thus, the huge cost of snow removal and street repair generated by an unusually severe winter in New York in 1961 called for such action. In like manner, floods or similar disasters usually produce costs too great for financing from current revenues—especially when taxpayers are struggling with the unusual private costs which arise simultaneously.

Essentially the point is that the full impact of major emergencies can be more easily absorbed if handled over a period of years. On the other hand, care needs to be taken to avoid the deferment payment of normal current costs to future years.

Historically, the nation's local governments probably have never faced a greater emergency than that imposed by the Great Depression of the 1930s. Soaring unemployment relief, usually a wholly local function until well into that depression, coupled with continuing fixed charges and declining tax collections produced unprecedented problems for most general purpose local governments. Initially there was an effort to meet these problems through cutting regular governmental costs and increasing tax rates. Emergency borrowing was used in many circumstances, with the expectation this would be only temporary in duration. But as the depression continued and mounted in severity, much of this debt was converted to long-term debt—unless the bond markets refused to accept the additional debt. With reduced assessments, debt limits contracted;

delinquent taxes piled up and efforts at collection were frustrated by a lack of sufficient bidders at tax sales. Eventually, the states and later the federal government were obliged to come to the rescue of local governments through a combination of actions. Yet, numerous local governments required a decade or more to work themselves out from under the obligations accumulated in that period.

Deficit Funding. Basically, the issuance of bonds to fund accumulated operating deficits is not a justifiable purpose of long-term borrowing. Even so, such action may be unavoidable because of an unmanageable accumulation of temporary debt; but, in times other than those of deep and protracted business depression, it stems almost invariably from financial mismanagement. If a deficit funding operation becomes necessary, it should be made an integral part of a constructive program of financial rehabilitation. Moreover, the term of the funding bonds should be kept to a minimum.

Notable instances of deficit funding in the period from World War II through 1960 were limited because conditions generally were propitious for the quick remedy of casual deficits; but a review of the finances of cities over 50,000 population in this period discloses a number of such operations of a relatively minor character and a few of a more conspicuous nature.

Borrowing for Revenue-producing Enterprises. The revenue-producing undertakings of local government are increasing and borrowing for such purposes has increased enormously. This development has had marked influence on local government structure, administrative organization, revenue systems, and instruments of borrowing. Both federal and state governments have participated in this development, bringing about new intergovernmental arrangements respecting local debt. Four factors, in particular, have influenced this trend.

First, the provision of urban water supplies and treatment of waste water have become more difficult and more expensive because of growing demands that press heavily upon readily available local financial resources.

Second, public ownership of certain other utilities has had a notable increase. Thus, for many years, there was an increase in the number of municipal electric and power systems; however, recent changes in technology, especially nuclear power, have tended to reverse this trend. Currently, much of the hydroelectric development is centered in Arizona, California, Nebraska, New York, South Carolina, Texas, Washington, and the Tennessee River Valley. On a much more limited scale, the development of a nationwide network of privately-owned natural gas transmission systems has resulted in the setting up of numerous, small municipal gas distribution systems. Contributing also to the expansion of local government ownership of public utilities has been the public assumption of responsibility for certain essential types of undertakings that were too marginal in character to attract private capital or, possibly, required some public subsidy. This group is represented by large rapid transit systems and a variety of air, marine, and motor terminals—the last including off-street parking facilities.

A third factor has been the development of public housing, a relatively new function of government in the United States and one which has produced a new type of debt obligation—local government bonds virtually guaranteed by the federal government. A few states and local governments also have issued bonds directly for middle-income housing or have guaranteed the bonds of local housing agencies.

The fourth factor has been the substitution of service-charge support for tax support of functions that appeared amenable to this charge, to adapt existing fee systems to the servicing of new debt, and to initiate new or expanded functions under arrangements that lent themselves to service-charge financing. A distinguishing characteristic of this development has been the increasing use of limited liability bonds for capital financing purposes, with the investor receiving an interest rate designed to compensate him for any additional risk involved. The most conspicuous manifestation of this trend are the widespread system of toll highways, bridges, and tunnels and the extensive use of sewer charges to finance sewage disposal systems. Among the rich variety of other undertakings whose revenue-producing potentialities have sometimes been used as a base for limited liability bonds, supported solely by the earnings of the project, are: airports, auditoriums, beach recreation facilities, causeways, college dormitories, student union buildings and faculty residences, dog pounds, exhibit areas, fair grounds, golf courses, heating plants, hospitals, incinerators, industrial plants, marinas and small boat basins, parking areas and garages, parks, recreation centers, spas, sports arenas, stadiums, and swimming pools.

Borrowing for Industrial Aid

"We have established, we think, beyond cavil" said the U. S. Supreme Court in *Loan Association v. Topeka* "that there can be no lawful tax which is not laid for *a public purpose*. It may not be easy to draw the line in all cases so as to decide what is a public purpose in this sense and what is not."[5] The Court was holding that $100,000 of bonds, issued by the City of Topeka under authority of a state law and presented to a company as an inducement to establish a local bridge manufacturing business, were not issued for a public purpose and, since the creation of debt involved a tax obligation, the city could not contract debt for a purpose for which it had no right to levy taxes. That borrowing must be restricted to public purposes is stated specifically in very few state constitutions, but this limitation has been held by the courts in almost all of the states.

What constitutes a public purpose for which local governments may tax, borrow, and spend is a question that has received a steadily widening interpretation with the growth of urbanism and public responsibilities in a community. One issue has involved the scope of municipal functions, particularly their permissible extension into the ownership and operation of utility and commercial projects, traditionally considered to be in the domain of private enterprise. Various questions respecting municipal operation of basic utilities were resolved before the turn of the present century, and, in the early 1900s such commercial undertakings as wood, coal and fuel yards, grain elevators, and food processing plants were sustained as public purposes in some areas with special economic

---

[5] 20 Wallace, 655 (1874). This decision was not based on any specific constitutional provision, but later the Court based the illegality of a tax for private purposes on the due process of law provision. *Fallbrook Irrigation District v. Bradley*, 164 U.S. 112 (1896).

problems. A California court held, and an Iowa court denied, that a municipal opera house was a public function. The municipal manufacture and sale of ice was ruled to be a public purpose in Georgia; when a Louisiana court held otherwise, the state constitution was amended to authorize municipal ice plants. In more recent years, such relatively new undertakings as low-rent housing, airports and off-street parking facilities have gained general acceptance as public functions. Less generally, approval has been given to such commercial undertakings as hotels, restaurants, and liquor stores.

Another issue has involved the public-purpose status of municipal borrowing in direct aid of private industry. The construction of public markets, piers, and docks in which space is rented for commercial purposes has long-established acceptance. One significant recent development has been an extension of this policy to municipal ownership and operation of certain facilities for the benefit of privately-owned undertakings "affected with a public interest"—primarily to air terminals; in a few instances, to bus and truck terminals; and, in New Orleans, to a railway passenger terminal. The acceptance of borrowing for air terminals as a public purpose now includes public financing for lease of hangars and overhaul facilities at the terminals to the airlines. Many years ago, municipal loans and grants for private railroad construction, involving no public ownership and operation, were defended as necessary for community advancement or as compatible with the age-old concern of government for the means of travel and transportation.

Over the past several years, the very justifiable interest of local governments in the economic development of their communities has been extended, in some areas, to attracting new industry by means of subsidies. Initially, these inducements took the form of property tax exemption for more or less extended periods; but, since World War II, there has been a rapidly growing use of industrial aid bonds to construct or acquire plants for lease to industrial concerns, to loan money to such concerns for plant construction, or even to acquire control of the concerns.

Railroad Aid Bonds. Back in the 1860s and 1870s, a great many local governments in the United States became involved in serious financial difficulties by incurring debt to aid private promoters of railroad construction. When much of this investment, supposedly for community advancement, turned out to be a total loss there was widespread default and repudiation of municipal debt that plagued both municipalities and investors for many years.[6] While a majority of state court decisions sustained such borrowing as being for a public purpose, the policy was widely repudiated by the people themselves. State after state amended its constitution to prohibit local governments from making gifts or loans of money, property, or credit to, or owning the stock of, private corporations and undertakings. (A similar prohibition previously imposed on the use of state credit has shifted the subsidizing of business and industry from the states to the local governments.) The constitutions of 35 states contained such provisions in 1960.

---

[6] For an account of municipal railroad aid bonds and their vicissitudes see A. M. Hillhouse, *Municipal Bonds, A Century of Experience*, (New York: Prentice-Hall, Inc., 1936), pp. 143-199.

Real Estate Aid Bonds. During the real estate boom of the 1920s, neither the principle that borrowing is restricted to public purposes nor the specific constitutional prohibitions on the loan of credit to private enterprise prevented the profligate use of special assessment bonds to aid the private promotion of land subdivision and development. Speculative developers were enabled to subdivide large tracts into building lots with only shoestring capital through dependence on bonds authorized by municipalities to finance streets, sidewalks, sewers, drainage, street lighting, and other improvements. As one authority has observed, "only a tenuous legal distinction may be found between the old railroad aid bonds and the millions of improvement bonds issued during the 1920s."[7] Many of these projects collapsed, and many of the bonds that financed them went into default, under the impact of the 1930s depression. In those states (such as Florida and North Carolina) where special assessment bonds had the backing of the municipalities' full resources, there was a disastrous undermining of municipal credit. Where the bonds were payable only from special assessments, many people, unable or unwilling to pay their assessments, stopped paying property taxes, forcing some local governments to assume responsibility for the defaulted bonds on a scaled-down basis in order to protect their credit position.[8]

Industrial Aid Bonds. Reminiscent of the municipal borrowing for railroad aid of a hundred years ago, municipalities are again borrowing to aid private industry. The usual procedure is for a municipality to acquire or build an industrial or commercial facility, sometimes install equipment, and rent it to a private concern. To finance the project, the municipality issues bonds, which may be either general obligation bonds or revenue bonds payable from the rentals. This method of inducing industrial concerns to locate in a community offers several financial advantages to such concerns: the lessee is freed from providing capital financing for the plant; his rental is tax-deductible as an operating cost; and the amount of the rental is influenced by the municipal owner's ability to finance the plant with tax-exempt bonds and frequently, freedom from paying taxes on the property.

This revival of municipal borrowing for industrial aid appears to have originated in Mississippi's adoption in 1936 of its Balance Agriculture with Industry (BAWI) program, which included enactment of a general law authorizing municipalities to issue general obligation bonds for industrial aid purposes. The movement spread through most other states.

The legal authorization for these projects has been by state constitutions, general acts, and special acts. By 1969 about three-fourth of the states had authorized the issuance of local government bonds to finance plants for lease

---

[7] Hillhouse. *op. cit.*, p. 67.

[8] There was some revival of this misuse of public credit in California in the 1960s. According to the *Wall Street Journal* of September 27, 1961, "California officials are concerned over a recent increase in the number of special districts initiated by real estate promoters. Officials fear that some bond issuers may be unduly optimistic about future capability of producing taxes. It's given speculators a way of developing land without putting up any money of their own, while unwary investors often believe they are buying bonds backed by the state of California, its cities or counties complains an official of the state's attorney general's office."

to private concerns. Some states adopted provisions permitting, with voter approval, the issuance of general obligation bonds, with the totals in Louisiana and Missouri limited to 20 percent and 10 percent, respectively, of the local government's assessed valuation. Other states permitted only revenue bonds to be used for this purpose. These laws have been challenged in the courts on two counts: (1) that they authorize the issuance of bonds for a private purpose, and (2) that such bonds violate constitutional prohibitions against gifts or loans of money or credit to private corporations. A large majority of the courts have held that industrial aid bonds are issued for a public purpose, with the reasoning substantially that of the Mississippi court in 1938 in the leading case of *Albritton v. City of Winona* (178 So. at 804)—". . . care of the poor, the relief of unemployment, and the promotion of agriculture and industry are undoubtedly proper governmental purposes, and the building of plants and leasing them to private enterprise, since it serves such objectives, is also for a public purpose." Negative rulings have stressed that, in the issuance of such bonds, the private purpose is paramount and that the plan is a threat to free enterprise.[9] Most courts have found that industrial aid bonds are not a gift or loan of credit to private enterprise. In the instance of revenue bonds, the courts have emphasized that the municipal credit and taxing power are not involved; but one of the prime purposes of having the necessary bonds issued by, and in the name of, a municipality is to make them more readily salable on the market. Thus, the credit of the municipality is extended in aid of the project. In sustaining general obligation bonds, the courts have held that the prohibition does not apply to gifts or loans that serve a public purpose or to the employment of private corporations to perform a public service.[10]

Local governments have a clear responsibility for promoting the economic growth of their communities, but their use of industrial aid bonds for this purpose is a policy of questionable prudence. Thus, the implications of large-scale employment of municipal bonds needs comprehensive examination. Unless we are very careful, we will be financing an ever-increasing portion of construction and even of normal acquisitions from the proceeds of tax exempt bonds. Not only will this have a significant adverse impact upon federal income tax revenues but also it will act to dilute the market for tax exempt bonds to the point that much of the advantage of such tax exempt status will be lost.

---

[9] The Nebraska court said: "It is true, of course, that the city may be benefited by the location of the company in the city . . . But general benefit to the economy of a community does not justify use of public funds of the city unless it be for a public as distinguished from a private purpose. This is simply a case where the city is attempting to use the powers, credits and public moneys of the city to purchase land and erect industrial buildings thereon for use of a private corporation for private profit and private gain. It serves no public or municipal purpose." (*State ex rel. Beck v. City of York*, 164 Neb 223, 82 N.W. 2d 269 (1957).) In the words of the Idaho Supreme Court in 1960, ". . . It is obvious that private enterprise, not so favored, could not compete with industries operating thereunder. If the state-favored industries were successfully managed, private enterprise would of necessity be forced out, and the state, through its municipalities, would increasingly become involved in promoting, sponsoring, regulating, and controlling private business, and our free private enterprise economy would be replaced by socialism . . ." (*Village of Moyie Springs v. Aurora Mfg. Co.*, 82 Idaho 337, 353 P. 2nd 767 (1960).)

[10] *Ibid.*

Once industrial aid bonds became fashionable, there was a huge upswing in this type of financing. By 1969, the total amount of state and local industrial aid bonds issued in a single year reached $1.5 billion, with single issues of as much as $130 million. The Congress became concerned and, in 1969, adopted legislation which severely circumscribed the power of state and local governments to issue tax-free bonds for industrial aid purposes. Under the existing law, the maximum amount of such debt available to a single corporation or person within the same political jurisdiction is $5 million in any three-year period—except in the case of pollution control bonds where the amounts are generally unlimited. These, and other restrictions, are imposed to help discourage the use of this financing mechanism on a broad scale. Even so, large amounts of such financing continue.

Subsidies and preferential treatment may be a major attraction to industries of a marginal, peripatetic type, but they are of much less interest to the stable, progressive type that seek locations for long-term growth. The latter are concerned primarily with the advantages of location in relation to markets, raw materials and labor supply—only the last of which is subject to much local influence; but, they are interested, also, in the kind of environment a community offers. A municipality can make its best contribution to the encouragement of industry in its area by creating the kind of environment that responsible, progressive industry needs. Among the specific essentials are a well-enforced zoning plan; a street system and traffic regulation that provide good mobility; availability of adequate water supply and sewage and waste disposal facilities; dependable fire, police, and other protection services; school, health and recreational facilities; a standard building code, etc., that provide for employees an attractive place of residence; and a reasonably competent, economical local government that is intelligently cooperative. When a community uses its borrowing power for these purposes—for urban renewal projects as needed and, perhaps, for the development of an industrial park—it is likely to accomplish more for its long-term economic advancement than by building industrial plants for rent.[11]

Actually, so long as some state and local governments use the device of industrial aid bonds, the competitive situation among localities more or less requires extensive use by other governments.

ECONOMIC EFFECTS OF LOCAL BORROWING

Local government borrowing that runs into several billions of dollars a year has economic effects nationally as well as on the individual local borrowers. Some of these economic implications have been indicated in discussing the purposes of borrowing; a few need elaboration.

---

[11] For a review of the influence of industrial aid bonds in Mississippi, see Martin Schnitzer, "Mississippi's BAWI Program," *Mississippi Business*. February, 1961, pp. 1-6. For a summary of objections to the industrial aid program by various professional groups concerned with municipal finance, see John N. Mitchell, "Municipal Industrial Aid Bonds," *Municipal Finance*, May, 1961, pp. 163-168.

Immediate and Subsequent Local Effects

The local economic effects of local government borrowing are influenced by several factors, including the purpose, extent, and timing of such borrowing, and there is a wide contrast between the immediate and later effects. In economic terms the immediate effect of a local bond issue is usually inflationary. If, for example, borrowing is superimposed on the existing level of expenditures, there is a quick step-up in public spending without an increase in taxes. If it replaces some part of existing expenditure from current revenue, the level of public spending can be maintained with a reduction or levelling off in taxes that permits increased private spending. If the bonds are sold outside the community, as is usually the case, the purchase of the bonds absorbs little local spending power; and the deposit in local banks of bond proceeds supplied from outside sources increases local bank reserves and promotes easier local credit.

In the case of borrowing to finance construction, the initial impact of that portion of the bond proceeds spent locally is on local construction workers, contractors, and suppliers; but, part of this income moves quickly to the local consumer goods and service industries, giving a multiplying effect to the original stimulus. The nature of the stimulus, however, varies with the condition of the local economy. If times are dull for the construction industry, employment and income rise and some of the affluence is transmitted throughout the community without much change in the price level. On the other hand, if the industry already is functioning at capacity, the demand for labor, material, and equipment becomes highly competitive and the main effect is to force up prices—giving the local government less for its money.[12]

The local economy, however, receives only part, and sometimes a rather limited part, of the immediately stimulating effect. Some of the bond proceeds are spent for construction materials, equipment, and services in other parts of the country. This external stimulus, including the upward pressure on interest rates and contraction of bank reserves in the financial centers where the bonds are purchased, may be relatively negligible in one transaction by a single community; but, if similar borrowing policies are followed more or less simultaneously by many communities, the cumulative influence on the national economy can be very considerable—occasionally involving actions by the Federal Reserve System.

The subsequent economic effect on a local community is more or less the reverse of the immediate effect. Inflationary spending of the bond proceeds is replaced by annual mandatory principal and interest charges as the revenues are raised to pay for what the community has bought on the installment plan. How heavy the burden is depends largely on what benefits the acquisition is producing. If the nature of the benefits is such as to increase the taxable

---

[12] The initial impact of borrowing for other than construction purposes may vary considerably with the purpose. For example, the sale of bonds to fund an accumulated operating deficit would liquefy assets of the creditors involved and spread the effect of eliminating the deficit. Borrowing for poor relief in a depression would initially stimulate the consumer goods industry. In borrowing to purchase land for some future development, such as a park, the effect might depend on whether the purchase money went to local or outside owners and how far the loss of taxes on the acquired property was offset by the immediate appreciation in value of the surrounding property.

resources or income of the community or to decrease the cost of living and doing business in the community, or the cost of performance of public services for the community, the burden may be minimized or offset entirely. Borrowing for many purposes that are desirable from a community point of view produces less tangible or slowly realizable benefits and clearly imposes an increased burden on the current generation of taxpayers. Not to be overlooked, moreover, is the probability that the benefits will not be distributed to individuals in a community in the same proportions in which these individuals are required to support the costs of debt service.

The debt of most local governments, moreover, is similar to the external debt of a national government in that local governments usually pay the bulk of their debt service requirements to outside investors. Unlike the debt of the federal government, which may be said to be incurred by the people and owed to themselves (although with the borrowing and repayment process involving some redistribution of income), local debt involves a process not of redistribution of income within the community but can result in a loss of income by payments to other areas.

The ability of the people of a community to support borrowing for public goods and services is no more unlimited than their ability to support borrowing for private goods and services. If borrowing persists for purposes that do not produce benefits commensurate with the costs, several results ensue: (1) the rise of taxes and charges for debt service places a progressively heavier burden on the local population; (2) there is a growing tendency to skimp on operation and maintenance requirements because of the financial pressure of debt service; (3) interest rates are forced upward as the local government's bonds become less attractive for investment; and (4) the reserve of credit that should be available for emergency purposes disappears. In such cases borrowing can become an instrument of economic retrogression instead of economic progress.

Local Debt Policy and the National Economy

Government spending, taxing, and borrowing policies inevitably have a major influence on the national economy. The federal government has recognized a responsibility for directing such policies as far as possible to maintain a sustained high level of production and employment, reasonable price stability, and a satisfactory rate of economic growth. The success of such efforts is bound to be affected, in some degree, by whether they are helped or hindered by state and local government fiscal policies.

While a large part of the spending by local governments (and state governments) is vital to national economic growth, the general view is that their spending, taxing, and borrowing policies tend to foster economic instability by intensifying both inflation and deflation.[13] This has been very evident over

---

[13] See, among numerous commentators: A. H. Hansen and H. S. Perloff, *State and Local Finance in the National Economy*, (New York: W. W. Norton, 1944), pp. 59-69; John F. Due and Ann Friedlaender, *Government Finance: Economics of the Public Sector*, (Homewood, Ill.: Richard D. Irwin, Inc., 1973), 5th edition, pp. 574-576; P. E. Taylor, *The Economics of Public Finance*, (New York: Macmillan, 1953) rev. ed., pp. 130-131; and Mabel Newcomer, "State and Local Financing in Relation to Economic Fluctuations," *National Tax Journal*, June, 1954, pp. 97-109.

protracted periods of boom and depression, as will be shown later; but, in the moderate, short-range fluctuations of the economy, the fiscal policies of local governments tend to be compensatory rather than financially perverse. In the series of fairly sharp but temporary business recessions since World War II, local government finance appears, on the whole, to have had a countercyclical influence. While most local revenue systems are too inelastic to share in this influence, local spending in short recessions tends to remain stable or increase. There is no pronounced movement to cut general operating expenses or employment rolls and, when local governments have improvement bonds authorized but unissued, they frequently expedite their sale and spending of the proceeds to take advantage of the decline in interest rates and bids by contractors engendered by a recession. This local contribution to short-range stabilization, however, is largely fortuitous rather than the result of planning.[14]

That local financial policies are fiscally perverse over protracted periods of boom and depression has been evident in the major economic swings since World War I. In the generally prosperous 1920s, local governments encouraged inflation by borrowing, instead of taxing, for virtually everything that the law allowed, including even the lending of public credit for the promotion of private land speculation. In the 1930s depression, their borrowing power exhausted and their credit under suspicion, they were forced to add their weight to deflation by cutting wages, service, and outlays and by keeping taxes high to pay off debt and meet emergency requirements.[15] The period of World War II provided an exception, with the local fiscal policy more in keeping with countercyclical requirements. The reduction of debt was accelerated and, to a limited extent, reserves for deferred maintenance and capital purposes were created as an alternative to tax reduction. Much of this wartime anti-inflationary policy, however, was unavoidable rather than planned. Since World War II, local governments again have contributed to inflation, with expenditures increasing more rapidly than revenues. Debt has been used to balance these local government accounts. Looking at municipal budgeting comprehensively, instead of merely the plans for financing current expenses, local governments tend to maintain unbalanced budgets in long periods of prosperity by incurring more debt than they retire and then to produce budgetary surpluses in periods of deep depression by retiring more debt than they incur—the reverse of cooperation for economic stabilization.

Since economic stability is as advantageous to local governments as it is to the nation, there is a dual importance in examining why local government finance has failed to contribute to it beyond the limited area of short-range economic fluctuations, what the obstacles are to such contribution, and what means there are, if any, for their removal. The main reasons cited for the fiscally perverse

---

[14] A conclusion of two authorities who have studied this short-range countercyclical effect of municipal policy is that "because local finance moves up and down more slowly than GNP, it assists in the stabilization of minor recessions occurring during secular booms, and in the stabilization of minor upturns occurring during periods of long-run depression." (Morton S. Baratz and Helen T. Farr, "Is Municipal Finance Fiscally Perverse," *National Tax Journal*, September, 1959, pp. 276-284.)

[15] While federal government construction increased from $313 million in 1930 to $802 million in 1933, state and local construction declined from $2,545 million to $846 million.

character of financing by local governments are the nature of their responsibilities, the inelastic quality of their revenue systems, and the limitations on their fiscal powers. To these must be added the handicaps of a less than orderly governmental structure, the inadequacy of planning, the shortcomings of fiscal policy (particularly of borrowing policy) and the absence of any consistent, well-directed effort to coordinate federal-state-local fiscal policy with economic stabilization as a goal.

In the first place, local governments have the responsibility for providing adequately and continuously a wide assortment of basic public service functions. They cannot be expected, in furnishing police, fire and health protection, water supplies, education and the like, to reduce operating expenses in periods of prosperity and increase them in periods of depression. In practice, throughout both major upward and downward swings of the economy, they have followed the reverse of this pattern for most functions, increasing spending for operations in prosperity and cutting it in depression. The nature of the services, however, preclude drastic curtailment at any time, and one important service of some local governments—welfare—is countercyclical in its expenditure requirements. Thus, in contrast with the wide cyclical fluctuations of private industry the perverse effect of local government spending for operations is very moderate.

The perverse influence lies more in the timing and method of financing capital construction. Provision of local public services entails, from time to time, making large capital outlays. Often the timing of these outlays cannot be geared to any theoretical regard for the most appropriate phase of the business cycle, since the demand is likely to be most urgent in periods of industrial expansion, abnormal residential building activity, and general economic optimism. With the financing of such programs mainly by borrowing, bond issues for capital improvements tend to multiply in boom periods and almost to disappear in depressions.

A second obstacle frequently emphasized is the lack, in most local revenue systems, of built-in elasticity such as that provided the federal government by its heavy dependence on graduated income taxes, coupled with deduction and exemption policies, that expand and contract more widely than income. An income-elastic revenue system, however, is an amenity that, under prevailing financial policies, most local governments could not afford. In a severe and protracted decline in business, they are not in a position to slash costs ruthlessly and, therefore, must have available either large and liquid reserves or abundant credit. For the vast majority, neither is available. They tend to operate financially at all times under a system which virtually prohibits the accumulation of significant deficits or surpluses. They tend to enter deeply depressed periods with heavy fixed charges that leave little room for emergency borrowing. Moreover, the psychology in periods of economic adversity is to pressure local governments to tighten their belts.

Under any circumstances, the range of choices available to local governments in the determination of fiscal policy is sharply restricted as compared with the state and federal governments; but, in many states, the choices of local governments are further narrowed by restraints imposed by state constitutions and statutes. There are prohibitions against the accumulation of surplus, and the normal lack of fiscal flexibility sometimes is accentuated by tax rate and debt limits that not only lessen the opportunity for long-range planning but also force local governments into devious measures for meeting their fiscal needs. Even if local governments had more financial flexibility, many of them are too small or too limited in resources to make much of a contribution to national economic stabilization through their fiscal policy; but, there is much that can be done by the few thousand larger municipalities, counties, and school and special districts that account for the bulk of local government revenue, borrowing, and expenditure.

Beyond these, it must be kept in mind that significant portions of the federal government's budget consists of amounts payable to state, local, and foreign governments. Much of the elasticity in the federal government arises from changes in these policies—not from contraction or expansion of service programs actually provided by the federal government. To a lesser degree, this is also true of state governments.

THE BOUNDARIES OF SAFETY IN BORROWING

How much debt a local government may safely incur is not ascertainable by any precise formula. The answer depends on numerous factors, such as: the purposes for which the debt is incurred; the community's economic characteristics; the community's prospects for economic stability, growth, or decline; the adequacy of the municipality's revenue system; the competence with which debt is planned and managed; the amount of debt that overlapping governments incur; and the intangible factor of the people's willingness to support the debt issued.

The Performance Record

The history of extensive municipal borrowing in the United States covers little more than a century and is summarized in Table 25. In 1840, the total local debt was only about $25 million; but, by 1860, it had risen to $200 million and in the next decade it increased two and one-half times to $516 million in 1870. It did not reach the billion dollar level until the 1890s, but thereafter it rose rapidly, with a short interruption for World War I, to $16.4 billion in 1932. There was little net change in the years of recovery from the 1930s depression; restrictions on local construction during World War II resulted in a decline in the total to $13.6 billion in 1946—the level of the late 1920s. But, by 1957 the debt level had tripled, amounting to $39.3 billion. In the overall, total debt increased 13 percent in the 1940s, 173 percent in the 1950s, and 116 percent in the 1960s—making up for lost time and reaching $111.0 billion by 1971.

Total debt, in relation to the gross national product (GNP), showed a decline during the 1880s, but then rose steadily until the depression of the 1930s when borrowing continued at a stable rate while the GNP fell sharply, causing the total debt, interest, and "calculated debt service requirements" to double in

Table 25
LOCAL GOVERNMENT DEBT, INTEREST EXPENDITURE, AND "CALCULATED DEBT SERVICE REQUIREMENTS" IN RELATION TO THE GROSS NATIONAL PRODUCT FOR SELECTED YEARS, 1860-1971

Year	U.S. Totals for Local Governments				Local Government Amts./$1,000 of GNP		
	Total Debt At End of Fiscal Yr. (in billions)	Interest Expended During Fiscal Yr. (in billions)	"Calculated Debt Service" Requirements for Fiscal Yr.* (in billions)	GNP (in billions)	Total Debt	Interest Expenditures	Calculated Debt Service Requirements
1860	$0.20	$n.a.	$n.a.	$n.a.	$n.a.	$n.a.	$n.a.
1870	0.52	n.a.	n.a.	6.7	77.0	n.a.	n.a.
1880	0.82	n.a.	n.a.	9.2	89.2	n.a.	n.a.
1890	0.93	n.a.	n.a.	13.5	68.6	n.a.	n.a.
1902	1.88	0.07	0.16	20.8	90.2	3.3	7.8
1913	4.04	0.16	0.36	37.0	109.1	4.3	9.8
1922	8.98	0.39	0.77	74.0	121.3	5.2	10.5
1929	14.70	0.65	1.35	104.4	140.8	6.2	12.9
1932	16.37	0.73	1.54	58.5	279.9	12.4	26.4
1941	16.79	0.62	1.46	125.8	133.4	4.9	11.6
1946	13.56	0.47	1.18	210.7	64.4	2.2	5.6
1950	18.83	0.50	1.35	284.6	66.2	1.8	4.7
1952	23.23	0.58	1.68	347.0	66.9	1.7	4.8
1957	39.30	1.03	2.82	442.8	88.8	2.3	6.4
1960	51.41	1.49	3.85	503.2	102.2	3.0	7.7
1962	59.26	1.79	4.54	560.3	105.8	3.2	8.1
1965	72.48	2.19	5.54	681.2	106.4	3.2	8.1
1968	85.40	2.76	6.87	864.2	98.8	2.5	7.9
1969	94.00	3.13	7.40	930.3	101.0	3.4	8.0
1970	101.56	3.62	8.32	976.4	104.0	3.7	8.5
1971	111.03	4.14	9.22	1,050.4	105.7	3.9	8.8

n.a. Indicates data not available.

* In each case, the sum of interest expenditures and 5 percent of the total debt outstanding at the beginning of the fiscal year.

Source: For debt and interest amounts to 1960, Advisory Commission on Intergovernmental Relations, *State Constitutional and Statutory Restrictions on Local Government Debt* (Washington, D.C.: United States Government Printing Office, 1961), p. 18; for figures 1962 to 1971, Tax Foundation, Inc., *Facts and Figures on Government Finance* (New York: Tax Foundation, Inc. 1973), pp. 231, 253, and 33.

relation to the GNP during the three-year period 1929-1932.[16] In the interlude induced by World War II, while the GNP increased from $126 billion to $211 billion, borrowing remained stable and total debt decreased from a figure of $133 per $1000 of GNP to $64. Subsequent to 1946, GNP has risen steadily while total debt, in relation to GNP, peaked in 1965 and was at about the same level, $106 in 1971.

[16] "Calculated debt service requirements" are approximate figures for annual debt service derived by adding to interest expenditure five percent of the principal outstanding at the beginning of each year as the estimated requirement for retirement of principal.

At three rather widely separated intervals in the history of local government debt, borrowing in many localities exceeded the boundaries of safety and there were widespread defaults. In each instance, the immediate cause of the trouble was a sharp and deep business depression; but, in each instance, there was also a background of the reckless use of public credit. In the 1860s and 1870s, there were hundreds of municipal bond defaults, which reached their most virulent stage with the depression of 1873 and involved, it has been estimated, about one-fifth of all municipal debt.[17] Had the upsurge of local borrowing in this period concentrated on the public improvement needs of the rapidly growing towns and cities, widespread financial difficulties might have been avoided, despite the rudimentary character of municipal financial management; but, when local governments began lending their credit on a large scale for private railroad promotion, as has been noted earlier, trouble was inevitable. The bulk of the defaults in this period were on railroad aid bonds, and some of their weakening of municipal credit carried into the present century.

The next wave of municipal bond defaults centered in the panic and depression of 1893. According to Hillhouse, the percentage of places and the amount of debt in default were not so large as in the earlier period, although the defaults were more widely scattered geographically. Defaults on railroad aid bonds still predominated, largely because many such bonds, issued before the widespread ban on their use in the 1870s, were falling due in that depressed period.

For many years after recovery from that depression, most municipalities administered their rising debts without apparent difficulty. In the early decades of the 1900s, economic reversals were not protracted; orderly methods of municipal financial management and marketing of municipal bonds were developing; and the real estate boom of the 1920s brought soaring assessed valuations that greatly expanded local borrowing and taxing power. There were sporadic defaults, largely in speculatively developed western irrigation districts; but, municipal securities as a class acquired high status as investments.

The deep economic depression of the 1930s, however, precipitated debt defaults in thousands of counties, cities, towns, school districts, and special districts. Beginning in the late 1920s, the first municipal defaults occurred in Florida after the collapse of its fabulous land boom. Due to an accumulation of special assessment bond defaults in the cities and towns in the state of Washington, defaults piled up at a rapid rate in the early 1930s—the number of units in default reaching a peak of well over 3,000 in 1935.[18] In addition to actual defaults, many cities fell behind in deposits required to keep sinking funds at

---

[17] Hillhouse, *op. cit.*, p. 39.

[18] See Shanks, Sanders, Jr., "The Extent of Municipal Defaults," *National Municipal Review*, January, 1935, and Hillhouse, *op cit.*, pp, 12-30. In Florida, nearly one-half of all local governments defaulted; in eight other states the number of reported defaults ranged between 100 and 300. These states were Arkansas, California, (mainly irrigation districts), Illinois, Louisiana, Michigan, North Carolina, Ohio, and Texas. And, in some 20 other states, there were a considerable number of defaults. There appeared to have been no local defaults, or at least none of any significance, in eight states—Connecticut, Delaware, Maryland, Massachusetts, New Hampshire, Rhode Island, Vermont, and West Virginia—and very few in Georgia, Kansas, Maine, Nevada, New York and Virginia.

Table 26

**POST-WORLD WAR II LOCAL GOVERNMENT DEFAULTS,
BY PURPOSE OF ISSUE AND TYPE OF SECURITY**

Purpose of Issue	Type of Security	Number of Defaults
Toll facilities	Nonguaranteed	7
Marina facilities	Nonguaranteed	3
Water systems	Nonguaranteed	3
Industrial Aid	Nonguaranteed	2
Natural gas systems	Nonguaranteed	2
College dormitories	Nonguaranteed	1
Aerial tramway	Nonguaranteed	1
Irrigation districts	Guaranteed	6
Cities or counties	Guaranteed	4
Fire district	Guaranteed	1

Source: Jackson Phillips and Roger Baum, "Postwar Default Experience of Municipal Bonds," United States Congress, Subcommittee on Economic Progress of the Joint Economic Committee, *State and Local Public Facility Needs and Financing*, (Washington, D. C.: United States Government Printing Office, 1966), Vol. 2, p. 245.

proper levels. Had the great majority of debt been in serial form in the 1930s the number of actual defaults would have been much greater.

The immediate causes of these defaults included a decline in tax receipts to a point at which they were insufficient to cover both debt charges and maintenance of essential services; bank failures and frozen funds; handicapping legal restrictions on taxing power; poorly planned debt structures; and weak financial administration, added to the general economic woes. Less obvious, because it had its origin in the predepression years of boom and prosperity, was the chief underlying cause of the most serious defaults—the use of public credit to promote private real estate speculation.

In the municipal debacle of the 1930s, the majority of local governments were in only temporary difficulty and either cleared up their arrears with little delay or successfully negotiated limited refunding plans. A sizable minority, however, required very comprehensive debt reorganization, in some instances involving the scaling down of interest rates and even of principal. The public disillusionment was painful, but there was the undeniable fact that the vast majority of local governments had weathered the storm without financial disaster.

The number of state and local bond defaults in the two decades after World War II was the subject of a 1966 Congressional study. It found that there were only thirty known defaults in that period—and only four of these were municipal.[19] Other characteristics are shown in Table 26.

---

[19] The energy crisis of 1973-74 produced major declines in yields of motor fuel taxes and many of the toll roads and toll bridges felt sharp adverse effects of reduced motor vehicle usage. Whether these presage a new round of major stresses (and perhaps defaults) for revenue bonds supported from these sources is not yet known.

Constitutional and Statutory Limitations on
Local Government Borrowing

For more than a century the states have sought to impose suitable legal limits upon local government borrowing and to regulate borrowing methods and debt management. In a majority of the states some of the basic provisions are incorporated in the constitutions; in a minority statutory law has been widely used. The main features of these regulatory provisions may be summarized as follows:[20]

1. Limitation of the amount of debt that may be outstanding
2. Voter approval of bond authorizations
3. Mandatory levy of annual taxes sufficient for the payment of principal and interest
4. Establishment of certain principles of debt management
5. Prohibition of the gift or loan of money or credit to individuals and private associations and corporations (and, in some cases, to public corporations)

At this point, we are concerned primarily with the efficacy of the legal devices for keeping the amount of borrowing by local governments within bounds. The gradual erosion of the prohibition on the gift or loan of money or credit as it relates to private enterprise has been noted earlier, in the discussion of borrowing for industrial aid; the prohibition, with respect to public corporations, seems to be passing from the scene.

The Debt-to-Property Ratio. The device used almost universally by the states as a measure of permitted local borrowing is to establish a maximum amount of outstanding "tax-supported" debt that a local government may have in relation to the value of taxable property—usually measured by the local assessed valuation, the market value, or the state equalized valuation of taxable property. This method of control, which seemed quite logical when most local government revenue came from the general property tax, had its origin in the 1850s. Having no inherent long-term borrowing power, local governments looked to the state legislatures for authorization to incur debt; and, in this period, the taxpayers in some states became convinced that the legislatures could not be trusted with this responsibility and demanded constitutional restrictions on local borrowing. In 1857, Iowa placed in its constitution a limitation of five percent of the local assessed valuation on the debt that any local government could incur; but, it was not until the peak of local financial troubles in the 1870s that such action became widespread.

---

[20] Useful general studies of this subject include a report of the Advisory Commission on Intergovernmental Relations, *State Constitutional and Statutory Restrictions on Local Government Debt*, (Washington, D. C.: United States Government Printing Office, 1961), 98 pp.; *State Constitutional Restrictions on Local Borrowing and Property Taxing Powers* by Frederick L. Bird and Bettie Mann, (Albany: Government Affairs Foundation, Inc., 1964), 311 pp.; and *The Effectiveness of Debt Limits on State and Local Government Borrowing* by William L. Mitchell, (New York: New York University, 1967), 66 pp.

Table 27
ILLUSTRATIVE LIMITATIONS ON THE AUTHORITY
OF LOCAL GOVERNMENT TO INCUR LONG-TERM GENERAL
OBLIGATION DEBT

Constitutional Provision	Constitutional Provision and State Statute	State Statute	None
Arizona	Alabama	Arkansas[1]	Alaska
Georgia	Hawaii	California	Connecticut[2]
Indiana	Illinois	Colorado	Nebraska
Iowa	Michigan	Delaware[3]	Tennessee
Kentucky	Missouri	Florida[4]	
Louisiana	Montana	Idaho[4]	
Maine[4]	New York	Kansas	
New Mexico	North Carolina	Maryland[5]	
North Dakota	Oklahoma	Massachusetts[6]	
South Carolina	Virginia[4]	Minnesota[7]	
South Dakota	West Virginia	Mississippi	
Utah	Wisconsin	Nevada	
Washington	Wyoming	New Hampshire	
		New Jersey	
		Ohio	
		Oregon	
		Pennsylvania[8]	
		Rhode Island	
		Texas[1]	
		Vermont	

[1] School districts only.
[2] Restricted to 2¼ times tax receipts for most recent year.
[3] Applicable only to two counties.
[4] Municipalities only.
[5] Chartered counties only.
[6] Municipalities and school districts.
[7] Excluding Minneapolis, St. Paul, and Duluth.
[8] Philadelphia City is governed by Constitutional limit.

Source: Advisory Commission on Intergovernmental Relations, *State-Local Finances: Significant Features and Suggested Legislation*, (Washington, D. C., United States Government Printing Office, 1972), pp. 150-159.

As seen in Table 27, comprehensive limitations on the power of local governments to issue long-term, general obligation bonds are currently found in the constitutions of 26 states, supplemented by statutory requirements in half of these. Extensive statutory limitations are found in 14 states and limitations restricted to only one class of local government in another six. No limitations exist in three states and Connecticut restricts debt, not by rate, but at 2¼ times the tax receipts for the most recent year.

The legal device of limiting a local government's borrowing power to some percentage of the property tax base still carries great authority and prestige, but it has serious defects. Dependence on this device to permit local governments to use their credit adequately, but not excessively, is a demonstration of misdirected confidence in many jurisdictions. The defects tend to be greatest in those states which have made no real effort to modernize ancient formulae to take into account contemporary needs and contemporary assessment practices. Constitutions are difficult to amend; but, even in the minority of states that have worked assiduously to make their constitutional or statutory debt limit provisions meaningful and constructive, there remain certain deficiencies that may be inherent. The nature of the defects most commonly ascribed to the debt-to-property ratio indicates that some of them are easily remediable; others, only with great difficulty, if at all.

1. Percentages Are Arbitrary and Unrealistic. Although some states adjust the debt ceiling to allow for the varying needs of different classes and sizes of local governments, other states make no such distinctions or the adjustments are perfunctory. When the ratio for cities ranges among the states from one percent to 20 percent, and for school districts from one-half of one percent to 25 percent, there is no reason to believe that these divergent ratios are the product of careful study and analysis of the needs and fiscal abilities of local governments.

There is the additional complication that borrowing requirements vary not only among classes but also within classes of local governments, depending on rate of growth, population density, topography, and other economic, geographic, and demographic factors. Some states maintain rigid limiting ratios with no allowances for such factors, necessitating various makeshift arrangements. In many states, on the other hand, legal borrowing power is given considerable flexibility by such devices as two-level limits, with borrowing in the upper level requiring a popular referendum; provision, in a few instances (such as for school districts in New York), to exceed the debt limit by a special majority popular vote and approval by a state administrative agency; and exemption from the limit of debt incurred for revenue-producing undertakings, reflecting the traditional concept that debt limits are primarily for the protection of property taxpayers. In some states, self-sustaining debt is automatically exempt or is given additional range because of the basic importance of the purpose. There would appear to be ample justification for exemption of the self-supporting debts of basic municipally-owned utilities which might, alternately be privately owned; but, when it is extended to the debts of an increasing variety of public functions whose support has been shifted from taxes to service charges, the effectiveness of the limit is weakened. Debt does not vanish because of a change in the means of its financial support. As noted earlier, the exemption of general obligation special assessment debt in some states has caused trouble in the past.

2. Assessed Value Offers An Unreliable Guide. The measurement base to which the limiting ratio is applied, usually the most recent assessed valuation of taxable property, is unreliable because of the general practice of underassessment—in varying degrees. The law requires that property be assessed at its full value or at some specified fraction of full value; but, local assessors commonly set the level much lower than these standards and on a go-as-you-please basis that varies the level among local assessing districts in the same state. Even if the limiting ratios originally reflected careful study of the borrowing needs and fiscal capacities of local governments, their application is distorted by this usurpation of legislative power by the assessors. Several states, e.g., New York, have undertaken to remedy this defect by applying the limiting percentages to the full value of taxable property and assigning to an adequately equipped state agency the responsibility for determining full value for each local government.

3. *The Single Year Base is Inappropriate.* Use of the assessed valuation of a single year as a measurement base opens the door to manipulation of borrowing power by quick inflation of the base—an artifice that occasionally has played a disconcerting role in municipal debt history.[21] There is also the shortcoming that, since assessed valuations tend to expand in boom periods and contract in depressed periods, local governments may be induced to over-borrow in periods of inflation and may be unable to borrow in time of deflation. A few states—notably Massachusetts, New Jersey, and New York—try to minimize these defects by using a moving average of the assessed valuations of the last three or five years as a measurement base. Philadelphia uses 13½ percent of moving 10 year average.

4. *Failure to Apply Limits to Overlapping Local Governments.* Debt limits tend to be misleading and ineffective because they are applied to the debts of individual local governments rather than to the aggregate debt of the overlapping local governments serving a community. In the relatively few states where the structure of local government is simple, the formulation of a satisfactory debt limit should not be difficult; but, when the local public debt that must be supported by the same group of taxpayers and ratepayers is incurred by several layers of separate local governments, there is the problem of how to place a reasonable ceiling on the aggregate debt and apportion this overall limit among the component governmental units in line with their respective responsibilities and needs.

Only one state, South Carolina, has undertaken to impose a specific constitutional limit on the overall amount of local government borrowing generally. This limit encountered operational difficulties and has been vitiated by court action and by amendments granting exceptions to individual municipalities. Connecticut and New Hampshire provide by statute for what may be called overall limits, but they are among the states with simple local government structures. In most states, the aggregate of the separate debt limits for the overlapping local governments serving a community may be said to constitute an overall limit—subject to some exceptions where there are overlapping special districts with no designated limits. Studies of these aggregates suggest that, in some states, there has been inadequate attention to their significance.

5. *Outdated Limitations.* The failure of some states, mainly those with constitutional debt limits, to provide realistic limits that protect, but do not suppress, has led to methods of evasion that are costly; detrimental to local government structure, administrative organization, and fiscal management; and contributory to the weakening of fiscal responsibility. One aspect of this development is that constitutional debt limitations are rapidly losing jurisdiction

---

[21] In the land boom of the 1920s, several mushrooming subdivisions incorporated as municipalities and were able, by this device, to incur debt of $10,000 and more *per capita* and to make it legal for investment by savings banks because of its low ratio to assessed valuation. Some savings banks were eager purchasers—to their later dismay.

over local government debt. Vast amounts and confusing varieties of local debt are being created throughout a large part of the country which the courts have held not to be debt in a constitutional sense. But, all local government debt, regardless of the source of revenue for its payment, has an impact on the local community that needs to be evaluated as to its equity and economic effect.

6. *Lack of Limits Related to Needs.* Some of the criticisms of the prevailing method of restricting local government borrowing go beyond the defects in application of the debt-to-property ratio and question the validity of the method itself. What has troubled a number of critics is the emphasis placed on arbitrary limitation and the lack of attention to the appropriate use of borrowing. The point is often made, too, that the capacity to incur debt is measured by existing resources, although the ability to meet interest and repay principal must depend on future resources. The prospect for future economic growth, stagnation, or decline is clearly a vital consideration in planning the incurrence of debt, but would be difficult to include in any legal measurement formula. There is a frequently voiced belief that the value of property subject to *ad valorem* taxation is not a good measure of fiscal resources for the support of debt. While one can readily agree that it is a far from ideal index of a community's fiscal ability, it is the only annually recurrent measurement standard presently available for virtually all local governments. Part of the criticism arises from failure to distinguish between the use of property value as a measurement standard and its relation to the local revenue system. Some argue that it could serve as a reasonably good index of local resources, regardless of the system of revenue that may be in effect, if actual values were not clouded by the vagaries of underassessment. Others take the view that, where the property tax has become much less important in the local revenue structure, it has little place in a modern determination of capacity to pay.

Alternative Limiting Formulae

Among the alternatives that have been put forward from time to time is one that the measurement base for local debt limitation be shifted from property values to the revenues of the borrower. It has been suggested variously that debt be limited to some multiple of a local government's annual revenue, that annual debt service be limited to some percentage of annual revenue, or that the limiting percentage should apply only to interest payments. B. U. Ratchford, a well-known authority on public debt, has proposed that limitation be based on a forward-dated moving average of net revenue receipts for several years.[22] Noting the unavailability of individual income data as a measure of ability to support debt, he pointed out that governmental revenues are not inferior to total individual incomes as a measure of the debt load which a community may safely assume, since "the public receipts indicate the level of governmental services to which the people are accustomed and for which they are willing to pay." He has taken the position, also, that governmental revenue

---

[22] Ratchford, B. U.: "A Formula for Limiting State and Local Debts," *The Quarterly Journal of Economics*, LI (1936), pp. 71-89, and "State and Local Debt Limitations," *The Proceedings of the Fifty-First National Tax Conference* (1958), pp. 215-229.

is a better measure of fiscal ability than property values; that, as a measurement base, it is less subject to manipulation than assessed values; and that there would be less likelihood of a thriftless use of credit if the incurrence of debt beyond a normal range were conditioned on acceptance of a higher tax level before the debt was incurred.

Of especial interest is the new Pennsylvania treatment of debt limits established by Act 185 of 1972.[23] Under the 1968 revision of the Pennsylvania Constitution, the legislature was directed to shift the basis for expression of debt limitations from assessed value of property to locally generated revenues (with the exclusions listed below).

Under the new Act, municipalities and school districts are permitted to incur debt equal to 250 percent of the borrowing base, counties equal to 300 percent of the borrowing base. The only exceptions are the City of Philadelphia which has a separate debt limit and school districts of the first class (Philadelphia and Pittsburgh), where the limit is set at 100 percent of the borrowing base. In all cases, if public authorities are involved, the limit is increased by 50 percent of the borrowing base, except in Philadelphia.

The borrowing base consists of the average of all revenues of the governmental unit involved for the three preceding years, provided however, that the following are excluded: (1) subsidies or reimbursements from the state or federal government; (2) revenues, user charges, special levies, etc., pledged to specific self-liquidating debt; (3) interest on moneys in the sinking funds, reserves, etc., pledged or budgeted for the payment of outstanding debt; (4) grants related to specific projects; and (5) proceeds from the disposition of capital assets and other non-recurring items.

Only when the outstanding debt exceeds the limits is the governing body of the municipality, county, or school district obliged to submit debt proposals to the electorate. In the case of debt approved by the electorate, there are no limits.

Beyond the limit for "regular purposes," the local government's borrowing limit is increased by 100 percent of the borrowing base if the counties have not already assumed county-wide responsibility to finance certain types of projects such as public health service, air and water pollution control, sewage and refuse collection, and public transportation. If serious damage has been incurred as a result of flood, fire, riot, etc., an additional 50 percent of the borrowing base is authorized with approval of the Commonwealth Court.

If it is desirable to continue the long effort to limit, by formula, the amount of debt that a local government may incur, adoption of annual revenue receipts as a measurement base undoubtedly would, as Ratchford has said, eliminate some of the defects of the debt-to-property ratio. There would remain, however, such old problems as how to determine the right limiting percentages, how to provide needed flexibility, and how to close the loopholes for circumvention.

---

[23] See "Act 185 of 1972—Local Government Unit Debt Act" by Ellen Coggins in the *Pennsylvanian* (The Magazine of Local Governments) Vol. 11, No. 8, August, 1972, pp. 10-14 and Pennsylvania Economy League, State Division, League Letter, June 1, 1972—"Local Government Borrowing—A New Basis," 6 pp. for a fuller discussion of the new situation in Pennsylvania.

The traditional system of debt limits, always a rather crude method of restriction, has been breaking down through evasion and the increasing intricacy of governmental structure.

In the authors' view, the local debt situation has become too complex to be controlled safely and constructively by formalized debt limits.

The Referendum as a Means of Debt Control

The requirement that local government bonds be authorized by referendum has the sanction of long tradition. At least some use of this form of debt regulation is required in nearly all of the states, but there is wide variation among, and within, states as to which classes of local governments must use it, the kinds and purposes of borrowing for which it must be used, and the degree of its potential restrictiveness. The referendum device was originally adopted for the control of long-term, general obligation debt.

At the end of 1971 the constitutions of 18 states required a referendum for the issue of any long-term, general obligation bonds; constitutional provisions are supplemented by statutory requirements in several of these states. There are no referendum requirements in Indiana, Connecticut, Hawaii, Massachusetts (except, on occasion, for regional school districts), or Tennessee (except for industrial developments bonds). Most commonly, a simple majority vote of the qualified electors that vote on the question is required for approval; this situation occurs in 32 states. But in 11 states, either generally or for certain purposes, a special majority of from three-fifths to two-thirds is required. In Nebraska and North Dakota, a specified percentage of voter participation is required for the bonds of specified classes of governments. A variation provided in Arizona is the requirements of a referendum only for the incurrence of debt above a specified percentage of the assessed valuation. There tends to be less popular control of the incurrence of limited liability debt, payable only from some special fund or nonproperty tax. Quite commonly, such debt may be authorized by the governing body without a referendum and, when a referendum is required, approval is almost always by a simple majority vote.

The desirability of mandatory referenda for the authorization of borrowing is to be questioned. The use of this device shifts responsibility from elected representatives, who should be required to make, instead of evade, important decisions. And, too, it is a deterrent to the advancement of comprehensive, well integrated budgeting for capital and current expense purposes, which calls for versatile financing of programs rather than sporadic decisions on bond issues. That voters often give perfunctory attention to bond referenda is indicated by low voter participation, and the assumption that their understanding of the validity of the proposed borrowing is more profound than that of the responsible officials is doubtful.

Recent comments on the requirement for bond referenda were contained in the *National Civic Review* in May, 1972 which reported on a survey recently conducted by the *Weekly Bond Buyer*. This survey attributed current bond failures to voter apathy and rural conservatism. The survey also concluded that the new United States Supreme Court ruling on residence requirements, in

Table 28
STATES REQUIRING REFERENDUM FOR ISSUE OF
GENERAL OBLIGATION LONG-TERM DEBT BY LOCAL
GOVERNMENTS, 1971

| Requirements by | | | No Referendum Requirement |
State Constitution	State Constitution and State Statute	State Statute	
Alabama	California	Delaware	Connecticut
Alaska	Colorado	Illinois	Hawaii
Arizona[1]	Florida	Iowa	Indiana
Arkansas	Idaho	Kansas	Massachusetts[2]
Georgia	Kentucky	Michigan	Tennessee[3]
Louisiana	Nebraska	Minnesota[4]	
Maine	North Dakota	Mississippi[5]	
Maryland	South Dakota	Montana[6]	
Missouri	Wyoming	New Hampshire[7]	
New Mexico		Nevada	
North Carolina[6]		New Jersey[8]	
South Carolina[9]		New York[10]	
Virginia[11]		Ohio	
Washington[6]		Oklahoma[12]	
		Oregon	
		Pennsylvania[14]	
		Rhode Island[6]	
		Texas	
		Utah	
		Vermont	
		West Virginia	
		Wisconsin[13]	

[1] Only for debt exceeding specified limits.
[2] For some regional school district issues.
[3] For industrial development bonds.
[4] Excluding Minneapolis, St. Paul, and Duluth.
[5] Only on county and municipal bonds and then by petition.
[6] For selected issues.
[7] Not required in cities and counties.
[8] Except in selected school districts.
[9] Only in cities and towns.
[10] Except in selected school districts.
[11] For county debt only.
[12] Except for county hospitals.
[13] Applies only to school districts.
[14] Applies only to debt in excess of statutory debt up to specified maximum. (See text for comments.)

Source: Advisory Commission on Intergovernmental Relations, *State-Local Finances: Significant Features and Suggested Legislation*, (Washington, D. C., United States Government Printing Office, 1972), pp. 160-161.

limiting such requirements to 30 days, would have a favorable effect on bond referenda since migrants would be more service-oriented than cost-oriented. This, in combination with the wave of 18-year old voters, pointed to the greater success of bond votes.[24]

Interestingly, in January, 1973 the *National Civic Review* summarized the fall elections as follows:

> Most fiscal issues fared well in November but property tax referenda did not. According to a tabulation by the *Weekly Bond Buyer*, more than 75 percent of the bond issues passed, a total of $3.268 billion out of $4.31 billion on ballots throughout the country.[25]

An alternative to bond referenda is the careful preparation of capital programs, with adequate provision for public hearings before adoption and with provision for permissive referenda by petition.[26] These provisions safeguard the public interest and avoid delays and election expense when there is no serious controversy. In any event, there seems to be inadequate justification for bond referenda that require special majority votes and, therefore, establish a veto by minorities and that induce governing bodies to resort to less restricted types of borrowing that may be less appropriate and more costly.

An Alternative to Debt Limit Formulae

The amounts of local government debt that are excluded from constitutional and statutory limits requires the admission that traditional debt limit formulae have not worked as planned; that they are out-moded; that suitable alternatives must be developed if we are to cope with this situation satisfactorily. Among the remedies under consideration, the most fundamental—and possibly the most constructive—is abandonment of constitutional and statutory limits and their replacement by the same kind of debt control to which private corporations and individuals are subject—the ability to maintan good credit. The regulatory role of the states would still include determination of the purposes of borrowing and the general principles of debt management; and it necessarily would include provision of advisory services and determination of minimum credit standards as gauged by the bond market.

The Advisory Commission on Intergovernmental Relations, following a study of local debt restrictions in 1961, made the following recommendations:[27]

---

24 "New Residence Ruling May Affect Bond Votes," *The National Civic Review*, Vol. 61, No. Five, pp. 258-59.

25 "Most Bond Issues Passed in November," *The National Civic Review*, Vol. 62, No. One, pp. 43-44.

26 See *A Model County and Municipal Bond Law*, (New York: National Municipal League, 1953) p. ix and Allen D. Manvel, *State Constitutional and Statutory Restrictions on Local Government Debt*, Advisory Commission on Intergovernmental Relations, (Washington, D. C. 1961), pp. 72-74.

27 See Advisory Commission on Intergovernmental Relations, *State Constitutional and Statutory Restrictions on Local Government Debt*, (Washington, D. C.: United States Government Printing Office, 1961), pp. 3-5.

1. That State provisions with respect to long-term borrowing and indebtedness of local governments be comprehensive in their coverage; any
   conditions they place upon local borrowing power should apply uni-
   formly—or with well-considered, minimum distinctions—to all types
   of long-term debt.

2. That the authority to issue bonds be legally vested in the governing
   bodies of local governments subject to a permissive referendum only
   on petition, with participation in any such referendum available to all
   eligible voters and the results determined by a simple majority vote
   on the question.

3. The repeal of constitutional and statutory provisions limiting local
   government debt or debt service by reference to the local base for
   property taxation.

4. That the States consider measures to regulate long-term borrowing
   of local governments by reference to the net interest cost of prospective bond issues in relation to the currently prevailing interest rate
   on high quality municipal securities.

5. That states make available technical and advisory assistance to local
   governments with regard to their issuance of long-term debt.

The fourth recommendation may be said to be the protective substitute for
debt limits. The proposal is, in brief, that a local government would be pro-
hibited from selling bonds at a net interest cost rate that was above some
specified multiple of the latest reported average interest yield for high-grade
municipal bonds.[28] For example, the maximum permissible net interest cost rate
might be set at 1.4 times the going average interest yield for high-grade bonds.
This would mean that, if the latter were 3.00 percent, the net interest cost rate
ceiling would be 4.20 percent; if it were 5.0 percent, the ceiling would be 7.00
percent.[29] Properly set up, the plan would debar the sale only of bonds
of obviously speculative security. These might include the bonds of units with
markedly deteriorating credit, bonds of weak units of nondescript types having
little justifiable place in the local government structure, or limited liability bonds
designed to finance undertakings of marginal, or untested, earning power. That
the plan is intended to cover all types of long-term financing by local governments is one of its most significant features.

The proposed plan should not be adopted without careful testing and
analysis, but it is worth serious consideration because of its potential advantages.
It would, among other things, emphasize the need for maintaining good credit;
obviate the need for inventing evasive borrowing devices and creating unnecessary special districts and authorities; give flexibility for choosing the most appropriate borrowing instruments and discourage the use of limited liability bonds

---

[28] The net interest cost rate takes into consideration the interest rate or rates and premium
or discount from par in sale of the bonds. It should be computed on the basis of internal
rate of return; not on the basis of average net interest cost.

[29] Given the normal pattern of the re-offering yield curve, this would encourage
governments with low credit ratings to issue relatively short-term bonds and would inhibit
the issue of long-term bonds.

for unsuitable purposes; identify weak units in the local government structure that needed technical or financial aid or had no good reason for existence; and help to retard the increasing obscurity of the local government debt structure.

Defining the Limits of Local Borrowing Capacity

The limits of local borrowing capacity considered here are the economic limits, not the locally imposed limits. To be able to define such limits by precise formulae would be a great convenience; but, as noted in beginning this discussion of the boundaries of safety in borrowing, there are too many variables to permit such precision. There are useful guides, however, for the determination of reasonable boundaries for any community's public borrowing.

1. All Relevant Debt Must Be Considered. A local government's debt load, from an economic point of view, is not merely the debt that is supported by property taxes but all of the other relevant debt which the economy of the local community must support. When making comparisons where water, sewer, gas, and electric debt are involved, consideration must include weights for these; however, it is also necessary to take into account in inter-city comparisons the fact that the gas and electric systems of one community may be privately-owned, whereas they may be publicly-owned in another. Obviously, genuine comparisons require that the gas and electric debt of the municipality with publicly-owned facilities be excluded in comparisons with those communities which have no such facilities.

Moreover, where a municipality operates a facility, e.g., an airport or parking complex, for which a large part of the revenues generated are from the economy beyond the city's limits, it is essential that these revenues be pro-rated. Or, if in the case of a school district, the state agrees to pay 60 percent of the school debt service charges, only the remaining 40 percent is appropriately chargeable against the local economy. Or, if a local government is providing public housing with the debt service payments being paid by the federal government, it is inappropriate to include the housing debt in the economic analysis. Finally, if some of the municipality's water and sewer debt is incurred to provide services to the region, a credit for a portion of the debt service costs is appropriate. Conversely, if the city is using facilities of other governments, a contra-entry is desirable. Only when all of these adjustments have been taken into account is it feasible to determine the true relative economic burden being undertaken by different communities.

2. Aggregate Relevant Debt Must be Considered. In a small minority of communities in the United States, the local population is required to support the debt of just one local government; but, as has been shown in the discussion of debt limits, in most areas it must support, or help to support, the debts of from two to even a dozen or more superimposed or overlapping local governments. Thus, the true debt burden on the population living within the boundaries of a given local government is the direct debt of that government, plus the overlapping debt (i.e., this population's share of the debts of the other layers of local government), or the overall debt, as it is commonly called.

Investment bankers, security analysts, and astute investors interested in municipal bonds customarily require data on overall debt for appraisal purposes. Most local finance officers are familiar with, and well aware of, the significance of these composite figures that show the true local public debts of their communities. They often provide such figures in the prospectuses or financial statements prepared for the sale of bonds; but only infrequently include them in annual financial reports for the enlightenment of the general public.

3. Influential Variables. Some communities are so fortunate as to have borrowing needs that are very limited in relation to their resources for the support of debt; but, there are many with such pressing demands for major capital improvements that they must be very observant of the limit of safety beyond which the accumulation of debt might be detrimental to the local economy and to the community's ability to obtain credit at reasonable rates. This limit of safety varies with numerous factors, some of which can be influenced favorably by local government policy and action. A summary of the more important factors follows:

a. The weight of a local government's direct and overlapping debt, i.e., the debt load or debt burden, is commonly determined by relating the amount of the debt to the economic capacity to pay. The emphasis is on relation of debt to the local government's present resources; but, debt principal and interest must be supported by future resources. For this reason, some local governments are safe in incurring heavier debts than others in relation to their present resources. In other words, more debt can be incurred with impunity under some conditions than under others.

b. A local government whose resources are growing with the prospect of continuing to grow should be able safely to incur a heavier debt than a local government whose resources are static or declining.

c. A local government whose economy is cyclically stable can incur with impunity a heavier debt than one whose economy is very sensitive to changes in the business cycle—its revenues and operating expenses fluctuate less and its budgeting tends to be less difficult.

d. Borrowing can be heavier when it represents investment in capital assets that clearly strengthen the local economy and stimulate the growth of resources than when it comprises deadweight and doubtfully productive debt.

e. Skillful planning of the debt structure with respect to its impact on future budgets permits the incurrence of more debt than would otherwise be prudent.

f. The weight of the debt depends partly on the level of interest rates obtainable. More debt can be carried if interest rates can be held down by choosing the most appropriate borrowing instruments, planning bond issues (insofar as this is possible) to satisfy the prevailing market, and making intelligent efforts to promote their sale.

g. The amount of debt that can safely be carried depends materially on the quality of a local government's budgeting and forward-looking planning.

h. A community can shoulder a larger burden of debt if there is cooperative physical and financial planning among the overlapping local units
of government, as, for example, existed for many years between
Cincinnati and its overlapping school district and county.

i. A local government with an adequate and reasonably well-balanced
revenue system is much better equipped to borrow to the limits of
economic capacity than one which is dependent on a restricted and
narrowly based system of revenues. In the few states where constitutional tax rate limits apply to property taxes levied for debt service, the
rate limit is a species of debt limit, not mentioned earlier, that may
greatly understate economic borrowing capacity.

j. A community can incur a relatively heavy debt without undue concern if the people are clearly willing, as well as able, to pay for it.
There might well be general agreement, for example, that the replacement of a low-quality existing water supply with a new, high-quality,
but expensive, supply would be a long-range investment of such value
as to justify above-average spending in the public sector of the economy
even if it necessitated less spending in the private sector.

k. The weight of debt that a local government may incur with assurance
depends very measurably on whether state regulations and restrictions
as regards local finance are helpful or harmful.

4. The Investment Analyst's Point of View. In appraising the investment
quality of municipal bonds, the analyst has had to concern himself with a constantly widening variety of securities. In analyzing the various types of limited
liability bonds, such as bonds payable solely from the earnings of a municipal
enterprise or solely from a yield of some specified nonproperty tax, he has to
interest himself particularly in the adequacy of the specific supporting revenues
and the protective features of the bond contracts; but, when he undertakes to
study the general obligation bonds of local governments with taxing power
(which still comprise the greater portion of local government debt), he is concerned with the communities as a whole—what their resources are, how they
are governed, and how these local governments finance their responsibilities.

In evaluating the debt of a local government, the analyst is interested in
such factors as the purposes for which the local government borrows, what its
borrowing discloses about its financial policies, how it plans and manages its
debt, how much competence it shows in the overall management of its financial
affairs, and how much the state helps or hinders local finance. Because the analyst
also needs meaningful data on the debt load, he must: (1) use composite figures
to show a local government's overall debt; (2) be able to compare these with
the overall debts of other local governments; and (3) relate this overall debt,
as best he can, to the local government's economic resources.

The concept of overall debt has been previously defined. For purposes of
intergovernmental comparisons, the computation of overall debt requires certain adjustments and deductions; but, in arriving at net figures, the analyst has
to avoid such understatement of the actual debt load as would result, for example,
from deducting debt merely because it is supported by a benefit charge instead of a tax. In comparing a given overall debt with local economic and

financial resources, the analyst employs such measurements standards as are available. The various federal censuses, as well as other sources, supply valuable data on such pertinent factors as personal income, housing values, retail and wholesale sales, manufacturing, agriculture, and natural resources; but much of this information is available only at infrequent intervals and most of it is not clearly applicable to a host of small units of government. This leaves the assessed value of taxable property as the only really universal and annually recurrent measure of local resources, which, when adjusted to approximate full value, provides a fairly reliable base—particularly when supplemented by such other criteria as are available.[30]

The level at which the ratio of overall net debt to the full value of taxable property indicates a dangerously heavy debt load cannot be determined with any degree of certainty. Because of the variables noted earlier, this figure would differ from one local government to another.

---

[30] Because of haphazard underassessment, assessed valuations are, of themselves, unreliable indicators; but reasonably dependable approximations of full value have become more generally available as the result of sales ratio and appraisal studies by numerous states and the sales ratio studies of the United States Bureau of the Census.

14

Planning a Local Government
Debt Policy

The patterns of financing public improvements through the use of debt have varied considerably during this century. Thus, at the outset of the century, the predominant pattern of financing was through bonds payable over periods up to 50 years from the date of issue. The debt was term debt and provision for its payment was made through the accumulation of sinking funds.

Commencing in the 1920s and greatly accentuated in the 1930s, local governments moved to the use of bond issues with serial maturities—either equal annual principal installment bonds or equal annual burden bonds, i.e., bond issues for which the principal and interest requirements were substantially equal from year to year. In that period, too, a number of municipalities (of which Milwaukee was the most notable example among the larger cities) undertook policies designated as "pay-as-you-go" or, perhaps more properly, "pay-as-you-acquire." Under these policies, local governments either ceased the issuance of new debt and paid for all improvements from current resources or reserve funds or developed a mix involving greatly reduced reliance upon the use of debt. The popularity of this process continued during the 1940s; however, various factors resulted in a return to debt financing by almost all of these governments in the 1950s.

The memories of the problems arising from high fixed charges in the 1930s, when current income was greatly reduced, still lingers on; however, public officials now appear much more reconciled to the use of public debt as an instrument through which each generation of users of public facilities pays its share of "rental" in the form of debt service. Moreover, if one takes into account the fact that the repayment of principal and the payment of interest is ordinarily by means of dollars with less purchasing power than those used to acquire the facility, there is considerable logic to the proposition that the use of debt is preferable to a pay-as-you-acquire policy.

Yet, inasmuch as debt constitutes the anticipation of future revenue, a rule of prudence is required. Accordingly, no prudent person will obligate the full amount of his anticipated future income. Nor will any prudent investor accept proffered debt in amounts that place the debtor in jeopardy of default.

Frequently, the amounts of capital funds reasonably needed by a community substantially exceed its financial capacity. In these circumstances, it is necessary for public officials to make priority decisions which are likely to be extremely difficult and which are not always popular—either with residents or bondholders. The need for effective debt planning is greatest where there is a significant disparity between financial resources and the needed, or desired, public facilities. It is to the processes incident to the development of a debt policy and its execution that this chapter is devoted.

This chapter is not concerned with *ad hoc* policy-making which will produce a predetermined long-term debt pattern, discernible only after many bond contracts have been entered into over a period of years. In contrast with such a retrospective imputation of policy, this chapter treats rather of a "planned" debt policy reduced to writing.

Such programmed debt is prospective; "debt policy," in itself, implies a long-term plan which includes projections into the future of debt service requirements plus estimations as to the government's ability to support such debt service. The period to be covered by a statement of debt policy is debatable. A well-constructed debt policy statement takes into account virtually all pertinent factors as of a given time, at least in theory. Actually, because the development of such a policy requires taking into account and giving appropriate weight to each factor, it is not feasible to have a "permanent" debt policy because the factors are ordinarily in a state of flux. Accordingly, any debt policy statement should be made the subject of periodic review—perhaps at the outset of each new administration and, certainly, no less frequently than once each decade.

Any debt policy statement worthy of the name should be reduced to writing, in terms which are easily understood. Although the policy may be largely that of the "administration," it is desirable that, in its tentative form, an opportunity be afforded for general public discussion and, at a minimum, for councilmanic review, if not adoption thereby.

In addition, a distinction must be made between long-term policy planning and the planning of individual bond issues. The latter is implementation of the former. Whereas, debt policy has to be incrementally implemented at fairly frequent intervals, the authors assume that it is to be incrementally formulated only at infrequent intervals.

DEBT POLICY IN PERSPECTIVE

Those responsible for formulating debt policy work best against a background knowledge of the interrelationships between debt policy and other policies under which the local government is conducted and recognize the difficulties of drawing precise boundaries. We begin with exploring interrelationships.

Debt policy is but one part, albeit important, of overall financial policy. Debt is sometimes incurred for operating expenses (deficit financing), but generally for capital outlays. For the former, debt is usually a very poor choice, and for the latter, only one of several, but not always the most valid. In a particular situation, an overall financial decision to combine several methods of financing with debt, thereby minimizing borrowing, may be the most important alternative choice.

To help put debt policy in perspective as part of local government finance, it may be pointed out that, in multipurpose municipal governments, debt service costs are likely to range between 10 and 20 percent of the annual operating budget. Even in the highly capital intensive elements of municipal operations, e.g., public utilities, there is a large component of operating and maintenance cost. In the low capital intensive activities, e.g., health centers, public safety, and sanitation, the component of debt service is quite low as a percentage of total costs.

The point is: an unwise debt policy can lead to either an extravagant or a pennywise total financial administration if debt policy is not considered in context with other cost elements. Moreover, underdesigned or inadequately designed facilities can frequently lead not only to current high operating costs but also to early obsolescence and demand for early replacement.

The Role of Borrowing

As has been stated earlier, the role of borrowing is that of providing ready funds for immediate use through the anticipation of future revenues. It permits the timely acquisition of facilities. Without borrowing local governments would be obliged both to increase current tax loads and to forego, for substantial periods of time, the use of facilities deemed by officials and citizens as appropriate for meeting the local government's responsibilities.

Moreover, especially in the case of capital expenditures of an unusual size, borrowing permits the levelling out of the burden of payment which cannot easily be achieved by the pay-as-you-acquire device, except through the advance accumulation of large sums of money over a period of years.

Further, borrowing permits local governments to meet needs arising from disasters and requiring the immediate replacement of vital facilities. Through appropriate debt maturity schedules, the burden upon hard-pressed citizens who must replace their own losses can be minimized.

Borrowing also provides an answer in cases of rapid population expansion or the unexpected availability of grants which require matching by the local government. In many circumstances, large capital expenditures by local governments on a timely basis are essential for attraction or retention of important elements of the economic base of the community. Thus, in a contemporary world, each region is required to furnish airport terminal and field facilities; otherwise, economic development may pass the community by in favor of other places which provide such facilities.

During periods of inflation, borrowing in order to acquire facilities at lower prices than those likely to prevail a few years hence becomes an important consideration.

A small local government and a large one are not in exactly the same position as to borrowing. A small government may not require a major capital project each year. Since it cannot, in one tax period, raise enough revenues for the occasional big project, it must save up in advance or borrow to build the project and pay off the debt over a period of time. A large local government requires new capital projects and replacements every year. Lumpiness in capital outlays, however, comes primarily in amounts rather than from the occasional single project. Yet the big government may have to meet a special situation not unlike that of a small government and its infrequent major project. Several years ago, the threat to Kansas City, Missouri, that TWA might move its international headquarters unless the city built new airport facilities and the pressure upon Chicago to build the O'Hare Airport in order to remain the air capital of "Middle America", are two cases in point. Competition forced each of these cities to initiate a project so costly that it alone would have necessitated borrowing.

It is an overstatement, however, to claim that one of the roles of borrowing is to provide a steady flow of capital outlays and to stabilize tax rates. Borrowing cannot accomplish either; it can only assist a local government in making more orderly adjustments to change. Without borrowing, adjustments would be more costly in terms of time lags and economic losses.

The major constraints upon borrowing against anticipated revenues are the burden of debt service upon future taxpayers and the possibility of an increase in the relative size of debt service within the operating budget. If the latter occurs, competition with alternate expenditure opportunities becomes a reality.

Finally, the role of temporary borrowing for capital purposes requires comment. If this takes the form of bond anticipation notes, the role merges into that of borrowing for capital improvements because such notes are but an interim phase of long-term borrowing. Spend now for capital projects by anticipating bond proceeds, fund, and pay later constitutes the sequence.

Temporary borrowing for operating purposes may arise legitimately, either to meet an emergency or to provide operating cash during portions of the year when there is a temporary adverse cash flow, due to an awkward schedule of heavy tax payments late in the fiscal year. Short-term borrowing to meet cash shortages anticipates revenues soon to be received. Such a course is defensible, although obviously a re-arranged revenue calendar would obviate the necessity for repetitive borrowing of this character. On the other hand, acceleration in payments by taxpayers must be weighed carefully. The local government avoids interest costs; but the taxpayer is required to part with his money earlier and frequently the cost to him is greater than the saving to the local government because of the differential in tax-exempt and taxable interest rates.

Funding a deficit, i.e., converting the results of two, three, or more years of unbalanced budgets into long-term debt is usually quite inadvisable. Spending now for operating purposes in anticipation of bond proceeds to bail out deficit financing and the payment later for interest and principal on long-term debt are, in the investment market, cardinal sins outranked only by a bond default.

Determination of the Amount of Debt to be Contracted

How much debt can be prudently contracted by a given community?

The factors which influence this decision vary so greatly from place to place and from time to time that they defy any basic formula prescription—despite the fact that most local governments must carry out their debt operations under legally prescribed debt limits, which frequently have little relation to the reality of current circumstances.

Among the factors which make it inadvisable to set forth a standard for specific amounts of debt financing are:

1. Variations in the kinds and extent of public facilities to be financed
2. Magnitude of the annual payments required to service the debt
3. The degree of favorable impact which the facilities acquired from debt proceeds are likely to have upon the economy of the community
4. Basic economic capacity of the community
5. Degree of overlapping debt of other governmental units which depend upon the same economic base for support
6. Projected rates of growth in the economy of the community

Most of these items require no further comment; however, a few additional words are in order concerning the first two.

Kinds and Extent of Facilities to be Financed. Each community has many needs which are similar to those of most other communities. But differences in some of the basic characteristics of communities, e.g., topography and soil conditions, can produce widely differing dollar costs for providing the same degree of service to the community. Thus, drainage and street construction costs in New Orleans, coupled with partial responsibility for construction and maintenance of flood protection levees, act to increase unit costs tremendously. The scarcity of drained and flood protected land drives the price of land up to astronomical levels. Thereby, the cost of land for all improvements is greatly increased.

Or, in the great central cities of metropolitan regions, the costs of providing adequate rapid transit facilities impose burdens of debt unknown in the middle-sized or smaller cities. High crime rates may impose significant costs in providing physical facilities for the administration of justice, detention, and imprisonment of the convicted.

Other cities may have rapidly growing public school populations; or, still others may be confronted with stable total populations but geographical shifts within the community which result in the underutilization of facilities built some years previously along with demands for early duplication in the newly developed communities.

Moreover, one community may be obliged to provide airport and water-borne commerce terminal facilities for the entire region, while the suburban areas are not obliged to participate in activities from which all benefit.

Accordingly, it is not feasible to develop specific, universally applicable standards for determination of need.

The Amount of Debt Service Requirements. It is highly significant that debt limits are almost universally expressed in terms of the amount of the principal of the debt. Actually, attention should be directed to a combination of the following factors:

1. The amount of the debt outstanding
2. The amount of authorized and unissued debt
3. The maturity schedule of the debt
4. The rate of interest payable upon the debt
5. The amounts of debt service reserves (excluding sinking funds) which are required to be developed and the pattern of such development

To illustrate elements of the differential impact in two cities which have different amounts of debt outstanding, contracted at different times and repayable according to different schedules, consider the following:

	City A (A newer city)	**City B** (An older city)
1. Amount of debt		
a. Outstanding	$40,000,000	$50,000,000
b. Authorized but unissued	15,000,000	5,000,000
c. Sub-total	55,000,000	55,000,000
d. Accumulated debt service reserve	3,000,000	4,000,000
e. Net total	52,000,000	51,000,000
2. Annual requirements		
a. Principal payments		
(1) On issued debt	2,000,000	2,000,000
(2) On debt to be issued	600,000	200,000
(3) Total principal	2,600,000	2,200,000
b. Interest requirements		
(1) On issued debt		
a. At average of 5 percent	2,000,000	
b. At average of 4 percent		2,000,000
(2) On debt to be issued		
a. At average of 6 percent	900,000	300,000
(3) Total interest	2,900,000	2,300,000
c. Debt service reserve deposits	300,000	50,000
d. Total annual requirements	$5,800,000	$4,550,000

When one looks at debt in light of these differences, it is clear that the older city has the advantage in the sense that it has already provided for many of its permanent facilities and will require relatively small amounts of debt in the near future as compared with the newer city. Moreover, given the fact that the older city has contracted its debt at significantly lower interest rates (at earlier times with a lower interest rate market), the amount of annual debt service is in favor of the older city, even though it has substantially the same amount of outstanding debt as the newer city.

Another facet of the error involved in considering only the principal portion of the debt arises from a general lack of understanding of the fact that the value of a bond consists of the sum of:

a. The present worth of the principal payable at a future date
b. The present worth of the interest payable at numerous future dates

To illustrate, consider the value of two bonds in a market in which the value of the particular government's credit is 5 percent for debt due 20 years from date. The government has outstanding one bond with a coupon rate of 6 percent and another with a coupon rate of 4.50 percent. The present value of the two bonds is as follows:

	6 Percent Coupon Bond	**4.50 Percent Coupon Bond**
Present values of principal of $1,000	$ 372.43	$372.43
Present value of semi-annual interest	753.08	558.54
Total value @ 5.00 percent yield rate	$1,125.51	$930.97

Applying the same concept to equal amounts of principal due on two bond issues of the same government, in the case of Issue "A," which was sold January 1, 1965, an amount of $1,000,000 of the issue matures January 1, 1995, and bears a 3.65 percent coupon rate. Issue "B," sold January 1, 1973, contains a $1,000,000 maturity also for January 1, 1995, and bears a coupon rate of 6.50. Assuming that the latter bond was reoffered at par, thereby representing the current market judgment of the interest rate appropriately applicable to the 1995 maturity, the following represents the present worth of the two amounts.[1]

	Present Worth of Two Issues	
	Issue "A" (3.65 percent)	Issue "B" (6.50 percent)
Present worth as of January 1, 1973 of $1,000,000 principal due January 1, 1995	$146,756	$146,756
Present worth as of January 1, 1973 of interest due July 1, 1973 through January 1, 1995	479,129	853,244
Total present worth of outstanding debt of two maturities	$625,885	$1,000,000

The present worth of the outstanding debt of $2,000,000 due January 1, 1995, amounts to $1,625,885, rather than to the face value of $2,000,000.

Therefore, if one is properly to judge the amount of debt outstanding, he must reduce all future payments of principal and interest according to the specific yield rates applicable to each maturity. Thereby, the actual value of the debt can be brought into proper focus. Short of application of such a method, one continues to look at the aggregate amount of outstanding debt, which may be substantially misleading.

In economic terms, therefore, the value of the outstanding debt changes from time to time as the effective interest rates in the market change when applied to the debt of a given local government. The owners of such debt obligations must take these variations in value into account in their regular business transactions. Therefore, a chief financial officer should also take them into account. He may be able to demonstrate that the outstanding debt of his city is substantially less in actual terms than commonly accepted through statement only in terms of par value. In comparisons with other cities, this can mean that he has a lesser amount of actual present value per capita debt than other comparable cities, even though his city has a larger amount of par value debt outstanding.

Relating Debt Policy to Economic Capacity

Physical requirements for capital outlays (the "demand" side) must be matched with the financial resources of the government and the economic capacity of the community (the "supply" side). Because resources are always

---

[1] This pricing ignores the effect of the capital gains tax, if any.

at least relatively scarce, the supply side tends to be (but is not always) the major determinant in fixing the level of capital outlays.

A debt policy statement should take into account the government's ability to support a capital program. However, accurate measurement of such economic capacity is an exceedingly difficult task and the capacity must be viewed over a period of time, retrospectively and prospectively, in order to give balance to the position developed. In many respects, capacity is a relative matter—relative to the general public attitudes in other communities and in the nation. Moreover, economic capacity is an ever-changing situation and must be frequently reviewed, especially for evidence that there is a weakening in the economy which may make it desirable to reduce previously planned capital outlay programs.

The following brief sketch of some of the measurement components is not intended as a step-by-step approach nor as a model. Its purpose is rather to help the reader visualize the difficulties which face the staff responsible for developing a workable methodology.

1. The Level of Capital Outlays: The determination of the amount of capital outlays which can be financed out of tax-supported debt is one major calculation. The level can be established for the next five or six years (the time-span of the capital improvement program), but projections of debt service requirements must be made over a longer period (the life-span of the proposed bond issues). One approach is to weigh the relative merits of three alternative amounts to be financed from tax-supported debt. For example, if we assume that the actual level of annual outlay over the last several years has been about $17.5 million, the proposed new level might be set alternately at $15, $20, or $25 million. Beginning with the debt already outstanding, the first calculation is to determine whether the new debt, added year by year over the five- or six-year period, would be within any restrictive debt limit and, if so, the amounts of unused debt margin which would remain. This requires: (1) calculating the amount of the debt limit for each year after projecting the base (assessed valuation, adjusted assessed valuation, tax receipts, etc.) and (2) computing the debt outstanding each year under each alternative and subtracting these amounts from the debt limit to arrive at the annual unused debt margin.

The staff must next consider the government's ability to support the debt service requirements over the next five or six years under each of the alternatives. First, three new debt service schedules should be prepared, combining the present schedule[2] *seriatim* with the proposed new debt service requirements under each of three assumptions. In these calculations, proposed new debt service should include the amounts annually scheduled for retirement under the assumptions being made for the new debt plus interest at a rate determined in light of recent sales and prospective market conditions. Too little attention is given to the interest rate factor. Thus, a capital program level that was prudent in the 1966-1967 period of relatively low interest rates may well have become unrealistic during the inflationary and high interest cost years which followed.

---

[2] Municipalities customarily calculate and place in their debt records a complete debt service schedule on each new issue at the time of issuance.

Next, computations should be made to determine whether the debt service requirements under each alternative fall within the city's "ability-to-support" such debt. The computations require projection of the city's operating and capital budget needs, total city revenues, city population, and the overlapping and underlying debt of all the local governments whose debt falls upon the economy of the city involved.

The next calculation is a projection of debt service requirements under each alternative over the entire life of the presently outstanding debt, plus the new debt assumed to be issued in the period under consideration. At this point, the shape of the debt service curve for the future becomes of substantial importance. It should generally be downward, following the peak represented by the final issue of the debt under consideration. Peaks in future years suggest that there are significant difficulties ahead.

Assuming that three basic alternatives have been projected, a choice must then be made among the three. Or, if all prove unsatisfactory, the whole process must be undertaken anew in search of an acceptable alternative. All debt must fall within the limits prescribed by law. In some cases, this refers to the amount of debt actually outstanding; in others, it is actual outstanding debt plus authorizations for debt currently unissued that is chargeable against the debt limit. Annual debt service must be within the government's ability-to-support such debt throughout the life of the debt. Many factors must be weighed fully before a final decision is reached. As the calculations are studied, value judgments must be made in light of: the leeway under legal constraints; the margin of safety required for emergencies; the need for flexibility in future action; the reasonableness of estimates as to growth in economic base, population, revenues, and operating expenditures; the possibility of new revenue sources; the competitive use by overlapping local governments of the same tax base; and the probable degree of stability of the community under adverse economic conditions.

2. Self-supporting Projects: The relative degree of reliance upon self-supporting debt is important. Provided the capital improvement program includes capital projects which can appropriately be financed by the issuance of self-supporting debt, each project must be analyzed separately and a projection made for each to determine whether the debt can be completely retired and serviced from the enterprise's net revenues or from special assessment levies. Special assessment projects require an investigation of the legality and feasibility of the projected benefit district and the ability of the property within the district to support a levy in addition to other levies, general and special, already borne by the property. For projects to be financed by revenue bonds, the requirement for ability-to-support must extend over the entire life of the debt. The prospects for customer growth must be examined along with the possibility of need for additional capital investment subsequent to required expansion. The standard test applied is the margin of coverage for debt service from projected net revenues after operating expenses (including repairs and maintenance) and certain reserves have been deducted from gross revenues. For safety purposes, the more speculative or untried the enterprise, the wider the margin must be. Margins of coverage may run as low as 1.10 or 1.20 for time-tested undertakings, like water and electric services. For projects of greater risk, margins of 3.0 to 4.0 are not uncommon if the market is to accept the debt favorably.

3. Special Local Factors: Taking special local factors into account is also necessary. A separate determination should be made of any additions which can be made to the level of capital outlays, as computed above, because of the existence of certain practices or special legal provisions. Examples which can be cited include:

a. Some local governments regularly allocate annual surpluses from operating funds to capital reserve accounts. Such amounts can be estimated for the future and worked into the long-term operating programs of such governments

b. Policy may require that proceeds from the sale of any property owned by the government go into a capital reserve fund to be made available for new capital projects

c. State or local law may permit the levy of a special millage to develop a capital reserve account

d. State or local law may require that a portion of each capital project be financed from current revenues

Policies of this type, which are essentially elements of a pay-as-you-acquire policy, tend to reduce the level of capital outlays to be financed from tax-supported debt.

In addition to the above calculations of what the community can afford, the finance staff must estimate the amount of outside assistance. Private and endowment fund gifts and contributions from other local governments on a cooperative capital project are occasional sources. State and federal grants constitute, of course, the largest portion of outside aid for capital programs. Since these grants are usually for specific purposes and must be matched on the basis of local funds, the nature of the local policy decision depends in each case upon whether the local government would have built the project without the outside aid. If the facility is to be built in any case, the grants are a substitute for local funds and release them for other capital requirements. If this is not the case, the policy decision is one of priorities—that is, whether to divert funds from other projects or to increase total funding in order to satisfy the matching requirements. If one dollar of local money will attract one dollar of state or federal aid, the project's cost to the local government will be only 50 percent of total construction costs. This may automatically place the project in a high priority position. The problem then becomes one of determining whether the city should match these outside funds, with full recognition of the consequences of this decision.

Into this scale of values, a proper evaluation requires determination not only of debt service costs but also of associated operating and maintenance costs.

Once a local government has achieved confidence in its ability to project its capital program requirements and associated financing arrangements over a five- or six-year period, it is recommended that it experiment with longer periods, e.g., ten or fifteen years. Naturally, the longer into the future that projections are made, the greater the degree of risk of inaccuracies in the assumptions used. Thus, a projection made in 1964 could not have anticipated (even on a six-year program) the tremendous changes in the price levels wrought by inflation and the rapid increase in interest rate levels associated with new debt issues.

The Use of Revenue Bonds

Broadly construed, any debt which is not tax-supported can be considered revenue debt. (See Chapter 15 for a discussion of the classification of debt.) Indeed, some bonds which are, in fact, tax-supported through lease arrangements are normally classified as revenue bonds, e.g., the debt of Pennsylvania local and state school building authorities.

The revenue bond in its present general form was invented around the turn of the century and came into common use about 25 years later. The essential characteristic of a genuine revenue bond is that the credit being pledged is from the net revenues of a revenue-producing facility, or group of facilities.

In many instances (some may argue in most instances), the total cost of borrowing money is greater for revenue bonds than for tax-supported debt, especially for general obligation debt with the full faith and credit of the local government's unlimited taxing power.

The authors of this volume are not in full agreement concerning the wisdom of a course of action which relies to the maximum degree on full faith and credit general obligation bonds. For the benefit of the reader, two views are therefore set forth:

Position No. 1: Maximization of the Use of General Obligation Bonds. The view in support of the maximum use of general obligation bonds and living within legal constraints is as follows:

In order to meet their capital improvement needs, local governments must live under the debt limits which have been prescribed. However, with state legislatures sometimes reticent to increase such limits sufficiently to enable local governments to meet their needs, many local governments have resorted to various versions of the revenue bond. These are sometimes issued by the government itself and sometimes by instrumentalities, e.g., a local authority created for this purpose. Because this approach has become so common, revenue bonds are likely to be accepted by some without careful evaluation. As a result, higher costs frequently result. In evaluating such a decision, the local government should also consider these alternatives:

1. *Adoption of the revolving concept of credit:* By drastically shortening the average life of general obligation debt, i.e., by more rapid retirement, the unused debt margin is made more rapidly available for new borrowings. Volume is dependent upon rapid turnover. Like a revolving fund, the unused debt margin is rapidly used up and also rapidly replenished. For each bond issue, this means less total interest.

2. *A requirement for substantial down payments:* If down-payments are used to reduce the amount of debt required, a gradual increase in the magnitude of such down payments would reduce the size of each bond issue.

3. *Expanded use of special assessments:* By a combination of pay-as-you-go, special assessment levies, and bonded debt, a city could achieve a flow of capital outlays for a long period before a major interruption ensues. A program wherein outlays are consistent with replacement needs and

requirements for new projects would tend to reduce the size of backlogs after cessation of the major interruption. Peak demands for new
debt incurrence are difficult to fit within restrictive debt limits.

4. *Securing noncash credits in redevelopment:* Maximizing the use of noncash contributions under urban renewal projects helps to free dollars
   for other purposes.

5. *Use of excess funds from municipal enterprises:* Use of surpluses from
   profitable self-supporting enterprises will help to reduce debt requirements for general purposes.

6. *Acceleration of revenue collections:* Acceleration of the calendar for
   payment of taxes and other revenues and timing of certain expenditures
   later in the year reduces the requirement for short-term borrowing—
   and, where such borrowing is charged against the debt limit, makes
   available additional general obligation borrowing capacity.

7. *Partial deferment of capital program items:* A "stretching out" of large
   capital projects or rearrangement of the capital program will reduce
   current demands for capital funds. This process will involve a tight-
   ening of the project priority process to assure that the proceeds of
   bond issues are not used for "marginal" projects.

If debt limits in more states were amended to exclude the general obligation
debt of completely self-supporting enterprises in determining available borrowing capacity (or the exclusion of that portion which is partially self-supporting),
the problem of living under restrictive debt limits would be eased, and the necessity for local authorities and similar devices solely to avoid restrictive debt limits
would be decreased. A major step in this direction was taken by the Commonwealth of Pennsylvania in Act 185 of 1972—after several decades of unrealistically
restrictive debt limit policies which were directly responsible for the creation
of hosts of local financing authorities in that state.

*Position No. 2: Diversification in the Use of General Obligation and Revenue
Bonds.* The basic views of those who hold to the proposition that there is a
very useful role for revenue bonds are set forth in the following:

There was a time when students of public debt stated unequivocally that
revenue bonds were always more costly than tax-supported bonds. For some,
this reaction was based upon fact; for some, on emotion; and for some, upon a
failure to understand the situation fully. Moreover, there may be circumstances
in which the use of the cheapest borrowing route available is not necessarily
the best choice!

Let us consider two cities, each with a total outstanding debt of $100,000,000,
distributed in the manner indicated on the following page.

This means that of the $50 million of revenue debt of City "B," $21.5 million is, in fact, supported by the economy outside the city. Assume that both
of these cities are central cities of their metropolitan regions. Further, assume
that in common with most central cities, the strength of the economy is not as
great as that of the remainder of the region.

Distribution of Debt in Two Cities

	City A	City B
1. General obligation debt		
a. General purposes	$ 50,000,000	$ 50,000,000
b. Water utility	20,000,000	—
c. Sewer utility	10,000,000	—
d. Parking	10,000,000	—
e. Airport	10,000,000	—
Total general obligation debt	$100,000,000	$ 50,000,000
2. Revenue debt		
a. Water utility	—	20,000,000
b. Sewer utility	—	10,000,000
c. Parking	—	10,000,000
d. Airport	—	10,000,000
Total revenue debt	—	$ 50,000,000
Grand total	$100,000,000	$100,000,000

Let us further assume that all of the water, sewer, parking, and airport debt is self-supporting, regardless of the security pledged. Also assume that the following portions of the revenue in support of these bonds were derived from nonresidents:

	Percent	Amount
Water	25	$ 5,000,000
Sewer	35	3,500,000
Parking	50	5,000,000
Airport	80	8,000,000
		$21,500,000

In light of these assumptions, the reaction of the effective bond analyst to the two situations may well be:

As to City "A." The overall debt is $100,000,000. All of it is chargeable against the taxing power of the city. All of it is general obligation debt. If the population is 333,000, this means a *per capita* debt of approximately $300. Although a bond analyst may be aware that some of the debt service is supportable by population outside the city, he may give this scant attention in his valuation.

As to City "B." If City "B" has done a proper job in placing the facts before the investment community, everyone is aware of the source of support for the revenue debt. The net debt, therefore, chargeable to the economy of the city becomes $78,500,000 ($100,000,000 less $21,500,000). Accordingly, the effective *per capita* debt is only about $235, assuming a population of 333,000.

Moreover, even if the revenue debt should carry a higher interest rate than the general obligation debt in the case of City "B," the low amount of general obligation debt of that city should entitle it to a better rating than

City "A," because the risks in the case of the general obligation debt are less. Finally, by the use of revenue debt, City "B" is properly assigning to non-residents the cost of the debt related to servicing them.

Under these circumstances, who can say with accuracy that the use of revenue debt is actually a higher cost avenue of funding?

A final consideration is that City "A" by use of its general obligation pledge is actually extending to its richer neighbors the use of its full-faith-and-credit pledge for these enterprise undertakings.

These two views have been set forth to bring into balance the discussion of the use of revenue bonds vs. general obligation bonds. The authors express no overall conclusion. Rather, this material should stimulate a full and careful evaluation of all the facts in the development of a modern debt policy.

Borrowing at the Lowest Interest Costs

To meet the criterion of economic efficiency a city will strive to secure the use of borrowed money at the lowest effective interest cost. The only way in which to assure that the bond issues are being sold at the lowest actual net interest cost is by use of the "present value" method. A variant of this method is widely used in Canadian cities; however, it has been consistently used over a period of years by only two local governmental jurisdictions in the United States—the Department of Water and Power and the Department of Aviation of the City of Los Angeles. The City of Philadelphia adopted this method in 1972 and a few other jurisdictions have now followed.[3]

The actual rates of interest paid are determined by a combination of the general market levels, the security behind a given issue, the pattern of maturity of the debt, and the credit standing of the city. The city can do something about each of these, except the general interest level prevailing in the market. It is part of the finance officer's responsibilities to strive to improve the city's credit rating. He must also determine how much of the city's resources will be pledged in support of each bond issue.

It is possible to improve the city's credit rating by holding the amounts borrowed to very low levels. If, however, this makes it impossible for the city to meet essential capital needs, "means" will have been put ahead of "ends," and the approach would prove, in the long run, to be penny-wise and pound-foolish. The social costs of not meeting capital requirements would then run higher than the actual amount saved by obtaining lower interest rates. Another aspect of securing the best credit rating available lies in a professional presentation of all the pertinent facts to rating agencies and investors.

Some may argue that the finance officer should time his offerings to take advantage of the "best market"; however, it is the authors' view that few persons can predict with sureness when the best markets will occur. Rather than

---

[3] For a fuller discussion of the present value method see Moak, Lennox L., *Administration of Local Government Debt*, (Chicago: Municipal Finance Officers Association, 1970), pp. 267-74; 304-311.

attempt to outguess the market, except to avoid obvious disruptions brought on by national or international events, the best course is to borrow when funds are needed. For most local governments, this will result in securing an average rate consistent with prevailing general market conditions.

Perhaps the following will help to sharpen the divergence of views on the matter of the rapidity with which debt should be retired:

1. *Advantages of Rapid Debt Retirement:*

    a. Interest costs are reduced because:

       (1) For any given level of capital program spending, rapid debt retirement improves the credit rating by reducing the amount of outstanding debt.

       (2) Given the normal characteristics of the bond market, the effective average net interest rate for shorter maturities is less than for longer maturities.

    b. Short life bonds permit more frequent issuance of new debt, and the financing of a larger capital program, where such is desirable.

    c. The discipline imposed by heavier annual debt service payments arising from shorter maturities will act to discourage projects of doubtful value.

    d. Considerations of "intergenerational" users of facilities can be accommodated by charging an annual "use charge" on all municipal facilities and applying the proceeds first to debt service and then to pay-as-you-go financing.[4]

2. *Advantages of Spreading Debt Retirement Over the Life of the Facilities*

    a. There is an automatic adjustment of the annual costs to correspond more closely to the annual cost of the use of facilities.

    b. The higher total interest costs are more than offset by advantages accruing to the taxpayers and citizens arising from a reduction in total payments to the government. In other words, the opportunity afforded the taxpayer by permitting his continued use of funds for a longer period of time, e.g., a return of 8 percent may be greater than the savings to the city, e.g., 5 percent.

    c. The debt limit should be set in terms of annual debt service, rather than the artificiality of only the principal portion of the debt. In such cases, the extended period of amortization would constitute the only feasible means of sustaining a given level of capital improvement activity.

    d. Given the general trend toward deflation of the value of the currency, the reality of costs, in terms of purchasing power for the taxpayers, is substantially less than the apparent costs represented by traditional statements of debt service.

---

[4] One fallacy here appears to be that, in time, all debt would be retired and the accumulation of the annual "use charges" may act to induce higher than necessary levels of capital spending—or, more likely, diversion to higher levels of operational costs.

DEBT POLICY AND IMPLEMENTATION

Of necessity, implementation of debt policy is incremental, bond issue by bond issue, and throughout every phase of the debt management cycle. In policy formulation, therefore, the broad guidelines will extend from the initial planning of an issue's terms to the final payment of the last debt service installment.

Obviously, the largest number of policy decisions are made when the bond issue is authorized because, at this stage, most of the details of the bond contract which will govern over the issue's entire life must be determined. But, policy decisions outside the contract have to be contemplated and covered in principle by the long-term debt policy—for example, the circumstances or conditions under which the following should be used: frequency and size of issues; negotiated sales vs. competitive bidding; use of bond anticipation notes; investment fund (pension, sinking and other) support of the market for a new issue; callable vs. non-callable bonds; registered vs. coupon bonds; and other detailed considerations. Again, while bond proceeds are in hand, the municipal debt policy should require appropriate temporary investment of the funds.

Debt servicing is normally a routine operation governed primarily by the bond contract. But, policy questions arise even here—such as accelerating debt retirement through exercise of the call feature, or using the call feature to convert the balance outstanding into a lower interest-bearing security, or retiring the bonds by purchase on the open market prior to maturity. It is a test of the wisdom of the policy if deviations follow the general planned direction and fall within the range set for planned flexibility as, and when, conditions change.

Flexibility and Debt Policy

Flexibility comprehends an ability to adjust financial actions of the future to pursue the local government's best interests. But, it does not mean complete freedom. To assure a suitable degree of future flexibility planning is required in advance of today's commitments. The policy statement should attempt to anticipate the types of conditions which are likely to arise and the manner in which it is planned that each of these will be handled.

The function of these procedures is not to induce a high degree of inflexibility into debt policy. Rather, the intent is to help assure that those responsible for debt policy will have taken each of the significant factors into account. Among the factors which may inhibit future flexibility are:

1. Persistent heavy reliance upon temporary borrowing, which can impair local markets for shorter term bonds and in some instances, absorb needed borrowing capacity within legally established limits
2. Funding of relatively short-life (five to ten years) equipment and improvements
3. Use of available borrowing capacity for funding of accumulated operating deficits
4. Use of very long life bonds, which are only slowly retired. Thereby, restoration of borrowing capacity through debt retirement is very slow
5. Failure to include call provisions in debt when issued, thereby making more difficult the achievement of savings from refunding in favorable markets and also precluding potential readjustments in maturity schedules

6. Excessive use of serial bond maturities. The maturity requirements on serial bonds can be merciless during periods of adverse economic conditions. The maturity schedule, once established, is rigid. Use of term bonds with sinking fund or with flexible redemption provisions provides much greater potential for movement
7. Excessive earmarking of revenues for debt service. Examination of the debt structure of some local governments reveal high degrees of earmarking of revenues for specific purposes and debt associated with such purposes. Earmarking for operating purposes is difficult to overcome because of legal and political considerations; earmarking for debt purposes imposes a much greater degree of inflexibility because of the long-term contracts expressly or impliedly involved

Some Effects of Debt Policy

A debt policy statement would hardly attempt to spell out the ramifications of the economic, social, and political effects which flow from borrowing. But the policy-makers should work with an understanding of the major effects and their implications or, at least, with enough knowledge to know at what points to seek professional advice.

As regards economic effects, the emphasis will be, of course, upon the local economy. At the project construction stage, the inflow of new capital (and a portion, often substantial, of the bond money will normally have been raised outside the municipality) will generate new income, shared in by laborers, suppliers of materials, contractors, and others. Over the life of the bond issue, the necessity for making interest and debt retirement payments outside the municipality will set up a contra flow. This means that, for sustained growth, the project constructed must, directly or indirectly, increase the economic productivity of the community over the life of the issue. The wisdom of capital project decision-making, is, therefore, of first importance. Capital programming can, by design, stimulate local economic growth; that is, a local government may deliberately build certain projects to attract institutions, or new industrial establishments, or may improve health and education through capital outlays which, in turn, make the area more inviting to new firms and skilled workers, or raise the productivity of firms already there and of individuals now in, or entering, the labor force. On the other hand, failure to build the right projects may, directly or indirectly, retard economic growth.

If borrowing by the local government is for purposes involving matching funds, an addition to the outside capital inflow during the construction period is made. This new money from outside is not entirely a gift. State and federal taxes which fall upon the local economy will, over a period, reflect some of the costs. However, there will usually still be a net gain to the community vis-a-vis not participating in available grant programs. Over the life of the project, at least no direct outflow is required for interest and principal upon the aid share of project costs. Certainly, for some communities, borrowing to match state and federal capital construction money is a profitable venture.

Some economists have placed emphasis upon using local government debt and overall financial policy for countercyclical purposes. Without a massive job of coordination by the federal government, it is difficult to see how this macro-economics approach could be implemented. In economic upswings, the acceleration of borrowing and capital outlays by local governments in the whole country may stimulate economic activity but later exacerbate inflationary pressures. In mild recessions, local borrowing and capital outlays, because of an adjustment time lag, can be countercyclical. But, in a deep downswing with a similar time lag, the great decline of borrowing and the retardation of municipal capital construction make the depression more disastrous. On the other hand, to expect local governments to hold back on construction during recovery and upswing periods when requirements for replacements and new improvements run high and to go against the psychology of serious downswings is asking more than most local political leaders can deliver. Federal, rather than local finance, must make the major effort if public construction is to be a countercyclical tool.

Many economic effects have social consequences. The two are closely interrelated, although economic and social effects are not synonymous. Local economic growth means a rising standard of living for many in the community. Certainly, non-growth capital expenditures should be scrutinized for social costs and social benefits.

Social effects may be looked at from the standpoint of the whole community; spatially, by neighborhoods; or by income or racial groups. Some in the community benefit directly or indirectly from a particular capital project; others do not benefit or benefit to a lesser extent. Some contribute more to debt service than others. Inequities are a difficult social effect to analyze. Social benefits and social costs are not yet measurable with precision. It is useful also to remember that, because of population mobility, social consequences cross political boundaries. For example, the impact of poor educational facilities in one community will probably be felt in others.

Some political effects of debt policy stand out clearly. One is easily documented from history. Municipal borrowing supported almost exclusively by the property tax was the main cause of debt limits—whether placed in the state constitution, statutes, or charters. In turn, debt limits have given rise to a vertical fragmentation of local government, with one taxing district piled upon another. The process is still going on, but with one variation; namely, local authorities have been added to new overlying taxing districts. Revenue bonds of the former, like taxes, must be serviced from the local income stream.

Municipal debt policies have also shaped state-local relations—as evidenced by the establishment of state boards or commissions to supervise local borrowing and by legislative efforts to control municipal debt automatically by statutory provisions.

Debt policies have also been a principal cause in many communities for organization of the fiscally conservative and for their pressure tactics.

One might also mention a probable, but yet unrealized, political consequence. Abuse of the tax-exempt feature through the issuance of industrial aid bonds, together with an overemphasis upon the revenue bond, may yet bear bitter fruit. Potential loss of the tax status of municipal bonds by court action has, in terms of the political impact upon an already weakened state sovereignty, not been clearly weighed. Actions by Congress and the United States Treasury Department have also had significant impact on the use of industrial aid bonds. More recently, Treasury regulations have made deep inroads upon the freedom of local governments in the investment of proceeds of bond issues and tax anticipation notes, under the view that arbitrage on such proceeds should be avoided.

Timing of Policy Information

A successful shift to a planned debt policy may well be a difficult and painful process. Normally, a shift must arise out of a felt need, a crisis, or a danger point in debt management when a changed direction is drastically needed and recognized by both top management and the local council. One can visualize such a crisis or danger point: a mark-down in credit rating; two or more unsuccessful bond referenda; a banker-group's refusal to extend large temporary loans; a succession of peak years in debt service requirements with outcries from property taxpayers over steep increases in rates, or a temporary bond default.

The proposal for a planned debt policy might well be embodied in a staff, or consultant's, report on the impending or actual crisis, which traces the recent history of debt management, the serious situation, the immediate remedies necessary, and, finally, the need for a shift to a planned debt policy to avoid a repetition of trouble. Ideally, approval of these recommendations by the governing body should quickly be followed by presentation from the chief finance officer of such a long-term policy in draft form while the air of crisis still pervades. To have a well-considered proposal ready, the chief finance officer might well have devoted considerable time and effort in preparation of such a policy long before the crisis, but with the report held in abeyance until the time when it would be acceptable and its adoption could be dramatized. A propitious time must be seized like a tide in flood, or else the policy never gets launched, or loses the initial crisis-generated impetus.

CONCLUSION

This chapter has dealt with the fundamentals of debt policy. To the authors, the implications of these fundamentals for long-term policy planning appear strong. The reader may disagree. A local government can continue to make bond-contract decisions without a long-term debt policy, explicit or even consciously implicit. The core of any disagreement is whether a rational, workable debt program is more apt to result from a planned, or an *ad hoc*, approach to debt policy.

A planned debt policy will be inclusive of all types of bonds and borrowing instruments, whether tax-supported or self-supporting; all parts of the local government; and of the whole cycle of debt management, down to and including the work of the final project inspection team. However, a debt policy should be no more complex than it has to be. Complexity may add to inflexibility.

A planned debt policy does not, itself, mean rigidity or lack of change. Flexibility in future actions should be provided for; that is, the statement of policy should recognize types of conditions under which deviations will be justified and expected. A long-term plan, in any case, constitutes only broad, directional guidelines. The plan cannot bind future administrations and legislative bodies; it can only attempt to establish reasoned bases for future action by expounding the "why" of the guidelines recommended.

The debt policy statement should emphasize the types of commitments which, over a period of time, can destroy flexibility in debt management. It should also include references to the legal and market constraints which enter into policy formulation.

In recent years local governments have used both the revenue bond and the authority as means to avoid restrictive debt limits. Determination of the level of capital outlays which the local government can afford to finance out of borrowing is one of the most important debt policy decisions.

A planned debt policy can contribute to a more orderly shift in levels of tax rates and eliminate much of the lumpiness in capital expenditures, but it cannot, over a long period, stabilize tax rates, nor can it provide an even flow of capital outlays. Business cycles, spurts in local expansion, wars, inflation, and other forces place limitations upon its stabilizing effects.

A planned debt policy is not a panacea. It cannot wipe out all the mistakes of the past, but it can set in motion a directional change which will ameliorate their effects.

15
The Instruments of Borrowing

Once relatively simple and limited in variety, the instruments of local government borrowing are becoming increasingly varied and complex. Four influences are primarily responsible for this trend: the growing diversity in the purposes for which local governments borrow; the expanding classes of borrowers; the invention of borrowing media to circumvent constitutional borrowing restrictions; and the use of varying debt forms in some areas to lessen a popular aversion to borrowing. The identifying terminology employed has not kept pace with this multiplication of borrowing instruments and is not as precise as it might be; but, for practical purposes, reasonably satisfactory classification and definition are possible. The various debt obligations may be classified in three general ways—already indicated, to some extent, in the discussion of the purposes of borrowing: (1) according to the length of term, (2) according to the method of retirement, and (3) according to the nature of the security pledged and the revenues earmarked for payment of the debt.

DEBT CLASSIFIED ACCORDING TO LENGTH OF TERM

Debt obligations may be divided into two broad classifications as to length of term, designated as (1) temporary debt, unfunded debt, short-term debt, or floating debt; and (2) funded debt, bonded debt, or long-term debt.

Temporary Debt

This classification includes borrowing to finance current operations or to finance capital facilities, usually with the intent of subsequently issuing long-term debt. The former may be in anticipation of the collection of budgeted revenues or for emergency purposes not covered in the budget. The instruments of such borrowing have a terminology that varies in different localities; the more general titles are bank loans, tax anticipation notes, revenue anticipation notes, warrants, registered warrants, and deficiency notes. Sometimes, there are special designations for borrowing in anticipation of the collection of revenues of past years, such as delinquent tax notes or tax lien certificates. These formal instruments do not represent all forms of temporary operating debt, which also include accounts payable, claims, and bank overdrafts.

Most of these formal borrowing instruments carry definite maturity dates but this is not true of registered warrants, which may be defined as follows:

Warrant. An order drawn by the legislative body or an officer of a governmental unit upon its treasurer directing the latter to pay a specified amount to the person named or to the bearer.[1]

If a warrant is payable on demand, its use is quite similar to a bank check. If, however, it is payable only from revenue expected to be available at some later time, it is a form of short-term borrowing. Such warrants are registered when issued, or by the paying officer, and are payable in the order of their registration when funds become available. The customary practice is to make them interest-bearing from the date of registration. When not interest-bearing, they are usually traded on a discount basis. In some states, registered warrants are the only available type of formalized, short-term borrowing in anticipation of the collection of revenue.

Another form of temporary borrowing for operating purposes, only infrequently used in recent years but of some historical interest, is the use of scrip. This is an emergency type loan, involuntary in character, that was resorted to rather extensively by local governments in the depression of the 1930s when property tax deliquency was high and bank loans were unavailable. It was used particularly to pay employees in order to conserve limited cash and to provide some form of paper which was usable where money was in short supply. Various kinds of scrip were used, some of them unsatisfactorily. The most successful type was issued against delinquent taxes. It was issued in various denominations to make it potentially a circulating medium, was redeemable when such taxes were paid, and was accepted by the issuer in payment of taxes and utility services. Detroit, for example, issued scrip, bearing interest at four percent, and had no difficulty in redeeming it; while Milwaukee, for several years, paid its employees partly in non-interest bearing scrip that circulated without a discount because of its acceptance at face value by local merchants.

Temporary borrowing for capital financing purposes takes the form of bond anticipation notes, capital notes, and special assessment notes. Their forms and uses have been described in the preceding chapters on debt.

Long-term Debt

Funded, or long-term, debt is usually designated bonded debt, although other terms are occasionally used, such as certificates of indebtedness, time warrants, debentures, and, in the instance of New York City's sinking fund bonds, corporate stock. A bond may be defined as

A written promise to pay a specified sum of money, called the face value or principal amount, at a specified date or dates in the future, called the maturity date(s), together with periodic interest at a specified rate.

---

[1] This and all subsequent definitions cited in this chapter are taken from The National Committee on Governmental Accounting. *Governmental Accounting, Auditing, and Financial Reporting* (Chicago, Municipal Finance Officers Association, 1968), pp. 151-172.

Interest customarily is payable semiannually from the date of issue, which is the official date on the bond from which the interest begins to accrue and not necessarily the date on which the bonds were sold. In addition to these formal instruments of long-term borrowing, some local governments incur long-term debt in the form of leases and installment contracts.

DEBT CLASSIFIED ACCORDING TO METHOD OF RETIREMENT

Bonds may be classified with respect to the plans for their maturity as term bonds or serial bonds. The distinguishing feature is that an issue of term bonds matures on one date, while an issue of serial bonds matures in periodic—usually annual—installments. These two basic types of bonds are subject to numerous variations in the plans and methods for their retirement.

One variation applicable to both types is whether an issue is callable or noncallable. A callable bond is

A type of bond which permits the issuer to pay the obligation before the stated maturity date by giving notice of redemption in a manner specified in the bond contract. Synonym: *Optional Bond.*

An issue may be callable in part or in its entirety, and redemption may be at par or at some specified premium. A noncallable bond is one that is not subject to redemption prior to the date of its maturity.

Both types of bonds may be in the form of coupon bonds or registered bonds. Coupon bonds have coupons attached, one for each interest payment indicating the amount and date of payment. They carry no designation of ownership and the interest and principal are payable, respectively, to the person presenting the coupons or bonds. A registered bond may be defined as:

A bond whose owner is registered with the issuing governmental unit and which cannot be sold or exchanged without a change in registration. Such a bond may be registered as to principal and interest or as to principal only.

The interest and principal for registered bonds are paid by check to the registered owner and title can be transferred only by endorsement. For many decades, coupon bonds were usually issued in denominations of $1,000; however, in recent years, denominations of $5,000, or greater, have become more popular. Registered bonds are issued in denominations to suit the investor and may range to large amounts. Coupon bonds often have the privilege of registration, only as to principal or as to principal and interest. If they are registered as to interest as well as principal, the coupons are detached and interest is paid by check to the registered owner. Alternatively several coupon bonds may be surrendered in exchange for one registered bond. Coupon bonds have the advantage of being more marketable and more readily usable as collateral, while registered bonds are given protection against loss and theft.

1312 Local Government Finance

Serial Bonds

Serial bonds mature in regular installments—usually annually—which are fixed at the time of issue of the bonds. The law may require equal annual principal installments, ordinarily referred to as *straight* serial bonds. Or it may permit equal annual debt service serial bonds. In that case, maturities and interest are arranged in a manner that the total of interest and principal payments in one year is approximately equal to that in each of the other years. This arrangement is sometimes referred to as *annuity* serials. Other patterns of maturity are also used.

The serial bonds have become very popular during the past 40 years particularly as they avoid the necessity for sinking fund management, with the possibilities of mismanagement due to incompetence, venality, or both. Also, the average interest costs on serial bonds *at the time of sale* is calculated to be less than on term bonds with sinking funds. (However, this can be an illusion if sinking fund earnings rates exceed rates payable on the bonds sold.)

Table 29 compares a straight serial issue and serial annuity issue, both in the amount of $1,000,000, both carrying an interest rate of three percent, and both maturing annually in one to ten years. For the former, the annual debt service requirement ranges downward from $130,000 to 103,000; for the latter, it holds at approximately $117,000. The fact that the total interest paid for the former is appreciably lower than that for the latter merely indicates that the money actually is being borrowed for a shorter period. The average life of the straight serial issue illustrated is 5.5 years; that of the serial annuity issue is 5.745 years.

It is to be noted that the total interest payable on the serial annuity bonds exceeds that payable on the straight serial bonds by $7,350. Nominally, therefore, the serial annuity bonds are about 4.45 percent more expensive than the straight serial bonds. However, it is also to be noted that the amounts to be paid in the early years under the serial annuity bonds is considerably less than the amount payable under the straight serial bonds.

In these circumstances, it is appropriate to point out that the present worth of principal, and the principal payments at a 3 percent rate, are identical—$1,000,000 in both cases. Most persons take into account only the gross amount of the money being paid; they fail to take into account the *time* at which it is paid. The value of money is a function of three factors: (1) the period during which the principal is available for use; (2) the interest rate; and (3) the times at which the payment of principal and payments of interest occur.[2]

The possibilities for variation in installment payment patterns are virtually unlimited. Schedules for the payment of principal can be arranged to produce rising annual debt service, gradually to abruptly declining annual debt service, and fluctuating annual debt service. Examples of all of these variations can be found, usually designed for some special purpose. The fluctuating and nondescript types are classed together as irregular serial bonds. They include the

[2] See Moak, Lennox L., *Administration of Local Government Debt* (Chicago: Municipal Finance Officers Association, 1970) pp. 297-312.

Table 29

A COMPARISON OF DEBT SERVICE ON STRAIGHT SERIAL AND SERIAL ANNUITY BONDS[1]

	Straight Serial Bonds			Serial Annuity Bonds		
Year	Principal	Interest	Total	Principal	Interest	Total
1	$100,000	$30,000	$130,000	$87,000	$30,000	$117,000
2	100,000	27,000	127,000	90,000	27,390	117,390
3	100,000	24,000	124,000	93,000	24,690	117,690
4	100,000	21,000	121,000	95,000	21,900	116,900
5	100,000	18,000	118,000	98,000	19,050	117,050
6	100,000	15,000	115,000	101,000	16,110	117,110
7	100,000	12,000	112,000	104,000	13,080	117,080
8	100,000	9,000	109,000	107,000	9,960	116,960
9	100,000	6,000	106,000	111,000	6,750	117,750
10	100,000	3,000	103,000	114,000	3,420	117,420
Total	$1,000,000	$165,000	$1,165,000	$1,000,000	$172,350	$1,172,350

[1] Bonds are $1,000,000, 10-year issues, at 3 percent

peculiar type that has an abnormally large final maturity, commonly called a balloon maturity; this type may be a combination of serial bonds and a term issue for which retirement plans have been made; or, it may merely represent the postponement of making adequate provision for retiring the bonds. Bonds having their first installment of principal deferred for several years are termed deferred serial bonds. Their function is to delay the beginning of full-scale debt payments. Such delay, as a general rule, is regarded as poor debt policy and management, and numerous general bond laws forbid deferment of more than a year or two. Situations do arise, however, in which deferment is an aid to good financial planning.

Term Bonds

In a term bond issue, all bonds mature on a single date; they are usually retired through sinking funds, although the method in which sinking funds are required to operate varies. A sinking fund, or debt service fund, may be defined as:

A fund established to finance and account for the payment of interest and principal on all (or a portion of) debt, serial and term, other than that payable exclusively from special assessments and revenue debt issued for and serviced by a governmental enterprise. When applied solely to a term bond issue, a sinking fund is understood to be a fund in which money is regularly deposited at a rate, which taken together with interest earnings thereupon will be sufficient to "sink," i.e., pay off, the debt at maturity.

In recent years, the more customary method of providing for the retirement of term bonds, particularly limited liability bonds issued to finance revenue-producing undertakings, is to apply money paid into the sinking fund directly to redemption of the bonds by call or purchase. This obviates the need for the long-term investment of sinking funds. To effectuate this method of term bond retirement, the standard procedure is to make a specified portion of the bonds of an issue callable each year for sinking fund purposes. The technique for this method of sinking fund operation varies somewhat, but may be illustrated by the following example:

> The bulk of the funded debt of the Port of New York Authority consists of term bonds; but, for each issue, there is a schedule of mandatory periodic retirement. For example, the $30,000,000 Consolidated Bonds, Fourth Series, were dated April 1, 1955, and are due April 1, 1985, but portions are to be retired prior to maturity, by purchase or call, by the dates and in at least the principal amounts shown in the following schedule[3]:

Relative Advantages of Serial and Term Bonds

Serial bonds are now used almost universally by general purpose governments and tax-supported, special purpose local governments. Sinking fund bonds, once in common use, have been ruled out by law or practice except in a very few places (notably New York City which is still authorized to issue sinking fund bonds for water supply, rapid transit, and dock purposes). The virtual discontinuance of the use of sinking fund bonds by local governments has been a constructive step in debt management for most local governments. It is not unusual for local governments to neglect the levy of taxes for sinking fund purposes and many of them lacked skill in managing sinking fund invest-

---

[3] The minimum retirement requirement disclosed in this schedule is $1,000,000 annually in 1965-1974, $1,500,000 annually in 1974-77, and gradually increasing annual amounts thereafter reaching $2,000,000 in the last three years. Some degree of flexibility is provided. The Port Authority could accelerate retirement by purchase in periods when bond prices declined, and, to the extent that it had retired bonds in excess of the minimum schedule, it could retard retirement in emergencies or in periods of high bond prices. When necessary to meet the mandatory retirement schedule, the bonds were subject to redemption on 30 days' notice on each October 1 beginning in 1965 at par, plus accrued interest to the date fixed for redemption. Otherwise, they were callable, in whole or in part, on any interest payment date on or after April 1, 1959, at a declining scale of prices ranging downward from 103 percent of par value initially to 100 percent on April 1, 1968 and thereafter.

By October 1	Par Value	By October 1	Par Value	By October 1	Par Value
1965	$1,000,000	1972	$ 8,000,000	1979	$18,300,000
1966	2,000,000	1973	9,000,000	1980	20,100,000
1967	3,000,000	1974	10,500,000	1981	22,000,000
1968	4,000,000	1975	12,000,000	1982	24,000,000
1969	5,000,000	1976	13,500,000	1983	26,000,000
1970	6,000,000	1977	15,000,000	1984	28,000,000
1971	7,000,000	1978	16,600,000	1985	30,000,000

ments. Also, sinking fund bonds may not provide as much flexibility in debt planning as do serials; however, there is still much to be said in favor of the term bond with sinking fund, when properly planned and administered.

Serial bonds, because of the range in their possible maturity patterns, are a useful, flexible instrument for long-term financial planning and have a marked financial advantage for the borrower. The annual maturities of each issue broaden the potential market by serving the requirements of a variety of investors and can be planned, to some extent, to take advantage of the differentials normally prevailing in the yield curve between short-term and long-term interest rates. Serial bonds do have a particularly demanding kind of rigidity, however, because maturities must be met regularly every year to avoid default. On the other hand, a temporary lag in sinking fund accumulation can be remedied without serious injury to a local government's credit.[4]

The use of term bonds with stated, single maturity dates that actually are retired in installments, by purchase or call as sinking funds accrue, has become quite common in the financing of revenue-producing enterprises by obligations payable only from the earnings of the projects. This device, because it avoids some of the rigidities of both sinking fund and serial bonds, has proved particularly useful in financing new undertakings whose prospective earnings are largely, or entirely, a matter of estimate and are likely to follow varying growth patterns. The usual procedure in planning such a bond issue is to: (1) set a stated maturity that allows some leeway for revenue to fall short of estimates, (2) devise a schedule of annual payments into a sinking fund that is geared to estimated earnings and adds up to the total amount of principal by the date of maturity, and (3) provide for the prompt application of sinking funds, as they become available, to the retirement of bonds. Customarily, there are provisions for the development of reserve funds and the acceleration of bond retirement as revenues permit. This type of term bond has some resemblance to serial bonds in its provision for periodic retirement, but avoids some of the rigidity of fixed annual maturities. In some instances, the bond contract defines failure to meet the annual sinking fund requirement as an event of default; but, more commonly, it provides that such failure does not constitute default if there has been full compliance with recommendations of the consulting engineers respecting rates and charges. The obvious advantage to the borrower of such flexibility is some-

---

[4] The possible effect of this rigidity was emphasized in the acute period of the 1930s depression when many local governments were forced, by sharply rising tax delinquency and scarcity of bank credit, to default temporarily on serial bond principal. Cook County, Illinois, and some of its overlapping local governments, plagued by property tax troubles that antedated the depression, experimented with a term bond alternative to serial bonds. While use of this procedure has been discontinued, the bulk of Cook County's long-term borrowing was term in form for a number of years. Of each term issue, an equal amount became callable each year on a specified interest payment date or on any interest payment date thereafter. A tax was required to be levied each year, sufficient to pay the interest and that portion of the principal that became callable in that year. The county treasurer was required to call bonds for redemption as funds became available from such tax levies and to call all of each installment before calling any part of any subsequent installment. This arrangement had a safeguarding flexibility in that the call of bonds could be retarded if tax collections were delayed and could then be accelerated correspondingly as collections improved.

what offset by the loss of the financial advantages, noted earlier, that are possessed by serial bonds.

Where term bonds are issued dependent upon development of a sinking fund for their retirement, it is frequently feasible to invest the assets of the sinking fund in taxable securities of equal, or better, quality which have a higher yield than the tax-free bonds being issued. In this way the effective interest cost to the issuer is reduced.

DEBT CLASSIFIED ACCORDING TO PURPOSE

Two important special classes of bonds, as related to purpose, are funding bonds and refunding bonds.

Funding Bonds. Bonds issued to retire outstanding floating debt and to eliminate deficits.

The items funded may be judgments or accumulations of bank loans, tax notes, accounts payable, etc. that are too unwieldy to be provided for in the budgets of immediate years. The term is improperly used to describe improvement bonds that fund bond anticipation notes.

Refunding Bonds. Bonds issued to retire bonds already outstanding. The refunding bonds may be sold for cash and outstanding bonds redeemed for cash, or the refunding bonds may be exchanged with holders of outstanding bonds.

Refunding bonds have two general uses, to continue and extend the life of maturing bonds for the payment of which no provision has been made and to take the place of callable bonds that have been called for redemption in order to achieve a reduced interest cost during the remaining life of the issue.

DEBT CLASSIFIED ACCORDING TO THE
SECURITY PLEDGED FOR REPAYMENT

As to their legal security bonds are of two general classes—general obligation bonds and special, or limited obligation bonds. Within these two broad classes, there are many types and subtypes of debt obligations. The development of so wide a variety of types becomes less bewildering when it is appreciated that many of them are merely devices for the evasion of state constitutional restrictions on local government borrowing. The following will clarify the distinctions as to the nature of the security and the sources of revenue for repayment for local government debt:

In the minds of the investor, the investment dealer, public officials, and others concerned with public debt, a full-faith-and-credit pledge represents not only the best and broadest pledge that the issuing government can make but it also continues to connote that the issuing government has pledged the full use of its taxing and other general revenue-producing power to making available the funds necessary to pay the interest and principal of the debt and to abide by any terms of law or of contract which have a bearing upon the security of the debt.

In the past, it has generally been assumed to mean that, in the case of local governments, the security is backed by authority to levy unlimited ad valorem taxes. More recently, the term has been applied to some debt that has not been secured by the power of unlimited ad valorem property taxation in support of portions of the full-faith-and-credit debt; other tax sources have been supplied as substitutes.[5]

Using the Bureau of the Census classification of nonguaranteed debt as representing all of the debt of local government that is not full-faith-and-credit obligation, it is appropriate now to consider the various subclasses within this category.

Revenue debt secured solely by net earned revenues

Revenue debt secured by net earned revenues plus a mortgage on the revenue-producing properties and/or mortgages on other property, e.g., municipal parking garages which have parking meter revenue as well as direct revenues on a pledge of municipal parking lots

Debt that is revenue in form but which is secured by a limited general property tax, by proceeds of a tax other than a general property tax, by excise taxes, or by legislative appropriations

Debt that is revenue in form but which in fact is secured by lease arrangements where the leasehold is payable from tax funds, e.g., Pennsylvania school authority debt

Special assessment debt

Industrial-aid debt secured by lease-rentals of lessee[6]

General Obligation Debt

General obligation debt still comprises the bulk (56 percent in 1970-71) of the long-term debt of local governments although it has been losing position to other types. It is used for all of the purposes for which local governments issue bonds. For the payment of such bonds, local governments pledge their full faith and credit and financial resources. Traditionally, general obligation debt has been payable, in the first instance, from the property tax; but, in practice, it is sometimes paid from other sources of revenue.

Because of the traditional reliance of local governments on *ad valorem* property taxes, the investment community has placed great emphasis on the property tax as security for the debt issued by such governments. Despite the gradual movement of many of the more progressive local governments to other forms of local taxation and despite the high degree of reliance by school districts and some other districts on various forms of aid from the state and federal gov-

---

[5] Moak, Lennox L., *op. cit.*, p. 51.

[6] *Ibid.*, p. 60.

ernment, one still finds that investors and rating agencies are prone to look almost exclusively to the right to levy an unlimited property tax as a condition for classification of a local debt as being *general obligation* in character.[7]

The emphasis here is also upon the right to levy an *unlimited* property tax. In the absence of such a right for unlimited levy in support of the debt, most persons in the investment community will withhold the classification of *general obligation*.

The term "general obligation" is frequently found in the bond resolutions of special purpose bonds or special purpose agencies; however, the use of the term in this connection should not be confused with the widely accepted meaning of *general obligation debt*. The use of the term "general obligation," in these special situations indicates that the issuer is pledging its full financial powers in support of the debt; however, a closer analysis of the facts will reveal that, in most such circumstances, the pledge is either not backed by taxing power or by very limited taxing power.

Self-supporting Debt. In many communities, various kinds of local government debt is, in fact, general obligation debt; however, for various purposes—primarily to determine the used borrowing capacity of the issuer debt that is fully (or sometimes partially) self-supporting is deducted from the gross debt in arriving at the amounts of debt chargeable against the debt limit. The fact that the debt may be serviced, on a *de facto* basis, from the net revenues of local utilities or other revenue-generating facilities does not, within itself, alter the nature of the pledge being offered to the investor. In other words, if the facility revenues prove insufficient, there is still an obligation on the issuer to meet the debt service from taxes and other general revenues.

Multiple Security Debt. Local governments sometimes find it necessary, or desirable, to undertake enterprises that, by their nature, can be only marginally self-supporting or require an initial investment for facilities to serve long-range needs that cannot be made immediately self-supporting. The dual-security type of bond may serve such purposes well. As a rather general practice, obligations secured by the full faith and credit of municipalities that are issued to finance self-supporting undertakings, but carry no specific pledge of the earnings of the undertakings, are, nevertheless, paid from such earnings. Water systems provide the most common illustration. The use of available water revenues for debt service may be a matter of local policy; but, in some states, it is a statutory requirement and, in numerous instances, it is required by local charter.

In a number of situations, debt is secured, first, by the revenues or the property of a utility or other revenue-producing facility and, secondly, by the general obligation pledge of a local government with full taxing powers. This kind of double security, in effect, differentiates this type of debt from other

---

[7] Many decades ago, this was also true in classifying the debt of state governments; however, with the withdrawal of the states from the general property tax field, investors have gradually accommodated themselves to the fact that general obligation debt at the state level does not have to be secured by a property tax. Perhaps, in due course, they will take account of the more generalized revenues of many local governments.

revenue debt for which the sole security is the net revenues and/or property pledged in support of the revenue debt. The double security also guarantees to the holder that, if the revenues of the facility are sufficient to service the debt, the holder will be paid promptly—even though tax-supported, general obligation debt of the issuer may be in trouble due to the availability of tax proceeds to service such debt. Occasionally, one finds a combination of elements of support for the debt, e.g., some combination of net revenues and state and/or federal grants or guarantees, coupled with the local general obligation support.

In this type of debt, one approaches the self-supported, general obligation debt which has been previously described.

Limited Tax Debt

Limited tax debt is ordinarily understood to be local government debt which is supported by a limited property tax. The limit is normally in terms of the tax rate which may be levied in support of such debt. It is more likely to be found in special districts than in general purpose governments.

The intent of this policy is to limit the amount of debt that may be incurred, rather than to restrict the power of local governments to pay for it after it has been incurred. Just how detrimental to a local government's credit a property tax limitation may be depends on a number of factors, such as the severity of the limit, the amount of other revenue resources available, the ability of the local fiscal officers, and the community's economic outlook. The only satisfactory method of measurement is price comparison of the unlimited and limited tax bonds of the same government.

Special Tax Debt

Special tax bonds are limited obligation bonds payable solely from specified nonproperty tax revenues. In many states, elements of local government debt are secured by portions of the state motor fuel tax allocated to local governments. In some states, this debt may be backed by sales taxes, gross receipts taxes, or other special taxes. This type of debt obligation is one of the devices developed to evade constitutional borrowing restrictions; but, the courts in only a small minority of the states have held that it does not constitute debt in a constitutional sense and, generally speaking, it has not been used extensively by local governments.

The use of special tax bonds instead of full faith and credit bonds to finance general improvements tends to be more expensive in interest cost; to handicap sound budgeting because of the earmarking of important revenues; and to freeze, over long periods, revenue sources that should be amenable to change when desirable.

Revenue Debt

Revenue bonds have been issued by municipalities to finance the acquisition or improvement of virtually every type of project, large or small, that can be made to pay its way from user charges. The objects of such borrowing have ranged from water systems to swimming pools and skating rinks, from all kinds of major transportation and terminal facilities to parking lots and small boat basins, and from such other basic utilities as sewage disposal, electric and gas systems to minor enterprises such as markets, auditoriums, and athletic fields. A relatively new, and debatable, use of municipal revenue bonds in several states (commented on previously in the discussion of the purposes of borrowing) is that of financing the construction of industrial plants for lease to private industry.

There is no uniformity of practice, however, in the capital financing of revenue-producing undertakings. Many local governments that operate self-liquidating enterprises make no use of revenue bonds, while others have issued such bonds for several different purposes.

There is no generally accepted definition of the term *revenue debt*. To some in the investment community, it means any kind of debt supported solely by property taxes. In a narrower sense, as used here, revenue debt is understood to be debt that is supported by one or both of the following:

1. The net revenues of a governmentally owned local utility or other revenue-generating facility, e.g., water, sewer, gas, electric, or telephone utility or other revenue-producing facilities such as parking garages, airports, toll bridges, and amusement undertakings. Net revenues are understood to mean the revenues remaining after the operating and maintenance charges have been met from the gross revenue.
2. The property used in any of these undertakings.

When the term is used in the *Bond Buyer* or by the Securities Industry Association it likely will include many other kinds (and sometimes all other kinds) of local government debt beyond general obligation debt.

Some local governments issue revenue bonds secured by the combined revenues of two or more enterprises administered by a single department, such as the combined water and sewer revenue bonds of a number of local governments. A variation of the policy is to strengthen the security of bonds issued for a new enterprise of possibly marginal earning power with a supplementary pledge of the surplus earnings of an established enterprise.

When a local government elects to finance the capital requirements of an enterprise by means of bonds whose security is dependent solely upon the earnings of the enterprise, it commits itself to managing the enterprise, setting its fiscal policies, and segregating its financial operations and accounting in a manner that is satisfactory to the bondholders. This needs to be done, however, without unduly complicating the local government's administration and without diffusion of administrative responsibility.

In past years, the term *revenue bond* specifically meant an obligation issued to finance a revenue-producing enterprise and both principal and interest were payable exclusively from the revenues of that enterprise; although, in some areas, loans in anticipation of revenue also were called revenue bonds. More recently, the term has also been applied to various other kinds of debt obligations that have been invented to circumvent constitutional restrictions on borrowing, including bonds payable only from the proceeds of some nonproperty tax or payable indirectly from property taxes or other government revenue through a rental device.

The nature of revenue bonds is considerably clarified by an understanding of the circumstances under which they originated and developed. In the second half of the nineteenth century many of the states, starting with Iowa in 1857, adopted constitutional limitations on the incurrence of debt by local governments. Almost immediately, efforts were initiated in those states where the limitation was severe and inflexible to devise means of circumventing the limitations that the courts would sustain. Since the 1870s, the courts have been faced with endlessly proliferating questions respecting the validity of evasive borrowing devices. Certain devices gained quick approval in some courts and have come into general acceptance, though with varying qualifications. The status of others differs among the states.

The Special District

Use of the special district device accounts, in part, for the very rapid increase, in recent years, in the number of such districts in the United States. Most legislatures may create special districts under constitutional provisions authorizing them to establish municipal corporations, public corporations, and the like. Such districts may have legally unlimited borrowing power or they may have debt limits of their own; in any event, their creation can make constitutional debt limits quite meaningless. The courts have tended to rule that, even when a special district is coextensive with a municipality and has virtually the same government, its debt is not chargeable against the municipality's constitutional borrowing power.

Special Fund Doctrine

Very early in the search for ways of circumventing constitutional debt limits, the question arose as to whether bonds (or other evidences of indebtedness) payable only from, and secured only by, a special fund rather than by the full faith and credit of a local government constituted debt in a constitutional sense. This reasoning, which came to be known as the special fund doctrine, soon was applied to bonds made payable only from special assessments. Municipal revenue bond laws came slowly in most states and the courts in some jurisdictions tended not to be amenable to the revenue bond idea. By the early 1930s, about a third of the states had statutes or constitutional amendments, many of them limited in scope, authorizing municipalities to issue revenue bonds for one or more types of enterprises, and a scattering of municipalities in most of these states had issued such bonds, mainly for water systems but including a few electric systems and, in the instance of Louisville, Kentucky, a toll bridge.

Authority revenue bonds had almost as early an origin. In 1899, a special act of the Maine legislature created the Kennebec Water District, with no power to levy taxes. But, the real impetus to authority revenue bonds was the establishment of the Port of New York Authority in 1921 and its sale of bridge revenue bonds five years later. The operations of this famous bi-state agency directed attention to the possibilities for broadening the uses of revenue bonds through the creation of special districts without the power to tax but with the right to own and operate revenue-producing enterprises and to finance them with revenue bonds.

The severe economic depression of the 1930s and the federal government were instrumental in bringing about, in a very few years, an extraordinary expansion in the utilization and purposes of revenue bonds. The contributing factors were a nationwide shrinkage in assessed valuations of taxable property which curtailed, or wiped out, the general borrowing margins of local governments; a heightened resistance of taxpayers to incurrence of new debt which might add to the tax burden; and the strong desire of the federal government to stimulate the construction of public works, especially of the self-liquidating type, through grants and loans. Financing by revenue bonds seemed to offer a means of action, but it immediately became evident that adequate and appropriate legal authority for the broad use of revenue bonds was lacking in the great majority of states. Soon, with the prospect of matching federal grants, there was wholesale enactment of revenue bond laws, leaving only a few states without at least some sort of authorizing statute. In this period, the federal government, through the Reconstruction Finance Corporation and Public Works Administration, made well over a thousand loans to state and local units of government in some 39 states for a wide variety of projects on the security of revenue bonds. Likewise, federal influence and federal aid soon became responsible for the creation of local housing authorities and for the choice of revenue bonds as the chief medium for financing the construction of local housing.

This effort by the federal government to get quick cooperation from the state and local governments in counterdeflationary action had the incidental effect of opening a veritable Pandora's box of borrowing instruments. The interest of investment bankers and investors was stimulated, creating a broad private market for new revenue bond issues as well as for those held by federal agencies. Numerous municipalities switched from full faith and credit bonds to revenue bonds to finance their well established self-liquidating enterprises because the latter could be issued without encumbering their limited general borrowing powers, or without a referendum, or with only a simple majority instead of a larger majority popular vote.

The accelerating trend toward the use of revenue obligations is indicated by the fact that of the $99.3 billion of long-term debt outstanding in 1970-71, as reported by the Bureau of the Census, $36.8 billion, or 38 percent, was classified as nonguaranteed debt—obligations for which local governments have not pledged their full faith and credit. In 1944, the first year in which the Census Bureau used this classification in its reporting, nonguaranteed obligations comprised only 13 percent of the outstanding long-term debt. Nonguaranteed debt was 21 percent of long-term debt in 1952 and has exceeded 30 percent of the long-term debt of local governments since the early 1960s.

Underlying much of the expansion of revenue bond financing and its state-to-state variations has been the application of the special fund doctrine by the courts. There were constitutional restrictions on local government borrowing to be dealt with in well over half of the states as previously shown in Tables 27 and 28. The general position of the courts has been that constitutional debt limitations were established to prevent the excessive use of property taxes and, therefore, did not apply to debt payable only from a special fund that would receive no property tax support.

Executory and Installment Contracts

Another method of circumventing debt restrictions is the use of executory and installment contracts. The use of continuing contracts for the provision of services and supplies—such as a long-term agreement with a private water company to provide water service to a local government at a specified annual charge or the long-term lease of a building at an annual rental—very early raised the question of whether the aggregate of these future charges created a present debt. The preponderance of judicial opinion has been that it does not, under the executory contract principle that the obligation of the local government to pay does not become a debt until the service is furnished. A different situation exists with contracts involving the lease financing of capital facilities. In the late 1800s, when municipalities were becoming increasingly interested in owning and operating water and electric systems, a scheme that emerged to evade debt restrictions was for a municipality to contract with a private agency to construct a system and agree to lease it over a period of years at an annual rental payable from current revenue. The contract might include an option to purchase for an amount equal to the aggregate of annual rentals or a provision for the municipality to acquire title upon payment of all of the rentals. Where the lease is obviously a purchase agreement, the courts have tended to hold that the aggregate contract rental is debt, but, there have been decisions to the contrary in several states.

Enterprise Revenue Bonds

Revenue bonds, in the long-accepted meaning of this term, are bonds issued to finance the construction, acquisition or improvement of a revenue-producing facility, with their principal and interest requirements payable solely from the revenues of the facility. Most commonly, they are secured only by a pledge of such revenues; but, in some states, as has been noted, they may be secured also by a mortgage on the property that is financed from the proceeds of the bonds. This disarmingly simple definition relates to an instrument of borrowing by local governments that has become infinitely complex in its purposes and forms.

Enterprise revenue bonds have been used more or less extensively by municipalities in most states, by some counties in at leaast a dozen states, and by some special districts having taxing power.[8] They may be issued directly by those local governments as limited obligations payable from a special fund; or occasionally, by an autonomous department or board; or indirectly, by operating authorities that are not separate local governments but merely subsidiary agencies of individual local governments. They have been used also by authorities that have some, or all, of the characteristics of separate special purpose governments without taxing power, usually created to provide facilities or utility

---

[8] Counties, because of their generally limited enterprise-type functions, have not made extensive use of revenue bonds, but such bonds have been issued for water systems, electric systems, gas distribution systems, and miscellaneous other purposes by a number of counties—particularly in the South, Midwest, and West. Several special districts with the power to issue bonds supported by taxes have shifted from the use of such obligations to limited obligation revenue bonds or have used revenue bonds for special purposes.

services for areas that are more extensive than those served by any one existing local government.

The availability of the revenue bond device has enabled local governments to proceed with the construction of many kinds of facilities which might otherwise have been difficult to build in a timely manner. For example, Chicago, Illinois, Kansas City, Missouri, and many other cities have used revenue bonds to develop adequate aviation facilities. Had they held back pending approval of general obligation debt sufficient to finance these undertakings, many opportunities would have been lost.

On the other hand, not all facilities constructed from the proceeds of revenue bonds have proved a success. Perhaps the best known default in this respect is one involving the Calumet Skyway Bonds issued on a revenue basis by the City of Chicago to build an expressway in the southern portion of the city.

Special Assessment Debt

Public improvements that are of special advantage to some specific section of a community rather than to the community as a whole are sometimes financed entirely, or in part, by the levy of special assessments on the benefited property. Special assessments are not levied *ad valorem*, but in proportion to benefits, as variously determined. When the assessments are paid in installments, as is permitted when the amounts are substantial, bonds may be issued to pay for the improvement with bond principal and interest payable from the collection of assessment installments and interest. A local government which has no public sewerage system may elect to issue debt which is based upon special assessments on the benefited property (or a combination of special assessments and net revenues from the operation of the facilities).

Of the two general classes of special assessment bonds, one class is payable, in the first instance, from special assessments but is additionally secured by the local government's full faith and credit. The other class is secured solely by the lien based on deferred installments; the local government acts merely as the agent of the bondholders for enforcing the liens and does not guarantee payment of the bonds.

This limited type of special assessment obligation has numerous variations. In its most rudimentary form, the individual bonds represent obligations of specific pieces of property and are, in odd denominations, corresponding to the amount of the deferred assessment payable on each property. More commonly, the bonds are issued as a lien on the property of an improvement district and made payable from a fund into which all assessment collections from the district are paid. The basic security for such bonds tends to be poor as the assessment lien on the property is subordinate to the lien of *ad valorem* taxes; losses to bondholders have been very large. They are marketable, if at all, at considerably higher interest rates than the guaranteed type of special assessment bonds and sometimes are given directly in payment to contractors, who necessarily adjust their project bids for the probable discount at which they must sell the debt. A financially undesirable type of obligation, it has one somewhat dubious advantage in that the courts have long been in agreement that, under the special fund doctrine, it does not constitute debt in a constitutional sense.

Special assessment debt was used very widely by local governments for many types of improvements prior to 1930—streets, street lighting, sewers, storm sewerage, sidewalks, and a long additional list. However, with the default of large amounts of special assessment debt in the late 1920s and, especially, in the 1930s, there has been a great reluctance in the market to accept large amounts of this type of debt. Moreover, with new types of development controls, many local governments require developers to install most of the kinds of facilities which were previously supported by special assessments. In some instances, special assessment debt is supported by a general obligation pledge and becomes a part of the multiple security type of general obligation debt discussed above.

Financing Authority Debt

A portion of today's revenue debt has been issued by regularly constituted, general purpose governments. In addition, a very large portion of revenue debt has been tied to the creation of authorities to which are entrusted the performance of selected public functions. Some of the best known authorities are state or interstate in character, e.g., the Port Authority of New York and New Jersey, the Massachusetts Port Authority, and the Delaware River Port Authority. Yet, numerous parking and other authorities, as well as redevelopment authorities, have issued debt which is supported by the net revenues of enterprises operated by such authorities.

The authority device has been widely used in some states (especially in California, Illinois, and Pennsylvania), as a means of circumventing processes involving debt limits or the ownership and management of property. Where the authority device is used for this purpose, the debt issued by it is frequently secured by lease rentals paid to the authority by governmental units with taxing powers. In other words, instead of a school district incurring debt and constructing a school building, it will contract with a school building authority to perform this task. In these circumstances, the debt incurred is in the name of the authority rather than in the name of the school district. Essentially, the investor is purchasing the bonds based upon the leasehold that has been secured by the school district. In Pennsylvania, additional security is pledged through a requirement that any state funds due the local school district shall be set aside to meet these debt service costs in event of default by the district.

In like manner, other forms of financing are frequently arranged on this type of basis. Usually, such financing authorities are not charged with the operation of the facilities or the provision of any public service beyond the financing operations involved.

This type of credit is usually of a lesser grade than the credit which exists in the governmental unit that is the lessee of the facilities; however, in the absence of reasonable debt limits or in the presence of unreasonable other conditions, it is necessary that public business continue to be carried out—even when more costly than through a more rational alternative.

More recently, the financing authority mechanism is being used to finance various kinds of community facilities where ownership and operation is in a nonprofit corporation, not a part of the local government involved. Thus, one finds a proliferation of authorities at the state level of government to facilitate the financing of facilities of institutions of higher learning and at the local level for financing hospitals, nursing homes, and other types of health facilities.

The latest of these numerous techniques for evading debt restrictions is the financing, or building, authority. These so-called authorities operate no facilities or services; they are nothing but borrowing mechanisms. The usual procedure is for a local government to create a public corporation or authority with power to enter into a contract with the creating unit by which it agrees to construct a public building or other facility which the creating unit agrees to rent. The authority then issues bonds payable from the rental revenue, with the agreed rental payments sufficient to pay the costs of the authority and the principal and interest requirements of the bonds. The rental may be made payable from the local government's current revenues (including property taxes) or from a special fund consisting of service charges or sundry nonproperty tax revenue. The local government takes title to the property when the debt has been retired. In states where the courts have sustained this procedure, a local unit of government can levy a tax or service charge to pay a rental designed to service the debt, with complete disregard of constitutional restrictions.

The financing authority device has met a very mixed reception by the courts, ranging from outright disapproval in some states to various types of approval in others. The special fund doctrine and the executory contract theory both play a part in such judicial support as financing authorities have received. Under the special fund doctrine, the bonds of the authority are held to be exempt from debt limits because they are payable from rentals rather than property taxes. The local unit of government is held not to incur debt because; (a) under the executory contract theory, future rent is not presently debt; or (b) in some instances, the rental is payable from a special fund that is not fed by property taxes. Upon consideration of this method of justification, it is difficult to avoid the conclusion that financing authority bonds represent borrowing by subterfuge, which the courts, quite aware of the underlying urgencies for capital improvements, manage to sustain.

Industrial Aid Debt

Commencing with Mississippi's program in the 1930s, the use of state and local government taxing and/or borrowing powers to finance industrial development has spread widely among the states. The program has included a variety of elements, ranging from outright subsidy by state or local governments from tax funds to partial financing through the use of tax-exempt securities.

The program did not become of major financial significance until the 1960s. By the end of that decade, a very significant portion of total financing by state and local governments was for the purpose of facilitating the financing of industrial facilities through the use of tax-exempt bonds. The trend became so pronounced that, in 1969, Congress placed substantial limitations upon the amounts of such bonds which could be used in respect to any specific private individual, partnership, or corporation. Even so, the Congress itself shortly found this device desirable to facilitate the financing of air and water pollution abatement activities in industry to remove debt limits, insofar as these specified activities were concerned.

In most instances, industrial aid debt is sold in the market as bonds. However, in some cases, it is arranged through a local authority with local banks in the form of more or less conventional mortgage financing.

Housing Authority Debt

Under the United States Housing Act of 1949, the so-called "new housing authority bonds" were authorized. The debt issued by local housing agencies to finance federally aided, low-rent housing is guaranteed as an unconditional obligation of the United States government in the sense that payments will be made to the local agencies in amounts sufficient to meet the interest and principal payments upon such debt. For all practical purposes, these obligations become tax-exempt, general obligation debt of the United States although the debt is legally issued in the name of the numerous local agencies in the various states.

There is no pledge of local tax support for such debt. The security is a combination of the net revenues of public housing projects and annual contributions made by the Department of Housing and Urban Development under its contracts with local public housing agencies (or directly with municipalities or counties in a few states).

Usually, the initial financing of a new public housing undertaking in this program is through temporary notes while the facilities are being constructed. The Department of Housing and Urban Development arranges for periodic sales of such notes and also for the periodic sale of bonds through which the long-term financing is arranged.[9]

---

[9] Although all bonds in this program have the same security, the underwriters customarily offer them to investors in three or four groups having small differentials as to yields. These small differences in yields are due, in part, to variations in the value to investors of state tax exemptions but also appear to be influenced, without valid justification, by the varying characteristics and general credit of the communities represented in the group of bonds being reoffered.

16

Accounting

To comprehend the operation of local government accounting systems, the principal objectives that such an accounting system is expected to serve must first be identified. A good accounting system must provide a basis for:

1. Accountability by officers and employees for the money and other local government property for which they are custodians or managers.
2. A system of controls in relation to the use of money and property with a view to prior determination that the expenditure of money and use of property are in accordance with law, local ordinances, and any rules or regulations governing these matters.
3. Reporting to other administrative officers, the governing body, and the citizens and taxpayers of the community concerning the exercise of stewardship. Also, where appropriate to provide an accounting to other governments as may be required.
4. Providing information to administrative and executive officers of the government in a form, frequency, and timeliness needed for management decisions and the supervision of the programs and activities for which such administrative and executive officers are responsible.
5. Providing accurate and timely information to creditors (bondholders and others) concerning the financial status of the local government.
6. Providing current information concerning the profitability of municipal enterprises.

The design and operation of an accounting system which performs these manifold activities satisfactorily is indeed a major contribution to the successful administration of any local government.

THE NATURE AND PRINCIPLES OF ACCOUNTING FOR LOCAL GOVERNMENT

Textbooks on municipal or local government accounting must, of necessity, cover aspects of three types of accounting: governmental accounting, commercial accounting, and institutional accounting—because the principles of all three are applied in local government. The first is nonprofit accounting, with principles

329

and standards set primarily by the National Committee on Governmental Accounting.* Under this type, falls the bulk of municipal accounting. Local governments, however, operate numerous business enterprises, some to provide services at cost to other municipal departments; some, such as a water plant, to sell services to the public. These enterprises (internal and external) follow commercial accounting principles and standards which have been set by separate standard-making bodies. And, if a local government operates a library, a hospital, and a community college or university, these institutions are each governed by still other principles and standards formulated by other bodies.

The nature of local government accounting stems directly, of course, from the primary objective or purpose of the government; namely, to render those services which its citizens effectively demand. Effective demand is manifested in appropriations to spend, as authorized by the citizens' representatives. The state has laid the ground rules for its political subdivisions, including the type of services they may perform, and may also mandate a portion of effective demand and provide resources therefor.

Local government administration places its major efforts in the planning, programming, and the providing of services. Because the resources are legislatively authorized and are destined for public purposes, the primary responsibility of local government accounting is to provide essential information and controls for assurance to the local legislative body, the state, and the local taxpayers that the government has carried out executive and legislative intent. Financial accountability for every dollar of revenue and legal compliance with all pertinent restrictions and limitations as well as the positive mandates must be facilitated by the accounting system—and its end-product, financial reports. The first and primary function of local government accounting, therefore, is to facilitate legislative and citizen control of the government's "business."

Whereas controls are devised for both the revenue and the expenditure sides of the budget, the multiplicity of types of service and the preponderance of personnel and activities involved in service performance means that local government accounting is heavily weighted on the expenditure side. Payroll accounting, purchasing and inventory controls, property controls, construction project accounting, and the bulk of budgetary accounting all emphasize outgo.

However, local government accounting serves another important function; i.e., the assistance given by the accounting system to management. It is still a secondary function, but one that is rapidly moving to a co-equal position. Management must live within all imposed directives and the rules of the game. Its drive is to provide the optimum in quantity and quality of services, given the relatively scarce resources with which the job must be done. The pressure and effective demand for programs and services is always greater than the resources available. Under any given economic climate, management may strive to "stretch the dollar" in order to hold taxes to reasonable levels; but, in ordinary and more favorable times, the drive for efficiency is to provide more and better services from the number of dollars made available. The managerial approach

---

* The name of the National Committee on Governmental Accounting was changed to National Council on Governmental Accounting in 1974.

to municipal accounting has therefore been added to the fiscal-accountability, legal-compliance approach. Both approaches are essential if local government administration is to reach a high order of achievement.

To understand the nature of local government accounting a quick look should be taken of "what it is not." This is best seen by an overall contrast with its opposite, commercial accounting. In private business, expenditures result in the production of goods or services which are then sold. Expenditures, therefore, generate revenues (income) which flow back into the business and from which profits are derived. Profits become the ultimate and crucial test of the wisdom and efficiency of the expenditures—whether made for production or for promotion of sales. The profit and loss statement, the end-product report which commercial accounting provides, places the final emphasis on net income measurement.

Local government presents a sharp contrast. In the main, its expenditures do not generate revenues. Expenditures provide services which normally have no price tag but are dispensed without payment of a fee which flows back as revenue dollars. Revenues are generated in order to finance expenditures and provide services, and the bulk of local government revenue generation is a separate process and, essentially, a compulsory process. If one moves into a local community, he must pay. As a home owner, car owner, dog owner, the pursuer of a business or profession, user of a subway or toll bridge, etc., he has no choice but to pay. There is no legal requirement that taxes and benefits derived from services be equated. Many taxes are on the ability-to-pay principle. Therefore, revenues derived are no test of the wisdom and efficiency of the expenditures made, and no profit and loss statement provides the final acid test. Local government financial statements are designed to show that all the money went for designated public purposes, that operations were within the budget, and that all was done within all the rules laid down. If the managerial approach has been added, accounting will also produce efficiency reports; but, there is no single standard like profits. Separate standards against which performance is measured have had to be devised for multiple programs and activities. These are public administration's answer to its inability to measure benefits in terms of sales dollars and to the lack of a single standard, such as profits.

Local government accounting is, therefore, nonprofit accounting. It is fiscal accountability accounting, financial position accounting, and budgetary accounting to show that resources were expended in strict compliance with legislative authorizations and restrictions and that revenues and expenditures were brought into balance. It is also now becoming performance-standard accounting. The control purpose was long dominant, but local government accounting has become more useful in planning and programming and in evaluating performance and appraising results in terms of managerial efficiency criteria. At its best, local government accounting is financial accounting and managerial accounting welded into a single system. Management is expenditure conscious (cash or accrued) for budget compliance purposes, but cost conscious for other purposes. The latter does not mean that the business-cost approach has been adopted. It has rather been adapted, with substantial modifications, to fit a nonprofit undertaking. The adaptation will be detailed further, later in this chapter.

Principles of Governmental Accounting

In the mid-1930s the National Committee on Municipal Accounting published a *Tentative Outline of Principles of Municipal Accounting*.[1] From time to time, publications of this committee have included revisions of the initial statement. In fact, in due course, the name of the committee itself was changed to the National Committee on Governmental Accounting and, in 1974, to National Council on Governmental Accounting.

The essence of the principles enunciated by the committee have now become the key features of desirable local government accounting systems. Stated in the form of "principles" they constitute a useful framework for describing the basic elements of local governmental accounting and, more importantly, they help to promote the adoption of uniform practices. The most recent comprehensive treatment of this subject by the Committee is contained in *Governmental Accounting, Auditing, and Financial Reporting*.[2]

Like similar guides in public administration—on assessment principles, budget principles, etc.—statements of accounting principles designate the generally accepted, the consensus as to what is "sound," as viewed by a body of experienced practitioners and theorists. They are not propounded as immutable, scientific laws or rules, but only as the best collective judgment of the experts. The limitations of the normative element are recognized; and, if these guides are to remain useful, it is also recognized that they will have to be revised as required, in accordance with inevitable improvements in the subject area and changes in expert opinion. It is also recognized that there are circumstances under which some of the principles do not apply, or apply only in a modified form. Hopefully, in this and other areas of public administration, a method of empirical testing can be developed which will someday supply a more solid foundation for the "principled" and the "unprincipled."

DIFFERENCES BETWEEN GOVERNMENTAL AND COMMERCIAL ACCOUNTING

In this section, the authors seek to ease the transition to governmental accounting for those who come trained in commercial accounting. This discussion emphasizes a number of basic differences between the two, many of which can be attributed to the lack of the profit test in governmental accounting.

1. Local governmental accounting is compartmentalized to ensure that revenues authorized from particular sources are expended for the purposes designated by law or administrative directive. These are public

---

[1] National Committee on Municipal Accounting, *Tentative Outline of Principles of Municipal Accounting*, (Chicago: National Committee on Municipal Accounting, Bul. No. 1, Jan., 1934), 4 pp.

[2] The National Committee on Governmental Accounting, *Governmental Accounting, Auditing, and Financial Reporting*, (Chicago: Municipal Finance Officers Association, 1968), 234 pp.

monies destined for public purposes. Each fund is an accounting entity (and usually a legal entity) which facilitates control for legal compliance. By contrast, commercial accounting is without this detailed public accountability for sources and uses of funds and free from such compartmentalization. Commercial firms collect their resources according to their skill in the market and, in the main, spend their resources as they choose. Earmarking of revenues is the exception rather than the rule. Governmental units have no such independence.

2. The legal framework which surrounds all phases of governmental finance introduces a high degree of inflexibility which extends much beyond fund accounting. Within funds, each appropriation item is a maximum limit restriction on the use of fund resources. Moreover, laws and legal manifestations of authority take precedence over accounting principles, if any conflict arises. Sometimes unsound financial and accounting practices for governments have even been written into law, thus greatly hindering the adoption of improved accounting methods. Commercial firms are often regulated by law as to their financial reports but, internally, their methods of accounting are primarily determined by management.

3. In commercial accounting, the budget assumes importance but merely as a guide or measure; in governmental accounting, the budget is a legal dictate as to the proper sources and uses of funds. The contrast is between a flexible budget and a legally authorized budget. Management of the former seeks to maximize sales revenue and to keep unit costs down, thereby maximizing profits. But, expenditures are not limited; they can be stepped up to increase production and sales. The public administrator focuses on compliance with expenditure restrictions and on maximizing service within a balanced budget (actual revenues and actual expenditures). Variances, above predetermined maximum expenditure figures, are not allowed. One important distinctive feature, therefore, of governmental accounting is that, in order to facilitate compliance, budgetary accounting is superimposed upon proprietary accounting and the two are integrated. Estimated revenues and actual revenues are recorded for comparative purposes in the same subsidiary revenue accounts; and appropriations (i.e., estimated expenditures) are recorded with actual expenditures in appropriation/expenditure ledger accounts. Internal management reports concentrate upon comparisons between what was authorized and actual progress under the budget.

4. In a private corporation, capital and surplus accounts are maintained to show the owners' equity in the business. There are no equity accounts in governmental accounting; and, there is no consolidated surplus figure. The surplus accounts are reckoned by individual funds and, within governmental accounting, are current in nature. The *unappropriated surplus* account (or fund balance) within a fund during the operating period is a mixed proprietary and budgetary account. At the end of the year after the books are closed, it is a true proprietary account and represents uncommitted resources free for appropriation.

The closest analogy in commercial accounting is the retained surplus account; but, even this is different in that retained earnings represent profits. The two are similar in that both identify an excess or deficiency of inflow over outflow.

5. Most of the funds in governmental accounting are current funds, i.e., they carry no capital assets nor fixed liabilities. Their resources are expendable, either in the current period or, as in the bond fund, over two or more fiscal periods. Their balance sheets, therefore, are current balance sheets and arrive at current balances or surpluses. General fixed assets are segregated into a self-balancing group of accounts; similarly, general bonded debt and other fixed liabilities constitute a second self-balancing group. The two are kept separate and used only for control purposes. No capital balance sheet is prepared, and no capital surplus is calculated. In most circumstances, creditors of governments cannot reach general fixed assets because of their dedication to a public purpose; creditors rely instead upon taxing power. Therefore, a capital surplus figure, even if prepared, would have no meaning as to solvency. This is in sharp contrast to commercial accounting.

6. Financial statements in municipal accounting differ in other respects from those prepared in commercial accounting. Mixed budgetary and proprietary statements dominate during the year, followed by proprietary condition statements at the end of the fiscal year. Each fund or fund group has its own balance sheet and operating statement. There is no consolidated balance sheet for the municipality as a whole, and no consolidated operating statement.[3] Operating statements arrive at a surplus or deficit (revenues over expenditures) and not a profit or loss, and are not designated as profit and loss statements.

7. Governmental accounting has necessarily developed its own terminology —but to a greater extent for operating statement accounts than for balance sheet accounts. In operating statements, revenues are classified by fund, collecting agency, and source. Expenditure classifications are more elaborate, namely, by fund, organizational unit, function, program or activity, character, and object. These classifications are more standardized and formalized than those for income and expenses in commercial accounting.

8. Governmental financial accounting concentrates upon expenditures within the fiscal period as authorized by the budget, but generally neglects cost concepts. Several examples may be cited. General fixed assets are not depreciated; capital outlays, therefore, are treated as expenditures in the fiscal period when made. When a general fixed asset is destroyed or sold at a loss, the loss is not reflected in any current

---

[3] This should not preclude the development of a modified consolidated operating statement to be presented in relation to public debt. This is especially true where the assets of several funds are available to meet debt service requirements. Thus, where all debt is general obligation debt of the local government and the assets of not only the general fund but also of the funds maintained for water, sewer, gas works, airports, etc., are available to meet debt service, it is appropriate to present the total picture. In fact, to fail to do so is depriving the community of proper representation of the financial facts involved.

fund since it does not affect the current budget. A third example involves inventories of materials and supplies. If stores are not requisitioned from central stores when needed for use, they are treated as expenditures when the liabilities are incurred and not in the period of requisition or use. Expenditures are recorded on a cash basis of accounting, or an accrued expenditure basis, but not on an accrued cost basis. Commercial accounting, on the other hand, is interested in full costs, i.e., expenses which are directly related to producing income in the current period plus all accrued costs—which includes consumption of inventory and the depreciation of capital assets which helped to generate current income. Business management is full-cost conscious; municipal management is partial-cost conscious. Since expenditures in local governments, in the main, do not generate revenues, management is not under the necessity of matching all costs with the revenue collected or accrued within a given period. Emphasis, therefore, is placed upon legal compliance, budget balancing, and fiscal accountability rather than upon a precise measurement of net income.

9. Accruals in governmental accounting serve several control purposes: to combine with encumbrance or commitment accounting in order to avert the danger of exceeding appropriation limits; to obtain an accurate comparison between actual and authorized expenditures and between actual and estimated revenues; and to arrive at a statement of the budget surplus at the end of operations which is both accurate and timely.

On the whole, local governments rely on a mixed, or modified, accrual basis of accounting. Practices vary widely among governments. In some, certain revenues are accrued as soon as the amounts due are known. Thus, some tax revenues, e.g., property taxes, can be accrued when the tax bills are prepared. Other revenues, e.g., fines and forfeitures, are on a cash basis because the precise amounts due are not known in advance of the circumstances which require the payments. On the outgo side, most cities are on an accrued expenditure basis, but not a full accrual basis. The trend toward a modified accrual basis has helped cities to improve cost allocations but the accruals are normally not comprehensive; they are essentially current and not long-term. Convenience often determines the extent to which cities record accrued expenditures and the amounts are often small. Again, because measurement of net income is not the goal, the results from accruing items may not be considered worth the effort. In the case of servicing bonded debt, accrued interest at the end of a period cannot legally be recorded because the full contractual amount is an appropriation of the next fiscal period. By contrast, commercial accounting's preoccupation with determining profit and loss results in a strict adherence to the accrual basis so that income will be accurately matched with the costs incurred in generating the income.

10. Depreciation in commercial accounting is, of course, one important application of the accrual basis. But depreciation of general fixed assets is not the practice in governmental accounting. Emphasis is upon the control of such assets rather than upon costing their contribution to

operations or upon their present value. The reasons for this are discussed elsewhere in this chapter (in the section on depreciation). Many cities, however, do apply depreciation to fixed assets in working capital funds, trust funds, and utility funds. The tax reason for depreciation in utility funds is absent because municipally-owned enterprises are not subject to state or federal corporate income taxes. But, depreciation is useful in setting utility rates and also facilitates comparisons of these operations with privately-owned utilities.

11. In government, the pinpointing of responsibility, or managerial accounting, has not been emphasized to the extent that it is now found in private industry. There has been a recent movement, however, among municipal accountants toward more accurate costing; and, as a result, more ways are being found to adapt cost controls to the needs of municipal management.

Beyond the foregoing, there are many other differences between commercial and governmental accounting, e.g., the treatment of premiums and discounts on bonds sold; the conversion of receivables from a current to a delinquent status; the actuarial basis of the sinking fund reserve in municipal accounting; and the recognition of judgments.

INSTITUTIONAL ACCOUNTING

Two important examples of institutional accounting, which are found within local government, are accounting for its hospitals and for community colleges or universities. From the outstanding features of each, the reader can readily see how they differ from municipal accounting, as a whole. Both engage in fund accounting but each has a separate standard-setting agency. Standards and principles have been devised to fit both publicly owned and private, or endowed, institutions. The objective is a common accounting approach for all types of hospitals and for all types of institutions of higher learning in order to obtain reporting comparability.

Features of Hospital Accounting. Among the distinctive features of hospital accounting are:

1. The plant fund arrives at a net figure for capital invested in the plant, but also has a separate section for current assets accumulated for plant improvement, replacement, and expansion. The plant fund, therefore, contains capital assets and long-term liabilities but also shows current assets dedicated for plant purposes.

2. Depreciation on fixed assets is recorded as an operating expense in the general fund, and allowances for depreciation are shown in the plant fund. Entries have been devised to accomplish this whether depreciation is funded in whole, in part, or not at all. This is accepted practice, although not universal, depending largely on relations with third-party contractors. Some accept depreciation expense on equipment, but not on buildings, or, only in part, on both.

3. Endowment funds are important in the fund structure. An agency fund group is also found, although the alternative of handling all agency transactions through the general fund is acceptable.
4. Budgetary accounting is often integrated with proprietary accounting; but, if permitted by regulation or by law, the better practice suggests a separate group of budgetary accounts.
5. A strict accrual basis is recommended by the American Hospital Association. This, plus the handling of depreciation, underscores the objective in hospital accounting of arriving at total cost figures.
6. Hospital accounting has also made real progress in measuring unit costs of the services provided. Cost centers are utilized. Books and up-to-date periodical literature on cost finding are available.
7. Within the uniform chart of accounts published by the American Hospital Association, accounts and notes receivable are combined. Provision is made for uncollectable receivables (losses from bad debts) to be treated as a deduction from revenue and not as an expense, as is done in commercial accounting.
8. Billings to patients are recorded as revenue in full, and allowances and adjustments are then recorded and classified under deductions from revenues.
9. The operating statement is closer to commercial accounting than to governmental accounting. It arrives at a net operating deficit, or net nonoperating income, but also contains a section to show how the overall deficit has been met by contributions and other outside sources.
10. On the whole, hospital accounting (although on a fund accounting basis) is somewhere between commercial and governmental accounting— with a strong pull by its cost-consciousness and managerial approach toward commercial accounting.

Features of College and University Accounting. On the whole, college and university accounting is much closer in its practices to governmental accounting than to commercial accounting. This relationship is evidenced by the form of the operating statements and the statements of surplus usually found in college and university reports. This closer kinship to governmental accounting is in contrast to hospital accounting. Both are engaged in nonprofit fund accounting, but hospitals have increasingly adopted features of commercial accounting.

Among the characteristics of college and university accounting are:

1. The fund structure differs from both governmental accounting and hospital accounting. Special revenue funds, loan funds, and endowment funds—including annuity funds (a special type of endowment fund)— loom very important. Agency funds are found. Auxiliary enterprises (such as cafeteria, campus stores, etc.) are often numerous and are recorded in current revolving funds.
2. Plant funds constitute a group, or one fund with three sections: improvements and replacements (current assets earmarked for expansion, repairs, and replacement); retirement of indebtedness (assets accumulated for debt retirement); and investment in plant, which, as the capital sec-

tion for educational plant, shows excess of capital assets over long-term liabilities and the sources which provided the educational plant.

3. Depreciation is generally not taken on educational plant, but is calculated on fixed assets used in auxiliary enterprises (which are income-producing or completely self-supporting) and on depreciable property assets in endowment funds, if the fund principal is to be kept intact.

4. Budgetary accounting is integrated with proprietary accounting, but there is a growing tendency to eliminate the recording of encumbrances. The budget so integrated usually covers only the current funds.

5. Fixed assets are found in auxiliary enterprise revolving funds, endowment funds (i.e., real estate for investment purposes), and the plant fund. Properties of the auxiliary enterprise revolving fund and endowment real estate (provided they constitute a part of the educational plant) are often shown both in their fund and in the plant fund. This means that some capital assets in the plant fund will be offset by allowances for depreciation.

6. Strict accruals are not recorded as in commercial and in hospital accounting. The term "modified accrual basis" in this area of institutional accounting, however, does not signify that revenues are on a cash basis and expenditures on an accrual basis.

7. Especially weighty features of college and university accounting are: accounting for investments in endowment funds and accounting controls to ensure adherence to the restrictions which donors place upon the uses of principal and upon expendable income.

8. Developments in the measurement of unit costs and in the managerial approach have not been as noteworthy as those which have occurred in hospital accounting.

ACCOUNTING STRUCTURE

Governmental accounting structure can be viewed as built around four central pillars: funds or fund groups; two major nonfund, self-balancing groups of accounts; a unified records system; and basic accounting classifications.

Funds. A fund is an accounting entity and, usually, a legal entity, with resources, and can "do business' or have transactions with other fund entities within the municipality. A fund is also an accounting compartment with a whole group of self-balancing accounts (balance sheet and operating statement accounts). Records are kept by funds. Separate statements are prepared for the major funds, and combined (but not consolidated) fund group statements are often feasible for the smaller funds. This means a series of balance sheets and other accounting statements for the municipality, rather than consolidated statements:

> . . . the purpose of combined fund balance sheets is to show in a single statement the financial condition of the several funds into which the financial organization of a governmental unit may be divided. An apparent accomplishment of this purpose is sometimes attained by the preparation of what might be termed a "consolidated balance sheet," in which like items of all

funds are consolidated into one amount and the resulting totals are organized into balance sheet form. This arrangement of financial information obscures the fund-entity principle which is vital in governmental accounting. On account of fund restrictions upon the use of assets and the variable nature of fund liabilities and net worth, such a consolidated statement is regarded by many as having little real value. There are, however, two generally accepted forms of combined balance sheets, one being a columnar arrangement and the other a series of vertically arranged balance sheets, one for each fund or type of fund operated by the governmental unit.[4]

The National Committee on Governmental Accounting has recommended eight standard fund designations:[5]

General Fund   Enterprise Funds
Special Revenue Funds   Intragovernmental Service Funds
Debt Service Funds   Trust and Agency Funds
Capital Projects Funds   Special Assessment Funds

This compartmentalization of resources, transactions, and statements is known as fund accounting and is one of the dominant characteristics of governmental accounting.

The local government budget cuts across some funds and fund groups, with the result that funds appear as major divisions in the budget as well as in the annual financial report.

Funds contain earmarked resources. It is important, however, to distinguish between a fund and an appropriation which is also earmarked:

1. As an accounting entity and compartment, a fund is more than one account; it is a group of self-balancing accounts. Some funds contain both budgetary and proprietary accounts. An appropriation is a single account and always a budgetary account.

2. An appropriation account is part of a fund group of accounts. There must be a fund out of which an appropriation can be made, so the existence of the fund precedes the appropriation.

3. Appropriations are usually annual or, in some instances, biennial. There are also a few continuing appropriations and appropriations for specific amounts but without limits as to time. By contrast, funds are not authorized periodically; they tend to be continuing. Some funds continue in existence for years; the general fund is, for all practical purposes, "permanent;" others may be closed out after their special purpose has been served.

4. There is also a difference in the power to create. Appropriations are authorized (created) by local legisative action only. On the other hand, funds may be created by the state constitution, a state statute, the local charter, or by local law or ordinance. In some cases, a fund may

---

[4] Mikesell, R. M. and Leon E. Hay. *Governmental Accounting* (Homewood, Ill.: Richard D. Irwin, Inc. 1969) Fourth Edition, p. 509.

[5] National Committee on Governmental Accounting, *op cit.*, pp. 7-8.

be administratively established. This is particularly true for enterprise, agency, trust, and special revenue funds.

Sometimes, the title of an appropriation item uses the term "fund." For example, there may be an appropriation designated as the "Mayor's Fund," a "Contingency Fund," or a "Petty Cash Fund." These appropriation items create only single accounts; the use of the term "fund" in these instances is unfortunately confusing.

Nonfund Accounts. Two nonfund, self-balancing groups of accounts, the general fixed asset group and the general long-term debt group of accounts, constitute the second central pillar of the accounting structure. Although accounting compartments, they are not funds because they do not contain resources which can be appropriated nor the basic accounts within the balance sheet equation. The GFA group contains fixed assets but no liabilities, reserves, or surplus accounts. The GLTD group contains no asset accounts and, therefore, no surplus account. These two groups provide one compartment where general fixed or capital assets are segregated and a second compartment where general long-term liabilities are segregated. This segregation accomplishes three important purposes: (1) it permits the operation of most funds as current funds, with only current assets and current liabilities; (2) general fixed assets and general long-term liabilities are completely segregated from each other, thereby avoiding a meaningless general capital surplus figure; and (3) each group brings together, in one accounting compartment, related accounts for control purposes—in one case, general fixed asset accounts which serve inventory, location responsibility, and other control purposes and, in the other case, general long-term debt records which must be kept in great detail so that prompt debt servicing can be monitored.

Within a local government, there are usually fixed assets which are not general assets of the government but belong to a particular fund, such as a utility or a trust fund; there are also fixed or long-term liabilities which are not general obligations of the government, but constitute special assessment debt or self-supporting revenue debt. The following table shows which funds and nonfund groups carry capital assets and capital liabilities. Also shown, for a further understanding of the fund structure, are those funds which normally contain investments; those within which capital construction activities may take place; and those which may have responsibility for servicing long-term debt (i.e., interest and principal payments).

Interest and principal for all general obligation bonds (unless they are serviced *entirely* out of special assessment levies or from enterprise earnings) are handled in the debt service funds group. If retirement of general obligation bonds is by sinking funds, such funds are also a part of this fund group. All special assessment bonds (both general-special and special-special) are serviced directly from special assessment funds. Both types of utility or other enterprise bonds (revenue bonds and general obligation bonds) if serviced entirely out of utility or enterprise earnings, are treated as fund debt (for accounting purposes) and are serviced out of funds in the enterprise group.

Many interfund transactions take place and require accounting entries. Such entries reflect services performed, sales, loans, the transfer of assets, contribu-

Table 30
SPECIAL FEATURES OF FUNDS AND NONFUND GROUPS

Funds	Contains			Executes	
	Fund capital or fixed assets	Fund long-term or fixed liabilities	Invest-ments	Construc-tion projects	Debt servicing
General			x		
Special revenue			x		
Debt service			x		x^1
Capital projects	x^2	x	x	x	x
Special assessments	x^2		x	x	
Trust and agency	x^3	x^3	x		x^3
Intragovernmental service	x	x^4		x	x
Enterprise	x	x	x	x	x

Nonfund Groups	General capital or fixed assets	General long-term or fixed liabilities
General fixed assets	x	
General long-term debt		x

^{1} Not for special assessment or enterprise debt.
^{2} Only for construction work in progress.
^{3} Possible for trusts only.
^{4} Only for inter-fund capital advances.

tions of capital or profits by one fund to, or from, another. An asset account "due from other funds," and a liability account "due to other funds," in the fund balance sheets are constant reminders of transactions between funds.

Other transactions which cannot be classified as "interfund" constitute, nonetheless, intrastructural connecting links. These transactions are recorded in current funds but, concurrently, require complementary entries in the general fixed assets group or the long-term debt group. Three illustrations will suffice:

1. When general obligation bonds (serial or term) mature, the liability, which has now become current, is set up in the debt service fund group. Concurrently the long-term liability must be taken out of the GLTD group.

2. When a capital construction project, financed from the proceeds of general obligation bonds is completed, the current accounts in the capital projects fund group are closed, and the capital asset is recorded in the general fixed assets group.

3. A general fixed asset is sold. In the general fund, the proceeds are recorded in a revenue account or in a replacement reserve account. Concurrently, the asset is taken out of the general fixed assets group of accounts.

One further connection exists between current funds and the two major nonfund groups. An intragovernmental service fund (formerly designated as a working capital fund) may carry its own capital assets and long-term liabilities; yet, since they are both "general," they may be shown again in the general fixed assets and general long-term debt groups, respectively. Such an intrastructural link is easily overlooked. Footnotes in the two nonfund groups should call attention to this duplication. Similarly, general-special assessment debt, double-barreled revenue bonds, and general obligation enterprise debt completely serviced by utility earnings will all be shown from the beginning as special assessment or enterprise fund debt liabilities. Such debt, however, because of the general obligation contingency, may be repeated in the long-term debt group. If so, the contingency nature should be emphasized in any financial report, and the duplication explained by footnotes.

Unified Records.   These constitute the third central pillar in the accounting structure. In order to have information "on the forest" as well as "on the trees" the general ledger contains summary accounts (posted as totals); the supporting details are kept in subsidiary ledgers with many different names. The summary accounts are controlling accounts because they contain a total figure for each posting, against which the summation of detailed subsidiary entries must reconcile. One summary account may control an entire subsidiary ledger; while several may each control particular segments of a single ledger. A good example of the latter is found in the accounts which control parts of the appropriation/expenditure ledger. The general ledger also contains some nonsummary or detailed accounts when the transactions in each are so few as not to justify the creation of a subsidiary ledger.

Basic Accounting Classifications.   Basic classifications of balance sheet accounts and operating statement accounts together comprise the fourth central pillar of the accounting structure. Usually, these are set forth in a chart of accounts in the municipal accounting manual. Many account titles for balance sheet accounts differ from those in commercial accounting, but the differences are much more pronounced in the classifications of revenues and exepnditures. The addition of budgetary account titles is responsible for some of the differences; more importantly, a government's revenue sources and expenditure purposes bear little resemblance to those of a business.

Revenues in municipal accounting are classified by fund and by source and, sometimes, by collecting agency. Expenditure classifications are more elaborate—detailing:

Fund	Activity
Organizational unit	Character
Function	Object
Program	

Recapitulation of figures by individual bases of classification are often published. More frequently, one recapitulation will combine several bases in one table by use of stub and columnar cross-classifications.

The National Committee on Governmental Accounting by standardizing terminology and by drafting and promulgating standard account classifications has helped to bring about a certain uniformity among municipalities in the use of terminology and in account titles. Whether or not a municipality has adopted the National Committee's classifications, within the municipality itself, a common basic classification will be used in account titles, titles of budget items, and nomenclature in both financial and audit reports.

SOME CONNECTING LINKS BETWEEN ACCOUNTING AND OTHER SEGMENTS OF FINANCE

In the foregoing the place of governmental accounting within the larger accounting subject area was contrasted with commercial and institutional accounting. The perspective attempted here is narrower. We look, first, at the connecting links between municipal accounting and certain nonaccounting segments of municipal finance and, secondly, by introversion, at the interrelationships among types and subtypes found within governmental accounting.

Uniform classifications of revenue and expenditure accounts constitute a major connecting link of local governmental accounting with budgeting and reporting. Account titles become appropriation items and reporting nomenclature. Accounting and reporting are further linked by a uniform classification of balance sheet accounts. Postauditing is facilitated not only by uniformity in classification of all accounts but also by uniform standard principles and standard terminology. Uniformity and standards ease the transition from accounting documents and records to budget presentations, all types of financial reports, and to auditing.

Further links between accounting and budgeting are important. At the budget formulation stage, expenditure estimates are justified by well-planned work programs which are translated into total costs through work-unit cost figures developed in the accounting records. Similarly, revenue estimates are based, in part, on recent recorded experience. At the execution stage, budget control is accomplished largely through budgetary accounting. It thus becomes difficult to mark the point where budgeting ends and accounting begins. Budgetary and proprietary accounts (i.e., estimates and actuals) are integrated so that much of accounting is actually a part of budget execution. In fact, intelligent action taken in the execution of the budget program is based upon accurate accounting information respecting the progress of commitments, expenditures, revenue collections, the treasury's cash position, and borrowing.

A frequent obstacle to a quick grasp of an operating budget document is the fund breakdown within the budget. Standard fund titles constitute one bridge to understanding, but are not sufficient. An important addition is a brief statement in the budget preface as to the fund groups which are included in the main (or general) budget, those excluded, and those covered in any annexed or special budgets. As for the capital budget, if it is to be implemented annually through the operating budget, the primary link is in the operating budget's character classification of expenditures. The fund location of capital projects depends on the method of financing.

Governmental accounting is also closely linked with treasury management, pension or retirement system administration, purchasing, property management, and public works administration. Cash accounting is a most important segment of treasury management. Accounting for investments plays a role in both treasury management and pension or retirement system administration. If purchasing is centralized, stores accounting (including requisitioning and inventory control) forms an informational basis for stores control and purchasing decisions. Property management is partly fixed asset accounting and inventory control; and, within public works planning, construction, and repairs and maintenance, one finds cost accounting and project accounting.

If local utilities are under independent boards, or, if a local public authority (e.g., a municipal parking authority) has been erected, the finances of such offshoots may, or may not, have a connecting link with the government's finances and finance administration. If such a connection exists, it is usually found in payments *in lieu* of taxes, contributions to the general fund, or in the mechanics of debt servicing. Such an intra-local fiscal relationship would, of course, be reflected in the government's accounts.

ELEMENTS OF THE MANAGERIAL
APPROACH TO ACCOUNTING

The "managerial approach" is a subject which was briefly broached in explaining the nature of local governmental accounting. If a local government has adopted this approach (or "managerial accounting" as some writers prefer), its accounting system has been so designed that end-products are a maximum service to management. Although conventional financial accounting has always served management, this relatively new approach in governmental accounting not only shifts the emphasis but thereby adds a new substantive dimension. The important features of this approach can be summarized as follows:

1. By placing more emphasis upon the production of information for planning and programming than found in financial accounting, it seeks to establish a balance between this role and accounting for control purposes.
2. Its approach to control is markedly different. The older approach is upon legal compliance and fiscal accountability. Managerial controls are added to these and center upon standards and the preparation of reports which highlight significant variances from such standards.
3. A greater emphasis is placed upon internal management reports and upon experimentation with and innovations in the types of information which will be supplied to management at various levels.
4. Although the managerial approach does not always require the accrued-cost basis, the emphasis is on performance standards and on unit costs,

the promotion of cost-consciousness, and, wherever feasible, the approximation of the full cost basis.

5. The cost approach is linked with decision-making and, often, with program/performance budgeting.

Development of the managerial approach has accompanied and contributed to a better understanding of financial decision-making. Under this approach, statements and reports anticipate questions which the decision-makers must resolve and focus the information so as to facilitate solutions. Dedicated to the aim of producing precisely the information needed and when needed, the managerial accountant, by imagination, experimentation, and innovation must keep abreast of management. He must continue to study the nature, timing, and other aspects of decision making. This is a large order. Management makes decisions in formulating policy to be recommended to the legislative body; in programming; and in controlling operating units and subordinates in order to ensure that planned programs are efficiently executed. Many decisions are current; others long-run, such as those which involve capital construction planning and long-term debt financing. Decisions may be final or may include alternatives. If management tends to think in terms of alternatives to solutions, the accounting office must be prepared to supply data for proposed alternatives. Later, after results are known, the wisdom of the choice among alternatives may be reappraised. Management and staff have placed decision making on a more scientific basis and have begun to accumulate documented experience, rather than "hunch" experience.

This approach is linked also to program/performance budgeting. Development of this newer brand of budgeting required the development of newer techniques. The one succored the other, as did the developments in decision-making. Managerial accounting provides the information for planning and programming and supplies both the workload estimates (expected demand level) and the unit costs to convert these into dollar requests. Accounting has helped budget management make obsolete the older approach of planning new budget requests by adding "x" amount to last year's expenditures.

As mentioned above, the managerial approach to control is through variance reports. Reports are designed so that management, by focusing on variances, i.e., the exemptions, can save time. The manager need not see the numerous statements which reflect the expected. Where variances occur, analysis will indicate to what extent they are pure efficiency variances or a mixture of controllable and such noncontrollable elements as price changes.

The managerial approach will not supersede financial accounting, but, under an optimal system, new processes will be devised to collect and utilize both statistical data (as to units of performance and service provided) and cost data. Both will be linked with standards within new internal management reports. These will originate in cost centers or program responsibility centers. The full-cost approach, however, is not absolutely required; partial costs, or an approximated approach, may prove satisfactory. Some attempts have been made to substitute a partial-cost system for the financial accounting system. This is most difficult. The municipality might better, in the authors' view, add managerial accounting with the possibility that, in time, it can be adjusted and improved to satisfy all the needs of the old as well as the new approach. An alternate solution would be to begin adjusting the financial accounting system so that emphasis shifts in the managerial direction. When feasible, a forward step would be the establishment of cost centers and responsibility centers. Expenditure data, supplied by activities and programs and related to performance data, would be one step nearer to a performance-cost system. Expenditures are only partial costs, but might include the bulk of controllable costs. At least, this approach would provide a learning stage, and a more refined approach could be scheduled for a later date.

We are not prepared to say that there are no weaknesses in the managerial approach. One speaks of "controlling costs," but it is actually people who must be controlled. The establishment of managerial accounting and use of its end-products require the education and enthusiasm of management and staff. With standards, there must be sanctions (rewards and punishment) because some performance and cost results will be highly satisfactory and some painfully unsatisfactory. Work-unit performance standards and cost standards must periodically be revised to keep pace with changes and, ultimately, must have the concurrence of those persons affected.

The stress in this chapter on the managerial approach requires, in the authors' view, no defense. In municipal management today, the better administrators wish to be more than "compliers" with the law. Their drive, training, and philosophy of management demand more sophisticated statistical and accounting information than conventional accounting can supply. They seek more effective controls, surer guides to higher levels of efficiency, and have become impatient with pedestrian reporting. Unfortunately, the managerial approach has been neglected in municipal accounting literature. One has to go to commercial accounting texts to find an adequate elaboration of managerial (responsibility and performance) accounting and instructive contrasts with financial accounting.

BASES OF ACCOUNTING

Closely associated with the managerial approach is the basis, or the bases, of accounting. A basis of accounting is the approach adopted for identifying those points in the cycle of transactions at which accounts recognize the availability of resources, the commitment and use of funds, and the consumption or application of resources. On the inflow side, two bases have been adopted: the cash basis and the accrued revenue basis. On the outgo side, four bases are used: the cash, obligation, accrued expenditure, and the accrued cost. These are pure basis-types, but later the hybrid bases and combinations of bases will be mentioned. The following table will serve to clarify what is meant by "identifying points in cycles" and to connect the corresponding bases.

Under a strict accrual basis, revenues are taken into account as soon as they are earned or levied or when tax bills are prepared, regardless of the fiscal period in which they are collected. In practice, however, not all revenues will, or can, be accrued. Accrual of revenue from minor sources may not be deemed worth the trouble. Others cannot be accrued because the amounts, or

Table 31
THE BASES OF ACCOUNTING

Transaction phase	Point in time when recorded	Recognized as (and basis)
In the inflow cycle		
1. Receipt of tax or other revenue without prior recording	When cash is received	A cash receipt (cash basis)
2. Tax or revenue due and definite amount known	When tax or revenue is earned, levied, or billed	An accrued revenue (accrued revenue basis)
In the outgo cycle		
1. Placing an order for goods or services	When goods or services are ordered or contracted for	An obligation (obligation basis)
2. Receipt of the goods or services ordered	When goods are received or the service performed; the liability incurred; or the invoice received	An accrued expenditure (accrued expenditure basis)
3. Payment made	When cash is paid	A cash disbursement (cash basis)
4. Goods or services applied or consumed	When goods or services are used in the program, activity, or project	A cost of work performed or service rendered (accrued cost basis)

the fact that payment is due, are not known in advance of actual collections—traffic fines, for example.

Most discussions of the bases of governmental accounting on the outgo side leave something to be desired. The "accrual basis" presented is the accrued expenditure basis, and no hint is given that there is a second accrual basis. Establishment of the superiority of the accrual basis (i.e., the accrued expenditure basis) over the cash basis leaves the newcomer to governmental accounting with the unfortunate impression that the former is the ultimate in accuracy and desirability. This he may later question if he moves into federal accounting where the more sophisticated accrued cost basis is frequently used. Governmental accounting should not (1) neglect the managerial approach where costs are differentiated from expenditures; or (2) fail to warn the student that in federal accounting he will find another segment of governmental accounting where different materials and concepts are developing which are relevant to all levels of government.

In the above table, the bases are presented as pure types. Combinations and hybrids, however, are so frequent as to be regarded as normal. First, it should be noted that the obligation basis is a part of budgetary accounting. Since budgetary and proprietary accounting are integrated in municipal accounting, the obligation basis parallels whatever proprietary accounting basis on the outgo side is used. Three "tandem" combinations thus exist: obligation-cash; obligation-accrued expenditure; and obligation-accrued costs.

Secondly, a local government may record its inflow on a cash basis, but accrue its current expenditures and incurred obligations. Under another approach, the inflow side resembles the accrual basis in form, but remains on the cash basis in substance. This occurs, for example, when the asset account, property taxes receivable, is recorded at the time of levy but is offset by a 100 percent reserve for uncollected taxes; or by a 95 to 98 percent reserve for uncollected taxes plus a two to five percent allowance for uncollectable taxes. This offset approach has the advantage of establishing the asset account as a control over collections, but without accruing revenues. Both of these examples which use the cash basis on the inflow side and the accrued expenditure basis on the outgo side should, in the authors' view, be classified under the "modified cash basis." Some authors, however, would classify them under a second hybrid type, the "modified accrual basis."

Thirdly, we prefer to reserve the term "modified accrual basis" to those cases in which the municipality accrues both revenues and expenditures—but only the large items or only when the accrual is convenient. The term, "strict accrual basis," within financial accounting, can then be applied to those cases in which all transactions on both sides are accrued, insofar as accruals are feasible and legal.

Fourthly, the local government may have moved close to the accrued cost basis, but still fall short of it. Some outgo transactions may remain on the accrued expenditure basis. This hybrid type may be expected when the managerial approach is being adopted in stages.

It should be understood that accounting on a more refined basis will produce all the information available under the less refined. For example, a system on either one of the pure accrual bases continues to provide cash receipts and disbursements figures. Also, a system on the accrued cost basis will still yield accrued expenditure data.

The four bases on the outgo side will be more clearly visualized if they are compared on several counts: provision of information; methods of financial control under each; differences in the measurement of management performance; type of situations where a particular basis has special applicability; and the major weaknesses of each basis.

Under three bases (cash, obligation, and accrued expenditure), the information provided for budget planning and for the justification of budget requests before the legislative body is incomplete and subject to possible manipulation. More specifically:

1. The estimation process may begin with an assumption that previous levels of appropriation were adequate for the agency's needs. Information is not readily available to challenge this assumption effectively.
2. Basing new budget requests on prior experience invites continuous pressure to keep prior experience at a high level; otherwise, the budget base for the next period is undercut. There is pressure to commit all obligational authority whether the need for goods or services requires full commitment or not and, at year's end, to speed up the process of converting obligations into accrued expenditures or cash disbursements. The temptation to manipulate and thereby prove that last year's budget was "needed" is a very powerful one.

3. When important shifts in demand for program services (an increase or decrease) are forecast, it is difficult to translate the shifts into dollar estimates without accurate unit costs.
4. Finally, in asking for new obligational authority, there is no recognition that unusual amounts of noncash resources carried over from preceding periods are available to reduce the need for new appropriations.

The accrued cost basis can supply the cost information for breaking the crude, and sometimes vicious, circle of formulating budget requests on the basis of the prior year's budget level. Under the accrued cost basis, management can develop the cost figures necessary to support any anticipated level of activity. The temptation to overobligate and overexpend in order to maintain a budget base is removed. The temptation to forecast too high a level of activity or to manipulate unit cost data remains, but accrued cost accounting produces better checks against manipulation than any other accounting basis.

Under all four bases, the primary overall financial control is budgetary and may be exercised at the point of commitment against allotments or appropriations. The budgetary obligation basis, which parallels each of the above proprietary bases, is an upper-limit control but does not extend beyond the commitment. Detailed operating controls throughout the stages in which the obligation is being fulfilled rest upon proprietary accounting bases and include control of cash receipts and disbursements by means of a cash-flow schedule; establishment of taxes receivable as a control over collections; and the use of program or cost centers where a partial-cost approach with accrued expenditures can be introduced. In the latter case, inventory and property accounting are essential. A more complete operational control, however, can be established if full or accrued costs are accumulated at program or cost centers. This basis best reflects all resources used and the financial status of the program. Stores inventory, property, and capital asset accounting—all in monetary terms—bring resources carried over from prior years under control and are integral parts of the full-cost approach.

Under all the bases except accrued costs, performance is rated primarily by the manager's ability to live within the budget. This may be supplemented under the accrued expenditure basis by partial unit cost measurements if program cost centers are used. Management must likewise live within the budget under the accrued cost basis, but can now be judged more precisely by the standards used to develop the cost-based budget and by performance under these standards. At the programming stage, the administrator must justify his estimates by showing that they are realistic and that they are reasonable costs per unit, in light of his own standards and the experiences of others doing the same job. At the execution stage, he is held to the performance goals which he set for himself. Management is thus judged by both the ability to forecast and plan and the ability to live up to the plan. It should be noted that unit costs are used not only to determine the budget level when a shift in demand for program services is forecast, but also to rate management performance. Measurements in terms of cost set the tone and give precision to cost consciousness in government operations. Under the cash basis, reliable unit costs cannot be developed. They are affected by random fluctuations in collections as well as by any deliberate withholding of payments to reduce unit costs. Under the accrued expenditure basis, the unit cost figures are partial. The contributions of noncash resources, including capital assets, are ignored, and the receipt period is erroneously equated with the period of use or consumption.

Situations in which a particular basis has special applicability are considered in the following:

For the very small local unit, a modified cash basis is often the most practical. Without accruing revenues, property taxes and other receivables which are due can be placed on the books for control purposes until they are collected and offset 100 percent by a small reserve for uncollectables plus a large reserve for uncollected receivables. Recording of cash disbursements will also produce reasonably satisfactory figures, if bills are paid promptly and inventories and prepaid items do not fluctuate much from the prior period's end.

In financial accounting (where proprietary and budgetary accounting are normally integrated), it is desirable that actual revenues and expenditures be recorded in order that the budget plan and its execution can be best compared. This is accomplished by accruing revenues and expenditures as far as practicable. Expenditures are recorded in the period within which provision has been made for them (rather than in the period of use or consumption), and revenues are recorded, as far as practicable, within the same period as the expenditures for which they were provided. This period matching is to determine how successfully the financial plan was achieved.

When, however, the managerial approach is added as a new dimension, accrued costs must be provided, as well as accrued expenditures, and a cost-based budget introduced. This means that, in the planning of the budget, new obligational authority must take into account all available resources carried over into the budget period under consideration, and accounting controls must be established over both the new and the old resources, including property accounting controls in monetary terms. Resources carried over may include opening inventories, prepaid expenses, unfilled orders, and work-in-progress. Accrued costs recognize the postponability of some costs and reflect, as costs within the period, all goods and services used or consumed. These costs, in turn, are matched by resources—applied to both new revenues and old resources available.

The accrued cost method provides the only accurate method of determining costs; however, application of this method involves a degree of sophistication rarely found in local governmental accounting. For example, under the accrued cost method, the accounts should reflect actual costs, as follows:

Personal Services: Cost at time of rendition, including full allowance for fringe benefits that accrue in respect to the personal services actually rendered.

Contractual Services: Recorded in relation to the project upon which used and on the basis of the time period during which used, regardless of which year's appropriation accounts they may be charged against.

Materials and Supplies: Recorded when used, not when acquired. Involves adjustments in central stores pricing to realistic bases, including cost of operations and administration thereof.

Equipment: Recorded on a basis which reflects the appropriate "rental" charge which, in turn, reflects depreciation, interest, and operating costs.

Structures and Land: Interest on investment, depreciation (where applicable), and other elements that would be represented should same be rented in connection with the project or activity being priced.

To summarize, important determinants which might enter into the choice of a basis of accounting include: the size of the governmental unit; the promptness with which bills are paid; the size of inventories and other available resources carried over and their fluctuation from one year's end to another; whether or not contracts are obligated in full when entered into; the length of the normal time lag between (1) the placement of an order and delivery of the goods or services and (2) the delivery date and use or consumption; the length of the usual capital construction period; the degree of emphasis placed on financial accounting and upon managerial accounting; the demand for unit cost information in a particular operation; and, if personnel costs constitute the major cost element, the choice of times for recognizing the cost of vacation leave—especially when earned in one period and taken in a subsequent period, usually at higher pay rates.

Each accounting basis has some weakness, although accounting becomes more refined as we move from the cash basis to the modified cash basis, to the modified accrual basis, to the accrued expenditure basis, and finally to the accrued cost basis. Most middle- and larger-sized local governments now use a system under which obligations are recorded at the time incurred. There is a tendency, within financial accounting, to refer to this as the "strict accrual basis." The danger in this view is the temptation to equate expenditures and costs. This transition cannot be done with assurance. Accrued expenditure figures may fall short of accurate costs or, in some cases, exceed full costs allocable to a period, because the period of use or consumption is postponed beyond the period of receipt, or because certain capital assets are recorded as expenditures when acquired, or recorded later as expenditures through the periodic retirement of debt, which was incurred to acquire the capital assets. The substitution of periodic debt retirement in lieu of periodic depreciation is often the practice. Another situation may arise where the accrued expenditure basis does not provide an accurate cost figure. Accrued expenditures include expenditures against current appropriations and those which arise from liquidating prior years' encumbrances, but exclude use, within the fiscal period, of inventories and other prepaid items carried over from a preceding period. This is good financial accounting but may not provide management with the information needed in planning and decision-making.

There are no theoretical weaknesses in the accrued cost basis as applied to governmental accounting. However, some practical drawbacks arise and militate against its use. Recognition of the resources carried over upsets the simple comparison of appropriations and current expenditures. Property controls and a cost-based budget are required which means a more sophisticated accounting system. If management does not use the added managerial data, or uses it unwisely, the cost and inconvenience are not justifiable. With a cost-based budget, management is given greater flexibility and responsibility. This fosters greater efficiency provided rewards and sanctions function well. The accrued cost basis is no automatic guarantee of improved management.

Another way to show the differences between accounting bases is to illustrate by figures each step of the reconciliation process. The following is an over-simplified version, but one which at least indicates the basic approach:

1. Cash disbursements plus any increase in the balance of accounts payable, or minus any decrease, equal total accrued expenditure
2. Total accrued expenditures plus any increase in the balance of undelivered orders (unfilled obligations), or minus any decrease, equals total obligations
3. Total accrued expenditures minus any increase in inventories carried over, or plus any decrease, and plus any unfunded costs, e.g., depreciation and vacation leave, equal total accrued costs

Moving from a cash basis (both sides) to an accrual basis (both sides) is not an unusual transition for a small municipality which is attempting to improve its accounting. A trial balance is taken and a balance sheet prepared as of an agreed cut-off date, and the next day the new system is placed in operation. This requires, in the main, setting up in the general ledger the necessary current asset accounts and current liability accounts with allowances for uncollectable receivables. General current asset and liability accounts are normal adjuncts of accrual accounting. Subsidiary ledgers will be required, namely, a property tax ledger, a receivables ledger, and a voucher register. After the cut-off date, all revenues and all expenditures (wherever practicable and legal) will be recorded as they are earned or incurred and not when received or paid. If budgetary accounting was not in effect and is to be added also, a subsidiary revenue ledger and an appropriation/expenditure ledger will be necessary. The latter will introduce the obligation basis.

That depreciation is part of the accrued cost basis has already been noted. The transaction cycle for a capital asset differs in length from that of current goods and services. First, the time lag between the order or contract phase and the phase when the capital asset, either in segments or as a whole, is received is usually much longer. Construction may extend over a two- to five-year period. Secondly, and more importantly, the capital asset is normally used or consumed over many years. As the capital asset is used, the cost is accrued as depreciation. Since depreciation presents special problems in governmental accounting, it is treated in the following section as a continuation of the bases of accounting.

Depreciation

Depreciation of general fixed assets has not been customary in government accounting. Several arguments have been advanced for the correctness of this approach: (1) many expenditures in government finance do not generate revenues; therefore, in any given period, there is no compelling rationale for allocating all costs which pertain to the revenues accumulated in that period. In business, the profit or loss reckoning acts as a curb on expenses; activities which do not generate revenues come under close surveillance. In governmental accounting, a profit or loss calculation is not possible; therefore, matching full costs with revenues serves no control purpose; (2) in municipal finance, all expenditures must be authorized by appropriations. Since depreciation is a noncash expense, recording it as an expenditure would result in an unbalanced budget. If, in order to preserve budget balancing, depreciation were funded by appropriations, the municipality would face all the attendant problems of investing the replacement funds; (3) since general fixed assets are not used as the basis for credit analysis, there is no necessity to report them at a current depreciated value, i.e., at original acquisition cost or value minus an estimated offset depreciation figure. As assets dedicated to a public purpose, they cannot be taken by creditors; bondholders base their appraisal of ability-to-pay primarily on taxing power or generation of earned revenue.

Implicit in any opposition to the introduction of depreciation into general fixed asset accounting are the reasons listed above. It must be underscored, however, that these reasons relate to municipal financial accounting. We have placed great emphasis in this chapter upon giving the managerial approach (i.e., managerial accounting) a co-equal place in municipal finance administration. Consistent with this emphasis, depreciation and equipment rental should be recorded as a part of full-cost information. Fortunately, depreciation can be recognized without impugning views which relate to financial accounting, because depreciation is part of the dimension added by the managerial approach.

Depreciation of general fixed assets can be accomplished in any one of three ways:

1. The accounting structure and organization for property management can be arranged to simulate business arrangements. A working capital fund can own all mobile equipment and include depreciation in its rental charges to operating units which use the equipment. With central garages and motor pools, this financial and accounting arrangement is already a fact in some cities. Appropriations to the operating agencies for rental charges, therefore, permit the allocation of full equipment costs to the user activity or function. The working capital fund builds up equipment replacement resources. Such an arrangement places equipment on an accrued cost (usage) basis analogous to materials and supplies requisitioned from central stores when all costs of central stores operations are included in pricing.

The same simulated business arrangement can be extended to all municipal buildings which are general fixed assets. A working capital fund or a trust fund can own all the buildings and collect a rental charge (on a full-cost basis) from all units which utilize space. Appropriations for rented space enable the building fund to finance repairs and maintenance and to accumulate replacement resources. A similar arrangement might be extended to furniture and other major depreciable items of office equipment.

This simulated business arrangement, unfortunately, stops short of a complete solution. It cannot produce depreciation costs figures for all general fixed assets. The major exceptions would be sidewalks, streets, traffic and street lights, expressways, and bridges. This approach, at least, would (a) provide full-cost information for a much larger area of decision-making than now possible; (b) concentrate depreciation accounting for general fixed assets within two funds; and (c) introduce a partial pay-as-you-go basis into capital financing.

2. By another method, depreciation accounting can be applied to all general fixed assets. Developed initially in hospital accounting, it is easily adapted to municipal accounting.

For each general fixed asset or group of small depreciable assets, such as typewriters, a noncash depreciation expense is recorded in the general or other fund where the asset is being used.[6] A corresponding, unfunded, offset reserve entry is recorded at the same time in the general fixed asset group of accounts. To illustrate:

General Fund

Dr. Depreciation Expense—Bridges _____

   Cr. Fund Balance   _____

General Fixed Asset Group

Dr. Investment in Fixed Assets—
       from Bonds   _____

   Cr. Estimated Depreciation—
       Bridges   _____

These entries, for example, would record accrued depreciation on all bridges under the Department of Public Works. The detailed amount for each bridge would be journalized as the basis for recording an offset estimated depreciation figure on each subsidiary ledger card for bridges within the general fixed asset group of accounts.

The above entries should be made at the end of the year. Within the general fund, should be the credit to unappropriated surplus as an offset against a noncash and nonappropriated debit when "Depreciation Expense—Bridges" is closed out (either directly or through an accrued costs account). The net effect on the fund balance account is zero. What is accomplished is a recording of depreciation expense in the accounting records as a noncash expense. As a nonappropriated item it is essentially a "statistical cost" (to borrow a term from federal accounting) which will be allocated to activities and program, depending upon the cost center structure. It enters into work-unit costs, into alternative decision-making, and into budget planning; however, it is taken out in arriving at the final budget appropriation request for an activity or program.

Unless full costs are considered in such decision-making, the choice between proposals may rest on a false foundation. One proposal may include the use of considerable equipment; another, less equipment but more labor. Space utilization may also be different among the competing proposals. Comparisons require estimated full costs, and these estimates must rest on past recorded experience. Further, when the efficiency of several cost centers is being analyzed, the different mixes of factors necessitate full cost data if meaningful comparisons are to be made.

---

[6] Noncash signifies that no funding takes place.

3. A third method of recording depreciation places the whole process on a memorandum basis. This means that no double entries are made in the general or other funds where the general fixed assets are used. Within the general fixed asset group, however, a memorandum record is kept on a subsidiary ledger card for each asset. These records can be grouped, or regrouped, for purposes of analysis—by cost centers, operating units, etc.—and the figures added to other costs in order to obtain full cost figures. Also, the data may be used in arriving at depreciation totals by programs, by classes of fixed assets, and for general fixed assets as a whole. This third method may be designated the "memoranda cost" method.

The National Committee on Governmental Accounting is not opposed to the memoranda cost method.[7] However, the authors see certain superior advantages of the second or "statistical cost method."

1. Formal double entries more nearly ensure that the information will be recorded accurately. Summary entries in the current funds supply a check against figures in the GFA group of accounts.

2. The statistical cost method lists depreciation in the current fund records, and there is an advantage in having the full cost figures available as a part of the accounting figures for each regular activity, program and cost-center. To take one example, it is possible to add depreciation to other accrued cost data and to arrive at full cost statements. It is feasible to differentiate in such statements between cash costs and non-cash costs.

The depreciation figures recorded under either the second or third method, or through some combination of the first with the second or third, could serve several additional purposes:

1. The current depreciated value and the estimated remaining life of usefulness of individual capital asset items constitute information which could be utilized by the budget staff or the capital planning staff. A factual basis would exist for the scheduling of particular capital replacements, for estimating salvage or trade-in values, and for supporting the establishment of a more rational equipment replacement program— or any other replacement program. A firmer basis for insurance coverage and for insurance adjustments would also be available to the property control officer.

2. Total current depreciated values of capital assets by major activities and by functions could also be utilized in the development of capital investment standards. Under one approach, city planners now use various professional standards prepared by functional specialists to calculate the needed level of capital plant and equipment. This is true even though many of the functional standards are not in terms of *per capita* or per pupil dollar investment. If depreciation figures were kept on all general fixed assets, capital budget specialists could begin to develop the govern-

---

[7] See R. M. Mikesell and Leon E. Hay, *Governmental Accounting*, (Homewood, Ill.: Richard D. Irwin, Inc., 1969), Fourth Edition, p. 740.

ment's own experience as to proper capital levels in each major activity and functional area. It is impossible now to establish such standards for different activities or functions or to attempt to make some kind of valid comparison between cities, so long as reported fixed asset figures are on an original cost or acquisition basis (adjusted only for betterments, losses, and retirements), and are unrelated to a common period of time. Historical costs so adjusted are not adaptable to the development of investment standards. If the city's capital plant and equipment in each major activity and functional area are assigned a dollar value at different points in time—on a current depreciated basis and over a long period—trend lines (adjusted, if desired, for changes in the value of the "construction dollar") could be computed. These figures, adjusted for total population increases and school population increases, could become the basis for useful projections. If done for groups of cities, and for a period of time, we could begin to generalize as to experience standards in capital planning.

3. Total annual depreciation expense figures could make a contribution to the determination of an overall level for the current capital improvement program. A case can be made for the view that the minimum, or floor, for the total capital improvement program for the next year should be established by the total amount of the estimated current depreciation of the government's total capital plant and equipment, adjusted by some factor for the difference between depreciation and replacement costs, and further adjusted for estimated population increases or decreases. However, this latter adjustment may have more validity for remaining years in the 5, 6, or 10-year program than in the year to be included in next year's current budget. The public would understand an argument to program enough new improvements or replacements to keep the total investment in total capital plant and equipment intact. The minimum protects the capital inheritance from the past and precludes a move backward, even if the community is too conservative in its financing to move forward. However inadequate a minimum (or floor) may be, it is at least a lower-limit guideline for capital planning—more of a guideline than may currently be available. Conceivably, by applying this approach over a period of time, we might develop in capital programming and capital budgeting the factual basis for a refinement of this proposal. It seems reasonable to hope ultimately for a verified, so-called "principle of establishment of a minimum capital improvement program." Until a factual basis can be built, the authors suggest a tentative, hypothetical approach:

a. That in a stable community the minimum (or floor) of the total capital improvement program be set at the total of the last full year's depreciation of all depreciable capital assets (plant and equipment), adjusted by a factor which may be different for each capital item (or a composite) to bring depreciation costs in line with replacement costs.

b. That in a growing community the adjusted total (detailed above) be converted to a *per capita* basis (or a per pupil basis for that part of the total represented by school plant and equipment), and that a further adjustment upward be applied for anticipated population increases (or school population increases).

c. That in a community with a declining population, the same conversions described in (b) be made, but that an adjustment downward be calculated for anticipated further population decreases (or school population decreases). Where the decline in the community is not based on population, but on economic viability or status (for example, movement of a high-grade residential suburb to a lower grade as measured by the average income of home-owners in the area), other conversion and adjustment factors would have to be applied.

In these ways, the planning of capital improvements could be upgraded and the amounts requested could be defended on a factual basis. In addition, the need for both increases and decreases could be readily identified.

17
Auditing

The role of auditing[1] in local government finance is becoming increasingly more important, not only because local government operations are expanding but also because there is a growing need for developing new means for reviewing the end-results. In 1968, the National Committee on Governmental Accounting defined auditing as:

The process of examining documents, records, reports, systems of internal control, accounting and financial procedures, and other evidence for one or more of the following purposes:

(1) To ascertain whether the statements prepared from the accounts present fairly the financial position and results of financial operations of the constituent funds and balanced account groups of the governmental unit in accordance with generally accepted accounting principles applicable to governmental units and on a basis consistent with that of the preceding year;

(2) To determine the propriety, legality, and mathematical accuracy of a governmental unit's financial transactions;

(3) To ascertain whether all financial transactions have been properly recorded; and

(4) To ascertain the stewardship of public officials who handle and are responsible for financial resources of a governmental unit.[2]

Historically in local government the audit function has been largely restricted to ascertaining that the balance sheet represents a proper statement of the government's financial condition; a determination that money received has been properly recorded and deposited to the government's accounts and that expenditures made are in accordance with authorizations under state law, local ordinances, and directives which govern the use of funds.

---

[1] As used in this chapter, we are basically concerned with postauditing. By definition, the steps leading to review and payment of accounts are deemed to be a combination of accounting and treasury functions—even though auditors in many local governments are assigned a role in the preaudit process.

[2] National Committee on Governmental Accounting, *Governmental Accounting, Auditing and Financial Reporting*, (Chicago: Municipal Finance Officers Association, 1968), p. 127.

These continue to be very important elements of the audit function; however, postaudit operations are gradually expanding into other areas. Moreover, audit techniques have been modified significantly as local governments have moved to greater use of the computer for recording financial data and for making computations for billings and payments.

Some students of public finance believe that the postaudit function needs to be extended to embrace performance auditing, which would greatly expand the field. It would include: (1) determination as to whether expenditures by agencies out of appropriations had conformed to the implicit contract which arose when appropriation grants were given and promises made by agencies to perform certain work and achieve certain goals; and (2) the use of management efficiency and effectiveness standards to measure the performance and achievements by each government agency.

An additional factor is the tremendous increase in the number and scope of audits of local governments performed by state and federal agencies. This was inevitable with the unprecedented increase in transfer payments to state and local governments and in the number and complexity of intergovernmental financial relationships. Except for federal general revenue-sharing, the typical pattern of state and federal grant programs is to require varying degrees of audit of the eventual use of grant funds. Frequently, such audits are performed by state or federal audit personnel. In fact, in some local governments, when funds are derived from a combination of federal, state and local sources, audits by each governmental level have resulted. Such repetitive auditing of the same transactions poses problems.

Because of the foregoing factors, and the degree of accuracy required in the auditing process, the National Committee (now Council) on Governmental Accounting, the Committee on Auditing Procedure of the American Institute of Certified Public Accountants, and the Office of the Comptroller General of the United States have each focused on and promulgated principles and recommended practices in governmental auditing. The standards recommended by the Comptroller General go beyond setting the criteria for propriety and efficiency and deal with the concept of program results. The standards recommended by all three are generally applicable for use by auditors working from any governmental level.

ORGANIZATION FOR AUDITING

Patterns of organization are a product of many factors, including compliance with any laws which govern auditing; local historical precedents; the volume and type of work to be performed; the quality of personnel available; and the personal preferences of the head of the auditing function.

In establishing an auditing organization, the most important ingredient is to assure that the principal postauditor has a remarkable degree of independence from the chief executive and others whom he is required to audit. A lack of such independence is likely to impair the quality of the audit, its findings, comments and recommendations.

It is difficult to guarantee full independence of the principal auditor. The pervasive political, personal, and economic considerations cannot be fully excluded from the process of selection of the auditor and from his conduct of the auditing functions. Despite this, it is desirable that the fullest attempt be made to secure a high degree of independence. Among the factors involved are:

1. Decision as to an auditing department vs. reliance upon outside auditors
2. The method of selection of the auditor
3. The qualifications of audit personnel
4. Protection against loss of independence through control of monetary and staff resources necessary for conduct of the audit function.

Auditing Department vs. Outside Auditors

Opinion varies widely concerning the pattern which offers the best way by which to perform the postaudit function. On the one hand, there is the regularly organized department within the overall local governmental structure. On the other hand, there are several possibilities for use of auditors outside the regular local government structure.

1. *The Auditing Department.* Most of the larger local governments which have responsibility for local performance of auditing depend upon a regular department within the government. This pattern is now found in New York, Chicago, Philadelphia, Detroit, and Richmond, Virginia, to name a few.

   Where the auditing department is responsible for both preaudit and postaudit, the use of a regular local department is a requirement because the preaudit must take place on a recurring basis. The advantages of the use of a local department include:

   (a) Development of a professional staff which maintains a comprehensive knowledge of the organization, procedures, and personnel of the local government, as well as of the laws and regulations under which the affairs of the local government are conducted.

   (b) Availability of the staff of the auditing department on a year-round basis for consultation with officials in both the executive and legislative branches.

   (c) Conduct of portions of the postaudit function on a more or less continuous basis, thereby avoiding the major compression of the workload into a few weeks or months. Moreover, this arrangement helps to discover at earlier dates lapses from standards of proper conduct of public business, rather than allowing months to go by before discovery is made.

   As a practical matter, the very small governments cannot rationally utilize a regular department both because of lack of sufficient workload and the difficulty of securing qualified audit personnel, for what amounts to part-time employment. Middle-size local governments can opt for the auditing department arrangement, except those that are required by law to elect an independent auditor. It appears, however, that relatively few have an audit department.

2. *Outside Auditors.* Reliance upon outside auditors takes three basic forms:

(a) *The State Government Audit.* A number of state governments require that the financial affairs of some, or all, of their local governments be audited by state personnel employed for that purpose. Among the states which pursue this course, for at least a portion of their local governments, are Ohio, New Jersey, and Louisiana.

State personnel to perform the audits of local government can provide useful links between the state and its localities. Provision can be made so that the audits performed by state personnel will comprehend all of the special audits required in connection with state categorical grants and other payments to its local governments. Thereby duplication of audits can be avoided.

On the other hand, depending upon the political responsiveness of the state officer who is in charge of auditing, the state audit personnel can be used to harass local government officials who are politically in opposition to the prevailing political officer(s) at the state level.

In some situations, especially in New Jersey, the close relationships between the local governments and the Department of Community Affairs (including prior approval of municipal budgets, etc.) offer an opportunity for gathering of information through audit by the state agency which is useful in performance of oversight and regulation of certain aspects of local government finance. Even there, however, many of the local governments use independent specially certified municipal accountants.

(b) *Contractual Auditors.* Most postaudits of local government finance are performed by independent auditors under contract with the local government being audited. The typical pattern is to engage a firm of certified public accountants to perform the postaudit. This arrangement has advantages of independence, competence and economy in most middle-sized and smaller governments. On the other hand, there is a disadvantage if the audit personnel has insufficient knowledge of local government accounting and law, and practices which are frequently quite different from those in private business.

New Jersey has attempted to overcome this obstacle by requiring special certification of municipal accountants. This procedure helps to assure that the municipal accountants are fully familiar with the law and the requirements of the Department of Community Affairs which supervises municipal finance.

(c) *Auditing Committees.* An historic practice in the smaller local governments is to have the governing body appoint a committee of citizens to review the accounts and file a kind of audit report on the local government's financial transactions. In earlier times, this was frequently the only procedure available. Recently, it is being supplanted by other forms of audit.

In making the choice, consideration must be given to relative cost as well as effectiveness. Unfortunately, there have been no comprehensive independent studies which provide objective data and guidance in this matter.

Selection of Auditor

The method of selection of the auditor is of major importance in helping to assure that the auditing process will be independent of inappropriate influences.

1. *Selecting Head of Auditing Department.* Selection must be by either election or appointment.

   (a) Under Jacksonian principles, one depends upon popular election to assure that the auditor is provided full independence. Although this may be good theory, the importance of political party arrangements in the nomination and election of officials raises major questions concerning the degree of independence which popular election of the auditor provides.

   Clearly in those states which hold partisan elections and in which there is a real contest between the parties, the method of sponsoring of candidates in each of the parties is an important part of the nomination and election processes. Moreover, persons who stand for election to the position of auditor frequently have ambitions for higher political office and may easily permit these ambitions to be a ruling factor in certain of the actions taken as auditor, either to protect friendly office holders or to chastise unfriendly ones.

   Even so, in a large local government, it can be argued that the conduct of the audit function must necessarily have political overtones, and that only an elected officer has the degree of understanding of the political aspects of audit work to enable him to use this to secure proper results. This consideration has helped to dictate the popular election of the auditor in New York, Philadelphia, and some other large cities.

   Among the problems involved in selecting an auditor by election is one which arises from his being elected at the same time, and for the same term, as other local officials. Some cities have overcome this problem by requiring that the auditor be elected at a different time and/or for a different term.

   (b) *Appointment.* The appointment of the head of the auditing department immediately opens the question as to who shall exercise the appointing authority. In Chicago the Mayor appoints the auditor. This enables the auditor to act with considerable independence of the other departments of city government; however, it can have the effect of limiting the degree to which the auditor feels free to criticize publicly other officers in the government and almost assures no criticism of the mayor's conduct.

   In Detroit the auditor is appointed by the council for a single term of 10 years and is ineligible to accept any other municipal office. He may be removed only for cause. This gives him considerable independence but, except for a person approaching retirement age, it means that arrangement for other employment at the end of the term must be made.

Whatever the form of the appointment and qualifications required as prerequisite to appointment, there are normal forces at work in which one may be preferred over another for reasons other than his superior qualifications. Even the use of independent nominating panels have not fully overcome these kinds of pressures.

2. *Selection of Contract Auditors.* The selection of contract auditors leaves wide open the making of choices among qualified individuals or firms. Each of the national accounting firms is likely to have an interest in the appointment if it has an active office in or near the local government. Moreover, numerous local or regional firms are readily able to assert their qualifications to perform the audit.

Inasmuch as the process does not lend itself to bidding, the result is frequently selection on the basis of personal acquaintance, or political preferences by members of the local legislative body that makes the appointment.

With the absence of bidding, competitive proposals invited from accounting firms deemed qualified can be of assistance to the members of the local governing body. Such proposals can assist in defining the scope of the work to be performed, estimates of the compensation payable, the audit schedule and the content of the audit report.

If the scope of the audit is sufficiently defined and if the auditor is acquainted with the magnitude of the work required, fixed fee arrangements may be feasible, perhaps with re-opener clauses in cases of unusual situations that require attention in depth.

Qualifications of Auditing Personnel and Financial Independence

It is axiomatic that if the audit is to be performed satisfactorily the audit personnel shall be qualified to do the work and that sufficient man-days be allowed to enable them to perform the work thoroughly. In the case of local auditing departments, it is desirable that the law require auditing personnel to have sufficient qualifications,[3] and that the auditing department have substantial independence in determining the size of the staff and the budget required to do the work satisfactorily. If the chief executive or the legislative body can throttle the audit operation through insufficient appropriations, the audit tends to lose much of its independent status.

SCOPE OF THE AUDIT

Whereas determination of the method of selecting the auditor occurs only intermittently, the determination of the scope of the audit is subject to more frequent review and decision. Such determinations of scope are to be made in the light of contemporary circumstances.

---

[3] One way is to require a certain percentage of certified public accountants. Another is to impose a minimum qualification on all audit personnel, e.g., minimum academic training and experience in accounting.

The National Committee on Governmental Accounting has defined the scope of the audit, where performed by professional auditors under contract, thusly:

A most important part of the audit contract is a clear indication of the financial operations the auditor is to include in his engagement and what limitations, if any, are imposed on procedures to be carried out by the auditor. If the audit is to cover all funds, agencies, and operations of a governmental unit, this should be clearly indicated. On the other hand, if the engagement is to be limited to certain funds, the funds to be audited must be clearly identified in the contract. If the governmental unit receives or holds assets for another governmental unit, such as property taxes collected by a municipality for an independent school district, the audit contract should specify the auditor's responsibilities for examining such assets as a part of his engagement.

If an audit of a governmental unit is to be fully effective as an instrument of financial management, it should be contracted for on such a basis that, in the absence of conflicting legal requirements and limitations, the auditor can express an unqualified opinion in his audit report. This Committee recommends that all governmental units provide for postaudits which contemplate an unqualified opinion and that the audit contract in such cases make explicit this expectation. It must be recognized, however, that some governments, with adequate legal authority and because of particular circumstances, may wish to restrict the audit engagement in some way which will preclude the auditor from giving an unqualified opinion. Where any such restriction is to be in effect, it should be clearly specified in the audit contract so that there will be no misunderstanding on the part of the governmental unit or the independent auditor when the audit engagement is completed.

Under normal circumstances, postaudits are performed on an annual basis and cover the financial transactions of a single fiscal year. However, there are instances where other periods of time may be covered. These include a period of several years where a unit has never before had an audit or after a lapse of several years without an audit; a part of a year when there is a change in the fiscal year of a governmental unit; or an audit warranted by special non-recurring circumstances during a fiscal period. Regardless of what time period is to be covered by the audit, it should be clearly indicated in the audit contract.

A final element in the scope of the audit services being contracted for is that of statements, records, and facilities to be provided for the independent auditor by the governmental unit. Under normal circumstances the governmental unit should have closed out the accounts and prepared preliminary statements and schedules for all funds as suggested elsewhere in this volume. If this has not been done and the auditor is required to perform these additional tasks, provision for this work and the additional expense involved should be made in the audit contract. Where the governmental unit agrees to provide working space and/or certain personnel services to the auditor, the audit contract should contain a detailed explanation of what these services and facilities are to be.[4]

---

[4] National Committee on Governmental Accounting, *op. cit.*, pp. 129-30.

AUDITING PROCEDURES

The National Committee on Governmental Accounting has set forth the basic procedures which should be used in the performance of audits. Although these are not repeated here, it is appropriate to call attention to some of the principal procedures treated by the Committee.[5]

1. *Statutes, Charters, and Other Legal Enactments.* Governmental accountability, in its broadest terms, is implicit in the conduct of any public service. As applied to the auditing process, this accountability is often specified in legislative enactments. Therefore, the auditor should begin with the enabling legislation governing the function or activity and any implementing legislation or legal opinions subsequently affecting it. Intergovernmental cooperation is required in making available to the local government auditors any statutes pertinent to these functions and activities in which federal or state moneys are involved. Because legal enactments are generally lengthy, a careful test checking of such legislation should be undertaken.

2. *Bond Ordinances and Bond Contracts.* A review of any bond ordinances and bond contracts pertinent to a specific function will give the auditors valuable background information for use in the auditing process.

3. *Funds Maintained.* A determination of the full fund structure maintained by the local government is basic to the auditing process since on this determination rests the propriety of receipts recorded, payments made, etc.

4. *Audit Instructions from Other Levels of Government.* For the functions and activities in which the resources of another level of government are involved and for which the audit is required by the superior level of government, the local auditors will need specific instructions regarding the requirements of the federal or state agency.

5. *The Bases of Accounting.* The auditors should describe the accounting bases used by the local government and its individual functions and activities. If there are any changes made in the accounting system from that covered in the financial report of the previous year, such changes should be carefully set forth in the new report. If these have a significant impact upon the statement of fund condition at the close of the year, the fund condition of the previous year should be restated in order that comparison can be made easily between the two years treated on the same basis.

6. *Internal Control.* The auditing process should identify the system of internal control of the entity being audited and should determine whether or not that system is effectively accounting for revenues, expenditures, resources and liabilities. An evaluation should then be made of the system of internal control to indicate to what extent it can be relied upon in auditing. Internal controls should point out any irregularities or improprieties; the auditing process is primarily a test of these procedures.

---

[5] *Ibid.*, pp. 131 et seq.

Upon concluding the foregoing procedures, the auditor can undertake the next steps in the auditing process which will produce his final certification or report.

In determining the scope of an audit, an evaluation should be made of the particular needs of its users. The National Committee on Governmental Accounting sets forth the requirements of a general audit (vs. a special audit), and provides a rather extensive checklist, involving:

1. Some twenty categories of revenues, recommending for each a review of:
   a. Its authorization (for rates charged, etc.)
   b. The status of current and delinquent revenues
   c. The accuracy of finance records
   d. Its distribution to the proper funds
2. Nine payment categories, requiring a check as to their:
   a. Promptness and propriety
   b. Authorization and correct recording
   c. Accuracy
3. Twelve types of assets requiring for each a written verification of items disposed, cash in bank, security of such cash, whether or not bank accounts are properly maintained, and inventories of fixed assets.
4. Ten types of liabilities, recommending for each a determination as to when it was authorized and recorded as a liability and a written verification of payments made and balance due.
5. Equity accounts requiring a check of fund balances to determine whether they are separately stated and have suitable reserves.[6]

THE AUDIT REPORT

Even among the large cities there is, in many instances, no separate report of a postauditor. The auditor's certification is included in the annual financial report. Depending on the structuring of the local government, the auditor's certification or report may be addressed to the chief executive or the local governing body. The date for completion of the annual audit should be set by law, usually within 90 to 120 days after the close of the fiscal year; thus making it available for timely use by management and legislative officials. To this end, the audit should be made available to the various officials of the local government, the public, and the various levels of government which have made resources available to the governmental entity being audited.

The Comptroller General of the United States has succinctly covered the content of the audit report in the following requirements:

1. Be as concise as possible but, at the same time, clear and complete enough to be understood by the users.
2. Present factual matter accurately, completely, and fairly.
3. Present findings and conclusions objectively and in language as clear and simple as the subject matter permits.

---

[6] *Ibid.*, pp. 141-146.

4. Include only factual information, findings, and conclusions that are adequately supported by enough evidence in the auditor's working papers to demonstrate or prove, when called upon, bases for the matters reported and their correctness and reasonableness. Detailed supporting information should be included in the report to the extent necessary to make a convincing presentation.

5. Include, when possible, the auditor's recommendations for actions to effect improvements in problem areas noted in his audit and to otherwise make improvements in operations. Information on underlying causes of problems reported should be included to assist in implementing or devising corrective actions.

6. Place primary emphasis on improvement rather than on criticism of the past; critical comments should be presented in balanced perspective, recognizing any unusual difficulties or circumstances faced by the operating officials concerned.

7. Identify and explain issues and questions needing further study and consideration by the auditor or others.

8. Include recognition of noteworthy accomplishments, particularly when management improvements in one program or activity may be applicable elsewhere.

9. Include recognition of the views of responsible officials of the organization, program, function, or activity audited in the auditor's findings, conclusions, and recommendations. Except where the possibility of fraud or other compelling reason may require different treatment, the auditor's tentative findings and conclusions should be reviewed with such officials. When possible, without undue delay, their views should be obtained in writing and objectively considered and presented in preparing the final report.

10. Clearly explain the scope and objectives of the audit.

11. State whether any significant pertinent information has been omitted because it is deemed privileged or confidential. The nature of such information should be described, and the law or other basis under which it is withheld should be stated.[7]

AUDIT CONFERENCES

One of the principal standards requisite to a fair and full audit report is a comprehensive conference on the preliminary draft of the report with the principal supervisory officer of the governmental unit or sub-unit being audited.

If the auditor has determined that there are matters which have not been carried out in accordance with the law or good accounting procedures, it is necessary that he call this to the attention of the proper officials at an early date in order that steps can be taken promptly to take corrective action, or disciplinary action where required.

---

[7] Comptroller General of the United States, *Standards for Audit of Governmental Organizations, Programs, Activities and Functions,* (Washington, D.C.: U.S. General Accounting Office, 1972), pp. 7-9.

These kinds of conferences have the added value of giving the officials responsible for the functions being reviewed an opportunity to correct any misunderstanding which the auditor may have unwittingly gained in the course of the audit. If the audited official has information which has not theretofore come to the attention of the auditor, these conferences offer an opportunity and a responsibility for him to add to the knowledge of the auditor before a final report is prepared.

IMPLEMENTATION OF RECOMMENDATIONS

Each office or department to which a recommendation in the audit report refers should be obliged to make a report thereupon to the chief executive, and, where appropriate, to the governing body:

The report should cover at least the following points:

1. Is the statement of facts which led to the recommendation correct? If not, what are the substantive errors in the auditor's report?
2. Does the operating official believe that the recommendation offers an appropriate remedy to the situation requiring correction?
3. Is the operating official proceeding with implementation of the recommendation? If not, why not?
4. As of what date is it intended that full compliance with the recommendation be effected?

Suitable follow-up by the chief finance officer and the chief executive's office should be made, with periodic reports to the auditor concerning progress made in putting approved recommendations into effect.

18

Measurement in
Local Government Finance

Local government administrators and many analysts outside "city hall," have learned to think in terms of benchmarks or measurement standards—some precise, others of the rule-of-thumb variety. This chapter seeks to examine their meaning and inherent limitations and to explore their application in budgeting, efforts to achieve maximum efficiency, routine managerial decisions, credit analysis, and the interpretation of local finance data. This chapter unavoidably cuts across other chapters; yet, treatment of the subject in one place and in more depth is required for a fuller understanding of the quantitative approach to local government finance and financial management.

We recognize that quality standards are important in service areas and play a major role in the purchasing function; but, the emphasis here is upon quantitative measurement. Within this delimitation, it would be possible to describe measurement as, basically, "quantitative research." But, we have used the term in a more rigorous sense, namely, as the application of yardsticks to programs, performance or results, effects, and to other "products" of financial administration.

Measurement is more than counting. The count itself is likely to provide little assistance until matched against a standard. Some financial measures are expressed first as a ratio and then compared with a standard ratio. Other measures require a translation of output into unit costs—dollar or man-hour costs—and a comparison with standard unit costs.

In interpreting measurements in local government finance, the danger of relying on one or two units must, first and foremost, be recognized. We live in a business-oriented society in which the custom of relying upon the profit-per-share measurement has become ingrained. When attention shifts to local government finance, the normal business-oriented person instinctively looks for a similar, single, comprehensive unit of measurement. But, it just does not exist. To judge a general purpose local government, e.g., a city, one must work within a multiplicity of measures because the municipality provides a wide range of services without related service-charge financing. It is a nonprofit organization. Even in the limited areas where it may operate a business (such as a water plant or a gas distribution system), the guidelines may be a mixture of both profit and nonprofit objectives. The tax rate, expenditures *per capita*, total debt *per capita*, or a closing cash surplus or deficit in the budget—any one of these may be seized upon by the uninitiated; but each, within itself, is wholly inadequate as an overall measure. In local government finance one is obliged to use a whole series of measures which cannot be merged mathematically into a "composite." This is both baffling and challenging because the weight given to each is still a matter of judgment. The greater the experience, the more likely the validity of the judgment.

LEGAL LIMITATIONS AS STANDARDS

Measures which show compliance with tax rate limits and debt limits may indicate something as to the finances of a governmental unit; but, on the whole, these limits are not satisfactory standards for other than legal purposes. The unused debt margin, for example, is calculated and reported at the time a new general obligation bond issue is offered. If the proposed new issue plus debt outstanding use up 50 percent of the debt limit or, in another situation, substantially exhaust all general borrowing power, this legal fact is significant for management and may also be significant for the bond market. But, few (if any) debt limits provide a satisfactory criterion regarding how much tax-supported debt the municipality can reasonably support, or should issue.

As upper limits, tax rate and debt limits are poor financial standards—first, because they are an *en masse* and, frequently, arbitrary approach. For example, the same property tax rate limit will often apply to all school districts regardless of type (elementary or high school), size, pupil population, or wealth. If the limit is "tight" for some local units, they may be prevented from adopting sound solutions to their problems. If "loose," the limit will have little bearing on financial decisions. Even in credit rating and investment analysis, limits have a negative rather than a positive meaning. The fact that a local government has a small unused debt margin is no indication that the debt burden is too heavy. A value judgment that the debt limit is too tight, or too loose, for this class and size municipality is more determinative than a precise standard, or upper limit, written into law.

Such upper limits are also unsatisfactory standards because they suffer from obsolescence over the years. These limits were originally designed to protect the property taxpayers. As automatic, indirect checks on expenditures, and as an assurance that beyond a certain point local governments will have to look to nonproperty taxes for new local revenues, these limits are cherished safeguards. Once written into a state constitution, a city charter, or the state statute books, they become almost sacrosanct, and enjoy a long life. Limits adopted decades ago become outmoded and require modernization. This, however, is often most difficult politically.

Where there are overlapping and underlying taxing and borrowing districts, overall summations are made of the potential total debt burden and total property tax burden which assessed and nonexempt property within a given district might have to bear. These calculations are of interest to property taxpayers who live within a multi-level local government structure, but these overall summations are not standards in themselves. They have, however, influenced the derivation of three ratios which are described and evaluated in the following section which deals with the standards used in credit analysis.

Another legal standard which must be considered under financial measurement is the standard for property tax assessment. In some jurisdictions it is 100 percent of true or market value. But, this standard is generally not obeyed, nor do the courts ordinarily enforce it. An administrative measure of an acceptable level of compliance has by long usage and custom been recognized as a legal substitution. A state board of equalization (or board of equalization and assessment) is required, in some states, to determine in each taxing district the average level of assessments (i.e., the average ratio of assessed to true or market values) and to publish this ratio as an assessment equalization ratio. Unless successfully contested, the state's administratively determined ratios have the force of law and are used by those responsible for equalizing the burden of overlapping property tax rates. Where a county property tax, for example, is to be spread over a number of subordinate taxing districts—each of which has its own assessment machinery—the state-determined assessment equalization ratio (rate) becomes, for all the subordinate taxing districts, the basis for adjustments upward (or downward) to a common level of assessed to true or market value.

These ratios can also be used by analysts in comparing the property tax bases of different units of local government which are located within the same state. For example, if the analyst wants to use *per capita* or per pupil adjusted assessed valuation figures in his analysis, he will use the state equalization rates in translating assessed valuations into adjusted assessed valuations.

STANDARDS USED IN CREDIT ANALYSIS

A few standards, derived from experience, are in use by credit-rating agencies, investment bankers, and large institutional investors. They fall into three groups:

1. Those applicable to general obligation bonds
2. Those applicable to revenue bonds
3. Other

General Obligation Bonds

Six standards which may be applied to general obligation bonds are:

1. Net direct and overlapping tax-supported debt per capita. General obligation bonds are tax-supported debt in the sense that the bondholder may look to their being serviced out of taxes. It is important here to differentiate between those general obligation bonds which are, in fact, tax-supported from those which are tax-supported only in law. For example, in the city of Philadelphia as of June 30, 1973, all the outstanding debt of the city was general obligation debt; yet, a practical classification showed that 53.7 percent was self-sustaining.

Some general obligation bonds are backed by the unlimited power to tax property; others are limited tax bonds, subject to a tax rate limit. Net means the gross tax-supported debt minus any sinking fund assets for meeting the principal payments on such debt. Direct debt is debt of the city proper; overlapping debt means an estimated share of the tax-supported debt of other local governments in the multi-level structure which constitutes a burden upon property which lies within the city. Overlapping debt consists of:

   a. Districts coterminous with the unit being considered, e.g., a city which is served by a school district with a separate debt structure, but identical boundaries
   b. Districts larger than the city, but fully embracing the city, *e.g.*, a county government
   c. Districts serving a part of the city but also serving areas outside the city, e.g., a drainage district which serves only a portion of the city or a special improvement district, smaller than the city but wholly embraced by the city's limits

The effort in this ratio is to calculate the total local debt burden which must be serviced out of the economic resources lying within the city's boundaries.

Evaluation. This *per capita* ratio is not difficult to compute if other districts are coterminous or if they wholly embrace the unit under consideration. But they are very difficult to compute in other situations. They supply a relative figure for comparison with other governments; but, do not show the true capacity to support debt. Debt is paid by people but out of income, or sometimes accumulated wealth. In a residential suburb of upper-middle income, or quite wealthy, inhabitants, this debt ratio might safely be in the $1,000-$5,000 *per capita* range, whereas in a suburb where only low-income workers lived, $500 or less *per capita* might be the safe upper limit.

2. Net direct and overlapping tax-supported debt to adjusted assessed valuation. This ratio uses the same debt figures as in the first standard, but relates this estimated debt burden to the approximate or full market value of taxable property within the boundaries of the local government. Assessed valuation is adjusted upward according to the ratio of assessed to market valuation.

Evaluation. Obtaining a reliable figure for this ratio is more difficult than for the first. The percentage of market value at which property *on the average* is being assessed is more often than not based on informed judgment. In a few states, e.g., New York, a state board publishes, by taxing districts, equalization rates which are derived from sample real estate transactions.

If reasonably accurate, this measure may be superior to a *per capita* ratio because the debt burden is being related directly to the most important taxable base within the community. For a majority of local governments, the property tax is still the most important tax, supplying 30 percent or more of total revenues. Yet, it must be recognized that this ratio is losing some of its earlier significance as more and more reliance is placed on other revenues. In such situations, this ratio must be supplemented by a measure of the elasticity of nonproperty tax revenues.

3. Percentage of current property tax delinquency. To arrive at this ratio, which shows the effectiveness of current property tax collections, the property tax delinquency at the fiscal year's end is related to the total levy of that year.

To get the cumulative delinquency, one would have to add to current delinquencies all past unpaid taxes with outstanding interest and penalties. The total could be expressed as a percentage of an average levy over a three- to five-year period, or of the most recent levy.

Evaluation. The ratio would be better stated as a range, e.g., three to five percent. In prosperous times, if year-end delinquency is higher than three or five percent, a warning flag is up for many bond analysts. Questions may be raised as to whether or not enforcement may be lax, or the date established for the sale of tax liens as well as other features of the property tax collection law may require modernization.

This ratio (in common with ratio #2) has a reduced significance in a governmental unit which has moved to a substantial reliance on nonproperty tax revenues. Moreover, the time relationship of the deadline for payment of taxes constitutes an important variable. Thus, a governmental unit whose deadline occurs on the final day of the fiscal year is at an obvious disadvantage vis-a-vis one whose deadline falls six or eight months before the end of the fiscal year.

4. Percentage of debt service on tax-supported debt to total revenues, or, as a segment of the total operating budget. Standard (upper limit): 25 percent.

Current debt service means payments of both interest and principal and may properly include any debt service reserve fund requirements. If the bonds are sinking fund bonds, payments into, rather than payments out of, the sinking fund (retirement fund) are treated as part of debt service (i.e., current amortization payments as opposed to retirement payments). Some analysts relate the annual debt service to the total operating budget; others, to total revenues since the budget may be distorted by the inclusion of proceeds from the sale of bonds or by short-term borrowing receipts. Still other analysts supplement the above calculation by a second, hypothetically constructed one. To current annual interest requirements is added five percent of all general bonded debt outstanding. The result is the debt burden that would fall on current revenues, if the debt were being retired orderly and regularly over a 20-year period. This added calculation corrects a distorted result (i.e., a low percentage) which would be arrived at under the regular computation provided debt retirement was being deferred completely for several years or, in the judgment of the bond analyst, was spread over too long a period.

Evaluation. The debt service ratio is the best of the first four measures for two reasons: (1) the true debt burden is the weight of the debt service upon the current revenue stream, and (2) this ratio is not tied to the property tax.

This is not to say that the applications of this ratio, nor the ratio itself, are free from criticism. It is usually applied to an individual governmental unit; whereas, in fact, this calculation should be supplemented by an overall calculation which expresses the debt service of all the local governments in the multi-level structure as a percentage of the total revenues of these local governments. The reason is that, if debt service—a contractual overhead cost—creates a budgetary crisis in one local government, the revenue action which it takes to remedy the situation will usually affect the unit under analysis along with others in the layer-cake structure. The overall approach should not be restricted to the first two ratios. Yet, the debt service to revenue ratio can be very misleading when revenue consists, in large part, of grants-in-aid or when large portions of the debt service relate to capital intensive operations.

In addition, the debt service ratio related only to the current year does not supply a broad enough perspective. The debt service schedule may be very irregular with peaks and valleys of retirement payment and may, therefore, show high or low ratios for the particular year studied. It would be safer to compute this ratio based on averages for the past three years plus the current year, and on estimates for the next three to five years. The calculations for the future provide an added perspective.

It is also recommended that the ratio be calculated using actual, rather than budget, figures. The latter present two difficulties. Because budgets cut across fund lines, it is often difficult, from published financial reports containing fund budgetary statements, to make certain that one has arrived at the total budget figure. Excessive reliance on general fund statements is a common mistake. In the second place, local governments include, within the receipts side of the budget, the proceeds of bond issues and short-term loans and, on the outgo side, all capital outlays from bond proceeds and amounts for the repayment of bank loans. It is safer and easier to relate debt service to total revenue figures.

5. Average life of tax-supported debt outstanding. Standard: 10½ to 15 years. This ratio may be expressed in years or as the percentage which annual retirement and/or amortization represents of the total debt outstanding (e.g., 7.14 percent instead of 14 years). Analysts who use this measure reason that credit is a revolving power; the more rapidly a local government retires its debt, the stronger its position in returning to the market again for new capital requirements. A 10½-year average life is considered satisfactory; a 20- to 30-year average is excessive, given the great demand for capital borrowings today. Fifteen years is a safe upper limit.

Evaluation. This fifth ratio is not widely used by analysts; but, because of the heavy demand in most governmental units for vast new improvements, wider application may be justified. If new debt is to be incurred rapidly, it is important that old debt be retired rapidly, unless the government began its rapid debt growth with a low level of debt outstanding. This ratio is forward-looking and expectations in the future are highly pertinent to credit analysis.

However, when term bonds with sinking funds are used, there is a significant difference in the meaning of average life as contrasted to the average life of serial bonds. One must take into account the sinking fund assets and future earnings thereupon in order to secure a comparable statement regarding serial and term debt.

6. Shape of the debt service curve. An effective measure is a graphic presentation of the annual debt service schedule, calculated through the final retirement date of all general debt currently outstanding. Many hold that the curve should be sharply downward if debt is to be retired rapidly and if room for servicing new debt is to be left in future budgets. This position has merit when dealing with metropolitan governmental units; however, for highly specialized units, e.g., an airport authority, there may be sound arguments for level debt servce over a period of years. A level debt service obviously means that each new borrowing raises the level of the burden rather than simply replacing (in whole or in part) the debt just retired.

Evaluation. This ratio is also forward-looking. Although it does not show the weight of the debt service burden, it projects into the future the pattern within which new debt service must be planned. It will also "red flag" peak years when debt service will create special problems. Although not usually done, this graphic measure should be supplemented by a composite, overall debt service schedule for all the underlying and overlapping local governments in the community.

On the whole, investment analysts have progressed by refining the old ratios in rating general obligation bonds:
   a. Gross debt has been superseded by net debt
   b. Tax-supported debt has been substituted for total debt
   c. In the fourth ratio, revenue figures are replacing budget figures
   d. There is a tendency to use several ratios rather than place reliance upon any single one
   e. And most importantly, overall debt (direct debt plus overlapping debt) is replacing the use of direct debt only

Revenue Bonds

The standards used in rating revenue bonds are related to the measure of profits or receipts against debt service requirements, or the excess of the depreciated value of the capital plant over the amount of bonded debt outstanding.

1. Debt service coverage. This measure is usually expressed as the ratio of annual net profits, net operating revenues, or net receipts (if from dedicated taxes) to the total annual debt service; e.g., 2 to 1 or 1.5 to 1. The net operating revenues or net profits available for debt service are calculated by taking the gross revenue of a revenue-producing enterprise, minus operating expenses (which exclude interest but include the sum authorized under the bond indenture or resolution to be set aside for repairs and maintenance). If the revenue bond is supported by some dedicated or earmarked tax (or nontax revenue), net receipts are derived by deducting refunds from gross receipts.

A coverage ratio might best be expressed within a range because the coverage will vary according to a number of factors:
   a. The financing may be for a new facility or enterprise with no record of earnings. Or, the revenue bonds may be for an enterprise which has already demonstrated its earning power and should now be modernized or expanded. When no earnings record is available, reliance must be placed upon engineering estimates of usage and earnings, rendering the analysis speculative, because engineering estimates sometimes turn out to be overly optimistic.
   b. The degree of essentiality of the public facility has an important bearing upon the coverage believed necessary. Generally, the higher the essentiality, the lower the coverage ratio.

   c. Stability of the debt service coverage is also important. Experience
      over a three-to five-year period provides a sounder basis for judgment
      than calculation from the latest year's figures.
   d. The general market reputation of a type of revenue bond, based on
      past investment experience, may classify it as speculative. This usually
      means a higher coverage requirement. The bonds of some transit au-
      thorities, airports, auditoriums, stadiums, and port facilities may fall
      into this category.
   e. The extent to which one, two, or three years of debt service have
      been accumulated in reserves should be determined. A reserve cushion
      tends to lower the coverage ratio.
   f. The issuer may also influence the coverage deemed necessary. A revenue
      bond issued by a well-known municipality will, other things being
      equal, require a smaller coverage than one by a local authority created
      for the purpose of building and operating a similar facility.
   g. If the so-called revenue bond is double-barrelled, i.e., backed addi-
      tionally by the full faith and credit of a taxing body, the required
      coverage will be lower.

   Evaluation. Coverage ratio analysis in the revenue bond field can be a
dangerous soporific. A prudent analyst will compute the ratio as a first approach
and then go forward with a thorough analysis of all aspects of the facility.
Market analysis, economic analysis, accounting, engineering, and legal requirement may have to be drawn upon in weighing the factors which might affect
prompt payment of all debt service requirements. The existence of competitive
facilities, elasticity of demand for the priced services, the predicted reaction of
revenue sources to war conditions and to declines in economic conditions, the
growth potential of the area served—these are but some of the factors.
   It is probably dangerous for writers to suggest standard coverage ratios.
Even though they are hedged in terms of ranges and the proviso, "other things
being equal," they may be taken literally by some and applied without
qualification.
   2. Excess of depreciated value of capital plant over debt. There is a high ratio
of capital plant to total initial bonded investment in municipally owned utilities,
airports, and a few other revenue-producing enterprises. With the exception of
an initial capital contribution by the city, the total capital plant investment is
almost always financed by bonded debt. Equity is a stock-ownership concept;
but a few analysts have extended it to revenue bonds; and defined it as the excess
of depreciated value of capital plant over the bonded debt outstanding. Since
municipally owned utilities are tax-exempt, it frequently happens that debt is
retired much more rapidly than the actual depreciation of plant, with the result
that the remaining revenue bondholders find themselves secured by the earnings
of a capital plant valued currently at perhaps from 60 to 40 percent of capital
liabilities. This they consider as "aging" of the bond security. Since the mortgage
provision in municipal revenue bonds is not common, this ratio seems useful only
as an index that the municipal utility has proved itself a successful, self-liquidating
venture. In effect, it is a shorthand approach which can be arrived at in other
ways.

Other Considerations

Finally, two standards which may be used in credit analysis fall into a general grouping which may be designated as "other." These are the budget balancing concept and the use of management ratios.

1. A balanced budget. Budget balancing does not have the same meaning at the local government level as it has at the federal level. The federal government, because of its vast taxing powers, is expected to pay for all of its capital expenditures out of current revenue (or increases in the national debt). Local governments, with more restricted revenue powers, by convention, are not expected to pay for all of their capital outlays out of current revenues. Balancing, however, requires that current revenues be sufficient to meet current operating expenses (including interest) plus debt retirement and/or amortization. To some, it also includes a five to ten percent contribution out of current revenues for capital improvements. (Such a down payment may be required by statute.)

2. Management ratios. Some bond analysts draw upon management ratios—especially the overall property tax rate, stability of major revenue sources, capital deficiency ratios, and those which are part of "Debt Management."

Finance administrators, of necessity, use legal limitations and market standards as management benchmarks. In all areas of local government finance, state laws must be obeyed and, when bond issues are planned and sold, market conventions must be observed and investor values considered. Progressive management, however, has gone beyond these externally imposed standards. A wide range of ratios have grown out of managerial experience. Some are useful in the planning and programming stages; others, during program execution; and still others, for reevaluation before the next administrative cycle begins.

These ratios are rules-of-thumb, not precise scientific measures; yet, they are useful when used critically. Most of these may be catalogued and grouped according to the area of financial activity in which they are being used. No one financial manager will use all of them, nor will he, because of his own experience, agree as to the utility or validity of some.

Management literature has made much of the concept of "management by exception" or "management by significant variances." It has long been recognized that an experienced manager will conserve his time and energy by focusing upon those areas and problems where variances indicate that developments require his attention. Not all variances, however, which signify trouble spots arise from quantitative standards. Calendars, project construction schedules, project specifications, ethical codes, personnel rules, procedural standards, etc. perform the same benchmark function in program management.

The Critical Usage of Ratios and Standards

Ratios and standard measures must be applied with caution. Analysis or management by slide rule is dangerous. A particular measure must be applied in an atmosphere of healthy skepticism. It may be wise to explore its limitations as well as to draw on its strengths. Also, alternative measurement tools should not be overlooked; another ratio, or a combination of two or more ratios, may be more meaningful than the one initially chosen. It should further be emphasized that:

1. Market standards on municipal debt are flexible. They are generally stated on the conservative side since this is the safer procedure and, when generalized, are often put at a level more applicable to the smaller or medium-sized governmental units than to the larger ones. The latter must seek to determine the level at which the standards are applied to them by a majority of investment analysts.

2. Legal limitations should not be confused with standards of good practice. For example, debt limits in New York State for city governments are too restrictive for the largest cities, which are not permitted to have independent city school districts with separate borrowing power, and too liberal for most of the remaining cities.

3. As a rule-of-thumb, benchmarks are but the beginning of an analysis—a rough starting point and no more.

4. The precise meaning of each measure and the rationale behind each require re-examination. It is quite clear in some cases that those who devised the standard never intended it to be used for other than a special purpose, and under specific circumstances.

5. In general, there is more agreement by management on the validity of the ratio approach than there is on the precise standard in each case against which the computed ratio is applied. Some standards must necessarily be shown as a range because experience varies for different sizes and different types of local government.

NEEDS AND THE CRITERION OF EFFICIENCY

Needs, requirements, and efficiency are terms which frequently arise in budget literature. Needs, and the measurement of needs or requirements, are part of the terminology used in the older approach to budgetary decision making. Unfortunately, this normative approach, which begins with standards of what the city ought to have and proceeds to compute the deficiencies within individual functions and programs, still has much support. In theory, but only partly in practice, this older approach has been superseded by Herbert Simon's "criterion of efficiency."[1]

As applied in the budgetary process, the criterion of efficiency is the key to a rational approach in establishing budgetary requirements (appropriations). Usually, application of this criterion requires four fundamental steps:

1. Delineation in operational terms of program objectives which, if rational, will be consistent with the local government's overall goals.

2. A tentative determination of the level of goal attainment or level of program adequacy for each program. Because of the relative scarcity

---

[1] Simon, Herbert A., *Administrative Behavior*, (New York: The Macmillan Company, 1957), 2nd. ed. Chapter 9, pp. 172-197.

of resources, not all program objectives can be met in full; some portion of programs must be postponed and the majority pared (to varying degrees) in order to bring total expenditures within the available resources. This means that a compromise level of attainment must be determined for most programs. Short of Utopia, attainment of objectives is always a matter of degree. The central budget staff and top management must decide the tentative amounts to be allocated to each program. When these decisions have been reached, notifications of tentative dollar allocations can go to department heads and to program supervisors.

3. The tentative amount allocated to each program is next tested by application of the criterion of efficiency. This process of measurement of efficiency is a probing, predictive process which attempts to answer such questions as:

   a. Is it possible to attain the compromise level of program adequacy, given the tentative allocation of resources?
   b. Which of the feasible alternative approaches to the utilization of resources will optimize results?

   If there is a single program objective, the program director begins to make a series of estimates regarding different ways to apply the alternative allocation of funds. The goal is to maximize anticipated results; given the limited resources.

   Under even the best alternative, it may be found that a small addition to funds will be required if the compromise level is to be reached. The program director will also be prepared to report to his superiors the program level which he can attain under the tentative allocations. If the goals are multiple, the problem is more complex. One approach is to break the program into sub-programs and to develop hypothetical allocations for each.

4. The process of efficiency measurement carried out by the program directors at the program level will produce refinements which will assist the central budget staff and the final decision-makers in making adjustments in the levels of program adequacy and in the allocation of funds before finalization of the budget proposals.

This last go-round on levels of adequacy and final budget figures may, of course, not be decided wholly by the efficiency approach to needs. What is posited here is the ideal contribution to the decision-making process by the several operational levels; rationality throughout; and basic acceptance of the wisdom of abiding by the criterion of efficiency. Actually, some department heads and other agency heads may not fully accept the efficiency approach and, therefore, introduce pressures and other power plays which make budget formulation something less than a rational process.

Setting Program Objectives

The starting point in the whole efficiency approach is, as stated above, a delineation of program objectives. The procedure begins with overall goals (which do not necessarily change each year) and moves from this broad frame-work to the more precise objectives of individual programs. Programs must be made as explicit and as definitive as possible; translated into operational terms; and, wherever possible, stated so that the measurement of results can be quantita-tive. The latter is not always possible, especially when services resulting from expenditures are intangible and indirect. Often, it is essential to have (and to define) immediate, intermediate, and ultimate goals. The justification for ex-penditure estimates is their contribution to the attainment of program goals. The ends to be achieved, the values to be maximized—these must be clarified and sharply delineated, if they are to serve as guidelines. Rationality is compromised, of course, to the extent that conflicts exist among program objectives and are allowed to persist.

Level of Program Adequacy

Determining the level of program adequacy is a useful concept. For a particular program, it is expressed as a percentage of the optimum which would have been programmed to meet full program objectives but for scarce resources and the subsequent assignment of priorities among programs competing for such resources. If, at the execution stage, efficient performance still results in a less than satisfactory level of governmental services, the fault lies in the level of adequacy finally programmed and authorized. If appropriations, for example, indicate a 75 percent level of program adequacy and this level is attained, efficiency has been achieved. At the programming and legislative authorization stages, the focus is on both the level of program adequacy and on anticipated efficiency; but, at the execution stage, the focus is primarily on efficiency.

Level of adequacy is a relative term; in the foregoing, it is a value judgment expressed as a percentage of the optimum requirements needed to carry out a program's full objectives. Normally, it is an agreed upon lower level of goal attainment; it is a measure of compromise—a compromise dictated by scarce resources and a system of priorities. It results from an answer to a question as to how much the local government can afford to program for this purpose—but not the only answer.

Budget requests are almost always in excess of available resources. Top management and central budget staff must take the generalist approach, looking at all programs and placing their requests in perspective. With changing times and conditions, program emphases shift. The administrative and budget staffs make many tentative decisions as to what new emphases shall be undertaken, the extent to which established programs should be de-emphasized, and the places where reductions from the prior year's level and from request levels can reasonably be made. A tentative allocation of resources to each program is a process of establishing priorities and of making value judgments as to relative deficiencies in program levels which the local government can live with. From experience, judgments must be made as to the level of goal attainment which can be expected in a particular program, if a certain sum is allocated.

Tentative levels of program adequacy are subject to adjustment during the next stage within the efficiency approach; i.e., after the criterion of efficiency has been applied in each program. Sometimes, the program supervisor can effectively show that the tentative allocation will not produce the level of attainment which is anticipated by top management, or that such a level would produce results which the central budget staff has overlooked. At this stage come a whole series of compromises—decisions as to the shifting of funds from one program to another in the final allocation of funds—and new acceptances as to the results anticipated from the respective levels of goal attainment. The levels of adequacy finally programmed, and usually authorized, are adjusted levels. The whole process has resulted in compromises, adjustments, and settlement for something less than the ideal. "Level of program adequacy" is a better term than "adequacy" because the latter suggests an absolute, rather than a relative, satisfaction with the goal attainment desired.

Measurement of Efficiency

Using the efficiency approach to arrive at program requirements, the third step is a direct application of the criterion of efficiency. Measurement at the budget formulation stage is predictive, a process of estimating what input (or combination of inputs) is required to obtain a certain result or results (i.e., output or combinations of outputs). With a level of goal attainment (adequacy) tentatively set for each program, and with a tentative budget figure allocated for the purpose, the program supervisor should estimate the results which could be obtained by different ways of using the tentative resources.[2] This process should resolve quantitatively several questions:

1. By what combination of inputs could the tentative level of program adequacy be reached, given the tentative allocation of budget funds?
2. If the budget figures are inadequate for the tentative level of program adequacy, how much more, in resources, would be needed to attain this level?
3. If no combination of inputs within the budget figure would produce the tentative level, what estimated level could be attained with the budget allocated?
4. If a combination of inputs can be found which would (on an estimated basis) permit an accomplishment in excess of the level tentatively established, how much of the tentative allocation of budget resources could be reallocated for some other program?

The terms "output," "performance," "results," "achievement," and "accomplishment" are being used here interchangeably. If a program is made up of a number of subprograms, the level of program adequacy will normally require a combination of results or outputs. Solutions to the problem of devising measurable units of output usually require a thorough knowledge of the activities within each program and subprogram and technical statistical talent. Output is sometimes in the form of physical products; but, more often, governmental

---

[2] If program objectives can be more sharply delineated than formerly, the program supervisor should have a better chance of improving his predictive (estimating) ability. At least, a sharper delineation of goals—immediate, intermediate, and ultimate—may spark his imagination in developing alternative approaches to achieving objectives.

operations provide services—some tangible and others intangible. Services are often difficult to measure in a meaningful way. But this is a challenging area and both direct and indirect quantitative measures have been devised.[3] If program goals are identified by stages—immediate, intermediate, and ultimate—measurement is more feasible. For example, a new recreation program for teenagers may involve partial conversion into tennis courts of a neglected park area. The immediate program goal is efficient construction. Standard costs for a certain type tennis court (with which the recreation department has had experience) fix the target. After construction is completed, the intermediate goal (or the new immediate goal) would probably be maximum usage by the teenage clientele of the courts during daylight hours within the seasonable months.

All operating costs (supervision, instruction, maintenance and repair, etc.) can be related to usage figures. Attainment of the ultimate goal (perhaps reduction of juvenile delinquency through this and other approaches) may, however, defy (or seem to defy) estimation and actual measurement. Despite this, discouragement with measuring this final end-product should not provoke condemnation of the criterion of efficiency and its role in budget-making. In a succeeding section measurements beyond efficiency are considered in order to appraise, in the final analysis, and over time, the validity of an undertaking such as building tennis courts and operating them, given the ultimate goal of their service contribution to the reduction of juvenile delinquency. This ultimate value test is most important for the policy-makers. Nonetheless, efficiency in attaining the first two end-products—construction of physical units and management by the recreation department so as to continue to attract the clientele, as planned, and within cost limits—are both important to management because of its responsibility to make the most of the dollars once the policy-makers have authorized a program. Any difficulties in measuring the ultimate value of the program should not detract from the desirability and usefulness of efficiency measures at the first two stages.

Input is normally measured in terms of dollars (cost of input) or man-hours of effort. Alternative uses of resources may involve different combinations of input labor (technical and nontechnical), utilization at one time or at successive stages, or different combinations of labor, materials, and equipment.

The criterion of efficiency requires: (1) a maximization of output with a given input and (2) minimization of input in the attainment of a given output, provided that labor as one input factor is not exploited. This is to say that the means cannot be treated as neutral.

Implicit in this discussion of optimization of *anticipated* results through alternative uses of tentatively allocated resources are two related types of efficiency: technical and economic. Technical efficiency is an engineering concept; it means maximizing output from the input of resources available. Economic efficiency includes technical efficiency and is achieved by the choice and employment of an optimum combination of inputs (given scarce resources) in attaining an output level or by the achievement of an optimum combination of outputs from the

---

[3] Cf. Takasaki, Richard S., "Measuring Efficiency In Government," *Municipal Finance*, May 1962, Vol. 34, No. 4, pp. 145-149.

utilization of scarce resources, however utilized. Optimum here means the best possible economic or value combination from the choices open. At the budget formulation or decision-making stage, the focus (and this has to be stressed) is upon predictive technical or economic efficiency and not on actual achievement which is measurable only at a later stage.

At the budget formulation stage, the predictive/estimation process is undertaken by: (1) program supervisors; (2) department heads; and (3) the central budget staff and top management.

If budget requests originate without the benefit of a tentative allocation of resources, the process begins with the program supervisor and is continued at successive levels. The order of the process is reversed if the central budget staff initiates the budget process by tentative allocations to programs. In some jurisdictions, the estimates come up the hierarchical scale and, after all estimates are in, and total resources are estimated, the program supervisors are asked to apply the criterion of efficiency all over again. This does not mean that all their first efforts were wasted. They will have acquired data for defending alternative levels of program adequacy, and completed much of the background work for a further examination of other approaches, given a lower level of program adequacy and of resources tentatively allocated.

Admittedly, application of the criterion of efficiency has been described in model terms. Often the budget is constructed incrementally from the "bottom up" without benefit of clear, overall objectives. If the process begins with top management, the spelling out of goals and levels of program adequacy may fall short of setting a proper value framework for program supervisors. In addition, other authors have stressed ways in which practice does not match the Simon model. Simon visualized, within democratic institutions, a division of labor between the legislative body and the administration in setting objectives and values. This is often imperfectly attained.[4] Jesse Burkhead also warns against expecting too much from the application of the criterion of efficiency within the public budgeting process.[5] Still, the model sets sights for improved delineation of program objectives and for continued efforts to measure some service outputs which have defied measurement to date.

Generalist vs. Specialist Approach

The efficiency approach is also referred to by some as the "generalist" approach. This is an appropriate secondary designation because it emphasizes the role of overall management: the recognition of scarce resources; the use of broad objectives as a starting point; translation of these into program goals; deciding what can be deferred, what is urgent, and what must be maintained at a steady level; establishment, on the basis of such decisions of reasonable levels of goal attainment, program by program; and, finally, a process of adjustment after each program supervisor has had an opportunity to apply the criteria of efficiency,

---

[4] See W. H. Brown Jr., and C. E. Gilbert, *Planning Municipal Investment: A Case Study of Philadelphia*, (Philadelphia: University of Pennsylvania Press, 1961), p. 205.

[5] Burkhead, Jesse, *Government Budgeting*, (New York: John Wiley and Sons, Inc., 1956). p. 37.

to defend retention of his tentative level, or to justify a markup of either funds or of the level of program adequacy.

Under this approach needs and requirements are relatives, not absolutes. Needs are conditioned by available resources. This approach fosters quantitative data which supply a firmer base for estimation than prior budget levels. It is an overall, but not an arbitrary, across-the-board approach. Rather, it proceeds by steps which involve successive levels. At the top, tentative value-judgment priorities are made, but there is feedback from operating levels. The final recommended utilization of resources is the result of a give-and-take process. The total goal is maximization of the utility of a wide variety of municipal services, given a relative scarcity of resources.

This approach takes into account the government's own special circumstances, is flexible, and is not bound to an outside set of standards. Therefore, it can produce answers in new areas where there are no recognized standards.

The specialist approach is older than the efficiency or generalist approach. It assumes that needs or requirements can be objectively measured. Professional associations—such as the American Public Health Association, the National Recreation Association, the American Library Association, the National Board of Fire Underwriters, etc.—have come forward with standards to be used in such measurements. However, we must consider them as ideal objectives which these special groups deem appropriate. Generally, they do not constitute satisfactory standards for measuring current objectives or performance in given local situations. Standards for operating personnel and the level of current services as well as for capital facilities and equipment have often been set. The functional/program standards are normatives or "what ought to be." The gaps between these standards and what the local government has already attained constitute the deficiencies or needs. Therefore, under such a system, the starting point is not the relative scarcity of resources. Rather, it is someone's judgment of the ideal. Another major difficulty is that each functional area has its own bias. For example, the education experts want schools stressed; consequently their standards are set high. The professional association in the recreation field naturally sees recreation facilities as a very high priority. The National Board of Fire Underwriters wants a fire department equipped to cope with the biggest of conflagrations. It would be expecting too much of a professional, functional association to view its standards within the broad perspective of all service areas.

Although this is essentially an external, model approach, decision-makers (e.g., the city planners) usually temper these with knowledge of the special circumstances of their particular community. This approach becomes more meaningful when this tempering is done well; but, basically, it is less flexible than the generalist approach. Other shortcomings of this approach can be summarized as follows:

1. The standards are on a functional basis. Some, but not all, can be translated onto a program basis.
2. The standards in each functional area disregard the relative claims of other functions. Given relative scarcity of resources, this approach supplies no methodology for adjusting initial value-judgment priorities to levels of program adequacy.

3. This approach is more useful for a long-term master plan and for long-term budgeting than for making decisions regarding the current operating budget because the standards are often at levels toward which the municipality is moving over a period of time.

The specialist approach takes two other forms which should be differentiated from the emphasis upon professional, functional standards. First, street and highway engineers have devised a system of "sufficiency ratings" for individual streets and highways which are based on traffic flow studies, accident rates, and case studies of traffic bottlenecks. Another approach to street and highway requirements is based on cost-benefit calculations. Both are specialist approaches but rest on careful engineering research of the special circumstances.

Secondly, rating scales have been devised by consultants who are experts in particular functional areas. These consultants survey the needs and make recommendations for the improvement of a department responsible for the function. Surveys of police organizations, for example, often use rating scales with a maximum number of points. This form of the specialist approach is quite similar to the methods of some of the professional, functional associations. The distinction is that most of the consultants' scales are not published and have not achieved the standing of those promulgated by professional associations.

Combinations of the efficiency approach and the specialist approach are found in practice. The two are not completely incompatible and can be complementary. Unfortunately, in some municipalities, cutbacks in budget requests, at times, degenerate into power struggles. Misuse of the functional standards may then become a part of such struggles which reduce rationality within the budget-making process. The loyalty and dedication of the program supervisor to a single program and of the department head to the functional department and its group programs may produce narrow protagonists. Sometimes, the top administrator and the local legislative body, given the controversial atmosphere, cannot ignore these standards because citizen pressure groups—with high value preferences for libraries, schools, etc.—have been organized in support of particular requests.

When a longer-range view is taken, these functional standards, rating scales, and other methods of the specialist approach no doubt contain, on balance, a net positive social value. Even though some are a bit utopian, they give a push toward, and supply constant support for, a higher standard of public services which many an affluent community can afford. The specialists (e.g., the state department of education, parent-teachers associations, etc.) will often have an influence, direct or indirect, in establishing the level of program adequacy, an important step in the generalist approach. The central budget staff and top management are often undoubtedly influenced, consciously or unconsciously, by the professional standards. In any given budget-making period, available resources are scarce for all practical budgetary purposes, but pressures for individual program expeditures can, over time (and sometimes within a relatively short time), raise the level of resources available. Scarcity is a relative and not an absolute term. That resources can only be levied, or raised, at a certain level is itself a value judgment, and one often dictated by those who, like the functional standard-makers, have a special bias of their own. External pressure which challenges the scarcity judgment may well introduce a healthy counteracting force.

Measurement Beyond Efficiency

If the criterion of efficiency is defined to include the effects, or consequences, of an expenditure input which are both indirect and remote in time from such input and which require a different measurement methodology, a severe strain has been placed upon the concept. In the authors' view, there is merit in not overloading one concept, particularly if it results in confusion where there should be clarity. For this reason, the measurement of such effects, or consequences, should be designated as "measurements beyond efficiency."

There are, in fact, three differences which, in combination, appear to justify the segregation of effects, or consequences, from the criterion of efficiency, and place their measurement within another supplementary, but separate, category:

1. Differences as to what is being measured
2. Differences in the methodology of measurement
3. Differences in the uses to which the measurements can be put

1. Differences as to what is being measured. Measurements of efficiency in achieving a goal (whether immediate, intermediate, or ultimate) are often terminal — this measurement embraces all; there are no left-overs. This, for example, is the case with measurement of the unit cost of preparing tax bills and comparison with a standard. To attempt to trace the effects, or consequences, of this efficiency would have little meaning. Such, however, is not always the case. Beyond the performance or achievement measured, there may be effects which have indirect and more remote, but nonetheless significant, consequences. These are often related to an ultimate goal. Measurement of these left-overs, against an ultimate goal are termed "measurements beyond efficiency." Take, for example, expenditures in order to prevent school dropouts. A program may, in fact, keep potential dropouts in school and stimulate some of them sufficiently to graduate with a vocational skill. Measurements of efficiency against these immediate and intermediate goals relate the input costs against an output of definite social value—more schooling for some and graduation for others who are better prepared for the labor market. But, beyond this, lies an ultimate goal— that this vocational training enable the graduate to find a permanent niche in the labor force as a skilled workman. Whether his preparation was sufficient in depth and in a skill which has marketable value (at least over a predictable future), only time will tell. The program expenditures may have met the early criterion of efficiency well; but, after five years, the more remote effects of the program costs may be so poor as to require a complete re-examination of the program's direction (the types of skills taught) and its depth (the quality and length of instruction).

Indirectness, remoteness in time, and relation to a goal not already included under an efficiency measurement are the differences which are being measured. Indirectness standing alone is not decisive. One cannot say that results equal direct benefits and effects equal indirect benefits. Also, such qualified terms as "ultimate effects," "the more remote effects," and "final consequences or effects" should be avoided because effects and consequences, without qualifying adjectives, already include remoteness and the ultimate.

2. *Differences in the methodology of measurement.* Upon reflection, it should be clear from the school dropout illustration, given above, that the more remote and indirect effects require different measurement techniques. The results are continued attendance in school and, for some, graduation; a much more difficult effect now has to be measured. Case studies of a suitable sample of graduates would be required to determine effects after five years. Multiple causation may have to be analyzed and segmented before it can be concluded that the course content and quality of instruction of the vocational school were important causative factors. For the future policy direction of the vocational program, the precise isolation and matching of causes and effects is most important. Fundamental decisions rest on these measurements, i.e., the kinds of skills to be taught, the length and caliber of the instruction, and the methods for ensuring that students have the necessary aptitudes for, and adequate interest in, the skills which they choose.

3. *Differences in the use to which measurement can be put.* Operationally, the results of efficiency measurements are often reported monthly. Therefore, they serve an operational control and a current function. By contrast, measurements beyond efficiency are usually so remote in time that they are of little or no use for operational control purposes. Their contribution is to long-run policy-making. They constitute an overall (as opposed to an operational) type of control in that they help to fix directions and to choose major approaches.

For establishing priorities among programs and defending budget requests, measurements beyond efficiency are often satisfactory because they relate to ultimate policy goals. They are, however, less useful for predictive purposes than are efficiency measurements because they are less precise and less repetitive. Efficiency measures which are done again and again often permit predictions close to the bull's eye. Measures beyond efficiency may, at times, indicate that "if you shoot in that direction you will at least hit the target somewhere." Again, they may only provide an indication of which weapons have the power to strike within range of the target.

Discarded Terminology

In the authors' view, more progress can be made in measuring the finance and service activities of local government if we carefully define terminology and discard certain terms which make precision in measurement more difficult. Harmless, but superfluous, terms add to confusion.

It has become customary in writing of local government finance to speak of estimating needs and of the measurement of needs. The belief is rather widespread that needs can be objectively measured. Actually, need is not an absolute but a relative term derived from relating program objectives to the resources available. As a community's resources rise, its standard of public living tends to rise. In many contexts, the term also has a normative meaning, i.e., the resources which a program or organizational unit "ought to have." Because it is difficult to apply quantitative measurement to a normative, the concept of "measurement of needs" and the word, "needs," should be discarded and "level of program adequacy" should be substituted for "program needs." We can then speak of determining the level of program adequacy. Budgetary appropriations, or requirements, then result from an interrelation of program objectives and available resources. The criterion of efficiency tests the validity of the dollar figure allocated to achieve the level of program adequacy.

The term "demands" for program services can also be avoided. "Budgetary requests" rather than "expenditure demands" seems preferable. Demands suggest that pressure groups have been at work and that the legislative body has summated the figures as a demand schedule and arrived at the outgo side of the budget. "Demands," as an economic term, fits the market place; but, in the public sector, the budgetary process performs the function which, in the private sector, is served by the market adjustment of supply and demand. The same objection could be interposed to the use of "effective demand." After citizens have voted affirmatively for a bond issue, an effective demand for the capital improvement to be financed has arisen. Citizens in other ways translate their wishes into an effective mandate. Nonetheless, the budget terms "appropriations" and "expenditure authorizations" seem more appropriate in public budgeting than market place terms. Serious confusion could result from an attempt to carry over into the public sector a term heavily laden with special meaning in the private sector.

"Effectiveness" and the concept of "measurement of effectiveness" are terms which should be discarded because they detract from a clear understanding of the goal of efficiency. "Effectiveness" has sometimes been used to mean the attainment of a high level of performance regardless of the cost involved, whereas efficiency means achieving the maximum output for a given dollar input. Thus, management could be efficient without being effective (because of limited resources), and could be effective without being efficient (because achievement, although at a high level, was costly). This is a possible comparison but we think it an unfortunate one. "Regardless of the cost involved" introduces a highly artificial condition into municipal management. Financial resources are almost always scarce relative to the services to be performed. The science of management is not being advanced by measuring performance or results without counting the costs. Efficiency is the concept to be stressed, not performance regardless of costs. It is better to begin with the assumption of scarce resources and to consider effectiveness and efficiency as synonymous. As a synonymous term (which may also be misleading because some attach to it a different meaning), it would best be dropped from management terminology on both counts.

"Adequacy of results" is another term we have rejected, while attempting to establish the usefulness of the concept of "level of program adequacy." It has been stressed earlier that, in the interest of clarity, the focus should be on level of adequacy at the programming and authorization stages, but upon efficiency at the execution stage. To introduce another measure, "adequacy of results," at the execution stage is confusing. To conclude that management has been efficient, but that results are inadequate, is to raise a question for which no standard has been set, and which is no longer relevant at this stage. If management has been efficient in achieving the level of program adequacy adopted, no more can be asked. To try to make adequacy of results an absolute measure of accomplishment perpetuates the same mistake as introducing the word, "effectiveness," as meaning accomplishment regardless of the cost involved.

"Adequacy of program" is also rejected because the expression connotes an absolute. "Level of program adequacy," on the other hand, connotes a relative. The addition of the word, "level," makes the significant difference.

The terms "output," "performance," "accomplishment," "benefits," and "results" appear frequently and interchangeably in the literature and appear to be widely accepted as synonymous. The authors recommend that all be retained because, at times, they permit nice shades of meaning to be made. Differences in the product of government or the need for more precise matching of the input and output justify the multiplicity of terms to cover output. Some government services are tangible, other intangible; some are directly measurable, and others measurable only indirectly. When "costs" are the input, the term, "benefits," is customarily used on the output side.

Results may be tangible or intangible, and direct or indirect, and such qualifications are appropriate. The use of the term, "ultimate results," however, is not recommended since this could easily be confused with "effects" or "consequences." It should be clear from the measurement whether or not it is terminal.

It is to be underscored, however, that the words "effects" and "consequences" be segregated from the above and reserved for measurement beyond efficiency. No single criterion is sufficient to separate these two terms from "output," "results," etc. (terms used in applying the criterion of efficiency), but the criteria, in combination, appear weighty enough to justify differentiation. We must admit that "effects" and "consequences" are synonymous; one term, therefore, should be dropped when this type of measurement beyond efficiency becomes better recognized.

MEASURES OF FISCAL CAPACITY

The measurement of fiscal capacity is not done in a vacuum. An operational decision may have to include: the purpose of the proposed measurement, the factors which are most relevant, the period of time over which predictive measures will be made; and other considerations. For example, fiscal capacity may be measured for the purpose of determining the maximum resources which can be allocated for a new capital improvement program without reducing the present operating budget level. To continue the example, if we assume that the capital program extends over four to six years, measurement would have to focus on three time periods:

1. Resources presently available (i.e., for the first year of the capital budget)

2. Resources potentially available in periodic installments for each of the remaining years of the capital program

3. An estimate of the general ability to support bonded debt with maturity dates which extend beyond—and often far beyond—the capital program period

Some measures of fiscal capacity pertain to the economic framework of the community and others to the more restrictive boundaries of the tax and revenue bases. In most applications the measure of fiscal capacity requires the use of both the broader and the narrower measurements. For example, in a preceding section on the standards used in credit analysis, one ratio (net direct and overlapping tax-supported debt to adjusted assessed valuation) related debt to one aspect of the economic base. Another ratio, (the percentage of current property tax delinquency) was concerned with the tax base. The purpose of all the applications in that section is abundantly clear, namely to determine whether an added debt burden could be reasonably supported.

Upon reflection, it will also be clear that measurements of fiscal capacity precede and supply the basis for some financial policy decisions. After the nature and extent of fiscal capacity have been measured (including resource availability by time periods), then—and only then—can the policy-makers determine precisely, and with confidence, how the resources which become available periodically might best be committed. Fortunately, the process of measuring fiscal capacity produces the background data needed in selecting the best method, or combination of methods, of financing.

This section, however, is not concerned with the role of measurement in financial decision-making nor with the many applications of fiscal capacity measures but rather with their systematic classification coupled, for some measures, with a statement of their strong and weak characteristics.

Economic statistics for many of the measures which follow are not available on a city basis. If interest centers on the city per se, reported county figures or metropolitan area figures will have to be adjusted to the city's economic base.

Measures of the Economic Base

One of the best indices of a community's wealth is the tangible property values *per capita*. The focus is on all tangible property values, real and personal, whether taxable or nontaxable. Tax-exempt property is included because, although not a part of the tax base, it is, nonetheless, a part of the economic base.

To inventory all tangible property values, one begins with total assessed valuation and adjusts the figure to estimated full valuation. If the assessment rolls do not supply assessed values for tax-exempt properties, an estimate should be made. If the property tax and the assessment process include only real property, or real property plus some classes of personal property, estimates will have to be made for each class of tangible personal property omitted. The number of automobile registrations will supply a starting point for this important category. Household furnishings can be estimated by a rule-of-thumb addition to assessed valuation of all homes.

Final figures for total tangible property values should then be reduced to a per pupil basis for school districts and to a per capita basis for all other local governments.

The handling of stocks, bonds, notes, mortgages, insurance policies, and other intangible personal property values presents a significant difficulty in this type of analysis. A considerable portion of these, especially mortgages and other paper in relation to real property, constitute a duplication of the real property values. On the other hand, large portions of these items represent a claim upon income which may be independent of real property in the community. Much of it will be based upon future earnings of individuals and businesses; large amounts will relate to economic activities outside the boundaries of the local government under consideration. Finally, it is usually very difficult to secure information concerning such wealth. Therefore, for practical purposes, evaluation in a typical community of intangible wealth must be treated as tangential information.

The per capita resources of banks and other financial institutions are a second index of the community's wealth. Aside from bank buildings, home or branch office buildings, their furnishing, and investment in real properties, most resources of financial institutions are intangibles. Moreover, in many communities branch banking cuts across political lines and it is not feasible to allocate the intangible wealth of such institutions to the respective communities which they serve.

Even so, the wealth of such institutions constitute an important element of the community's economic base because they mobilize resources and supply credit. They also lessen the dependence of the community upon outside credit institutions. Reported sources vary slightly according to the types of institutions which include commercial banks and trust companies, savings banks, savings and loan associations, life insurance companies, and property insurance companies.

A third category of resources which is an index to a community's economic wealth is that of human resources. In this regard, indices are necessary for both the total population and the labor force, with information being provided as follows:

1. Total population classified by:
    a. Age
    b. Level of education
    c. Employment
        (1) Civilian employment as a percentage of the total population
        (2) Percentage of the civilian labor force unemployed
2. Labor force classified by:
    a. Type of occupation: unskilled, semi-skilled, skilled, clerical, and professional
    b. Major industry

Another index of wealth is personal income per capita, disposable income (personal income minus all direct personal taxes) per capita, and the distribution of taxable personal income by adjusted gross income classes.

Measures of economic activity are useful as indirect evidences of wealth and income and, in a few cases (such as retail sales), are parts of a nonproperty tax base. Statisticians need to be highly selective and use only a limited number of measures from the following listing in gauging economic activity:

Water-borne cargo tonnage	Military expenditures
Freight carloadings	Value of construction
Trucking tonnage	Building permits
Motor vehicle registration	Retail sales
Gasoline consumption	Department stores sales
Number of tourists	Postal receipts
Kilowatt hours produced	Bank deposits
Average daily water consumption	Newspaper circulation
Value added by manufacturing	Enrollment in local institutions
Industrial payrolls	of higher education

In measuring the economic base, account may be taken of the trade-and payments-flow. This title is used to designate an approach which has been used by city planners and others. The central idea is that a community (or a metropolitan area) is similar to a nation trading with the outside world. Its economic viability depends upon its maintaining a balance of payments (taking into account all visible and invisible exports and imports, i.e., goods, services, and capital). One of the earliest systematic statements of this approach appeared in a study by Professors Robert M. Haig and R. C. McCrea.[6] In the 1930s and 1940s, Homer Hoyt, urban land economist and consultant, was the most prominent exponent of economic base studies.

Since there are no ports of entry and embarkation, and no central bank for balance-of-payment settlements for an urban region, the economist or city planner who applies this approach must improvise and attempt to do indirectly that which he cannot measure directly. One of the difficult problems is fixing the boundaries of the economic area to be studied. Economic and political boundaries do not usually coincide. The availability of relevant statistics which can be adjusted for the base chosen is another problem. One approach has been to make local economic surveys in order to distinguish basic activities (city forming) from nonbasic activities (city servicing) and to apportion "mixed" activities. Employment and payroll data by classes of business have played an important role in such analyses. The original concepts as to what activities make a city grow and become more viable as an economic unit have been questioned. Some planners and urban economists have turned from this approach and centered their interests in the economics of regional development, applications of the location theory, and small area income analyses.[7]

---

[6] Robert M. Haig and R. C. McCrea, *Regional Survey of New York and Its Environs,* 1927, Vol. 1, 111 pp.

[7] The economic base approach is explained in greater depth in Charles M. Tiebout, *The Community Economic Base Study,* (New York: Committee for Economic Development, 1962), 84 pp. and *The Economic Base of American Cities* by Edward L. Ullman, Michael F. Dacey, and Harold Brodsky, (Seattle, Washington: The University of Washington Press, Revised Edition, 1971), 118 pp.

Finally, measurement of the economic base should include projections of economic stability and economic growth. The former may be gauged by the economic classification of the city, the amount of diversification of its industry, the trend in commercial failures, the trend in unemployment, the trend in unused industrial plant capacity, etc. Projections of economic growth should include the trends in per capita gross income, per capita disposable income, and population growth.

In using these data one must be sensitive to some of the transitory elements of valuations of wealth. Thus, in the 1929-1937 economic depression valuations at market tended greatly to understate the long-term economic capacity of most communities. Conversely valuation of housing immediately following World War II at market would have tended to overstate values. In a sense, therefore, some smoothing out of the curves may be appropriate.

Measures of the Tax Base

A tax base is the stipulated object, or fact, to which the tax rate is applied, and must be connected with the subject of the tax (i.e., the taxpayer). The base and the rate are the tax determinants. Examples of tax bases include the assessed valuation of property, gross wages, gallons of beer, package of cigarettes, and the value of retail sales.

Each tax has its own base, and measurement of that base is a separate problem from measurement of the base of another tax. Technically, we can talk of a total tax system, but of a total tax base only if there is but one tax. One cannot summate a series of tax bases because some are valuations, some are things, some are transactions, etc. Despite this, the expressions, "broadening the tax base" and "measurement of the tax base," are often used in an aggregative sense. In general the following measures, with some limitations, can be used:

1. *The overall productivity of the total tax system:* This measure is represented by per capita tax collections and per capita taxes as a percentage of per capita income.

2. *Limitations on broadening the tax base:* Local governments, for one reason or another, are unable to tap many components of the economic base which lie within their boundaries. Among the limitations are:

   a. *Legal limitations:* In some cases, the state, through exemptions, narrows the tax base available to the local governments. In others, the state reserves to itself the right to tax and will not authorize local governments to reach some forms of wealth, income, or economic activity.

   b. *Administrative limitations:* For some proposed taxes, the cost of collection at the local level would be excessive because of the many opportunities for evasion or avoidance. In other cases, the tax base itself is vulnerable. A local retail sales or gasoline tax base, for example, might be greatly reduced because of the ease of making purchases outside the local government's boundaries in tax-free territory.

    c. *A political limitation:* Where two or more overlapping/under-
lying governments use the same tax base, there comes a point in the
overall tax structure at which increased use of the base by one
local government restricts the action of another. Political tolerance
reaches a breaking point and this fixes an overall upper limit.

    d. *Competitive limitation:* Where jurisdictions are in competition with
each other for the location of industry, employment or other economic development one frequently finds that the levels of local taxation become factors in the process of competition. A "favorable"
tax rate in the one jurisdiction is used to attempt to entice decision-
makers to locate in the jurisdiction. This process is likely to have an
influence upon the jurisdiction with the higher tax rate and inhibit
the rate of growth in tax rate that otherwise might have occurred.

3. *Property tax base:* Almost all tax bases, especially the property tax,
are under frequent attack from various sources. In recent years, the
property tax has been a favorite target. Unless other major sources of
revenue are supplied, the viability of the local government revenue
system depends on the maintenance of a very broad property tax base.

4. *Stability of the local tax system:* Diversification tends to provide some
stability. The revenue "mix," or extent of diversification, is expressed
in several ways:

    a. The percentage ratio of nonproperty taxes to total revenues

    b. The percentage ratio of nontax local revenues to total revenues

    c. State and federal aid as a percentage of total revenues

    d. Measurement of tax elasticity with changes in income payments:
This measure can result in the classification of taxes as very stable
taxes, e.g., licenses, rigidly administered property taxes, and a poll tax;
taxes whose yields vary roughly in proportion to income payments,
e.g., the general sales taxes; and taxes with high sensitivity to income
changes, e.g., the individual and corporate net income taxes

5. *Rate of tax base growth:* This measure may be calculated by a combination of direct and indirect means such as plotting population growth,
determining the rate of growth in taxable assessed valuations, calculating
the probable extension of the local government's boundaries, projecting
the potential increase in receipts from tax sources which have not been
used to their full capacity, and estimating the productivity of unused
tax sources which are available to the local government—both those
already authorized and those which have a fair chance of authorization.

A Comparative, Composite-index Approach

A final approach attempts to relate an individual local government's fiscal
ability to other local governments in the same population class or within the
state. This involves a ranking process. Certain indices are selected, including
measures of both the economic base and the tax base, and a weight assigned to
each index. Local governments are ranked according to each index, the weights
applied, and the results combined into a weighted composite index (which is no
more than a weighted sum of the ranks). A slightly more sophisticated statistical

Table 32
COMPUTATION OF RELATIVE, COMPOSITE-INDEX OF FISCAL ABILITY

Governmental Unit	Estimated Taxable Property Value Per Capita[a]	Per Capita Personal Income	Retail Sales Per Capita	Per Capita Property Tax Collections	Per Capita Nonproperty Tax Collections	Per Capita State and Federal Aid[b]	Weighted Composite Index
(WT)	(3)	(3)	(1)	(1)	(2)	(2)	
A	% of median	% of median	% of median	% of median	% of median	% of median	
B							
C							
D							
E							
F							
G							
H							
I							
J	% of median	% of median	% of median	% of median	% of median	% of median	
etc.							
Average (Median)	$_____	$_____	$_____	$_____	$_____	$_____	

WT = weight assigned each series.

a Assessed valuation adjusted to estimated full or market value.

b Average over the last five-year period.

application of the same general approach begins with computing a median for each governmental unit, and its fiscal ability is then judged according to its relative standing, or rank, in the composite index column.

The index is basically the sum of the percentages of the median for each of the individual series, weighted in accordance with the compiler's judgment of the relative importance of each component series. The weights used should always be made explicit. The hypothetical example in Table 32 gives the bare bones of this approach.

SOME OTHER CONSIDERATIONS

In some of the preceding sections, the authors have attempted to put measurement within an operational framework. Theoretical concepts sometimes require more precision: a sharpening in order to produce a cutting edge for the practitioner. The foregoing discussion has attempted:

1. To identify the stages within the decision-making process where measurement has particular relevance
2. To indicate the levels within the hierarchical structure, typical of large cities, where divisions of labor are found in measurement application and, at each level, to indicate the function of measurement in meeting allocated managerial responsibility.

In this process, the three goals in measurement—the immediate, intermediate, and the ultimate—were set forth in order to delineate the time dimension within which measurement takes place.

The criterion of efficiency has been supplemented by measurement beyond efficiency, underscoring the problem of testing expenditure directions, the need for ultimate goals, and the value of periodic reassessment or reappraisal.

Measurement in public administration necessitates consideration of two associated and integral areas: the use of comparative financial data derived from the process of measurement and the organizational requirements of the measurement process.

Misuse of Comparative Financial Data

Two types of comparison—between or among local governments and comparison at two points in time of a governmental unit's financial position—frequently involve the misuse of reported figures or of some measurement ratio.

First, comparative data between two local governments or among a group can easily be misinterpreted. It is legitimate, for example, to take all cities 250,000 to 500,000 population and rank them according to a certain financial measure, or measures, provided the major pitfalls in interpretation are made quite clear. One illustration will suffice. Assume a comparison of state aid per capita for this group of cities. Questions which should be resolved before any, but the most superficial, conclusions can be drawn include:

1. Is any one of the cities in the group a combined city-county government?
2. Does the city government proper have the school function or is this function in an independent city school district?
3. Are health and welfare the responsibilities of the city or of the county?
4. Have any of the states in which these cities are located centralized certain functions in the state government itself which, in others, are still the responsibility of the cities?
5. Does any state in the group provide a share of some state-collected tax for a particular city function which the other states subsidize by a grant-in-aid?

Comparative city financial data frequently are presented without the proper kinds of interpretative framework, or background data. The reader is left to color the data with his own biases. If, for example, he has children and is very much interested in public schools, but "opposed to a welfare state," he may be proud that his community has higher per capita school costs. His pride or displeasure might even be reversed, or somewhat modified, if the full reasons for the differences between the two communities were known. Again, to use another example, he may derive satisfaction from a lower per capita debt figure for his community, compared with others, without adequate knowledge of the explanation.

Historical comparisons of a governmental unit's finances at two points in time, unless carefully qualified, can present only half truths. The following illustrations indicate the possible pitfalls.

1. Per capita total expenditures of a governmental unit today may be compared with 10 years ago. However, qualifications which are needed
   to assure a valid comparison may include:
   a. Conversion of the two figures to a dollar which has comparable
      purchasing power at both dates
   b. A listing of new services which citizens now require which were
      not provided 10 years ago
   c. A shift, in the interim, between the city and some other local govern-
      ment of responsibility for certain service activities
   d. Inclusion today, but not 10 years ago, of expenditures mandated by
      the state, or performed as an agent of the state, for which the
      state provides the revenue

2. Net direct tax-supported debt per capita today and 10 years ago is a
   relevant comparison. Again, the figures will not be understood completely without a disclosure of the following:
   a. Whether new taxing districts have been created to relieve the govern-
      mental unit of the necessity of incurring new general obligation debt
   b. The extent to which new capital requirements have been met by a
      shift to revenue bonds, issued either by the government directly or
      by a new local authority with power to issue revenue bonds only
   c. The shift of capital requirements to another level of local government
      —for example, transfer of the city airport to the county or to a tri-
      county authority
   d. A shift of the burden of some improvements to special assessment debt
      ("special-specials") which is not included in tax-supported debt
   e. A marked change in the value of the dollar which distorts the state-
      ment of values in the two periods

3. A comparison may be made of the property tax rate today and 10
   years ago. This comparison cannot be understood without knowing at
   the same time:
   a. Whether the city chose, in the interim, to raise taxes by a revalua-
      tion of assessments upward rather than by disturbing the level of
      rates or to raise rates and lower the level of assessment
   b. The local rates may have changed because of a shift of some im-
      portant service between levels of local government without changing
      the overall tax rate of the property owner—for example, the govern-
      mental unit may have shifted a major function such as hospitals, to
      the county
   c. Local property tax rates have been kept on an even keel by a shift
      to special assessment levies for some major capital improvements, or
      to revenue bonds financed by sewer rentals or other service charges.

"Let the figures speak for themselves" is a dangerous and irresponsible attitude on the part of city hall, the newspapers, and other media that publish
comparative data for public consumption. Local finance and the pattern of local
government structure vary from state to state and local finance itself may vary
among governmental units, even within the same state. With high degrees of

population mobility and the changes at work in local government finance, it is asking too much of the general public to understand the bare figures.

Aside from mobility, the general public approaches local government finance with varied degrees of sophistication and ignorance. The highly sophisticated often support citizens' bureaus of government research or belong to organizations which, with paid staff and interested committees and subcommittees, follow certain aspects of local finance very closely. They make use of at least some of the measures herein discussed. The property tax is often the center of interest. In devising meaningful measures, a local government should keep in mind these organized, well-informed groups and their data requirements, as well as a much larger group whose level of understanding is without the benefit of staff assistance.

Organization for Measurement

In a medium-sized or large governmental unit, the task of studying measurement units and their imaginative usage should be in the hands of a professional statistician. This is usually a one-man job unless some related day-to-day operating responsibility is also assigned. The statistician will draw heavily upon the work of others, including the financial and cost accountants, the purchasing agent, the budget staff, and operating personnel. Recognition of this activity and recruitment of the proper individual is more important than his precise location in the organizational structure. One defensible location is in the internal audit section reporting directly to the chief executive. If, however, the budget division is attuned to technical assistance and not obsessed with central control, the statistician might be "in budget." Performance budgeting and efficiency studies lean heavily on measurement devices. The activity might be combined with that of statistical coordination (which would include coordination of reporting) to assure that the operating departments, the planners, accountants, and the current and capital budget staffs are working with consistent data and presenting the best information to management and to the public.

CONCLUSION

Despite the array of measurement tools presented in this chapter, it is true that only a modicum of scientific effort has been put into this important area. Progress since the Ridley and Simon book, *Measuring Municipal Activities*,[8] has been disappointingly slow.

Experimentation and research by those on the job is one badly needed approach. In some cases, a more intensive application of statistical methodology and cost accounting, or cost analysis techniques, would convert rules-of-thumb and standards which are in an early, experimental stage into more useful benchmarks. Lines of inquiry which might profitably be pursued include:

1. A reclassification into more meaningful categories and subcategories of programs, activities, and operations. Sharing of experiences among local

---

[8] Clarence E. Ridley and Herbert A. Simon, *Measuring Municipal Activities*, (Chicago: The International City Managers' Association, 2nd. ed., 1943), 115 pp.

governments of the work which program and performance budgeting have stimulated could be stepped up.

2. Cost analysis techniques might be used more frequently in the development of unit cost standards for program areas where regular cost accounting is too expensive and, therefore, impractical.

3. Depreciation accounting for general capital assets will have to be accepted if justification of overall levels of capital outlays and capital deficiency ratios by programs are to be placed on a more scientific basis.

4. Finally, imaginative and intensive work on the measurement of the "effects" of municipal programs appears essential if management in local government is to become more of a science. For example, expenditures are being made on multitudinous approaches to juvenile delinquency. If effects attributable to individual causes could be statistically isolated and measured, policy-makers would have a guide to expenditure priorities. With advancements already made in correlation analysis by the statistics profession, it is reasonable to expect that many problems of multiple causation in the area of local government could be resolved.

Aside from research by staff and operating heads who are close to the administrative problems which must be faced, research by university bureaus and individual social scientists is also required. Work might begin with more precise statements and delineations of some of the measurement problems to be resolved.

19

State Supervision of
Local Government Finance

There are two distinct methods by which state governments carry out programs of supervision over local government finance: (1) through departments or agencies whose supervisory activities are oriented towards selected aspects of substantive or procedural financial matters, e.g., budgeting, accounting, procurement, and debt; and (2) through departments or agencies of the state government whose supervisory activities are based on programs, e.g., education, health, and highways.

These two kinds of state supervision of local government finance have important overlapping elements and also important elements of distinctive emphasis and method. The concern of this chapter is primarily with the former type; however, some attention is also devoted to the latter.

Much detailed legislation governing local finance has been adopted—restrictive, permissive, prohibitive, and mandatory. All can be found embedded in general or special municipal finance laws, tax legislation, bond laws, education and highway aid legislation, and in other segments of statutory law. In a few states, even the state constitution is not free from such detail. These legal measures are not self-executing. Long ago, the states found it necessary to establish administrative supervisory agencies to assure that there would be legal compliance and that local finance officials would face accountability for their actions, or their failure to act. To the basic roles of enforcement and policing, some states, at an early period, added supportive roles of administrative services and technical assistance. The state stands *in loco parentis* to its political subdivisions; like a parent it may punish; but, it may also stand ready to assist with money, instruction, or advice.

Administrative supervisory measures or approaches are important in making things work. However, they are not substitutes for sound legislative policies on local government finance. A state can have a good supervisory agency; but, if its local finance policies are not sound, local governments will eventually pile up financial difficulties and, in the end, the supervisory work will have proved of little long-run consequence.

All of this must be seen in perspective. Despite the wide diversity found in the fifty states, there are also some common approaches: the boundaries of the term, "state administrative supervision of local government finance," are difficult to draw. Included are all types of administrative controls and all forms of tech-

nical assistance (such as services, advice, information, instructional materials, etc.).
Normally excluded from this term are: state-local cooperation unless it is on an
administrative level; financial aids and loans unless supervision accompanies them;
and statutory or constitutional directives, prohibitions, or restrictions unless
there is actual enforcement through a supervisory agency, as differentiated from
enforcement through the courts.

Despite certain attempted exclusions, state administrative supervision of local
government finance cannot be neatly separated from other aspects of state-local
fiscal relations. Supervision, like other aspects of administration, is not wholly
neutral; it has inevitably become interwoven with the substance of interlevel
fiscal relations. A state supervisory agency may, or may not, establish broad
policies in such relations. Even if its direct policy-determination role is limited,
it can significantly influence the development of legislative policy. To a substantial degree, it can mold the meaning of legislative policy by the quality
of its implementation. Supervision is frequently a necessary aspect of state-local
fiscal relationships. Its importance can easily be overestimated, particularly when
enmeshed in the home rule philosophy. On the other hand, its importance and
potentialities can also be easily underestimated.

FACTORS DICTATING A STATE INTEREST IN THE
SUPERVISION OF LOCAL GOVERNMENT FINANCE

One might rationally inquire why, over time, a situation has developed
whereby the states exercise so pervasive an influence over the delivery of services
by local governments. By contrast, the nation during its colonial period and its
early history depended very heavily upon local governments to provide significant
elements of direct services to the people.

The principal reasons for the interest of state governments in the finances
of local governments are summarized below.

Local Governments Are Creatures of the States

Although the historical development of local government, both in America
and in England, shows clearly that many local governments were not altogether
the creatures of the "mother government," the fact remains that, as constitutional law has developed in the United States, the local governments are dependent
upon the states for their legal existence. Except where ordained otherwise by
state constitutions, local governments are subject to an almost plenary exercise
of state legislative power in the definition of their structure, functions, and powers.

It is not surprising, therefore, that the states have enacted legislation for the
creation of administrative arrangements under which local government finances
are subject to state regulation and supervision.

Historical Interest in the Property Tax

Historically, one of the earliest steps taken by state governments toward
supervision of local financial operations was in relation to the administration of

the local property tax, due largely to the fact that the states themselves relied substantially upon state property taxes administered by local officials. The interest of the state was pecuniary in the protection of its own revenue. Over time, matters of equity among taxpayers in different communities developed. Also, in matters of public utility taxation, statewide administration provided a uniformity deemed necessary by corporations engaged in these activities.

Development of Standardized Information and Practices

A significant factor in the development of state standards for performance of local government financial functions, e.g., budgeting, accounting, and auditing, has been to permit the gathering of information on a basis which will enable the legislature to review the effects of policies which it has previously adopted, to adjust such policies, and to develop new policies as circumstances require.

Supervision of Execution of Standards

State legislatures (and administrative agencies operating under the authority entrusted to them by the legislatures) have prescribed numerous standards in various fields in the interest of providing a minimum level of operation in relation to moneys made available by the state. Inasmuch as these standards were not self-executing, it became desirable, from the point of view of the state, to establish procedures for the policing of the financial and other activities of the local governments. In a sense, the local governments were being required to "toe the mark" that had been set by the states and their regulatory agencies.

Protection of the Public Credit

One of the fields in which state governments have generally prescribed comprehensive protection to local governments has been in the creation and administration of public debt. This interest by the states was, in part, a reaction to the unwise actions of local governments in entering into long-term debt contracts of doubtful wisdom in the subsidy of railroad building. This interest was augmented by local government defaults in meeting their obligations during periods of economic adversity—1873, 1893, 1913, and the 1930s.

The states were encouraged in these actions by local property owners who sought protection against unreasonable tax levies, or defaults which endangered the value of their property. Moreover, as the state governments began to enter the credit markets for substantial financing, they found that imprudent borrowing programs by their local governments were easily converted into adverse market positions for state securities.

Regulations over debt gradually expanded in several directions: amounts of debt that could be outstanding, limitations on the term for which debt could be issued; requirements for the orderly accumulation of reserves for repayment of the debt (or later through requirements for the use of serial bonds), and limitations as to the amounts of tax levies which could be devoted to debt service.

Enforcement of state legal provisions governing debt has been largely by private initiative—either through the legal actions of local taxpayers or through the requirements of bond counsel in connection with the marketing of new debt. However, in some states, e.g., New Jersey and North Carolina, state supervision has been through direct action by state agencies.

Protection Against Excessive Tax Rates

An important factor in extending state supervision to the finances of local governments arose from the demands of local taxpayers that they be protected from the unrestrained levy of local taxes in support of current budgets. Here, state supervision took the form of limits on tax rates and requirements for improved budgeting, accounting, and auditing.

Despite the limitations on debt and tax rates, one continues to find that, during periods of high level economic activity, a spirit of optimism is likely to characterize the mood in most communities—a spirit capitalized upon by the groups interested in securing the benefits arising from high levels of capital improvements. Even where there were constitutional limitations, state legislatures were able to avoid these either through the creation of overlapping governments or, more recently, through the creation of authorities or governmental corporations which have the right to incur debt outside the constitutional limits that may be imposed.

Mismanagement at the Local Level

Whether in large or small jurisdictions, the opportunities for mismanagement by officials in power are legion—despite the restrictive statutes. Such mismanagement may be due to ineptitude or to outright corruption. The culminating effect of the long, dreary history of mismanagement inevitably brings with it demands for more aggressive supervision by the state government.

The dearth of professionally trained personnel to manage the financial affairs of local governments has been, and continues to be, a significant factor in abetting those who strive for greater state supervision of local finance.

Expansion of State Support of Local Government

Through the years, the degree of dependence of local governments upon grants-in-aid and other forms of support from state governments has expanded in geometric proportions. States are now generally providing about half the revenues in support of local public education programs and are now expanding such aid to numerous other aspects of local government. With states making such large amounts of financial aid available to local governments, it is hoped that their direct pecuniary interest in seeing that the money is used in accordance with law and regulations will give additional emphasis to state supervision.

Interdependence of Revenue Systems

Following 1945, a number of states markedly expanded the rights of local governments to levy taxes—sometimes allowing the local governments to levy any tax not being used by the state itself—and, in some instances, permitting the duplication of the same tax at the state and local level either by independent levies (e.g., the sales tax in Louisiana and the real estate transfer tax in Pennsylvania), or by allowing local governments to levy incremental elements of a state tax with state collection and payments to the local governments involved.

This has led to a high degree of competition between some states and their local governments which has, in turn, induced the states to provide greater degrees of supervision over local financial operations.

TYPES OF STATE SUPERVISION

The elements of state supervision of local government finance consist of a number of steps which act directly to circumscribe the exercise of discretion by local governments in the field of finance. The first grouping of such steps may be denoted as elements of supervision. This grouping consists of such items as:

1. Mandatory requirements involving minimum levels of performance at either the procedural or substantive levels, or both
2. The "shall nots"—the formal limits with respect to debt, taxes, expenditures, etc.
3. Coordination—which requires a careful distinction between that which takes place in the presence of power sufficient to require coordination vs. cooperation, which is presumed a voluntary act
4. The threat, or actuality, of direct takeover of management during periods of local fiscal emergency
5. Enforcement of terms of "voluntary" contracts because, although local governments may choose not to enter into contracts with state governments, once a local government does enter into such contracts with state agencies, these are ordinarily enforceable by administrative or judicial action

As distinguished from the foregoing group of steps, one finds a number of other activities of state governments which, within themselves, do not constitute supervision. However, the use of this second group of activities by skilled operatives may have as much effect—or even more—than some kinds of supervision included in the first grouping. In the second grouping we include such items as:

1. Provision of technical assistance and advice
2. Cooperative training programs
3. Joint planning
4. Joint development of proposed legislative programs affecting local government finance

Our concern in this chapter is solely with the first grouping of supervisory activities, partially because these are more easily defined and partially because they rest upon laws or regulations which can be enforced against the recalcitrant local government. The major areas of finance activities supervised by the states are: accounting, operating budget processes and content, purchasing, debt, financial reporting, and auditing. In addition to the foregoing, New Jersey has made a start in supervision of various aspects of capital programming and capital budgeting.

The State Supervisory Agencies

The exercise of supervisory powers is likely to be spread among a number of state government departments and agencies. Thus, working under the provisions in the school code, the supervision of local governments may be vested in the department of education; matters relating to public health may be assigned to the department of health; those relating to roads and mass transit may be assigned to the department of transportation; etc. The controls which are exercised primarily in relation to the functional objective of the supervisory agency may include major supervision; or, they may consist of only minor financial supervision. Thus, the supervision by a state department of education is more likely to extend to the details of handling local school finance than to close supervision of the elements of regulation relating to public health.

Against these kinds of financial controls exercised by educational, health, and transportation agencies, and the like, there are the more general kinds of financial controls which, in recent years, are tending to be gathered into a state department of community affairs or similar state agency. Here, one is more likely to be concerned with finance as such, rather than as incidental to functional supervision.

Some types of supervisory activity require direct, on-site contacts or inspections in the field. Others can be accomplished, in whole or in part, at the state capital by the issuance of information bulletins and memoranda, the preparation of uniform manuals, or by direct orders and regulations—the latter requiring an audit to ascertain compliance.

Before considering the types of supervision, it is necessary to identify the various diversities among the states:

1. Differences as to location (or locations) within the state governmental structure of the responsibility for finance supervisory activities
2. The specific classes of local governments in each state to which individual supervisory activities apply—for example, debt supervision in Kentucky extends only to counties
3. The different circumstances under which exemptions are granted, even though the specific requirements fall upon all local governments
4. The supervisory methods, or combinations of methods, in use
5. The types of sanctions employed
6. The approximate degrees of effectiveness in specific areas

Where there are one or more large cities in the state (i.e., cities of 300,000 population or more), their accounting systems might well be exempted from some, or all, of the state's requirements.

Where a multiplicity of funds is required because of the statutory earmarking of funds, the state supervisory agency should, over a period of time, restore the general fund to its rightful place through advice to the legislature.

Supervision of the Budgeting Function

State supervision of budgeting takes on many different hues and gradations, ranging from the comprehensive kinds of controls exercised by the Department of Community Affairs in New Jersey, to the very limited forms of control exercised by Pennsylvania, and on to those states which make no effort of consequence in their general concern with local government budgeting—except, perhaps, in selected fields such as education.

One approach to state supervision of budgeting substitutes the judgment of the state supervisory agency for that of the local governing body in selected circumstances. State review may result in substantial modifications in locally prepared budgets. Submission of local budgets to the state supervisory agency may be mandatory; required only under certain delineated circumstances, e.g., formal petition by local citizens; or nonexistent.

A second approach leaves expenditure control primarily with the local governing bodies. This approach may require that all local budgets be submitted annually to the state capital; but, review is for statutory compliance. Modifications are ordered only in cases of noncompliance. In other states, budgets are not reviewed at the state capital; compliance with statutes is a matter covered by the postaudit. The emphasis, in some states, is upon technical assistance. Budget forms or manuals are provided and a state staff is available to assist the local governments in improving their budgetary practices.

States vary as to the minimum standards set by statute. A given state may prescribe one or more of the following requirements:

1. Appointment by the local governing body of a budget officer in order to fix responsibility for compliance
2. Use of a prescribed budget format or of uniform titles for revenue and appropriation items
3. A budget balanced in accordance with the provisions of a cash basis budget law; or an accrual basis budget law
4. Inclusion of appropriations for all expenditures mandated by state statutes
5. Preparation of a budget within some statutory limitation regarding tax levies
6. Inclusion in the budget of all capital projects—with provision for coverage by authorized bonded debt or by adequate current revenues

Uniform titles for revenue estimates and appropriation items usually conform to the classification of revenues and expenditures prescribed for local accounting. The titles may be inserted only in a standard budget form, but the preparation of a uniform budget manual has a distinct advantage. The manual permits explanations, amplifications, and statements of principles and provides more satisfactory material for short instruction courses. The reasons for the budget-balancing requirement are several. First, the property tax has been used as a deficiency tax, i.e., it is levied in an amount sufficient to meet the differential between projected expenditures and the total resources available from non-property tax sources. In perhaps a majority of local governments, this means that the requirement that current revenues (or revenues plus carryover surpluses) cover operating expenditures invokes a form of overall expenditure control spearheaded by organized property taxpayers. In the second place, balancing the proposed budget is at least the first step in preventing an operating deficit. The appropriations are all maximum expenditure estimates. A deficit, in actuality, can occur only because nonproperty tax revenues were overestimated; property tax delinquencies were underestimated; or supplemental appropriations were authorized later without providing for additional revenues. These contingencies are anticipated and covered in state cash or accrual basis budget laws by a requirement that an actual operating deficit be covered in the next year's budget. Third, a balanced budget sets overall targets for revenues and expenditures. If actuals exceed the original estimates (the targets, or standards, set), comparisons are shown in reports and variances highlighted. These become matters for questioning by the electorate, the local government body, and, at least in some states, by the state supervisory agency.

If local budgets are reviewed at the state capital for statutory compliance or, if this type of review is under consideration, it is reasonable to ask—why cannot compliance be left entirely to the postaudit? Proponents of budget review argue as follows:

1. This approach allows the supervisory agency to detect noncompliance much earlier. Knowledge that a postaudit will be made has an important preventive value, but noncompliance often arises because of the carelessness or ignorance of new officials. Similar to preaudit, the budget review results in timely preventive or curative action either at the beginning of, or during, the budget year.

2. Budget review substantially reduces the amount and, therefore, the expense of audit report writing. Noncompliances corrected need not be reported; or, if so, only a list of items which have already been corrected is needed. Audit reports can also omit the presentation of budget figures and financial statements. Incorporation can be by reference to pages in the budget document and the financial report on file, or to items in a reporting schedule. Since budget and reports have to be prepared by local governments for their own use, the requirement of filing places on them no real burden. Savings in audit report writing is, therefore, a net savings.

3. Some of the matters which can easily be checked in the budget document are: compliance with the budget balancing provision in a cash or accrual basis budget law; adherence to any restrictions as to estimating nonproperty taxes or nontax receipts; compliance with legal rate limitations on the property tax or any nonproperty tax; and compliance with salary and wage rate laws.

Arguments have also been advanced for state review of local budgets to ensure the inclusion of all mandatory expenditures and the adequate provision for proposed capital projects (sometimes involving a mandatory down-payment) by authorized debt or current revenues. Proponents of local budget review at the state level cite a number of advantages for this type of review:

1. The review ensures that the small municipalities at least meet minimum standards in the use of this planning and control instrument. This is a form of mass compulsory "education."
2. Budget review, more quickly than any other approach, enables the state agency to know where advice and technical assistance are needed.
3. If comparative data are mandated, the budget is the best possible material from which the state agency can determine whether the local unit is planning well and living up to its financial program.
4. As noted above, budget review is a better approach than the postaudit for checking on some compliance matters.

The requirement that budgets be filed annually imposes upon the state the obligation to provide adequate staff for review purposes and to make constructive use of the information. New Jersey calls in its audit staff from the field to assist with the review. Discussions between the office staff and the auditors are beneficial to the work of both groups. If there is to be compliance with the filing requirement, the legislature must provide sanctions. The New Jersey agency is authorized to impose a fine if the filing date is not met. Some states withhold aid monies until this, and other, reporting requirements are met.

Annual filing is not burdensome to a municipality since preparation of a document is part of the normal budget process.

Supervision of the Accounting Function

Four of the major finance activities supervised by states are closely interrelated: accounting, budgeting, financial reporting, and auditing. Two uniform classifications of accounts—one for balance sheet accounts and the other for operating statement accounts (revenues and expenditures)—constitute the major connecting link. The close interrelationship is one justification for placing in a single state agency the responsibility for supervising all four functions.

Provisions for uniform accounting normally include uniform terminology, uniform principles of accounting, and uniform classifications of balance sheet and operating statement accounts. In all three categories some states have adopted, in the main, the standards recommended by the National Committee on Governmental Accounting. Others have gone their own way, or used only some of the Committee's recommendations.[1]

Uniform accounting is often embodied in an accounting manual. A codification system assists in the organization and presentation of the manual, but the code is not an essential element in uniformity. Most governmental accounting

---

[1] The trend toward use of the National Committee on Governmental Accounting's recommendations has been accelerating in recent years and probably will increase since the American Institute of Certified Public Accountants in its publications now specify the use of the National Committee's volume, *Governmental Accounting, Auditing, and Financial Reporting.* Under recent legislation in Florida a uniform system of accounts is required and officials there have specified the National Committee's standards. The Michigan law providing for uniform accounting systems for local governments specifically refers to MFOA and the National Committee in its law. Colorado, Iowa, North Carolina, and Washington are among the other states which have specified use of the National Committee's standards.

experts recommend that uniformity not go beyond the three categories cited above. To prescribe the forms, exact procedures, and the precise format for presenting statements introduces rigidity and leaves no flexibility for local accountants or accounting consultants who desire, within a uniform framework, to innovate and develop a system that fits the peculiar needs of the local administrators and governing bodies.

The manual will usually illustrate typical entries and explain the reasons for certain recommendations. If forms and statements are included, it is recommended that they be for illustrative purposes only. Since it is important to keep the uniform system up to date, some states use looseleaf manuals.

Some good reasons can be advanced for uniform accounting:

1. Compliance with the law under state aid statutes and accountability for state funds are more nearly ensured by a uniform system that brings order and, at least, minimum standards into local record-keeping.
2. A well devised accounting system lays a foundation for competence in local finance administration, and the basic elements in a uniform system constitute at least the first steps in laying such a foundation.
3. Uniform accounting greatly facilitates the publication of comparable financial statistics for each class of local government within a state.
4. If the state agency has responsibility for supervising local budgeting, uniform accounting is almost an essential prerequisite. A foundation for improved accounting has to be laid before a budget manual and improved budgeting are feasible.
5. Uniform accounting simplifies the task of a state supervisory agency which provides technical assistance in municipal accounting, including sponsorship of in-service training courses.
6. If the state agency has responsibility for auditing municipal accounts, uniform accounting makes possible a more efficient use of audit manpower. If private accounting firms contract for such audit work, the same is true. Staff can more quickly adapt themselves to municipal accounting work if individual systems rest on basic uniformities.

Some states have made uniform accounting mandatory for one or more classes of local governments. In a few states, the supervisory agency is promoting uniformity through accounting manuals and technical assistance; but, use of this service or acceptance of the state's recommendations is optional.

A single uniform accounting manual will not fit all classes of local government. For example, the cash basis may be more feasible for the smaller units, such as villages, than the accrual or modified accrual basis. Furthermore, the fund structure and revenue and expenditure classifications for a school district are quite different from those for a city. It is feasible, however, to provide comprehensive, but collapsible, revenue and expenditure classifications which will fit all sizes of governments within a particular class.

Supervision of the Purchasing Function

State administrative supervision of local purchasing is usually limited in nature. Statutes generally require competitive bidding for purchases above a certain dollar value. Statutes also spell out restrictions as to conflicts of interest for local officials and employees. Simply stated, the local government is restricted from purchasing goods or services from a supplier or contractor in which the concerned local officials or employees have a substantive financial interest. The statutes and the courts seek to protect the local government against a conflict of interest situation where a local officer or employee might use his public position for private profit-taking.

In such legal compliance matters, the responsibility of the state supervisory agency is to assure that the postauditors of local governments check for any violations. This is facilitated by the inclusion of the conflict of interest regulations within the audit specifications.

A state purchasing agent rarely exercises administrative supervision over local purchasing agents. In a few jurisdictions, he is required to render a limited form of technical assistance. For example, he may be required to send to the purchasing officers of counties or school districts, a monthly, or quarterly, list of prices paid by the state for items commonly purchased by such public bodies. This service establishes for these local units some price benchmarks. Local purchasing agents may also consult the catalogues of manufacturers and other suppliers on file in the state capital. In rare instances, counties may be required to report to the state purchasing agent prices paid for items over a certain dollar value.

Cooperation in purchasing is promoted by a few statutes. Local governments, or certain classes, are given the option of participating in state contracts for certain major items. To illustrate, at the time the state is asking for competitive bids on automobiles and trucks, local governments may be invited to include their requirements. Where local units are numerous, mandatory buying through the state would impose a heavy administrative responsibility on the state agent.

In certain instances, the state purchasing agent should conduct an annual training institute or conference for local purchasing agents.

Supervision of Debt Operations

The degree of state control over the debt practices of local governments is much more widespread than, perhaps, any other form of state control over local government finance, except in the case of school districts. The elements of state control are likely to extend to most of the following items with respect to debt:

1. The kinds of debt which may be incurred
2. The amounts of debt to be incurred, especially general obligation debt and revenue anticipation notes
3. The terms and conditions under which revenue debt may be incurred
4. The provisions as to the levy of taxes and charges for retirement of the debt and the payment of interest thereon.
5. Repayment schedules and maximum life of different kinds of debt
6. Maximum interest rates which may be paid
7. Requirements for voter approval
8. Procedures to be complied with in the authorization of debt
9. Debt reporting

These are but a few of the aspects of state control imposed. The extent and character of these controls over debt are extremely varied. In some instances, such controls are limited to legal expressions which are left to local officials, taxpayers, bond counsel, and the courts to enforce. In other situations, most actions involving the creation of debt are subject to prior review and approval by state agencies. In the case of North Carolina, the state's role is extended to the actual conduct of sales of long-term debt for all of the local governments in the state.

Supervision of Financial Reporting

Some states require that all local governments (or certain classes) annually report financial data to a state supervisory agency; but, because of a lack of funds or staff, the states may not publish the data. Much of the information, however, is used for supervisory purposes. About a third of the states go one step further and prepare an annual volume of local government financial statistics. California, New Jersey, New York, and Rhode Island are noteworthy. The reporting requirement is a form of supervisory control; the publication, a type of technical assistance.

Methods of obtaining the data vary. The states which publish an annual volume normally use a standard reporting form for each class of local government. Those agencies which need figures solely for administrative and research purposes may require only that a financial report be published locally and filed at the state capital on, or before, a designated date. Others prescribe a basic minimum format and mandate the inclusion of certain types of data.

There are substantial reasons for a state requirement that all local governments provide figures annually on their finances:

1. The state supervisory agency needs such information in meeting its responsibility for ensuring compliance with the state's finance laws
2. Analysis of the individual reports will bring to light those situations which require technical assistance or special remedial action
3. The requirement that annual reports be filed is complementary to that of requiring annual budgets because, with both, the supervisory agency can review proposed financial programs and the actual results. This permits better judgment as to the quality of financial administration
4. If the state agency does some, or all, of the auditing of local accounts, the annual budget and financial report of the local government to be audited help the auditor to isolate particular areas for investigation and may also save time in the field
5. If local budgets and financial reports are available in the state capital, credit-rating agencies and researchers have a central place for obtaining information on local finance and ease in obtaining credit information is of special importance for smaller units of government which must enter the bond market

There are also important reasons why a state government should take the next step and publish annual financial statistics regarding all of its local governments.

1. The process of preparing a statewide statistical report produces *per capita* figures, aggregates, and comparative analyses. Only by statistical manipulation of the raw data can the state supervisory agency arrive at a thorough understanding of local finance trends in the state. A generalized view as to what is happening is not enough.

2. The state supervisory agency needs precise information not only for the proper direction of its energies but also for policy advice on bills before the legislature.

3. The agency has a responsibility to keep the governor and the legislature informed on the status of local finance within the state and upon trends which are developing.

4. Local officials, from time to time, are called upon to compare their results with those of other local units in the same population group. The annual publication of a statistical volume would provide a reliable sourcebook for such a purpose.

5. Taxpayers' groups, large institutional investors, researchers, and others also require financial data on local governments. If the state processes the original data and publishes its results, a valuable technical service has been performed. It is a proper division of labor for the state governments to assume reporting responsibility for the host of small political subdivisions and leave to the United States Bureau of the Census the preparation of nationwide comparative data on the larger units.

One word of caution is derived from the experience of a few states. If the supervisory agency does not, from time to time, update its reporting form or its reporting requirements, the accounting practices of some of the smaller local units will be retarded. For many of them, the mandated report to the state becomes the model for its account titles and for the information which it is essential to record.

Supervision of the Auditing Function

Some states have used auditing as an opportunity for technical assistance; but the primary purpose of state auditing of local accounts, or state supervision of the requirement that there be a postaudit, is to ensure compliance with state laws and to enforce fiscal accountability. State aid monies are handled by local finance officers. The state also knows that fiscal accountability is a fundamental ingredient in sound local finance administration.

State supervision in this area may take one of several forms:

1. A state supervisory agency may be charged with the auditing of all local governments within the state—exempting in some jurisdictions, however, the big cities

2. The state may require that all local governments be audited annually (or biennially) but provide, at the same time, the options of an audit by: the state staff, a certified public accountant, or a public accountant licensed by the state specifically for municipal purposes

3. The state may provide no audit service for local governments but require that an audit report, prepared by an independent auditor, be filed annually (or biennially) with the state supervisory agency

Where audits are performed by independent auditors, the state may provide a standard audit contract, including audit specifications. In order to ensure compliance and to guard against abnormal audit fees, the state may require prior approval by the supervisory agency of each individual contract.

What are the weaknesses in requiring that all local governments (with but a few exceptions) be audited by the state staff?

1. If the number of local units in the state is large, the state staff may find it impossible to audit each local unit more frequently than every two to five years. A lapse of more than two years between audits would appear to be unacceptable.

2. Under the above circumstances, there is little time for auditors to provide technical assistance. Their efforts must, of necessity, be concentrated upon checking for legal compliance and for accountability.

3. If a determined attempt is made to provide an adequate number of staff members in order to meet the mass problem each year (or every two years), the result is apt to be a mediocre staff. A small, highly competent, and well paid staff will probably be sacrificed in the process of spreading available appropriations in order to acquire more staff members.

4. Where the state accepts responsibility for auditing all local governments, there is generally little time for follow-up to ensure that exceptions are corrected and recommendations implemented. Sanctions are apt to be applied only in the most flagrant cases. In some jurisdictions, sanctions are already weak and difficult to invoke, except in cases of embezzlement, fraud, or other serious breaches of public trust.

5. The weakness of the state audit staff approach is, of course, compounded if exemptions are not allowed for the big cities.

Much of the literature which discusses state supervision in the auditing area is devoted to four or five subjects: the advantages and disadvantages of the state audit service vs. the use of private, independent auditors; allocation of the cost of a state audit between the state and the audited local unit; control by the state over audit contracts with accountants; and the evils of a competitive bidding requirement. As regards location of the audit staff within the state government structure, if there is to be a state service, the authors recommend only that responsibility for the supervision of accounting, budgeting, reporting, and auditing not be separated. The close interrelationship of all four areas is a strong reason for the centralization of responsibility.

It is important, however, to raise an additional question, namely, as to the form of the audit report prepared by an independent auditor and filed with the state agency. The state's primary interest, insofar as the use of locally generated revenue is concerned, is to learn of the independent auditor's exceptions (whether violations of statutory requirements or of good accounting practices); his recommendations for correcting such exceptions; and his recommendations for improvements of procedures or the accounting structure. It follows, therefore, that the state agency should require only a summary of the audit along with an annual financial report prepared by the local finance officer but checked by the independent auditor and bearing his certification. It would be a waste of taxpayers' money and of filing cabinet space within the state agency if the private audit report, or that of the state staff, were permitted to duplicate the annual financial report which the local unit must file.

On the other hand, where the local use of state funds is involved, it frequently becomes necessary for the state personnel to assume the responsibility for those elements of the audit relating to determination of the degree of local compliance with state regulations or contracts between the state and local government. The state agency's efforts to interest the state professional accountant's society in the progress of local government accounting within the state; the ready accessibility of annual budgets, financial reports, and audit reports in the state capital; and the agency's work in promoting elements of uniform accounting and budgeting all have a direct, or indirect, connection with improved local government auditing practices.

STATE SUPERVISION THROUGH TRANSFER PAYMENTS AND CONTRACTS

The traditional controls and supervision by state governments over local government finance have been much enhanced by the additional powers secured under programs of transfer payments to local governments, i.e., grants-in-aid, and contracts between the state and local governments in undertakings of mutual interest and concern.

Transfer Payments

The aid of state governments to local governments through transfer payments has increased rapidly in recent decades. Normally, these grant-in-aids payments are for specific purposes and the terms under which they are available normally require the recipient local governments to submit to substantial degrees of supervision by state departments and agencies—far beyond the degree to which controls are normally imposed in relation to activities of local governments which are not subject to state aid.

In a few instances, states have made block grants to local governments; however, the experience to date has been quite limited.

Minimum standards are normally set, often including personnel standards; state funds must sometimes be matched; capital projects must receive prior state approval; and inspections and audits follow to ensure that the conditions of the grants are being met. Withholding of grant monies if the local government fails to meet conditions is a strong sanction.

Through specific grants and supervisory controls, many states have raised local standards in important functional areas, especially in education, health, welfare, and highway/street construction. The states have a poorer record in housing, slum clearance, planning, and urban renewal. But, on the whole, state aids constitute one of the brightest spots in state government and in state-local relations. Standards have been raised in important service areas with a minimum of local resistance. There have been grumblings and friction; but, on balance, local officials have retained areas for initiative and discretion and the state grants have permitted many local governments to render services which would not have been possible otherwise. The grant system has equalized educational and other opportunities and distributed the cost burden over a broader tax base.

One of the major dangers to local governments involved in the states making categorical grants is the degree to which this process permits the states to intrude upon the judgment of local officials—all in the form, or guise, of setting minimum standards.

Obviously, the state legislature cannot itself determine all of the standards appropriate for the administration of categorical grants. In like manner, the top officials of the state departments to which the functions are entrusted are ordinarily too busy with other concerns to enable them to monitor all of the minimum standards that are being imposed. Accordingly, there is a discernible tendency to yield to the pressures of professional committees of one kind or another which, under the justification of improving the public service, are really more concerned with the adoption of standards which may appropriately be viewed as self-serving for the professional groups involved.

Thus, the educators may impose unnecessarily rigid standards in matters of class size, pupil-teacher ratios, school building requirements, and on through a long list of items. On a *prima facie* basis, each of these is justified on the basis that it contributes to better education for the children; however, such standards are frequently set without adequate and *objective* research as to the relationship of such standards to improved educational attainment by the pupils or without sufficient understanding, or taking into account, of the impact upon the local economy.

State-Local Contracts

Closely related to the increase in transfer payments is the development of various kinds of projects carried out under joint agreements by the states and local governments—ordinarily, with the legal right of either party to refuse to join in the contract, but with the state holding the whip-hand inasmuch as it can refuse to allocate state funds for projects of interest and importance to the concerned local governments unless the local governments agree to the terms which have been established by the state officials or employees.

Moreover, inasmuch as the state officials are dealing with a large number of local governments, there is a tendency for the state to develop "standard" contract terms which are likely to be offered to the local governments on a take-it-or-leave-it basis with little opportunity, except for the larger local governments or those with especially powerful political relationships, to negotiate terms which take account of considerations which are important to local officials and citizens.

These contract arrangements extend not only to joint projects but also to projects where the state, or a state agency, is arranging the long-term financing—

even when the full responsibility for repayment rests with the local governments. Thus, in Pennsylvania, the State Public School Building Authority can have very important inputs into the kinds of school structures to be financed for local school districts and, obviously, the costs associated therewith.

OTHER CONSIDERATIONS

Beyond the kinds of controls that have been discussed above, there are a number of other kinds of state-local relationships which warrant comment here. Some of these are controls and some are of a different character.

Supervision in Emergency Situations

When a municipality, or other taxing district, has mismanaged its financial affairs with a consequent default (or a threatened default) on its debt, there is ample precedent for the state to step in and substitute temporary state control for local control until financial health has been restored. During the Great Depression, three out of four types of state remedial legislation provided for administrative intervention: (1) special emergency measures placing particular local units under administrative receivers; (2) administrative receivership laws, applicable to any local units that might default; and (3) receivership legislation which was applicable to special districts only (e.g., irrigation districts). The fourth type of statute authorized court receiverships.

Some of the statutes which applied broadly to any local unit that might default are still in force. In light of past experience, this seems desirable. The Federal Bankruptcy Act serves the useful purpose of preventing minority creditors from blocking a settlement which is acceptable to the majority and which the court deems equitable. But, this is not enough. Federal legislation cannot provide for an active leadership in financial rehabilitation, but state legislation can. For example, in order to forestall needless suits against the defaulting unit, a state administrative body can go into the federal court having jurisdiction over the petition under the Bankruptcy Act and ask for a stay of all proceedings in order to give the state body an opportunity to improve finances prior to the formulation of a debt adjustment plan.

State administrative agencies during the depression assisted municipalities which were in financial trouble even when a state receivership was not required. Two states, Oregon and North Carolina, aided some of their local units with technical surveys to determine their future ability to pay debt which had already been incurred, while maintaining reasonable operating services. In a larger number of states — Michigan, Montana, New Jersey, North Carolina, Ohio, Pennsylvania, and Texas—local refunding operations proceeded under the supervision, and with the approval, of a state administrative agency.

It should be added that experience with state intervention in local financial crises antedated the Great Depression. In order to follow this development, one might begin with the 1870s.[2]

---

[2] Hillhouse, A. M., *Municipal Bonds—A Century of Experience*, (New York: Prentice-Hall, 1936), pp. 321-360.

Technical Assistance

If the state supervisory agency is to supplement controls with a technical assistance program, two arguments may carry weight with the legislators who must provide the authority and the appropriations. First, technical assistance from the state capital is one way to pool and share scarce expert talent—talent which local governments need only occasionally or part-time. A budgeting specialist, for example, from the state agency could keep very busy assisting units which are preparing capital budgets or program budgets for the first time or revising their budgetary accounting system or procedures. A second argument is by analogy from the field of education. As stated earlier, minimum standards set by control measures are a form of mass education; auditors checking for compliance and accountability are enforcing bare minimums. But backward, individual local governments and some progressive ones that would like to do an outstanding job are analogous to the dull and the very bright students. Both types require special attention. No school and no supervisory agency is doing its job if all are treated as having the same capabilities. Minimum standards (mass education) and technical assistance (special attention) are both responsibilities. Technical assistance is not "frosting on the cake," but the second half of the supervisory function.

From the standpoint of staff morale and effectiveness, the positive approach through technical assistance, i.e., "going the extra mile" when needed or requested, has a high value. This also, over time, may have weight with the legislature.

Effective use of the staff for technical assistance requires a combination of methods. Sometimes an audit staff member in the field may be used. The advice or expert help, needed or requested, can be given while the routine audit is being performed. Some requests can be anticipated and instructional materials prepared. When needed, they can be applied by any staff member in the field. For some complicated problem, an *ad hoc* consulting team from the state agency should work with the municipality. More often than not, a single specialist will be sufficient.

A portion of technical assistance can be statewide in nature. A management advisory service, for example, can act as a clearinghouse for new ideas and developments; answer individual inquiries and disseminate the replies when the answers have wide applicability; prepare technical bulletins on current problems; report on examples of cooperation among neighboring local units; inform local units of new bulletins, reports, or services available from some branch of the state or federal government; and publish financial statistics and analyses of trends.

The Federal Government's Interest in State Administrative Supervision

Indirectly, the federal government should benefit from any state administrative supervision which effectively improves the caliber of local finance administration. As federal aid to local governments increases, improvements in local administration should mean better utilization of the allocated federal resources by the recipient units.

The federal government now channels financial aid *via* two distinct methods: (1) directly to the recipient local units (e.g., federal aid to airports and revenue sharing) and (2) through the state governments, with state responsibility for enforcing the standards laid down by Congress and the federal agency involved (e.g., hospital construction funds under the Hill-Burton Act).

Today, local housing authorities and urban renewal and redevelopment agencies are audited directly by auditors of the Department of Housing and Urban Development (HUD). Here, again, we can conceive of a satisfactory protection of the federal subsidy monies through audit contracts with state audit agencies. If HUD prescribed audit specifications, the state auditors could audit according to federal requirements. The General Accounting Office staff, in conjunction with HUD representatives, could periodically check as to the effectiveness of performance under the audit contract. At present, the General Accounting Office must perform such tests upon the work of the HUD field auditors.[3]

As federal aid to local governments increases—regardless of whether it is channeled directly, or through the states—cogent reasons exist for concentrating federal money allocated to auditing in a process that will bolster state audit field staffs. This alternative appears more attractive than constantly increasing the number of federal agency auditors.

Exemption of the Large Cities

This matter is best seen as a whole rather than piecemeal under each area—accounting, budgeting, etc. In fact, the problem is often attitudinal, rather than technical.

Certain exemptions of big cities from state supervision are justifiable. The major, and almost the sole criterion, is whether the big city is being asked to conform to standards which are not suitable—either because the standards do not fit a large unit or because the big city is much more advanced in its methods and procedures than those prescribed by the state. No large city should be forced into a Procrustean bed designed for the small or average-size local unit. Neither should a city's progress be blocked by less advanced ideas emanating from the state capital.

But, where the state supervisory requirements are compatible with good management, it is to the big city's interest to comply and to work cooperatively with the state agency. The rationale for this has already been discussed in a preceding section.

Often, the big cities are annoyed with, or hostile to, officials and agencies at the state capital for any one of a number of reasons, and this annoyance or hostility carries over to state administrative supervision. Inequities in the ap-

---

[3] Currently there is a concentrated effort toward the "single audit" concept whereby an audit conducted by either an independent auditor, a state audit agency, or the General Accounting Office, would be used by all those governmental agencies having an interest in the audit. Basic to this has been the setting of standards by the General Accounting Office in its *Standards of Audit of Governmental Organizations, Programs, Activities and Functions*, to which reference has already been made extensively in Chapter 17. This effort is also augmented by various OMB Circulars, e.g., A-73 and A-102, and by the release by the American Institute of Certified Public Accountants of its *Audits of State and Local Governmental Units*.

portionment of state legislatures has, in the past, meant that the big city has often been shortchanged by a rural, or a rural-suburban, dominated legislature; however, this problem of apportionment is now largely solved through court dominated reapportionment plans.[4] Added to this, the political party in power in the state capital is often not the party which controls city hall. Sometimes, state officials do not try to cooperate with the cities or to visualize the problems which they must confront. Evidence exists, for example, that state agencies responsible for apportioning state aid and distributing local shares in state-collected taxes do not always try to assist the local governments in estimating revenues to be derived from these sources.

Some state officials are known to suffer from hierarchical snobbery and to practice the usual "one-upmanship." In turn, those in city hall play the same game. Because of urban sophistication, the size of their operations, and, some-times, a deserved lack of respect for those in state supervisory positions, they also practice snobbery. They deem themselves above supervision and want a treatment different from that accorded the smaller units. Finally, there are the usual conflicts of personalities.

Home Rule and Administrative Supervision

Although, in a few isolated instances, home rule chartered cities have been specifically exempt from some forms of state financial supervision, the rationale of such exemption is unclear. The home rule movement has been a struggle for freedom from arbitrary kinds of supervision imposed through acts of the legislature which, in effect, are limited to a single municipality;[5] freedom to choose the form of local government which the local citizens want; freedom to maintain flexibility in a few other policy areas, including, but not limited to, finance; and the possession of a home rule charter as an outward symbol of local autonomy. To pose any real conflict between the doctrines of home rule and state financial supervision would require an extension of the doctrine of home rule beyond its traditional boundaries.

In a larger sense than the technical meaning of home rule, state administrative supervision has helped to achieve a substantial protection of the so-called "grass roots of democracy." This has already been alluded to earlier. Administrative supervision has enabled states to leave operational responsibility of many activities with the local governments and, therefore, close to the people affected. Without effective supervision of delegated responsibilities and an agency to smooth over and to prevent friction between the parent state and its political subdivisions, there may have been a greater centralization of functions within

---

[4] Ironically, for many of the older cities, this change comes too late. For decades, many of these cities were underrepresented in relation to their population. With the growth of the suburban areas, some had, during the mid-1960s, begun to be slightly overrepresented— just at the time that the new systems of reapportionment came along and denied them of their somewhat favored positions in relation to population.

[5] For a description of one of the most flagrant episodes of state legislative punishment of a city, see Lennox L. Moak and Helen R. Moak, "The Rape of New Orleans," *National Municipal Review*, Vol. 37, No. 8, Sept. 1948, pp. 412-415.

the hands of the state. In several important functional areas, clear lines can no longer be drawn between what is a state responsibility and what is a local responsibility and this result, rather than a clean-cut centralization of functions, is a major achievement. Education, highways, health, and social welfare—to name important segments—are joint responsibilities. Effective state supervision has made this possible, established a healthy pattern for the future, and preserved something more important than technical home rule. Administrative supervision has also permitted both the states and the federal government to use the local governments as the administrative agents for execution of their own programs, thereby making unnecessary a great proliferation of state and federal offices.

Quality of Leadership

The quality of leadership provided by a state supervisory agency is important, second only to the character of the substantive municipal finance policies which are to be enforced, especially at a critical time when municipal finance laws are being reshaped and supervisory approaches redirected. We too often underestimate the power and lasting influence of a single individual. It is unfortunate that there is no coveted national prize to honor such constructive contributors to state and local government.

A significant aspect of quality leadership is also the staff which the supervisory head assembles and directs. A small, well balanced, professional staff should include accountants, a statistician, management and other public administration specialists, a political scientist, a public finance economist, computer technicians, and lawyers. Ideally, a majority of the staff will be managerially oriented and will have had some public administration training or background. In some supervisory agencies, the atmosphere is overly legalistic. This stems from an historical emphasis upon legal compliance and controls, with an unfortunate underemphasis upon leadership through service and technical assistance. The natural gravitation of lawyers to the state capital has not always been counterbalanced by an aggressive recruitment of other types of professional talent.

To command the respect of the local officials being supervised, the state agency has to be on its toes. It must provide the means and time for the staff to keep abreast of new developments because supervisory manuals and approaches can become outdated all too quickly. Progressive changes and innovations are signs of effective leadership and, as one experienced official has quipped, "supervision of the living by the dead is certainly not good state supervision."

CONCLUSION

First and foremost to be noted is that although administrative supervision is important, the basic local finance policies established by the constitution and by legislative enactment are far more important. Whatever the constitution prescribes and the legislature decides constitute the policy framework within which the supervisory administrators and staff must operate. If, therefore, the supervisory agency, in a given state, is to function constructively, the agency head and others interested in local finance must work to get sound municipal policies written into state legislation. To this responsibility of initiating legislative proposals should be added the requirement that all proposed legislation which would affect local government finance should be referred to the supervisory agency for study and recommendation.

Of the work done by state supervisory agencies, the most essential appears to be in the areas of accounting and budgeting. Effective activities include the promulgation of uniform accounting and uniform budget manuals, technical assistance in these two areas, and state agency review of budgets for sound practices and for legal compliance—but not for substitution of the state agency's judgment for that of the local governing body. New Jersey has established one interesting pattern for these approaches.

Basically, a state supervisory agency has two potential approaches: (1) sanctions, and (2) technical assistance. However, its capacity for effectiveness in either of these is very largely dependent upon the sufficiency in quantity and adequacy in quality of its staff. Analogous to mass education, effective state supervision includes controls and discipline, but also includes special assistance for both the less inventive and the creative local units which want to go much beyond minimum requirements.

The states, the big cities, and the federal government all have a stake in maintaining the quality and effectiveness of state administrative supervision. These stakes, although not identical, stem essentially from enlightened self-interest. The relative degree of future supervision arising from grants-in-aid cannot be forecast at this point. The tendency toward block grants and special revenue sharing now present can result in reduced amounts of such supervision. However, special interest groups generally push for categorical grants and these tend to increase requirements for supervision.

The pattern of state supervision of local finance, at any given time, is the result of many annual, or biennial, legislative additions and adjustments from the past. Periodically, therefore, it is important that a hard look be taken in this whole area to see whether the pattern, as a whole, still makes sense and is workable. A reexamination may also be required whenever policy changes in local government finance are adopted. Each state must do its own soul searching; but, something can usually be learned from the mistakes and successes of other states.

No official agency has been given the responsibility for surveying periodically the fifty states and their administrative supervisory practices. To date, knowledge has been left largely to an occasional excursion into this area by some academician. There is a need for a central clearinghouse of information on this and other aspects of stae-local fiscal relations. By default, as is true in other matters, this function on a regular basis will, no doubt, be eventually assumed by the federal government.

In some states, proposals for a Department of Local Government or a Department of Community Affairs have been made and, in a few, these proposals have been adopted. Generally, the thrust is to consolidate into a single agency the principal activities of the state government relating to local governments; however, even where these kinds of departments exist large portions of state-local relations are conducted by the traditional state departments—health, highways, education, and others.

The creation of such new departments can provide a new thrust in the state's concern with the problems of local governments—assuming that the organic change is accompanied by other changes in state government attitudes and actions. However, there is always the danger that mere administrative reorganization at the state level will be taken for substantive change, thereby creating a situation in which old inadequate practices in state-local relations are continued. Along with these changes, there should be an attempt toward the creation of new systems of local government, competent to cope with the problems arising in almost all metropolitan complexes. Indeed, if the forces of reaction gain control of a state's department of local government or community affairs, there is even less likelihood of moving toward significant remedies.

Finally, in state supervision, the quality of leadership and the caliber of the staff are much more important that the precise location of the supervisory activities within the state government structure. The concept, or image, which the supervisors have of their role, their attitudes, motivation, and system of priorities—these will be reflected in their efforts and accomplishments. The suggested model comprises an advisor to the legislature, a coordinator within the state executive branch, a control supervisor, and a technical consultant. Today, there is little quarrel as to the essentiality of state supervision. The problem is how, and with what spirit, it shall be done.

20

Financial Reporting

Effective financial reporting involves not only presentation of the bare financial facts but also provision for integration and interpretation that will enable interested persons easily to comprehend the significant aspects of the local government's financial operations.

Emphasis here is dual; it is not restricted to the accountant's view. Yet in no manner should the reporting process eliminate those matters of importance to the accountant and the auditor.

From the accountant's point of view, it is necessary to set forth in the manner that has been recommended by the National Committee on Governmental Accounting all those statements essential to make a full disclosure of the facts of operation for the fiscal year. The audience for such reports is basically those persons technically prepared to comprehend the significance implicit in the financial data presented. The audience includes accountants, investors, researchers, public employees and officers in other governments, and students of public finance and public administration. Except where the postauditor has taken some exception to the presentation in the financial report, there is ordinarily little of major interest to the ordinary citizen beyond whether a surplus or deficit occurred in the principal operating fund or funds for the year just closed.

However, there is a second audience consisting of the general public and of the reporters, editorial writers, and others of the mass media for whom a somewhat different type of reporting is needed. The elements of the overall financial picture which may be of interest to these segments of the community include:

1. A summary of the operating budget in its proposed form, in its originally adopted form, and in its finally amended form—if there have been significant changes during the course of the fiscal year
2. The capital budget and the capital program in their proposed, originally adopted, and finally amended forms
3. The reports of completed financial operations—which may take the form of a single comprehensive report or of a series of specialized reports, sometimes by different officials when the financial functions are performed on a widely decentralized basis, especially if several elected officials are involved.

The format and content of the operating budget have been discussed in Chapter 5. Little elaboration is required here as to the document itself. Some

427

local governments find it helpful to public understanding if a summary version of the operating budget, either in proposed or approved form is published. Such summaries are distributed widely throughout the community, especially among the elements of the community that have a special interest in local government and local governmental finance. This group would include the leaders who normally help to formulate public opinion.

Generally, citizens can more easily comprehend the proposed capital program and capital budget because it deals with specific public improvements. It can be more meaningfully illustrated with pictures, drawings and maps than can the operating budget.

INTERIM FINANCIAL REPORTING

For purposes of internal control and public accountability, regularly scheduled reports should be issued by the responsible financial officials throughout the fiscal year. Ordinarily a combination of monthly and quarterly reports will be appropriate. Such interim reports need not be elaborate; they may be inexpensively reproduced and bound. But they should be informative. They should comment upon the progress to date and any impending problems regarding:

1. Revenues anticipated and received during the reporting period compared with original expectations in the budget preparation process
2. Status of appropriations, allocations, and allotments during the reporting period with comments as to prospects during the remainder of the fiscal year.
3. Revenues and expenditures of enterprise funds
4. Combined balance sheets for all appropriate funds or groups of funds
5. Forecast of fund condition and cash position of each fund as of the end of the fiscal year, especially operating and debt service funds

Because this type of reporting is integral to budgetary administration and cash management, and can be successfully used in public relations, it should be timely—being published within a few days after the close of the period to which it relates. Suitable press releases should be prepared for the media emphasizing the high points of interest to the community.

INTEGRATED ANNUAL FINANCIAL REPORTING

The basic technical accounting content of the annual financial report has become largely standardized along the lines recommended by the National Committee on Governmental Accounting.[1] The Committee proposes that the contents of an *introductory section* include a title page, a listing of the principal officials of the governmental unit supplemented by an organization chart for the

---

[1] National Committee on Governmental Accounting, *Governmental Accounting, Auditing, and Financial Reporting*, (Chicago; Municipal Finance Officers Association, 1968). See especially pp. 106-126.

government, the table of contents, a letter of transmittal (including details of any changes in financial policies and the significant aspects of financial management), the opinion of the independent auditor or other postauditing agency, and, if the local government has attained the distinction of receipt of a Certificate of Conformance from the Municipal Finance Officers Association, or a note to that effect.

The *financial section* of the annual financial report should, according to the Committee, contain the fund statements and schedules for individual funds and classified fund groups and a minimum of four combined statements: (1) a combined balance sheet for all funds, (2) a statement of expenditures and encumbrances compared with authorizations for specified funds, (3) a statement of estimated and actual revenue for specified funds, and (4) a statement of cash receipts and disbursements for all funds. It recommends three combined schedules: (a) delinquent taxes receivable, (b) bonds payable, and (c) investments—each by fund. Finally, the Committee recommends inclusion of a *statistical section* presenting data for periods of ten or more years on seventeen varying aspects of local government finance, including tax rates, assessed valuations, the computation of direct and overlapping debt, and numerous other items.

Assuming these requirements are satisfied, there remains a major job to be done in developing additional materials which will facilitate understanding of the contents of the accounting statements and schedules. Today, the usefulness of financial reports is very much limited by the fragmentation of responsibility for different financial activities within individual local governments. This fragmentation is accentuated by the complicated structuring of urban government itself within a given geographical area; and by the lack of benchmarks and frames of reference within which financial reports can be interpreted.

The Local Government's Annual Financial Report

Where a number of different local governmental units serve the same basic political community, i.e., where there are a number of corporations, authorities, and special entities, a needed service can be performed through a rational integration of the annual reports of these agencies into a single document along with a comprehensive narrative which helps to bring the full picture into focus. The comments below may be useful in helping to organize such a reporting system.

The Introductory Section. Where basic data arises from various independent reports for units serving the same political community, some proposed guidelines for the general integration of reporting are:

1. A brief description of the governmental structure, with notations concerning each independent or quasi-independent authority, nonprofit corporation, and separate reporting office. This list should indicate the organic and functional basis of the related agencies and their formal or informal ties to the prinicipal local government.
2. A section which undertakes to inter-relate the financial reports of these various units insofar as this is feasible within resources available.
3. References to pages in the annual financial report where the accounting fund structure (funds or groups of funds) is set forth together with a

column which shows the equivalent titles in the standard terminology recommended by the National Committee on Governmental Accounting.

4. Identification of the accounting basis (or bases) used by the local government(s).

5. An indication of the fiscal year of the parent local government and any deviations therefrom by any reporting unit.

6. A listing of the names of all overlapping and underlying local governmental units and authorities.

The objective of the integrating sections of the principal local government's annual financial report should be to provide as clear, comprehensive, and comprehensible picture, as is feasible, of the total local government finances for the political community.

The annual financial report should include a section which traces any changes which have been made during the fiscal year by formal amendment (or administrative transfers, where permitted) in the originally adopted annual operating budget, or the approved capital program and approved capital budget. For example, this section would contain a schedule listing the types of capital expenditures and the sources of their authorization in the operating budget, the capital budget, or by an action subsequent to the approval of, or independent of, the approval of both of the foregoing.

A Description of Budgeting and Capital Programming and Capital Budgeting Processes. The annual financial report of the principal local government should provide a succinct description of the basic processes involved in the preparation, consideration, adoption and amendment of the annual operating budget, the capital program and the capital budget. To the extent that the processes are organically related, the descriptive material should clearly indicate the linkages. The annual financial report of the prinicipal local government should include a summary comparison of the operating budgets of each operating fund for several years, rather than only for the current and immediately preceding fiscal years.

Connecting Links with the Capital Program and Capital Budget. It is desirable that the annual financial report of the prinicpal local government include information that helps the reader to understand the inter-relationships between the operating budget and the capital program and the capital budget. To this end, it is desirable that:

1. Information be provided concerning the types of capital expenditures that are met from operating funds and the extent to which such expenditures are reflected in the capital program and capital budget

2. Comparisons, over a period of years, of the levels of capital budget authorizations and commitments thereunder

A Financial Report for Overlapping Units of Local Government

Since local governmental structure in many urban centers is of a layercake variety, an integrated presentation of the financial operations of these overlapping governments is useful to those who seek to understand the complexities and significance of urban finance. Of course, no single local government—except where a regional agency with appropriate responsibilities is operable—can undertake this process. If it is to be provided, the responsibility will doubtless have to fall to an appropriate agency of the state government.

In the eyes of many, the proposal here is visionary. Yet, the proposal is for one report, essentially financial in nature and on an annual basis, pertaining to the financial operations of the various units of local government combined. It would differ in coverage (and somewhat in form) from the conventional annual financial report because of its wide use of statistical tables, rather than conventional accounting presentations. It would draw some data from financial reports at each level, including reports by purchasing agents, treasurers, and other agencies.

No attempt would be made to integrate and publish planning data from the operating budgets and capital programs and capital budgets of the respective local governments. Whereas a strong case can be made for cooperative capital planning of certain types of facilities this does not require publication of an integrated capital program and capital budget document for the entire region.

A suitably developed regional agency, or an agency of the state government, would have the responsibility for preparation of such reports, one covering each of the important urban regions within the state. In the final analysis, it might be the state government that has to provide such services because only it has the direct power to require submission of data annually on a timely basis and in a uniform manner. However, it is to be remembered that many of the most important urban regions in the United States cut across state boundaries. Under these circumstances, the regional planning commissions which have been established may offer a more workable substitute.

One of the advantages to the use of state agency facilities is to help bring home to responsible state officials the irrationality of local government structure in many urban regions. Perhaps, over time, such a process might provide a nucleus of appreciation of the need for change.

The staff assigned by the responsible regional or state reporting agency would have to include administrative personnel, computer technicians, and statisticians in a centralized location to compile, analyze, and supervise the publication of data which have been collected by field representatives located in strategic urban centers. The field representatives would initially be responsible for making adjustments to accommodate any singularities in the local data and for acquainting local officials with the new reporting system. Some technical problems would confront the staff, such as lack of a common fiscal year among the local units involved and nonconformity in financial terminology in many states. In establishing such a reporting system, the regional and state officials may be able to secure considerable assistance from various federal officials.

An introduction to the integrated financial report could explain its purpose, limitations, ultimate goal, and any technical points which are essential for proper interpretation. The statistical information to be presented in such an integrated report might be developed along the following lines for each overlapping unit of government and as a total figure for the full family of local governmental units:

1. Assessed taxable valuation adjusted to full market value
   a. Amounts
   b. Per capita

2. Properties exempt from the property tax
   a. Adjusted assessed valuation
   b. Percentage distribution by type of property
   c. Percentage distribution by type of exemption, e.g., educational, religious, etc.
3. Property tax rates per $1,000 of adjusted taxable assessed valuation
4. Revenue sources
   a. Amounts of revenue by major type plus an "all other" group
   b. Percentage distribution by type
5. Aid from state government
   a. Amounts, by type and total
   b. Percentage distribution by type
6. Aid from the federal government
   a. Amounts by type and total
   b. Percentage distribution by type
7. Operating expenditures
   a. Total amounts
   b. Excess over originally approved budget
   c. Total per capita
   d. Amounts by functions
   e. Percentage distribution by function
   f. Percentage distribution by identifiable programs
8. Capital expenditures
   a. Total amounts
   b. Percentage distribution by sources, e.g., general obligation bonds, revenue bonds, operating revenues, and other sources
   c. Percentage distribution by functional purpose
   d. Percentage distribution by type of government—general government and types of public service enterprise

Other areas which could be included are: capital projects programmed and projects completed; net general obligation debt; net revenue bonded debt; bond authorizations; cash balances; and temporary borrowing.

Because experimentation would be necessary for a state or regional agency to bring this annual reporting process to a high level of development, it might be wise to progress by stages, adding a block of new segments each year until the whole range of financial activities is covered.

STANDARDS OF REFERENCE

Along with the integration of the annual financial report comes the need for parallel development of standards of reference that could be widely applicable. At the technical level, once agreement has been reached concerning the initial gathering and uniform classification of data, computer technology now available makes it feasible to process the data with promptness. Moreover, it can be processed for the derivation of norms which in turn can lead to development of useful guidelines. These guidelines would fall far short of being standards, yet they might facilitate adjustments of standards which have periodically been developed on an arbitrary basis or for the gradual development of standards in areas where they have not heretofore been feasible. Of course, just as in the case of the data published by the Bureau of the Census, considerable financial editing will be required, especially in the case of the very small governmental units where it becomes more difficult, if not meaningless, to apply detailed standardized classifications.

If a few state governments began experimentation with integrated reporting, one might expect that maximum progress would result if the federal government paralleled this work with research on the interpretation of these integrated reports.

The most obvious candidates for statistical compilation and analysis are:

1. Overall net tax-supported debt
2. Overall net self-supporting debt
3. Overall property tax rates on an adjusted full value basis
4. Overall state aid
5. Overall federal aid

For illustrative purposes, the following data with regard to overall capital outlays and capital assets might be considered for analysis and determination of a norm:

1. Percentage distribution of sources of funds for capital outlays—from the proceeds of general obligation bonds, proceeds of revenue bonds, accumulated capital reserves, special assessments, current budgeted revenues, state aid, federal aid, and gifts
2. Percentage distribution of capital outlays between general government and public service enterprises—with a further breakdown for the latter to show the types of enterprises
3. Calculation of the amounts of capital outlays corrected to a stable construction dollar basis and reduced to: an overall per capita amount, per capita for general government only; per customer for public service enterprises, and per pupil for educational purposes
4. Derivation of the ratio of local governmental outlays for capital purposes to capital expenditures in the private sector in the same time period and geographical area
5. Determination, from past experience, of the depreciation rates which need to be applied to capital equipment and to various structures and substructures (water and sewer mains, etc.), in the overall municipal public sector. Work in this field would have to provide corrective factors for replacement costs and proper interpretative materials to facilitate understanding
6. Estimation of the present depreciated value of capital assets dedicated to general government and assets used in public service enterprises with these subsequently reduced to per capita and per customer bases as appropriate. Along with this depreciated value based on cost, it is necessary to consider a parallel presentation taking into account replacement costs
7. Determination of the ratio of new overall capital outlays to estimated depreciation and obsolescence being generated in respect to the old capital investments

8. Identification of the effects of the "cost of government" if accounting records were kept on an accrued cost basis rather than on an accrued expenditure basis, especially if depreciation were treated as a cost rather than capital cost being reflected as an expenditure when made or as annual debt service payments. In each case computations would have to extend over a long enough period to ascertain the norms and deviations therefrom

CONCLUSION

The annual financial report as we know it today has been devised almost exclusively for technically oriented people, with a major emphasis upon the single class of the investor and his agents: bond dealers and credit rating agencies. These groups represent a very important clientele of the annual financial report; however, they do not represent the full clientele. To the extent that the annual financial report neglects very important other segments of the community, there is a need for modification.

The present emphasis derives in part from the fact that private financial reports are necessarily directed to the investor, because they largely relate to profit-oriented operations. But in the case of public business, the customer, the taxpayer, full-time and part-time citizens, and those concerned with social progress justify a kind of reporting that will be useful to them in the performance of their roles in our society. Therefore, we need to move to an early correction of the imbalance now present.

Financial reporting is an essential part of holding public officials and other public servants responsible for a proper stewardship of the funds which have been entrusted to them for performance of public functions. It is no longer sufficient that the niceties of conformity to the rules governing financial transactions be observed. We are interested in the results of what the money bought as well as whether it was handled in accordance with legal requirements and administrative regulations.

What appears to be required at this juncture is a shift in emphasis to a statistical approach which would not supersede, but rather would take an equal place with the accounting approach. The computer makes it possible to develop a wide range of statistical statements which may well stand on an equal footing with the conventional balance sheets and operating statements. The financial/social statistician can begin with a whole list of questions to which the taxpayer, citizen, investor, community leader, and social scientist seek answers. They can work backwards and forwards to the kinds of records, accounting or statistical, which will produce the required information.

This kind of approach to the new annual financial report can lend a vitality to it that no amount of accounting materials can provide. The problems to be encountered are almost innumerable; the techniques necessary to provide the new kinds of reporting are only partially known and understood. However, a new beginning by the generation of students of public finance and public administration which will shortly succeed that of the authors of this volume appears warranted!

A

C

E

R